Knowing Why

127 MORE Evidences That the Book of Mormon Is True

Cover Images: From top to bottom and left to right; *Stone carving at El Tajin Veracruz Mexico* © Thomas Aleto, courtesy of Flickr.com; *Moroni Delivers the Plates to Joseph Smith* © Jorge Cocco; *Dawn on the Land of Desolation* © James Fullmer; *Agnus Dei* © Francisco de Zubarán, courtesy of Wikimedia Commons; *Mayan Calendar* © Jasmin Gimenez Rappleye, courtesy of Book of Mormon Central; *Hill North of Shilom* © James Fullmer; *Lake Atitlan* © Steven Newton, courtesy of flickr.com; *2 Nephi 31* © Jorge Cocco; *Engraving of Dante Alighieri and Beatrice Portinari Gaze into the Highest Heaven* © Gustave Doré, courtesy of Wikimedia Commons; *Moroni 6* © Normandy Poulter and the BYU Virtual Scriptures Group; *75th Anniversary of Music and the Spoken Word* © MoTabChoir01, courtesy of Wikimedia Commons; *Mother, Tell Me* © Megan Rieker, courtesy of Book of Mormon Central; *Moroni* © Normandy Poulter and the BYU Virtual Scriptures Group; *Jesus Washing the Feet of Apostles* © Wolfgang Sauber, courtesy of Wikimedia Commons; *I Am the Light of the World* © James Fullmer; *4 Nephi* © Normandy Poulter and the BYU Virtual Scriptures Group; *Mormon* © Jorge Cocco; *Teancum* © James Fullmer. *Background Image* © Book of Mormon Central; *Replica of the Gold Plates by David A. Baird* © Daniel Smith

Cover design copyright © 2019 by Covenant Communications, Inc.

Published by Covenant Communications, Inc.
American Fork, Utah

Copyright © 2019 by Book of Mormon Central
All rights reserved. No part of this book may be reproduced in any format or in any medium without the written permission of the publisher, Covenant Communications, Inc., P.O. Box 416, American Fork, UT 84003. This work is not an official publication of The Church of Jesus Christ of Latter-day Saints. The views expressed within this work are the sole responsibility of the author and do not necessarily reflect the position of The Church of Jesus Christ of Latter-day Saints, Covenant Communications, Inc., or any other entity.

Printed in South Korea.
First Printing: October 2019

26 25 24 23 22 21 20 19 10 9 8 7 6 5 4 3 2 1

ISBN-13: 978-1-52441-160-2

Knowing Why

127 MORE Evidences That the Book of Mormon Is True

Edited By

John W. Welch, Neal Rappleye, Jasmin G. Rappleye, Jonathon Riley, and Taylor Halverson

With Contributions From

Neal Rappleye, Stephen O. Smoot, Jonathon Riley, Ryan Dahle, David J. Larsen, Jasmin G. Rappleye, and Jared Riddick

Covenant Communications, Inc.

Table of Contents

Acknowledgments

At Book of Mormon Central, we are indebted to many who have helped make our work possible. First and foremost, we express gratitude to Lynn and Dow Wilson for their founding role in getting Book of Mormon Central off the ground and for their continued support of our goals and initiatives. Without the Wilsons, there would be no Book of Mormon Central. Our deep appreciation is also extended to the Perry family for their support and commitment to help more people experience the power of the Book of Mormon in their lives. We would also like to thank John S. and Unita W. Welch and many other generous donors for their contributions and support.

Many thanks go to Alan Minor, who provides us with office space and allowed us to absorb much of his personal library into the beginnings of our in-house library.

Book of Mormon Central is greatly indebted to many individuals, without whom our work would not be possible. They have enabled the work of Book of Mormon Central to go forward, and we greatly appreciate the time, talents, and resources they have contributed to our cause.

In addition to our full-time staff, several others have assisted in the production of these KnoWhys on a part-time, contract, or volunteer basis, and they deserve our recognition and gratitude. Juan Pinto provided valuable research for several of the KnoWhys as a part-time research assistant in the summer of 2016. Holly Boud has greatly assisted in editing and PDF typesetting of several KnoWhys as a part-time editor. Angel Sturgill has worked with our video and digital publishing staff to gather useable images for the videos, PDF, and web versions of each KnoWhy. Nick Galieti has lent his voice talent and audio recording skills in providing a podcast version of each KnoWhy. Scott Christopher and Amanda Cook also provided their voice talent for the narration of our KnoWhy videos, and Robert Starling has assisted in the writing of scripts for these same videos. Sketch art for several KnoWhys was provided by Jody Livingston. Normandy Poulter and the BYU Virtual Scriptures group also provided us with a number of commissioned art peices. James Fullmer, Jorge Cocco, and Anthony Sweat have graciously allowed us to use their artwork, and we also appreciate the contributions of all those who submitted art to us for our Book of Mormon art contests; their works, along with other illustrative resources, have been used to greatly enhance the visual appeal of each KnoWhy. Mark Alan Wright has also frequently shared with Book of Mormon Central staff insights that he has kindly allowed us to use in KnoWhys, and we have strived to give him proper attribution for these.

Throughout these KnoWhys, we have drawn upon the work of past and present Book of Mormon scholars, such as Hugh Nibley, John L. Sorenson, Royal Skousen, John A. Tvedtnes, and Brant A. Gardner. The scholarship of these and many others forms the backbone of the insights we seek to highlight and bring to life. We are inspired by their love of the Book of Mormon and the dedication they have shown to better our understanding of this important work of scripture. We are indebted to them and owe much to the product of their labor. Truly, we stand on the shoulders of giants.

We express our gratitude to Ruth Schmidt, who selflessly gave of her time to help prepare this manuscript for publication and has been a steady presence at Book of Mormon Central over the years. Brant A. Gardner helped prepare the original manuscript we submitted to Covenant for consideration. Finally, we would like to extend our appreciation to Kathy Jenkins and the talented team at Covenant Communications for all the work they have done in bringing our KnoWhys to a print medium. They have been a joy to work with, and we look forward to continuing a productive publishing relationship with them in the future.

PEER REVIEWERS

Peer reviewers volunteer to review KnoWhys on a weekly basis, providing valuable feedback on accuracy, academic rigor, and readability for a lay audience. This is something they do on their own personal time, in addition to whatever full-time work and family obligations to which they are committed. They have been diligently working to improve our KnoWhys, and we greatly appreciate their time and expertise.

Introduction

"I know the Book of Mormon is true."

Many Latter-day Saints hear this statement on a monthly basis during fast and testimony meetings, as well as on numerous other occasions. Our culture places a premium on knowing what is true. As we prepared to launch Book of Mormon Central, we wanted a central part of our mission to be knowing the Book of Mormon with all our heart, mind, and strength. As we discussed what we hoped to accomplish, however, we felt we needed to convey something more than just knowing the Book of Mormon is true. We determined that it was important to illustrate why.

In an address to CES teachers and instructors on February 26, 2016, Elder M. Russell Ballard taught that asking why is important to learning and gaining gospel knowledge:

> One of the most important questions people may ask is "Why?" When asked with a sincere desire to understand, "Why?" is a great question. It is the question missionaries want their investigators to ask. Why are we here? Why do bad things happen to good people? Why should we pray? Why should we follow Christ? It is often the "why" questions that lead to inspiration and revelation.[i]

Knowing why something is the way it is goes deeper than simply knowing that it is. It involves identifying reasons or evidence that support what we know. It was in the spirit of knowing why that we launched Book of Mormon Central's KnoWhy series on January 1, 2016. A KnoWhy is a short essay—supplemented by a podcast, video, images, and related social media content—about some brief historical, archaeological, cultural, linguistic, literary, legal, devotional, or prophetic insight in the Book of Mormon. It shares something to know and explains why that thing is worth knowing. Since we launched in 2016, we've published more than 540 KnoWhys on our website. In our first *Knowing Why* book, we published, with some updates, the first 137 of these, primarily related to the first half of the Book of Mormon (1 Nephi–Alma 29). For this second volume, we've taken another 127, this time primarily related to the second half of the Book of Mormon (Alma 30–Moroni 10), and reedited and updated them, some more extensively than others.

Individually, these pieces are about very specific topics: knowing why Alma wrote using chiasmus (chapter 13), knowing why Nephi prophesied near the main highway (chapter 50), knowing why the Savior said Isaiah's words were "great" (chapter 85), or knowing why Ether begins with a long genealogy (chapter 103). In many cases, we profess less-than-definitive answers, but rather offer some reasons for why these things might be as they are in the Book of Mormon. As a collective body, these KnoWhys provide more than possible answers to specific questions. Combined, they are about knowing why the Book of Mormon is so amazing, knowing why it is beautiful, knowing why it speaks to our hearts and minds so powerfully, knowing why it is so uniquely inspiring, and ultimately knowing why the Book of Mormon is true in so many ways.

Of course, the ultimate reason anyone knows the Book of Mormon is true is because, in accordance with the promise made by Moroni, they prayed to the Father in the name of His Son Jesus Christ and received an affirmative answer through the power of the Holy Ghost (see Moroni 10:3–5). We do not intend to supplant, but rather to supplement and facilitate this central reason with many additional reasons to believe. Elder Neal A. Maxwell often taught that reasons do not take the place of faith and testimony, but they do create an intellectual and spiritual environment in which faith and hope may flourish.[ii] We seek to follow the example of Elder Jeffrey R. Holland, who spoke of having "a thousand elements of my own testimony of the divinity of the Book of Mormon."[iii] We have not yet provided a thousand, but here we offer 127 reasons to know why the Book of Mormon is true—and we continue to provide more online at bookofmormoncentral.org.

We hope that within these pages you will find some reasons to call your own and that you too can know why the Book of Mormon is amazing, beautiful, and true.

John W. Welch
Neal Rappleye
Taylor Halverson

i. M. Russell Ballard, "The Opportunities and Responsibilities of CES Teachers in the 21st Century," Address to CES Religious Educators, February 26, 2016, online at lds.org; reprinted as "By Study and by Faith," *Religious Educator* 17, no. 3 (2016): 1–11, quote on p. 6.

ii. See, for example, Neal A. Maxwell, "All Hell is Moved," Brigham Young University devotional, Nov. 8, 1977, speeches.byu.edu; Neal A. Maxwell, "Discipleship and Scholarship," *BYU Studies 32*, no. 3 (1992): 5–9.

iii. Jeffrey R. Holland, "Safety for the Soul," *Ensign*, November 2009, online at lds.org.

The Book of Mormon and the Restoration

1

Why Did Moroni Deliver the Plates on September 22?

"At length the time arrived for obtaining the plates. . . . On the twenty-second day of September, one thousand eight hundred and twenty-seven, having gone as usual at the end of another year to the place where they were deposited, the same heavenly messenger delivered them up to me." (Testimony of the Prophet Joseph Smith, front of 2013 edition of the Book of Mormon; cf. Joseph Smith—History 1:59)

THE KNOW

The emergence of the Book of Mormon from its hiding place began on September 21, 1823. That night, the angel Moroni appeared to a young Joseph Smith and told him that "God had a work for [him] to do" (Joseph Smith—History 1:33). That work would involve translating "a book deposited, written upon gold plates, giving an account of the former inhabitants of this continent"—what we know today as the Book of Mormon (Joseph Smith—History 1:34).

The next day, on September 22, Joseph went to the hill and "made an attempt to take [the plates] out" but was forbidden by Moroni, who reminded him that "the time for bringing them forth had not yet arrived." Joseph would have to wait "until four years from that time" but was to "come to that place precisely in one year from that time" and to return each year "until the time should come for obtaining the plates" (Joseph Smith—History 1:53).

Moroni's annual visits occurred generally around the time of the Israelite harvest festival season.[1] The initial visit on September 21 in 1823 coincided with that year's celebration of the Feast of Tabernacles. In 1824, September 22 was the eve of the Jewish New Year (Rosh Hashanah) and the beginning of the fall festivals. In 1825, September 22 was precisely Yom Kippur (the Day of Atonement). In 1827, when Moroni finally delivered the plates to Joseph (see Joseph Smith—History 1:59), September 22 coincided exactly with Rosh Hashanah, also known as the Feast of Trumpets.[2]

This important festival season, celebrated in the fall of each year, goes back to the days of ancient Israel (see Leviticus 23), and scholars have found extensive evidence of its observance in the Book of Mormon.[3] Over time, many key themes were associated with the New Year and with the harvest festival in general. Lenet Hadley Read explained:

> The Feast of Trumpets signifies the time of Israel's final harvest; the Day of Remembrance of God's covenants with Israel; the announcement of revelation or truth; and preparation for God's

holiest times, including the Messianic Age.[4]

Other themes include solemn admonitions and warnings, covenant making, remembrance, sacrifice, prophecy, a new beginning, and God's involvement in history.[5]

THE WHY

Though it is hard to be certain whether all these themes were part of the New Year celebrations in Old Testament times, they were all part of long-standing Jewish customs and traditions by the time the Book of Mormon came forth. When the Book of Mormon's message and purpose—along with Moroni's counsel to Joseph during his September visits—are compared with these holy festival themes, one can see a number of interesting connections.

For example, Moroni's visits to young Joseph Smith included solemn words of admonition and warning to all the world (see Joseph Smith—History 1:42, 46). The coming forth of the Book of Mormon can also be seen as initiating the final harvest of souls,[6] renewing God's covenant with Israel,[7] offering a new revelation of truth,[8] and being clearly tied to the second coming of Jesus the Messiah.[9]

No bolder statement could be made about God's involvement in history than that of an angel delivering a historical record full of interactions with God—including the stunning account of the divine and risen Lord Jesus Christ ministering personally to the Nephites (see 3 Nephi 11–27).[10] Perhaps most relevant of all, the coming forth of the Book of Mormon launched a new beginning—the dawning of a day when the heavens are opened again.

No doubt many likely reasons can be suggested for the timing of Moroni's visits to Joseph Smith each year in late September and for his particular insistence that Joseph wait four years before recovering the plates. For example, that waiting period allowed Joseph Smith time to mature a bit more, to be married, and to be periodically instructed by Moroni.

But perhaps most striking of all, one further reason could have been so that his instructions would closely coincide with the sacred Israelite autumn festival season, with Moroni delivering the plates exactly on Rosh Hashanah. The number of meaningful ways in which the messages and purposes of the Book of Mormon coincide with the themes of Rosh Hashanah and the Jewish high holy days suggest that this timing was no coincidence, but that Moroni had carefully and deliberately scheduled his meaningful visits. For these reasons, there was no better day on which to commence the coming forth of the Book of Mormon than Rosh Hashanah, September 22, 1827.

FURTHER READING

Christopher Kirkland, "The Relationship Between Rosh Hashanah and Mormon Temples," *Mormon Writers*, September 21, 2015, online at https://medium.com/mormon-writers.

Lenet Hadley Read, "The Golden Plates and the Feast of Trumpets," *Ensign*, January 2000, online at lds.org.

Terrence L. Szink and John W. Welch, "King Benjamin's Speech in the Context of Ancient Israelite Festivals," in *King Benjamin's Speech: "That Ye May Learn Wisdom,"* ed. John W. Welch and Stephen D. Ricks (Provo, UT: FARMS, 1998), 160–174.

Lenet Hadley Read, "Joseph Smith's Receipt of the Plates and the Israelite Feast of Trumpets," *Journal of Book of Mormon Studies 2*, no. 2 (1993): 110–120.

2

Why Did Joseph and Oliver Seek Authority to Be Baptized?

"And now behold, these are the words which ye shall say, calling them by name, saying: Having authority given me of Jesus Christ, I baptize you in the name of the Father, and of the Son, and of the Holy Ghost. Amen." (3 Nephi 11:24–25)

THE KNOW

On May 15, 1829, during the process of translating the Book of Mormon, Joseph Smith and Oliver Cowdery "went into the woods to pray and inquire of the Lord respecting baptism for the remission of sins" (Joseph Smith—History 1:68).[11] In response, the Lord sent John the Baptist to confer upon them the Aaronic Priesthood, to instruct them concerning the nature of its authority, and then to command them to ordain and baptize each other (see Joseph Smith—History 1:68–72).[12]

Some may wonder what in the first place initiated Joseph and Oliver's concern about baptism and the authority necessary to perform it. In 1834, Oliver Cowdery recalled, "No men in their sober senses, could translate and write the directions given to the Nephites, from the mouth of the Savior, of the precise manner in which men should build up His Church, . . . without desiring a privilege of showing the willingness of the heart by being buried in the liquid grave, to answer a 'good conscience by the resurrection of Jesus Christ.'"[13]

This statement indicates that it was the Book of Mormon itself, and specifically the Savior's instructions concerning baptism found in 3 Nephi 11, that led to this important event in Church history.[14] Considering how frequently baptism and authority are discussed in the Book of Mormon, 3 Nephi may have only been the final impetus that sent them into the woods to pray.

Mosiah 18 was probably the first instance in the translation process that prominently featured information about priesthood authority, baptism, and the founding of a church of Christ.[15] It states that Alma baptized "having *authority* from the Almighty God" (Mosiah 18:13), and "whosoever was baptized by the power and *authority* of God was added to his church" (Mosiah 18:17; emphasis added). Moreover, "Alma, having *authority* from God, ordained priests" among his followers (Mosiah 18:18; emphasis added).

Mosiah 18 was only the beginning, though. Church historians Michael H. MacKay and Gerrit J. Dirkmaat explained, "In an almost cadence-like repetition, Smith dictated additional accounts of baptism week after week," and throughout this process "the necessity of baptism [was revealed] nearly every day."[16]

For example, Alma the Younger ordained priests and elders in the church at Zarahemla "by laying on his hands according to the order of God" (Alma 6:1).

In Alma 13, the translators frequently came across the term *priesthood* and would have learned that those who obtained it were "called with a holy calling, and ordained with a holy ordinance" (Alma 13:8). And from Alma 49:30 they would have understood that repentance, baptism, and ordination are required before one can be "sent forth to preach among the people."

The importance of receiving authorized and properly administered baptism would have been especially pronounced, though, in the account of the Savior's ministry found in 3 Nephi. As in Joseph Smith's day, the proper mode of baptism was disputed anciently among the Nephites (see 3 Nephi 11:28).[17] This led the Savior to explicitly describe and clarify the process.

Jesus taught, "And now behold, these are the words which ye shall say, calling them by name, saying: Having authority given me of Jesus Christ,[18] I baptize you in the name of the Father, and of the Son, and of the Holy Ghost. Amen. And then shall ye immerse them in the water, and come forth again out of the water" (3 Nephi 11:24–26).[19]

According to Daniel C. Peterson, "The passage [in 3 Nephi] that features ordination for authority to baptize was probably translated within, at the most, five weeks of the report of Alma and the waters of Mormon."[20] Thus because of the rapid pace of the translation, the translators would have, in just more than a month's time, come across multiple references to baptism and priesthood authority—topics that culminated in importance during the Savior's ministry in 3 Nephi.[21]

THE WHY

Recognizing that conferral of priesthood authority in this dispensation was sparked by translating the Book of Mormon and pondering its message is instructive. Richard L. Bushman reported that during the translation process, Joseph and Oliver paused "occasionally to talk over the unfolding story of the Nephites."[22] Such discussions indicate an intent interest in the ancient record and a willingness to study its revelations out in their minds (see D&C 9:8).

Elder Joseph B. Wirthlin taught, "We are constantly reminded through the scriptures that we should give the things of God much more than usual superficial consideration. We must ponder them and reach into the very essence of what we are and what we may become."[23] By studying out and pondering the revelations already given in the Book of Mormon, Joseph Smith and Oliver Cowdery discovered what they could become—bearers of the holy priesthood of God.

Lucy Mack Smith even recalled that in response to their interest, these young translators received a direct revelation to go into the woods to pray: "One morning they sat down to their work, as usual, and the first thing which presented itself through the Urim and Thummim, was a commandment for Joseph and Oliver to repair to the water and attend to the ordinance of Baptism."[24] The process of spiritual growth is thus "revelation upon revelation, knowledge upon knowledge" (D&C 42:61), the prior things preparing and pointing the way toward greater knowledge, instruction, and authority (see Alma 12:9–11; cf. Abraham 1:2).

Not only did Jesus Christ and prophets in the Book of Mormon frequently teach about baptism and priesthood authority,[25] but, as described by Scott H. Faulring, they "directly linked the baptismal ordinance with membership in the Lord's church."[26] It is thus not entirely surprising that this sacred text inspired those translating it to seek guidance about how to restore Christ's church anew in the "dispensation of the fullness of times" (D&C 112:30).

From the pages of the Book of Mormon, and especially from the words of the resurrected Savior, Joseph and Oliver came to know they needed to obtain a remission of sins, a covenant to bind them to the Lord and to one another, and the authority to bring others into this covenant. Because no one on the earth held that authority, John the Baptist "delivered the anxiously looked for message, and the keys of the gospel of repentance!"[27] Describing the profound importance of this event, Oliver Cowdery exclaimed, "What joy! what wonder! what amazement!"[28]

FURTHER READING

Saints: The Story of the Church of Jesus Christ in the Latter Days, Volume 1: The Standard of Truth, 1815–1846 (Salt Lake City, UT: The Church of Jesus Christ of Latter-day Saints, 2018), 65–68.

Michael Hubbard MacKay and Gerrit J. Dirkmaat, *From Darkness unto Light: Joseph Smith's Translation and Publication of the Book of Mormon* (Salt Lake City and Provo, UT: Deseret Book and BYU Religious Studies Center, 2015), 130–134.

John W. Welch, "The Book of Mormon as the Keystone of Church Administration," in *A Firm Foundation*, ed. David J. Whittaker and Arnold K. Garr (Salt Lake City and Provo, UT: Deseret Book and BYU Religious Studies Center, 2011), 15–58.

Daniel C. Peterson, "Authority in the Book of Mosiah," *FARMS Review 18*, no. 1 (2006): 149–185.

Scott H. Faulring, "The Book of Mormon: A Blueprint for Organizing the Church," *Journal of Book of Mormon Studies 7*, no. 1 (1998): 60–69, 71.

Larry C. Porter, "The Restoration of the Aaronic and Melchizedek Priesthoods," *Ensign*, December 1996, online at lds.org.

3

Why Did the Lord Quote the Book of Mormon When Reestablishing the Church?

"And now behold, these are the words which ye shall say." (3 Nephi 11:24)

THE KNOW

On April 6, 1830, Joseph Smith and more than fifty others gathered in the log home of Peter Whitmer Sr. in Fayette, New York, to reorganize Christ's Church on the earth in modern times.[29] Joseph and his associates had been anticipating and preparing for this day well in advance of that time. Nine months earlier, in June 1829, as they were finishing up the translation of the Book of Mormon, the Lord told Oliver Cowdery to "rely upon the things which are written," meaning the Book of Mormon, "for in them are all things written concerning the foundation of my church, my gospel, and my rock" (D&C 18:3–4).[30]

In response to this revelation, Oliver began drafting the "Articles of the Church of Christ," a first effort to set forth the basic administrative and procedural standards for the Church.[31] According to historian Scott Faulring, "more than half of Cowdery's Articles are either direct quotations or paraphrases with slight deviations from the Book of Mormon."[32] This document was eventually replaced by Doctrine and Covenants 20, which was revealed to Joseph Smith between April and June 1830.[33] As with Oliver's "Articles," much of what was contained in that revelation was similar to what is found in the Book of Mormon.[34]

For example, the sacrament prayers, found in Doctrine and Covenants 20:77, 79, quote almost verbatim from the Book of Mormon.[35] The two are so similar that, as John W. Welch has noted, the first known printing of Doctrine and Covenants 20 simply states: "And the manner of baptism and the manner of administering the Sacrament are to be done as is written in the Book of Mormon,"[36] rather than spelling out the full text of those prayers.[37] Both the words of the sacrament prayers and the instructions on how to administer the sacrament come from the Book of Mormon nearly verbatim (D&C 20:76; Moroni 4:1–2).[38]

The procedures for baptism also show the same heavy reliance on the Book of Mormon, as illustrated by a side-by-side reading (see table on p. 9).[39]

Other examples and more general similarities could be cited.[40] As Welch noted, in both the Doctrine and Covenants and the Book of Mormon, "leaders of the Church are told to keep a list of the names of all members, numbering those who have been baptized and to blot out the names of those expelled from the Church."[41]

Other similarities laid down in the Book of Mormon include leaders being "called" of God (see 1 Nephi

2:22; Jacob 2:3; Moroni 6:4; 7:2; 8:1); the purpose and conduct of meetings (see Moroni 6); the principle that buildings for worship should be simply decorated (see Mosiah 11:7–10; Mormon 8:37); strength from fasting together (see Alma 6:6; 4 Nephi 1:2; Moroni 6:5); singing together (see Alma 6:6; 4 Nephi 1:2; Moroni 6:5); preaching as led by the Holy Ghost (see Moroni 6:9); meeting one day every week (see Mosiah 18:25); and holding conferences (see Mosiah 2–5; Alma 5, 7).[42]

THE WHY

The similarities between Doctrine and Covenants 20 and texts in the Book of Mormon show the importance of the Book of Mormon to the Restoration. They also show that the Lord organized His Church in a similar way in each dispensation. The Lord told Joseph, "I will establish my Church yea even the church which was taught by my disciples in the days of old."[43] The points of contact between these texts show that He did just that.

Reading the Doctrine and Covenants and the Book of Mormon side by side shows that Joseph relied on the Book of Mormon in reestablishing the Church. This reliance on the Book of Mormon allowed him to make the Church similar to Christ's ancient Church in both the Old and New World. This is a reminder to modern readers of the Book of Mormon that Christ's Church today is remarkably similar to His Church in ancient times, and that God is indeed "unchangeable from all eternity to all eternity" (Moroni 8:18).

The organizing principles of Christ's Church did not originate in modern times. They are the same as they were in ancient times and are found in the Book of Mormon. As Welch has noted, the Book of Mormon's "ordinances and administrative principles are not just convenient or optional things to do in a would-be church of Christ. They provide the essential and integral organizational principles and framework upon which the Church of Christ is truly established."[44]

FURTHER READING

John W. Welch, "The Book of Mormon as the Keystone of Church Administration," *Religious Educator 12*, no. 2 (2011): 83–117, reprinted in *A Firm Foundation: Church Organization and Administration*, ed. David J. Whittaker and Arnold K. Garr (Salt Lake City and Provo, UT: Deseret Book and BYU Religious Studies Center, 2011), 15–58.

Scott H. Faulring, "An Examination of the 1829 'Articles of the Church of Christ' in Relation to Section 20 of the Doctrine and Covenants," *BYU Studies 43*, no. 4 (2004): 57–91.

John A. Tvedtnes, *The Most Correct Book: Insights from a Book of Mormon Scholar* (Salt Lake City, UT: Cornerstone Publishing, 1999), 291–316.

Scott H. Faulring, "The Book of Mormon: A Blueprint for Organizing the Church," *Journal of Book of Mormon Studies 7*, no. 1 (1998): 60–69, 71.

Doctrine and Covenants 20:72–74	**3 Nephi 11:23–26**
The person who is called of God . . .	Behold, ye
shall go down into the water	shall go down and stand in the water,
with the person who has presented himself or herself for baptism, and	and in my name shall ye baptize them. And now behold, these are the words which ye
shall say, calling him or her by name: Having been commissioned of Jesus Christ, I baptize you in the name of the Father, and of the Son, and of the Holy Ghost. Amen. Then shall he immerse him or her in the water, and come forth again out of the water.[45]	shall say, calling them by name, saying: Having authority given me of Jesus Christ, I baptize you in the name of the Father, and of the Son, and of the Holy Ghost. Amen. And then shall ye immerse them in the water, and come forth again out of the water.[46]

Alma

4

Why Was Korihor Cursed with Speechlessness?

"Now when Alma had said these words, Korihor was struck dumb, that he could not have utterance, according to the words of Alma." (Alma 30:5)

THE KNOW

At the end of the seventeenth year of the reign of the judges (approximately 75 BC), there arose an anti-Christ named Korihor, who "began to preach unto the people against the prophecies which had been spoken by the prophets, concerning the coming of Christ" (Alma 30:6). Mosiah's reforms determined that "there was no law against a man's belief; for it was strictly contrary to the commands of God that there should be a law which should bring men on to unequal grounds" (Alma 30:7). However, the situation with Korihor was unique. Much like the case involving Nehor (see Alma 1),[47] the problems involving Korihor's case raised important questions in Nephite jurisprudence.

> Did equality mean that a person could not only believe whatever he wanted but also say whatever he wanted? If a person did not believe that Jehovah was God, could he be punished for profaning the name of Jehovah or speaking insolently against him? In other words, did freedom of belief (or disbelief) entail freedom of expression specifically articulating or reflecting that belief? This important question had been neither contemplated nor addressed in the law originally established by King Mosiah a generation earlier.[48]

Because of the seriousness of these issues, Korihor was eventually brought to stand trial before Alma and the Nephite chief judge (see Alma 30:29). In the course of their verbal sparring, Korihor, who denied the existence of God,[49] demanded of Alma, "If thou wilt show me a sign, that I may be convinced that there is a God, yea, show unto me that he hath power, and then will I be convinced of the truth of thy words" (Alma 30:43).

Alma's response to this challenge was decisive: "Thou hast had signs enough; will ye tempt your God? . . . This will I give unto thee for a sign, that thou shalt be struck dumb, according to my words; and I say, that in the name of God, ye shall be struck dumb, that ye shall no more have utterance" (Alma 30:44, 49). Immediately after this, "Korihor was struck dumb, that he could not have utterance, according to the words of Alma" (Alma 30:50).

This clear display of divine power compelled Korihor into confessing his errors and humbling himself to some extent before God (see Alma 30:51–54). His confession, however, was incomplete, and his promise of future good behavior was evasive. Despite begging for the curse to be lifted, Korihor was dismissed and "cast out," or shunned, in Zarahemla. Thus reduced to begging, he soon went to Antionum and there, among the Zoramites, he was trampled to death (see Alma 30:56, 58–59).

THE WHY

Korihor was shown a sign because he challenged Alma to prove the existence of God: "If you wilt show me a sign, that I may be convinced that there is a God, yea, show unto me that he hath power" (Alma 30:43). Being willing to undergo an ordeal was often seen in ancient trials when the parties had reached a point of stalemate.[50] Being the defendant, Korihor would have seen any failure by Alma to produce compelling evidence as a vindication of Korihor's entire case.

That Korihor was cursed with speechlessness is shocking enough. That the curse remained upon him even after he acknowledged his error might be even more difficult for modern readers to tolerate. But the chief judge had asked Korihor to answer four questions following the cursing (Alma 30:51), and Korihor responded to only parts of them, and his response was halfhearted. Korihor then turned to Alma and asked him to pray to God to remove the curse (Alma 30:54).

Perhaps anticipating objections to this outcome among those who had admired Korihor, Alma explained that "if this curse should be taken from thee thou wouldst again lead away the hearts of this people; therefore, it shall be unto thee even as the Lord will" (Alma 30:55). With justifiable precautionary reasons, Alma declined to petition God to change this outcome, and the curse remained on Korihor.

Korihor's specific affliction also makes sense when read in the light of ancient religious and legal practices. As explained by John W. Welch, "The speechlessness of Korihor . . . was precisely the kind of sign or restraint that people in the ancient world expected a god to manifest in a judicial setting, especially in the face of false accusations."[51] This is confirmed by the recovery of numerous ancient spells that deliberately aimed to invoke the divine curse of speechlessness on revilers and blasphemers (which Korihor clearly was).

> While the use of such a curse may seem somewhat unusual or sensational to modern readers, the pronouncing of curses or spells was common in the ancient Mediterranean world, and their most frequent use was in fact in the legal sphere. In recent decades, more than one hundred Greek and Latin "binding spells" or curses have been recovered from tombs, temples, and especially wells near law courts. They were inscribed on small lead sheets, folded up and pierced through with a nail where they were placed in hopes that a deity from the underworld would receive them.[52]

Korihor's punishment, it appears, was in line with ancient legal procedure for cases such as this. Welch, therefore, sees this outcome as "a good example of divinely executed talionic justice: his curse befits his crime." Indeed, Korihor's punishment was fully suitable: "Because he had spoken evil, he was punished by being made unable to speak."[53]

With all this contextual information in mind, readers can appreciate Mormon's concluding thoughts on the pitiful outcome of Korihor's case. With his penchant for moralizing on important incidents in Nephite history, Mormon summarized, "And thus we see the end of him who perverteth the ways of the Lord; and thus we see that the devil will not support his children at the last day, but doth speedily drag them down to hell" (Alma 30:60).

FURTHER READING

John W. Welch, *The Legal Cases in the Book of Mormon* (Provo, UT: BYU Press and the Neal A. Maxwell Institute for Religious Scholarship, 2008), 273–300.

Gerald N. Lund, "An Anti-Christ in the Book of Mormon—The Face May Be Strange, but the Voice Is Familiar," in *The Book of Mormon: Alma, the Testimony of the Word*, ed. Monte S. Nyman and Charles D. Tate Jr. (Provo, UT: BYU Religious Studies Center, 1992), 107–128.

How is the Name *Zoram* Connected with Pride?

"Yea, and he also saw that their hearts were lifted up unto great boasting, in their pride." (Alma 31:25)

THE KNOW

It doesn't take long for readers of the Book of Mormon to come across the name *Zoram* (see 1 Nephi 4:35). Zoram was Laban's important servant, the official guard of the treasury that housed sacred records. He chose to become a free man by joining Lehi's family and journeying with them to their promised land.

Not much is revealed about Zoram except that he was a "true friend" to Nephi[54] and that, despite having been an outsider to Lehi's group, he became one of the seven founding tribal heads of Lehi's people.[55] Although Zoram was apparently a righteous man, some of his descendants caused problems for the Nephites,[56] and it seems that Mormon may have used a pun on Zoram's name to emphasize this point.

After analyzing the name *Zoram* in light of ancient Semitic languages, Matthew L. Bowen suggested that it "could . . . plausibly denote 'the one who is high/exalted' or 'He of the Exalted One'."[57] Although *Zoram* was likely meant to be a praiseworthy name, Nephite authors instead associated it with pride and vanity. Evidence for this connection can be found in a number of Book of Mormon passages, but it is perhaps most apparent in the story of Alma's mission to the Zoramites.

When Alma and his missionaries arrived in the land of Antionum, they found that the Zoramites had perverted the righteous traditions of the Nephites. This included the offering of vain prayers on an elevated platform called the Rameumptom (see Alma 31:21). From this platform, which was "high above the head" (Alma 31:13), the richly dressed Zoramites boasted about their supposedly holy and elected status. Notably, the term *ram* at the beginning of **Ram**eumptom is probably the same basic element in *Zo**ram***, which means "high" or "exalted" in Hebrew.[58] The dual presence of *ram* in this context makes the possibility of intentional wordplay especially likely.

An additional line of evidence can be seen in the fact that Alma, on two separate occasions, contrasted the Zoramites' prideful behavior with righteous themes of being "lifted up." In the first instance, Alma compared the hearts of the Zoramites, which were "**lifted up** unto great boasting, in their pride," with his own righteous prayer, in which he "**lifted up** his voice to heaven" (Alma 31:25–26; emphasis added). In the second instance, Alma counseled his son Shiblon to not be "**lifted up** unto pride" or "pray as the Zoramites do" (Alma 38:11, 13; emphasis added). He contrasted this with the promise that Shiblon would be "**lifted up** at the last day" if he remembered to put his "trust in God" (Alma 38:5; emphasis added).[59]

Yet further evidence for an intended wordplay comes from the way that the names *Cezoram* and *Seezoram* (each sharing the *-zoram* name element) are associated with being proud and lifted up. It was in the context of the assassination of a chief judge named Cezoram that the people "began to seek to get gain that they might be **lifted up** one above another" (Helaman 6:15–17; emphasis added). Likewise, it was during the reign of Seezoram that the Nephites were "**lifted . . . up** beyond that which is good" (Helaman 7:26; emphasis added). Thus, during the tenure of these leaders—each with *Zoram*-associated names—the Nephites began to be lifted up in wickedness much like the prideful Zoramites.[60]

THE WHY

In light of these and other textual evidences, it seems apparent that the Zoramites came to be associated with the "high" and "exalted" connotations of their own name. Yet, instead of being high or holy in a positive way, they were "lifted up" unto gross pride and vanity. In particular, the Zoramites became a symbol of the type of pride that stems from greed, materialism, worldly success, and a false sense of personal or collective righteousness.

Sadly, the same pride that led to the downfall of the Zoramites eventually infected the Nephite nation as a whole. In a letter to Moroni, Mormon declared, "Behold, the pride of this nation, or the people of the Nephites, hath proven their destruction except they should repent" (Moroni 8:27).[61] Latter-day readers should be especially concerned about this type of pride because it is also rampant in our own day. To modern readers, Moroni wrote,

> Behold, I speak unto you as if ye were present, and yet ye are not. But behold, Jesus Christ hath shown you unto me, and I know your doing. And I know that ye do walk in the pride of your hearts; and there are none save a few only who do not lift themselves up in the pride of their hearts, unto the wearing of very fine apparel, unto envying, and strifes, and malice, and persecutions, and all manner of iniquities; and your churches, yea, even every one, have become polluted because of the pride of your hearts. (Mormon 8:35–36; emphasis added)

It should be understood that ancient Hebrew authors didn't use puns only for amusement. Instead, the use of wordplay was often meant to help establish and reinforce important narrative themes. In this case, the story of the Zoramites, including the clever pun on the name *Zoram*, can help us remember the dangers of boasting in our own strength or being lifted up in the pride of our hearts. It was this type of pride that led the Zoramites and Nephites to destruction.[62] And if we are not careful, the same pride will lead societies in our own time to the same dismal fate.

President Dieter F. Uchtdorf taught, "Pride is the great sin of self-elevation. It is for so many a personal Rameumptom, a holy stand that justifies envy, greed, and vanity."[63] How can we ensure that we don't fall into the same prideful condition as the Zoramites and Nephites? One way is to deflect praise and glory away from ourselves and toward God. For example, when an individual called Jesus "Good Master," Jesus "said unto him, Why callest thou me good? there is none good but one, that is, God" (Matthew 19:17). Likewise, Ammon the Nephite missionary was once warned about boasting in himself, yet Ammon explained that he was actually giving all his praise to "the Most High God" (Alma 26:14).

As we keep our focus on the Lord's goodness and away from our own achievements, the Lord will help us see our true eternal value and worth as His children. In this condition, we won't feel we need to lift ourselves up in pride. This is because, like Shiblon, we can trust that the Lord will do all the lifting for us—meaning He will graciously lift us up unto eternal life—if we keep the commandments and faithfully "put [our] trust in God" (Alma 38:5).

FURTHER READING

Matthew L. Bowen, "'See That Ye Are Not Lifted Up': The Name Zoram and Its Paronomastic Pejoration," *Interpreter: A Journal of Mormon Scripture 19* (2016): 109–143.

Parrish Brady and Shon Hopkin, "The Zoramites and Costly Apparel: Symbolism and Irony," *Journal of the Book of Mormon and Other Restoration Scripture 22*, no. 1 (2013): 40–53.

Sherrie Mills Johnson, "The Zoramite Separation: A Sociological Perspective," *Journal of Book of Mormon Studies 14*, no. 1 (2005): 74–85, 129–30.

6

Why Did Mormon Emphasize the Zoramites' Costly Apparel?

"Behold, O my God, their costly apparel, and their ringlets, and their bracelets, and their ornaments of gold, and all their precious things . . . and behold, their hearts are set upon them." (Alma 31:28)

THE KNOW

When Alma and his missionary companions journeyed to Antionum,[64] they found that the dissenting Zoramites "did worship after a manner which Alma and his brethren had never beheld" (Alma 31:3). The Zoramites had constructed a "Rameumptom, which, being interpreted, is the holy stand" (Alma 31:21). Mormon described it as being "high above the head; and the top thereof would only admit one person" (Alma 31:13).[65]

From this elevated position, "they did offer up, every man, the selfsame prayer unto God" (Alma 31:22). This rote prayer repeatedly emphasized the Zoramites' superior status as elected and chosen by God (Alma 31:16–18). It condemned the religious traditions of the Nephites as "foolish" (Alma 31:17). And it boldly declared "that there shall be no Christ" (Alma 31:16).

In a stirring lament, Alma declared this practice of worship to be "gross wickedness" (Alma 31:26).[66] Interestingly, he also described specific features of the "costly apparel" of these affluent Zoramite worshipers: "their ringlets, and their bracelets, and their ornaments of gold, and all their precious things which they are ornamented with" (Alma 31:28).[67] Parrish Brady and Shon Hopkin noted that "the Rameumptom . . . provided a perfect opportunity for the individual at the top to show off his or her attire and adornments to the rest of his community."[68]

In the next chapter, readers learn that the poor among the Zoramites were "cast out of the synagogues because of the coarseness of their apparel" (Alma 32:2). When Alma and Amulek saw that these poor Zoramites were prepared to hear their message (Alma 32:6), they repeatedly "highlight[ed] the tension caused by outward appearances compared to a true state of being chosen."[69]

Mormon, who surely picked up on this theme in Alma's and Amulek's teachings, then wove in further references to clothing throughout the rest of the narrative about the Zoramites. For instance, after the poor class of Zoramites were expelled from Antionum, the people of Ammon took them in and "did clothe them" (Alma 35:9). At this point, the narrative tension is "reversed as the obedient and humble truly began to prosper in the land, while the proud and wicked began to lose their material blessings."[70]

Later, during the war chapters in the book of Alma, Mormon reported that the wicked Zoramites had allied themselves with the Lamanites, who "were naked, save it were a skin which was girded about their loins" (Alma 43:20).[71] Although the Zoramites themselves didn't dress like the Lamanites, they were clearly linked with the army that had inferior battle attire. In contrast, the Nephites—and by inference, any of the poor Zoramites who joined their army—were prepared with "breastplates and with arm-shields, yea, and also shields to defend their heads, and also they were dressed with thick clothing" (Alma 43:19).

When the Nephites defeated the Lamanites in battle, the leader of the Lamanite army denied that God had intervened and instead attributed their loss merely to the outward superiority of the Nephite armor (see Alma 44:9). This reasoning is noticeably similar to the Zoramites' perception that outward clothing was somehow a key factor in determining worthiness and righteousness.

Yet the Book of Mormon demonstrates that even after the Lamanites tried to copy the Nephite mode of armor, they still failed to attain a military advantage (see Alma 49:6–12).[72] As Brady and Hopkin concluded, "The ferocious battle between the Nephites and Lamanites in Alma 43–44 provides a stunning array of contrasting images, ironies, and tensions based on the metaphor of clothing, all of which are resolved by the end of the story line."[73]

THE WHY

This narrative demonstrates the tragedy that can befall any group that willfully removes itself from the true Church of Christ and then replaces authorized worship with its own worldly priorities. It seems that the Zoramites may have initially separated themselves from the Nephites for political and social reasons.[74] Yet what likely began as a movement to correct perceived injustices ended up severing them from the "true fold of God" and from the "true vine," which is Jesus Christ (1 Nephi 15:15).

Left to themselves, the Zoramites quickly perverted Lehi's foundational teaching about the Lord blessing and prospering the righteous (see 2 Nephi 1:9).[75] Instead of inward righteousness naturally yielding outward blessings, they assumed that outward appearances, wealth, and prestige could somehow yield inward righteousness, as well as God's favor. This led to their gaudy apparel, self-promoting forms of worship, and exclusionary rituals.[76]

As modern societies increase in wealth and prosperity, they become susceptible to a similar preoccupation with riches, appearance, and materialism. Elder Joe J. Christensen taught, "Our prosperity brings some real challenges because many are getting rich, more of us are waxing fat, and as a result of greed, selfishness, and overindulgence, we could [like the Zoramites] lose the Spirit and literally kick ourselves out of the Church."[77]

What is the solution to combat this growing tide of materialism? Alma taught the poor Zoramites, "it is well that ye are cast out of your synagogues" and that "because of your exceeding poverty . . . ye are necessarily brought to be humble" (Alma 32:12). Yet he emphasized that an even better solution than being compelled to be humble by outward circumstances is to freely choose humility and repentance because of an inward desire to follow Christ (Alma 32:14). Amulek then affirmed that if they were truly righteous, "their garments [which were then coarse and unseemly] should be made white through the blood of the Lamb" (Alma 34:36).

Brady and Hopkin found that the "story of the poorly adorned Zoramites contrasts powerfully with that of their well-clothed brethren, whose tale ends in complete humiliation and failure steeped in bitter irony, while Mormon demonstrates that in the end the obedient will indeed prosper in the land."[78] The poor Zoramites were cared for and clothed by the people of Ammon, they were clothed in protective battle attire by Captain Moroni, and in the end they would be clothed in white garments by Jesus Christ. All those who similarly repent and humble themselves before the Lord will be similarly blessed, protected, and "clothed with purity, yea, even with the robe of righteousness" (2 Nephi 9:14).

FURTHER READING

Matthew L. Bowen, "'See That Ye Are Not Lifted Up': The Name Zoram and Its Paronomastic Pejoration," *Interpreter: A Journal of Mormon Scripture 19* (2016): 109–143.

Parrish Brady and Shon Hopkin, "The Zoramites and Costly Apparel: Symbolism and Irony," *Journal of the Book of Mormon and Other Restoration Scripture 22*, no. 1 (2013): 40–53.

Sherrie Mills Johnson, "The Zoramite Separation: A Sociological Perspective," *Journal of Book of Mormon Studies 14*, no. 1 (2005): 74–85, 129–30.

7

Why Did Alma Repeat the Lord's Name Ten Times While in Prayer?

"And he lifted up his voice to heaven, and cried, saying: O, how long, O Lord, wilt thou suffer that thy servants shall dwell here below in the flesh, to behold such gross wickedness among the children of men?" (Alma 31:26)

THE KNOW

Despite repeated efforts by Alma, the social tensions among the Nephites continued to mount. Sometime before Korihor began to preach among the Nephites, "a people . . . had separated themselves from the Nephites and called themselves Zoramites" (Alma 30:59).

When Korihor was cast out, he sought refuge among the Zoramites, but they trampled him to death instead (see Alma 30:59).[79] It seems that this fate, however, alerted Alma to the way "the Zoramites were perverting the ways of the Lord" (Alma 31:1). The dissension of the Zoramites especially alarmed Alma and other Nephite leaders, because they feared "the Zoramites would enter into a correspondence with the Lamanites" (Alma 31:4).

Hugh Nibley explained, "It was felt that the hostility of the Zoramites and their proximity to the Lamanites posed a definite threat to Nephite security, and that was why Alma . . . gave top priority to the Zoramite mission."[80] Alma was firm in his conviction that "the preaching of the word had a great tendency to lead the people to do that which was just"; Alma maintained that it even had a "more powerful effect upon the minds of the people than the sword, or anything else" (Alma 31:5).[81] So Alma put together an all-star team of missionaries and "went . . . among the Zoramites, to preach unto them the word" (Alma 31:7).[82]

Given the threat level, Alma knew they would need the strength of the Lord to aid them in their mission. So all nine missionaries gathered, and Alma, no doubt acting in his role as high priest, invoked the Lord's name ten times (Alma 31:26, 30–35).[83]

According to Rachel Elior, professor of Jewish philosophy, the Jewish oral traditions in the Mishneh describe "the Day of Atonement service in detail, counting ten occasions on which the Ineffable Name was pronounced" by the high priest.[84] Significantly, "The Ineffable Name was enunciated during the confession in the formula 'O the Name,' and when the High Priest prayed for atonement, the Name was said in the formula of an oath or invocation: 'O by the Name . . . , atone, I pray you . . . '."[85]

This is reminiscent of Alma's formulaic repetition of "O Lord," followed variously by declarations of the people's sins and wickedness and petitions for strength in Christ, through whom atonement comes. For instance, Alma prayed, "*O Lord* God, how long wilt thou suffer that such wickedness and infidelity shall be among this people? *O Lord*, wilt thou give me strength, that I may bear with mine infirmities. For I am infirm, and such wickedness among this people doth pain my soul" (Alma 31:30; emphasis added).

Alma shifted in terminology from *O Lord* to *O God* while describing the Zoramite worship practices, attesting to the intentionality of Alma's tenfold repetition of *O Lord* in his high priestly prayer. John W. Welch reasoned that Alma consciously shifted terminology to avoid profaning the sacred name while describing apostate practices.[86] Moreover, "that shift is marked by the second occurrence of *O Lord*, which is the only instance of the expanded *O Lord God* in this text, indicating that the Lord Jehovah is indeed the true God."[87]

When he was finished, Alma "clapped his hands upon all them who were with him . . . [and] they were filled with the Holy Spirit" (Alma 31:36). BYU religion professor Alonzo Gaskill explained, "The laying on of hands is the standard symbol in antiquity for the transference of power, authority, or blessings," and hence, "Alma's act here . . . [was] an act that equipped his eight brethren for their work."[88]

THE WHY

Alma and his companions were in a desperate situation: they needed to restore cohesion to the Nephite society through gospel conversion, or there was a risk of war. Under these circumstances, Alma's repetition of the Lord's name ten times likely reflects his urgency to bring down the power of God upon him and his companions. For ancient Israelites, the number ten symbolized perfection or completion.[89] By calling on the Lord's name ten times, Alma called on His perfect power to aid them in their mission.

Alma's prayer also sought to calm and comfort his fellow missionaries at that desperate time. "O Lord, wilt thou comfort my soul, and . . . also my fellow laborers who are with me . . . yea, even all these wilt thou comfort, O Lord. Yea, wilt thou comfort their souls in Christ" (Alma 31:32). By invoking the name of the Lord ten times, Alma probably hoped to remind them of the Day of Atonement as well as the recently passed jubilee year and the associated joy and peace that followed.[90]

On the Day of Atonement, Alma and his companions, along with the rest of the Nephites, would have renewed covenants and remembered the Atonement of Christ. Not only would this reassure them of God's promises, it would make them eager to bring those same blessings and covenants to the Zoramites (see Alma 31:34). With everyone being one with God, all can then be united or reunited with each other. Most importantly, the atoning reconciliation with God would remind all of them that the souls of the Zoramites were precious to God, and thus should be equally precious to them (Alma 31:35).

Just as Alma did in their time of need, readers today can call upon the name of the Lord when seeking strength, power, comfort, and blessings.

FURTHER READING

Alonzo Gaskill, *Miracles of the Book of Mormon: A Guide to the Symbolic Messages* (Springville, UT: Cedar Fort, 2015), 252–256.

John W. Welch, "Counting to Ten," *Journal of Book of Mormon Studies 12*, no. 2 (2003): 42–57, 113–114.

Hugh Nibley, *Since Cumorah, The Collected Works of Hugh Nibley: Volume 7* (Salt Lake City and Provo, UT: Deseret Book and FARMS, 1988), 293–296.

Rodney Turner, "A Faith unto Salvation (Alma 31–33)," in *Book of Mormon, Part 2: Alma 30 to Moroni*, ed. Kent P. Jackson (Salt Lake City, UT: Deseret Book, 1988), 16–27.

Why Did Alma Use Creation Imagery in His Sermon on Faith?

"And thus, if ye will not nourish the word, looking forward with an eye of faith to the fruit thereof, ye can never pluck of the fruit of the tree of life." (Alma 32:40)

THE KNOW

When Alma taught the gospel to the Zoramites in the land of Antionum, he included a masterful discourse on the nature and nurture of faith, as recorded in Alma 32. This chapter is well-known to Latter-day Saints, who have cherished it for its presentation of eternal gospel truths.[91] This text is replete with profound teachings, such as Alma's insistence that "faith is not to have a perfect knowledge of things; therefore if ye have faith ye hope for things which are not seen, which are true" (Alma 32:21).

To illustrate how Alma 32 is "a learned text" and a "highly sophisticated sermon," biblical scholar David Bokovoy explored how this passage utilizes biblical elements in the development of its ideas. Specifically, "Alma's sermon on faith and the word contains a variety of advanced literary allusions to the Genesis creation accounts."[92] This would put Alma in good company, as Nephi and other Book of Mormon prophets likewise quoted or alluded to prophets such as Zenos and Isaiah throughout their writings and discourses.[93]

For instance, Bokovoy points out that "Alma's statement that a testimony is 'light' and that 'whatsoever is light, is good' clearly reflects God's initial act of creation in Genesis 1:3–4: 'And God said let there be light, and there was light. And God saw the light, that it was good.'"[94]

The use of *good* throughout Alma 32:28–39 to describe the seed reflects the language of Genesis 1, which speaks of God pronouncing the various stages of creation "good" (*tov* in Hebrew) upon their completion (Genesis 1:4, 10, 12, 18, 21, 25, 31).

Additionally, Alma prominently used the imagery of the tree of life bringing forth the fruit of eternal life: "But if ye will nourish the word, yea, nourish the tree as it beginneth to grow, by your faith with great diligence, and with patience, looking forward to the fruit thereof, it shall take root; and behold it shall be a tree springing up unto everlasting life" (Alma 32:41). This imagery finds close alignment with Genesis 2:9: "And out of the ground made the Lord God to grow every tree that is pleasant to the sight, and good for food; the tree of life also in the midst of the garden, and the tree of knowledge of good and evil."

What is remarkable is the wording in Alma 32, which uses the verb *spring* to describe the action of the tree of life after faith has taken root. As Bokovoy explained, the Hebrew verb used in Genesis 2:5 and 3:18 "translated in the KJV [as] 'to bring forth' literally means 'to spring up.' This Genesis passage seems to be echoed in Alma's invitation to his audience to nourish the seed so that it may become a tree 'springing up unto everlasting life' (Alma 32:41)."[95]

The multiple instances where Alma 32 draws from the creation imagery found in Genesis 1–3 "conceptually associates Alma's discourse on faith with the original purpose of human creation. In essence, Alma is saying we were created to cultivate faith."[96]

Jenny Webb likewise sees Alma 32 as "succinctly encapsulate[ing] the plan of salvation." She explained how "the process of becoming humble, seeking repentance, finding mercy, and enduring to the end was a pattern established by Adam and Eve" in the early chapters of Genesis.

These are precisely the main doctrinal points of Alma 32, which culminates—as Adam and Eve soon learned (see Moses 5:1–12)—with the fundamental truth that "redemption can only come through faith in Christ."[97]

THE WHY

Book of Mormon prophets understood how crucial it was to always return people to the foundational doctrines of the plan of salvation. While preaching in the apostate city of Ammonihah, Alma emphasized the plan of salvation—including the Creation, Fall, Atonement, and Resurrection—in a temple context that hearkened back to the narrative of Adam and Eve (see Alma 12). [98]

Similarly, Ammon taught King Lamoni "the plan of redemption, which was prepared from the foundation of the world" (Alma 18:39). Aaron likewise "did expound unto [Lamoni's father] the scriptures from the creation of Adam, laying the fall of man before him, and their carnal state and also the plan of redemption, which was prepared from the foundation of the world, through Christ, for all whosoever would believe on his name" (Alma 22:13).

What Alma apparently realized was that in order to call the apostate Zoramites to repentance, he would have to return to the very beginning—to the Creation. The Zoramites had separated themselves from the Nephites, leaving behind the temple in the land of Zarahemla in the process (Alma 31:2–3).

To win back the Zoramites, Alma drew from the Creation imagery of Genesis 1–3. This makes sense, as Genesis 1–3 is a text associated often with the temple, which explains why it could have easily been of service to Alma in his desire to revitalize their consciousness of the temple and its blessings.[99]

Individually, "readers . . . can appreciate this learned text at an even deeper level by identifying the ways in which Alma's discourse invokes biblical creation to encourage audiences to develop the type of faith that brings everlasting life."[100] Although Alma's words in Alma 32–33 were originally addressed to the Zoramites of his time, Alma 32 is still highly relevant for readers today. "Alma uses both forms of creation in the Bible's opening chapters . . . to encourage his audience to exercise faith in the present through reflections upon the primordial past. Using this process, Alma instructs his audience to develop the type of faith that leads to everlasting life, thus fulfilling the measure of their creation."[101]

FURTHER READING

David E. Bokovoy, "The Word and the Seed: The Theological Use of Biblical Creation in Alma 32," *Journal of Book of Mormon Studies 23* (2014): 1–21.

Jenny Webb, "It Is Well that Ye Are Cast Out: Alma 32 and Eden," in *An Experiment on the Word: Reading Alma 32*, ed. Adam S. Miller (Provo, UT: Neal A. Maxwell Institute for Religious Scholarship, 2014), 43–56.

9

What Were the Nephite Articles of Faith?

"Believe in the Son of God, that he will come to redeem his people, and that he shall suffer and die to atone for their sins." (Alma 33:22)

THE KNOW

Alma's discourse on faith as recorded in Alma 32 is continued in Alma 33 and culminates with a declaration of faith. This seven-part statement of belief in Christ focuses on the atoning mission of Jesus as God's divine son and builds on the foundation laid by Alma about the nature of faith and testimony in Alma 32.

Alma prefaced this concise declaration of his basic articles of faith by recalling the story of the Israelites wandering in the wilderness (see Alma 33:19–20). As recorded in Numbers 21, the children of Israel began to complain against Moses, resulting in God sending "fiery" or poisonous serpents to humble them. To cure those who were bitten by these serpents, Moses erected a bronze serpent on a pole so that "every one that is bitten, when he looketh upon it, shall live" (Numbers 21:9).

In retelling this account, Alma emphasized that the bronze serpent was a type of Christ (see Alma 33:19), and he likened its miraculous healing powers to the importance of having faith in the Savior's redeeming powers. "O my brethren, if ye could be healed by merely casting about your eyes that ye might be healed, would ye not behold quickly, or would ye rather harden your hearts in unbelief, and be slothful, that ye would not cast about your eyes, that ye might perish?" (Alma 33:21).

With this scriptural and rhetorical backdrop in place, Alma concluded his words to the multitude of poor Zoramites, who had come out of Antionium to hear his message (see Alma 32:4). Speaking clearly and powerfully, Alma invited them to "plant *this* word" (Alma 33:23; emphasis added) as the seed of faith in their hearts, namely:

> Believe in the Son of God, that he will come to redeem his people, and that he shall suffer and die to atone for their sins; and that he shall rise again from the dead, which shall bring to pass the resurrection, that all men shall stand before him, to be judged at the last and judgment day, according to their works. (Alma 33:22)

According to Alma, the articles of faith include: (1) belief in the Son of God; (2) belief that He will redeem His people; (3) belief that He will suffer and die; (4) belief that He will perform the Atonement; (5) belief that He will rise from the dead; (6) belief that He will bring to pass the resurrection of the dead; and (7) belief in the final judgment (see chart).[102] These articles of faith are consistent with what was stated by several other prophets who similarly clustered and emphasized many of these particular gospel teachings in their own sermons and writings throughout the Book of Mormon. Of those, Alma's statement on this occasion is the most complete and concise. [103]

THE WHY

As summarized by John W. Welch and J. Gregory Welch, "One may well imagine that Alma and his followers could have personally recited this declaration in explaining their faith, in much the same way as members of the church today use the Articles of Faith in stating the fundamental elements of their faith."[104] These articles of faith—what one might well call the core of the Nephite Creed[105]—constitute, according to Alma, specifically the "word" spoken of in Alma 32 that followers of Christ should plant in their hearts. "And now, my brethren, I desire that ye shall plant this word in your hearts, and as it beginneth to swell even so nourish it by your faith" (Alma 33:23).

This key point clarifies why Alma 32–33 should be read as one complete whole. Originally, these two chapters were not divided. The chapter division between these chapters might mislead some readers into thinking these two chapters are unrelated.

When these two chapters are read as one, Alma's logic and testimony becomes clear. If one is to develop faith by planting a seed, as explored in Alma 32, then one must understand what one is to believe in the first place, as clarified by the Nephite articles of faith in Alma 33. In other words, Alma first explains *how* to believe (see Alma 32) and then outlines *what* to believe (see Alma 33).

Each step in this sequence of true and growing faith is essential. Of ultimate importance for faithful believers is to realize that, because of the universal effect of Christ's personal suffering, death, and resurrection, every individual will stand re-embodied before the Lord, "to be judged at the last and judgment day, according to their works" (Alma 33:22). It is important to plant and nourish the right seed in order to grow the desired plant.

Thus it is significant that both Alma 32 and Alma 33 end with the imagery of the tree of life (see Alma 32:42; 33:23). This, for believers, is the supreme symbol of Christ's incarnation, love, eternal mission, and resurrection. It is also the overarching symbol that unites Alma's discourse on faith. As this word begins to swell and grow, Alma promises, "behold, it will become a tree, springing up in you unto everlasting life" (Alma 33:23). The seed of this tree that faithful men and women are to plant in their hearts is belief in the atoning Messiah and His mission, as captured and encapsulated by Alma in his articles of faith.

FURTHER READING

John W. Welch, "Ten Testimonies of Jesus Christ from the Book of Mormon," in *Doctrines of the Book of Mormon: The 1991 Sperry Symposium*, ed. Bruce A. Van Orden and Brent L. Top (Salt Lake City, UT: Deseret Book, 1992), 223–242.

Elaine Shaw Sorensen, "Seeds of Faith: A Follower's View of Alma 32," in *The Book of Mormon: Alma, the Testimony of the Word*, ed. Monte S. Nyman and Charles D. Tate Jr. (Provo, UT: BYU Religious Studies Center, 1992), 129–139.

Nephite Declaration of Faith

1 We "believe in the Son of God,

2 that he will come to redeem his people,

3 and that he shall suffer and die

4 to atone for their sins;

5 and that he shall rise again from the dead,

6 which shall bring to pass the resurrection,

7 that all men shall stand before him,
to be judged"

Alma 33:22

© Copyright Book of Mormon Central

10

Why Must There Be an Infinite and Eternal Sacrifice?

"There can be nothing which is short of an infinite atonement which will suffice for the sins of the world." (Alma 34:12)

THE KNOW

The Zoramites denied the need for the Atonement (Alma 31:16–17). Hence, when preaching in their city, Amulek stressed the importance of "a great and last sacrifice," a sacrifice that, he said, "must be an infinite and eternal sacrifice" (Alma 34:10). Amulek went to great lengths to explain what this sacrifice—the Atonement—was not: "not a sacrifice of man, neither of beast, neither of any manner of fowl; for it shall not be a human sacrifice" (Alma 34:10).[106] This clarification likely reflects specifically ways in which the Zoramites had "pervert[ed] the ways of the Lord in very many instances" (Alma 34:11).

Both the Israelites and Nephites lived among cultures that performed vicarious sacrifices for the sins of individuals and communities. Jewish studies lecturer Dr. Elaine Goodfriend explained, "Vicarious punishment—when the penalty for a wrong is suffered by someone other than the perpetrator—is found in" some Mesopotamian laws.[107] Ze'ev Falk noted, "in Babylonian and perhaps also in Hittite law, the principle of talion was applied not only to the criminal himself but also to his dependents."[108]

In contrast to some practices of their neighbors, Israelite law did not allow for vicarious punishment, but instead insisted that "every man shall be put to death for his own sin" (Deuteronomy 24:16; cf. Ezekiel 18:20).[109] Similarly, Amulek asked the Zoramites, "Now, if a man murdereth, behold will our law, which is just, take the life of his brother?" The answer was straightforward: "there is not any man that can sacrifice his own blood which will atone for the sins of another" (Alma 34:11).

In their divergent state of apostasy, the Zoramites may thus have adopted some kind of religious system that practiced vicarious blood sacrifices. Ancient Mesoamerica provides a potential cultural backdrop. There, "Maya kings voluntarily shed their blood as an offering on behalf of their people."[110] This came in the form of bloodletting, a practice where the king "used thorns, stingray spines, and obsidian blades to draw blood from" sensitive parts of the body.[111] While this is a different conceptual background than that of the Babylonian laws in the Old World, it was still a system wherein a man would "sacrifice his own blood" vicariously for his people.[112]

There were also other forms of sacrifice practiced in Mesoamerica. Brant A. Gardner explained, "Mesoamerican culture also offered parallel examples of animal sacrifices as part of their worship and even human sacrifice."[113] Mark Alan Wright reasoned, "The peoples of the Book of Mormon would have been familiar with the types of sacrifices being offered by their surrounding Mesoamerican neighbors, which often comprised burnt offerings of animals, such as deer or birds."[114]

Amulek explained, "For it is expedient that there should be a great and last sacrifice; yea, not a sacrifice of man, neither of beast, neither of any manner of fowl; for it shall not be a human sacrifice; but it must be an infinite and eternal sacrifice" (Alma 34:10). Wright noted, "It is significant that the three things that Amulek is expressly telling the apostate Zoramites not to sacrifice are the three most common things that were offered by Mesoamerican worshipers: human, beast, and fowl."[115]

Micah, an Israelite prophet, also apparently mentioned these three forms of sacrifice. He asked if he should "come before the Lord" with "burnt offerings, with calves of a year old?" He asked whether "the Lord [would] be pleased with thousands of rams" or if he should "give my firstborn for my transgression, the fruit of my body for the sin of my soul?" He answered, "the Lord require of thee, but to do justly, and to love mercy, and to walk humbly with thy God" (Micah 6:6–8).

Recognizing that birds were often given as "burnt offerings," Amulek seems to be reversing the order of Micah's rhetorical questions, after which he launches into an exposition of justice and mercy (see Alma 34:15–16). Amulek, therefore, seems to be employing a technique called Seidel's Law to invoke Micah's words and remind his Zoramite audience of the true purpose of animal sacrifice under the Mosaic law.[116]

THE WHY

As pious Israelites, the Nephites would have practiced various forms of animal sacrifice as part of the law of Moses. They did so, however, with an awareness that such sacrifices were only a type and a shadow, "every whit pointing to that great and last sacrifice . . . [of] the Son of God, yea, infinite and eternal" (Alma 34:14). In the Nephite view, "The law of Moses was as one grand prophecy of Christ inasmuch as it testified of the salvation to be obtained in and through his atoning blood."[117]

In their apostasy, the Zoramites rejected the infinite and eternal Atonement of Jesus Christ. Influenced by the surrounding culture, it seems they instead treated animal sacrifice as a full substitute for the Atonement, perhaps going so far as to have adopted other local sacrificial customs, such as bloodletting and human sacrifice.

Amulek, therefore, made it a point to explain that "there is not any man that can sacrifice his own blood" on behalf of others (Alma 34:11), as would be the case with even a king while bloodletting. Nor could any kind of blood sacrifice—beast, fowl, or human—cleanse the Zoramites, nor anyone else, of their sins (see Alma 34:11–14). Not only does logic work against the Zoramite view, but so did the symbolism of the law of Moses that prohibited the taking of one mortal life in punishment for the wrongdoing of another.

For any sacrifice to have eternal force and effect, that sacrifice must be more than mortal and temporary. Tad R. Callister explained:

> The word infinite, as used in this context, may refer to an atonement that is infinite in its scope and coverage, . . . to an atonement that simultaneously applies retroactively and prospectively, oblivious to constraints and measurements of time . . . to an atonement that applies to all God's creations, past, present, and future, and thus is infinite in its application, duration, and effect.[118]

"Nothing short of the shedding of the blood of both an infinite and perfect Being could"[119] accomplish this kind of ever-enduring and all-reaching sacrifice. "Accordingly," explained Callister, "the Atonement is 'infinite' because its source is 'infinite'."[120]

Just as certain particular cultural factors apparently had enticed the Zoramites to pervert the ways of the Lord, so also may social trends today entice some to twist, distort, wrest, or otherwise skew true gospel principles to fit fashionable ideologies. Avoiding these temptations requires both individuals and communities to do as Alma taught, and Amulek reiterated: "plant the word in your hearts, that ye may try the experiment of its goodness" (Alma 34:4). Only by letting the eternal word of Christ take root can the everlasting gospel then become the guiding light that enables all to see past the temporary fashions of the day.

FURTHER READING

Mark Alan Wright and Brant A. Gardner, "The Cultural Context of Nephite Apostasy," *Interpreter: A Journal of Mormon Scripture 1* (2012): 25–55.

Rodney Turner, "The Infinite Atonement of God," in *Book of Mormon, Part 2: Alma 30 to Moroni, Studies in Scripture: Volume 8* (Salt Lake City, UT: Deseret Book, 1988), 28–40.

11

Why Was the Zoramite Defection so Disastrous?

"And thus the Zoramites and the Lamanites began to make preparation for war against the people of Ammon, and also against the Nephites." (Alma 35:11)

THE KNOW

At the end of Alma 30, the Book of Mormon reports that a group of Nephite dissenters, known as the Zoramites,[121] was responsible for Korihor's death (see Alma 30:59).[122] After receiving news that "the Zoramites were perverting the ways of the Lord,"[123] Alma gathered an elite group of missionaries to "preach unto them the word of God" (Alma 31:1, 7). Yet despite efforts to reclaim these apostates, the Zoramites "cast out of the land" any who believed in the words of these missionaries (Alma 35:6). The Zoramite problem immediately escalated into a series of all-out wars in the land of Zarahemla.

When the people of Ammon took in these exiled believers, the Zoramites stirred up the Lamanites to anger, and together they made "preparations for war against the people of Ammon, and also against the Nephites" (Alma 35:11). While Alma and the Nephites "greatly feared that the Zoramites would enter into a correspondence with the Lamanites, and that it would be the means for a great loss on the part of the Nephites" (Alma 31:4), the Zoramites clearly felt threatened by the missionary effort of Alma and his companions, "for it did destroy their craft" (Alma 35:3). As Brant Gardner has aptly explained:

> Religion provided the formal underpinnings and outward presentation of the political structure. In the Zoramite case, the whole purpose and end of the religio-political structure was to maintain a social hierarchy. Egalitarian gospel principles, if adopted, would have destroyed the Zoramite social and political structure (not to mention their religion).[124]

Ultimately, the Zoramite defection was a major catalyst for seven years of armed conflicts between the Nephites and the Lamanites; the account of these is often called "the war chapters" in the book of Alma.[125] Those wars were led by Amalickiah and his brother Ammoron and their chief captains, all of whom were Zoramites (see Alma 48:5; 54:23).

Geographic clues in the Book of Mormon can help readers understand why this turn of events was so disastrous. The "Zoramites had gathered themselves together in a land which they called Antionum, which was east of the land of Zarahemla, which lay nearly bordering upon the seashore" (Alma 31:3). With a Lamanite presence already in the south and west (see

Alma 22:28), this development led to the Nephites being precariously situated between two major Lamanite forces (see map on p. 29).[126]

Such a state of affairs is not without scriptural precedent. During Lehi's time, Israelite leaders failed to heed the words of the prophets, and in consequence were geographically and politically caught between two major world powers—the Egyptians to the south and the Babylonians to the north. Acting out of fear, and in direct defiance of Jeremiah's prophetic counsel, King Zedekiah chose to ally Israel with Egypt.[127] This poor decision eventually led to a Babylonian invasion, which ended with Zedekiah being exiled into Babylon after the execution of his family.[128]

THE WHY

Like the kingdom of Judah in Lehi's time, the Nephites were vulnerable to enemy incursions on two separate fronts. Understanding the high stakes that were involved in this situation—meaning both the worth of souls among the Zoramites as well as the need to maintain them as military allies—can help readers better empathize with Alma's great sorrow after the Zoramites rejected his message:

> Now Alma, being grieved for the iniquity of his people, yea for the wars, and the bloodsheds, and the contentions which were among them; and having been to declare the word, or sent to declare the word, among all the people in every city; and seeing that the hearts of the people began to wax hard, and that they began to be offended because of the strictness of the word, his heart was exceedingly sorrowful. (Alma 35:15)

This episode also demonstrates the relationship between a society's political well-being and the degree of heed it gives to the words of the prophets. As the military conflicts unfold in the Book of Mormon, it becomes increasingly clear that the greatest threat to the Nephite civilization was internal wickedness and dissension, rather than external enemies. In an editorial comment, Mormon later emphasized that it was Captain Moroni's "first care to put an end to such contentions and dissensions among the people; for behold, this had been hitherto a cause of all their destruction" (Alma 51:16).

Such a pointed statement should serve as a strong word of caution to modern societies fraught with their own competing social interests and political intrigues. Social justice can be achieved only when all people respect one another's rights of religious liberty and mutual dignity, and Zion can be achieved only when faithful people unitedly heed the words of God's true messengers. Although missionary efforts are not always successful, modern readers are, like Alma, still obligated to "try the virtue of the word of God" because "it [has] a more powerful effect upon the minds of the people than the sword, or anything else" (Alma 31:5).

FURTHER READING

Parrish Brady and Shon Hopkin, "The Zoramites and Costly Apparel: Symbolism and Irony," *Journal of the Book of Mormon and Other Restoration Scripture 22*, no. 1 (2013): 40–53.

Brant A. Gardner, *Second Witness: Analytical & Contextual Commentary on the Book of Mormon,* 6 vols. (Salt Lake City, UT: Greg Kofford Books, 2007), 4:488–494.

Stephen D. Ricks and William Hamblin, eds., *Warfare in the Book of Mormon* (Salt Lake City and Provo, UT: Deseret Book and FARMS, 1990).

Lands of the Book of Mormon
by
James H. Fullmer
based on the scholarship of
John L. Sorenson in,
"Mormon's Map"
• - Settlement (town, village, city)
★ - Capital city
▲ - Mountain or Hill
ABC - Land
Ablom
hill Cumorah
MORON
Shem
hill Shim
Jordan
ANTUM
DESOLATION
Boaz
Teancum
Desolation
Mulek
Over into
Up to the land of...
Down to the land of...
Landscape terms
Bountiful
Mulek
Gid
Omner
Morianton
Jershon
Moroni
Lehi
BOUNTIFUL
Nephihah
hill Onidah
ANTIONUM
SIRON
Jared
Hagoth
Ammonihah
river Sidon
Noah
ZARAHEMLA
Melek
hill Amnihu
Wilderness of Hermounts
Zarahemla
Gideon
Judea
MINON
Cumeni
Manti
hill Riplah
Zeezrom
Antiparah
valley of Alma
Helam
AMULON
ISHMAEL
NEPHI
Jerusalem
waters of Mormon
Mormon
MIDDONI
Ani-Anti
Nephi
mount Antipas
Shilom
Lehi
SHEMLON
FIRST INHERITANCE

12

Why Is the Presence of Chiasmus in the Book of Mormon Significant?

"And now it shall come to pass, that whosoever shall not take upon him the name of Christ must be called by some other name; therefore, he findeth himself on the left hand of God. . . I say unto you . . . that ye are not found on the left hand of God, but that ye hear and know the voice by which ye shall be called, and also, the name by which he shall call you." (Mosiah 5:10–12)

THE KNOW

The discovery of chiasmus in the Book of Mormon is one of the most significant scholarly contributions to understanding and appreciating the Nephite record.[129] John W. Welch discovered the presence of chiasmus on August 16, 1967, while on his mission in Germany,[130] and his publications since that time have steadily thrown much light on this matter.[131]

Chiasmus is a structural form that has been used in both poetry and prose for thousands of years in a variety of cultures and languages. "Chiasmus can be defined most simply as an inverted type of parallelism."[132] *Parallelism* is a literary technique where "the component elements of one line correspond directly to those of the other in a one-to-one relationship."[133] For example, a verse in the Psalms reads:

As a father has *compassion* on his children,
so the Lord has *compassion* on those who fear him" (Psalm 103:13 NIV).

Parallelisms and chiasms are pervasive literary features of ancient Hebrew texts.

Chiasmus (named after the Greek letter *chi*, χ) is a form of inverted parallelism where the elements are ordered and then repeated in reverse (a-b-b-a). Chiasms can be simple or complex, and can be structured along both vocabulary or thematic elements. A scripture well-known to Latter-day Saints is a good example of a simple chiasm:

(A) And he shall turn the heart of the fathers
  (B) to the children,
  (B') and the heart of the children
(A') to their fathers. (Malachi 4:6)

Chiasmus (as well as other forms of parallelism) appears throughout the entirety of the Book of Mormon, both in prose and poetic passages.[134] One of the chiastic passages Welch initially discovered occurs in King Benjamin's speech.[135] In this passage, "King Benjamin is interested in contrasting those who remember the covenantal name with those who do not, or contrasting those who know the voice by which they will be called with those who must be called by some other name."[136]

(A) And now it shall come to pass, that whosoever shall not take upon him the *name of Christ*
(B) must be *called* by some other name;
(C) therefore, he findeth himself on the *left hand of God*.
(D) And I would that ye should *remember* also, that this is the name that I said I should give unto you
(E) that never should be *blotted out*,
(F) except it be through *transgression*
(F') therefore, take heed that ye do not *transgress*,
(E') that the name be not *blotted out* of your hearts.
(D') I say unto you, I would that ye should *remember* to retain the name written always in your hearts,
(C') that ye are not found on the *left hand of God*, but that ye hear and know the
(B') voice by which ye shall be *called*, and also,
(A') the *name* by which he shall call you. (Mosiah 5:10–12)

Not only individual verses but whole chapters and even entire books in the Book of Mormon are structured as chiasms.[137] For example, Alma 36 is structured as an intricate chiasm with Jesus Christ as its central focus.[138]

THE WHY

Understanding the use of chiasmus in the Book of Mormon can benefit readers in many ways. First, chiasmus in the Book of Mormon demonstrates that the text is quite orderly, complex, rich, and aesthetically pleasing. "The presence of chiasmus in the English text of the Book of Mormon supplies significant evidence that the book is more beautiful than people had previously thought."[139] It deserves attention for its literary qualities in addition to its doctrinal significance.

Likewise, chiasms in the Book of Mormon show the training, care, diligence, and authorial intent of the writers. They focus readers' attention on specific narrative and doctrinal points of emphasis in skillful and fulfilling ways. They provide evidence "that these texts were purposefully written to center on certain key ideas and turning points."[140] They help attentive readers follow the structure and interrelatedness of carefully developed passages.

Chiasmus in the Book of Mormon also provides a glimpse into Nephite society and culture, and it reveals close affinities with ancient Israelite and Maya poetic and authorial methods.[141] "There can be no question that chiasmus was used heavily in ancient Israelite writing at and around the time of Lehi," Welch explained.

Chiasmus may thus be seen as evidence for the Book of Mormon's antiquity. After all, "if the Book of Mormon did not contain chiasmus, one would undoubtedly count this against the book as a glaring deficiency." The fact that so many deftly rendered chiasms are found in the Book of Mormon, therefore, lends support for the book's claim of Israelite and ancient American origins.[142]

Several studies have shown it is highly unlikely that chiasmus appears in the Book of Mormon by chance.[143] While all chiasms are not created equal, many Book of Mormon chiasms are highly deliberate and skillfully executed. Therefore, "As evidence of Book of Mormon authorship, the discovery of biblical-style chiasms in the Book of Mormon strongly tends to reduce the probability that Joseph Smith or any of his contemporaries could have written the book."[144] Even on the unlikely chance that they had heard of chiasmus,[145] there still remained the inordinate challenge to compose these well-constructed chiastic passages, without the use of any notes, during the rapid dictation process in the spring of 1829.[146]

As explained by Welch in his groundbreaking 1969 publication, "Since the Book of Mormon contains numerous chiasms, it thus becomes logical to consider the book a product of the ancient world and to judge its literary qualities accordingly."[147] Chiasmus in the Book of Mormon may, therefore, help readers more deeply appreciate the literary brilliance of the book while simultaneously increasing confidence in its authenticity as an ancient text and elevating faith in its concerted testimony of Jesus Christ, who is without doubt the central figure of this sacred record.

FURTHER READING

John W. Welch, "What Does Chiasmus in the Book of Mormon Prove?" in *Book of Mormon Authorship Revisited: The Evidence for Ancient Origins*, ed. Noel B. Reynolds (Provo, UT: FARMS, 1997), 199–224.

Boyd F. Edwards and W. Farrell Edwards, "Does Chiasmus Appear in the Book of Mormon by Chance?" *BYU Studies 43*, no. 2 (2004): 103–130.

Boyd F. Edwards and W. Farrell Edwards, "When Are Chiasms Admissible as Evidence?" *BYU Studies Quarterly 49*, no. 4 (2010): 131–154.

13

Why Was Alma Converted?

"Yea, I say unto you, my son, that there could be nothing so exquisite and so bitter as were my pains. Yea, and again I say unto you, my son, that on the other hand, there can be nothing so exquisite and sweet as was my joy." (Alma 36:21)

THE KNOW

No other event had a greater impact on Alma's life than the transformative three days he spent racked with torment after being rebuked by an angel.[148] The themes of that experience permeate his sermons,[149] and at least three different accounts of it survive in the Book of Mormon (see Mosiah 27; Alma 36, 38). Detailed comparison of these accounts strongly suggests that all three are, in significant part, first-person accounts from Alma himself.[150] Of these accounts, Alma 36 stands out as the most complete and well composed.

John W. Welch noted, "The abrupt antithetical parallelisms" of Alma's original words in Mosiah 27:29–30 "have been rearranged into one masterfully crafted chiastic composition in Alma 36."[151] This repurposing of the spontaneous phrases spoken by the young Alma as he retold the story of his conversion to his son Helaman a number of years later offers strong evidence that the structure of Alma 36 was deliberate and purposeful.

Welch, who discovered chiasmus in the Book of Mormon as a missionary in Germany in 1967,[152] first published the chiastic structure of Alma 36 in 1969 (see chart on p. 33).[153] Since that time, the structure of Alma 36 has received continued attention and analysis, detailing not only the overall chiasm, but also laying out several substructures.[154]

Of interpretive importance, careful observers have found that the climax of a strong chiastic structure is usually found at its midpoint. As Nils Lund set forth, "The centre is always the turning point. . . . At the centre there is often a change in the trend of thought, and an antithetic idea is introduced, [which is a] shift at the centre. . . . Thus, the climax is at the centre, not at the end, where we should expect it."[155] This feature of a deliberately composed chiasm, clearly present in Alma 36, helps readers discern the key point of the whole passage.

Though some have questioned the absolute chiasticity of the account,[156] both criteria-based evaluations and statistical analyses further indicate that the chiastic structure in Alma 36 is unlikely to be an accident.[157] Welch concluded, "After evaluating hundreds of proposed chiasms in a wide variety of lengthy texts, I have found that only a few texts unmistakably rate as planned, successful chiasms. Alma 36 is one of the best."[158]

Chiasmus in Alma 36

My son give ear to ***my words*** (v. 1)

Keep the commandments and ye shall ***prosper in the land*** (v. 1)

Do as I have done (v. 2)

Remember the captivity of our fathers (v. 2)

They were in ***bondage*** (v. 2)

He surely did ***deliver*** them (v. 2)

Trust in God (v. 3)

Supported in ***trials, troubles, and afflictions*** (v. 3)

Lifted up at the ***last day*** (v. 3)

I ***know*** this not of myself but ***of God*** (v. 4)

Born of God (v. 5)

I sought to destroy the church (vv. 6–9)

My limbs were paralyzed (v. 10)

Fear of being in the ***presence of God*** (vv. 14–15)

Pains of a damned soul (v. 16)

Harrowed up by the memory of sins (v. 17)

I remembered ***Jesus Christ, a son of God*** (v. 17)

I cried, ***Jesus Christ, son of God*** (v. 18)

Harrowed by the memory of sins no more (v. 19)

Joy as exceeding as was the ***pain*** (v. 20)

Long to be in the ***presence of God*** (v. 22)

My limbs received strength again (v. 23)

I labored to bring souls to repentance (v. 24)

Born of God (v. 26)

Therefore ***my knowledge*** is ***of God*** (v. 26)

Supported under ***trials, troubles, and afflictions*** (v. 26)

Trust in him (v. 27)

He will ***deliver*** me (v. 27)

And ***raise me up at the last day*** (v. 28)

As God brought our fathers out of ***bondage*** and captivity (vv. 28–29)

Retain a ***remembrance of their captivity*** (v. 29)

Know ***as I do*** know (v. 30)

Keep the commandments and ye shall ***prosper in the land*** (v. 30)

This according to his ***word*** (v. 30)

© Copyright Book of Mormon Central

THE WHY

Producing a well-written, elegant chiasm is challenging and difficult. According to Welch, "If an author uses chiasmus mechanically, it can produce rigid, stilted writing (a poor result from an author misusing or poorly implementing any artistic device)."[159] This is not the case with Alma 36, which smoothly transitions from one point to the next until reaching its climatic center point and then effortlessly unwinding down the same path.[160]

> Alma … does not simply stick a list of ideas together in one order and then awkwardly and slavishly retrace his steps through that list in the opposite order. His work has the markings of a skillful, painstaking writer, one completely comfortable with using this difficult mode of expression well.[161]

Grant Hardy noted that Alma's "account moves from public to personal to private and then back again."[162] Throughout the whole account, Hardy noticed the remarkable detail that "God is present in every phase." Hardy thus thought "the order and purposeful design of Alma 36 suggests a world in which God . . . is in control, where the lives of individuals fit into some overarching . . . plan."[163]

Central to that plan is Jesus Christ and His atoning power. While Alma on some occasions placed emphasis on the angelic encounter,[164] it was not the appearance of the angel that caused Alma's change of heart. Indeed, the chiastic structure in Alma 36 eloquently and effectively guides the reader most centrally and emphatically toward Alma's direct, personal encounter with Jesus Christ. Welch noted:

> The structure of the chapter powerfully communicates Alma's personal experience, for the central turning point of his conversion came precisely when he called upon the name of Jesus Christ and asked for mercy. Nothing was more important than this in Alma's conversion—neither the appearance of the angel, nor the prayers of his father and the priests. Just as this was the turning point of Alma's life, he makes it the center of this magnificent composition.[165]

The point of this remarkable literary structure underscores the dramatic turnaround in Alma's life, answering most assuredly the question, *Why was Alma converted?* That conversion occurred when Alma remembered his father speaking of "the coming of one Jesus Christ, a Son of God, to atone for the sins of the world." His father's declaration caused Alma to call out, "O Jesus, thou Son of God, have mercy on me, who am in the gall of bitterness, and am encircled about the by everlasting chains of death" (Alma 36:17–18).

From that turning point, the chiastic pattern takes on what Noel B. Reynolds termed a "reverse polarity between the parallel units of text."[166] While once "harrowed up by the memory of [his] many sins" (Alma 36:17), he was "harrowed up by the memory of [his] sins no more" (Alma 36:19). Where once there were "the pains of a damned soul" (Alma 36:16), there was now a "soul . . . filled with joy as exceeding as was [the] pain!" (Alma 36:20).

The reversal here proceeds out from the central point until Alma's effort "to destroy the church of God" (Alma 36:6) is juxtaposed with his new, unceasing effort to "bring souls unto repentance" (Alma 36:24). From this reversal, Welch reasoned, "The message is clear: Christ's atonement and man's responding sacrifice of a broken heart and willing mind are central to receiving forgiveness from God."[167]

It is hard to imagine any literary form being used more effectively than this extended chiasm to articulate the transformative effect of the Atonement in the lives of individuals all around the world. Many have felt as Alma felt. As a result, Alma 36 naturally and powerfully resonates with readers everywhere.[168] After reading Alma 36 with Welch, prominent biblical scholar David Noel Freedman remarked, "Mormons are very lucky. Their book is very beautiful."[169] After extensive study of Alma 36, Welch concluded:

> This text ranks as one of the best uses of chiasmus one can imagine. It merits high acclaim and recognition. Despite its complexity, the meaning of the chapter is both simple and profound. Alma's words are both inspired and inspiring, religious and

literary, historical and timeless, clear yet complex—a text that deserves to be pondered for years to come.[170]

FURTHER READING

John W. Welch, "A Masterpiece: Alma 36," in *Rediscovering the Book of Mormon: Insights You May Have Missed Before*, ed. John L. Sorenson and Melvin J. Thorne (Salt Lake City and Provo, UT: Deseret Book and FARMS, 1991), 114–131.

John W. Welch, "Chiasmus in Alma 36," *FARMS Preliminary Report* (1989).

John W. Welch, "Chiasmus in the Book of Mormon," in *Book of Mormon Authorship: New Light on Ancient Origins*, ed. Noel B. Reynolds (Provo, UT: BYU Religious Studies Center, 1982), 33–52.

14

Why Was a Stone Used as an Aid in Translating the Book of Mormon?

"And the Lord said: I will prepare unto my servant Gazelem, a stone, which shall shine forth in darkness unto light." (Alma 37:23)

THE KNOW

Alma's words to his son Helaman, as recorded in Alma 37, contain the somewhat perplexing reference to Gazelem,[171] apparently an unspecified servant who should perform a special work for God. Alma prophesied, "And the Lord said: I will prepare unto my servant Gazelem, a stone, which shall shine forth in darkness unto light, that I may discover unto my people who serve me, that I may discover unto them the works of their brethren, yea, their secret works, their works of darkness, and their wickedness and abominations" (Alma 37:23).

As this is the only reference to Gazelem in the Book of Mormon, readers are somewhat at a loss as to whom this passage refers or what it is talking about. Joseph Fielding McConkie and Robert L. Millet have asked, "Is Gazelem the seer stone or the servant? It is difficult to tell from the passage and depends very much on the placement of a comma in the sentence. Perhaps it could refer to both. . . . Though this name or title of Gazelem may be used in regard to any seer who utilizes seer stones, it seems in this instance to be a direct reference to Joseph Smith the Prophet."[172]

While Gazelem is perhaps the name of the individual using the stone prepared by God, the issue is far from settled. Royal Skousen has traced Mormon interpretations of this passage to the lifetime of Joseph Smith himself, where both the Prophet Joseph Smith and the stone were variously identified as Gazelem.[173]

Joseph Smith would easily fit the identity of Gazelem. As several historians and scholars have discussed, Joseph used both the Nephite interpreters (later called the "Urim and Thummim") that were discovered with the plates and his individual seer stone in the translation of the Book of Mormon.[174] The topic is also discussed in official Church publications, even by General Authorities who have written on this topic.[175]

Unfortunately, the historical sources on Joseph's use of these instruments during the translation are sometimes contradictory or ambiguous. For example, even eyewitness participants in the translation of the Book of Mormon sometimes confused the terminology in their descriptions of the event. "These two instruments—the interpreters and the seer stone—were apparently interchangeable and worked in much the same way such that, in the course of time, Joseph Smith and his associates often used the term 'Urim and Thummim' to refer to the single stone as well as the interpreters."[176]

Despite these ambiguities, it is clear that Joseph utilized sacred instruments—in this case seer stones that he found or the interpreters, which Moroni gave him—that had been prepared by the Lord for the purpose of translating the Book of Mormon. It cannot be disputed that the Prophet did in fact utilize divinely prepared instruments as mediums for inspiration in the translation of the Book of Mormon and some early revelations (such as D&C 3, 6, 7, 11, 14, 17).

THE WHY

Many people today have come to outright dismiss the existence of miracles or supernatural forces. Claims that cannot be explained scientifically or rationally are often treated as mere superstition, especially in the secular West. It's therefore understandable why many have a hard time accepting that the Lord would prepare seemingly "magical" or wondrous stones for Joseph Smith to use in translating the Book of Mormon.

Joseph Smith's use of such stones needs to be situated in its historical and theological context. The practice of using stones or glass as media to receive divine revelation is a documented practice in many modern and ancient cultures, including among the ancient Israelites and the ancient (as well as modern) Maya.[177] In Joseph Smith's own day, so-called "folk magic" was practiced in rural parts of the United States. This included the use of stones, rods, and other instruments to communicate with spirits, find hidden treasures protected by supernatural guardians, look for lost objects, or even discover sources of water.[178] The Smith family participated in this culture, and Joseph himself had a reputation as a village seer even before he retrieved and translated the plates.[179]

It is crucial to keep in mind, however, that there still exists much debate among anthropologists and historians about how to properly define "magic" (as opposed to the more conventional "religion"), as practiced by both ancient and modern people. The men and women who participated in these supernatural practices typically did not find them to be in conflict with their own Christian faith. After all, prophets in both the Old and New Testament, including Moses and Elijah, Peter and Paul, and of course Jesus Himself, possessed powers or instruments that were used to perform great wonders.[180] Well-known is the biblical practice of casting lots, which had a clear supernatural dimension (cf. 1 Nephi 3:11).[181]

Claims of "a magic world view" having heavily influenced Joseph Smith should therefore be approached very cautiously.[182] Legitimate questions still remain as to just how involved Joseph actually was in this type of folk culture and how much it actually impacted him.[183] Nevertheless, Latter-day Saint theology allows for the Lord to communicate to His children through culturally embedded methods (see 2 Nephi 31:3; D&C 1:14).[184] Furthermore, the Book of Mormon itself speaks specifically about the Lord preparing "means" (physical instruments) through which He would channel His power, including sacred stones that would aid seers in translating ancient records by the gift and power of God (Mosiah 8).[185]

We may ultimately never fully understand the nature or process of the Book of Mormon's translation, including why the Lord prepared sacred stones for Joseph the Seer to utilize. Nevertheless, the fact remains that Joseph consistently and repeatedly testified, and many witnesses close to the process confirmed, that he translated the plates by the gift and power of God. A sound understanding of the history behind the translation of the Book of Mormon can answer some questions or otherwise be faith promoting in some regards.[186] A spiritual testimony of Joseph Smith's calling as a seer, including a burning testimony of the divine nature of the Book of Mormon, however, comes only from God, through the power of the Holy Ghost.

FURTHER READING

Saints: The Story of the Church of Jesus Christ in the Latter Days, Volume 1: The Standard of Truth, 1815–1846 (Salt Lake City, UT: The Church of Jesus Christ of Latter-day Saints, 2018), 31–64.

Richard E. Turley Jr., Robin S. Jensen, and Mark Ashurst-McGee, "Joseph the Seer," *Ensign*, October 2015, 49–54.

Michael Hubbard MacKay and Gerrit J. Dirkmaat, *From Darkness unto Light: Joseph Smith's Translation and Publication of the Book of Mormon* (Provo and Salt Lake City, UT: BYU Religious Studies Center and Deseret Book, 2015).

Roger Nicholson, "The Spectacles, the Stone, the Hat, and the Book: A Twenty-first Century Believer's View of the Book of Mormon Translation," *Interpreter: A Journal of Mormon Scripture 5* (2013): 121–190.

Did Alma Counsel His Sons During the Feast of the Passover?

"And now my son, Shiblon, I would that ye should remember, that as much as ye shall put your trust in God even so much ye shall be delivered out of your trials, and your troubles, and your afflictions, and ye shall be lifted up at the last day." (Alma 38:5)

THE KNOW

After their ministry among the Zoramites, Alma "caused that his sons should be gathered together, that he might give unto them every one his charge, separately, concerning the things pertaining unto righteousness" (Alma 35:16). On this occasion, Alma's exhortation to his sons may be linked to an ancient Jewish practice associated with the Passover. Gordon C. Thomasson and John W. Welch related:

> According to traditions at least as early as the time of Christ and probably earlier, after gathering his family the father then instructed his sons and answered their questions. His words were not fixed but were "to fit the knowledge and understanding of the child" and were supposed "to spell out the sequence of sin, suffering, repentance, and redemption."[187]

Although it is unknown how early this particular practice began, the Feast of the Passover was long celebrated as an important time for family gatherings, eating of the pascal lamb, and remembering the traditional texts associated with God's deliverance of Israel from servitude in Egypt. Furthermore, it is important to note that scholars understand this Passover ceremony developed over time from earlier wisdom traditions. It is possible that Alma's exhortation to his sons could have thematically descended from early strains of these same interweaving wisdom traditions.[188]

What makes the link between Alma's words to his three sons and this Passover tradition particularly striking is that, according to some Jewish customs, the sons asking questions often played out different roles and characters.[189]

The first was a wise son, who quoted from Deuteronomy, asking: "What mean the testimonies, and the statutes, and the judgments, which the Lord our God hath commanded you?" (Deuteronomy 6:7). Alma's eldest son, Helaman, clearly stands out as the favored or wise son, and it is notable that in addressing him, Alma "mentions 'wisdom' at least eight times in Alma 37."[190]

The second was a wicked son, who quoted from Exodus, asking: "What mean ye by this service?" (Exodus 12:26). Thomasson and Welch explained:

> This son is depicted in the Jewish literature as one guilty of social crimes, who had excluded himself from the community, and believed in false doctrines. According to Jewish practice, he is to be told, in a manner that will "set his teeth on edge," that he will be punished for his own sins.[191]

Obviously, this description applies fittingly to Corianton, who struggled with moral transgressions and found several false doctrines attractive.[192]

Finally, a third son would ask, "What is this?" (Exodus 13:14). "Israelite tradition said that the uninformed son who asked this question needed to be taught the law and given preventative instruction to keep him well away from any risk of breaking the law."[193] Along these lines, Alma informatively warned Shiblon concerning the problems of pride, overbearance, unbridled passions, idleness, and the apostate practices of the Zoramites.[194]

Although it is uncertain if Alma's exhortation to his sons directly coincided with the Nephite observance of Passover, the method and content of his instruction is certainly reminiscent of its themes, including suffering in captivity and affliction, crying for deliverance, the appearance of a powerful angel, and deliverance from darkness and bitter pains.[195] The timing is also appropriate: just as Israelites returned home to celebrate Passover, Alma and his missionary team had just returned to Zarahelma, having completed their efforts to bring the Zoramites in Antionum back to the faith (Alma 35:14).

THE WHY

The way that Alma's sermons tie into the ancient traditions of the Jewish Passover provides evidence of his conscious awareness of and adherence to the righteous "traditions of [his] fathers" (Alma 3:11). Moreover, recognizing the sacred, ceremonial nature of these fatherly moments of heartfelt testimony, instruction, and exhortation may help explain the remarkable sophistication and elegance of the literary and rhetorical forms used by Alma on this occasion.[196]

The Passover tradition was intended to help Israel remember the Lord's hand in leading them out of Egyptian oppression. Likewise, Alma's words to his sons were filled with exhortations to remember sacred things. For example, Alma's chiastic discourse to Helaman began precisely with the very admonition to "do as I have done, in remembering the captivity of our fathers" (Alma 36:2) and ended similarly by reaffirming that Alma had "always retained in remembrance their captivity" (Alma 36:29). In this context, Alma even specifically mentioned the Israelite exodus when stating, "I will praise him forever, for he has brought our fathers out of Egypt" (Alma 36:28). Alma's words and commandments to his sons were thus highly suitable for the time of Passover. Speaking on such an occasion would only have enhanced the serious momentousness of that occasion.

Similar to the various exodus narratives among the Nephites,[197] the Church today has its own parallels to ancient Israel's miraculous deliverance. President Russell M. Nelson taught, "Both groups shared many miracles that are memorialized annually. The celebration of Passover relates to the travels of the ancient Israelites. And each July we repeat legendary stories of our pioneers."[198] Such observances in our day can help readers of the scriptures appreciate and relate to the solemn impact of the words Alma spoke centuries ago.

Like Alma's sons, modern members of the house of Israel of all kinds have a duty to "always retain in remembrance" the hand of the Lord in their own divine deliverance (Alma 36:29).

FURTHER READING

Gordon C. Thomasson and John W. Welch, "The Sons of the Passover," in *Reexploring the Book of Mormon: A Decade of New Research* (Provo UT: FARMS, 1992), 196–198.

16

Why Was Corianton's Sin so Serious?

"Know ye not, my son, that these things are an abomination in the sight of the Lord; yea, most abominable above all sins save it be the shedding of innocent blood or denying the Holy Ghost?" (Alma 39:5)

THE KNOW

Rather striking in Alma's words to his young-adult son Corianton (Alma 39–42) is the uncompromising denouncement of sexual sins. "Thou didst do that which was grievous unto me," Alma lamented to his then wayward son. "For thou didst forsake the ministry, and did go over into the land of Siron among the borders of the Lamanites, after the harlot Isabel" (Alma 39:3). The implications are clear: Corianton had committed grievous sexual sins.

Readers of Alma 39:5 have understandably identified sexual transgression as a "sin next to murder."[199] Seeing here the infamy of sexual transgression comes directly from Alma's rhetorical question to Corianton: "Know ye not, my son, that these things are an abomination in the sight of the Lord; yea, most abominable above all sins save it be the shedding of innocent blood or denying the Holy Ghost?" (Alma 39:5)

Certainly all sexual transgressions are serious matters that should be entirely avoided and quickly repented of if committed, and indeed some sexual sins are more serious than others.[200] Reading Alma 39 more closely reveals some additional insights regarding Corianton's behaviors.

As pointed out by Michael R. Ash and B. W. Jorgensen, for instance, it appears Corianton's sin was more than just sexual immorality.[201] They argue that Corianton's sin was a composite of several elements, specifically sexual immorality by a priesthood leader that caused him to abandon his ministry and therefore neglect the spiritual needs of his flock, thereby leading them into apostasy. In effect, Corianton metaphorically "murdered" the testimonies of those he was commissioned to bring unto Christ when he was lured away by Isabel (cf. Alma 36:14).

This understanding of Corianton's particular situation is strengthened by the fact that in Alma 39:5, Alma speaks of "*these things*" (plural) being "an abomination in the sight of the Lord." Apparently "these things" included not only Corianton committing sexual sin, but purposefully neglecting "the ministry wherewith [he] wast entrusted" (Alma 39:4). Perhaps, then, "the more serious infraction was the resulting spiritual damage inflicted upon others who had witnessed Corianton's sinful actions."[202]

If Corianton's *only* sin was committing sexually immoral acts, then it's curious why Alma did not focus on that in the rest of the chapter. Instead of warning against sexual immorality, the remainder of

Alma 39 focuses on such topics as "a description of the unpardonable sin—to knowingly deny the Holy Ghost."[203]

Apostasy is a sin of unfaithfulness that was seen in some ways by Old Testament prophets as conceptually similar to adultery.[204] Alma associated the unpardonable sin of denying the Holy Ghost with leading others into apostasy. This he did by explaining that "whosoever murdereth against the light and knowledge of God, it is not easy for him to obtain forgiveness" (Alma 39:6). "Denying the Holy Ghost is unforgivable," Alma's logic goes, "but those who murder 'against the light and knowledge of God' can receive forgiveness, albeit with great difficulty."[205]

In light of the entirety of Alma 39, it is clear that Corianton was not just guilty of sexual sin, but was also "guilty of leaving his mission to chase a harlot (either literally and/or figuratively). This harlot has damaged many testimonies already, and Corianton's actions have also led some of the people to destruction instead of to God."[206]

THE WHY

Corianton's sin was a composite crime of sexual immorality and leading others into apostasy through neglecting the ministry, being unfaithful to his priesthood calling, and setting a poor example. The crime of leading others into apostasy through sinful behavior was, in Alma's view, next to shedding innocent blood and denying the Holy Ghost in seriousness. Given that he himself was once guilty of that particular crime (see Mosiah 27; Alma 36), Alma's pleading with Corianton to repent is all the more powerful (see Alma 39:9–13).

To be clear, sexual immorality is an enormously harmful sin that can result in excruciating spiritual and temporal consequences. Both ancient and modern prophets have unequivocally condemned sexual immorality and related vices, and the Book of Mormon repeatedly warns all readers against adultery, fornication, whoredoms, lasciviousness, and sexual sins of all kinds (see Jacob 3:12; Alma 16:18; Alma 45:12; 4 Nephi 1:16). These and any other types of wickedness become all the more serious when combined with any other dereliction of spiritual or religious duty.

Happily, Corianton did repent and soon returned successfully to the ministry alongside his brothers (see Alma 49:30). This shows that repentance and forgiveness is possible for even severe sins, and that God is always willing to receive again those who forsake their transgressions (see D&C 58:42–43).

FURTHER READING

Michael R. Ash, "The Sin 'Next to Murder': An Alternative Interpretation," *Sunstone*, November 2006, 34–43.

B. W. Jorgensen, "Scriptural Chastity Lessons: Joseph and Potiphar's Wife; Corianton and the Harlot Isabel," *Dialogue: A Journal of Mormon Thought 32*, no. 1 (1999): 7–34.

Why Was Corianton so Concerned about the Resurrection?

"What becometh of the souls of men is the thing which I have inquired diligently of the Lord to know; and this is the thing of which I do know." (Alma 40:9)

THE KNOW

After censuring Corianton for his immoral and detrimental conduct (see Alma 39:1–3), Alma perceived that his son's "mind [was] worried concerning the resurrection of the dead" (Alma 40:1). Corianton's concern is somewhat startling, though, considering that his father, Alma, was a prophet and the high priest over the land (see Alma 5:3). Why would the son of a prophet struggle to understand one of the most fundamental doctrines of the gospel?

One likely possibility is that Corianton was exposed to religious philosophies that either dismissed or corrupted the true doctrine of the Resurrection. Early in the Book of Mormon, Lehi and his son Jacob taught the reality of the Resurrection explicitly (see 2 Nephi 2:8; 9:6).[207] It seems, though, that sometime between the death of Jacob and the reign of King Mosiah, a portion of the people rejected this teaching.[208]

For instance, the way Abinadi emphasized the Resurrection when he confronted King Noah and his priests suggests that this doctrine was not being correctly or sufficiently taught among the people in the city of Nephi.[209] Likewise, when Alma the Elder strove to perpetuate Abinadi's teachings, many of the rising generation "did not believe what had been said concerning the resurrection of the dead" (Mosiah 26:2).[210]

As a rebellious youth, Alma the Younger himself likely rejected the reality of the Resurrection and was "numbered among the unbelievers" before his miraculous conversion (Mosiah 27:8). These types of textual clues indicate that some outside teaching or philosophy may have been competing against the true doctrine of the Resurrection.

What is more certain is the way Nehor negatively influenced attitudes toward this doctrine. Unlike Korihor, who completely denied the existence of God (see Alma 30:2), Nehor introduced the concept that the "Lord had created all men, and had also redeemed all men; and, in the end, all men should have eternal life" (Alma 1:4). Nehor's divergent theology obviously had influenced the young Corianton's views of resurrection and judgment, and yet it conflicted with the eternal laws of justice and judgment embedded in the true doctrine of the Resurrection (see Alma 42:22).[211]

Despite his trial and execution,[212] Nehor's enticing doctrines became popular among the people—so much so that his philosophy was formally designated as "the order of Nehor" (Alma 14:16; 24:29). Unfortunately,

Nehor's heresy was promulgated by the Amlicites,[213] who, by the time of Corianton's ministry, had gained prominent influence.[214]

THE WHY

Recognizing the historical controversy that surrounded the doctrine of the Resurrection can help readers better understand the root cause of Corianton's confusion. His concern over this doctrine was not likely due to casual curiosity or mere inquisitiveness. It seems, rather, that he was surrounded by philosophical and theological ideologies that directly contradicted a foundational tenet of his father's religion. Corianton's immoral behavior can also be meaningfully correlated to his concerns and doubts that threatened his faith in Jesus Christ, the reality of His death, the Resurrection, and the final judgment.[215]

These topics had been of great concern to many people, not only to Corianton but also to Alma. Charting the development of the doctrine of resurrection in the Book of Mormon can also help us appreciate the new contributions of Alma's teachings to his son. As noted earlier, Alma himself had once been an unbeliever. In order to satisfy his own questions or concerns about this issue, he had "inquired diligently of the Lord" (Alma 40:9). In response, the Lord sent an angel to enlighten him. From this experience, Alma was able to add the following insights to what was already written about the Resurrection in the Book of Mormon:

- No one is resurrected until after the coming of Christ (see Alma 40:2).
- There is a specific time appointed when every person will be resurrected, but only God knows that time (see Alma 40:4, 9).
- There will likely be multiple times of resurrection, since there will be righteous people who live and die after Christ dies and is resurrected (see Alma 40:5, 8).
- Alma believed that the righteous who lived before the time of Christ would be resurrected with Him (see Alma 40:20).[216]

It is uncertain what Corianton's specific beliefs were prior to his father's exhortation, but thematically speaking, Alma's treasured instructions to Corianton helped him understand the systematic nature and crucial functions of the resurrection. Alma had clearly taught on several occasions that an essential part of the gospel was believing that through the resurrection all men shall eventually stand before God in their bodies to be judged according to their works while in the flesh (see Alma 33:22; 40:22–26). Recognizing that Corianton and others were questioning and were worried about this very thing, Alma then patiently guided Corianton through the logical argument that explained the meaning of the word *restoration* (see Alma 41:2–15) and defended the balance of justice and mercy inherent in this system (see Alma 42).[217]

Similar to Corianton's environment, modern society faces a host of misguided philosophies and false teachings that can threaten faith in true doctrines. Alma's brilliant exposition powerfully demonstrates that true knowledge of sacred things cannot be inherited and is obtained only through diligent seeking and sincere prayer. In all of this, modern readers can learn much from Alma's example of helping a loved one find meaningful answers to difficult and productive questions.

FURTHER READING

A. Keith Thompson, "The Doctrine of Resurrection in the Book of Mormon," *Interpreter: A Journal of Mormon Scripture 12* (2016): 101–129.

Douglas J. Merrell, "The False Priests of the Book of Mormon," in *Selections from the Religious Education Student Symposium 2005* (Provo, UT: BYU Religious Studies Center, 2005): 87–94.

See John Hilton III and Jana Johnson, "Who Uses the Word *Resurrection* in the Book of Mormon and How Is It Used?" *Journal of the Book of Mormon and Other Restoration Scripture 21*, no. 2 (2012): 30–39.

18

How Did Alma Explain the Meaning of the Word *Restoration*?

"And now, my son, I have somewhat to say concerning the restoration of which has been spoken; for behold, some have wrested the scriptures, and have gone far astray because of this thing." (Alma 41:1)

THE KNOW

In order to help Corianton understand the fairness and justice inherent in the doctrine of the Resurrection,[218] Alma expounded on what he called "the plan of restoration" (Alma 41:2). The usage of the term *restoration* marks a notable shift from the previous chapter, wherein Alma almost exclusively referred to this doctrine as the "resurrection."[219] The transition in terminology seems to signal that a more nuanced and developed explanation was underway.

Concerning the meaning of the word *restoration*, Alma explained that "some have wrested the scriptures, and have gone far astray because of this thing" (Alma 41:1). This allusion likely referred to those who were "after the order and faith of Nehor" (Alma 14:16). Before his execution,[220] Nehor

> testified unto the people that all mankind should be saved at the last day, and that they need not fear nor tremble, but that they might lift up their heads and rejoice; for the Lord had created all men, and had also redeemed all men; and, in the end, all men should have eternal life. (Alma 1:4)

The way Alma's discourse directly addressed these assumptions about universal salvation indicates that Corianton subscribed to Nehor's heretical teachings. For example, Alma cautioned his son to "not suppose, because it has been spoken concerning restoration, that ye shall be restored from sin to happiness" (Alma 41:10). Alma supported his reasoning by further defining and elaborating on the meaning of restoration:

> the meaning of the word restoration is to bring back again evil for evil, or carnal for carnal, or devilish for devilish—good for that which is good; righteous for that which is righteous; just for that which is just; merciful for that which is merciful. (Alma 41:13)

An ancient legal principle known as *talionic justice* embodies this sentiment. John W. Welch explained, "Talionic justice achieved a sense of poetic justice, rectification of imbalance, relatedness between the nature of the wrong and the fashioning of the remedy, and appropriateness in determining the measure or degree of punishment."[221] Essentially, this was the famous law of an "eye for an eye" and a "tooth for a tooth" that was divinely revealed in the Old Testament and applied broadly throughout the ancient Near East (see Exodus 21:24).[222]

Not only did Alma's explanation to Corianton aptly utilize this ancient legal principle, but he structured his sermon in a chiastic form,[223] similar to legal parallelisms found in Mosaic law. For instance, in Leviticus 24:17– 21 we read:

And he that killeth any *man* shall surely be put to death.
And he that killeth a *beast* shall make it good: beast for beast.
And if a man cause a *blemish* in his neighbor; as he hath done so shall it be done to him;
Breach for breach,
Eye for eye,
Tooth for tooth,
As he hath caused a *blemish* in a man, so shall it be done to him again
And he that killeth a *beast*, he shall restore it:
And he that killeth a *man*, he shall be put to death.[224]

Alma's sermon on *restoration* provides a striking parallel:

The meaning of the word *restoration* is to bring back again
evil for evil, or carnal for carnal, or devilish for devilish—
(a) *good* for that which is (a') *good*;
(b) *righteous* for that which is (b') *righteous*;
(c) *just* for that which is (c') *just*;
(d) *merciful* for that which is (d') *merciful*.
(d') see that you are *merciful* unto your brethren;
(c') deal *justly*,
(b') judge *righteously*,
(a') and do *good* continually.
And if ye do all these things, then shall ye receive your reward;
(d) Yea, ye shall have *mercy* restored unto you again;
(c) Ye shall have *justice* restored unto you again;
(b) Ye shall have a *righteous* judgment restored unto you again
(a) And ye shall have *good* rewarded unto you again.
For that which ye do send out shall return unto you again, and be restored;
therefore, the word *restoration* more fully condemneth the sinner, and justifieth him not at all. (Alma 41:13–15)[225]

"The twist here is clever: after listing four pairs of terms, Alma pairs two lists of four terms and reverses their order at the same time."[226] Notably, this chiasm focuses mostly on the positive aspects of restoration. It is true that evil, carnal, and devilish behavior will in some way return to afflict the sinner, but in this instance Alma chose instead to emphasize the blessings of goodness, righteousness, justice, and mercy that will be restored to the righteous. Although he was very explicit and emphatic in his denunciation of sin, Alma ultimately wanted Corianton to "let the justice of God, and his mercy, and his long-suffering have full sway in [his] heart" (Alma 42:30).

THE WHY

Some readers may view the legal statutes of the Old Testament as irrelevant or obsolete, but Alma's exhortation demonstrates that their fundamental principles are eternally relevant. Clearly, a divine implementation of talionic justice will be the guiding principle of restoration as it relates to final judgment and the Resurrection. For example, people will receive forgiveness as they have forgiven (see Matthew 6:12), and people will be judged by the way they have judged others (see Matthew 7:1). Awareness of this principle can deepen appreciation for how, even though the application of truth may vary, "God is the same yesterday, today, and forever" (Mormon 9:9).

Alma's use of chiasmus to illustrate this principle is also instructive. What better way to demonstrate the inverse principles of divine justice than by using an inverse form of poetic parallelism? As Welch explained, "an elaborate and elegant chiastic structure embodies the very notion of the talion."[227] Therefore, both the form and the content of Alma's sermon converge on a singular, overarching principle of divine justice: "that all things should be restored to their proper order" (Alma 41:2). Such a profound and elegant truth must have stood in stark contrast to the unbalanced and incoherent program of salvation promoted by Nehor.

FURTHER READING

John W. Welch, *The Legal Cases in the Book of Mormon* (Provo, UT: BYU Press and Neal A. Maxwell Institute for Religious Scholarship, 2008), 335–381.

John W. Welch, "Chiasmus in the Book of Mormon," in *Book of Mormon Authorship: New Light on Ancient Origins,* ed. Noel B. Reynolds (Provo, UT: BYU Religious Studies Center, 1982), 33–52.

Richard O. Cowan, "A New Meaning of 'Restoration': The Book of Mormon on Life after Death," in *The Book of Mormon: Alma, The Testimony of the Word,* ed. Monte S. Nyman and Charles D. Tate Jr. (Provo, UT: BYU Religious Studies Center, 1992), 195–210.

19

Why Does Alma Mention "the Plan" Ten Times in His Words to Corianton?

"Therefore, according to justice, the plan of redemption could not be brought about, only on conditions of repentance of men in this probationary state." (Alma 42:13)

THE KNOW

Alma 42 concludes Alma the Younger's powerful, four-chapter exhortation to his son Corianton. After explaining the consequences of sin and expounding on the Resurrection (see Alma 39–41), Alma perceived that Corianton was still troubled and confused concerning the justice of God. In particular, Alma noted that Corianton tried "to suppose that it is injustice that the sinner should be consigned to a state of misery" (Alma 42:1). In order to help his son reconcile himself to God's justice, Alma explained how the balance of justice and mercy is integral to "the great plan of salvation" (Alma 42:5).[228]

A feature of Alma's discourse that may be easy to overlook is the symbolic use of the number ten. In many ancient civilizations, including the Israelite civilization, certain numbers were considered to hold sacred meaning or importance. For example, John W. Welch explained that the number ten "conveyed a tight cluster of symbolic messages associated with the divine realms, namely, completeness, perfection, worthiness, consecration, testing, justice, reverence, atonement, supplication, and holiness (to mention ten)."[229] It seems likely that this sacred use of numbers was preserved in the plates of brass and perpetuated by Nephite prophets as part of their literary tradition.[230]

Evidence from the earliest Book of Mormon manuscripts indicates that its original chapter units were divinely revealed to Joseph Smith,[231] and in the 1830 edition of the Book of Mormon, Alma 39–42 comprised a single, cohesive chapter.[232] It may well be significant, therefore, that within these chapters Alma referred to the plan of redemption (or its variants, such as the "plan of salvation" or the "plan of happiness") precisely ten times.[233]

During this period, Alma was the high priest over the Church and likely fulfilled temple responsibilities similar to those found in the Old Testament (see Alma 5:3).[234] This is notable because the number ten features prominently in temple architecture and ritual formula:

> When the temple of Solomon was built, it also contained many features that came in tens. The height and width of the cherubim in Solomon's temple were both ten cubits . . . [the] diameter of the brazen sea was ten cubits . . . the brass altar was ten cubits high; ten candlesticks were made of

> gold; and ten tables were placed, five on each side.[235]

We know that Nephi's temple, which was probably a model for later Nephite temple worship,[236] was itself constructed "after the manner of the temple of Solomon" (2 Nephi 5:16). Thus, it makes sense that Alma, being the high priest in charge of temple worship, would have been aware of this number's sacred meaning and purposefully utilized it to help his son comprehend the plan of salvation.

Alma's tenfold invocation of the plan of salvation could also be connected to his high priestly role to determine worthiness in relation to the Ten Commandments. Welch proposed that "the Ten Commandments may have functioned somewhat like a list of modern temple recommend requirements to determine who might ascend into the mountain of the Lord, or the temple (see Psalm 24)."[237] In this way, Alma's exhortation could be seen as symbolically bringing Corianton to stand trial before God for violating one of those sacred commandments. Alma wanted Corianton to take advantage of the time for repentance that is mercifully allowed under God's overarching plan of happiness.

Furthermore, Alma's exhortation to Corianton doesn't contain the only discernable example of sacred numerals found in the Book of Mormon.[238] Of particular relevance is another tenfold repetition of the word *plan* found in Alma 12. In that case, the first three uses of the term are in reference to Zeezrom's "subtle plan" to deceive the people and turn them against Alma and Amulek (see Alma 12:32–33). In contrast, the last seven uses (seven itself being a sacred priestly number[239]) all refer to the "plan of redemption" (see Alma 12:25–33). The occurrence of negative examples or contexts of a repeated item being supplanted or overpowered by a greater number of positive usages is not an isolated phenomenon and can be found elsewhere in the Book of Mormon.[240] It therefore seems more than coincidental that both Alma 12 and Alma 39–42 use the same pattern of tenfold repetition to expound on the same sacred topic—the plan of redemption. [241]

THE WHY

Corianton had bought into the wrong "plan" (as had Zeezrom in Alma 12), so in order to turn his son back onto the true path, Alma's sermon needed to state the totality of the true plan. Even if someone isn't aware of this tenfold thread, the subconscious effect of its tenfold repetition allows the spirit to gather momentum to a very satisfying conclusion and convincing admonition. Alma's words had a very beneficial effect on Corianton.[242] This emphatic element may be one of the reasons why these words left such an indelible impression on his son and still leave such a powerful impact on readers today.

Understanding the numeric symbolism in parts of the Book of Mormon can also deepen comprehension of the scriptures and the prophets who wrote them. For example, identifying Alma's symbolic repetition of "the plan of redemption" helps readers recognize how significant this concept might have been to him. He likely saw God's plan as a perfect or complete solution to his son's moral confusion and wayward behavior. Not only does Alma repeat the concept exactly ten times, but in Alma 39–42 he uses five connotative variations to describe it: *plan of redemption*, *restoration*, *salvation*, *mercy*, and *happiness*.

Readers should be cautious to not assume that every instance of a sacred number, whether explicitly mentioned or implied through repetition, is symbolically significant. Yet many of the text's attestations of symbolic numbers are so distinctive and cogent that it is difficult to see them as anything other than intentional. The fact that specific words, phrases, or concepts are repeated a sacred number of times in a meaningful context is evidence that the authors were familiar with ancient numeric symbolism. Exploring the sacred significance of numbers, therefore, reveals an insightful layer of subtle complexity in the Book of Mormon.

FURTHER READING

John W. Welch, "Counting to Ten," *Journal of Book of Mormon Studies 12*, no. 2 (2003): 42–57, 113–114.

Corbin Volluz, "A Study in Seven: Hebrew Numerology in the Book of Mormon," *BYU Studies Quarterly 53*, no. 2 (2014): 57–83.

John W. Welch, "Number 24," *Reexploring the Book of Mormon: A Decade of New Research*, ed. John W. Welch (Provo, UT: FARMS, 1992), 272–274.

Why Was Moroni's Young Age an Advantage?

"And Moroni took all the command, and the government of their wars. And he was only twenty and five years old when he was appointed chief captain over the armies of the Nephites." (Alma 43:17)

THE KNOW

After including in his record much of Alma's counsel to his three sons, Mormon picked up where he had left off in giving his historical narrative report "of the wars between the Nephites and the Lamanites" (Alma 43:3). Nearly all of the remainder of the book of Alma (see Alma 43–62) gives one detailed account after another of battles and strategies used during a period of extensive warfare. At the head of the armies at this pivotal time was one Moroni, who "took the command of all the armies of the Nephites" at the age of twenty-five, in the eighteenth year of the Nephite reign of judges (see Alma 43:16–17).

Despite his youth, Moroni proved to be an effective military commander. There seem to be two reasons for Moroni's success: (1) he implemented innovative defensive measures; and (2) he sought and followed prophetic counsel.

1. Innovative Defensive Measures

Douglas J. Bell, a former BYU professor and officer in the U.S. Army, succinctly listed Moroni's innovative leadership practices: "he creatively fortified his cities, designed body armor, and motivated every city with the Title of Liberty."[243]

One of the innovations mentioned is the protective armor with which Moroni equipped his men (see Alma 43:19).[244] Earlier mentions of armor are rare and vague.[245] David E. Spencer, a professor of counterterrorism and insurgency, suggested that prior to this point, individual soldiers were responsible for arming themselves.[246] This probably resulted in uneven or inadequate armor for the rank-and-file. Under Moroni's command, each soldier was equipped with a full ensemble of protective gear, which included breastplates, arm-shields, head-shields, and thick clothing.[247]

Moroni also built extensive fortifications with ditches, earthen walls, and palisades (see Alma 49–50).[248] Like armor, fortifications had been known among the Nephites at an earlier time, but they are only briefly mentioned and only in the Land of Nephi.[249] Mormon reported that Moroni's fortifications were "in a manner which never had been known among the children of Lehi" (Alma 49:8).

Moroni also rallied the people behind a righteous cause, and raised a battle standard on a pole to represent that cause (see Alma 46). Using a battle standard allowed for greater cohesion and unity on the battlefield.[250] Never before was the use of a battle standard mentioned among the Nephites.

Each of these innovations may have been borrowed from nearby cultures or earlier practices that had previously been forgotten. For example, a similar ensemble of armor was known in pre-Columbian Mesoamerica.[251] We know that the Israelites and various pre-Columbian American cultures had comparable earthwork fortifications,[252] and in Mesoamerica, a proliferation of such fortifications can be confidently dated to the Late Preclassic period, coinciding with the time of Moroni.[253] Battle standards are also well attested to in many cultures from both the Old and New Worlds, including the Israelites and Mesoamerican peoples.[254]

2. Seeking and Following the Prophet

In addition to physical preparations, Moroni sought and followed the guidance of the Lord. Before going to rally the people with his battle standard, "he bowed himself to the earth, and he prayed mightily unto his God" (Alma 46:13). In the first battle under his command, he "sent certain men" to the prophet, Alma, "that he should inquire of the Lord whither the armies of the Nephites should go to defend themselves against the Lamanites" (Alma 43:23). As a result, the Lord revealed the activities of the Lamanite army, and Moroni was able put his troops in place to cut off the Lamanite soldiers.

Moroni was not the first to draw on a prophet for guidance in wartime (see Alma 16:5–6). In fact, he was part of a long-standing Israelite and ancient Near Eastern tradition.[255] While innovative in so many ways on the battlefield, he proved willing to continue righteous traditions like this one, much to his benefit and success.

THE WHY

Moroni's age likely played a crucial role in the Nephites' military successes. As a young military captain, he was particularly open to applying and adapting military technology that was present or emerging in wider society.[256] Similarly, younger leaders today may have an advantage in using innovative technologies to further the Lord's work. Elder David A. Bednar taught, "The youth can offer much to older individuals who are uncomfortable with or intimidated by technology."[257]

Not only did Captain Moroni help his soldiers physically and spiritually clothe themselves in the armor of God,[258] but he also demonstrated the importance of humbly heeding prophetic counsel. Rather than simply relying on his own gifts in military strategy, Moroni looked to Alma for divine revelation and guidance. John Bytheway, a prominent LDS author and youth speaker, insightfully commented, "Prophets know where the enemy will attack and can prepare us to meet the threat!"[259]

After demonstrating how heeding the words of a living prophet had blessed his own life, President Russell M. Nelson testified:

> Prophets see ahead. They see the harrowing dangers the adversary has placed or will yet place in our path. Prophets also foresee the grand possibilities and privileges awaiting those who listen with the intent to obey. I know this is true! I have experienced it for myself over and over again. [260]

Moroni followed divine counsel in wartime preparations and by so doing succeeded in the face of impossible odds. He not only preserved the Nephite people from a dangerous adversary, but he also secured his place in Nephite history. President Nelson directly declared of the millennial generation of the Church—those who are close to the same age as Moroni was when he assumed command of the Nephite armies—

> As a True Millennial whom the Lord can count on, you will make history too! You will be asked to accept challenging assignments and become an instrument in the Lord's hands. And He will enable you to accomplish the impossible.[261]

FURTHER READING

Neal Elwood Lambert, "Moroni[1]", in *Book of Mormon Reference Companion*, ed. Dennis L. Largey (Salt Lake City, UT: Deseret Book, 2003), 556–557.

Joe J. Christensen, "Captain Moroni, an Authentic Hero," in *Heroes from the Book of Mormon* (Salt Lake City, UT: Bookcraft, 1995), 128–133.

Thomas R. Valletta, "The Captain and the Covenant," in *The Book of Mormon: Alma, "The Testimony of the Word,"* ed. Monte S. Nyman and Charles D. Tate Jr. (Provo, UT: BYU Religious Studies Center, 1992), 223–248.

H. Dean Garrett, "Inspired by a Better Cause," in *The Book of Mormon, Part 2: Alma 30 to Moroni*, ed. Kent P. Jackson, *Studies in Scripture: Volume 8* (Salt Lake City, UT: Deseret Book, 1988), 69–79.

Why Would Zerahemnah Not Swear an Oath to Moroni?

"Behold, here are our weapons of war; we will deliver them up unto you, but we will not suffer ourselves to take an oath unto you, which we know that we shall break." (Alma 44:8)

THE KNOW

Just before the so-called "war chapters" of the book of Alma (see Alma 45–62) is the account of a clash between the Nephite and Lamanite military commanders Moroni and Zerahemnah, respectively (see Alma 43–44). After affirming that the Nephites did "not desire to be men of blood" (Alma 44:1), Moroni commanded their foe "in the name of that all-powerful God" (Alma 44:5) to "deliver up [their] weapons of war unto" the victorious Nephites (Alma 44:6). If Zerahemnah would do as commanded, his life and the lives of his men would be spared (see Alma 44:6).

Zerahemnah's response was terse and adamant: "Behold, here are our weapons of war; we will deliver them up unto you, but we will not suffer ourselves to take an oath unto you, which we know that we shall break, and also our children; but take our weapons of war, and suffer that we may depart into the wilderness; otherwise we will retain our swords, and we will perish or conquer" (Alma 44:8). Believing he had been defeated through Nephite ingenuity rather than divine intervention, Zerahemnah was willing to concede the immediate battle but refused perpetual surrender (Alma 44:9).

After another round of negotiations (see Alma 44:10–11), Zerahemnah suddenly attacked when Moroni briefly let his guard down. However, the Lamanite commander was halted when "one of Moroni's soldiers . . . smote Zerahemnah that he took off his scalp and it fell to the earth" (Alma 44:12). Immediately thereafter,

> the soldier who stood by, who smote off the scalp of Zerahemnah, took up the scalp from off the ground by the hair, and laid it upon the point of his sword, and stretched it forth unto them, saying unto them with a loud voice: Even as this scalp has fallen to the earth, which is the scalp of your chief, so shall ye fall to the earth except ye will deliver up your weapons of war and depart with a covenant of peace. (Alma 44:13–14)

Utterly defeated and moments away from death, Zerahemnah finally covenanted with Moroni and withdrew what was left of his now unarmed and humiliated army, never to be heard of again (see Alma 44:19–24).

It is important to note that Moroni invoked the name of God in the brief covenant-making ceremony he enacted with Zerahemnah (see Alma 44:4). Invoking the name of a deity to witness and ratify a covenant or oath was standard procedure in ancient Near Eastern oath-making ceremonies. The understanding anciently was that if a party failed to keep the covenant, then that party would face divine retribution. This might explain why Zerahemnah initially refused to make an oath he knew he couldn't (or wouldn't) keep. He may have feared God at least enough to anticipate divine wrath should he fail to keep the covenant, even if he disbelieved it was God who granted the Nephites victory (see Alma 44:9).

Whatever the case on Zerahemnah's part, the subsequent action of Moroni's soldier who lifted up the Lamanite commander's scalp makes perfect sense from an ancient perspective. Scholars have identified a pattern of oath-making in the ancient Near East that involves what is commonly called a *simile curse.*[262] As found in Hittite and Semitic cultures, simile curses involved one party in a covenant forewarning the precise penalties that should befall the other parties if they were ever to break the pact.

These penalties were framed in the form of a simile: "If so-and-so does not keep this covenant, then may he be destroyed just or even as this object shall be destroyed." When simile curses were given, the party giving the terms sometimes demonstrated what would happen by dramatically destroying some kind of object, animal, or figure that symbolized the doomed party.

For example, an eighth century BC Aramaic treaty contains a clear example of a simile curse. "Just as this wax is burned by fire, so shall Mati[el be burned by fi]re. Just as (this) bow and these arrows are broken, so may Anahita and Hadad break [the bow of Matiel] and the bow of his nobles. And just as a man of wax is blinded, so may Mati[el] be blinded."[263]

The Hebrew Bible also contains an example of a simile curse. In 1 Kings 14, the prophet Ahijah was commanded by God to foretell divine retribution for the wicked king Jeroboam. "Therefore, behold, I will bring evil upon the house of Jeroboam," God promised, "and will take away the remnant of the house of Jeroboam, as a man taketh away dung, till it be all gone" (1 Kings 14:10; compare 2 Kings 21:13). Simile curses are found in a number of Hittite texts, such as a series of oaths Hittite soldiers made as part of their military service.[264] Curses against those who break or alter the terms of suzerain-vassal treaties are also included in some Hittite texts written on bronze plates.[265]

THE WHY

The nature of oaths and oath-making in the Book of Mormon closely follows an ancient Near Eastern pattern.[266] This includes a sometimes life-or-death seriousness when it comes to making and keeping covenants and oaths. A close reading of Alma 44 reveals that Moroni's interaction with Zerahemnah followed the same pattern.

Latter-day Saint scholars have noted that the pronouncement of the Nephite soldier who scalped Zerahemnah follows the simile curse formula almost perfectly: "Even as this scalp has fallen to the earth, which is the scalp of your chief, so shall ye fall to the earth except ye will deliver up your weapons of war and depart with a covenant of peace" (Alma 44:14).[267] From an ancient perspective this simile curse would have greatly reinforced the life-or-death seriousness of the covenant Moroni had commanded Zerahemnah to enter, and would have given Zerahemnah even more reason not to agree with Moroni's demand without absolute certainty of keeping it.

The elements of Alma 44 combine to show that both the Nephites and Lamanites, including even the wrathful Zerahemnah, respected the seriousness of oaths, especially oaths sworn in God's name. This in turn demonstrates "the rich complexity of the Book of Mormon" as well as its ancient provenance.[268]

FURTHER READING

RoseAnn Benson and Stephen D. Ricks, "Treaties and Covenants: Ancient Near Eastern Legal Terminology in the Book of Mormon," *Journal of Book of Mormon Studies 14*, no. 1 (2005): 48–61, 128–129.

Mark J. Morrise, "Simile Curses in the Ancient Near East, Old Testament, and Book of Mormon," *Journal of Book of Mormon Studies 2*, no. 1 (1993): 124–138.

Terrence L. Szink, "Oath of Allegiance in the Book of Mormon," in *Warfare in the Book of Mormon*, ed. Stephen D. Ricks and William J. Hamblin (Salt Lake City and Provo, UT: Deseret Book and FARMS, 1990), 35–45.

22

How Did Seeking a King Get in the Way of Sustaining a Prophet?

"And now it came to pass that after Helaman and his brethren had appointed priests and teachers over the churches that there arose a dissension among them, and they would not give heed to the words of Helaman and his brethren." (Alma 45:23)

THE KNOW

At the beginning of Alma 45, Mormon provided a special heading summary,[269] sometimes referred to as a *colophon*,[270] which reads: "The account of the people of Nephi, and their wars and dissensions, in the days of Helaman, according to the record of Helaman, which he kept in his days" (Alma 45, chapter heading). Although still in the book of Alma, Mormon's helpful summary reveals that a shift in the source text has taken place and emphasizes that Helaman will unfortunately have to face wars and dissensions during his ministry.

After preparing Helaman as his successor, Alma mysteriously disappeared while journeying toward the land of Melek (see Alma 45:18–19).[271] While Mormon doesn't reveal how Helaman felt about this sudden loss of his father or his new burden of responsibility, the text immediately reports that Helaman went forth to "declare the word" and "establish the church again in all the land" (Alma 45:20, 22).

Unfortunately, Helaman's diligent efforts were promptly rejected by a substantial segment of the people:

> And now it came to pass that after Helaman and his brethren had appointed priests and teachers over the churches that there arose a dissension among them, and they would not give heed to the words of Helaman and his brethren. But they grew proud, being lifted up in their hearts, because of their exceedingly great riches; therefore they grew rich in their own eyes, and would not give heed to their words, to walk uprightly before God. (Alma 45:23–24)

The animosity toward Helaman's spiritual reforms was so strong that these dissenters gathered together and were "determined to slay" him and his brethren (Alma 46:1). The culprit behind this movement was a "large and strong man" named Amalickiah, who, through flattery, had convinced many "lower judges of the land" to "support him and establish him to be their king" (Alma 46:3–5). Not only was he popular among society at large, but "there were many in the church who believed in the flattering words of Amalickiah" (Alma 45:7).

For those Nephites familiar with their own history, this state of affairs would have indeed seemed "exceedingly precarious and dangerous" (Alma 45:7). Less than twenty years earlier,[272] King Mosiah had, in allusion to King Noah, reminded them of "how much iniquity doth one wicked king cause to be committed, yea, and what great destruction" (Mosiah 29:17). In the deeper past, the early Israelites sought to pressure Samuel into anointing a king who would "judge [them] like all other nations" (1 Samuel 8:5).[273] Samuel similarly tried to warn the people about the excesses and abuses of power to which monarchs often succumbed (see 1 Samuel 8:11–18).[274]

It may also be noteworthy that during the approximate timeframe of Helaman's ministry, a fundamental political shift took place in ancient America. "Though the significance of the Preclassic-Classic divide can be overstated, the distinction does seem to reflect a transformation from one social and political order to another. . . . Elements of this system took root in various parts of Mesoamerica between 100 BC and AD 100."[275] During this transition, the "relationship between kingship and cosmos was re-articulated, even reconceived."[276] This suggests, perhaps, that the Nephites who supported Amalickiah were, like the Israelites in Samuel's day, influenced by the political movements of surrounding nations.

THE WHY

In the cases of Samuel and King Mosiah, the moral was not necessarily that kingship was or is inherently evil.[277] Rather those histories show that when the people would not take counsel from the Lord, their desire for worldly monarchs readily led to sorrow and destruction. In both narratives, the Lord, through an appointed prophet, counseled the people to either adopt or maintain a specific political system—in these cases, a system of judges.

In large part, then, it would appear that Helaman was rejected because the people allowed their own political agendas to supersede their faith in prophetic counsel. Especially from the perspective of Mormon, who himself saw much the same development among his own people, this loss of faithful loyalty and good judgment was tragic. As in Mormon's day, many members of the church in Helaman's day were not immune to flattery and desertion.

Mormon reported that Helaman's people "dissented even from the church" (Alma 46:7). Yet, as the Lord told Samuel anciently, "they have not rejected thee, but they have rejected me, that I should not reign over them" (1 Samuel 8:7). This same sentiment can certainly be applied to Helaman and his brethren, who "notwithstanding their exceedingly great care over the church" (Alma 46:6), failed to persuade the people to heed the Lord.

The rise of Amalickiah and the kingmen who supported him led the Nephite civilization into a decade of intermittent but steady warfare and destruction.[278] This terrible course of events helps demonstrate the importance of remembering the Lord in times of prosperity and peace, and it warns against rejecting prophetic teachings in favor of popular political ideologies. In the wake of these events, Mormon's lament provides a stirring warning to modern readers to not repeat such follies: "Thus we see how quick the children of men do forget the Lord their God, yea, how quick to do iniquity, and to be led away by the evil one" (Alma 46:8).

FURTHER READING

Joseph Fielding McConkie and Robert J. Millet, *Doctrinal Commentary on the Book of Mormon*, 4 vols. (Salt Lake City, UT: Bookcraft, 1987–1991) 3:321–327.

John A. Tvedtnes, "King Mosiah and the Judgeship," *Insights: A Window on the Ancient World 20*, no. 11 (2000): 2.

23 Why Did Moroni Quote the Patriarch Jacob about a Piece of Joseph's Coat?

"Even as this remnant of garment of my son hath been preserved, so shall a remnant of the seed of my son be preserved by the hand of God, and be taken unto himself, while the remainder of the seed of Joseph shall perish, even as the remnant of his garment." (Alma 46:24)

THE KNOW

To quell dissensions and treason among his fellow Nephites, many of whom were being persuaded by the flattery of Amalickiah (see Alma 46:10), Moroni undertook to rally Nephite morale and faithfulness. Accordingly, "He rent his coat; and he took a piece thereof, and wrote upon it—In memory of our God, our religion, and freedom, and our peace, our wives, and our children—and he fastened it upon the end of a pole" (Alma 46:12).

This banner, called the "title of liberty" (Alma 46:13), was used at first as a war banner for the Nephite forces (see Alma 46:19–20).[279] Following the well-attested ancient Near Eastern phenomenon of the simile curse, those soldiers who rallied around Moroni rent their own garments as a token of their covenant,[280] pledging that if they transgressed God's commandments "the Lord should rend them even as they had rent their garments" (Alma 46:21).[281]

While gathering support for the Nephite military cause, Moroni curiously invoked the words of the Old Testament patriarch Jacob, the father of Joseph of Egypt (see Alma 46:24). He prefaced his recitation of Jacob's words by reminding his comrades,

> Behold, we are a remnant of the seed of Jacob; yea, we are a remnant of the seed of Joseph, whose coat was rent by his brethren into many pieces; yea, and now behold, let us remember to keep the commandments of God, or our garments shall be rent by our brethren, and we be cast into prison, or be sold, or be slain. (Alma 46:23)

Moroni then went on to quote Jacob thus:

> Even as this remnant of garment of my son hath been preserved, so shall a remnant of the seed of my son be preserved by the hand of God, and be taken unto himself, while the remainder of the seed of Joseph shall perish, even as the remnant of his

> garment. Now behold, this giveth my soul sorrow; nevertheless, my soul hath joy in my son, because of that part of his seed which shall be taken unto God. (Alma 46:24–25)

To drive the point home and to reiterate the simile curse already annunciated, Moroni concluded by stating that even as a remnant of Joseph's seed had perished as had his garment, "even it shall be ourselves if we do not stand fast in the faith of Christ" (Alma 46:27).

Moroni's use of a war banner converges comfortably with martial practices found in ancient Israel and Mesoamerica. Among the Dead Sea Scrolls is the so-called War Scroll, which details how the Qumran community was to prepare for the great and final battle between good and evil. Included among the listed military equipment to be used were war banners with written text on them. "Rule of the banners of the whole congregation according to their formations. On the grand banner which is at the head of all the people they shall write 'People of God,' the names 'Israel' and 'Aaron,' and the names of the twelve t[ribes of Isra]el according to their order of birth."[282]

As explained by Kerry Hull, Mesoamerican cultures also utilized war banners in highly ritualized ways that are closely comparable to Moroni's title of liberty.[283] This unexpected convergence of linguistic and cultural data "is a striking endorsement for the validity of the text as an ancient document and provides evidence of a Mesoamerican cultural background for the Book of Mormon."[284]

THE WHY

Ultimately, Moroni's war banner and quotation of Jacob went together to effectively validate the Nephite cause. "Moroni pulled out all the stops with the title of liberty," Hull clarified. With his title of liberty, Moroni reminded his soldiers that they were fighting for three ultimate values: their God and religion, their liberty and peace, and their women and children.

Moroni's symbolic action also invoked the power of ancestral heritage and God's covenants with Nephite ancestors. "He provided legitimization for the covenant-entering ceremony by hearkening back to an apocryphal story of Jacob with a remnant of his son Joseph's coat."

> Since Lehi was a descendant of Joseph (1 Nephi 5:14), the archaic nature of the rite by their lineage ancestor would have garnered Moroni additional support. The innovative use of a standard to display the rent garment shows Moroni adapting to the circumstances and culture in which he lived. A banner, well-known as a symbol of warfare, motivation, and leadership in battle in societies around the world, was an eminently appropriate way to rally others to his cause.[285]

In addition, by explicitly calling upon the words of Jacob, the father of the house of Israel, promising that "a remnant of the seed of my son [Joseph shall] be preserved by the hand of God," Moroni renewed and extended Jacob's promise to his soldiers, who were themselves a remnant of the house of Jacob in a foreign land. It is hard to imagine a symbol that would have been more energizing and reassuring to Moroni's soldiers than this. That remnant had portended such ill, but in the end, it opened the door for God's preservation of the people of Israel as strangers in the land of Egypt.

FURTHER READING

Kerry Hull, "War Banners: A Mesoamerican Context for the Title of Liberty," *Journal of Book of Mormon Studies 24* (2015): 84–118.

Hugh Nibley, *An Approach to the Book of Mormon, The Collected Works of Hugh Nibley: Volume 6* (Salt Lake City and Provo, UT: Deseret Book and FARMS, 1988), 211–213, 218–221.

24

Why Did Mormon See Captain Moroni as a Hero?

"Yea, verily, verily I say unto you, if all men had been, and were, and ever would be, like unto Moroni, behold, the very powers of hell would have been shaken forever; yea, the devil would never have power over the hearts of the children of men." (Alma 48:17)

THE KNOW

Mormon, the warrior-historian-prophet who wrote the majority of the narrative contained in the book of Alma, had much to say about Moroni, the young chief captain over the Nephite armies. Mormon was writing nearly four centuries after the events of the so-called "war chapters" in the second half of the book of Alma. It seemed that Mormon had many records on which to draw when writing his history. However, he decided to make the figure of Captain Moroni a main focus. The heroic acts of Captain Moroni are discussed in nearly twenty chapters of the book of Alma.

In Alma 46–48, especially, readers can perceive that Mormon holds Moroni in very high regard and considers him an example that "all men" should emulate (Alma 48:17). Starting in Alma 46, Mormon clearly attempts to contrast Moroni and his archenemy Amalickiah, presenting each figure as the antithesis of the other. The following table has some specific points of comparison that Mormon included in his narrative:

Moroni	Amalickiah
"a strong and a mighty man" (Alma 48:11)	"a large and a strong man" (Alma 46:3)
appointed by "the voice of the people" and by judges (Alma 46:34)	desired to be king through flattery, dissension, fraud and deceit (see Alma 46:3–10; 47:1–35; 48:7)

unified his people for the cause of righteousness and to keep their covenants (see Alma 46:12–21; 48:7)	caused dissension among people by blinding their minds and stirring them up unto anger (see Alma 48:1–3)
rejoiced in the liberty and freedom of his country and people (see Alma 48:11)	"sought to destroy the foundation of liberty" (Alma 46:10)
recognized the Lord's hand, prayed for his people, and "was firm in the faith of Christ" (Alma 46:12–13; 48:12–13)	fought against the preaching of Helaman, led dissensions from the Church, and sought to destroy the Church of God (see Alma 46:3–10)
"did not delight in bloodshed," was willing to have his own blood spilled for his people, led his armies into battle and did not attack offensively (see Alma 48:11–16)	"did care not for the blood of his people," "did not come down himself to battle," attacked the Nephites, hoping to bring them into bondage, "or slay and massacre them" (Alma 49:7, 10–11)
"had sworn with an oath to defend his people, his rights, and his country, and his religion," led the people in making a covenant to fight for their freedom, rights, families, and religion (Alma 48:13; 46:19–28)	his chief captains took an oath that they would destroy the people of the city of Noah; Amalickiah himself "did curse God, and also Moroni, swearing with an oath that he would drink his blood" (Alma 48:13, 17; 49:27)

Many more points of contrast could be observed between these two figures. Mormon wanted to show what great damage "one very wicked man" (Alma 46:9) could cause, but also, in contrast, how one very righteous man, like Moroni, had the power to overcome all evil in the world if emulated by many (see Alma 48:17).

In addition, it is also worth mentioning that Mormon apparently tried to imitate Moroni's war strategies in his own time, including the fortification of cities (see Mormon 2:4; Alma 48:9) and trying to rally his people to "fight for their wives, and their children, and their houses, and their homes" (Mormon 2:23; Alma 46:12; 58:12).[286] Although not mentioned overtly, Mormon clearly had so much respect and admiration for Captain Moroni and what he had accomplished that he named his son after his hero.

THE WHY

Mormon, like Captain Moroni, was called to be a military leader at a young age (see Mormon 1:15; 2:1–2), at a time in which his people were similarly engaged in near-constant wars. His exposure to the records containing the history of Moroni showed him a time when the Nephites still had faith in God, were strengthened by the Spirit, and were led to victory because of their righteous desires. At the time when Mormon was abridging this part of the Nephite records, he could see that Captain Moroni's example was desperately needed among his people, and he longed to lead his people as Moroni did.

Mormon also longed for the time when his people, like the people of Nephi in Moroni's day, would recognize the error of their ways, turn their hearts back to the Lord, and be blessed. In Alma 50, Mormon briefly emphasized how good things were for the Nephites in the days when they still kept the commandments of God, likely contrasting that period with his own. He declared:

> And those who were faithful in keeping the commandments of the Lord were delivered at all times, whilst thousands of their wicked brethren have been consigned to bondage, or to perish by the sword, or to dwindle in unbelief, and mingle with the Lamanites.
>
> But behold there never was a happier time among the people of Nephi, since the days of Nephi, than in the days of Moroni, yea, even at this time, in the twenty and first year of the reign of the judges. (Alma 50:22–23)

Mormon likely had in mind Moroni's time when, in Mormon 2:8–13, he tells of how he had hope that his own people would turn from their wicked ways and qualify for the blessings of the Lord once more. Because of their losses and because of the curse that was upon the land, the Nephites of Mormon's time apparently "began to repent of their iniquity, and began to cry" unto the Lord. He recounted:

> And it came to pass that when I, Mormon, saw their lamentation and their mourning and their sorrow before the Lord, my heart did begin to rejoice within me, knowing the mercies and the long-suffering of the Lord, therefore supposing that he would be merciful unto them that they would again become a righteous people. (Mormon 2:12)

However, as a prophet of God, he soon understood the lamentable reality of his people's situation—that their response was not like the Nephites of yesteryear. Mormon exclaimed in disconsolation:

> But behold this my joy was vain, for their sorrowing was not unto repentance, because of the goodness of God; but it was rather the sorrowing of the damned, because the Lord would not always suffer them to take happiness in sin. (Mormon 2:13)

For many reasons and in many ways, Captain Moroni was a great hero to Mormon. He represented the golden days of the Nephite civilization, a time when the people still repented of their sins and qualified for the blessings of God and the strength that comes from having the Spirit present. Mormon did his best to emulate Captain Moroni and even named his own son after that great man.

Today, attentive readers can appreciate the numerous subtle signals that Mormon sent in his abridging of the war chapters of the book of Alma that are in the end purposefully echoed 150 pages later in Mormon's account of the painful conclusion of the Nephite demise. Mormon sincerely hoped that all of his future readers would understand what a powerful disciple of Christ Moroni was. Indeed, he declared that "if all men had been, and were, and ever would be, like unto Moroni, behold, the very powers of hell would have been shaken forever" (Alma 48:17) and the world would be a better place, concordant with the will of God.

FURTHER READING

Thomas R. Valleta, "The Captain and the Covenant," in *The Book of Mormon: Alma, The Testimony of the Word*, ed. Monte S. Nyman and Charles D. Tate Jr. (Provo, UT: BYU Religious Studies Center, 1992), 223–248.

Richard McClendon, "Captain Moroni's Wartime Strategies: "An Application for the Spiritual Battles of Our Day," *Religious Educator: Perspectives on the Restored Gospel 3*, no. 3 (2002): 99–114.

How Did Democracy Help the Nephites Withstand Their Enemies?

"And thus he was preparing to support their liberty, their lands, their wives, and their children, and their peace, and that they might live unto the Lord their God." (Alma 48:10)

THE KNOW

Mormon described Moroni as "a man that did not delight in bloodshed; a man whose soul did joy in the liberty and the freedom of his country" (Alma 48:11). Such language often resonates with modern readers who have embraced similar ideals of freedom, especially those democratic principles that form the basis of many modern constitutions.[287] Yet, while it may be tempting to imagine Nephite society as a mirror of the modern democratic republic, their institutional methods for preserving freedom and liberty were actually, in some important ways, quite different from modern secular democracies.

Richard L. Bushman remarked,

> Looking at the Book of Mormon as a whole, it seems clear that most of the principles traditionally associated with the American Constitution are slighted or disregarded altogether. All of the constitutional checks and balances are missing.
>
> When judges were instituted, Mosiah provided that a greater judge could remove lesser judges and a number of lesser judges try [corrupt] higher judges, but the book records no instance of impeachment. It was apparently not a routine working principle. All other limitations on government are missing.[288]

On the other hand, Ryan W. Davis, a political scholar, has concluded that Nephite society can still be seen as fundamentally democratic because of its freedom of conscience, the potential of "intra-agency checks" to balance its government, and the political voice given to its people.[289] "It is in this limited but important sense that the regime established by Mosiah should be considered a democracy."[290]

Furthermore, several democratizing forces were set in motion by King Benjamin's speech, including his narrowing of the gap between king and subjects (see Mosiah 2:20–26), affirming popular freedom through communal covenant (see Mosiah 5:8), and dispensing a new name to all the people at the time of his son's coronation (see Mosiah 3:8; 5:9).[291]

While the Nephites' institutional methods of preserving freedom were certainly different from most modern systems of government, several fundamental principles and intents seem to be considerably the same. For instance, Moroni's preparations for war were intended "to support their liberty, their lands, their wives, and their children, and their peace" (Alma 48:10). This political emphasis on freedom and liberty provides a sharp contrast with the Lamanites' aggressive pursuit of autocratic control (where a single ruler holds concentrated power).[292]

THE WHY

Exploring the political backdrop of Nephite military campaigns can help readers better understand their success over the Lamanites. After surveying numerous conflicts throughout Nephite military history, Davis concluded:

> The trend that emerges from this analysis is that short conflicts . . . favor the Lamanite autocracy, but extended conflicts are ultimately won by the Nephite democracy. We recall that the theoretical reason democracies are expected to succeed in conflicts is that they can direct greater resources over an extended period of time. While democracies may lose in the short term, "in every prolonged conflict in modern history, such states have prevailed over their illiberal rivals."[293]

This explains, in part, why Moroni fought so vigorously to preserve and protect the Nephite method of governance.[294] King Benjamin's political reforms had thus far strengthened and preserved Mosiah's and Alma's people from bondage and captivity (see Mosiah 29). Neglecting to defend such an institution would directly threaten their religious and personal freedoms.

This is not to say, however, that their safety ultimately depended on the arm of flesh or on the democratic system they fought to preserve. "The most basic lesson in the Book of Mormon's politics is simple: God makes all the difference."[295] Time and again, the promise to the people was that they would be divinely blessed and prospered according to their obedience to the commandments.[296]

In reference to Alma's teaching that God often works through "small and simple things" (Alma 37:6), Davis proposed that "another possible reading of the term simple is natural, or organic. God uses natural processes—those explainable without use of an appeal to divine intercession—to accomplish his purposes."[297] This reading may help shed light on one possible way the Lord would protect and preserve the Nephites. Rather than idly waiting for God to miraculously deliver the Nephites from their enemies, the Lord expected them to fight to preserve a governmental institution that would, by its very nature, secure their safety and freedoms.

Like Amalickiah and those who followed him, there are many parties today that similarly seek to undermine the sacred principles of individual freedom, conscience, civil duty, and accountability. After identifying three things that Church members can do to preserve their sacred freedoms and rights,[298] Elder Robert D. Hales taught:

> Our Savior's Second Coming is drawing nearer. Let us not delay in this great cause. Remember Captain Moroni, who hoisted the title of liberty inscribed with the words "In memory of our God, our religion, and freedom, and our peace, our wives, and our children." Let us remember the people's response: exercising their agency, they "came running together" with a covenant to act.
>
> My beloved brothers and sisters, don't walk! Run! Run to receive the blessings of agency by following the Holy Ghost and exercising the freedoms God has given us to do His will.[299]

FURTHER READING

Ryan W. Davis, "For the Peace of the People: War and Democracy in the Book of Mormon," *Journal of Book of Mormon Studies 16*, no. 1 (2007): 42–55, 85–86.

Richard L. Bushman, "The Book of Mormon and the American Revolution," in *Book of Mormon Authorship: New Light on Ancient Origins,* ed. Noel B. Reynolds (Provo UT: BYU Religious Studies Center, 1982), 201–202.

Hugh Nibley, *Since Cumorah*, in *The Collected Works of Hugh Nibley: Volume 7* (Salt Lake City and Provo, UT: Deseret Book and FARMS, 1988) 137–172.

26

Why Are There so Many War Chapters in the Book of Mormon?

"And it came to pass that the Lamanites . . . were exceedingly astonished at their manner of preparation for war." (Alma 49:9)

THE KNOW

The Book of Mormon is a book saturated with warfare. The grim reality for ancient peoples was that religious, political, and cultural ideologies were frequently enforced through war. Even before bloodshed broke out between the Nephites and the Lamanites in the New World, Lehi's party was exposed to a violent rivalry between Nephi and his brothers, Laman and Lemuel.

John W. Welch identified at least fifteen major wars or conflicts that spanned the history of Book of Mormon peoples (see chart below).[300] A fair portion of the book of Alma (see Alma 2–3, 16, 24–25, 43–62) sometimes provides excruciating details concerning the wars between the Lamanites and Nephites. Unforgettable is the tragic downfall of the Nephites at the battle of Cumorah, which resulted in unparalleled death and carnage (see Mormon 1–6).

As is true today, warfare in the ancient world took on ideological importance for both sides of a conflict. The ancient Egyptians, Hebrews, Greeks, and Romans all recorded or recounted tales of combat and war that took on nationalistic and mythic significance for them as a people.[301] "Scribes often recorded the results of these wars in accounts usually intended to exalt the king and/or the nation's god(s)," Boyd Seevers observed. "The biblical authors normally write about warfare for some theological purpose, such as illustrating faith—or lack thereof—in God by some Israelite leader or the nation as a whole."[302]

The same is true of the ancient Maya. Archaeological investigations have determined conclusively that the Maya, Aztec, and other Mesoamerican cultures were often steeped in warfare that carried great cultural and practical significance.[303] Warfare "occupied a prominent place in the mind and practice" of ancient Mesoamerican peoples. Just as it did for the Nephites, "warfare, whether real or imagined, played an important role in shaping values, meanings, and identities in the lives of the Maya, and such cultural notions, in turn, affected how war was fought or avoided."[304]

This was precisely Mormon's intention in capturing the history of Nephite warfare. Much more than simply reporting these wars like a modern journalist—unbiased, impartial, and striving to remain morally neutral—Mormon infused (sometimes stereotypical) moral and theological significance into his war narratives.[305] Thus Mormon's lament at the end of his record that his people were slaughtered because of their having "departed from the ways of the Lord" (Mormon 6:17). Or his forceful denunciation of Amalickiah, the Nephites' chief enemy some centuries before Mormon's time, as a wicked usurper, conspirator, apostate, and traitor who "by his fraud, gained the hearts of the people" (Alma 47:30).

Mormon's focus on Nephite troop tactics, weaponry, fortifications, and the like might also easily be explained by the simple fact that Mormon himself was a military leader as much as a historian or prophet. With a professional interest in military matters, it makes sense that Mormon would knowledgeably spend time describing the finer details of Nephite military history—especially when these details augmented his narrative, such as when Nephite innovations in armor and fortifications granted them victory over their Lamanite foes (see, for example, Alma 44:8–9; 50:10–12).[306]

THE WHY

When viewed in an ancient context, it begins to make sense why the Book of Mormon would focus so closely on war. As explained by Welch,

> Wars and the politics of war were an integral part of history in the Book of Mormon. . . . Most military events in the Book of Mormon have both religious and political importance. The Nephites did not dichotomize their world between church and state as we do. Ancient peoples generally viewed war as a contest between the gods of one people and the gods of another.[307]

In addition to providing a glimpse into Nephite and Lamanite political and religious culture, the war chapters in the Book of Mormon can also provide evidence for the book's historicity. "One powerful dimension of historicity of the Book of Mormon is the sheer complexity of the record. The amazing achievement of the Book of Mormon is not the fact that it is a big book containing numerous chapters on warfare, but the stark reality that those chapters are complicated and consistent." Not only the book's *complexity*, but also its *realism* is evidence in favor of its historicity.[308] "The human and social events recorded in the Book of Mormon are realistic. They make sense in light of the way people and nations in fact behave."[309]

These factors combine to make the war chapters in the Book of Mormon powerful for a number of reasons. They not only provide important information on the history of the Nephites and Lamanites, but also give modern readers a window into Mormon's thinking on how and why he presented the history of his people the way he did.

War tactics and atrocities, whether conventional or terrorist, continue to plague the world today. The causes of war and armed conflict, the sources of contention and violence, still preoccupy and perplex the minds and hearts of nations everywhere. While Mormon and his peoples proved unable to stave off the horrors of their own annihilation, they wrote their record as a witness and a warning to help people today all over the world learn wisdom. Its prophetic teachings—of faith in Christ, sincere repentance, obedience to righteous covenants, generous love for all mankind, and concern for children and future generations—offer messages of hope, peace, and eternal rest in the presence of God. Though ancient, the messages of the Book of Mormon could not be more relevant to the urgent needs of today's modern world.

FURTHER READING

Brant A. Gardner, *Traditions of the Fathers: The Book of Mormon as History* (Salt Lake City, UT: Greg Kofford Books, 2015), 311–324.

John W. Welch, "Why Study Warfare in the Book of Mormon?" in *Warfare in the Book of Mormon,* ed. Stephen D. Ricks and William J. Hamblin (Salt Lake City and Provo, UT: Deseret Book and FARMS, 1990), 3–24.

R. Douglas Phillips, "Why Is So Much of the Book of Mormon Given Over to Military Accounts?" in *Warfare in the Book of Mormon*, ed. Stephen D. Ricks and William J. Hamblin (Salt Lake City and Provo, UT: Deseret Book and FARMS, 1990), 25–28.

Richard Dilworth Rust, "Purpose of War Chapters in the Book of Mormon," in *Warfare in the Book of Mormon*, ed. Stephen D. Ricks and William J. Hamblin (Salt Lake City and Provo, UT: Deseret Book and FARMS, 1990), 29–32.

Wars in the Book of Mormon CHART

Date	War	Location	Reference
500 - 100 B.C.	Early tribal wars	Land of Nephi	Jacob 1:10, 14; Enos–Omni
160 -150 B.C.	Wars of King Laman's sons	City of Nephi and the land of Zarahemla	Omni 1:24; Words of Mormon 1:13–14; Mosiah 9–10
87 B.C.	War of Amlici	Zarahemla, hill Amnihu, and river Sidon	Alma 2–3
81 B.C.	Destruction of Ammonihah	Ammonihah, west of Zarahemla	Alma 16:1–11; 24:1–25:14
77 B.C.	War of the Ammonite secession	Zarahemla, the land of Jershon	Alma 28
74 B.C.	Zoramite war	Between Antionum and Jershon	Alma 43–44
72 B.C.	First Amalickiahite War	Ammonihah, Noah, the east coast near narrow neck of land	Alma 46:1–50:11
67 - 61 B.C.	Second Amalickiahite war (seven years' war)	Throughout land of Zarahemla	Alma 51–62
52 B.C.	Rebellion of Paanchi	City of Zarahemla	Helaman 1:1–13
51 B.C.	War of Tubaloth	Cities of Zarahemla and Bountiful	Helaman 1:14–34
38, 35 - 30 B.C.	War of Moronihah	Land of Zarahemla	Helaman 4
26 - 19 B.C.	War of Gadianton and Kishkumen	The entire land, but centered in the land of Zarahemla	Helaman 6:15–11:20
A.D. 13 - 22	War of Giddianhi and Zemnarihah	From Zarahemla to Bountiful	3 Nephi 2:11–4:28

Date	War	Location	Reference
A.D. 30	Rebellion of Jacob	Land of Zarahemla	3 Nephi 6:14–7:14
A.D. 322, 327 - 328	Final Nephite wars, phase I	Land of Zarahemla and northward	Mormon 1:6–2:9
A.D. 346 - 350	Final Nephite wars, phase II	Land of Zarahemla, Jashon, and Shem	Mormon 2:16–3:1
A.D. 361 - 385	Final Nephite wars, phase III	The narrow neck of land and all the land northward	Mormon 3:4–6:15

Wars in the Book of Mormon TIMELINE

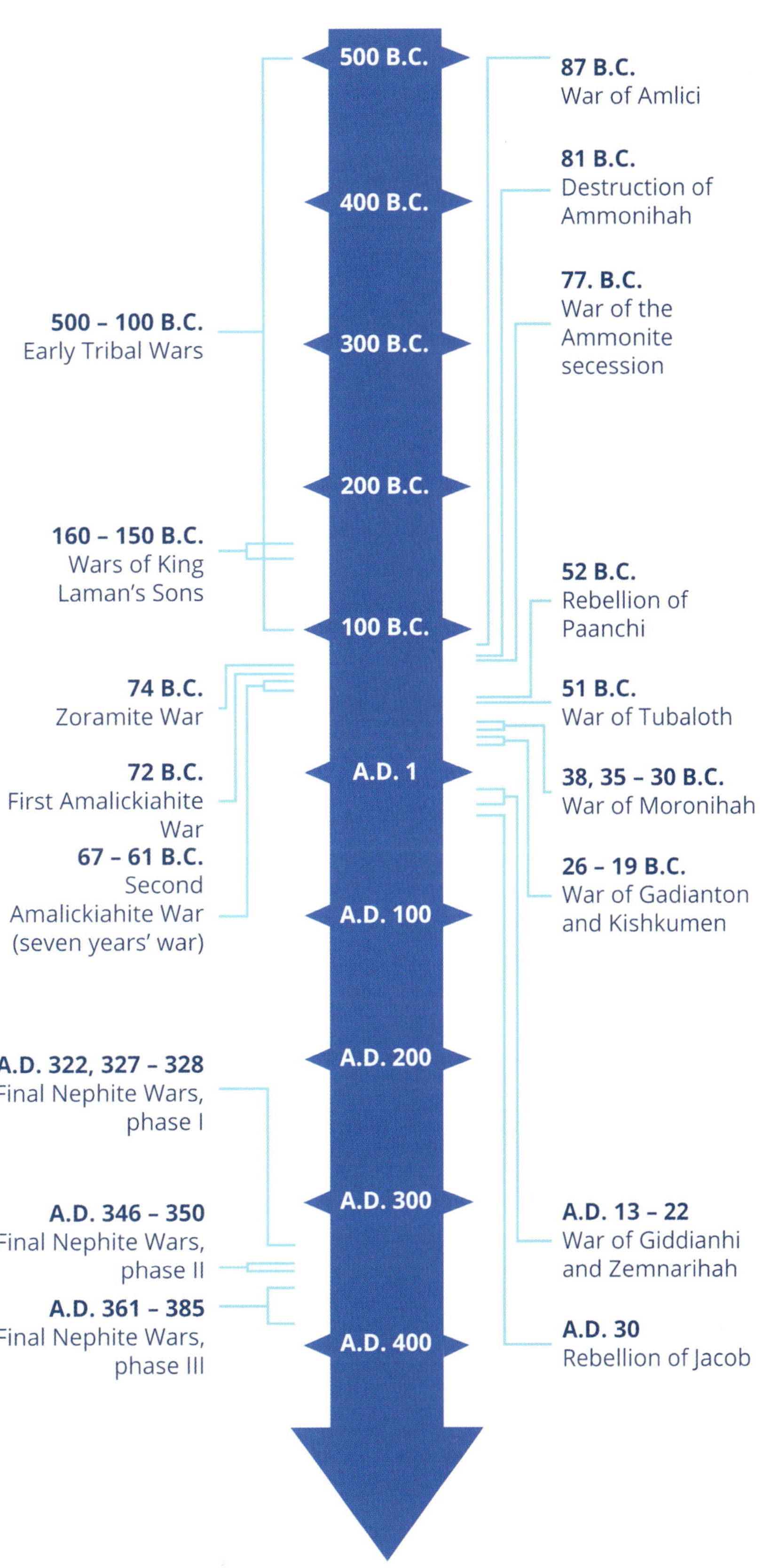

© Copyright Book of Mormon Central

27

What Was the Nature of Nephite Fortifications?

"Thus Moroni did prepare strongholds against the coming of their enemies, round about every city in all the land." (Alma 50:6)

THE KNOW

Around the year 75 BC, warfare between the Nephites and the Lamanites began to evolve. Only in recent years had the commander of the army become separate from the highest political official. That commander was a young man named Moroni, who employed innovative strategies of defense in warding off invading Lamanite armies.[310] One of those innovations was extensive fortifications throughout the land of Zarahemla (Alma 50:1–6).

While there are some mentions of fortifications previous to this time,[311] the nature of Moroni's forts seems to be different from those of earlier times. Lamanites reacted to them with "uttermost astonishment" because such "never had been known among the children of Lehi" (Alma 49:8). Descriptions of those fortifications indicate the following features:

1. Earth/dirt was "heaped" up into a "ridge" or wall "round about" the city; sometimes a "breastwork of timbers" was used to reinforce the inside of the earthen wall; in at least one instance, stone was also used to build the wall (see Alma 48:8; 49:4, 18; 50:1; 53:3).
2. Naturally, the displacement of dirt created a "ditch . . . round about" the outside of the wall or bank (Alma 49:18).
3. A timber palisade, picket, or parapet was built on top of the earthen wall (see Alma 50:2–3).
4. Towers were built above the timber picket, with bastions ("places of security") atop the towers, from which defenders of the city could safely "cast stones . . . and slay him who should attempt to approach near the walls" (Alma 50:4–5).[312]

Fortifications of a similar nature are known among many ancient cultures, including some in pre-Columbian America.[313] According to Ross Hassig, "during the Late Formative," also called the Late Preclassic period, "the general sophistication of warfare in Mesoamerica increased."[314] This naturally "spurred the development of defensive architecture" during this time period.[315]

A pair of Mesoamerican archaeologists agreed. "Defensive features" on archaeological sites "appear to have been more prominent, though far from prevalent, during the Late Preclassic (300 BC to AD 250)," noting, "significant transformations in conducts of war appear to have taken place during the Preclassic period."[316] John L.

Sorenson documented a minimum of fifty-six Late Preclassic fortifications, as opposed to only five from earlier time periods.[317]

More than just documenting the rise in fortifications, however, Sorenson made note of their features in each period. Features documented at Late Preclassic fortifications include: (1) earthen barriers and occasionally even stone walls; (2) a ditch or moat; (3) a wooden palisade; and (4) isolated guard posts and towers from which stones and other projectiles could be launched at invaders.[318]

For example, the defensive earthworks at Becan (ca. AD 100) involved a ditch with an average width of sixteen meters and an earth embankment approximately eleven meters high on average from the bottom of the ditch. Archaeologists suspect a wooden palisade was built atop the embankment, from which stones and perhaps other projectiles were thrown at enemy attackers.[319]

The few fortifications that predate the Late Preclassic period do not have all these features,[320] while fortifications from later periods have a variety of additional features. Thus, in Mesoamerica, fortifications most consistent with those of Moroni in the mid-first century BC are those that date to that general time period. Similar fortifications are also known in pre-Columbian North America, although currently none in that region are known to date to Book of Mormon times.[321]

THE WHY

As the frequency and complexity of war increased, there became a greater need for the Nephites to fortify themselves against Lamanite attacks. Under these circumstances, Moroni did not settle for simple or basic fortifications. As Latter-day Saint author and educator John Bytheway pointed out, "it wasn't just heaps and timbers, but heaps, timbers, pickets, and towers that created places of security."[322] Comparison with the defensive features in contemporary Mesoamerica suggests that Moroni employed all the available methods of his time to protect and fortify his people.

Today, the temptations of the adversary grow subtler and more sophisticated. Following Moroni's example, readers today can and should use all the available means to protect themselves against "the temptations and the fiery darts of the adversary" (1 Nephi 15:24).

Elder M. Russell Ballard taught, "there is not one great and grand thing we can do to arm ourselves spiritually." Instead, Elder Ballard explained, "True spiritual power lies in numerous smaller acts woven together in a fabric of spiritual fortification that protects and shields from all evil."[323] These include prayer, scripture study, and following the living prophets, who are the current "watchmen" positioned atop the towers.[324]

Each feature of our spiritual defense is designed to further ground individuals and communities upon the rock of Christ, the only true defense and refuge from evil, suffering, and temptation in this fallen world (see Helaman 5:12).

FURTHER READING

David E. Spencer, *Captain Moroni's Command: Dynamics of Warfare in the Book of Mormon* (Springville, UT: Cedar Fort, 2015), 20–32.

John L. Sorenson, "Fortifications in the Book of Mormon Account Compared with Mesoamerican Fortifications," in *Warfare in the Book of Mormon*, ed. Stephen D. Ricks and William J. Hamblin (Salt Lake City and Provo, UT: Deseret Book and FARMS, 1990), 425–444.

John L. Sorenson, "Digging in the Book of Mormon: Our Changing Understanding of Ancient America and Its Scripture," *Ensign*, September 1984.

Why Would Pahoran Not Allow the Law to Be Amended?

"But behold, Pahoran would not alter nor suffer the law to be altered; therefore, he did not hearken to those who had sent in their voices with their petitions concerning the altering of the law." (Alma 51:3)

THE KNOW

Soon after Pahoran had been appointed as the chief judge (see Alma 50:39–40), the Book of Mormon reports that "there began to be a contention among the people . . . for behold, there were a part of the people who desired that a few particular points of the law should be altered" (Alma 51:2). These political activists were called "king-men" because they desired to "overthrow the free government and to establish a king over the land" (Alma 51:5).

When "Pahoran would not alter nor suffer the law to be altered" (Alma 51:3), the king-men "were desirous that Pahoran should be dethroned from the judgment-seat" (Alma 51:5). On the other hand, those who supported Pahoran "took upon them the name of freemen; and thus was the division among them, for the freemen had sworn or covenanted to maintain their rights and the privileges of their religion by a free government" (Alma 51:6).

While modern societies typically view laws as provisional products of human creation, ancient civilizations often saw them as immutable decrees publically promulgated and sent forth by divinely appointed rulers.[325] Moses, for example, received the Ten Commandments on "tables of stone, written with the finger of God" (Exodus 31:18), which in turn were covenantally accepted by the people.[326]

That these divinely etched tablets were to be transported and memorialized in a sacred vessel, known as the ark of the covenant, only solidified their physical and symbolic permanence (see Exodus 25:10–16).[327] Other ancient societies similarly wrote on non-perishable materials, such as stone or metal, in order to establish the durability of laws, treaties, or decrees.[328]

John W. Welch explained:

> Accordingly, in the ancient world, law was much more than a matter of pragmatic policy or economic regulation. Law was an expression of the divine will, the highest ideals of a civilization, the necessary order of life, and the fundamental substance of justice and reality.[329]

Understanding that ancient peoples typically held their laws "in the highest esteem possible" might help explain why Pahoran and his freemen were so opposed to the king-men's effort to alter the law.[330]

Furthermore, ancient law was typically perceived as a binding component of a covenantal relationship.[331]

The stated reason for the freemen's support for retaining their current law was that they had "sworn or covenanted to maintain their rights and the privileges of their religion" (Alma 51:6). This likely refers most directly to their covenant to uphold Moroni's title of liberty (see Alma 46:19–21),[332] but it might also reflect an earlier commitment to support the laws and government Mosiah established (see Mosiah 29:37–39).[333]

THE WHY

Recognizing that legal statutes in the ancient world were often seen as permanent, divinely inspired, and covenant-related can help readers better contextualize the political factionalism found in Alma 51. This dispute was about far more than a suggested alteration of legal minutiae. Rather, the king-men's radical proposal to reverse King Mosiah's inspired system of judges would have encroached upon both political and religious fundamental norms and freedoms.

Unfortunately, the modern world faces similar threats to culturally crucial and religiously sacred freedoms. Elder D. Todd Christofferson concluded:

> My friends and fellow citizens, we live in challenging times. Religious freedom is indeed under fire. And things may get worse before they get better. But these are our times. This is our moment to defend our fundamental freedoms. With courage, conviction, and civility . . . each one of us can make a profound difference.[334]

In their perilous circumstances and in the context of ancient laws associated with religious covenants, Moroni was granted legal permission from the governor and the voice of the people "to compel those dissenters" to carry out their legal obligation "to defend their country" (Alma 51:15).[335] When those dissenters "did lift their weapons of war to fight against the men of Moroni" (Alma 51:18), many were killed. The rest were given a choice either to simply yield "to the standard of liberty" (Alma 51:20) or to be held in long-term prison under threat of death until eventually there would be time for their trials (see Alma 51:19).

Thankfully, our modern circumstances—although requiring no less boldness—call for civility and patience rather than force or compulsion, and in most places in the world we have the fortunate luxuries of time and resources to be able to respect human rights and constitutional protections. Thus, all people are encouraged "to teach and defend eternal truth in the way that our Heavenly Father desires, while at the same time exemplifying the respect, compassion, and deep love that Christ exemplified."[336]

Modern Latter-day Saints and patriots of other faiths see the established laws, rights, and duties of the United States Constitution—as well as many other similarly modeled constitutions or freedom-enabling governments—as being divinely inspired and consonant with God's will (see D&C 101:76–80).[337] While legal changes can and must occur in all societies, those modifications do not justifiably occur by civil disobedience and political opportunism. Therefore, like the freemen in Pahoran's day, all people who are so benefited are similarly and naturally obligated to defend their fundamental rights and privileges by following the guidance of patriotic leaders in carrying out the righteous will of the "voice of the people" (Alma 51:7).

FURTHER READING

John W. Welch, *The Legal Cases in the Book of Mormon* (Provo, UT: BYU Press and Neal A. Maxwell Institute for Religious Scholarship, 2008), 3–18.

RoseAnn Benson and Stephen D. Ricks, "Treaties and Covenants: Ancient Near Eastern Legal Terminology in the Book of Mormon," *Journal of Book of Mormon Studies 14*, no. 1 (2005): 48–61, 128–29.

John A. Tvedtnes, *The Book of Mormon and Other Hidden Books: Out of Darkness unto Light* (Provo UT: FARMS, 2000).

29

Why Did Mormon Speak of Pulling Down Pride?

"And it came to pass that Moroni commanded that his army should go against those king-men, to pull down their pride and their nobility and level them with the earth." (Alma 51:17)

THE KNOW

On several occasions, Captain Moroni spoke of pulling down the pride of the political elite who were unwilling to fight for their country. For instance, when a group of dissenters known as king-men attempted to overthrow the government, Moroni "commanded that his army should go against those king-men, to *pull down their pride and their nobility* and level them with the earth" (Alma 51:17; emphasis added).[338]

Some may wonder where the imagery of pulling something down comes from and how it might be related to political power, pride, or nobility. First, to *pull down*, *bring down*, *break down*, *throw down*, or *cut down* something in order to destroy or humble it occurs in many biblical passages.[339] In many cases, the things that are brought low are inherently high or prideful, such as false idols, altars, lofty trees, towers, buildings, armies, mighty kingdoms, and noble rulers. Typically, the high thing is brought low to the earth, to the grave, into captivity, or even to a pit symbolic of hell. The Book of Mormon uses much of the same imagery.[340]

Perhaps Moroni recalled that a great and spacious building in Nephi's vision represented the "pride of the world" and that "it fell, and the fall thereof was exceedingly great" (1 Nephi 11:36).[341] Or maybe he was thinking of the "pomp" of Lucifer, who had "fallen from heaven" and was "cut down to the ground" (Isaiah 14:11–12). Whatever the case, his warning that the proud would be leveled to the earth seems to be right at home with a number of other scriptures dealing with the consequences of pride.

Studying the Book of Mormon in an ancient American setting may offer even more ways to view Moroni's language. Like ancient Near Eastern rulers, Mesoamerican kings often sat on elevated thrones, which literally and symbolically raised them above their subjects.[342] This may help explain why Moroni, after repeatedly condemning wicked rulers for sitting idly on their thrones, concluded by saying, "I seek not for power, but to *pull it down*" (Alma 60:36; emphasis added).[343] In other words, pulling down pride may have been a metaphor for pulling down a ruler from his throne.[344]

Yet thrones weren't the only raised objects that signified a ruler's status. Mesoamerican kings also erected large stones called "stelae" that, among other things, recorded their accomplishments.[345] These inscribed stones (also called "banner stones") were conceptually linked to cloth war banners called "flap staffs." The erection of stelae and the raising of flap staffs on towers were ceremonial actions that held political and ritual significance among various Mesoamerican societies.[346]

That such rituals were also important to Book of Mormon peoples can be seen by the fact that Moroni compelled the dissenters to "hoist the title of liberty [a perfect example of a 'flap staff'] upon their towers, and in their cities, and to take up arms in defence of their country" (Alma 51:20).[347] Thus, *pulling down* their pride was followed immediately by *raising up* a symbol of religious freedom. This suggests that Moroni's imagery of pulling down pride may have been an idiom that directly contrasted with the raising up of ceremonial objects symbolic of kingship.[348]

Interestingly, when one group of people conquered another in ancient Mesoamerica, the conquerors often pulled down or destroyed the monuments of past leaders and replaced them with their own.[349] Excavators at Piedras Negras, for example, found that an elaborately carved throne had been "willfully smashed and strewn about the chamber of the palace" after what was likely a "military attack."[350] In relation to the "proposed conquest of Tikal by Teotihuicanos and their Tikal allies," a stela depicting a "king stepping on a bound sacrificial victim" was ritually decapitated.[351]

At Cholula, a group of large stone stelae were "thrown down and intentionally smashed."[352] And in Copan, a stela inscription begins with a reference to the "toppling of the Foundation House."[353] David Stuart, an expert in ancient Mesoamerican inscriptions, interpreted this as "a possible metaphorical reference to the end of Copan's ruling line."[354] In light of these findings, Moroni's command that his army "pull down" the rulers' pride may have been more than mere metaphor: it may have referred to literally tearing down the monuments representing the king-men's nobel status.

THE WHY

The problem with the king-men in the time of Captain Moroni was that they felt their social status granted them special privileges. Their pride led them to selfishly stand by and watch as the common people bled and died on the battlefield to preserve their rights and freedoms. Moroni's stern rebuke and swift military action is a reminder that God will not always tolerate injustice. It also shows that the eventual fall of those who exercise unlawful dominion will be tremendous, which is dramatically visualized in the idea of prideful monuments being "pulled down."

President Ezra Taft Benson referred to pride as the "universal sin" and "the great vice."[355] Similarly, President Dieter F. Uchtdorf taught, "Pride is the great sin of self-elevation. It is for so many a personal Rameumptom, a holy stand that justifies envy, greed, and vanity."[356] Those in this state of self-elevation often become self-absorbed and calloused to others' needs.

The Book of Mormon teaches that the solution for anyone to get out of this condition is to willingly "humble yourselves even to the dust" (Alma 34:38). The "dust" of the earth provides a good metaphor because as one willingly lowers oneself in humility (such as bowing to the earth in prayer), he or she can remember that mankind was "created of the dust of the earth" and that "it belongeth to him who created you" (Mosiah 2:25).[357]

Ultimately, when we begin to comprehend our complete dependence on Jesus Christ—who both created us and atoned for our sins—we will begin to see why, in the end, "every knee shall bow, and every tongue confess before him" (Mosiah 27:31).[358] In one of the gospel's insightful ironies, those who refuse to humble themselves will, like Lucifer, be pulled down to the dust (see Genesis 3:14). In contrast, those who willingly humble themselves to the dust and obey God's commandments will be raised up into eternal life (see 3 Nephi 15:1).[359] As the prophet Alma taught, "Yea, he that truly humbleth himself, and repenteth of his sins, and endureth to the end, the same shall be blessed—yea, much more blessed than they who are compelled to be humble" (Alma 32:15).

FURTHER READING

Kerry Hull, "War Banners: A Mesoamerican Context for the Title of Liberty," *Journal of Book of Mormon Studies 24* (2015): 84–118.

Dieter F. Uchtdorf, "Pride and the Priesthood," *Ensign*, November 2010, 55–58.

Ezra Taft Benson, "Beware of Pride," *Ensign*, May 1989.

30

Why Did Teancum Slay Amalickiah on New Year's Eve?

"And thus ended the twenty and fifth year of the reign of the judges over the people of Nephi. And thus ended the days of Amalickiah." (Alma 51:37)[360]

THE KNOW

The rebellion of the king-men diverted the attention of Moroni and the Nephite military, creating an opportunity that Amalickiah used to seize control of some Nephite lands along the eastern seashore (see Alma 51:12–28). Teancum and his "great warriors" met Amalickiah's army, however, before they could reach Bountiful (see Alma 51:29–30). Teancum and his army pushed Amalickiah back, forcing him to retreat to the coast, where his armies set up camp for the night (see Alma 51:31–32).

After night fell, Teancum snuck into the Lamanite camp and "stole privily into the tent of the king, and put a javelin to his heart," thereby putting Amalickiah to death (Alma 51:34). Mormon dramatically reported that this was the final night of the twenty-fifth year of the reign of the judges (see Alma 51:37). The next morning, New Year's Day, the Lamanites awoke to find that "Amalickiah was dead in his own tent; and . . . Teancum was ready to give them battle on that day" (Alma 52:1). The Lamanites "were affrighted," retreated into a stronghold they had conquered from the Nephites, and appointed Amalickiah's brother Ammoron as king (see Alma 51:2–3).

The timing of this event was significant. In ancient Israel, where people were obligated to keep close track of the days of the months and years (see Leviticus 23), the New Year was traditionally celebrated as "a day of coronation of divine and earthly kings, a day of victory over chaos, a day of renewal of covenant and the reenactment of the king's enthronement. . . . This was the day when the king should have ceremonially conquered death and been reenthroned!"[361]

Taylor Halverson noted, "In the ancient Near Eastern culture, . . . New Year's Day was the time when the king of the land would sally forth to demonstrate his vitality and liveliness to successfully rule as a king for another year."[362] As one can imagine, awaking to find the king dead on such a day could not be a good sign. In fact, it was almost certainly interpreted by the Lamanites as a bad omen.

John L. Sorenson explained that in Mesoamerica, "Omens were regularly sought and frequently were tied to the events of the last, or first, day [of the year]." As such, "It would be highly characteristic of Mesoamericans to act as the Lamanites did upon the death of Amalickiah. To awaken on the first day of a new year to find their leader dead would have been far more unnerving to their omen-conscious feelings than we moderns may appreciate."[363]

Allen J. Christensen documented "that as part of their New Year's rites, ancient Maya kings engaged in ritual combat with evil lords who resided in the north." Christensen continued, "Their legitimacy and the continued survival of their kingdoms depended on the successful defeat of these powerful adversaries." These rites can be "traced continuously in time to at least the Late Preclassic period," placing it squarely within the time of Teancum and Amalickiah.

> It is therefore no accident that the Lamanite king Amalickiah chose New Year's to engage the Nephites in battle (Alma 51:32–52:1). The Nephite general Teancum took advantage of the situation by slaying Amalickiah on New Year's Eve, precisely when the underworld lords would have been believed to be their strongest. When the Lamanites awoke the following morning, expecting a divinely sanctioned victory, they found instead their king and protector dead. It is no wonder, then, that they fled in terror.[364]

THE WHY

Halverson felt that this story illustrated the importance of minute details. "The seemingly small details in the text of the Book of Mormon matter."[365] The exact date of the event is a seemingly minor point, but Mormon goes out of his way to include it. It was important: Teancum could have chosen no better day for his slaying for the maximum amount of negative impact on Lamanite morale.

Given the ancient Old and New World backgrounds, it seems likely that Teancum deliberately chose New Year's Eve for his nocturnal assassination. Daniel C. Peterson reasoned, "Given the importance of ancient kings for guaranteeing prosperity, good harvests and the proper order of the cosmos, and given their central role in military conflicts . . . the sudden loss of a king at the beginning of the New Year could be psychologically traumatic and disorienting, if not lethal."[366]

Halverson agreed: "A dead king was the sure sign of a disastrous future." Hence, no act could be more psychologically demoralizing to an opposing army than to find their king dead on New Year's Day. Teancum chose New Year's Eve to assassinate Amalickiah. He sought to win a massive psychological victory against the Lamanites by sending a message of disaster, despair, and fear.[367]

This is one of many examples that illustrate the importance for modern readers to not only pay attention to, but to investigate with heightened interest the seemingly trivial and yet often unexpectedly significant information in the Book of Mormon text.

FURTHER READING

Taylor Halverson, "In Cover of Darkness and the Turning of the New Year," *Deseret News*, January 1, 2015.

Daniel C. Peterson, "May Your New Year Begin Better than Amalickiah's," *Deseret News*, December 29, 2011.

Allen J. Christenson, "Maya Harvest Festivals and the Book of Mormon," *Review of Books on the Book of Mormon 3* (1991): 1–31.

31

How Old Were the Stripling Warriors?

"And they were all young men, and they were exceedingly valiant for courage, and also for strength and activity." (Alma 53:20)

THE KNOW

About a year into the great Nephite and Lamanite war, the sons of the Anti-Nephi-Lehies "who had not entered into a covenant that they would not take their weapons of war" instead "entered into a covenant to fight for the liberty of the Nephites" (Alma 53:16–17). Some have wondered just how old these "young men" were. While their fathers were still under oath to not take up arms again, these sons were old enough to fight but young enough to have not made that oath themselves.

While the exact timing of the covenant is difficult to devise from the Book of Mormon narrative, it seems to be shortly before the Lamanites attacked Ammonihah in the eleventh year of the reign of the judges (see Alma 16:1–4). This attack was precipitated by the Lamanite frustration from having slaughtered their own brethren among the Anti-Nephi-Lehies (see Alma 24–25:2). When the stripling warriors enlisted to aid the Nephite armies, it was the twenty-sixth year of the reign of the judges (see Alma 56:9). So the young men took up arms approximately fifteen years after their fathers had made their covenant.

In ancient Israel, "twenty appears to have been the age at which Israelite males became obligated to serve in the military" (see, for example, Numbers 1:3).[368] A handful of Latter-day Saint scholars have thus proposed that the "young men" under Helaman's command were around twenty years of age.[369] This would make them about five years old at the time their fathers covenanted to never take up arms again, likely too young to have joined their covenant-making ceremony.[370]

While twenty years old may have been the appointed age for military service, John W. Welch hinted, "Some of these volunteers may have been under the legal age for military service and for that reason were not serving in the regular Nephite army."[371] Helaman told Moroni that they were "very young" (Alma 56:46), and called them his "little sons" (Alma 56:30, 39), descriptions that suggest they were younger than the usual age of a soldier.

When Joseph Smith translated the Book of Mormon, the word *stripling* (see Alma 53:22; 56:57) meant "a youth in the state of adolescence, or just passing from boyhood to manhood; a lad."[372] Given that it was typical for young men to be married and starting a family by seventeen, this could indicate that some of these warriors may have been very young, perhaps between twelve and fifteen years of age.[373]

THE WHY

Visualizing an army of adolescents ranging from early teens, or even preteens, to about twenty adds emphasis to key points in the narrative. It heightens Helaman's fears "that my little sons should fall into [Lamanite] hands" and his reluctance to send them into battle (Alma 56:39). Hence, they must plead with him, "let us go," arguing, "God is with us, and he will not suffer that we should fall" (Alma 56:46).

Their notable youth also amplifies the greatness of their courage. In the face of an older, larger, more menacing army of blood-thirsty Lamanites, these striplings "did not fear death" (Alma 56:47). No wonder Helaman remarked, "Never had I seen so great courage, nay, not amongst all the Nephites" (Alma 56:45).

It also magnifies the miracle. After the battle, Helaman understandably feared "lest there were many of them slain" (Alma 56:55). Upon learning that all of them had survived, he marveled, "They had fought as if with the strength of God; yea, never were men known to have fought with such miraculous strength; and with such mighty power" (Alma 56:56). Realizing it was an army of teenagers who fought with such incredible strength gives us a greater sense of God's miraculous power.

For Mormon, this story must have been especially inspiring. Being only fifteen when he was appointed commander-in-chief of the whole Nephite army (see Mormon 1:15; 2:2), he would have been intrigued to learn about a whole army of youths who had fought at an earlier time in Nephite history. Learning about how their firm faith and exacting obedience to the gospel teachings of their mothers served to strengthen them in battle would have been stirring for the young commander. It possibly led him to reflect on his own experience and see how the Lord had guided and preserved him in battle from an early age.

Today, the story continues to inspire readers of all ages, but especially youths and young adults, who face an increasingly menacing world.[374] Like the stripling warriors, through faith, courage, and obedience, youth today can overcome challenges "with the strength of God" (Alma 56:56).

FURTHER READING

John A. Tvedtnes, "What Were the Ages of Helaman's Stripling Warriors?," *Ensign*, September 1992, 28.

32

Why Was Ammoron Determined to Avenge the Blood of His Brother?

"I am Ammoron, the king of the Lamanites; I am the brother of Amalickiah whom ye have murdered. Behold, I will avenge his blood upon you." (Alma 54:16)

THE KNOW

The Nephite defector Amalickiah is infamous for his treachery, fraud, and deceit. A descendant of Zoram (see Alma 49:25; 54:23), Amalickiah "used flattery and played on the ambitions of others to obtain a substantial following" before eventually assassinating the Lamanite king and launching war on the Nephites (Alma 46–50).[375] Amalickiah met his end when the Nephite warrior Teancum snuck into his camp and "put a javelin to his heart" while he slept (Alma 51:34).[376]

Amalickiah's legacy did not die with him, however. Amalickiah's brother Ammoron succeeded him as king of the Lamanites and did not hesitate to continue his fallen brother's warfare against the Nephites (see Alma 52). Like his brother, Ammoron had no love for his former brethren, and he demanded no less than total surrender or annihilation. "We will wage a war which shall be eternal, either to the subjecting the Nephites to our authority or to their eternal extinction," boasted Ammoron (Alma 54:20).

Ammoron's hatred for the Nephites also ran on a deeply personal level. In a heated letter to Moroni, the new Lamanite king vowed,

> I am Ammoron, the king of the Lamanites; I am the brother of Amalickiah whom ye have murdered. Behold, I will avenge his blood upon you, yea, and I will come upon you with my armies for I fear not your threatenings (Alma 54:16).

Ironically, Amalickiah had sworn that he would drink the blood of Moroni (see Alma 49:27; 51:9), but now it was Amalickiah's blood that needed to be avenged.

Besides feeling personally obligated to avenge the blood of his brother, Ammoron went back to the origins of tribal conflict in the earliest days of the Nephite–Lamanite split. "For behold, your fathers did wrong their brethren, insomuch that they did rob them of their right to the government when it rightly belonged unto them" (Alma 54:17). "I am a bold Lamanite," declared Ammoron, a former Zoramite, thus making it clear he had switched sides, adopting a new political and cultural identity (Alma 54:24).

The dynamics fueling Ammoron's worldview and objectives are complex. At a most basic level, this is a rather obvious example of tribalism and ethnic tension.

While political aspirations were undoubtedly tied up in Ammoron's declaration, it is important to note that he appealed to a deeply rooted tribal or clan rivalry as the motivation for his political goals. In perpetuating this tribal antagonism, Ammoron promoted an ideology fundamentally at odds with the egalitarian and anti-tribal ideals of Nephite prophets (cf. 2 Nephi 26:33; Mosiah 4:19; 4 Nephi 1:2, 17).[377]

An additional motivating factor for Ammoron may be related to the Hebrew judicial concept of "blood vengeance." In a world with no real equivalent to modern law enforcement, "one of the most important clan duties" in many ancient cultures was "for the nearest of kin to hunt down and carry out the death-penalty on a person that had slain a member of the sept or family."[378] Ancient Hebrew law allowed for this, granting the legal right and duty for a kinsman to avenge the blood of a murdered family or clan member (see Exodus 21:12–14; Numbers 35:16–28; Deuteronomy 19:4–13).[379]

This avenger of blood is called a *goel* in biblical Hebrew. Conventionally translated as "redeemer,"[380] one of the responsibilities of being an avenging kinsman (a *goel*) was to bring about justice, rectifying the intentional and hateful murder of a near family member by killing the murderer or a substitute.[381] At the same time, one suspected of wrongful homicide had the right to flee to a city of refuge, where a disinterested body of elders and Levites would hear the case (see Numbers 35:9–24; Deuteronomy 4:41–44).

Extending this legal procedure into the theological realm, Jehovah was, naturally, considered the divine *goel* (redeemer, avenger) of Israel as a whole (see Exodus 6:6; 15:13; Psalms 74:2; 94). He was expected to avenge Israel's blood shed by her physical and spiritual enemies and also to redeem Israel or buy her back from bondage, slavery, or debt servitude.

The language in Alma 54 surely suggests that Ammoron was familiar with this underlying institution of blood redemption. He saw himself as acting in a redemptive capacity. His threat to Moroni that he would specifically "avenge [his brother Amalickiah's] blood upon you" invokes and captures the thrust of the blood vengeance mechanism stemming from the earliest days of ancient Israelite history.

THE WHY

In a straightforward reaction, Ammoron threatened to hold Moroni personally accountable for the death of his brother, Amalickiah. Teancum was one of Moroni's warriors, and although he apparently acted on his own initiative, Ammoron would have naturally invoked his traditional rights and duties to avenge the death of his brother. He tried to do this by putting Moroni on notice that he was a hunted man.

Yet Ammoron himself acted rashly in making this threat. His motives were not based in measured legal steps. Why, for example, did he not seek the blood of the slayer, Teancum, who was still alive? The answer to this question probably lies in Ammoron's desire to escalate the situation, using the death of King Amalickiah as justifying a call for the death of a higher-ranking Nephite, like Moroni. This, however, was not a call for legal justice. Ammoron, assuming the role of divine avenger, would hardly have allowed Moroni to flee to an altar of refuge for protection and justice.[382]

Ammoron's reaction typifies one more way in which the war chapters in the book of Alma are composed as a portrait of stark opposites.[383] The righteous heroes Moroni and Helaman stand in contrast with the villains Amalickiah and Ammoron. Where Moroni was honorable, just, and righteous (Alma 48:17–18), Amalickiah was power-hungry, treasonous, and deceitful (see Alma 46:4–5; 47:30, 35). Where Moroni treated his enemies nobly (see Alma 44:1–7), Ammoron treated his enemies spitefully, and in this case vindictively (see Alma 54:16–24). This point was included by Mormon in his final record in order to paint for modern readers a clear picture of what good and bad leaders look like.

By studying Ammoron's personality, including his literal thirst for blood and vengeance, readers of the Book of Mormon are also warned to avoid allowing past grievances and old wounds to consume one with hatred and malice. Had Ammoron sought the true Redeemer's way of reconciliation instead of raw vengeance, it's very likely that thousands, including Ammoron (see Alma 62:35–36), would have been spared from years of bloody and senseless conflict.

FURTHER READING

Richard McClendon, "Captain Moroni's Wartime Strategies: An Application for the Spiritual Battles of Our Day," *Religious Educator 3*, no. 3 (2002): 99–114.

Brant A. Gardner, *Second Witness: Analytical and Contextual Commentary on the Book of Mormon*, 6 vols. (Salt Lake City, UT: Greg Kofford Books, 2007), 4:689–694.

Why Did Moroni Change His Mind about Exchanging Prisoners with Ammoron?

"Behold, I will not exchange prisoners with Ammoron save he will withdraw his purpose, as I have stated in my epistle; for I will not grant unto him that he shall have any more power than what he hath got." (Alma 55:2)

THE KNOW

Among several other literary genres,[384] Mormon's abridgment of Nephite history includes a handful of official letters and communications. Such epistles offer a unique view of characters' personalities and motivations because we get it firsthand from the authors themselves rather than as editorialized, secondhand abridgments.[385] An example of such is the exchange between Moroni and Ammoron.[386]

After retaking the city of Mulek and fortifying Bountiful (see Alma 53:2–3), Moroni received a written message from Ammoron, who desired to exchange prisoners (see Alma 54:1). Moroni accepted Ammoron's offer on the condition that he would "deliver up a man and his wife and his children, for one prisoner" (Alma 54:11).

Yet when Ammoron gladly agreed to these terms (see Alma 54:20), Moroni declared, "Behold, I will not exchange prisoners with Ammoron save he will withdraw his purpose, as I have stated in my epistle" (Alma 55:2). This turnabout may be somewhat perplexing for many readers. Why would Moroni set forth the terms for a prisoner exchange and then change his mind once Ammoron accepted his offer?

Richard Dilworth Rust explained:

> In cosmic terms, these letters between Moroni and Ammoron have to do less with exchange of prisoners than with the irreconcilable conflict between the powers of God and Satan, with Moroni appearing as the Christian champion. . . . For his part, Ammoron, a Zoramite who has rejected his faith and turned into a Lamanite, epitomizes the apostate who repeatedly leads attacks on the Nephites.[387]

More than simply setting the terms for an exchange of prisoners, Moroni's epistle was mainly focused on proclaiming the justness of the Nephite cause and warning Ammoron against continuing to pursue the conflict. "The first half of Moroni's letter builds on a rhetorical formula repeated four times: 'except ye repent and withdraw' (Alma 54:6, 7) or 'except ye withdraw' (Alma 54:9, 10) your armies and your murderous intentions, God's wrath and death will come upon you."[388]

When considered in this light, it becomes clear that Moroni's terms for the prisoner exchange were accompanied by an ultimatum to cease the war.

Ammoron's reply not only revealed his "perfect knowledge of his fraud" (Alma 55:1), but that he would gladly exchange prisoners so that, as he stated, "I may preserve my food for my men, and we will wage a war which shall be eternal" (Alma 54:20). In other words, Ammoron outright dismissed Moroni's warnings and showed that the prisoner exchange would only facilitate further warfare.

THE WHY

A careful reading of Moroni's epistle can help demonstrate that, rather than going back on his word, Moroni was likely justified in withdrawing his offer. Ammoron had utterly refused the most essential part of the bargain—to cease the war—and Moroni was certainly not going to "grant unto him that he shall have any more power than what he hath got" (Alma 55:2).

Because the text demonstrates Moroni's anger and frustration in response to Ammoron's actions (Alma 54:13; 55:1), some may read into this scenario that Moroni was simply a hotheaded and unwise negotiator. Yet Mormon, who likely had more access to material about Moroni than appears in the text,[389] consistently saw Moroni's choices and character in a favorable light.[390] Moreover, the narrative itself demonstrates that Moroni's choice to forego a prisoner exchange turned to the Nephites' favor, for they were able to not only rescue the captives, but also boldly arm even the women and children, results that Moroni had openly announced and predicted in his letter (see Alma 55:16–17).[391]

Whether or not Moroni's anger was a form of righteous indignation,[392] these epistles demonstrate that he was able to channel his passion toward defending and protecting his people as God had entrusted him to do. Likewise, modern prophets and apostles, with their admitted personal flaws or weaknesses, have been called by God to accomplish His own purposes. Elder David A. Bednar taught:

> I am blessed to observe on a daily basis the individual personalities, capacities, and noble characters of these leaders. Some people find the human shortcomings of the Brethren troubling and faith diminishing. For me those imperfections are encouraging and faith promoting.[393]

Mormon's assessment of Moroni's character can be a guiding star in helping readers assess his true worth and character.[394] Concerning his righteousness, Mormon declared, "Yea, verily, verily I say unto you, if all men had been, and were, and ever would be, like unto Moroni, behold, the very powers of hell would have been shaken forever; yea, the devil would never have power over the hearts of the children of men" (Alma 48:17).

FURTHER READING

Robert F. Smith, "Epistolary Form in the Book of Mormon," *FARMS Review 22*, no. 2 (2010): 125–135.

Richard Dilworth Rust, *Feasting on the Word: The Literary Testimony of the Book of Mormon* (Salt Lake City and Provo, UT: Deseret Book and FARMS, 1997), 150–154.

Sidney B. Sperry, "Types of Literature in the Book of Mormon: Epistles, Psalms, Lamentations," *Journal of Book of Mormon Studies 4*, no. 1 (1995): 69–80.

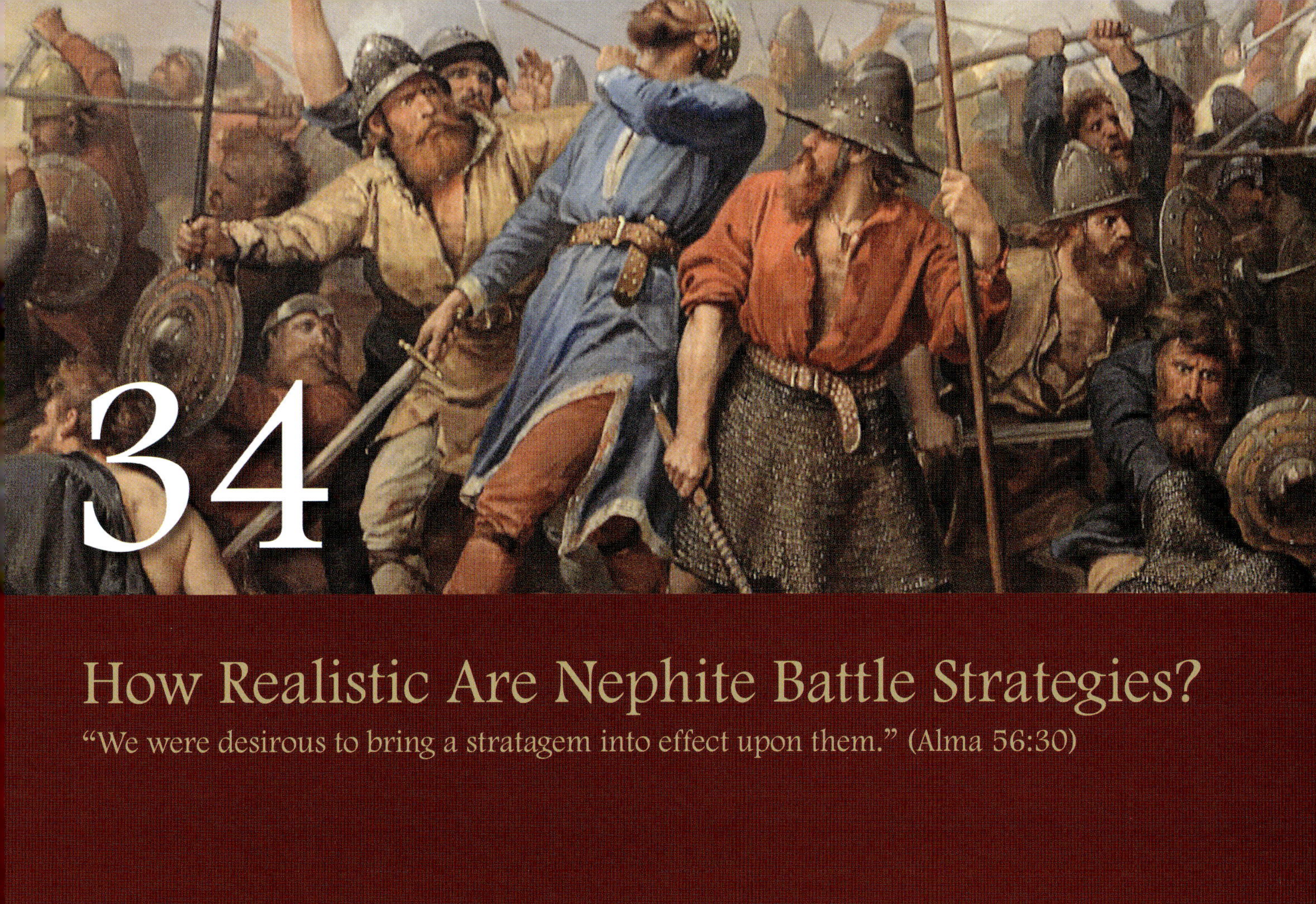

How Realistic Are Nephite Battle Strategies?

"We were desirous to bring a stratagem into effect upon them." (Alma 56:30)

THE KNOW

The Book of Mormon's rich accounts of warfare in the first century BC contain some of the most exciting and interesting material in the thousand-year narrative. The stories are replete with battlefield strategies, various military maneuvers, topographical awareness, innovative fortifications and weaponry, concerns over provisions, military intelligence, and even covert, late-night operations.

These narratives have captured the imagination of Latter-day Saints of all ages, from young boys in Primary to popular fiction writers. Perhaps less recognized, these chapters have also caught the attention of some with both academic and professional military expertise.[395]

Before Hugh Nibley was a popular BYU professor and scholar, he was a soldier in World War II.[396] After experiencing the horrors of war, he strenuously avoided the war chapters in the Book of Mormon.[397] When he finally turned his critical eye toward the military accounts, he quickly saw,

> It is real war that we see here, a tedious, sordid, plodding, joyless routine of see-saw successes and losses—brutally expensive, destructive, exhausting, and boring, with constant marches and countermarches that end sometimes in fiasco and sometimes in intensely unpleasant engagements.

Nibley felt this kind of war could be described only by someone who experienced it.

> The author writes as one would write—as only one could write—who had gone through a long war as a front-line observer with his eyes wide open. Everything is strictly authentic, with the proper emphasis in the proper place. Strategy and tactics are treated with the knowledge of an expert . . . it is all there.[398]

Several years later, former U.S. Army reserve officer John E. Kammeyer concluded, "the Book of Mormon does indeed depict warfare on three levels: it is realistic war, it is realistic Iron Age warfare, and it is realistic Mesoamerican warfare."[399] Consistent with these conclusions, William J. Hamblin, a military historian, also concluded "the Book of Mormon [warfare] uniquely reflects its dual heritage of the ancient Near East and Mesoamerica."[400]

Morgan Deane, a published military historian,[401] also served in the U.S. Marine Corps. Bringing this unique set of expertise to his study of the Book of Mormon, Deane remarked, "[Military] Leaders in The Book of Mormon responded in realistic and organized fashion."[402]

After careful study of the maneuvers in Alma 56, David E. Spencer, an academic and professional with expertise in defense studies and experience in the U.S. Army, concluded, "These seemingly sudden, illogical actions . . . speak volumes about the authenticity of the text and the military expertise of the author, as when all of the clues provided in the text are examined in depth, the logic becomes apparent."[403]

THE WHY

Many aspects of military theory are universal across time and space. Nonetheless, proper understanding and expertise in the strategy and tactics of war requires years of study, extensive training, and real-life experience. Joseph Smith lacked that kind of background,[404] yet several modern readers with just such qualifications have found that the Book of Mormon accounts of wartime strategy are strikingly realistic.

According to Spencer—who has been involved in creating battle scenarios for training purposes—this kind of accuracy was beyond the ability of Joseph Smith to fabricate.[405]

This is the sort of unconscious consistency in war accounts that would be almost impossible for someone writing a made-up story—as Joseph Smith has been accused of—to get right. And yet the Book of Mormon gets them right repeatedly.[406]

The realism of the Book of Mormon's crucial accounts about warfare carries with it many equally authentic lessons that are critical for our day.[407] The horrors of inhumane militarism carries with it a stark warning for modern societies. No one knew this better than Mormon, the Nephite prophet, historian, and commander-in-chief. Kammeyer rightly concluded that if Mormon's record presents real, authentic accounts of devastating wars and rightly attributes them to wickedness, then "we have to take seriously the book's assertion that survival of a society depends on obedience to God."[408]

FURTHER READING

David E. Spencer, *Captain Moroni's Command: Dynamics of Warfare in the Book of Mormon* (Springville, UT: Cedar Fort, 2015).

Morgan Deane, *Bleached Bones and Wicked Serpents: Ancient Warfare in the Book of Mormon* (self-published, 2014).

John E. Kammeyer, *The Nephite Art of War* (Far West Publications, 2012).

Hugh Nibley, *Since Cumorah*, *The Collected Works of Hugh Nibley: Volume 7* (Salt Lake City and Provo, UT: Deseret Book and FARMS, 1988), 291–333.

35

Why Did the Stripling Warriors Perform Their Duties "with Exactness"?

"Yea, and they did obey and observe to perform every word of command with exactness." (Alma 57:21)

THE KNOW

Helaman's stripling warriors are looked to by Latter-day Saints, especially Latter-day Saint youth, as examples of great faith and courage.[409] Their exploits are chronicled in Alma 53, 56–58. The stripling warriors were described as "young men . . . exceedingly valiant for courage, and also for strength and activity."[410] More than adept warriors, however, the sons of Helaman were "men of truth and soberness, for they had been taught to keep the commandments of God and to walk uprightly before him" (Alma 53:20–21).

During one skirmish with the Lamanites, the stripling warriors stood out among their Nephite comrades for their unflinching bravery and obedience at a crucial moment. Just as Ammoron's forces "were about to overpower us," Helaman reported, "behold, my little band of two thousand and sixty fought most desperately; yea, they were firm before the Lamanites, and did administer death unto all those who opposed them" (Alma 57:18–19). Just "as the remainder of [Helaman's] army were about to give way before the Lamanites, behold, those two thousand and sixty were firm and undaunted" (Alma 57:20).

Helaman directly attributed the last-minute Nephite victory to the faithfulness of his stripling warriors: "Yea, and they did obey and observe to perform every word of command with exactness; yea, and even according to their faith it was done unto them" (Alma 57:21). This dedication and diligence saved the Nephites from "critical circumstances" (Alma 57:16) that otherwise might very well have doomed the Nephite war effort.

The language in Alma 57 used to describe the sons of Helaman hearkens back to the language of another ancient military campaign: that of the Israelite conquest of Canaan as recorded in the book of Joshua. As the children of Israel were preparing for war with Canaanite enemies, the Lord commanded them through the prophet-general Joshua, "Be strong and of a good courage . . . that thou mayest observe to do according to all the law, which Moses my servant commanded thee: turn not from it to the right hand or to the left, that thou mayest prosper whithersoever thou goest" (Joshua 1:6–7).

This command to the Israelites was repeated throughout the campaign in Canaan (cf. Joshua 10:25; 23:6). It was conjoined with a promise that if the children of Israel were strictly faithful and obedient to all the Lord's commandments, He would lead them, fight for them, deliver them from their enemies, and prosper them in the land of promise (see Joshua 1:8, 23). The book of Joshua retells several instances where the Israelites were routed because of their disobedience to the Lord (see, for example, Joshua 7). The clear intention of these accounts was to show the dangers of rebellion, disobedience, and apostasy, especially during precarious times when exacting obedience to God was necessary for collective success and national salvation.

THE WHY

On a strictly pragmatic level, the success or failure of a military campaign largely depends on the effectiveness of the combat force. Victory is dependent on troops that are disciplined, loyal, obedient, and quick to execute their commander's orders. Helaman's stripling warriors more than proved their combat effectiveness in their quick, decisive, and unflinching bravery and loyalty in the face of opposition.

On a spiritual level, this portrayal of the sons of Helaman may serve to reinforce an important doctrine in the Book of Mormon; namely, "Inasmuch as ye shall keep my commandments, ye shall prosper in the land . . . Inasmuch as ye will not keep my commandments ye shall be cut off from the presence of the Lord" (Alma 9:13). Beyond the mere acquisition of wealth, to "prosper" in a scriptural sense is to fulfill righteous desires or promises and, ultimately, to find safety in the Lord's presence.[411] This was true also for the ancient Israelites, who were promised both temporal and spiritual blessings in the land of promise should they "prosper" by keeping the Lord's commandments.

Likening the tenacity of the stripling warriors to modern followers of Christ, Elder David F. Evans of the Seventy remarked, "In life, it is when the rains descend and the floods come and the winds blow and beat upon us and on our house that we determine whether our faith is strong and whether we put our trust in God continually."[412] Like the ancient Nephites and Israelites, modern believers can find strength in following the Lord's commandments, especially in times of adversity.

FURTHER READING

Douglas J. Bell, *Defenders of the Faith: The Book of Mormon from a Soldier's Perspective* (Springville, UT: Cedar Fort, Inc., 2012), 89–105.

Jo Ann H. Seely, "Stripling Warriors," in *Book of Mormon Reference Companion,* ed. Dennis L. Largey (Salt Lake City, UT: Deseret Book, 2003), 746–747.

36

How Did Helaman's Army Maintain Faith While Being Cut off from Provisions?

"But, behold . . . we trust God will deliver us, notwithstanding the weakness of our armies, yea, and deliver us out of the hands of our enemies." (Alma 58:37)

THE KNOW

In his lengthy epistle to Moroni, Helaman reported that the Nephite armies on his front of the war had essentially reached a stalemate with the Lamanites (see Alma 58:1–2). Helaman wrote that after sending "an embassy to the governor of our land, to acquaint him concerning the affairs of our people," Helaman and his companions waited "to receive provisions and strength from the land of Zarahemla" (Alma 58:4).

Yet while the Lamanites were "receiving great strength from day to day, and also many provisions" (Alma 58:5), the Nephites "did wait in these difficult circumstances for the space of many months, even until [they] were about to perish for the want of food" (Alma 58:7). Eventually, they received food guarded by an "army of two thousand men," but Helaman lamented that "this is all the assistance which we did receive . . . to contend with an enemy which was innumerable" (Alma 58:8).

Prior to this time, Helaman's young warriors had received many provisions from their fathers (see Alma 56:27), who were obligated to provide "a portion of their substance to assist" the Nephites in maintaining their armies (Alma 43:13). These Ammonite fathers couldn't fight themselves because of their covenant to never "use weapons again for the shedding of man's blood" (Alma 24:18).[413] Interestingly, what we know of supplying armies in ancient America provides a striking resemblance to this narrative. John L. Sorenson explained:

> The logistics of maintaining a force in the field in Mesoamerica, either defensively or on the attack, was a serious challenge under ancient conditions. . . . Typically a supply of food was carried by soldiers on their backs from their home communities. . . . Supplies continually brought from the home base by a transport column were required or desirable.[414]

Similar to an ancient Mesoamerican environment, the Book of Mormon never mentions the use of animals for battle[415] or even to haul war supplies.[416] This likely indicates that the soldiers themselves had to carry heavy packs over long distances.[417] Whether the fathers of the stripling warriors personally delivered these supplies or whether they were simply dispatched by battle-capable Nephite warriors is ambiguous in the text.[418] What is clear is that for some reason the transport of these essential provisions to the Nephite and Ammonite soldiers had either been halted or otherwise deterred.[419]

THE WHY

Because of their increasing lack of food and supplies, Helaman wrote, "we were grieved and also filled with fear, lest by any means the judgments of God should come upon our land, to our overthrow and utter destruction" (Alma 58:9). Rather than letting these fears sink them into utter despair, the high priest Helaman helped his young warriors maintain their faith through prayer: "Therefore we did pour out our souls in prayer to God, that he would strengthen us and deliver us" (Alma 58:10). The Lord's response brought them deep relief and peace:

> Yea, and it came to pass that the Lord our God did visit us with assurances that he would deliver us; yea, insomuch that he did speak peace to our souls, and did grant unto us great faith, and did cause us that we should hope for our deliverance in him. (Alma 58:11)

At a time when they were temporarily cut off from needed food and military supplies, Helaman and his soldiers in balanced counterpoint received divine assurance that they were not cut off from the Lord's miraculous blessings and deliverance. In response to their asking, they received the spiritual gifts of faith, hope, and comforting knowledge. Such a story can provide solace and hope to any who find themselves temporally destitute or in spiritual peril.

There is also a lesson to be found in the response of Helaman and his men to the Lord's promised deliverance. Rather than idly waiting for God to provide for their needs, Helaman's armies maintained their faith as they took the initiative and successfully executed a military strategy to take over a Lamanite stronghold. Helaman recorded, "And thus we did go forth with all our might against the Lamanites, who were in the city of Manti" (Alma 58:13). Elder D. Todd Christoffersen taught, "Likewise, as we plead with God for our daily bread—for help in the moment that we cannot ourselves provide—we must still be active in doing and providing that which is within our power."[420]

Eventually, readers learn that it was because of the corruption of government officials in the very center of Nephite territory that had stalled provisions from reaching Helaman's men (see Alma 61:3–4).[421] Similarly, the essential supply lines of faith, spiritual blessings, and gifts—often facilitated by inspired leaders and loving family members—can be impeded when the heart of the recipient becomes hardened or corrupt. Elder L. Whitney Clayton taught:

> The promises of the gospel are uplifting and ennobling, even exalting. We receive those promises by covenants which are conditioned on our living lives of purity and morality. When we live right and seek to purify our hearts, we draw closer to God and the Spirit. The condition of our heart determines how much evidence of divinity we see in the world now and qualifies us for the eventual realization of the promise that the pure "shall see God." Ours is a quest for purity.[422]

FURTHER READING

Brant A. Gardner, *Traditions of the Fathers: The Book of Mormon as History* (Salt Lake City, UT: Greg Kofford Books, 2015), 311–320.

John L. Sorenson, *Mormon's Codex* (Salt Lake City and Provo, UT: Deseret Book and Neal A. Maxwell Institute for Religious Scholarship, 2013), 381–425.

37

Why Was Moroni's Correspondence with Pahoran Significant?

"And it came to pass that he immediately sent an epistle to Pahoran." (Alma 59:3)

THE KNOW

The concluding chapters of the book of Alma (see Alma 60–61) include a series of letters written between Moroni and the chief judge, Pahoran. The catalyst for this exchange was a Lamanite victory in taking the city of Nephihah: "And thus being exceedingly numerous, yea, and receiving strength from day to day, by the command of Ammoron they came forth against the people of Nephihah, and they did begin to slay them with an exceedingly great slaughter" (Alma 59:7).

The Nephite response to this attack was anything but positive. "They doubted and marveled also because of the wickedness of the people, and this because of the success of the Lamanites over them" (Alma 59:12). Moroni angrily wrote to Pahoran demanding help with the war effort (see Alma 60:24–25). Believing that Pahoran was abandoning his duty to both God and the Nephite cause (see Alma 60:20–23), Moroni threatened, "Except ye do bestir yourselves in the defence of your country and your little ones, the sword of justice doth hang over you; yea, and it shall fall upon you and visit you even to your utter destruction" (Alma 60:29).

Pahoran's response to Moroni is somewhat startling. After clarifying that an attempted coup had forced the government into exile (see Alma 61:3–5), the Nephite chief judge replied, "And now, in your epistle you have censured me, but it mattereth not; I am not angry, but do rejoice in the greatness of your heart" (Alma 61:9). Instead of becoming defensive, Pahoran deferred to Moroni's emotional outburst.

"My beloved brother, Moroni," Pahoran resolved, "let us resist evil, and whatsoever evil we cannot resist with our words, yea, such as rebellions and dissensions, let us resist them with our swords, that we may retain our freedom, that we may rejoice in the great privilege of our church, and in the cause of our Redeemer and our God" (Alma 61:14). Instead of firing back at Moroni for assuming the worst in him, Pahoran calmly explained the situation and urged continued resistance against both domestic and foreign threats to Nephite freedom.

This exchange between Moroni and Pahoran is revealing on a number of levels. For starters, it appears that the epistolary form used by Moroni and Pahoran follows some ancient conventions. Robert F. Smith explained that one noticeable thing about these and other Book of Mormon epistles "is that they never violate the ancient Hittite-Syrian, Neo-Assyrian, Amarna, and Hebrew format in which the superior correspondent is always listed first."[423]

The correspondence between Moroni and Pahoran also provides important glimpses into the personalities of these men. Although a man of great faith, it is clear that Moroni was also susceptible to anger, frustration, doubt, and misplaced outrage at those whom he assumed had slighted him. At the same time, Pahoran is revealed in his letter to be a man of patience in the face of being wrongfully accused. His "reply is a remarkable example of emotional restraint. By choosing not to take offense, he was able to communicate clearly and work toward resolving the problem."[424]

THE WHY

That Mormon preserved Moroni's letter to Pahoran in his abridgment is remarkable. It shows a level of honesty on Mormon's part, since he was willing to include information that portrayed Moroni, one of his heroes (see Alma 48:17),[425] in an unflattering light.

Readers can learn an important lesson from Moroni's shortcoming. Moroni's anxieties and frustrations were undoubtedly real. He and his army were facing serious Lamanite threats, and no assistance from the government was forthcoming. Nevertheless, he might have profited from giving Pahoran the benefit of the doubt and being careful not to jump to hasty conclusions or pass unwarranted judgment. His example cautions readers to be careful not to allow anger, doubt, or uncertainties to create a negative influence.

As Elder Dieter F. Uchtdorf taught, "Sometimes questions arise because we simply don't have all the information and we just need a bit more patience. When the entire truth is eventually known, things that didn't make sense to us before will be resolved to our satisfaction." Elder Uchtdorf accordingly recommended to "first doubt your doubts before you doubt your faith."[426] While Elder Uchtdorf was speaking specifically about those who question their testimonies of the gospel, his counsel can be applied to other areas, such as when doubting someone's sincerity or intentions, as in Moroni's case.

Also setting an important example for modern readers, ultimately Moroni reconciled with Pahoran, and "was filled with exceedingly great joy because of the faithfulness" of the chief judge (Alma 62:1). The two eventually put the entire misunderstanding behind them and united their forces in a successful bid to restore Pahoran to the judgment seat (see Alma 62:6–8).

FURTHER READING

Robert F. Smith, "Epistolary Form in the Book of Mormon," *FARMS Review 22*, no. 2 (2010): 125–135.

Larry W. Tippetts, "Toward Emotional Maturity: Insights from the Book of Mormon," *Religious Educator 11*, no. 2 (2010): 89–103.

Why Did Moroni Refer to Vessel Impurity in Condemning the Central Government?

"Now I would that ye should remember that God has said that the inward vessel shall be cleansed first, and then shall the outer vessel be cleansed also." (Alma 60:23)

THE KNOW

In a sharp-toned letter to Chief Judge Pahoran, Captain Moroni rebuked those central governmental officials who were responsible for the deprivations of their soldiers in the field. Yet nestled among a series of rhetorical questions, Moroni drew on a divinely stated law that is not found elsewhere in the Book of Mormon: "Now I would that ye should remember that God has said that the inward vessel shall be cleansed first, and then shall the outer vessel be cleansed also" (Alma 60:23).

It is likely that Moroni's argument here stems from his reading of legal instructions given to ancient Israel. Clay pots and various vessels were plentiful in Israelite civilization, and in order for people to eat ritually clean food out of them, these containers needed to be in a state of ritual purity. In Leviticus, the Lord established laws of impurity regarding dead animals (specifically creeping things like rodents and lizards) that might happen to contaminate various kinds of vessels by falling into them:

> And upon whatsoever any of them, when they are dead, doth fall, it shall be unclean; whether it be any vessel of wood, or raiment, or skin, or sack, whatsoever vessel it be, wherein any work is done, it must be put into water, and it shall be unclean until the even; so it shall be cleansed.
>
> And every earthen vessel, whereinto [literally, into the midst of] any of them falleth, whatsoever is in it shall be unclean; and ye shall break it. (Leviticus 11:32–33)

Another provision of the law stated: "When a man dieth in a tent: all that come into the tent, and all that is in the tent, shall be unclean seven days. And every open vessel, which hath no covering bound upon it, is unclean" (Numbers 19:14–15).

These regulations eventually raised a number of legal issues: did this rule of impurity apply only to a piece of pottery that had an inside and an outside—like a jar—but not a plate? Apparently yes; otherwise, how could the animal corpse fall "into the midst" of it (Leviticus 11:33)? Was it enough to be in the same space with the dead animal, or was impurity transferred to an open vessel only by actual contact? Evidently, no contact with an open vessel was required (see Numbers 19:15). Was the vessel rendered impure if the dead animal came in contact with the inside only? Apparently yes, for corpse contamination of the outside of a covered vessel did not render the pot impure. If only the outside of the container was contaminated, could it be purified simply by immersing it in water until the end of the day? Yes (see Leviticus 11:32). If the inside of an open vessel was contaminated, did it have to be smashed? Yes (see Leviticus 11:33). Clearly, these regulations were quite specific, and documents from Egypt show that pot impurity was of actual ancient concern.[427]

Implicit behind these rules is the assumption that the inside of a vessel was more susceptible to impurity than the outside. This distinction would logically account for the idea that cleansing the greater impurity inside a vessel would automatically purify the lesser impurity outside, and thus, for several reasons, it would make more sense to cleanse the inside of a vessel before the outside.

Understandably, these legalities could easily be imbued with symbolic importance. From the teachings of Jesus in the New Testament, it is clear that He was aware of rules regarding pot purity and their metaphorical significance. In one instance, Christ affirmed Isaiah's condemnation that "This people honoureth me with their lips [the outside], but their heart [the more susceptible inside] is far from me" (Mark 7:6).[428] Jesus then explained, "There is nothing from [outside] a man, that entering into him can defile him: but the things which come out of him, those are they that defile the man" (Mark 7:15).

Wrestling with these ancient issues, the Jewish schools of Hillel and Shammai at the time of Jesus argued about the order of cleansing a container, whether one should purify its inside or its outside first.[429] Jesus made use of this debate to draw a moral lesson when He condemned the Pharisees for being like people who purify the outside of a vessel, "but within they are full of extortion and excess. . . . Cleanse first that which is within the cup and platter, that the outside of them may be clean also" (Matthew 23:26). Similar sentiments related to inner vessel impurity can be found elsewhere in several early Christian or gnostic texts.[430]

THE WHY

When Captain Moroni required of Pahoran that "the inward vessel shall be cleansed first, and then shall the outer vessel be cleansed also" (Alma 60:23), he invoked legal provisions from the law of Moses that would have been known to Pahoran. Moroni built on the essential "inner-outer" dichotomy when he spoke of those in the inner "heart of our country . . . surrounded by security" (Alma 60:19), and those outside, "round about in the borders of the land" (Alma 60:22). He presumed that the inner part could become seriously contaminated quite easily, simply by idleness and dereliction of duty (see Alma 60:18, 22). He assumed that as soon as the inward vessel was cleansed, then would the outer vessel be consequently "cleansed also" (Alma 60:23). Thus, it made compelling sense to begin by cleaning up the situation in the inner capital city.

While Jesus took issue with those Pharisees who began by cleansing the outside of a vessel, Moroni knew of no one who was suggesting that the soldiers in the outreaches needed to be purified first. Still, the overall agreement between the arguments of Jesus and Moroni strongly suggest that they were drawing on the laws from Leviticus and Numbers. Moroni attributed these rules of pot purification unequivocally to God in order to heighten the impact of his metaphorical indictment. Whatever the explanation, the textual interaction of these texts demonstrates the value of studying the Bible and the Book of Mormon together.[431]

A unifying component in these statements and concerns about impurities can be found in ancient temple theology. Vessels used in the ancient Israelite temples needed to be kept pure,[432] which seems to be directly related to Isaiah's injunction to "be ye clean, that bear the vessels of the Lord" (Isaiah 52:11; 3 Nephi 20:41). Echoing this sentiment, Psalms 24:3–4 emphasized the need for both external cleanliness as well as internal purity: "Who shall stand in his holy place? He that hath clean hands, and a pure heart" (cf. 2 Nephi 25:16 and Alma 5:19).[433]

The innermost parts of the temple in Jerusalem were considered more holy than the outer portions, with the holy of holies as the most sacred and cosmically central of all.[434] The same principle applied in Zarahemla, the key temple city of the Nephites. Moroni's call for Pahoran to cleanse the inner city might also have carried an implication that the temple in Zarahemla had been desecrated by Pahoran's failure to support the soldiers in the field, some of whom had even died, along with women and children (see Alma 60:17).

Recognizing that "the Lord hath said he dwelleth not in unholy temples, but in the hearts of the righteous doth he dwell" (Alma 34:36), Moroni would also have hoped that Pahoran's heart would change so that God's Spirit could sanctify the deepest and most inward parts of his soul and impel him to action in behalf of Moroni's desperate situation.[435] And just as an individual must purify his or her heart in order to enter the presence of the Lord,[436] so too must a nation be pure in heart—and in the case of Moroni's people, pure in its central government—if God is to bless them together with peace and prosperity.[437]

FURTHER READING

John W. Welch, *The Sermon at the Temple and the Sermon on the Mount: A Latter-day Saint Approach* (Salt Lake City and Provo, UT: Deseret Book and FARMS, 1990), 42–46, 77–78.

Donald W. Parry, "Demarcation between Sacred Space and Profane Space: The Temple of Herod Model," in *Temples of the Ancient World: Ritual and Symbolism,* ed. Donald W. Parry (Salt Lake City and Provo, UT: Deseret Book and FARMS, 1994), 413–439.

39

Why Was Teancum Captured and Killed?

"But behold, the king did awaken his servants before he died, insomuch that they did pursue Teancum, and slew him." (Alma 62:36)

THE KNOW

Teancum played a pivotal role in the Nephite wars in the book of Alma. From his introduction in Alma 50, he is depicted as a brave, loyal, and righteous Nephite warrior. He was instrumental, for example, in the death of the treacherous Amalickiah (see Alma 51:33–37).[438]

His last appearance in the Book of Mormon occurs in Alma 61–62. "In about 60 B.C., when all the Lamanite armies and king Ammoron had fled to the land of Moroni and camped for the night, Teancum" was "exceedingly angry," and "in his anger" took it upon himself to bring an end to Ammoron, acting all alone. "Angry at the bloodshed and destruction wrought by Amalickiah and Ammoron, he slipped into the Lamanite camp and found Ammoron. His javelin killed Ammoron, but not before Ammoron woke his servants, who pursued and killed Teancum (Alma 62:35–36)."[439]

Teancum's bravery, while admirable, ultimately got the better of him. George Reynolds and Janne Sjodahl observed how Teancum's decision was undoubtedly "rash," and that his failing was that he did not keep in mind "his personal safety when he thought the good of his country required the sacrifice."[440]

This would not have been abnormal for Teancum. Brant Gardner explained how the Nephite general had "acted unilaterally and impulsively in the past (Alma 51:33– 34) and had probably fretted at being forced to play a waiting game on the eastern front for a couple of years." With this in mind, "it is perhaps not surprising that Teancum [took] matters into his own hands."[441] What is also not entirely surprising was the unfortunate outcome, given the circumstances.

THE WHY

The untimely demise of Teancum can serve as a cautionary tale for readers of the Book of Mormon. While getting angry or upset is an understandable response when circumstances are out of our control, this example from Teancum warns about the potential dangers of acting out of anger. Unlike when he coolly and carefully planned the timing for killing Amalickiah, in killing Ammoron Teancum was upset and not able to clearly weigh the substantial risks of the situation. Unlike the first foray, when he took a servant with him (see Alma 51:33), this time he went alone. Having scaled a wall, carrying a cord, and not finding Ammoron quickly, the best Teancum could do was to throw a javelin at him, hitting him close to his heart (see Alma 62:36), whereas he was able to stab Amalickiah with precision at close range (see Alma 51:34). Under these circumstances, while Lehi and Moroni bitterly mourned the loss of a valiant and true friend, the final epitaph given to Teancum by Mormon was terse: "But behold, he was dead, and had gone the way of all the earth" (Alma 62:37).

President Thomas S. Monson warned, "We are all susceptible to those feelings which, if left unchecked, can lead to anger. We experience displeasure or irritation or antagonism, and if we so choose, we lose our temper and become angry with others."[442] Readers of the Book of Mormon can appreciate the examples in its pages that illustrate the dangers of becoming angry. They can likewise learn from these examples how to avoid or overcome such.

For instance, at the beginning of the Book of Mormon, Nephi and his brothers were cruelly mistreated by Laban, who himself became "angry" with Nephi's brother Laman when the latter requested the brass plates (see 1 Nephi 3:11–14). Laman in turn became "angry" with Nephi when the resulting outcome was less than favorable (1 Nephi 3:28). Nephi had many opportunities to become angry and dissatisfied with things but instead remained composed and rational. This permitted him to seek and find inspiration from the Spirit of the Lord, which ultimately led to him succeeding in his mission to retrieve the brass plates (see 1 Nephi 4).

None of this is meant to impugn Teancum's righteous example. He undoubtedly deserved all of the praise Mormon afforded him in his moving eulogy: "he had been a man who had fought valiantly for his country, yea, a true friend to liberty; and he had suffered very many exceedingly sore afflictions" (Alma 62:37). Nevertheless, Teancum's overconfidently acting on his own initiative serves as a powerful warning to modern readers of the Book of Mormon.

FURTHER READING

Brant A. Gardner, *Second Witness: Analytical & Contextual Commentary on the Book of Mormon,* 6 vols. (Salt Lake City, UT: Greg Kofford Books, 2007), 4:755–766.

Ted L. Gibbons, "Teancum," in *Book of Mormon Reference Companion*, ed. Dennis L. Largey (Salt Lake City, UT: Deseret Book, 2003), 752–753.

40

How Does Chiasmus Teach Us to Reverse the Pride Cycle?

"And they began to grow exceedingly rich. But notwithstanding their riches, or their strength, or their prosperity, they were not lifted up in the pride of their eyes." (Alma 62:48–49)

THE KNOW

One way that the Book of Mormon provides a valuable view of history is that it records the spiritual condition of various peoples over the course of many generations. Mormon, as the primary abridger and editor of this lengthy record, was particularly aware of how the Nephites' degree of pride or humility cycled over time.[443] One of Mormon's historical summaries in particular stands out because it emphasizes how the typical transition from receiving blessings to engaging in prideful behavior was avoided.[444] This summary, found in Alma 62:48–51, uses a chiasm to emphasize this point:[445]

A And the people of Nephi began to **prosper again in the land**,

B and began to multiply and to **wax exceedingly strong** again in the land.

C And **they began to grow exceedingly rich.** But notwithstanding their riches, or their strength, or their prosperity,

D (a) they were **not lifted up** in the pride of their eyes;

(b) neither were they slow to **remember** the Lord their God;

D' (a) but they did **humble** themselves exceedingly before him.

(b) Yea, they did **remember** how great things the Lord had done for them,

C' that he had delivered them from death, and from bonds, and from prisons, and from all manner of afflictions, and he had delivered them out of the hands of their enemies. And they did pray unto the Lord their God continually, insomuch that **the Lord did bless them**, according to his word,

B' so that they did **wax strong** and

A' prosper in the land.

While the outer layers of this chiasm concern the prosperity that the people were experiencing, the central elements (D and D') emphasize what the people did to avoid the pride that usually follows such prosperity. In each central element, the concept of being humble or "not lifted up" is coupled with the people's remembrance of God's blessings, suggesting a direct relationship between these concepts.[446]

Notably, this chiasm alludes to words in Lehi's famous prophecy about prosperity, which were picked up on by other Nephite prophets and repeatedly expressed throughout the Book of Mormon.[447] As the following chart demonstrates, in many of these restatements, the concepts of remembering or forgetting are directly related to prospering in the land or being cut off from the Lord's blessings.

Mosiah 1:7	"And now, my sons, I would that ye should **remember** to search [the scriptures] diligently, that ye may profit thereby; and I would that ye should keep the commandments of God, that ye may **prosper in the land** according to the promises which the Lord made unto our fathers."
Alma 9:13-14	"Behold, do ye not **remember** the words which he spake unto Lehi, saying that: Inasmuch as ye shall keep my commandments, ye shall **prosper in the land**? ... Now I would that ye should **remember**, that inasmuch as the Lamanites have not kept the commandments of God, they have been **cut off from the presence of the Lord**.
Alma 37:13	O **remember, remember,** my son Helaman, how strict are the commandments of God. And he said: If ye will keep my commandments ye shall **prosper in the land**—but if ye keep not his commandments ye shall be **cut off from his presence**.
Alma 50:20	Blessed art thou and thy children; and they shall be blessed, inasmuch as they shall keep my commandments they shall **prosper in the land**. But **remember,** inasmuch as they will not keep my commandments they shall be **cut off from the presence of the Lord**.

Readers should also be aware that the inner and outer sections of the chiastic structure found in Alma 62:48–51 closely mirror the same inner/outer sections in the famous chiastic masterpiece found in Alma 36:[448]

	Alma 62	Alma 36
Outer Element (First)	62:48. And the people of Nephi began to **prosper again in the land,** and began to multiply and to wax exceedingly strong again in the land.	36:1. My son, give ear to my words; for I swear unto you, that inasmuch as ye shall keep the commandments of God ye shall **prosper in the land**.
Inner Element (First)	62:49. they were not lifted up in the pride of their eyes; neither were they slow to **remember the Lord their God**	36:17. I **remembered** also to have heard my father prophesy unto the people concerning **the coming of one Jesus Christ, a Son of God,** to atone for the sins of the world.

Inner Element (Last)	62:50. Yea, they did **remember** how great things the Lord had done for them, that he had **delivered them from death**	36:18. Now, as my mind caught hold upon this thought, I cried within my heart: O Jesus, thou Son of God, have mercy on me, who am in the gall of bitterness, and am encircled about by the everlasting **chains of death**. 19. And now, behold, when I thought this, I could **remember** my pains no more;
Outer Element (Last)	62:51. And they did pray unto the Lord their God continually, insomuch that the Lord did bless them, according to his word, so that they did wax strong and **prosper in the land**.	36:30 But behold, my son, this is not all; for ye ought to know as I do know, that inasmuch as ye shall keep the commandments of God ye shall **prosper in the land**;

THE WHY

The way that the chiasm in Alma 62:48–51 connects to other passages that discuss Lehi's promise of prosperity, as well as its shared inner/outer elements with Alma 36, suggests that its structure is both sophisticated and intentional. Recognizing a chiastic structure focuses our attention on words and key themes that their writers wanted us to note in particular. This helps us better understand the original intent of the Book of Mormon's authors, which we otherwise might not have absorbed so completely.[449]

Chiasmus can also emphasize a reversal. At the turning point, the text reaches a climax or pinnacle and from that point it reverses its path and returns to the point of departure. In the process of this thought pattern, the reader is able to see the original idea in a new light. In this way, chiasmus helps listeners turn around and go in a better direction. A famous chiastic proverb says, "Those who fail to prepare, prepare to fail." This saying has power precisely because it stops people in their tracks and turns them around.

Typically, the Nephites experienced pride, wickedness, and destruction after periods of righteousness and blessings. In this instance, however, remembering the Lord helped them avoid this negative cycle. They steadily increased in both righteousness and prosperity without having to be humbled first by war, famine, or some other type of destruction. The underlying chiastic structure in Alma 62:48–51 helps readers similarly stop their regression into the pride cycle and reverse the course that heads to disaster. It shows how remembering the Lord—particularly the way He has blessed us—can help us retain humility in times of prosperity, just as the Nephites did.

Readers today can learn much from this chiastic message. While there is still much poverty in the world, many societies have been blessed beyond anything that previous generations have known. Technology and science have led to advances in food production, medicine, communication, transportation, health practices, and many other unprecedented blessings.

If we are not careful, however, we will face the same types of humbling tragedies recorded in the Book of Mormon. As Elder Joseph B. Wirthlin taught, "There is something about prosperity that brings out the worst in some people."[450] Fortunately, the chiasm in Alma 62:48–51 shows that remembering the Lord and keeping His commandments brings out the best in people, even in times of great prosperity. By entering into sacred covenants to remember the Savior,[451] and then by keeping those covenants, we can remain humble and grateful, even during the most prosperous of times.

FURTHER READING

Gerrit W. Gong, "Always Remember Him," *Ensign*, May 2016.

Joseph B. Wirthlin, "Journey to Higher Ground," *Ensign*, November 2005.

Louis Midgley, "To Remember and Keep: On the Book of Mormon as an Ancient Book," in *The Disciple as Scholar: Essays on Scripture and the Ancient World in Honor of Richard Lloyd Anderson*, ed. Stephen D. Ricks, Donald W. Parry, and Andrew H. Hedges (Provo, UT: FARMS, 2000), 95–137.

Nephite Cycle of Righteousness
Mormon's Warning for Us Today

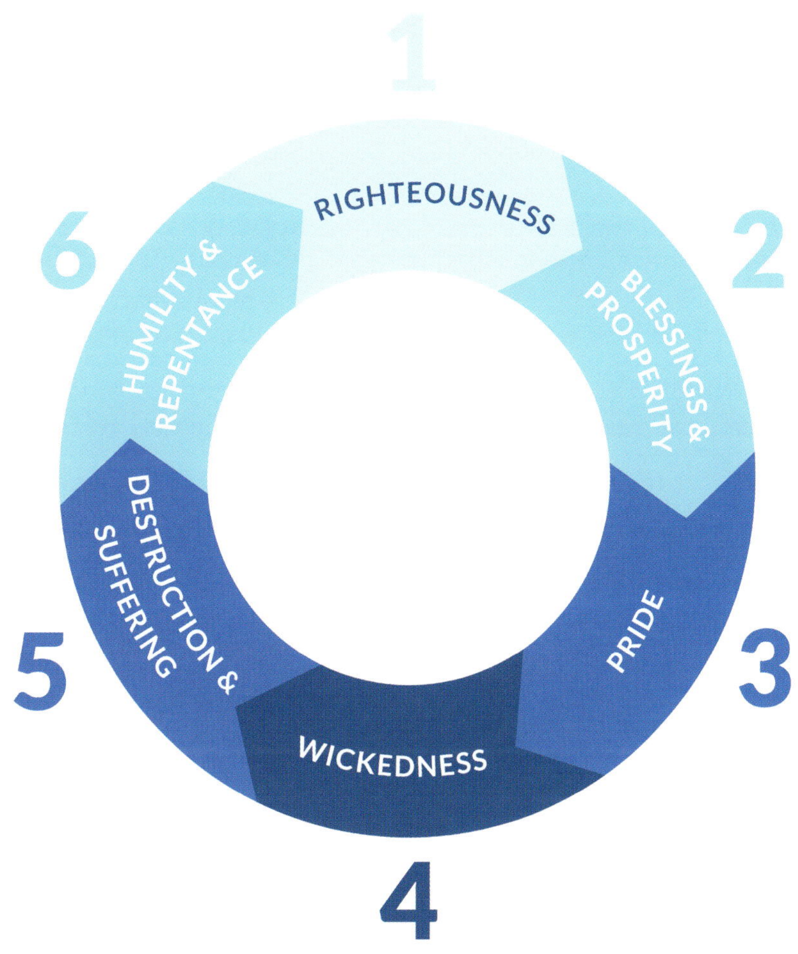

Why Did Mormon Mention Hagoth?

"And it came to pass that Hagoth, he being an exceedingly curious man, therefore he went forth and built him an exceedingly large ship." (Alma 63:5)

THE KNOW

At the conclusion of the extended conflict between the Nephites and the Lamanites, Mormon reported that a "large company of men, even to the amount of five thousand and four hundred men, with their wives and their children, departed out of the land of Zarahemla into the land which was northward" (Alma 63:4).

Next, the reader learns that "an exceedingly curious" man named Hagoth "went forth and built him an exceedingly large ship. . . . And behold, there were many of the Nephites who did enter therein and did sail forth with much provisions, and also many women and children; and they took their course northward" (Alma 63:5–6).[452] During the next year, Hagoth built even more ships, and when the first ship returned, "many more people did enter into it; and they also took much provisions, and set out again to the land northward" (Alma 63:7). Exactly what type of ships Hagoth built is uncertain; the only detail we have is the description of his first ship as "exceedingly large" (Alma 63:5).[453]

Mormon concluded his narrative about migrations on this somber note:

> And it came to pass that they were never heard of more. And we suppose that they were drowned in the depths of the sea. And it came to pass that one other ship also did sail forth; and whither she did go we know not. And it came to pass that in this year there were many people who went forth into the land northward. (Alma 63:8–9)

A careful reading of these events shows that in the space of two years Mormon reported at least five notable migrations—three by sea, two by land,[454] and all of them "northward."[455] Although brief, Mormon's sampling of these migrations helps the reader catch a glimpse of an expanding Nephite civilization. While nothing is said further concerning the matter, Mormon's mentioning that "Hagoth built even more ships" implies that further seafaring migrations may have been on the horizon.[456]

THE WHY

The uncertainty concerning the final destination of Hagoth's voyagers (and potentially Hagoth himself, assuming he accompanied the second journey of his ship),[457] has captured the attention of Book of Mormon readers for generations.[458] Several Latter-day Saint prophets and General Authorities have believed Hagoth's seafarers were progenitors of various peoples of the Pacific Islands.[459] Thus, for many Polynesians the story about Hagoth and the possibility of other Lehite voyages by sea has significantly influenced perceptions of cultural identity and heritage.[460] Officially, though, The Church of Jesus Christ of Latter-day Saints claims no specific revelation or position on these matters.[461]

While the fate of Hagoth's travelers is not known, the very fact that their journeys are mentioned at all is relevant to interpreting the Book of Mormon. Mormon was very selective about what things he included in his narrative,[462] which suggests that digressing into details about these migrations must have served some overarching narrative goal.

Wherever they went and whatever their relationship with the indigenous peoples in the Pacific, Hagoth's oceanic voyagers certainly open up the possibility for the Lehite lineage to have been dispersed to locations far away from the central locus of the Book of Mormon narrative.[463] Thematically speaking, this helps readers recognize that even among the Nephites, the scattering of Israel was still taking place.[464] Indeed, nine years after Hagoth set sail, large numbers of Nephites migrated a "great distance" to the north (Helaman 3:3), and Mormon's description of their multiplying and spreading abroad to the south, north, west, and east uses language similar to the covenantal promise given to Jacob in Genesis 28:14, indicating that he saw these migrations as part of that larger Abrahamic narrative.

Furthermore, the fact that ships were being built at all and that Nephites were feeling a need to relocate suggests that population growth and industry were being restored after the lengthy war between the Nephites and the Lamanites.[465] This renewed economic prosperity accompanied by a northward expansion helps set the stage for the next phase of Nephite history. As John L. Sorenson explained:

> Other major realignments took place during the Expansion phase. Cultural, and probably genetic, interchange continued between the main Lamanite and Nephite centers. . . . As the Book of Mormon narrative approached AD 30, the picture of society throughout the "promised land" occupied by Lehi's descendants was one of factional fragmentation and perhaps increasing cultural differentiation within a highly variegated set of environments. It was evidently difficult for the component peoples to maintain stable social and cultural conditions.[466]

In other words, expansion and prosperity helped pave the way for increasing social complexity and eventual instability. Sorenson's analysis helps demonstrate that the story about Hagoth and the other voyages northward was not merely a casual digression into historical trivia. On the contrary, Mormon (who would have had a personal interest in the land northward, where he grew up[467]) presented this information to help readers better conceptualize the large-scale transportations and important transformations happening among the Nephite and Lamanite civilizations.[468] No narrative takes place in a historical vacuum, and the more that readers understand the historical backdrop of the Book of Mormon, the more real and meaningful its sacred stories will become to them.

FURTHER READING

Mark Alan Wright, "Heartland as Hinterland: The Mesoamerican Core and North American Periphery of Book of Mormon Geography," *Interpreter: A Journal of Mormon Scripture 13* (2015): 111–129.

John L. Sorenson, *Transoceanic Voyaging: How Ancient America Became Civilized* (unpublished manuscript, 2013).

Tyler Livingston, "The Book of Mormon and Mesoamerican Travels 'Northward,'" *Book of Mormon Archeological Forum*, January 2011.

Helaman

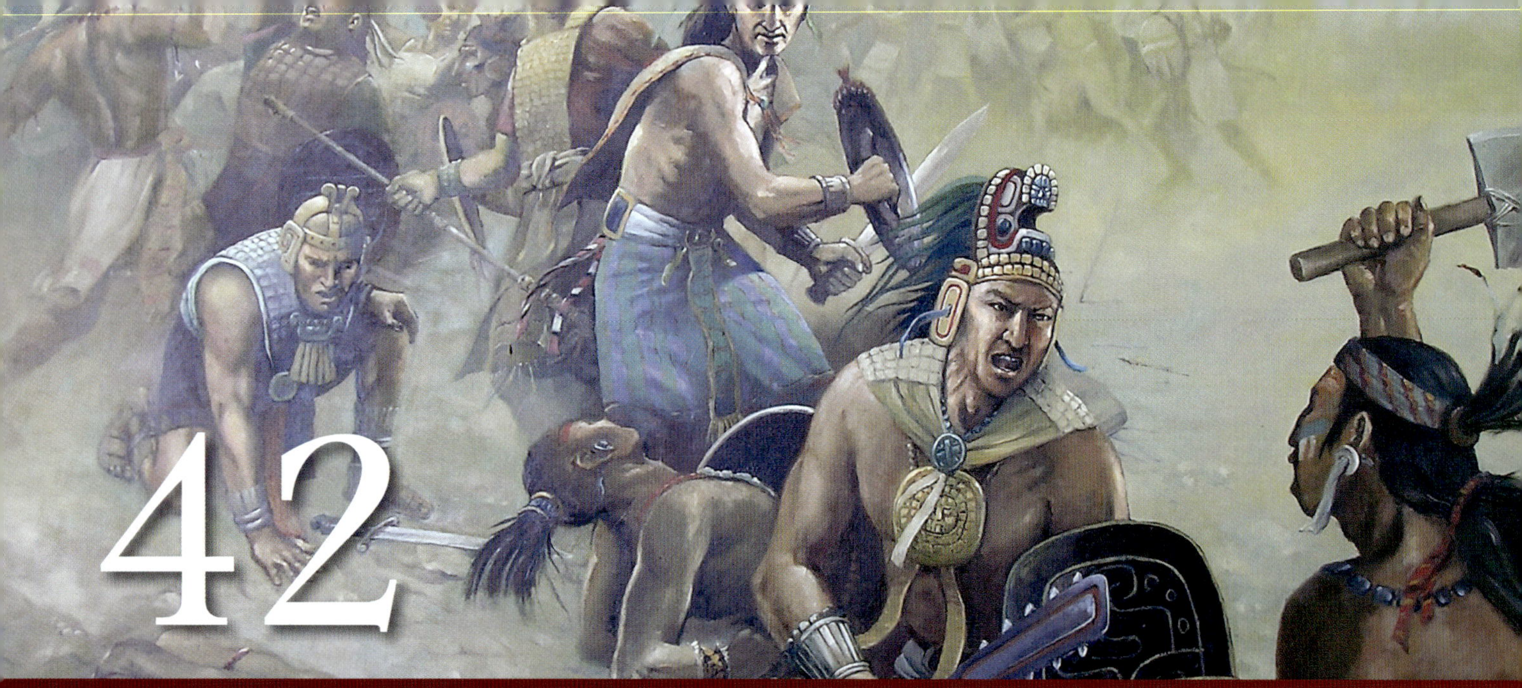

How Was a Void in Leadership Dangerous for the Nephites?

"Therefore there began to be a serious contention concerning who should have the judgment-seat among the brethren, who were the sons of Pahoran." (Helaman 1:2)

THE KNOW

At the "commencement of the fortieth year of the reign of the judges," Mormon ominously reported that "there began to be a serious difficulty among the people of the Nephites" (Helaman 1:1). Key leaders such as Helaman (see Alma 62:52), Moroni (see Alma 63:3), and Shiblon (see Alma 63:10) had all recently died.

Because of that void, when Pahoran passed away during the fortieth year of the reign of the judges (see Helaman 1:2), at least one cause for their alarm becomes apparent: within five years, the Nephites had lost several of their finest and most admirable leaders—men who had been pivotal in holding their nation together during the long defensive military campaign against the Lamanites.

As might be expected, the death of Chief Judge Pahoran caused no small disturbance among the people. The position of chief judge was much more like a king than many readers may realize,[469] and when Pahoran died, his three sons—Pahoran, Paanchi, and Pacumeni[470]—all "did contend for the judgment-seat; therefore, they did cause three divisions among the people" (Helaman 1:4).

This scenario almost precisely matches what King Mosiah feared would happen if he didn't transform the Nephite monarchy into a system of judges (see Mosiah 29:7). Richard L. Bushman, however, noted that Mosiah's reforms weren't altogether successful: "The institution of judgeships, rather than beginning a republican era in Book of Mormon history, slid back at once toward monarchy."[471]

On the other hand, Brant A. Gardner explained that monarchical successions could actually be somewhat beneficial:

> An advantage of monarchies in which the dead king has an adult son is the clarity of the process, with the son having a divinely sanctioned mandate to replace the father.[472]

Unfortunately, the situation after Pahoran's death was a full realization of Mosiah's fears without the advantageous stability that monarchical successions sometimes provide.

According to Gardner:

> Not only was the chief judge's death a time of transition, but it was the first time that the surviving chief judge had not declared his ruler. . . . Complicating things even more, the

> crisis of succession came at a time of increasing internal divisions among the Nephites. Pahoran's death became a spark that ignited already-smoldering divisions.[473]

Recognizing that this leadership vacuum presented an opportunity for an insurgency, the secret band of Kishkumen (which soon became the band of Gadianton) began to assert their influence. After Pahoran, the son of Pahoran, was chosen by the voice of the people as chief judge (see Helaman 1:5), Paanchi did not accept this decision.

As he was "about to . . . rise up in rebellion," Paanchi was apprehended, convicted of rebellion, and executed (see Helaman 1:7–8). Paanchi's followers then enlisted "one Kishkumen" who "murdered Pahoran as he sat upon the judgment seat" (Helaman 1:9).

Pacumeni was then chosen to fill Pahoran's place as chief judge, but he was shortly thereafter killed during a Lamanite invasion of Zarahemla (see Helaman 1:21). After this, Helaman, the son of Helaman, was appointed chief judge, and Kishkumen then attempted to assassinate Helaman.[474]

From this narrative of intrigue and social unrest, we can see that the Gadianton robbers played a crucial role in destabilizing the Nephite government. Gardner concluded:

> Above and beyond the simple reporting of history, Mormon is including this event because from it he traces the beginnings of secret combinations in the Nephite society. For Mormon, this covenant among conspirators is more important than the actual murder. Political assassinations will become a defining trait of the Gadianton robbers.[475]

THE WHY

It is imperative that modern readers of the Book of Mormon recognize how dangerous the Gadianton robbers were to the safety and stability of Nephite society. Mormon wrote, "And behold, in the end of this book ye shall see that this Gadianton did prove the overthrow, yea, almost the entire destruction of the people of Nephi" (Helaman 2:13).[476]

This episode at the beginning of the book of Helaman demonstrates and warns that such secret societies thrive on a society's internal division and are prone to target key leaders and political figures, especially at times of transition in power or weakness in leadership.

Moroni thus directly warned latter-day readers about the rise of secret combinations:

> Wherefore, the Lord commandeth you, when ye shall see these things come among you that ye shall awake to a sense of your awful situation.
>
> For it cometh to pass that whoso buildeth it [a secret combination] up seeketh to overthrow the freedom of all lands, nations, and countries; and it bringeth to pass the destruction of all people, for it is built up by the devil, who is the father of all lies. (Ether 8:24–25)[477]

Thankfully, when it comes to the leadership, governance, and succession in the presidency of His Church, the Lord Himself has established crucial safeguards and protections. President Russell M. Nelson declared:

> The calling of 15 men to the holy apostleship provides great protection for us as members of the Church. . . . The Church today has been organized by the Lord Himself. He has put in place a remarkable system of governance that provides redundancy and backup. That system provides for prophetic leadership even when the inevitable illnesses and incapacities may come with advancing age. Counterbalances and safeguards abound so that no one can ever lead the Church astray.[478]

Despite the complexities and dangers of the modern world, despite the rise of secret combinations and modern-day Gadianton robbers, despite the vulnerability that nations and their leaders may face in the increasing chaos and turmoil—despite all of these things, those who place faith in Jesus Christ can trust that His established Church and His appointed leaders are safeguarding the keys of the kingdom.

As Elder Gary E. Stevenson declared, "Yes, the keys are safely in the possession of prophets, seers, and revelators."[479] This thought should give comfort and solace to all who have faith in Christ, for in these latter days Zion has been established "for a defense, and for a refuge from the storm, and from wrath when it shall be poured out without mixture upon the whole earth" (D&C 115:6).

FURTHER READING

Richard Dilworth Rust, "'I Know Your Doing': The Book of Mormon Speaks to Our Times," *Ensign,* December 1988.

Hugh Nibley, *Lehi in the Desert/The World of the Jaredites/There Were Jaredites,* in *The Collected Works of Hugh Nibley: Volume 5* (Salt Lake City and Provo, UT: Deseret Book and FARMS, 1988), 253–282.

Daniel C. Peterson, "The Gadianton Robbers as Guerrilla Warriors," in *Warfare in the Book of Mormon,* ed. Stephen D. Ricks and William J. Hamblin (Salt Lake City and Provo, UT: Deseret Book and FARMS, 1990), 147–173.

Why Was Helaman's Servant Justified in Killing Kishkumen?

"But behold, the servant of Helaman, as they were going forth unto the judgment-seat, did stab Kishkumen even to the heart, that he fell dead without a groan." (Helaman 2:9)

THE KNOW

Shortly after the assassination of Chief Judge Pahoran and the death of his son Pacumeni, Helaman, the son of Captain Helaman, was appointed as chief judge (see Helaman 2:2).[480] But the job was becoming an increasingly risky one. Persuaded by the flattery of "one Gadianton, who was exceedingly expert in many words" (Helaman 2:4), Kishkumen, who assassinated Pahoran, also "went forth towards the judgment-seat to destroy Helaman" (Helaman 2:6). Just when he was about to assassinate Helaman, one of the chief judge's servants, having discovered the plot, stabbed "Kishkumen even to the heart, that he fell dead without a groan" (Helaman 2:9).

This story may be shocking to many readers, who may expect the servant to have taken Kishkumen prisoner so he could face trial. In a previous situation, Mormon felt it necessary to explain why enemy soldiers were detained without a trial, yet he gave no explanation in this case.[481] A careful reading of Mormon's narrative, however, suggests he viewed killing Kishkumen as the correct decision.

In Helaman 2, Mormon uses the rare phrase "out by night." This phrase appears only three times in the Book of Mormon: when Nephi kills Laban (see 1 Nephi 4:22), when Teancum kills Amalickiah (see Alma 51:33), and just before Helaman's servant kills Kishkumen (see Helaman 2:6). Ancient Israelite authors often used a rare word or phrase like this from an earlier story as a way of alluding back to the previous story.[482]

Comparing the connected stories allows the reader to use information from one to answer questions about the others.[483] Assuming Mormon used this ancient literary technique, the stories of Nephi and Teancum may explain why Helaman's servant killed Kishkumen instead of taking him prisoner.

For example, when Teancum was "out by night," he killed Amalickiah so silently "that he did not awake his servants." He did this by stabbing him in the heart (see Alma 51:33–34).[484] Helaman's servant also stabbed Kishkumen in "the heart," killing him so silently "that he fell dead without a groan" (Helaman 2:9). This comparison suggests that Kishkumen had to be killed because an attempt to take him prisoner would have been loud enough to alert his friends, just like anything other than a silent killing would have awakened Amalickiah's servants (see Alma 62:36).

This conclusion is supported by the fact that Kishkumen was part of a secret combination. When dealing with a secret society, one never knows who is part of the conspiracy and who is not.[485] In ancient Assyria, when one of the king's servants attempted to expose a plot against him, he unknowingly reported it to a man who was in league with the assassins, and the servant was promptly killed.[486]

This threat may explain why Helaman's servant didn't somehow incapacitate Kishkumen and take him away to stand trial. It was impossible to know how many people were in on the conspiracy, and a co-conspirator could have been lurking around any corner. The only safe thing was to kill Kishkumen so quietly that his death did not alert anyone else who might have been nearby.[487]

When Nephi stumbled upon Laban, while "out by night," the Spirit told Nephi to kill him. When Nephi resisted, the Spirit told Nephi to "slay him, for the Lord hath *delivered him into thy hands*" (1 Nephi 4:12; emphasis added). This justification may refer to Exodus 21:13, which states that it is acceptable to kill someone "if a man lie not in wait, but God *deliver him into his hand*" (emphasis added).[488] The striking parallel between these texts indicates that the Spirit was legally authorizing Nephi to slay Laban.[489]

In the same way, Mormon may have been implying that the killing of Kishkumen was legal as well. Mormon specifically noted that the servant of Helaman killed Kishkumen only after he heard from his mouth "that it was his object to murder, and also that it was the object of all those who belonged to his band to murder, and to rob, and to gain power" (Helaman 2:8).[490] Simply becoming part of a conspiracy to overthrow the government appears to have been illegal during this period.[491] Thus the servant of Helaman could legally kill Kishkumen as a traitor.

THE WHY

The Book of Mormon sometimes contains details that can be confusing or unclear to modern readers. This is because ancient texts were written in a different style than most books today. Israelite literary scholar Hermann Gunkel noted, "In very many situations where the modern writer would expect a psychological analysis," the ancient Israelite author "simply presents an action."[492] Because of this, modern readers can understand the book better if they pay attention to ancient literary methods.

This ancient literary technique of using an earlier narrative to explain a later narrative reveals a higher moral justification for the servant's actions. The Spirit finally got Nephi to kill Laban by telling him, "It is better that one man should perish than that a nation should dwindle and perish in unbelief" (1 Nephi 4:13). Mormon likely expected his readers to recognize that the servant's motivation in killing Kishkumen was similar to Nephi's reasons for slaying Laban: it was better for Kishkumen to die than for the Nephite nation to dwindle and perish in the unbelief brought about by having a band of robbers in a position of power.[493]

A passage in Helaman 2:8–9 strengthens this notion: "And when the servant of Helaman had known all the *heart* of Kishkumen . . . the servant of Helaman . . . did stab Kishkumen even to the heart" (emphasis added). Knowing that the wicked hearts of Kishkumen and his band would corrupt the Nephites, the servant stabbed Kishkumen in his heart, the heart that Mormon just established was so evil.

As readers put themselves into the real-life situations recounted in the book, and as they comprehend the writing conventions of its authors and abridgers, they will understand its message more clearly. All this helps in affirming the justice and equity of this true testament of our Lord and Lawgiver, Jesus Christ.

FURTHER READING

John W. Welch, *The Legal Cases in the Book of Mormon* (Provo, UT: BYU Press and the Neal A. Maxwell Institute for Religious Scholarship, 2008), 313–322.

John W. Welch, "Legal Perspectives on the Slaying of Laban," *Journal of Book of Mormon Studies 1*, no. 1 (1992): 119–141.

When Did Cement Become Common in Ancient America?

"The people who went forth became exceedingly expert in the working of cement; therefore they did build houses of cement, in the which they did dwell." (Helaman 3:7)

THE KNOW

In the mid-first century BC, Mormon reported that some Nephite dissenters "did travel to an exceedingly great distance" into "the land northward," where they found "large bodies of water and many rivers" (Helaman 3:3–4). There was "little timber" in the region, and these people "became exceedingly expert in the working of cement," and thus built "houses of cement," and even built "many cities, both of wood and of cement" (Helaman 3:7, 9, 11).

Ancient American cement was made using limestone, and it has thus far been found only in Mesoamerica.[494] While some people were aware of pre-Columbian American cement in the early nineteenth century,[495] its origins, history, and development remained obscure well into the twentieth century.

In 1970, David S. Hyman was "not able to uncover clues relative to the origins of American cement manufacturing."[496] The earliest samples he had found dated to the first century AD but were so "technically well advanced" that Hyman was convinced there must have been earlier, less developed forms.[497]

Since that time, earlier examples have indeed been found. In a 1991 report, Matthew G. Wells documented that a "limey whitewash," which was "not structural" but "is believed to be a precursor to later structural developments," was in use as early as the ninth century BC.[498] During the Middle Preclassic period (ca. 800–300 BC), "the Maya of the lowlands had discovered . . . that if limestone fragments were burnt, and the resulting powder mixed with water, a white plaster of great durability was created."[499]

According to Mayan experts Michael D. Coe and Stephen Houston, it was not until the Late Preclassic period (300 BC–AD 250) that the Maya "quickly realized the structural value of a concrete-like fill made from limestone rubble" and lime-rich mud.[500] This led to "an explosion of activity around 100 BC."[501] One area where cement was used extensively was the city of Teotihuacán in central Mexico, which some Book of Mormon scholars consider to be in the land northward.[502]

These discoveries place the development and expansion of lime cement in Mesoamerica for structural building construction very close to the same period that the cement mentioned in the Book of Mormon becomes widespread in the northern lands.

THE WHY

Despite the fact that pre-Columbian cement had been known to some in the early nineteenth century, the

Book of Mormon was criticized for this point as recently as the early twentieth century. In 1929, Heber J. Grant related a story from his youth where a fellow with a doctorate "ridiculed [him] for believing in the Book of Mormon." This was because it mentioned that "people had built their homes out of cement and that they were very skillful in the use of cement."

This well-educated young man went on to declare, "There had never been found and never would be found, a house built of cement by the ancient inhabitants of this country, because the people in that early age knew nothing about cement."

The young President Grant responded by bearing impassioned testimony of the Book of Mormon:

> That does not affect my faith one particle. I read the Book of Mormon prayerfully and supplicated God for a testimony in my heart and soul of the divinity of it, and I have accepted it and believe it with all my heart. . . . If my children do not find cement houses, I expect that my grandchildren will.

His antagonist responded with more ridicule. "Well what is the good of talking to a fool like that."[503] Grant did not have to wait for future generations to validate the Book of Mormon on this point. Despite being well-educated, his friendly critic was misinformed—cement had already been found in pre-Columbian America. Still, as in so many other instances, as more is learned about cement in ancient America, the correlation with the Book of Mormon gets stronger.

John L. Sorenson observed, "The first-century-BC appearance of cement in the Book of Mormon agrees strikingly with the archaeology of central Mexico."[504] Both Sorenson and John W. Welch remarked, "No one in the nineteenth century could have known that cement, in fact, was extensively used in Mesoamerica beginning at about this time, the middle of the first century BC."[505] And it is more than the mere mention of cement. As Welch put it, "The dating by archaeologists of this technological advance to the precise time mentioned in the book of Helaman seems far from knowable to anyone in the world in 1829."[506]

While other examples of alleged anachronisms have revealed the value in being patient and waiting for new light from archaeology,[507] this example teaches another kind of lesson: sometimes, even well-educated and well-intended people can be wrong (as seen in 2 Nephi 9:28–29).

Rather than panicking at overconfident dismissals or jumping to presupposed outcomes, it is always wiser to continue to investigate the facts to the best of one's ability. In some cases, further time and patience may be necessary to bring additional clarity and understanding, but in other cases—as with cement—the concrete evidence that people can confidently build on is gratefully already available.[508]

FURTHER READING

Matthew Roper, "Exceedingly Expert in the Working of Cement (Howlers #9)," *Ether's Cave: A Place for Book of Mormon Research*, July 1, 2013.

John L. Sorenson, "How Could Joseph Smith Write So Accurately about Ancient American Civilization?," in *Echoes and Evidences of the Book of Mormon,* ed. Donald W. Parry, Daniel C. Peterson, and John W. Welch (Provo, UT: FARMS, 2002), 287–288.

Matthew G. Wells and John W. Welch, "Concrete Evidence for the Book of Mormon," in *Reexploring the Book of Mormon: A Decade of New Research,* ed. John W. Welch (Salt Lake City and Provo, UT: Deseret Book and FARMS, 1992), 212–214.

How Did the Nephites Become Weak in Such a Short Time?

"The Lord did cease to preserve them by his miraculous and matchless power, for they had fallen into a state of unbelief and awful wickedness." (Helaman 4:25)

THE KNOW

War and contention in the land of Zarahemla did not end with the Nephite victories over the forces of Amalickiah and Ammoron toward the end of the book of Alma. In a sadly recurring cycle seen throughout Book of Mormon history, pride, divisiveness, disaffection, sin, wickedness, corruption, and rebellion plagued the Nephites thirty years before the birth of Christ. Helaman 4 reports that within a decade, the Nephites had lost half the land of Zarahemla as well as much of their belief in the spirit of prophecy and revelation.

Mormon told this sad story that he knew not only from history but also from his own personal experiences four hundred years later. The forty-ninth and fiftieth years of the reign of judges (ca. 43 and 42 BC) had been celebrated as years of "great prosperity," Church growth, astonishing blessings, openness to all who "believe on the name of Jesus Christ," and "continual peace" and rejoicing (Helaman 3:23–32). But within only two years, the people were caught up with "exceedingly great pride" (Helaman 3:36). Soon Helaman, the son of Helaman, suddenly died, leaving his fairly young son Nephi in the judgment-seat. During this time, "there were many dissensions in the church, and there was also a contention among the people" (Helaman 4:1), and the government tottered.

A rebellious Nephite faction eventually joined the ranks of the Lamanites and succeeded in stirring up the latter into a war-frenzy (see Helaman 4:3–4). Battle commenced, with the result that the Lamanites captured all the land of Zarahemla and exiled the Nephite government and populace into the land of Bountiful (see Helaman 4:5–9).

The Nephites fought back, regaining half of their lands (see Helaman 4:10), but in telling this tragic story, Mormon lamented, "Now this great loss of the Nephites, and the great slaughter which was among them, would not have happened had it not been for their wickedness and their abomination which was among them; yea, and it was among those also who professed to belong to the church of God" (Helaman 4:11). The wickedness at this time included pride, oppressing the poor, mocking that which was sacred, denying the spirit of prophecy and revelation, murder, plunder, dishonesty, theft, adultery, contention, and desertion (see Helaman 4:12).

In a somewhat startling moment of self-awareness, the Nephites came to their senses and acknowledged their sins, problems, and weaknesses. The Nephites became greatly afraid when they "began to remember the prophecies of Alma, and also the words of Mosiah," as well as when "they saw that they had been a stiffnecked people, and that they had set at naught the commandments of God" (Helaman 4:21).

Additionally, the Nephites recognized that "they had become weak, like unto their brethren, the Lamanites, and that the Spirit of the Lord did no more preserve them; yea, it had withdrawn from them because the Spirit of the Lord doth not dwell in unholy temples" (Helaman 4:24).[509] The Nephites ultimately accepted their need to repent: "They saw that the Lamanites were exceedingly more numerous than they, and except they should cleave unto the Lord their God they must unavoidably perish" (Helaman 4:25).

THE WHY

The Nephites, although being a remnant of the Lord's chosen people, were not inherently safe from the sins and weaknesses of the world. Coming out of a period of prosperity and peace that included an increase in the Church's membership and prestige, many of the Nephites during the time recorded in Helaman 3 began to fall into the dangerous snares of pride. As Mormon recorded, in the fifty-first year of the reign of judges there appeared to be peace, but pride began to enter "into the hearts of the people who professed to belong to the church of God," and in the next year that pride "had gotten into the hearts of the people; and it was because of their exceedingly great riches and their prosperity in the land; and it did grow upon them from day to day" (Helaman 3:33, 36).

Thus, the Nephites quickly became their own worst enemies by allowing their spiritual successes, military victories, and material gains to grow into unchecked pride and soon into outright contention. Daniel C. Peterson perceived, "Wealth . . . carries with it major risks to the spiritual well-being of those who possess it. It can, in fact, come to possess *them*. Sometimes, oddly, those who have more than enough of worldly goods can become more obsessed with them than those who must struggle to make ends meet. So it was with the Nephites at this time."[510]

Perhaps this sad condition spread so rapidly because these material successes arose dramatically in an unregulated decade of post-war boom. Perhaps people felt insecure due to lingering worries about Gadianton terrorism. Perhaps disgruntled political partisans saw opportunities to expand their positions at times when the central government was young and inexperienced. Whatever the economic or political causes, their spiritual failures to act righteously and to keep the commandments of God exposed the Church and the people to impending disasters. Only when they repented could Moronihah "venture to lead them forth from place to place, and from city to city, even until they had regained one one-half" of what they had lost (Helaman 4:15–16).

Mormon's account of this time of Nephite history offers many sobering lessons for modern readers. The fact that these sins and problems began with Nephite members of the Church probably made these attractions and temptations all the more difficult to resist. This should warn all modern followers of Christ to be careful not to slip into an attitude of "all is well in Zion" (2 Nephi 28:21). Even devoted disciples are readily at risk if they assume they are immune to the dangers of pride, selfishness, and contention.

As President Thomas S. Monson warned, "We cannot afford to be complacent. We live in perilous times; the signs are all around us."[511] These same perils can easily be seen at times plaguing Nephite history, and therefore they serve as a reminder for modern readers to "beware of pride, lest ye become as the Nephites of old" (D&C 38:39).

FURTHER READING

Daniel C. Peterson, "Their Own Worst Enemies," in *The Book of Mormon, Part 2: Alma 30 to Moroni, Studies in Scripture*, Volume 8, ed. Kent P. Jackson (Salt Lake City, UT: Deseret Book, 1988), 92–106.

Why Did Helaman Compare Christ to a Rock?

"And now, my sons, remember, remember that it is upon the rock of our Redeemer, who is Christ, the Son of God, that ye must build your foundation; that when the devil shall send forth his mighty winds, yea, his shafts in the whirlwind, yea, when all his hail and his mighty storm shall beat upon you, it shall have no power over you to drag you down to the gulf of misery and endless wo, because of the rock upon which ye are built, which is a sure foundation, a foundation whereon if men build they cannot fall." (Helaman 5:12)

THE KNOW

Helaman 5 gives an account of how Nephi, the son of Helaman, gave up the chief judgment-seat to go with his brother, Lehi, to preach the word of God to the "stiffnecked" Nephite people (Helaman 5:1–4). The text implies that Nephi chose to do this because he remembered some words of counsel from his father, Helaman, who had implored his sons to *remember* several important ideas and principles—the word *remember/remembered* is used fifteen times in this chapter.

One of these important principles that they were to remember was "that it is upon the rock of our Redeemer, who is Christ, the Son of God, that ye must build your foundation" (Helaman 5:12). This phrasing is common in the scriptures and is highly reminiscent of the language of the first generation of Lehites, after whom Helaman's sons were named.[512] The first Nephi, the son of the patriarch Lehi, had often referred to the Lord as the "rock."[513]

This idea of Christ being a stone or rock that serves as a refuge or place of safety is also common in the Old Testament. Books such as Psalms, Isaiah, and Deuteronomy—which the Lehites would likely have had access to on the plates of brass—use similar language. The Psalmist, for example, wrote, "my God is the rock of my refuge" (Psalms 94:22), "thou art my rock and my fortress" (Psalms 71:3), and "For in the time of trouble he shall hide me . . . he shall set me up upon a rock" (Psalms 27:5).

Isaiah said that the Messianic king "shall be as an hiding place from the wind, and a covert from the tempest . . . as the shadow of a great rock in a weary land" (Isaiah 32:2) and that the Lord was "a refuge from the storm" (Isaiah 25:4).

It is interesting to note that the wicked are similarly told that they will need to hide themselves in the rocks in order to escape the wrath of the Lord when He comes to visit them in judgment. The Lord will bring a storm of lightning, hail, arrows, whirlwinds, and so on to punish the wicked. Isaiah warns the wicked to "Enter into the rock, and hide thee in the dust, for fear of the Lord" (Isaiah 2:10; cf. v.19; Revelation 6:15–16), and he says they will "be visited of the Lord of hosts with thunder, and with earthquake, and great noise, with storm and tempest, and the flame of devouring fire" (Isaiah 29:6). In Zechariah 9:14, the Lord is said to come specifically with "arrows" and with "whirlwinds."[514]

In these passages, it is the Lord who comes, in His wrath, with fire, hail, tempest, and fury, and it is the wicked who must hide in the rocks. Heleman effectively reverses this imagery, applying it to Satan's attack on the righteous: "when the devil shall send forth his mighty winds, yea, his shafts [arrows] in the whirlwind, yea, when all his hail and his mighty storm shall beat upon you" (Helaman 5:12).[515] This shouldn't come as a surprise, as Satan often impersonates or imitates God's different capacities.[516]

THE WHY

In the imagery of the Hebrew Bible, the rocks are a place of refuge and safety from storms, hail, and arrows in the whirlwind, and the Lord is ultimately the rock and refuge of Israel. Scriptures such as Isaiah 25:4 describe Jehovah as a place of refuge from the storm when times of trouble arise. Others, such as Isaiah 28, depict the Lord as the cornerstone of the temple, a sure foundation upon which to build. The imagery common to these passages, that the Lord is the Rock, inspires faith in the idea that despite all that the Adversary has to throw at believers, they can seek refuge and safety in Christ. They can be sure that if they build their lives upon Him, His Atonement, and His gospel, they will be building on a safe and secure foundation.

In Helaman 5:12, Helaman described a situation in which Satan, instead of the Lord, is coming in wrath with storm, hail, and arrows in the whirlwind, in order to attack not the wicked, but the righteous. Satan has co-opted this function of Deity and attacks the righteous with all his infernal power. Under these circumstances, Helaman desired that his sons Nephi and Lehi remember the important scriptural principle, one repeated many times in the words of prophets both from the Old World and the New, that Christ is the Rock—a place of refuge, safety, and stability. It is likely that Helaman would have expected that the imagery he used would have brought up many related scriptural passages to their minds, such as those discussed above.

Helaman's words share this common background together with Jesus's concluding parable of the wise man who built his house upon the rock. In 3 Nephi, Jesus declared that those who adhere to His doctrine and do the things that He commanded will be building upon His rock, "and the gates of hell shall not prevail against them" (3 Nephi 11:39; cf. 14:24; 18:12–13).

As Nephi and Lehi went out to preach the gospel among a hardhearted people, they knew that Satan would do his best to tempt, discourage, and destroy them. They chose to rehearse these powerful words of their father in order to remind themselves in whom they could trust and upon what foundation they could build their spiritual house so that it would never be moved out of its place.

Elder Neil L. Andersen of the Quorum of the Twelve Apostles recently admonished:

> Don't let the whirlwinds drag you down. . . . Build more firmly your foundation upon the rock of your Redeemer. . . . Embrace more deeply His love, His mercy and grace, and the powerful gifts of His Atonement. As you do, I promise you that you will see the whirlwinds for what they are—tests, temptations, distractions, or challenges to help you grow. And as you live righteously year after year, I assure you that your experiences will confirm to you again and again that Jesus is the Christ. The spiritual rock under your feet will be solid and secure.[517]

FURTHER READING

Ronald D. Anderson, "Leitworter in Helaman and 3 Nephi," in *The Book of Mormon: Helaman through 3 Nephi 8, According to Thy Word*, eds. Monte S. Nyman and Charles D. Tate Jr. (Provo, UT: BYU Religious Studies Center, 1992), 241–249.

Neil L. Andersen, "Spiritual Whirlwinds," *Ensign*, May 2014, 18–21.

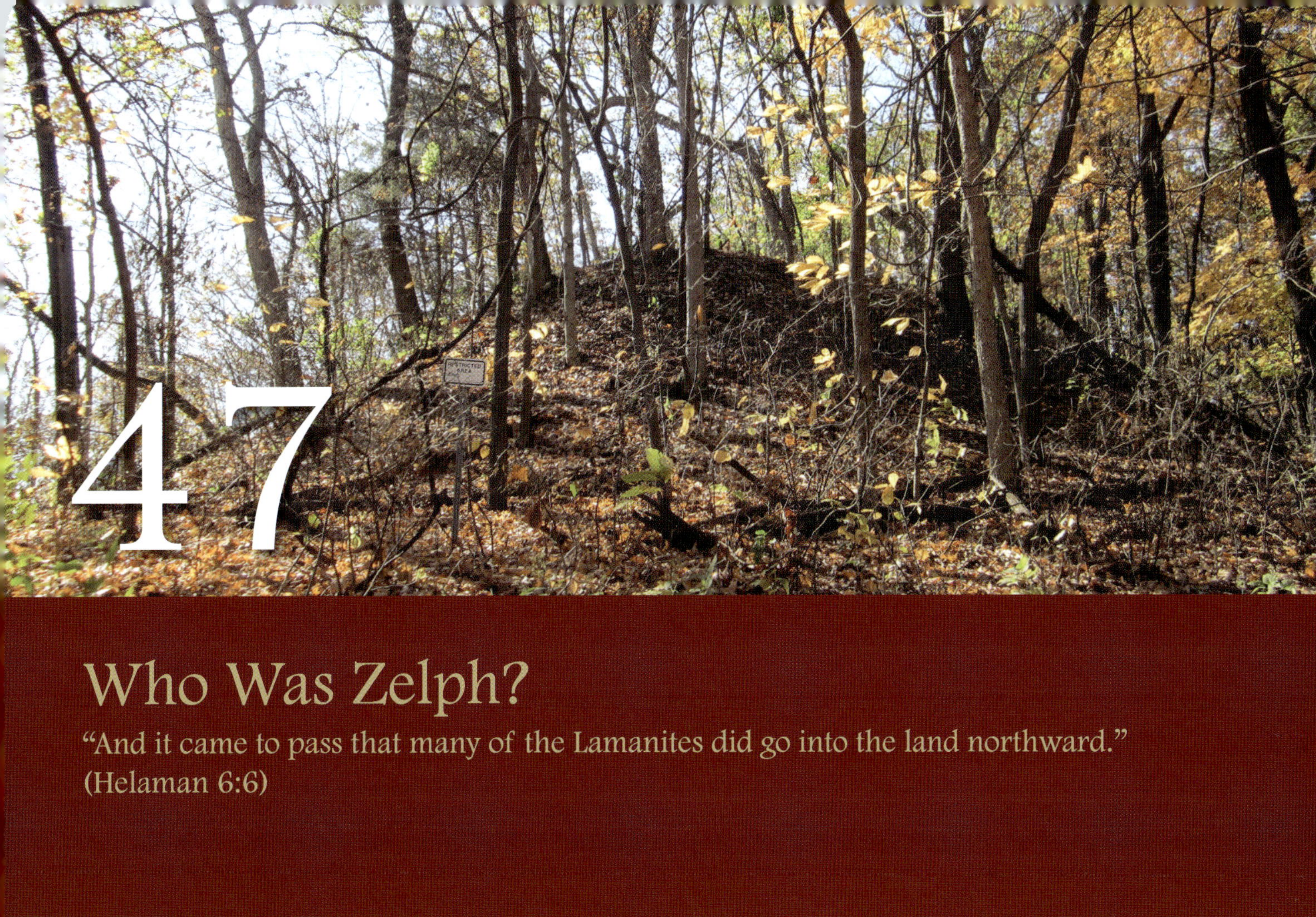

47

Who Was Zelph?

"And it came to pass that many of the Lamanites did go into the land northward." (Helaman 6:6)

THE KNOW

While marching with Zion's Camp in June 1834, Joseph Smith and the brethren "visited many of the mounds" that Wilford Woodruff speculated were "flung up . . . probably by the Nephites & Lamanites."[518] In a letter to Emma, Joseph Smith said they had been "wandering over the plains of the Nephites, recounting occasionally the history of the Book of Mormon." Joseph even said they were "picking up their skulls & their bones, as a proof of its divine authenticity."[519]

On one such occasion, several of the brethren remembered Joseph having identified the bones of a Lamanite warrior named Zelph, who had died in battle.[520] Archaeologists today recognize this event as the first documented archaeological excavation in the Illinois River Valley.[521]

Exactly who Zelph was or how his story relates to Book of Mormon events, however, remains uncertain. In an account published as part of the "History of Joseph Smith" in 1846, after Joseph Smith's death, Zelph was directly linked to the final battles fought between the Nephites and Lamanites in the fourth century AD:

> The visions of the past being opened to my understanding by the spirit of the Almighty I discovered that the person whose skeleton was before us, was a white Lamanite. . . . He was a warrior and chieftain under the great prophet O[n]andagus, who was known from the hill Cumorah, or Eastern sea, to the Rocky Mountains. His name was Zelph. . . . He was killed in battle, by the arrow found among his ribs, during the last great struggle of the Lamanites and Nephites.[522]

Despite this being written in the first person, Joseph Smith himself left behind no direct statements about Zelph. Because this account mentions Cumorah and a "last great struggle" between "Lamanites and Nephites," some have taken this as a prophetic statement about Book of Mormon geography.[523] However, when this account is compared against the manuscript history of the Church and the earlier sources on Zelph, the explicit connections to Book of Mormon places and events become tenuous. There are three crucial details that need to be carefully examined:

1. **"and Nephites":** None of the early accounts about Zelph, written by people in Zion's Camp, mentions the Nephites.[524] Furthermore, in the pre-publication manuscript, written in 1842–1843 under Joseph Smith's guidance and direction, "and Nephites" is crossed out.[525] While some of the early accounts say Zelph died in battle, most do not specify which groups the battle was between.[526] Heber C. Kimball said Zelph "fell in battle . . . among the Lamanites,"[527] perhaps meaning it was a battle between warring Lamanite factions.[528]

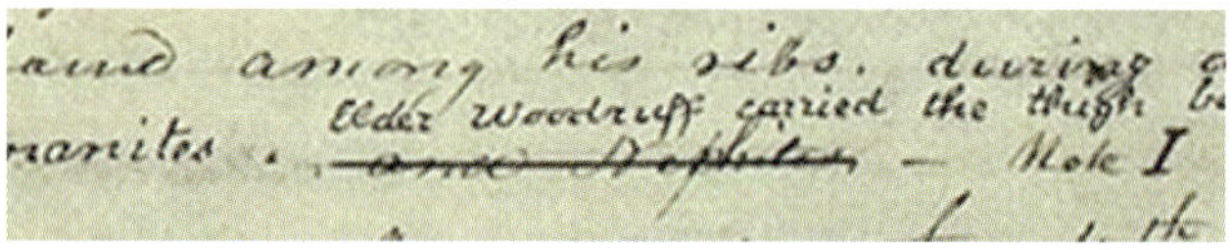
and among his ribs. during
Elder Woodruff carried the thigh
manites. ~~and Nephites~~ — Note I

2. **"the last great struggle":** As with "and Nephites," the word "last" is actually crossed out in the pre-publication manuscript prepared under Joseph Smith's direction.[529] Thus, when reading the pre-publication manuscript without the crossed-out phrases, we find only that Zelph, himself a Lamanite, "was killed . . . during a great struggle with the Lamanites."[530] This suggests that, like in the Kimball account, this was a battle between Lamanites.

Among the early sources, only Heber C. Kimball, in an account published in 1845, after Joseph Smith's death, associated Zelph with "the last destruction." However, as already mentioned, Kimball only described "the last destruction among the Lamanites," with no mention of Nephite involvement. It is thus unclear whether he had the final Book of Mormon battles in mind.[531]

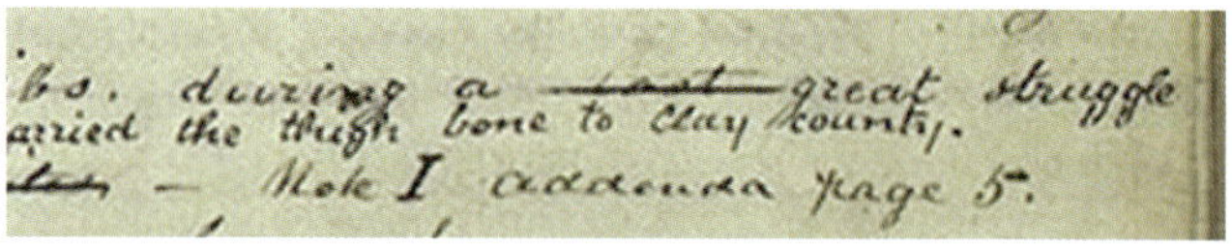
bs. during a ~~last~~ great struggle
arried the thigh bone to Clay county.
— Note I addenda page 5.

3. **"hill Cumorah":** Once again, in the pre-publication manuscript, "hill Cumorah" is crossed out, and thus Onandagus is only said to be "known from the eastern sea to the Rocky Mountains."[532]

Among the six early accounts, only Wilford Woodruff mentioned the Hill Cumorah, stating that "the great prophet . . . was known from the hill Cumorah to the Rocky mountains."[533] In the earlier account written by Rueben McBride, it was Zelph himself who was "known from the Atlantic to the Rocky Mountains,"[534] with no mention of the Hill Cumorah.

In sum, all the details connecting Zelph to specific Book of Mormon places or events in the "History of the Church" article are crossed out in the pre-publication manuscript and are poorly supported by the early primary sources (see table).[535]

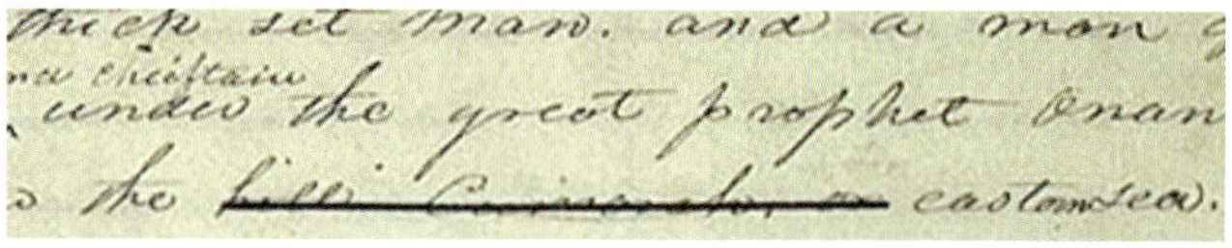
set man. and a man
a chieftain
under the great prophet Onan
the ~~hill Cumorah~~ eastern sea.

Select Details Mentioned in the Early (pre-1846) Primary Sources on Zelph

	Reuden McBride (June 1834)	Moses Martin (June 1834)	Wilford Woodruff (1834)	Levi Hancock (1834)	Heber C. Kimball (1843?)
Hill Cumorah?	No	No	Yes	No	No
"Last" Battle?	No	No	No	No	Yes
Nephites?	No	No	No	No	No
Warrior?	Yes	No	Yes	Yes	Yes
Lamanite?	Yes	No	Yes	Yes	Yes
Righteous?	Yes	Yes	Yes	No	No

THE WHY

Based on the pre-publication manuscript of the "History of the Church" and the most consistent details found in the early primary sources, it appears that Zelph was a righteous Lamanite warrior who died in battle, possibly an inter-Lamanite conflict (see table). After reviewing all the sources, historian Kenneth Godfrey reached a similar conclusion: "Most sources agree that Zelph was a white Lamanite who fought under a leader named Onandagus (variously spelled). Beyond that, what Joseph said to his men is not entirely clear, judging by the variations in the available sources."[536]

This makes Zelph difficult to situate in terms of Book of Mormon history. One possibility, put forward by Apostle John A. Widtsoe, is that "Zelph probably dated from a later time when Nephites and Lamanites had been somewhat dispersed and had wandered over the country."[537]

Historian Donald Q. Cannon concluded that these accounts "indicate that [Joseph Smith] believed that Book of Mormon history, *or at least a part of it,* transpired in North America."[538] While this may be true, we cannot be certain how Zelph relates to any specific Book of Mormon places or events, and therefore his story cannot be used as proof in support of any particular geography.[539] Cannon himself did not feel that Joseph Smith's statement pinned Book of Mormon geography down in North America, but rather "raises the feasibility of a connection between Central America and North America."[540]

A historical connection between peoples in Central and North America is supported by current evidence from anthropology,[541] and the Book of Mormon records that in the mid-first century BC, many Nephites and Lamanites migrated northward (see Alma 63:4–9; Helaman 3:3–8; 6:6). These northward travelers "were never heard of more" (Alma 63:8). Perhaps, as suggested by Mark Wright, Zelph and Onandagus lived among colonies of Lamanites in the land northward that fell outside the scope of Book of Mormon history.[542]

Ultimately, exactly who Zelph was remains a mystery today, and solid conclusions about the location of Book of Mormon places and events simply cannot be reached using his story. Yet like Kenneth Godfrey, we can "hope that someday we will understand more fully just how Zelph, Onandagus, and others not mentioned in the Book of Mormon fit into the divine scheme of things on this, the American continent."[543]

FURTHER READING

Kenneth W. Godfrey, "What Is the Significance of Zelph in the Study of Book of Mormon Geography?" *Journal of Book of Mormon Studies 8*, no. 2 (1999): 70–79, 88.

Donald Q. Cannon, "Zelph Revisited," in *Regional Studies in Latter-day Saint Church History: Illinois,* ed. H. Dean Garrett (Provo, UT: Department of Church History and Doctrine, Brigham Young University, 1995), 97–111.

Kenneth W. Godfrey, "The Zelph Story," *BYU Studies 29*, no. 2 (1989): 31–56.

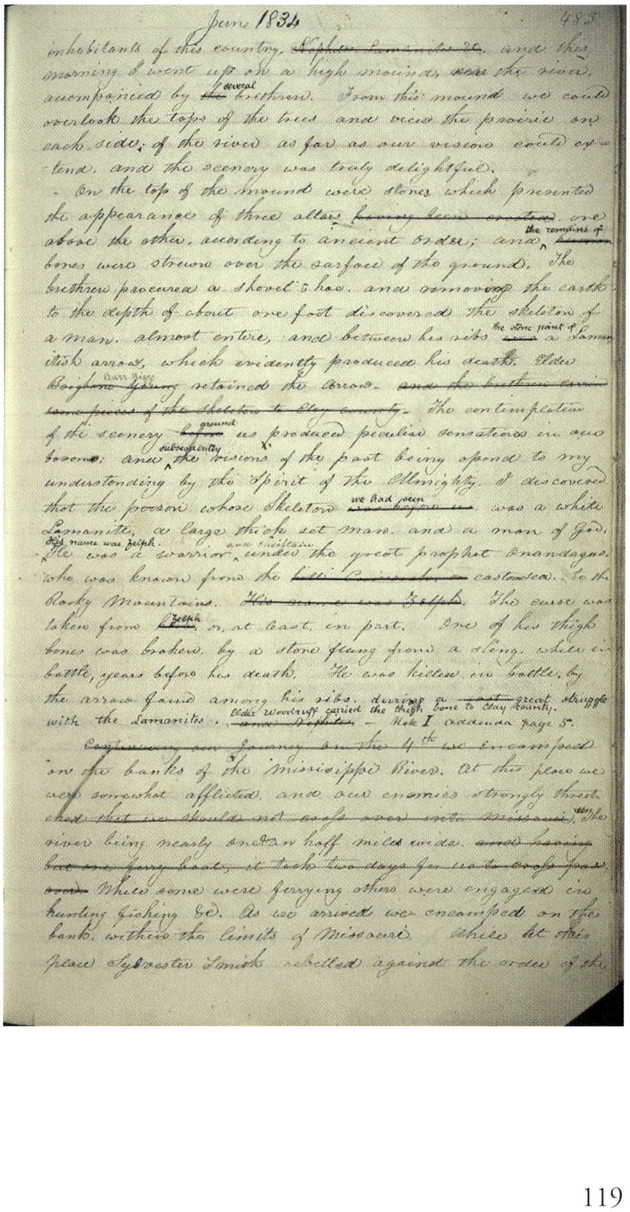

June 1834 483

inhabitants of this country, and this morning I went up on a high mound, near the river, accompanied by several brethren. From this mound we could overlook the tops of the trees and view the prairie on each side of the river as far as our vision could extend, and the scenery was truly delightful.

On the top of the mound were stones which presented the appearance of three altars, one above the other, according to ancient order; and the remains of bones were strewn over the surface of the ground. The brethren procured a shovel & hoe, and removing the earth to the depth of about one foot discovered the skeleton of a man, almost entire, and between his ribs the stone point of a Lamanitish arrow, which evidently produced his death. Elder ~~Brigham Young~~ Burr Riggs retained the arrow. The contemplation of the scenery around us produced peculiar sensations in our bosoms: and subsequently the visions of the past being opened to my understanding by the Spirit of the Almighty, I discovered that the person whose skeleton we had seen was a white Lamanite, a large thick set man, and a man of God. His name was Zelph. He was a warrior and chieftain under the great prophet Onandagus, who was known from the castern sea to the Rocky Mountains. ~~His name was Zelph.~~ The curse was taken from Zelph, or, at least, in part. One of his thigh bones was broken by a stone flung from a sling, while in battle, years before his death. He was killed in battle, by the arrow found among his ribs, during a great struggle with the Lamanites. Elder Woodruff carried the thigh bone to Clay County. — Note I addenda page 5.

on the banks of the Mississippi River. At this place we were somewhat afflicted, and our enemies strongly threatened. The river being nearly one & an half miles wide. While some were ferrying others were engaged in hunting fishing &c. As we arrived we encamped on the bank, within the limits of Missouri. While at this place Sylvester Smith rebelled against the order of the

48

Why Was Chiasmus Used in Nephite Record Keeping?

"Now the land south was called Lehi, and the land north was called Mulek, which was after the son of Zedekiah; for the Lord did bring Mulek into the land north, and Lehi into the land south." (Helaman 6:10)

THE KNOW

Although Mormon's editorial voice is quite noticeable at key junctures in many of the historical narratives found in the Book of Mormon, it should be recognized that he also often relied heavily on various types of underlying historical records.[544] John L. Sorenson has noted that Mormon "depended primarily on the writings on 'the [large] plates of Nephi' to formulate his narrative." The "fundamental format of the plates of Nephi was that of annals," which Sorenson described as "yearly summaries of salient events."[545]

Helaman 6:7–13 seems to be a strong candidate for one such yearly summary that Mormon copied directly from the large plates of Nephi. This is because the record contained in these verses (which reports on the sixty-fourth year of the Reign of the Judges) appears to be a purposefully crafted chiasm and functions on its own as complete literary unit.[546]

And behold, there was *peace* in all the land,
[Freedom of travel and trade in *both lands* is discussed]
they became exceedingly rich, both the Lamanites and the Nephites;
. . . exceeding plenty of . . . *precious* metals,
both in the land south and in the land north.
Now the *land south*
was called *Lehi*, and
the *land north*
was called *Mulek*,
which was after the son of *Zedekiah*
for the *Lord*
did bring *Mulek*
into the *land north*,
and *Lehi*
into the *land south*.
. . . all manner of gold in *both* these lands,
and of silver, and of *precious* ore
. . . and thus they did become *rich*
[Economic prosperity in *both lands* is discussed]
And thus the sixty and fourth year did pass away in *peace*.[547]

According to John W. Welch,

> This composition is remarkable in several ways. First, the report itself is beautifully executed. The overall structure is concentrically organized, and individual words, phrases, and

> ideas that appear in the first half are repeated with precision and balance in the second half. This entry exhibits both fine quality and admirable length.[548]

What Welch found most remarkable, though, was the center of the chiasm.

> Just as divine names often appear at the center of biblical chiasms, at the very apex of this passage in Helaman 6, the words *Zedekiah* and *Lord* stand parallel to each other. The parallelism between these two names is intriguing not only because Zedekiah was the king and adoptive royal son of Yahweh, the Lord, but also because the Hebrew word for *Lord (YHWH)* constitutes the final syllable, or theophoric suffix, –*yah*, at the end of the name Zedekiah. Thus the central chiastic structure in Helaman 6:10 actually would have worked better and would have been more obvious in Hebrew (or its related Nephite dialect) than in the English translation.[549]

THE WHY

Why was chiasmus used here? Because the spread of peace and prosperity is the major theme in this scriptural passage, it is meaningful that names designating Jehovah (Yahweh) are situated in its very center. This suggests that the original scribal record keeper (whoever it was) may have used chiasmus to emphasize the central role that the Lord God had played in providing the posterity of Lehi and Mulek with their numerous blessings and favorable circumstances in their two lands.[550]

In addition, the sixty-fourth year of the Reign of Judges was a most remarkable year. After more than a decade of hostility between the peoples in the lands of Nephi and Zarahemla, free and open opportunities for travel and trade were suddenly possible. Three years earlier, the extraordinary missionary successes of Nephi and Lehi, the sons of Helaman, facilitated much of this, as Helaman 5 glowingly reports.

The two-way traffic made possible by this brief window of peace and righteous sharing of ethical and religious values (see Helaman 6:4–6) was ideally suited to an inverted chiastic presentation of these reciprocal interactions—both "in the land south and in the land north" (Helaman 6:9) and, emphatically also, "in the north and in the south" (Helaman 6:12).

The chiastic structure of this year's report also draws double attention to the exceeding prosperity, gains, and riches (see Helaman 6:8–9) and the exceeding increases, well-being, and flourishing (see Helaman 6:12–13) among the people in both of these lands. Indeed, such a symbolic and purposeful (as well as accurate and elegant) approach employed in this record would have deeply impressed Mormon. All of this would have encouraged Mormon to incorporate this annal unaltered. As Sorenson explained,

> [Mormon's] primary criterion comes through repeatedly in his book. The aim was to ensure that his readers, especially the future inhabitants of the American promised land and particularly Lehi's descendants, grasp the significance for them of the promise and prophecy given to father Lehi: "Inasmuch as ye will keep my commandments ye shall prosper in the land." (Jarom 1:9)[551]

This well-crafted annal efficiently illustrates that central principle. Moreover, messages written in classic forms tend to radiate a sense of agelessness, not only to their immediate audiences but also to future generations. Modern readers, therefore, can also readily relate to the enduring truths enshrined in this chronicler's report, that peace and prosperity at all times are dependent on one's willingness to keep God's commandments. Notably, this promise was not only extended to Lehi and his posterity, but to "all those who should be led out of other countries by the hand of the Lord" (2 Nephi 1:5).[552]

Concerning the overall worth of this chiasm, Welch concluded, "Helaman 6:7–13 deserves to take its place among the finest examples of chiasmus found in the Book of Mormon."[553] Not only is this instance a model example of the ancient poetic form, but the fact that its central message is most impactful in ancient Hebrew is yet another evidence of the Book of Mormon's authenticity and divine imprimatur. As Welch put it, at several levels—verbally, historically, and theologically—"Joseph Smith would have had no way of consciously concocting this parallelism on his own."[554]

FURTHER READING

John L. Sorenson, "Mormon's Miraculous Book," *Ensign*, February 2016, 38–41.

John L. Sorenson, "Mormon's Sources," *Journal of Book of Mormon and Other Restoration Scripture 20*, no. 2 (2011): 2–15.

John W. Welch, "A Steady Stream of Significant Recognitions," in *Echoes and Evidences of the Book of Mormon,* ed. Donald W. Parry, Daniel C. Peterson, and John W. Welch (Provo, UT: FARMS, 2002), 345–347.

49

What Is the Difference between "Robbers" and "Thieves" in the Book of Mormon?

"And now behold, those murderers and plunderers were a band who had been formed by Kishkumen and Gadianton. . . . And they were called Gadianton's robbers and murderers." (Helaman 6:18)

THE KNOW

Although most readers probably haven't thought much about this detail, the Book of Mormon consistently discusses *thieves* and *theft* in a different way than it does *robbers* and *robbery*. Throughout the Nephite record, *robbers* are typically organized bands who separate themselves from society, oppose the government, and largely subsist by plundering their enemies. *Thieves*, on the other hand, seem to be community members who are guilty of stealing from fellow citizens. In simple terms, robbers were organized groups of "outsiders," whereas thieves were community "insiders" who acted alone.

Illustrating this distinction, John W. Welch and Kelly Ward have explained that "the Lamanites are always said to 'rob' from the Nephites but never from their own brethren—that would be 'theft,' not 'robbery.' It also explains the rise and fearful menace of the Gadianton society, who are always called 'robbers' in the Book of Mormon, never 'thieves.'"[555]

Although these differences may not seem important to modern readers, they were crucial throughout much of the ancient world. Drawing on the research of Bernard S. Jackson, Welch and Ward noted "how robbers usually acted in organized groups rivaling local governments and attacking towns and how they swore oaths and extorted ransom, a menace worse than outright war. Thieves, however, were a much less serious threat to society."[556]

We know that this distinction was important in the Bible because, just as in the Book of Mormon, its authors consistently referred to thieves and robbers by different names. Again, drawing on Jackson's analysis, Welch explained,

> In Hebrew, the terms *gazal* (to rob) and *gazlan* (robber) normally mean taking property openly and blatantly, while the words *ganab* (to steal) and *gannab* (thief) usually connote stealing in secret. Similarly the Greek term *kleptes* "is used to describe a stealthy person who, without violence, deprives another person of his property," whereas by contrast, "in the Old Testament and Apocrypha, a λῃστής *[lēstēs]* is always a brigand, a marauder, a member of a gang whose activity takes place out of doors. He

belongs to a troop that attacks caravans or settlements with weapons and robs them of their goods."[557]

THE WHY

It seems highly improbable that Joseph Smith, relying on his own American cultural background and knowledge, would have even have been aware that a distinction existed anciently between robbers and thieves. Although this distinction is consistent in the underlying texts of the Old and New Testaments, Welch has demonstrated that even the well-educated "King James translators used the words *theft* and *robbery* interchangeably."[558]

For instance, "the same phrase is translated inconsistently as 'den of robbers' and 'den of thieves' in Jeremiah 7:11 and Matthew 21:13. The same word (*lestai*) is translated sometimes as 'thieves' (Matthew 27:38), other times as 'robber' (John 18:40)."[559] If expert biblical scholars trained in ancient languages were ignorant of this important nuance, what chance would the uneducated Joseph Smith have of noticing it?[560]

Understanding the difference between thieves and robbers can also help us better grasp the significance of some events in Book of Mormon stories. For instance, readers may wonder why some individuals, like Zemnarihah, were executed without any trial or ordinarily due legal process. Welch has noted, "This treatment can be explained by Zemnarihah's status as a robber. Robbers in the ancient world were more than common thieves; they were outsiders and enemies to society itself. As such, the ancients reasoned, they were outlaws, outside the law, and not entitled to legal process."[561]

Thus, although it is a seemingly small detail, the Book of Mormon's distinction between thieves and robbers has significant implications. Its presence offers good evidence of the Book of Mormon's antiquity, as well as the attention paid by Nephite record keepers to technical legal terminology. It can also help readers better understand the drastic social and legal implications of the "robbers" who terrorized the Nephite civilization. More than mere thieves, these organized, oath-bound criminals were intent on overthrowing the Nephite government and subjecting the people to their rule.[562] As such, they were always treated as a serious military threat and swiftly punished as traitors or brigands.[563]

FURTHER READING

John W. Welch, "Legal and Social Perspectives on Robbers in First-Century Judea," *BYU Studies 36*, no. 3 (1996–1997): 141–153.

John W. Welch and Kelly Ward, "Thieves and Robbers," in *Reexploring the Book of Mormon: A Decade of New Research*, ed. John W. Welch (Salt Lake City and Provo, UT: Deseret Book and FARMS, 1992), 248–249.

John W. Welch, "Theft and Robbery in the Book of Mormon and Ancient Near Eastern Law," *FARMS Preliminary Report* (1985).

50

Why Did Nephi Prophesy Near "the Highway which Led to the Chief Market"?

"And behold, now it came to pass that it was upon a tower, which was in the garden of Nephi, which was by the highway which led to the chief market." (Helaman 7:10)

THE KNOW

Speaking about a time of peace and growing prosperity, Mormon recorded that both Nephites and Lamanites "did go into whatsoever part of the land they would" and "did have free intercourse one with another" (Helaman 6:7–8). Free trade naturally led to wealth (see Helaman 6:11–13), which soon gave way to pride (see Helaman 6:17). Pride then led to moral decline and eventually to "secret murders and combinations" (Helaman 6:38).

It is with this backdrop that Nephi delivered his well-known prophetic lament. Although seemingly unremarkable, Mormon's mention that Nephi was "upon a tower, which was in the garden of Nephi, which was by the highway which led to the chief market" (Helaman 7:10) is actually both relevant to the story and historically well attested.

Wallace Hunt explained, "If we look at Mesoamerica . . . we find that reference to a market (marketplace) is not only proper but crucial to Mormon's description of Nephi's praying and its effect upon the people."[564] According to Eric Thompson, "The present-day markets of highland Guatemala are enchanting, colorful, and thought-provoking, but they are but pale shadows of the markets in pre-Columbian times."[565] Sylvanus Morley and George Brainerd concluded that "the most important economic institution of the ancient Maya was the centralized market."[566]

Aside from a central or chief market, ancient Mesoamerican cities also had subsidiary markets that, together with the main market, worked as an organized trade network.[567] These market systems were typically coordinated so that on a certain day (or days) of the week, traders from outlying areas would buy and sell their goods at the central market. After this they would exchange these goods with other traders in neighboring market locations, who in turn would transport the goods to outlying settlements.[568]

It is also well known that an extensive network of highways traversed ancient America,[569] and some proposed sites for Mesoamerican markets, such as the Maax Na Marketplace in Belize, did indeed have a main road or causeway that led into a central market plaza.[570]

Furthermore, in some Mesoamerican cities "garden areas were cultivated immediately adjacent to single habitation complexes,"[571] and low-rising pyramidal towers were enclosed within private family compounds.[572] The convergence of these features in ancient Mesoamerica provides a very believable real-world context for Nephi's public statement.

Prophets in ancient Israel often staged a creative scene wherein they would act out or symbolically represent a central component of their prophetic message. For example, John W. Welch explained,

> When Jeremiah wanted to impress the people of Jerusalem with his prophecy that they would be yoked into bondage by the Babylonians, he draped himself with thongs and a yoke and thus went forth proclaiming his message of doom (see Jeremiah 27:2–11). Other similar symbolic or parabolic acts performed as prophetic oracles are found in Jeremiah 13:1–11 (hiding a waistcloth), Jeremiah 19:1–13 (smashing a bottle), 1 Kings 11:29–39 (tearing a garment into twelve pieces), 2 Kings 13:15–19 (shooting an arrow), and Isaiah 20:2–6 (walking naked).[573]

Welch suggested eight reasons for similarly seeing Nephi's prophetic lament as a sort of staged funeral sermon.[574] As people may have been wondering in this case who had died, Nephi asked them, "Why will ye die?" (Helaman 7:17). He then publicly rebuked them for their wickedness and then prophesied concerning the chief judge who had, unbeknownst to the people, just been murdered (see Helaman 8:27). Thus in response to both physical and spiritual death, Nephi conspicuously acted out a poignant funerary lament.

THE WHY

If this event was indeed so staged, then Nephi's choice to publicly mourn on a private tower next to the highway makes a lot of sense. His whole purpose would have been to make a scene, and the throngs of people on their way to a centralized market (perhaps on an appointed market day) would have provided a sizable audience.

When "the people came together in multitudes" (Helaman 7:11), Nephi was able to deliver the heart of his message as he boldly declared, "And ye have set your hearts upon the riches and the vain things of this world, for the which ye do murder, and plunder, and steal, and bear false witness against your neighbor, and do all manner of iniquity" (Helaman 7:21).

The irony of this rebuke would have been stinging, for the people—*at that very moment*—were likely on their way to buy and sell the riches upon which they had set their hearts and that they were seeking "to get gain that they might be lifted up one above another" (Helaman 6:17).

The news of such a strange and marvelous prophecy would surely have traveled along the same trade network that was otherwise distributing the wealth and riches that were leading to wickedness.

Nephi didn't have a modern conference center with a raised podium and a microphone. He didn't have the internet, television, or radio to transmit his message to his people. Instead, he had a tower next to a highway leading to a market. And while Nephi's message was initially intended for an ancient audience, there can be no doubt that his cry of warning was included for our day. To modern readers, Moroni stirringly declared,

> Behold, I speak unto you as if ye were present, and yet ye are not. But behold, Jesus Christ hath shown you unto me, and I know your doing. And I know that ye do walk in the pride of your hearts. . . . For behold, ye do love money, and your substance, and your fine apparel, and the adorning of your churches, more than ye love the poor and the needy, the sick and the afflicted. (Mormon 8:35–37)

For a modern world largely preoccupied with concerns about wealth and materialism, Nephi's prophetic lament remains an instructive and stirring warning against pride, greed, and spiritual indifference.

FURTHER READING

Wallace E. Hunt Jr., "The Marketplace," in *Pressing Forward with the Book of Mormon: The FARMS Updates of the 1990s*, ed. John W. Welch and Melvin J. Thorne (Provo UT: FARMS, 1999), 196–200.

John L. Sorenson, "Nephi's Garden and Chief Market," in *Reexploring the Book of Mormon: A Decade of New Research*, ed. John W. Welch (Salt Lake City and Provo, UT: Deseret Book and FARMS, 1992), 236–238.

John W. Welch, "Was Helaman 7–8 an Allegorical Funeral Sermon?" in *Reexploring the Book of Mormon: A Decade of New Research*, ed. John W. Welch (Salt Lake City and Provo, UT: Deseret Book and FARMS, 1992), 239–241.

Why Did Nephi Appeal to so Many Earlier Testimonies of Christ?

"All of our fathers, even down to this time . . . have testified of the coming of Christ, and have looked forward, and have rejoiced in his day which is to come." (Helaman 8:22)

THE KNOW

In trying to convince the people of Zarahemla to rectify the wickedness of their laws, Nephi appealed to the testimonies of those who long before had "testified of the coming of Christ" (Helaman 8:22). By doing so, he reminded the people of the laws of God. Corrupt judges were attempting to have Nephi put on trial (see Helaman 8:1), but Nephi turned the tables on them by symbolically bringing them to trial instead.[575]

Because they had rejected the law of Moses for their own unjust laws, the first witness he brought against them was Moses himself. After all, who could judge better than Moses if his laws were being negated? Nephi reminded them of the miracles Moses performed by the power of God (see Helaman 8:11) and then pointed them toward the most important part of the law of Moses: Christ. "Yea, did he not bear record that the Son of God should come? And as he lifted up the brazen serpent in the wilderness, even so shall he be lifted up who should come" (Helaman 8:14).

Nephi then called his second witness, the Psalms, which he quotes in Helaman 8:15: "And as many as should look upon that serpent should live, even so as many as should look upon the Son of God with faith, having a *contrite spirit*, might live, even unto that life which is eternal" (emphasis added). Here Nephi combined his comments on Moses with an allusion to Psalms 34:18–19, talking about how Christ saved the people in the wilderness and can still save them now: "The Lord is nigh unto them that are of a broken heart; and saveth such as be of a *contrite spirit*" (emphasis added).

His next witness was Abraham, the father of the covenant between Jehovah and His people: "Yea, and behold, Abraham saw of his coming, and was filled with gladness and did rejoice" (Helaman 8:17). This statement may have a common background with the version of Genesis 15:2 found in the Joseph Smith Translation and evidently on the plates of brass: "And it came to pass, that Abram looked forth and saw the days of the Son of Man, and was glad, and his soul found rest."[576] Nephi then listed Zenos, Zenock, Ezias, Isaiah, and Jeremiah in quick succession. This list gave him the symbolically significant number of seven named witnesses from the plates of brass to support his witness of Christ.[577]

Nephi then moved from the Old World to the New World, using the very people in the audience as witnesses against themselves: "Now we know that Jerusalem was destroyed according to the words of Jeremiah. O then why not the Son of God come, according to his prophecy? And now will you dispute that Jerusalem was destroyed? Will ye say that the sons of Zedekiah were not slain, all except it were Mulek? Yea, and do ye not behold that the seed of Zedekiah are with us, and they were driven out of the land of Jerusalem?" (Helaman 8:20–22).[578]

Because some people in the audience were descendants of Mulek, who left Jerusalem while it was being destroyed, they provided living witnesses to the truthfulness of Jeremiah's prophecy concerning the destruction of Jerusalem (cf. Omni 1:15). And if Jeremiah's prophecy about the destruction of Jerusalem was correct, Nephi argued, surely his prophecy about the coming of Christ was also correct.

Nephi continued drawing from New World prophets, citing Lehi, Nephi, and those who followed them as additional witnesses. Finally, he called the heavens and the earth to witness what he had said. "In this ye have sinned, for ye have rejected all these things, notwithstanding so many evidences which ye have received; yea, even ye have received all things, both things in *heaven*, and all things which are in the *earth*, as a witness that they are true" (Helaman 8:24; emphasis added). This juridical move likely reflects the ancient Israelite practice manifest in Isaiah 1:2: "Hear, O *heavens*, and give ear, O *earth*: for the Lord hath spoken, I have nourished and brought up children, and they have rebelled against me" (emphasis added). Nephi's indictment and calling of witnesses forms a superb example of what has been identified by many biblical scholars as a "prophetic lawsuit."[579]

THE WHY

Helaman 8 begins with the people nearly bringing Nephi to trial before local judges. But throughout this chapter, Nephi successfully called higher witnesses to testify against them before God instead. He formally put the people on divine trial and pronounced them worthy of "everlasting destruction" but suspended the judgment if they would repent (Helaman 8:26).

Nephi knew that "at the mouth of two witnesses, or three witnesses, shall he that is worthy of death be put to death" (Deuteronomy 17:6).[580] But Nephi emphatically called many more than the required number of witnesses, urging the people to reject their flawed legal system and return to the laws authorized by God. That law was grounded in the scriptures, which he referenced so frequently.[581]

There are times in the Book of Mormon when prophets needed to stand up and criticize negative trends they saw around them. Sometimes, as in Nephi's case, they stood alone. Many people might find themselves in a similar position in today's world. But Nephi reminded readers of the Book of Mormon that they are never really alone in pushing back against corruption within society. Modern readers can, like Nephi, appeal to the scriptures and personal revelation in resisting any negative trends around them.

FURTHER READING

John W. Welch, *The Legal Cases in the Book of Mormon* (Provo, UT: BYU Press and Neal A. Maxwell Institute for Religious Scholarship, 2008), 323–327.

M. Russell Ballard, "Learning the Lessons of the Past," *Ensign*, May 2009, 31–33.

Why Was Seantum Convicted without Any Witnesses?

"Then shall he confess unto you, and deny no more that he has done this murder. And then shall he say unto you, that I, Nephi, know nothing concerning the matter save it were given unto me by the power of God." (Helaman 9:35–36)

THE KNOW

In Helaman 9, Nephi the son of Helaman revealed, through revelation, that the chief judge Seezoram had been murdered by his brother Seantum. When Seantum was questioned, he was incriminated by the blood found on his clothes; he subsequently confessed to the crime.

Seantum was then condemned, and five people who had been falsely accused of the murder were set free. However, since the law of Moses traditionally required two or three witnesses for a conviction (see Deuteronomy 17:6), it is difficult to know how Seantum's conviction could have been legal. Thankfully, a story in the book of Joshua set a precedent that helps explain what happened in Helaman 9.

Shortly after the Israelite conquest of Jericho, the Israelites attempted to take over a city called Ai, but were soundly defeated (see Joshua 7:3–5). Wondering what was wrong, Joshua prayed to know why they had lost the battle (see Joshua 7:6–9). God told Joshua that someone had taken something from the city, even though everything was supposed to be either destroyed or consecrated to the Lord (see Joshua 7:10–11).[582]

Because of this, God refused to fight with them, and they lost (see Joshua 7:12). Joshua discovered through revelation that the culprit was an Israelite soldier named Achan (see Joshua 7:16–18).[583] When Joshua confronted Achan, he confessed to the crime, and Joshua sent people to find what Achan had stolen (see Joshua 7:19–22). Achan was then summarily executed (see Joshua 7:25).

In both Seantum's and Achan's cases, a person was condemned for a capital crime, even though he was the only witness. Thus, it would seem that the two-witness law had been violated in both of these instances.

However, Jewish legal authorities have noted that even though two witnesses were generally needed for a conviction, there was an exception to this rule. John W. Welch noted that the two-witness rule could only be overridden if the perpetrator incriminated himself and if two conditions were met:

1. The person confessed outside of court or the will of God was obviously manifest in bringing him to justice.
2. Physical evidence was produced that proved who committed the crime.

As Welch noted,

> Quite remarkably, Seantum's self-incriminating confession was precisely such a case on all counts, and thus his execution would not have been legally problematic. His confession was spontaneous and occurred outside of court. The evidence of God's will was supplied through Nephi's prophecy. The tangible evidence was present in the blood found on Seantum's cloak.[584]

Just as in the case of Achan, Seantum had been detected through revelation, he had confessed to the crime spontaneously outside of court, and obvious physical evidence corroborated that he had committed this criminal act.[585] Because the case met all of these conditions, it is likely that these factors could stand in the place of the two or three witnesses normally required.

THE WHY

Seantum could be convicted because other factors were present in his case, and Mormon was careful to mention each of those three factors with precision. Even though Seantum's conviction might otherwise seem irregular, it was consonant with the biblical precedent of Achan. The technically precise legality of this case demonstrates the stark contrast between the corrupt judgments of the Gadianton robbers who currently filled the judgment seat and the righteous judgments of God, delivered by Nephi.

It has been noted that as the influence of the Gadianton robbers continued to increase, "God's entrance into this proceeding demonstrated that he was aware of the corruption of political officials to the point of openly sustaining and validating the words of his prophets. In this case especially, righteous judgment equates with God's judgment."[586]

Thus, by revealing the scene of this homicide to the prophet Nephi, God forcefully made the point that He was still in control. No matter how well the people concealed their wickedness from others, they could never hide it from God.

Because the trial and execution of Seantum displayed so prominently God's awareness of the corruption of the wicked and His support for the righteous, as Welch explained,

> The case of Seantum would have sustained and encouraged the righteous few in this society in their adamant determination to resist civil corruption, to challenge and expose secret combinations, to induce confessions of secret wrongdoings, and to judge courageously and righteously themselves.[587]

Finally, in some situations, modern readers may need to be a lone voice for righteousness, even on occasions when surrounded by wickedness. As President Thomas S. Monson stated, "May we maintain the courage to defy the consensus. May we ever choose the harder right instead of the easier wrong."[588]

Surely the Lord's directing of the outcome in the trial of Seantum would likely have encouraged the small band of righteous Nephites living in a wicked society. This story can be equally encouraging to modern readers as they live in difficult times.

FURTHER READING

Thomas S. Monson, "Choices," *Ensign*, May, 2016, 86.

John W. Welch, *The Legal Cases in the Book of Mormon* (Provo, UT: BYU Press and Neal A. Maxwell Institute for Religious Scholarship, 2008), 313–322.

John W. Welch, "The Case of an Unobserved Murder," in *Reexploring the Book of Mormon: A Decade of New Research*, ed. John W. Welch (Salt Lake City and Provo, UT: Deseret Book and FARMS, 1992), 242–244.

Why Is There Temple Imagery in Helaman 10?

"And thus, if ye shall say unto this temple it shall be rent in twain, it shall be done." (Helaman 10:8)

THE KNOW

In Helaman 10, after revealing the murderer of the chief judge, Nephi the son of Helaman began to walk back to his house, pondering the wickedness of the people. As he was thinking about all that had just transpired, God reassured Nephi that his diligence did not go unnoticed (see Helaman 10:3–5). Suddenly, God stated that His words to Nephi were being given "in the presence of [God's] angels" (Helaman 10:6), and then it appears that God's declaration to Nephi was being given in a temple (see Helaman 10:8). These somewhat unexpected and often overlooked details suggest that Nephi was being shown a vision of the divine council inside a holy temple.

In ancient Israel, some prophets received visions in which they saw God's "divine council," a group composed of God and His "royal court" in heaven.[589] Accounts of these experiences have similar elements: the prophet has a pressing need for help, often related to knowing how to help a wicked group of people;[590] the prophet is in a temple or mountain setting;[591] the prophet sees the divine council, or a messenger from the council;[592] the Lord reassures the prophet and gives him knowledge;[593] and the prophet is then empowered and called to speak and act on God's behalf.[594]

Over the years, several Latter-day Saint biblical scholars have noted continuities between these Israelite throne manifestations and the revelatory experiences of Book of Mormon prophets.[595] Recently, David Bokovoy explained that elements like these "provide a type of template for depicting an official encounter between witness and worshipper in preparation for the introduction to advanced revelatory truths."[596]

Father Lehi had a divine council experience (see 1 Nephi 1:8–14), as did his son Nephi (see 1 Nephi 11:1–6).[597] In Nephi's case, the divine council experience in 1 Nephi 11 contains a detail that helps explain Helaman 10. It began as Nephi was "pondering" Lehi's account of his dream in his "heart" (1 Nephi 11:1). Nephi was then spiritually transported to a high mountain where he had his divine council experience.[598] The only other time something happened in the Book of Mormon as a character was "pondering" in his "heart" was the experience of this later Nephi, described in Helaman 10:3. According to the ancient Israelite writing style that Book of Mormon authors likely employed, this detail was a signal to the reader to read Helaman 10 in conjunction with and in comparison to 1 Nephi 11.[599]

This comparison indicates that the experience of Nephi the son of Helaman in Helaman 10 is yet another example of the sacred divine council experience. Nephi needed help, and was "pondering" how he could help eliminate "the wickedness of the people" (Helaman 10:3). He then found himself at a "temple" (Helaman 10:8) on a "mountain" (Helaman 10:9). Angels were present (see Helaman 10:6). The Lord reassured him by telling him that he was "blessed" because he had been keeping God's commandments (Helaman 10:4). God gave him religious truths and empowered him with the ability to "seal" and "loose" on "earth" and in "heaven" (Helaman 10:7). Finally, Nephi was called to speak and act on God's behalf, being told to "go and declare" God's words to the people (Helaman 10:11).

THE WHY

Seeing Nephi the son of Helaman as being admitted into the presence of the divine council explains the presence of angels, temples, mountains, and sealing in Helaman 10. As the leading Nephite prophet and high priest, Nephi would have been familiar with the Israelite temple traditions, having officiated over the main temple in Zarahemla, the temple used by King Benjamin, Mosiah, Alma, and Helaman.

Moreover, Nephi was "much cast down because of the wickedness of the people of the Nephites" (Helaman 10:3). Considering that he had narrowly escaped being put to death and that the Gadianton robbers had killed the chief judge, his great concern and need for divine guidance and reassurance was certainly a reasonable response.

Yet it was during this difficult time of personal obedience and sacrifice that Nephi not only heard God's voice (see Helaman 10:3) but had an expansive prophetic experience with the Lord and His heavenly host. Nephi's profound story reminds readers that sometimes the most spiritual experiences come only after the most painful experiences.

Referring to Christ's Crucifixion, Elder Joseph B. Wirthlin stated:

> Each of us will have our own Fridays—those days when the universe itself seems shattered and the shards of our world lie littered about us in pieces. We all will experience those broken times when it seems we can never be put together again. We will all have our Fridays. But I testify to you in the name of the One who conquered death—Sunday will come. In the darkness of our sorrow, Sunday will come. No matter our desperation, no matter our grief, Sunday will come. In this life or the next, Sunday will come.[600]

During what may have been one of Nephi's darkest moments, God blessed Nephi and swore an oath to Nephi in His own name that He would always be with him and answer his prayers.[601] This is a powerful reminder of God's personal care and covenantal reassurance in the darkest of times. This principle is as true for readers of the Book of Mormon and temple attenders today as it was for Nephi the son of Helaman shortly before the birth of Christ.

FURTHER READING

Stephen O. Smoot, "The Divine Council in the Hebrew Bible and the Book of Mormon," *Interpreter: A Journal of Mormon Scripture 27*, no. 2 (2017): 155–180.

David E. Bokovoy, "'Thou Knowest That I Believe': Invoking the Spirit of the Lord as Council Witness in 1 Nephi 11," *Interpreter: A Journal of Mormon Scripture 1* (2012): 1–23.

Taylor Halverson, "The Path of Angels: A Biblical Pattern for the Role of Angels in Physical Salvation," *The Gospel of Jesus Christ in the Old Testament* (Provo, UT: BYU Religious Studies Center, 2009).

Stephen D. Ricks, "Heavenly Visions and Prophetic Calls in Isaiah 6 (2 Nephi 16), the Book of Mormon, and the Revelation of John," in *Isaiah in the Book of Mormon*, ed. Donald W. Parry and John W. Welch (Provo, UT: FARMS, 1998), 171–190.

Is the Book of Mormon's Depiction of Guerrilla Warfare Realistic?

"And they did commit murder and plunder; and then they would retreat back into the mountains, and into the wilderness and secret places, hiding themselves that they could not be discovered, receiving daily an addition to their numbers, inasmuch as there were dissenters that went forth unto them." (Helaman 11:25)

THE KNOW

In many respects, the style of warfare depicted in the Book of Mormon is quite different from the mode of war familiar to most Americans in Joseph Smith's day.[602] One notable example is the starkly realistic account of guerrilla warfare found in the books of Helaman and 3 Nephi.

During the nineteenth century, it was commonly expected that opposing troops would formally array themselves for battle and engage in an all-out contest on a set-piece battlefield. Guerrilla warfare, on the other hand, operates on the principles of stealth, surprise, hidden base camps, small-scale skirmishes, strategic retreats, advantageous terrain, and—importantly—propaganda. These types of tactics, although foreign and even shameful to nineteenth-century thinking, were used repeatedly by the Gadianton robbers of the Book of Mormon.

Like many other revolutionaries, the Gadianton robbers started out as a marginalized political group.[603] After the "voice of the people" sided against them and their secret band was discovered, "they took their flight out of the land, by a secret way, into the wilderness" (Helaman 2:2, 11). Years later, Nephite dissenters revived Gadianton's "secret plans" and began to wage an extended war with the Nephites (Helaman 11:26).[604]

We are told that "they did commit murder and plunder; and then they would retreat back into the mountains, and into the wilderness and secret places, hiding themselves that they could not be discovered, receiving daily an addition to their numbers, inasmuch as there were dissenters that went forth unto them" (Helaman 11:25). As is the case in most historical examples, the robbers' hit-and-run guerrilla tactics worked exceptionally well against the more stationary Nephites and their regular armies (see Helaman 11:27–33).

Recognizing the clear parallels to modern military history, Daniel Peterson noted:

> Like those who later faced Marxist insurgencies in Cuba, China, and Vietnam, the Nephite and Lamanite authorities had to do something. They could not simply sit back and tolerate the depredations their Gadianton

> enemies practiced upon them. But they would learn, as would the French, the Americans, Batista y Zaldívar, Chiang Kai-shek, and General Westmoreland, that guerrilla forces are extraordinarily difficult to defeat and virtually impossible to dislodge from their chosen territory.[605]

Not only were the robbers difficult to root out militarily, but they were also hard to counter politically. According to military historian and Brigadier General Samuel Griffith, "Guerrilla leaders spend a great deal more time in organization, instruction, agitation, and propaganda work than they do fighting, for their most important job is to win over the people."[606] This agenda is clearly present in the behavior of the Gadianton robbers. On some occasions they almost seemed to "have become extinct" (Helaman 11:10), but apparently they were just biding their time, mingling among the people, secretly promoting their cause, and recruiting dissidents until they had enough support to wage another promising insurgency (see Helaman 11:24–34).

A firsthand glimpse of the political savviness of the Gadianton robbers can be seen in a letter from one of their leaders, Giddianhi. His epistle to Lachoneus attempts both to flatter and intimidate the Nephite governor and his soldiers.[607] After inviting the Nephites to "unite with us and become acquainted with our secret works," Giddianhi threatened to completely destroy them within a month if they didn't submit (3 Nephi 3:7–8). Yet, like a number of guerilla forces throughout history, these robbers transitioned into standard pitched-battle tactics too soon.[608]

The Nephites' first impulse was to "fall upon the robbers and destroy them in their own lands" (3 Nephi 3:20). But their prophetic chief captain, Gidgiddoni, warned them that such a course would lead to disaster—both militarily and spiritually. Instead, he proposed that "we will prepare ourselves in the center of our lands, and we will gather all our armies together, and we will not go against them, but we will wait till they shall come against us" (3 Nephi 3:21). This also involved gathering together their food and animals, leaving their lands completely desolate, in order to weather the siege (see 3 Nephi 3:22).

This tactic reversed the strategy that the robbers had been using against the Nephites all along. According to Peterson, "Gidgiddoni would force the Gadianton armies to attack the Nephites in the Nephites' own strongholds. Nephite fortified cities would effectively take the place of mountain base camps. . . . By yielding up territory in a classic 'strategic retreat,' he was, to borrow Mao's phrase, 'luring the enemy in deep.'"[609] The robbers ran out of food, could not besiege the city, and decisively lost the battle (see 3 Nephi 4:1–14).

THE WHY

In basic principles as well as nuanced subtleties, the Book of Mormon's depiction of guerrilla warfare is stunningly authentic.[610] Peterson described it as "a totally believable and coherent complex of military behaviors and responses."[611] This feature of the Book of Mormon is especially remarkable because it is so out of place coming from a nineteenth-century farmer like Joseph Smith.

While examples of guerrilla-style tactics have been used by different military groups throughout history, "only in our century have they been systematized in formal theoretical terms."[612] According to Peterson, the guerilla warfare displayed in the Book of Mormon

> goes considerably beyond anything Joseph Smith would have been likely to create out of his own imagination. It is not simply the Book of Mormon's precise portrayal of irregular warfare that is foreign to Joseph and his environment. Its realistic and wholly unromantic military narratives do not, it seems clear to me, come from the mind of that Joseph Smith, who, while he abhorred actual battle, loved parades and military pageantry, relished his commission as Lieutenant-General of the Nauvoo Legion, and, uniformed in elegant blue and gold, liked nothing better than to review the troops while mounted on his black stallion, Charlie.[613]

On another occasion, Peterson remarked that in "the Book of Mormon's portrayal of the Gadianton robbers we find a detailed, realistic depiction of a prolonged guerrilla struggle—lacking any trace of romanticism, uniforms, glamour, or parades, but matching up remarkably well with the actual conduct of such unconventional conflict."[614]

These findings provide good evidence that Joseph Smith was a true prophet. It also indicates that the Book of Mormon's account of secret combinations and their guerrilla efforts to destabilize and destroy governments is no idle tale. In fact, we are seeing it play out again before our own eyes as terrorist groups throughout the world seek to secretly recruit armies and topple governments. Concerning the Nephites' conflict with the robbers, political science professor Ray C. Hillam has noted, "It was not simply a contest of arms but of ideas."[615] The same is certainly true in our day as well.

If the most important goal of modern-day Gadianton robbers is, as Griffith put it, to "win over the people," then there is something each of us can do.[616] We can unite together, live the gospel, and share its joy and goodness with the world. For, as we learn in the Book of Mormon, the word of God "had more powerful effect upon the minds of the people than the sword, or anything else, which had happened unto them" (Alma 31:5).

FURTHER READING

Daniel C. Peterson, "The Gadianton Robbers as Guerrilla Warriors," in *Warfare in the Book of Mormon,* ed. Stephen D. Ricks and William J. Hamblin (Salt Lake City and Provo, UT: Deseret Book and FARMS, 1990), 146–173.

Ray C. Hillam, "The Gadianton Robbers and Protracted War," *BYU Studies Quarterly 15*, no. 2 (1975): 215–224.

55

Why Did Samuel Give Such Chronologically Precise Prophecies?

"Behold, I, Samuel, a Lamanite, do speak the words of the Lord which he doth put into my heart; and behold he hath put it into my heart to say unto this people that the sword of justice hangeth over this people; and four hundred years pass not away save the sword of justice falleth upon this people." (Helaman 13:5)

THE KNOW

During his extended address to the Nephites in Zarahemla, Samuel the Lamanite made two remarkably specific prophetic utterances. First, he declared, "four hundred years pass not away save the sword of justice falleth upon this people" (Helaman 13:5; cf. v. 9; Alma 45:10). Later, he said, "Behold, I give unto you a sign; for five years more cometh, and behold, then cometh the Son of God to redeem all those who shall believe on his name" (Helaman 14:2).

Such precise prophetic predictions are rare in scripture.[617] Even within Samuel's own discourse, there is another prophecy—the sign of Christ's death—where the exact timing is not mentioned (see Helaman 14:14, 20–27).[618] It seems likely, therefore, that when the exact timing is included in the record, the timing itself was somehow significant.

All ancient societies had important calendar units or time periods that were carefully marked.[619] Latter-day Saint Mesoamericanist John E. Clark noted, "The major cycle of Maya time was a four-hundred-year period called a *baktun*."[620] Each *baktun* was broken down into twenty units called a *katun*, a twenty-year cycle, and the *katun* was subdivided into units called a *hotun*, which was a five-year cycle.[621] According to John L. Sorenson, "Omens and prophecies . . . among the Maya were commonly phrased in terms of the beginning or ending of whole calendar units." [622]

In this light, it is significant that both of Samuel the Lamanite's time-specific prophecies correlate to the specific units of measurement within the Mesoamerican calendrical system.[623] As Clark put it, "Samuel the Lamanite warned the Nephites that one *baktun* 'shall not pass away before . . . they [would] be smitten' (Helaman 13:9)."[624]

Another Latter-day Saint Mesoamericanist, Mark Wright, suggested, "Samuel the Lamanite may have been making a *hotun* prophecy when he stated that in 'five years' signs would be given concerning the birth of Christ (Helaman 14:2)."[625] Interestingly, according to Sorenson, "In Yucatan at the time of the Spanish conquest, the ruler or his spokesman . . . had the duty to prophesy five years in advance what fate the next twenty-year *katun* would bring."[626] In similar fashion, Samuel the Lamanite prophesied the fate of the next *baktun* (see Helaman 13:5, 9), and apparently did so five years in advance (see Helaman 14:2).[627]

THE WHY

Mesoamerican anthropologist Prudence M. Rice explained, "Time is a cultural construct. Its units of measurement, meaning, and so on are unique in terms of legitimizing power and authority."[628] It is therefore highly significant that Samuel the Lamanite's chronologically precise prophecies each used time periods that were likely important within the broader cultural context of the Nephites. The use of these culturally important time periods likely served to legitimize Samuel's prophetic authority and credibility.

As Sorenson observed, "In Mesoamerican thinking, Alma's and Samuel's prophecies for an entire *baktun* would have been exceedingly profound statements."[629] Another Latter-day Saint Mesoamerican expert agreed: "Samuel's prophecy included such a powerfully evocative number that the people would doubtless have considered the entire prophecy highly symbolic."[630]

According to Wright,[631] part of that symbolism would have made the prophetic utterance relevant for Samuel's contemporary Nephite audience. Mesoamerican views of time were cyclical—meaning they expected certain events to repeat themselves over the course of each *katun* or *baktun*.[632]

Thus, a prophecy of destruction in four hundred years—in one *baktun*—could also be considered a warning of destruction in the here and now.[633] Indeed, Samuel warned that at that very moment, "the sword of justice hangeth over this people," that "the anger of the Lord is *already* kindled against you," and that the only way out was repentance followed by continuing faith in Jesus Christ (see Helaman 13:5–6, 30; emphasis added).[634]

Meanwhile, the *hotun* was a period commonly celebrated and commemorated, as was the *katun*.[635] Samuel's prophecy warned the people in advance that the next *hotun* would truly be a cause to celebrate—it would mark the birth of the Lord and Savior into the world. Mormon recorded that the coming of the sign did indeed bring "glad tidings unto the people" (3 Nephi 1:26). The occasion was no doubt honored and celebrated for *hotuns* and *katuns* to come, not only as marking the birth of Christ but also in commemoration of the miraculous timing of the sign—coming, as it did, just in time to spare the believers from being executed (see 3 Nephi 1:8–16).

This background also potentially explains why a specific time frame for the sign of Christ's death goes unmentioned in Samuel's prophecy. It did not come at the completion of an important unit of time, as did the birth of Christ (a *hotun*) and the ultimate fall of the Nephites (a *baktun*). Mormon, it seems, mentioned the specific time frame of these events when it coincided with time cycles deemed important within the surrounding culture. The prophetic use of highly symbolic time periods in Book of Mormon prophecy appears to be an example of the Lord speaking "unto men according to their language, unto their understanding" (2 Nephi 31:3; cf. D&C 1:24).[636]

FURTHER READING

Mark Alan Wright, "Nephite Daykeepers: Ritual Specialists in Mesoamerica and the Book of Mormon," in *Ancient Temple Worship: Proceedings of the Expound Symposium, 14 May 2011*, ed. Matthew B. Brown, Jeffrey M. Bradshaw, Stephen D. Ricks, and John S. Thompson (Salt Lake City and Orem, UT: Eborn Books and Interpreter Foundation, 2014), 252–253.

John L. Sorenson, *Mormon's Codex: An Ancient American Book* (Salt Lake City and Provo, UT: Deseret Book and Neal A. Maxwell Institute for Religious Scholarship, 2013), 192–195, 434–442.

John E. Clark, "Archaeology, Relics, and Book of Mormon Belief," *Journal of Book of Mormon Studies 14*, no. 2 (2005): 46–47.

56

Why Did Samuel Say the Lord "Hated" the Lamanites?

"But behold my brethren, the Lamanites hath he hated because their deeds have been evil continually, and this because of the iniquity of the tradition of their fathers." (Helaman 15:4)

THE KNOW

During Samuel's prophetic warning to the Nephites, he declared that his own people, the Lamanites, were a people whom the Lord "hath hated because their deeds have been evil continually, and this because of the iniquity of the tradition of their fathers" (Helaman 15:4). Such a seemingly harsh pronouncement can be difficult for modern readers to grasp, but in ancient societies, according to Raymond Westbrook, "Terms of affect such as 'love' [and 'hate'] are employed in servant-master/vassal-overlord relations."[637]

David Bokovoy explained:

> Scholars in recent decades have shown that in the biblical world the word love often represented a covenantal devotion to one's superior, while its opposite, namely hate, at times signified the status of an individual outside of this affiliation. While the connotation of these words for Westerners usually signifies an intense emotional charge, in the ancient Near East, love and hate often carried the aforementioned unique covenantal connotation.

Bokovoy concluded, "Thus, the words love and hate in the biblical world often carried a deliberate connotation of political alliance (or lack thereof)."[638]

Examples of this usage can be found throughout the Old and New Testaments.[639] In the time of Solomon, for example, Hiram, who was the king of a neighboring state, was described as "a lover of David" (1 Kings 5:1), when Hiram was simply serving under David.[640] Jesus taught, "No man can serve two masters: for either he will hate the one, and love the other; or else he will hold to the one, and despise the other. Ye cannot serve God and mammon" (Matthew 6:24; 3 Nephi 13:24). This either/or scenario is clarified when God and mammon are thought of as rival suzerains making competing demands on a vassal.[641] The vassal can only be loyal (show "love") to one, which necessarily would betray (show "hate" for) his or her covenant with the other.[642]

As another example of this concept in the Old Testament, Bokovoy referenced the Ephraimites, of whom the Lord declared, "I hated them . . . [and] I will love them no more" because of "the wickedness of their doings" (Hosea 9:15). Bokovoy noted, "in the context of ancient Near Eastern treaties these acts were tantamount to a political insurrection," thus, "the Ephraimites were removed from God's covenantal house or family."[643]

Samuel clearly placed the Lamanites—his own people—on the "hate" side of this divide, noting that their "deeds have been evil continually" due to the "iniquity of the tradition of their fathers" (Helaman 15:4). "Significantly," remarked Bokovoy, "Samuel uses the verb hate in the same context in which it appears in the book of Hosea. God hated the Lamanites in a parallel manner to the way he hated the Ephraimites: their evil acts had placed them outside the boundary of his covenantal relationship."[644]

THE WHY

Recognizing that the words love and hate were technical terms used in ancient covenantal expressions, and realizing that God's hatred, in its scriptural contexts, was about loyal covenantal allegiance (or its opposite) provides important clarification for Samuel's statement. As Bokovoy explained, "Samuel's message relates perfectly to the context of 'love' and 'hate' in the ancient sense of alliance."[645]

Moreover, when Samuel's words are read in their entirety, it becomes clear that he was actually aiming to demonstrate God's ultimate love toward the Lamanites, who were still people of covenant. Samuel described how "salvation hath come unto them" (Helaman 15:4), how they now "do observe to keep his commandments" (Helaman 15:5), how "they are striving with unwearied diligence" to preach the gospel (Helaman 15:6), how they "believe the holy scriptures" (Helaman 15:7), how they "are firm and steadfast in the faith" (Helaman 15:8), how "they have buried their weapons of war . . . because of their faith in Christ" (Helaman 15:9), and how "the Lord shall bless them and prolong their days, notwithstanding their iniquity" (Helaman 15:10).

In short, the Lamanites had rejuvenated their covenant status with the Lord, and Samuel hoped that he could inspire the backsliding Nephites to do the same.

Ultimately, the Lord extends His love, loyalty, and allegiance to all who come unto Him. In fact, the Book of Mormon repeatedly emphasizes God's eternal love and mercy for all His children, including the Lamanites.[646] In both the Old and New Worlds, Jesus commanded His disciples to be like God in doing likewise: "And behold it is written also, that thou shalt love thy neighbor and hate thine enemy; But behold I say unto you, love your enemies, bless them that curse you, do good to them that hate you, and pray for them who despitefully use you and persecute you" (3 Nephi 12:43–44; cf. Matthew 6:43–44).

Thus, when taken in its proper ancient scriptural context, Samuel's prophetic forewarning actually demonstrates the preeminence of God's eternal love for all His children—especially His willingness to forgive those who, like the Lamanites, have committed grave sins. As President Thomas S. Monson taught:

> Actually, love is the very essence of the gospel, and Jesus Christ is our Exemplar. His life was a legacy of love. The sick He healed; the downtrodden He lifted; the sinner He saved. At the end the angry mob took His life. And yet there rings from Golgotha's hill the words: "Father, forgive them; for they know not what they do"—a crowning expression in mortality of compassion and love.[647]

FURTHER READING

RoseAnn Benson and Stephen D. Ricks, "Treaties and Covenants: Ancient Near Eastern Legal Terminology in the Book of Mormon," *Journal of Book of Mormon Studies 14*, no. 1 (2005): 48–61, 128–129.

David E. Bokovoy, "Love vs. Hate: An Analysis of Helaman 15: 1–4," *Insights: A Window on the Ancient World 22*, no. 2 (2002): 2–3.

3 Nephi

57

How Does the Book of Mormon Help Date the First Christmas?

"Lift up your head and be of good cheer; for behold, the time is at hand, and on this night shall the sign be given, and on the morrow come I into the world." (3 Nephi 1:13)

THE KNOW

On December 25, Latter-day Saints join with many other Christians around the world in celebrating the birth of Jesus Christ, the Savior and Redeemer of all mankind. Yet most scholars agree that the exact date of Christ's birth is uncertain. Even Latter-day Saints and their General Authorities have expressed different views on the matter.[648]

Birthdates were not as important in the ancient world as they are today, and consequently the birthdays of most major figures in ancient history are unknown. It was not until the second century that early Christians began to discuss the timing of Christ's birth, and already by then there was already disagreement.[649] Such disagreement continued even as the celebration of Christmas on December 25 began to be fixed in the late third century AD,[650] and it wasn't until the sixth century that a calendar was made attempting to calculate time based on the date of Christ's birth.[651]

Given the lack of interest in Christ's birth early on and the uncertainty about its timing in later centuries, it is no wonder the question remains unsettled today. Scholars employ a wide range of sources—including the Gospel accounts, ancient historical works, astronomy, and archaeology—when trying to address this question. The year 4 BC is considered the *latest* possible date because Herod the Great died in the spring of that year, meaning the Savior must have been born sometime before then (see Matthew 2; Luke 1:5).[652]

An important factor to settling the timing of Christ's birth is determining the timing of His death in combination with the duration of His life.[653] While there remains some uncertainty, many scholars have concluded "that the first weekend of April AD 30 is the most likely time of the death of Jesus."[654]

Though scholars have scoured the Gospel accounts for clues, nothing in the New Testament provides definitive answers as to the length of the Savior's life.[655] Latter-day Saints benefit from having another source on the duration of the Savior's life: the Book of Mormon.

Since the Nephites began counting their years from the time the sign of Christ's birth was given (see 3 Nephi 2:8), and since they recorded the exact day they received the sign of His death in their calendar (see 3 Nephi 8:5), the Book of Mormon provides a fairly precise duration of the Savior's life.[656] The sign of Christ's death came "in the thirty and fourth year, in the first month, on the fourth day" (3 Nephi 8:5), so the Savior lived at least thirty-three years and four days by the Nephites' count.

Yet there remains some ambiguity. First, it is not certain how the Nephites counted those thirty-three years. Did they start counting from the *very day* the sign was given? Or did they wait for the next new year's day? Did they count the year in which the sign was given as year one, or begin the year after? There also remain questions about the length of a Nephite "year" at that time, and whether they were solar years (about 365 days), lunar years (about 354 days), or the tun years (360 days) used in Mesoamerica.[657]

With these considerations in mind, Latter-day Saint scholars Lincoln H. Blumell and Thomas A. Wayment have reasoned that the Book of Mormon "indicates Jesus lived between thirty-two and nearly thirty-four years."[658]

Combining the Book of Mormon with additional evidence from archaeology, astronomy, history, and ancient Jewish and Mesoamerican calendars, various Latter-day Saint researchers—such as Apostle Orson Pratt, researcher Randall Spackman, New Testament scholar Thomas Wayment, and archaeologist Jeffrey Chadwick—have reached different conclusions, ranging between spring in 5 BC to spring in 4 BC.[659]

THE WHY

While the Book of Mormon does not provide definitive evidence on the dating of Jesus Christ's birth, it does offer important additional information, especially to scholars within the Latter-day Saint tradition. Specifically, it provides a limited range for the lifespan of Jesus that, once anchored to a solid death date, limits the possible time span within which the birth of Christ must have occurred. If the proposed date of April AD 30 for the death of Jesus is correct, then possible birthdates for Christ are limited to sometime in 5 BC or in the early months of 4 BC.

No doubt scholars in and out of the Church will continue to investigate and debate the timing of the Savior's birth. While exploring this question, Latter-day Saint scholars and lay persons alike should appreciate and cherish this added resource on the Savior's birth, life, death, and teachings. The Book of Mormon truly is another testament of Jesus Christ, bringing clarity and understanding to every aspect of the Savior's life and teachings.

Latter-day Saint archaeologist Jeffrey R. Chadwick reflected this attitude when he wrote:

> As a Latter-day Saint, I am not only duty-bound but personally grateful to accept and present data from the Book of Mormon, the genuine historical reliability of which I am both spiritually and materially convinced, to corroborate the evidence of the New Testament and the other avenues explored.[660]

In the end, knowing exactly when Jesus Christ was born is not as important as knowing that He lived and that He is the Savior of the world, that He was born as "the light and the life of the world" (3 Nephi 11:11).

The Book of Mormon is absolutely clear on the overriding reality that the Lord Jesus did in fact condescend to come and dwell as a mortal among mankind, and to suffer and die, bringing to pass the resurrection and immortality of all the sons and daughters of God. Just as the sign announcing his birth brought light and deliverance to the Nephites,[661] He will bring light and deliverance to all who come unto Him.

FURTHER READING

Jeffrey R. Chadwick, "Dating the Birth of Jesus Christ," *BYU Studies Quarterly 49*, no. 4 (2010): 5–38.

Lincoln H. Blumell and Thomas A. Wayment, "When Was Jesus Born? A Response to a Recent Proposal," *BYU Studies Quarterly 51*, no. 3 (2012): 53–81.

John A. Tvedtnes, "When Was Christ Born?" *Interpreter: A Journal of Mormon Scripture 10* (2014): 1–33.

58

How Was There a Night without Darkness?

"For behold, at the going down of the sun there was no darkness; and the people began to be astonished because there was no darkness when the night came." (3 Nephi 1:15)

THE KNOW

When a Lamanite came into Zarahemla prophesying that there would be "great lights in heaven," leading to a night with "no darkness . . . as if it was day," and "many signs and wonders in heaven" (Helaman 14:2–6),[662] some Nephites were skeptical; some were even hostile (see Helaman 16:2).[663] In the next five years, both the skepticism and the hostility grew, and a date was set by which "all those who believed in those traditions should be put to death" if the sign failed to appear (3 Nephi 1:7, 9). Yet, as prophesied, "at the going down of the sun there was no darkness" and "it was as light as though it was mid-day" (3 Nephi 1:15, 19).[664]

Today, this prophetic sign remains difficult for some to believe. How could there be a night without darkness? Exactly how God produced such a sign is impossible to know for certain, but there are natural astronomical and atmospheric events that may shed some light on this matter.

Hugh Nibley suggested to his students once that this sign could have been caused by a supernova, comparing it to one in AD 1054 that "could be seen all over the world" and "was almost as bright as the sun."[665] Astronomers have documented a supernova in the eleventh century that, according to lead researcher Frank Winkler, provided enough light that "people could probably have read manuscripts at midnight by its light."[666]

Yet Samuel made it sound like the new star in the sky was a separate sign from the night without darkness (see Helaman 14:5).[667] In this regard, John A. Tvedtnes noted some possible similarities to the atmospheric effects caused by an explosion that took place in a remote part of Russia on June 30, 1908.[668] Known to scholars simply as the "Tunguska event," scientists are still unsure what exactly caused the explosion.[669] Its effect on the night sky, however, is well documented. As reported by NASA, "Night skies glowed, and reports came in that people who lived as far away as Asia could read newspapers outdoors as late as midnight."[670]

In the most comprehensive study on the event to date, Vladimir Rubtsov documented "atmospheric phenomena" in 155 different places,[671] spread across several days, beginning a few days before the explosion.[672] Tvedtnes reported, "For months afterward, there were spectacular sunrises and sunsets throughout the world, caused by the vast amount of dust thrown up into the atmosphere."[673] There were also "daytime anomalies such as intense and prolonged solar halos, mother-of-pearl clouds, and a Bishop's ring."[674]

It was the night of June 30, however, that was most spectacular. According to Rubtsov, "throughout a territory of about 12 million km^2, there was no night separating June 30 and July 1."[675] That evening, a Soviet astronomer "waited in vain for night to fall," and in Germany, "The intensity of the nighttime luminosity was considerable. . . . At 1.15 [a.m.] it was as light as daytime."[676] Despite covering a vast region, "no atmospheric anomalies occurred in the area of Tunguska" itself,[677] and the intensity of nighttime light "seemed to increase from East to West," thus indicating that it was brighter the farther away from the Tunguska explosion one went.[678]

THE WHY

A miracle can be defined as "a beneficial event brought about through divine power that mortals do not understand and of themselves cannot duplicate."[679] God uses miracles so that great benefits may be brought about for mankind "according to their faith" (see Mosiah 8:18; Alma 37:40). At the same time, Elder John A. Widtsoe, a member of the Quorum of the Twelve and himself a scientist, gave assurances that "This is a universe of law and order," and thus "a miracle simply means a phenomenon not understood, in its cause and effect relations."[680]

The phenomena and anomalies associated with the Tunguska event in 1908—with nightglows in the days before, with total day-like brightness the night after, and with continuing nightglows and even daytime effects in the days that followed—surprisingly demonstrate at least one possible naturalistic understanding of how God could have fulfilled Samuel's prophecy,[681] even if such astronomical and atmospheric observations cannot be fully understood or explained.[682]

Regardless of the actual method the Lord used to accomplish this miracle, the night without darkness was deeply symbolic and meaningful. Kimberly M. Berkey noted, "The excessive light surrounding Christ's birth acts as a kind of morning,"[683] the beginning of a new dawn welcoming the Savior into the world: the Light of the World had come,[684] introduced into the world by light.

Furthermore, just as with the appearance of the new star, any method for making night bright as day would have required a great deal of advance planning on the part of the Lord. Elder Neal A. Maxwell taught, "the so-called 'little star of Bethlehem' was actually very large in its declaration of divine design! It had to have been placed in its precise orbit long, long before it shone so precisely!"[685]

Elder Maxwell went on to explain that the Lord puts the same care and attention into the lives of His children. "His overseeing precision pertains not only to astrophysical orbits but to human orbits as well."[686] Just as the new star "was in its precise orbit long before it so shone," so are individuals "placed in human orbits to illuminate."[687]

FURTHER READING

Kimberly M. Berkey, "Temporality and Fulfillment in 3 Nephi 1," *Journal of Book of Mormon Studies 24* (2015): 53–83.

John A. Tvedtnes, "A Modern Example of Night without Darkness," *Insights: An Ancient Window 18*, no. 5 (October 1998): 4.

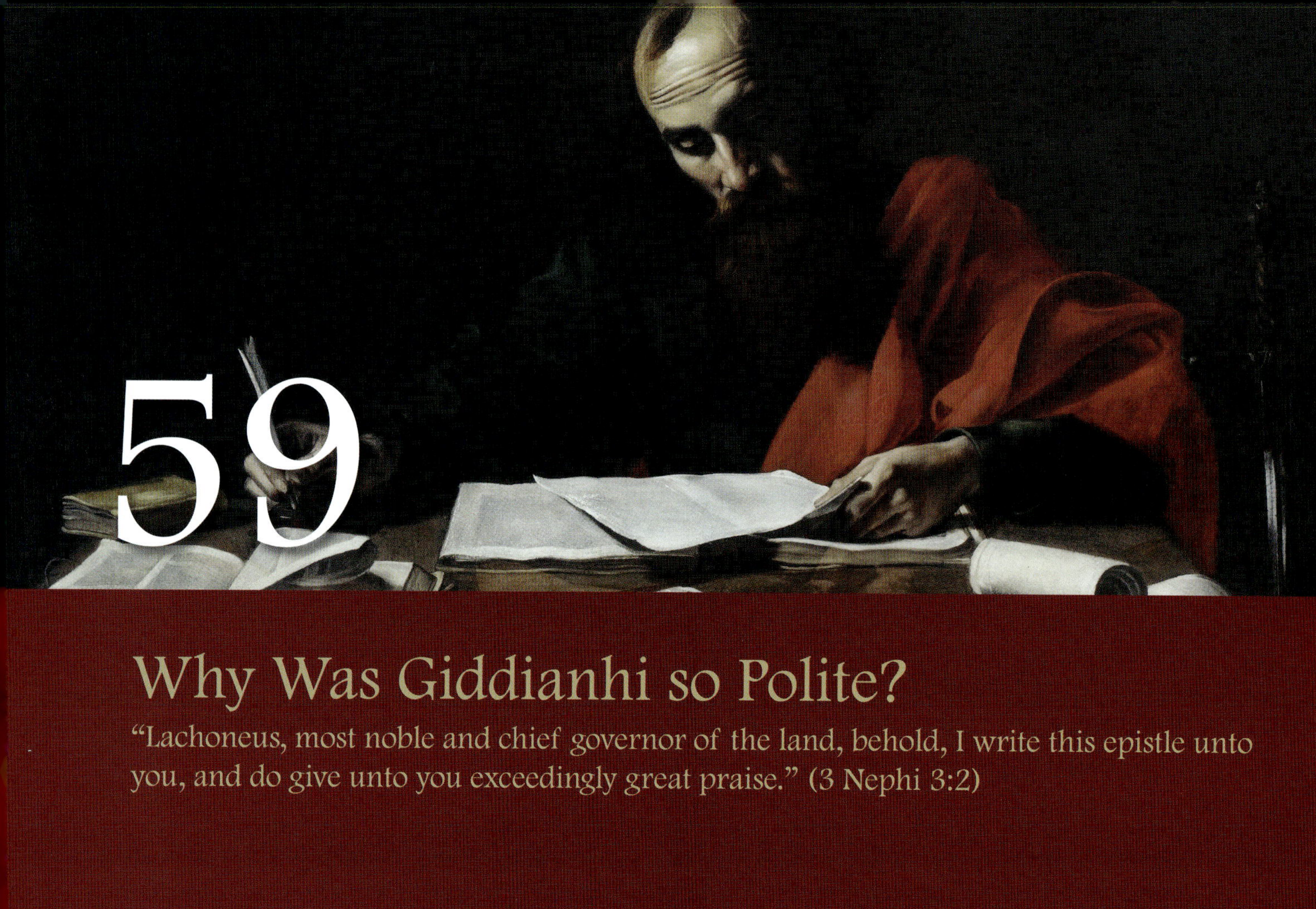

Why Was Giddianhi so Polite?

"Lachoneus, most noble and chief governor of the land, behold, I write this epistle unto you, and do give unto you exceedingly great praise." (3 Nephi 3:2)

THE KNOW

In the sixteenth year since the sign of Christ's birth, "Lachoneus, the governor of the land, received an epistle from the leader and the governor of [a] band of robbers," who was called Giddianhi (3 Nephi 3:1). Giddianhi began his letter graciously. "Lachoneus, most noble and chief governor of the land, behold, I write this epistle unto you, and do give unto you exceedingly great praise because of your firmness . . . yea, ye do stand well, as if ye were supported by the hand of a god" (3 Nephi 3:2).

Such a cordial tone coming from the leader of the Gadianton robbers is quite startling—and even more so when considering that his letter followed several uniquely ancient conventions of politeness. For example, in his introduction, he deferentially mentioned Lachoneus first, as was customary in the "ancient Hittite-Syrian, Neo-Assyrian, Amarna, and Hebrew format," as well as in the Book of Mormon itself.[688]

His letter also mirrors forms of politeness found in ancient Egyptian letters.[689] According to Kim Ridealgh, "when a subordinate individual writes to his superior, a longer formal introduction is necessary alongside more fawning language."[690] Such is clearly the case in Giddianhi's letter, where excessive praise and flattery saturate his opening remarks (see 3 Nephi 3:2–3).

Moreover, when making imperative requests, writers of ancient Egyptian letters would often introduce the request with the phrase "when my letter reaches you" as in the following example: "When my letter reaches you, you shall release this man."[691] According to Ridealgh, "These phrases seem to hold a deeper cultural significance and perhaps even reflect a form of 'politeness.'"[692]

Before issuing a formal request to Lachoneus, Giddianhi placed a similar self-referential emphasis on the written words of his letter: "Therefore I have *written this epistle, sealing it with mine own hand*. . . . Therefore *I write unto you*, desiring that ye would yield up unto this my people, your cities, your lands, and your possessions" (3 Nephi 3:5–6; emphasis added).[693]

Giddianhi's rhetoric also conforms more broadly to strategies recognized in politeness theory. For instance, throughout his letter he expressed praise for Lachoneus and his men,[694] reluctance for their impending conflict,[695] sympathy for their welfare,[696] in-group language (words and phrases familiar to a group),[697] offers for mutual cooperation,[698] and even acted as if he were a mediator between these groups, placing himself as a protector who could save the Nephites from his own robbers.[699]

When analyzed in light of the ground-breaking politeness theory developed by Penelope Brown and Stephen C. Levinson, Giddianhi's persuasive strategies and motivations are easier to identify and understand. Brown and Levinson summarized:

> Central to our model is a highly abstract notion of "face" which consists of two specific kinds of desires ("face-wants") attributed by interactants to one another: the desire to be unimpeded in one's actions (negative face), and the desire (in some respects) to be approved of (positive face). This is the bare bones of a notion of face which (we argue) is universal.[700]

When this model is applied to Giddianhi's letter, his praise, sympathy, use of in-group language, and attempts at cooperation can be seen as efforts to retain respect or gain approval from the Nephites (positive face).[701] And his expression of reluctance to send his men against the Nephites can be seen as a token desire not to impinge on the Nephites' need for freedom and independence (negative face).[702] Thus, in several ways, his letter provides textbook examples of persuasive strategies.

Moreover, because Giddianhi's epistle was liable to be read by multiple individuals, and perhaps even be made known to the general public, it can be reasonably categorized as "on the record" (or in public view).[703] According to Brown and Levinson, a speaker who goes "on the record" may strategically seek to "enlist public pressure against the addressee or in support of himself; he can get credit for honesty, for indicating that he trusts the addressee; he can get credit for outspokenness, avoiding the danger of being seen to be a manipulator; [and] he can avoid the danger of being misunderstood."[704]

Several of Giddianhi's strategies, such as boldness and upfront honesty about his intentions, seem to comply generally with this list. It is even possible that Giddianhi gave a countdown to impending destruction as a form of public pressure, a motivation for as many Nephites as possible to dissent from their own government and join his cause.[705]

THE WHY

Although efforts at persuasion aren't inherently evil, Giddianhi's use of rhetoric was clearly aimed at manipulating and gaining control over the Nephite nation. In ways that are both uniquely ancient and also culturally universal, his letter demonstrates what is meant by "flattery, and much power of speech, . . . according to the power of the devil" (Jacob 7:4).

Despite Giddianhi's attempts to ingratiate himself with the Nephites, he couldn't hide from them his ulterior motives, nor could he completely veil the actual import and consequences of what he was proposing—the end to their religious and political freedom.[706]

Ironically, Giddianhi's open and unabashed attempts at flattery and persuasion significantly backfired. Instead of being charmed or impressed, Lachoneus "was exceedingly astonished, because of the boldness of Giddianhi demanding the possession of the land of the Nephites, and also of threatening the people" (3 Nephi 3:11). And instead of cowering in fear, succumbing to Giddianhi's demands, or changing their minds about the justness of the robbers' cause, Lachoneus saw through these duplicitous formalisms, and the Nephites ultimately placed their faith in the Lord and followed Lachoneus until they achieved victory over Giddianhi and his robbers (see 3 Nephi 4:8–14).

To help readers similarly avoid flattery and deception in their own time, the Lord has made available the gift of discernment.[707] Elder David A. Bednar taught that the gift of discernment helps its recipients to "read under the surface" and "detect hidden error and evil in others."[708]

President Stephen L. Richards explained,

> Every member in the restored Church of Christ could have this gift if he willed to do so. He could not be deceived with the sophistries of the world. He could not be led astray by pseudo-prophets and subversive cults. Even the inexperienced would recognize false teachings, in a measure at least. . . . We ought to be grateful every day of our lives for this sense which keeps alive a conscience which constantly alerts us to the dangers inherent in wrongdoers and sin.[709]

FURTHER READING

Robert F. Smith, "Epistolary Form in the Book of Mormon," *FARMS Review 22*, no. 2 (2010): 125–135.

Sidney B. Sperry, "Types of Literature in the Book of Mormon: Epistles, Psalms, Lamentations," *Journal of Book of Mormon Studies 4*, no. 1 (1995): 69–80.

Why Did the Gadianton Robbers Wear a Lamb-skin?

"Behold, great and terrible was the day that they did come up to battle; and they were girded about after the manner of robbers; and they had a lamb-skin about their loins, and they were dyed in blood." (3 Nephi 4:7)

THE KNOW

When the Gadianton robbers came to battle against the Nephite army in 3 Nephi 4, their heads were shorn, they wore head plates, they had a "lamb-skin about their loins, and they were dyed in blood."[710] Their appearance must have been shocking, for the text declares that "great and terrible was the appearance of the armies of Giddianhi, because of their armor, and because of their being dyed in blood" (3 Nephi 4:7).

While the fierce appearance of the warriors would have been frightening, it may have been the lambskins and their being dyed in blood that was the most disturbing.[711] Early in the Book of Mormon, the Lamanites were known to shave their heads and dress only in a skin about their loins,[712] yet this scripture uniquely identifies the army as wearing a *lamb*skin, possibly a new choice in garment that was particularly appalling to the Nephites. Perhaps the Gadianton robbers had girded themselves with a "lamb-skin" and had dyed themselves in blood as a visual mockery of the sacrificial Lamb of God.

The terms *lamb* and *sheep* appear in the Book of Mormon text more than a hundred times, used most often in religious metaphors, such as with the phrase "Lamb of God."[713] While there is some evidence of sheep in the Americas,[714] it is also possible that the translated word *lamb* refers to a different animal found in the New World.[715] Whether the Nephites had sheep in the New World, or whether the word *lamb* refers to a different animal, the usage of *lamb* in the Book of Mormon is more often connected with Jesus Christ than it is to a specific species of livestock.[716]

Since the Nephites practiced the law of Moses, they would presumably have preferred to have an animal equivalent[717] to a lamb to perform sacrificial ordinances at the temple.[718] Thus, when 3 Nephi 4:7 describes the skin as a "lamb-skin," it may be a reference to the New World equivalent of a sacrificial lamb.[719] In fighting the armies of the Nephites, the Gadianton robbers' slaughtering and wearing the skins of an animal of holy sacrifice would certainly have been a jarring image for the Nephites.

The shock factor of the lambskin is heightened when put in the context of Mesoamerican intimidation tactics. The donning of animal pelts was intended to create a fearful spectacle,[720] so it may have been unexpected for the Gadianton robbers to appear in the skins of a nonaggressive herbivore, like a lamb. Brant Gardner explained, "Mesoamericans were well-known to wear animal skins, though the animal would typically be a ferocious jaguar, not a peaceful 'lamb.'"[721]

While this unusual choice of a lamb (or a similar animal) may not have been terrifying for surrounding Mesoamerican cultures, the blood-stained pelt of an innocent lamb was clearly "great and terrible" (3 Nephi 4:7) to the temple-oriented Nephites.[722] If the objective of the Gadianton robbers was to stun and terrify the armies of the Nephites, the sacrilege of a slaughtered sacred symbol would surely accomplish just that.

THE WHY

By dying their skin in blood, and girding themselves with a lambskin, the Gadianton robbers may have been making a mockery of the Lamb of God, whose blood was sacrificed for the sins of the world. In a temple setting, priests ritually executed lambs with solemnity and care. However, in this woeful battle, the Gadianton Robbers blasphemously slaughtered the animal and smeared themselves in blood.

In their quest for dominance and power, the Gadianton robbers trampled that which is sacred and holy to intimidate and terrify the opposing Nephites. Matthew Brown and Ethan Sproat have both argued that the "lamb-skin" in this episode may have strong connections to ancient temple clothing.[723] Perhaps the Gadianton robbers would wear ritualistic clothing to war, because in many ancient societies, the clothing represented power, the very thing the Gadianton robbers sought to usurp.[724]

Despite the terror that the army of Giddianhi tried to inflict, the impactful point is that the Nephites' reaction to the ghastly appearance of the army was not to fear, but to cry unto the Lord for deliverance: "the Nephites, when they saw the appearance of the army of Giddianhi, had all fallen to the earth, and did lift their cries to the Lord their God, that he would spare them and deliver them out of the hands of their enemies" (3 Nephi 4:8).

This story creates a masterful irony since the Gadianton robbers sought to subjugate others with the blood of lambs, but in turn were defeated by those who sought deliverance from the Lamb of God. Alma and Ether declared of followers of Christ: "their garments were washed white through the blood of the Lamb" (Alma 13:11; cf. 34:36; Ether 13:10–11). The garments of the Gadianton robbers were stained, rather than made white, in the blood of the lamb.

By crying unto the Lord their God, the Nephites were victorious in defeating the army of Giddianhi and repelling the forces of the adversary. One of Satan's most powerful tactics is fear; however, despite how horrific and grim life may sometimes appear, readers can garner hope and strength by crying to the Lord their God. Because the Lamb of God shed His blood for the children of men, all can find deliverance from sin and from life's trials.

FURTHER READING

David Rolph Seely and Jo Ann H. Seely, "Behold the Lamb of God," *Ensign*, April 2013.

Matthew Brown, "Girded About with a Lambskin," *Journal of Book of Mormon Studies 6*, no. 2 (1997): 124–151.

John W. Welch, "The Temple in the Book of Mormon: The Temples at the Cities of Nephi, Zarahemla, and Bountiful," in *Temples of the Ancient World: Ritual and Symbolism,* ed. Donald W. Parry (Salt Lake City, UT: Deseret Book and FARMS, 1994), 297–387.

Why Did the People Cut Down the Tree after Hanging Zemnarihah?

"And their leader, Zemnarihah, was taken and hanged upon a tree . . . and when they had hanged him until he was dead they did fell the tree to the earth." (3 Nephi 4:28)

THE KNOW

When the Nephites captured the Gadianton leader Zemnarihah, they summarily executed him by hanging, and the tree on which he was hanged was cut down (see 3 Nephi 4:28). Cutting down a tree after hanging someone on it may seem odd; however, evidence from Jewish law sources suggests this detail was an important ritual for cleansing the community.[725]

John W. Welch explained, "Although the practice cannot be documented as early as the time of Lehi, Jewish practice shortly after the time of Christ expressly required that the tree upon which the culprit was hung had to be buried with the body. Hence the tree had to be chopped down."[726] Welch believed "the rather striking similarities between these two sources . . . bespeak a common historical base."[727]

Cutting down and burying the tree would have eliminated any impurity created by contact with a dead body, but it also had a more vivid purpose.[728] Welch noted, "The punishment of Zemnarihah was related symbolically to his offense. He was hung in front of the very nation he had tried to destroy, and he was felled to the earth much as he had tried to bring that nation down."[729] 3 Nephi 4:29 states, "May the Lord preserve his people in righteousness and in holiness of heart, that they may cause to be felled to the earth all who shall seek to slay them because of power and secret combinations, even as this man hath been felled to the earth."

This statement is a reflection of a style of oath-making in the ancient Near East called a *simile curse*.[730] In simile curses, one party to a covenant would state the precise penalties connected to the violation of the covenant.[731]

These penalties were stated as similes. A Hittite text known as *The First Soldier's Oath* shows how seriously these oaths were taken in the ancient world:

> They lead before them a woman, a blind man and a deaf man and you say to them as follows: "Here (are) a woman, a blind man and a deaf man. Who takes part in evil against the king and queen, may the oath deities seize him and make (that) man (into) a woman. May they b[li]nd him like the blind man. May they d[eaf]en him like the deaf man."[732]

Simile curses appear in pre-Columbian America as well. In the Popol Vuh, a sacred text from ancient

America, two boys, when dealing with an enemy, cook a bird in an earth-covered pit and state that "in the same way, therefore, he (their enemy) will be buried in the earth."[733] When these examples are taken together, one can see that, in its ancient context, this seemingly unusual felling of a tree makes more sense.

THE WHY

Besides being an interesting reminder of the antiquity of the Book of Mormon, the detail about the tree is significant in other ways. The Nephites cut down the tree on which the robber had been hung, showing their strict observance of the law of Moses. This emphasis on lawfulness contrasts starkly with the killing of the robber, a man who lived his life outside the law. Thus, this detail could be seen as symbolic of the victory of Christ over the secret society and their socially disruptive and destabilizing brand of warfare that had plagued the Nephites for so long.

Additionally, the simile curse against "all who shall seek to slay [the people] because of power and secret combinations" (3 Nephi 4:29) would have been a powerful commitment against secret societies. When one realizes the weight such statements had in the ancient world, one can see that this was an ironclad commitment on the part of the people to seek out and destroy secret combinations. This is emphasized when one notes the exact wording of the declaration from the people: "May the Lord preserve his people in righteousness and in holiness of heart, that they may cause to be felled to the earth all who shall seek to slay them" (3 Nephi 4:29).

This statement was not a simple plea for God to take care of their problems for them. This simile curse would likely have served as a solemn covenant on the part of the people that they would put an end to the Gadianton robbers with God's help. And this is exactly what they did (see 3 Nephi 5:6).

Elder David A. Bednar explained this principle well when he stated that disciples of Christ are required "to ask in faith, which I understand to mean the necessity to not only express but to do, the dual obligation to both plead and to perform, the requirement to communicate and to act."[734] Just as these Nephites covenanted to combat and expunge the evil from among them, so modern readers should strengthen their resolve to root out the evil in their own lives and societies.

FURTHER READING

John W. Welch, *The Legal Cases in the Book of Mormon* (Provo, UT: BYU Press and Neal A. Maxwell Institute for Religious Scholarship, 2008), 313–322.

John A. Tvedtnes, "More on the Hanging of Zemharihah," in *Pressing Forward with the Book of Mormon: The FARMS Updates of the 1990s,* ed. John W. Welch and Melvin J. Thorne (Provo, UT: FARMS, 1999), 208–210.

John W. Welch, "The Execution of Zemnarihah," in *Reexploring the Book of Mormon: A Decade of New Research*, ed. John W. Welch (Salt Lake City and Provo, UT: Deseret Book and FARMS, 1992), 250–252.

62

Why Did Mormon Introduce Himself in 3 Nephi 5?

"And behold, I am called Mormon, being called after the land of Mormon, the land in which Alma did establish the church among the people." (3 Nephi 5:12)

THE KNOW

In 3 Nephi 5, Mormon digressed into a commentary about record keeping (see 3 Nephi 5:8–11, 14–19) and then surprisingly introduced himself (see 3 Nephi 5:12–13, 20). Readers may wonder, though, why Mormon chose this chapter of all places to reveal his identity to later audiences. Shouldn't an introduction have taken place at the beginning of the Book of Mormon?[735] After all, each of the writers of the small plates of Nephi—such as Nephi, Jacob, and Enos—introduced themselves as soon as they began to contribute to the record.[736]

It seems likely that Mormon may well have introduced himself at the beginning of the Book of Mormon in the 116 pages Martin Harris lost.[737] Brant A. Gardner argued:

> Mormon must have explained at the beginning of his record (the lost 116 pages or book of Lehi) who he [was] and what he [was] doing. He assumed that his relationship with the reader is so clear that he sometimes [did] not even identify himself in his continued editorial explanations.[738]

Yet if Mormon had already introduced himself somewhere in the book of Lehi, then why did he go out of his way to again reveal himself in 3 Nephi 5? One possible explanation is that Mormon's narrative was reaching a crescendo of importance. He would soon record Jesus Christ's visitation and ministry among His people, and to prepare the reader for this important revelation, Mormon sought to further disclose and establish himself as a reliable witness.

A careful analysis of Mormon's statements suggests that both his discussion of records and his self-introduction in 3 Nephi 5 can be seen as part of the same narrative goal—to legitimize both the record and the record keepers of the Book of Mormon. For instance, Mormon felt it important to mention that his source record for the book of 3 Nephi was written by Nephi, the son of Nephi,[739] and also that despite its brevity it was a "true account" (3 Nephi 5:9). His later comment that "we know our record to be true, for behold, it was a just man who did keep the record" (3 Nephi 8:1) further characterized Nephi as a reliable record keeper.

Mormon likewise certified his own record as being "just and true" (3 Nephi 5:18). He even felt it necessary to declare, "I do make the record on plates which I have made with mine own hands" (3 Nephi 5:11) and that his record of his own day was "of the things which I have seen with mine own eyes" (3 Nephi 5:17). This language was clearly intended to establish Mormon as a credible abridger and as a primary witness, perhaps analogous to the Eight Witnesses to the Book of Mormon who saw and hefted the plates for themselves.[740]

Yet not just any witness will do. A testator must be trustworthy and reliable. Thus Mormon declared, "I am called Mormon, being called after the land of Mormon" (3 Nephi 5:12). Matthew L. Bowen proposed, "Alma and his people consciously re-motivated the name 'Mormon' in terms of the covenant they made" and that the name may be etymologically associated with charity.[741]

If Bowen is correct, then Mormon likely emphasized his name and its history among the Nephites because it held connotations of pure and enduring love and because it linked him to the authority and covenant found in the "first church" established among his people "after their transgression" (3 Nephi 5:12).

Mormon further described himself as a "disciple of Jesus Christ" who had "been called of him to declare his word among his people" (3 Nephi 5:13). He made it clear that he was recording these things "according to the will of God," and that the production of his record was in response to prayers of "holy ones" who had preceded him (3 Nephi 5:14; cf. Enos 1:12–18). As a final stamp of approval on his authority, he declared himself to be a "pure descendant of Lehi" (3 Nephi 5:20).[742]

THE WHY

This juncture in the narrative of the Book of Mormon was ideal for Mormon's interjection. The people had just completed a major upswing and reversal (commonly referred to as a pride cycle), which then resolved itself into[743] a faithful period of righteousness (see 3 Nephi 5:1–3). Mormon's self-revealing digression can be seen as a strategically situated message to prepare readers to accept the recorded events of Christ's appearance to His people. In this light, Mormon wasn't so much concerned about what people would think of him but with how they would treat the culminating sacred story he was about to reveal.

In modern times, it is difficult for many people to believe what they haven't seen with their own eyes or felt with their own hands. And when confronted with the miraculous events reported in the Bible or Book of Mormon, they sometimes struggle to accept the testimonies and witnesses of others. Some people even go so far as to "declare that the Book of Mormon and other canonical works are not ancient records of scripture."[744]

All readers would do well to carefully read Mormon's personal testimony as a prelude to his account of Christ's ministry in the land of Bountiful. Mormon wanted his readers to know that he was a real person, that he really wrote on records that he made with his own hands, and that he recorded things he saw with his own eyes. He was a true disciple and witness of Jesus Christ, and the sources from which he compiled his own record were likewise written by trustworthy witnesses.

Most importantly, his record of Christ's ministry among His people is both spiritually essential and historically valid. Thousands of witnesses saw the face and felt the wounds and heard the voice of the resurrected Christ, and according to Mormon, "they know that their record is true for they all of them did see and hear, every man for himself" (3 Nephi 17:25). The standing invitation of the Book of Mormon, issued by Mormon's son and co-worker, Moroni, is that all those who "receive these things" and then "ask with a sincere heart, with real intent, having faith in Christ" concerning its message will gain their own testimony of its truth, goodness, and divinity by the power of the Holy Ghost (see Moroni 10:3–5).[745]

FURTHER READING

Matthew L. Bowen, "'Most Desirable Above All Things': Onomastic Play on Mary and Mormon in the Book of Mormon," *Interpreter: A Journal of Mormon Scripture 13* (2015): 27–61.

Brant A. Gardner, *Second Witness: Analytical and Contextual Commentary on the Book of Mormon,* 6 vols. (Salt Lake City, UT: Greg Kofford Books, 2007), 3:70–84.

63

Is There Evidence for Highways in Ancient America?

"And there were many highways cast up, and many roads made, which led from city to city, and from land to land, and from place to place." (3 Nephi 6:8)

THE KNOW

When abridging the record of 3 Nephi, Mormon reported on several civic-related building projects that occurred during a period of "great peace in the land" (3 Nephi 6:6). Along with the building of new cities and the repairing of old ones (see 3 Nephi 6:7), "there were many highways cast up, and many roads made, which led from city to city, and from land to land, and from place to place" (3 Nephi 6:8). Even after falling into disuse and disrepair, prominent highways often leave behind a large amount of non-perishable material. For this reason, readers may wonder if the remains of any ancient highways have been found in the Americas.

Notable systems of highways were indeed constructed by several ancient American societies,[746] and their remains have long been studied by archaeologists.[747] The ancient Maya, in particular, constructed and used highways (also known as causeways or *sacbeob*) in a manner that fits several details from the Book of Mormon. Concerning the features of these highways, Mesoamerican scholar Mark Wright explained:

> Although they varied in height and width, their construction was generally composed of rubble lined with large stones at the edges and large cobblestones in the interior, progressively getting smaller from bottom to top, finally gradating to fine gravel near the surface and topped with fine powdered limestone (called *sascab*), which was pressed smooth with stone rollers.[748]

The "66 feet (20 m) wide and up to 7 feet (2 m) high" road at Dzibilchaltun in the lowland Maya area was constructed in such a manner and dates close to the time when major networks of highway were being built in the Book of Mormon.[749] Commenting on this and similar structures, anthropologist John L. Sorenson remarked that such "massive construction surely qualifies as 'cast up'," as mentioned in 3 Nephi 6:8.[750]

Ancient Maya roads were often used to connect major districts or building complexes within sprawling cities. Metropolises like El Mirador, which thrived during Book of Mormon times, had numerous causeways that branched out from the city center like spokes on a wheel.[751] It's possible that the "highway which led to the chief market" near Nephi's garden tower was this type of major thoroughfare (Helaman 7:10).[752] Major sites had dozens of such roads. For instance, more than eighty causeways have been documented at Chichen Itza alone.[753]

In addition to inner-city causeways, longer highways connected main city centers with outlying satellite communities. Some, like the sixty-two-mile (one hundred km) Coba Yaxuna *sacbe*,[754] even spanned dozens of miles to reach other independent cities or settlements. These findings are consistent with statements in the Book of Mormon about the construction of "*many* highways . . . which led from city to city, and from land to land, and from place to place" (3 Nephi 6:8; emphasis added).[755]

Also of interest is that, according to anthropologist Justine M. Shaw, "Nearly all Maya causeways are straight" and "even when features of moderate size lie in the projected path of a *sacbe*, every effort is made to maintain the same line, even to the point of covering earlier constructions."[756] If Nephite highways adhered to this type of rigidly straight alignment, the resulting imagery would have nicely reinforced Alma's message to the people of Gideon:

> I perceive that ye are in the path which leads to the kingdom of God; yea, I perceive that ye are making his paths straight. I perceive that it has been made known unto you, by the testimony of his word, that he cannot walk in crooked paths; neither doth he vary from that which he hath said; neither hath he a shadow of turning from the right to the left, or from that which is right to that which is wrong. (Alma 7:19–20)[757]

Although hundreds of miles of these ancient "cast up" roads have been identified and studied throughout Mesoamerica,[758] a laser technology known as LiDAR has recently revealed previously unknown networks of highways.[759] This development shows just how easy it is for even prominent structures to go undetected beneath the dense jungle foliage in Mesoamerica.[760] It also suggests that many more miles of ancient highways are just waiting to be discovered under the forest canopy.

THE WHY

Most societies today value highways for their utility in transporting people and goods. Although the ancient Maya certainly used highways for these purposes, the primary reasons for their construction were likely political and religious in nature.[761] Shaw has suggested that highways offered "unique physical, symbolic, cosmological, social, and political ties" for the kin-based rulers who were most likely responsible for their construction.[762] She further pointed out that their "most likely intended purpose may be that of religion, most specifically for processions."[763]

This point is fascinating considering that King Lamoni seems to have planned a stately procession before his conversion. In Alma 18:9, readers learn that Lamoni "had commanded his servants . . . that they should prepare his horses and chariots, and conduct him forth to the land of Nephi; for there had been a great feast appointed at the land of Nephi, by the father of Lamoni, who was king over all the land."[764] If the Lamanites had built up prominent highways, Lamoni and his retinue of servants may have intended to use them for ceremonial purposes on their way to a politically, and possibly religiously, significant feast.[765]

With these details in mind, it is possible that the Nephites and Lamanites viewed highways much like the ancient Maya did—as symbolic "physical devices through which powerful forces flowed to connect material spaces and the peoples who populated them."[766] If so, this may actually help explain why the construction of major highways was mentioned in the Book of Mormon in the first place.

Samuel the Lamanite prophesied that "many highways shall be broken up" as a sign of Christ's death (Helaman 14:24). Mormon, always attentive to the fulfillment of prophecy, then mentioned the major construction of highways in 3 Nephi 6:8, as well as the fulfillment of Samuel's prophecy only two chapters later: "And the highways were broken up, and the level roads were spoiled, and many smooth places became rough" (3 Nephi 8:13).

If highways were seen as symbols of political and spiritual power that connected rulers and peoples together, then their destruction may have represented the severing of this power, as well as the breakdown of their society (see 3 Nephi 7:2). In turn, this haunting imagery, derived from the aftermath of major natural disasters,[767] set the stage for Christ's unifying ministry (see 4 Nephi 1:17).[768] With these possibilities in mind, Mormon's emphasis on the construction of highways in 3 Nephi 6:8 seems to be more than mere happenstance. It subtly sets up the fulfillment of Samuel's prophecy, while at the same time conveying a symbolic message that makes especially good sense in a Mesoamerican context.

It may be impossible to know whether or not the Nephites or Lamanites built or used any of the known ancient highways in Mesoamerica. Yet the physical forms and symbolic functions of these highways are remarkably consistent with what is described in the Book of Mormon. At the same time, they are not a feature of ancient American societies that was well-known or expected at the time of the Book of Mormon's translation.[769] For these reasons, the remnants of ancient American highways offer another intriguing evidence for the authenticity of the Book of Mormon.

FURTHER READING

"4 Ways the New Maya Discoveries May Relate to the Book of Mormon," Book of Mormon Central Blog, February 5, 2018, online at bookofmormoncentral.org.

Mark Alan Wright, "The Cultural Tapestry of Mesoamerica," *Journal of the Book of Mormon and Other Restoration Scripture 22*, no. 2 (2013): 4–21.

John L. Sorenson, *Mormon's Codex: An Ancient American Book* (Salt Lake City and Provo, UT: Deseret Book and Neal A. Maxwell Institute for Religious Scholarship, 2013), 356–357.

64

Why Did the Pride Cycle Destroy the Nephite Nation?

"And some were lifted up unto pride and boastings because of their exceedingly great riches, yea, even unto great persecutions." (3 Nephi 6:10)

THE KNOW

After eliminating the Gadianton robbers (see 3 Nephi 5:6), the Nephites were blessed with a period of peace and prosperity. But this was short-lived. Within only five years, the chief judge was assassinated, "and the people were divided one against another; and they did separate one from another into tribes" (3 Nephi 7:2). This sudden and rapid decline fits a common pattern found in the Book of Mormon:

The Lord blesses the Nephites; the Nephites become proud and sinful; prophets call the people to repentance; the people are punished; and, finally, the people are humbled and repent.[770] At this point the Lord blesses them again, they become successful, they become proud, and the pride cycle repeats itself.[771]

At first, one might wonder why the pride cycle finally ended up being so destructive. After all, one rarely thinks of pride as a major contributing factor in the collapse of nations. However, a key detail may reveal part of the problem: "there became a great inequality in all the land, insomuch that the church began to be broken up" (3 Nephi 6:14).

It appears that pride led to abuse of the poor, and that this abuse of the poor led to the destabilization of the church and of society.[772] As Mormon noted, "And some were lifted up unto pride and boastings because of their exceedingly great riches, yea, even unto great persecutions" (3 Nephi 6:10).

The ancient conquest of Canaan may provide a parallel. According to some archaeologists, surviving artifacts reveal that when the Israelites conquered Canaan, some Canaanites joined them. These Canaanites were the poor, marginalized members of society who joined the Israelites to fight their oppressive overlords.[773] For example, when the Israelites invaded Jericho, a woman named Rahab harbored the Israelite scouts, helping the invasion succeed.

As a prostitute, Rahab would have keenly understood what it meant to be an impoverished and disenfranchised member of society, and this may have made it easier for her to turn against the rest of the city (see Joshua 2:14–15).[774]

Ultimately, it seems that society in Canaan had marginalized the poor so much that when disaster struck (the Israelite invasion) they could not survive the blow and broke into feuding camps. It is possible that this is what happened to the Nephites as well.

The pride cycle had so badly fragmented the cohesiveness of society that when the chief judge was murdered, Nephite society could not withstand the blow and broke into tribes. Chief judges had been murdered before in Nephite history, but the pride cycle had finally polarized society so much that it could not withstand the strain. This assassination and other injustices seem to have happened at the worst possible moment, such that it tore the fragmented country apart.

THE WHY

Care for the poor has always been a core tenet of Christianity from the beginning: "Pure religion and undefiled before God and the Father is this, To visit the fatherless and widows in their affliction" (James 1:27). Yet it is easy to miss the full ramifications of what it means to care for the poor. In Canaanite and Nephite society, care for the poor may have helped preserve the country.

The Book of Moses records one case where this seems to have happened: a group of people, the city of Enoch, were blessed by the Lord, "and did flourish. And the Lord called his people Zion, because they were of one heart and one mind, and dwelt in righteousness; and there was no poor among them" (Moses 7:17–18). Far from letting their blessings cause them to become prideful, this group of people used their prosperity to eliminate poverty from their society. They let their prosperity strengthen their society rather than destroy it. On many occasions, the Nephites did this as well (see Mosiah 4:16–26; Alma 34:28–29; 4 Nephi 1:3), and modern readers can do the same today.

Elder Patrick Kearon taught:

> The Lord has instructed us that the stakes of Zion are to be "a defense" and "a refuge from the storm." We have found refuge. Let us come out from our safe places and share with (others), from our abundance, hope for a brighter future, faith in God and in our fellowman, and love that sees beyond cultural and ideological differences to the glorious truth that we are all children of our Heavenly Father.[775]

The story reminds modern readers of the Book of Mormon to avoid the pride that fragmented Nephite society and to actively care for the poor and needy.

FURTHER READING

Patrick Kearon, "Refuge from the Storm," *Ensign*, May 2016, 111–114.

Brant A. Gardner, *Second Witness: Analytical and Contextual Commentary on the Book of Mormon*, 6 vols. (Salt Lake City, UT: Greg Kofford Books, 2007), 5:280–285.

Lindon J. Robison, "No Poor Among Them," *Journal of Book of Mormon Studies 14*, no. 1 (2005): 86–97, 130.

Lindon J. Robison, "Economic Insights from the Book of Mormon," *Journal of Book of Mormon Studies 1*, no. 1 (1992): 35–53.

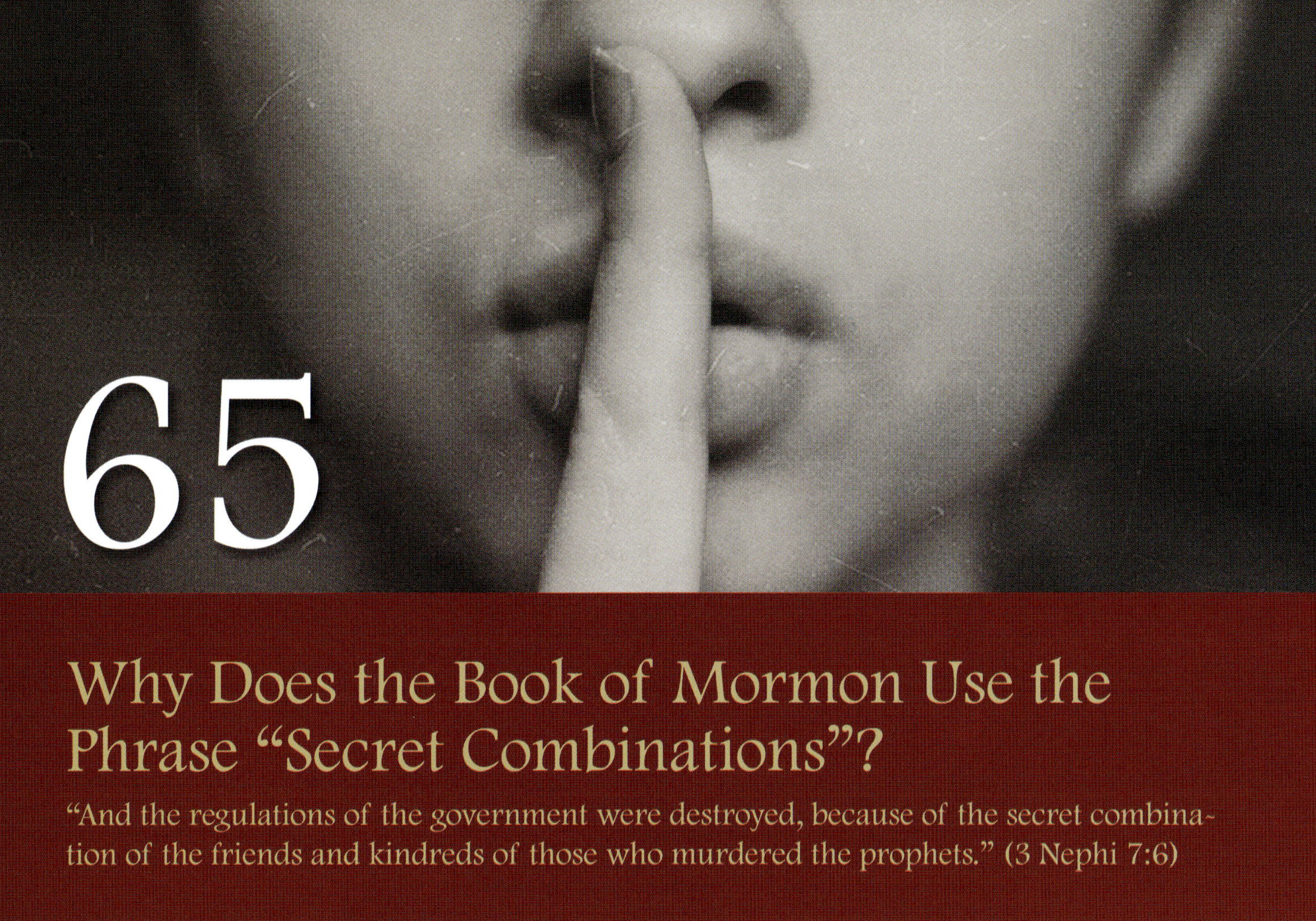

Why Does the Book of Mormon Use the Phrase "Secret Combinations"?

"And the regulations of the government were destroyed, because of the secret combination of the friends and kindreds of those who murdered the prophets." (3 Nephi 7:6)

THE KNOW

Throughout the Book of Mormon, the phrase *secret combinations* is used to describe the evil activities of secret, oath-bound societies like the Gadianton robbers. As Ray Hillam described, "secret combinations have existed since the days of Cain (Moses 5:51). Satan is their author (2 Nephi 26:22), power and gain are their motives (Ether 8:15, 25), and conspiracy is their method of operation (Helaman 6:22–24)."[776] In Helaman 2:13, Mormon indicated that the rise of secret combinations "did prove the overthrow, yea, almost the entire destruction of the people of Nephi."

Some have argued, though, that the secret societies in the Book of Mormon are merely fictional and were inspired by a well-known fraternity called Freemasons (or Masons).[777] As Daniel Peterson explained, "It has long been contended by critics of the Book of Mormon that its 'Gadianton robbers' are merely nineteenth-century Freemasons, transparently disguised."[778] As evidence of this claim, its supporters have pointed to a number of similarities between both groups, one of which being that "secret combinations" was used almost exclusively as a negative term for Freemasons around 1829.[779]

At least, this seemed like a potentially valid assumption, until online databases made it possible to search through a much larger number of nineteenth-century documents. In 2014, Gregory Smith found conclusive evidence from a variety of sources that "before, during, and after Joseph Smith's translation of the Book of Mormon, secret combinations was a general term in the United States for any clandestine group or plot, especially one in the political realm."[780] It wasn't at all the exclusive code name for Freemasons that some critics of the Book of Mormon had long maintained.

Adding to this argument for broader meaning, Webster's 1828 dictionary defines a *combination* in general terms as an "intimate union, or association of two or more persons or things."[781] It also notes that it can be used in both a positive and a negative sense.[7] Thus when the word *secret* is added before *combination*, it apparently helps clarify that this general term is being used in a negative, secretive sense.[782]

Yet even if "secret combinations" had exclusively referred to Freemasons around the time of the Book of Mormon's translation, it wouldn't mean that Joseph Smith had merely fabricated this aspect of its content. Many ancient societies had secret groups that were involved in oath-related conspiracies to get rich or influence the government.[783]

For instance, in Judea and elsewhere in the ancient Near East, robbers bound themselves with oaths to keep their hideouts and plans secret.[784] There is even good evidence that such societies existed in ancient Mesoamerica, and that they may have formed in the Early Preclassic Period (Olmec/Jaredite times).[785] Importantly, scholars who have studied secret societies have been struck by their similarities, even when they are from different locations and time periods in the world's history.[786]

It is therefore not surprising that the Gadianton robbers in the Book of Mormon share some similar features with the Freemasons of the nineteenth century.[787] Nor is it surprising that the Book of Mormon's 1829 English translation used "secret combinations" to describe them. It was a general term, often used to label Freemasons, but also used to describe a host of other secretive nineteenth-century groups, and a term that would apply equally well to secret societies all over the ancient world, including ancient America.

THE WHY

This situation demonstrates the need for patience and thorough investigation into issues that could otherwise trouble one's testimony or be the grounds for disbelief. Elder Neil L. Andersen taught, "Addressing honest questions is an important part of building faith, and we use both our intellect and our feelings. Not all answers will come immediately, but most questions can be resolved through sincere study and seeking answers from God."[788] On another occasion, Elder Andersen wisely counseled, "Will we understand everything? Of course not. We will put some issues on the shelf to be understood at a later time."[789]

This is precisely the approach that some Latter-day Saint scholars took when confronted with this issue. Daniel Peterson, one of the first to research this topic, suspected from the beginning that "secret combinations" wasn't an exclusive label for Freemasons in 1829. However, he couldn't initially locate the sources to prove it.[790]

Over the course of time, however, he and others uncovered document after document that supported his initial reservations.[791] And then, after decades of patiently waiting, modern search engines finally provided enough evidence to thoroughly and conclusively discredit the critical theory that Peterson had rejected all along. As Gregory Smith explained, "Now that a broader look at the literary culture of the early 1800s is more practical via digital search, Peterson's skepticism has been vindicated."[792]

In the case of "secret combinations," the information needed to fully dismiss this concern took a matter of decades from the time the issue was first raised.[793] Other causes for doubt may take much longer to resolve. And for some issues, the needed information may not be forthcoming until, as Elder Jeffrey R. Holland expressed, "Jesus descends as the ultimate infallible truth of all."[794]

The beauty of God's plan is that we don't have to wait for technological advancements and improved research methods in order to find answers to the questions that matter most. Through the power of the Holy Ghost, one can know the Book of Mormon is true without having to prove wrong every criticism that could possibly be raised against it.[795] As Elder Dieter F. Uchtdorf insightfully explained, "I wish I could help everyone to understand this one simple fact: we believe in God because of things we know with our heart and mind, not because of things we do not know."[796] This holds true for belief in the Book of Mormon as well.

FURTHER READING

Gregory L. Smith, "Cracking the Book of Mormon's 'Secret Combinations'?" *Interpreter: A Journal of Mormon Scripture 13* (2014): 63–109.

Nathan Oman, "'Secret Combinations': A Legal Analysis," *FARMS Review 16*, no. 1 (2004): 49–73.

Daniel C. Peterson, "Notes on 'Gadianton Masonry'," in *Warfare in the Book of Mormon*, ed. Stephen D. Ricks and William J. Hamblin (Salt Lake City and Provo, UT: Deseret Book and FARMS, 1990), 176–224.

Bruce W. Warren, "Secret Combinations, Warfare, and Captive Sacrifice in Mesoamerica and the Book of Mormon," in *Warfare in the Book of Mormon*, ed. Stephen D. Ricks and William J. Hamblin (Salt Lake City and Provo, UT: Deseret Book and FARMS, 1990), 225–236.

How Was Nephi, Son of Nephi, Similar to John the Baptist?

"And Nephi did cry unto the people . . . and he did preach unto them repentance and remission of sins. Now I would have you remember also, that there were none who were brought unto repentance who were not baptized with water." (3 Nephi 7:23–24)

THE KNOW

In the years before the coming of Christ to the Book of Mormon people, Nephi, son of Nephi and grandson of Helaman, performed a role much like that of John the Baptist. The language used to describe his manner of preaching and baptizing is reminiscent of that describing John the Baptist in the New Testament.

The miracles that he performed, especially those recorded in 3 Nephi 7, are similar to those that Jesus Himself would work during His ministry. This Nephi, who was the son of Nephi the high priest in Zarahemla, can be seen as a forerunner to the coming of Christ in the New World, much as John the Baptist, the son of the priest Zacharias in the temple of Jerusalem, was a forerunner in the Old World.

For example, Nephi was emphatic about baptism. Shortly after the sign of the birth of Christ, Nephi "went forth among the people, and also many others, baptizing unto repentance, in the which there was a great remission of sins" and confession of faults (3 Nephi 1:23, 25). Later, the record says that Nephi "did preach unto them repentance and remission of sins" (3 Nephi 7:23). This phrasing is very similar to what is said of John in Mark 1:4 (cf. Luke 3:3): "John did baptize in the wilderness, and preach the baptism of repentance for the remission of sins."

Nephi (and those he ordained) baptized all who had been brought unto repentance and they received a remission of their sins (see 3 Nephi 7:24–25). Likewise, John baptized all those who came unto him "confessing their sins" (Mark 1:5).

Shortly before the commencement of the ministry of Jesus in the Old World, Nephi was "visited by angels" and heard "the voice of the Lord" (3 Nephi 7:15). According to the Gospel of Luke, angels were involved in the events surrounding John's birth and he, too, was privileged to hear the voice of God.[797]

The Gospel of Mark's story of John baptizing Jesus leads into the narrative of Jesus beginning to preach and perform miracles. The text states that He did these things "with authority" (Mark 1:22, 27). He preached the gospel (see Mark 1:15), cast out unclean spirits (see Mark 1:23–26), and healed the sick (see Mark 1:30–34). Nephi performed many of the same prophetic acts preparing the way for the Messiah, including casting out "devils and unclean spirits" and raising his brother from the dead (3 Nephi 7:19). The record relates that "Nephi did minister with power and with great authority" (3 Nephi 7:17).

THE WHY

Readers may wonder why there are so many parallels between the New World ministry of Nephi, the son of Nephi, and the ministries of John the Baptist and Jesus Christ in the New Testament. Although most people are likely aware that Jesus called from among the Nephites twelve disciples just as He had in the Old World, readers may not have considered that Christ could have chosen a forerunner, like John the Baptist, to prepare the way for His coming in the New World as well.

John had been foreordained and sent by God as "my messenger before thy [Christ's] face, which shall prepare thy way before thee."[798] He had been foreseen as "the voice of one crying in the wilderness, Prepare the way of the Lord, and make his paths straight."[799] John was to serve as a type of Elias, a forerunner to prepare the way for the coming of Christ and the preaching of his gospel.[800] In much the same way, Nephi served as "an Elias," or forerunner, to prepare the Book of Mormon peoples for the visitation of Christ to their lands.

Furthermore, Nephi had been visited by angels and "had power given unto him that he might know concerning the ministry of Christ," making him an "eye-witness" of things that Jesus would do and say during His Old World ministry (3 Nephi 7:15, 18). Because of Nephi's "faith on the Lord Jesus Christ" (3 Nephi 7:18), he had the power to do similar miracles to those which he had seen Jesus do (see 3 Nephi 7:17). In this way he was serving, like John the Baptist, to truly "make ready a people prepared for the Lord" (Luke 1:17).

Similarly, there are those in this dispensation who have worked to serve a similar purpose, to prepare the way for the Second Coming of Christ. Joseph Smith, for example, was called by the Lord to restore His Church and proclaim His commandments to His people (D&C 1:17–18), and thereby "prepare the way whereby they may come unto [Christ] and call on the Father in [Christ's] name" (3 Nephi 21:27).

As Alma declared of the righteous people of Gideon, those individuals preparing for Christ's Second Coming can also walk "in the paths of righteousness . . . the path which leads to the kingdom of God" and earnestly "[make] his paths straight" (Alma 7:19).

FURTHER READING

John W. Welch, "Seeing Third Nephi as the Holy of Holies of the Book of Mormon," *Journal of the Book of Mormon and Other Restoration Scripture 19*, no. 1 (2010): 36–55.

Robert J. Matthews, *A Burning Light: The Life and Ministry of John the Baptist* (Orem, UT: Granite, 2000).

How Does the Book of Mormon Help Date Christ's Death?

"And it came to pass in the thirty and fourth year, in the first month, on the fourth day of the month, there arose a great storm, such an one as never had been known in all the land." (3 Nephi 8:5)

THE KNOW

The Book of Mormon records the precise day the Nephites witnessed the prophesied sign of Christ's death (see 3 Nephi 8:5).[801] This exceptional diligence on the part of Nephite record-keepers may help resolve at least two questions that New Testament scholars debate regarding the timing of Christ's death.

What Year Did Christ Die?

The first question relates to the year Christ was crucified. The New Testament accounts tie Christ's Crucifixion to a Passover festival during the governorship of Pontius Pilate (AD 26–36).[802] Using astronomical data to calculate the timing of the Passover, scholars have determined that the years AD 27, 30, and 33 "are the only years during the administration of Pontius Pilate when the eve of Passover, and Passover itself, fell within a three-day window of time prior to Sunday," the day of the Resurrection.[803]

Of these three years, based on additional factors involved in correlating the Gospel accounts to confirmable historical details, "Most scholars . . . believe that Jesus was killed in [AD] 30."[804] The issue is not definitively settled, however, and some scholars still "believe that he died in [AD] 33."[805]

Thanks to the diligence of Nephite record-keepers, the Book of Mormon helps to narrow down the length of Christ's life even further. Since Christ must have been born ca. 5–4 BC, this effectively rules out AD 27 as too short and AD 33 as too long to accommodate for Christ's death happening in the first month of the thirty-fourth year in the Nephite calendar (see 3 Nephi 8:5).[806] Thus, in the view of Latter-day Saint archaeologist Jeffrey Chadwick, combining the Book of Mormon with the additional evidence from the New Testament, archaeology, astronomy, and history makes AD 30 the correct year, "beyond any reasonable doubt."[807]

On What Day of the Week Did Christ Die?

The second question relates to the day of the week on which Christ was crucified. Long-standing tradition holds that Christ died on a Friday, and most New Testament scholars support this tradition.[808] A few scholars, however, have suggested that Christ actually died on a Thursday.[809] These scholars argue that a Thursday can better account for passages in the New Testament that speak of "three days and three nights" in the tomb (Matthew 12:40), and of the Resurrection occurring after three days (see Matthew 27:63; Mark

8:31), and Sunday being three days since the Crucifixion (see Luke 24:21).[810]

An important clue is John's description of the upcoming Sabbath as "an high day" (John 19:31), meaning it was the first day of the Passover.[811] Since certain festival days, such as Passover, were regarded as "Sabbaths," no matter what day of the week on which they occurred (see Leviticus 23: 7–8, 11, 15, 21, 24, 39),[812] this allows for the possibility that the Sabbath after the Crucifixion was not Saturday (the regular Jewish Sabbath), but the first day of Passover (a special "Sabbath," or "high day"), which most likely fell on Friday in AD 30.[813]

While the New Testament data does not decisively favor Thursday, the Book of Mormon adds some important information. Nephite prophets predicted that there would be three days of darkness coinciding with the time of Christ's death until His Resurrection (see 1 Nephi 19:10; Helaman 14:20–27). Nephite historians documented the fulfillment of this prophecy (see 3 Nephi 8:19–23; 10:9).

Due to the time difference between Jerusalem and the New World, "a Friday crucifixion leads to only two days of darkness in the New World" before Christ rose on Sunday morning.[814] A Thursday Crucifixion, however, "exactly fits the timing necessary for three days of darkness to have occurred in America prior to Jesus's resurrection" (see chart on p. 169).[815]

THE WHY

Readers should not be surprised that as a second witness of Jesus Christ, the Book of Mormon adds clarity to the timing of events in the Savior's life. All who embrace the Book of Mormon should appreciate the ways this sacred volume can illuminate the timing of an event as important as the death and entombment of Jesus Christ. Jeffrey R. Chadwick reflected this point of view when he wrote:

> As a Latter-day Saint, I am not only duty-bound but personally grateful to accept and present data from the Book of Mormon, the genuine historical reliability of which I am both spiritually and materially convinced, to corroborate the evidence of the New Testament and the other avenues explored.[816]

Openness and flexibility to new evidence and alternative interpretations should always be maintained, but the dating strongly supported by the Book of Mormon deserves serious consideration by all Latter-day Saints. If both the day and the year are correct, then the Savior died on Thursday, April 6, AD 30.[817] This gives profound significance to the timing of the Restoration of His Church, exactly 1800 years later.

Whatever the particulars in the timing of the Savior's death, no detail is more important, or inspiring, than the fact that by Sunday morning, the tomb was found empty, with angels declaring "He is not here: for he is risen" (Matthew 28:6; Mark 16:6; Luke 24:6). As President Monson taught, "No words in Christendom mean more to me than those spoken by the angel to the weeping Mary Magdalene and the other Mary when, on the first day of the week, they approached the tomb to care for the body of their Lord. . . . Our Savior lived again."[818]

President Gordon B. Hinckley taught, "The abject sorrow that comes with death, the bereavement that follows the passing of a loved one are mitigated only by the certainty of the Resurrection of the Son of God that first Easter morning. . . . In the hour of deepest sorrow we draw hope and peace and certitude from the words of the angel that Easter morning."[819]

He would show Himself to His disciples in Jerusalem, and then later that year, He appeared in glory to the Nephites as well (see 3 Nephi 11). Together, the Bible and the Book of Mormon forcefully testify that Jesus Christ lives! Modern prophets continue to testify "that Jesus is the Living Christ, the immortal Son of God."[820] No truth could be more beautiful, nor of greater eternal significance than this. Latter-day Saints should appreciate and cherish these added scriptural and prophetic witnesses of the Risen Lord.

FURTHER READING

Jeffrey R. Chadwick, "Dating the Death of Jesus Christ," *BYU Studies Quaterly 54*, no. 4 (2015): 135–191.

Lincoln H. Blumell and Thomas A. Wayment, "When was Jesus Born? A Response to a Recent Proposal," *BYU Studies Quaterly 51*, no. 3 (2012): 64–70.

David B. Cummings, "Three Days and Three Nights: Reassessing Jesus's Entombment," *Journal of Book of Mormon Studies 16*, no. 1 (2007): 56–73, 86.

Thursday Crucifixion

Friday Crucifixion

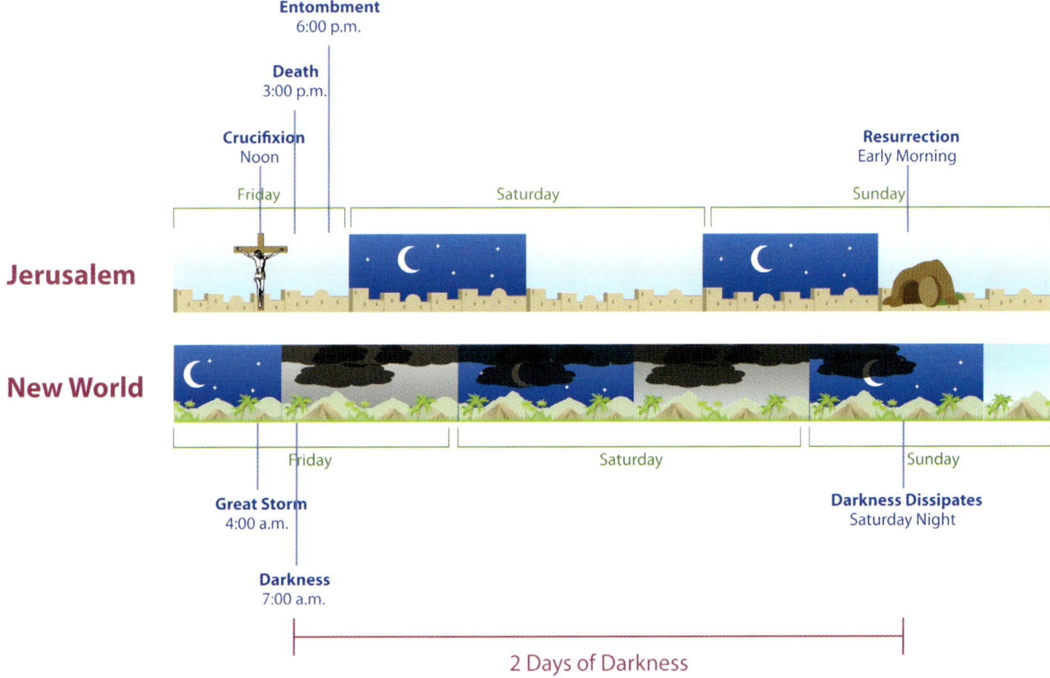

What Caused the Darkness and Destruction in the Thirty-fourth Year?

"And it came to pass that there was thick darkness upon all the face of the land, insomuch that the inhabitants thereof who had not fallen could feel the vapor of darkness." (3 Nephi 8:20)

THE KNOW

In the thirty-fourth year, Mormon carefully documented "a great and terrible tempest . . . terrible thunder . . . exceedingly sharp lightnings" and "thick darkness," even a "vapor of darkness" that could be felt and that prevented the lighting of fire (3 Nephi 8:6–7, 20–22). This had been predicted in detail by prophets such as Nephi son of Lehi, Zenos, and Samuel the Lamanite.[821]

In the 1960s, Hugh Nibley compared these Book of Mormon accounts to descriptions of earthquakes and volcanic eruptions.[822] Since that time, several other scholars, including many professional geologists, have examined these accounts and widely agreed that the three-day darkness and other destructive forces described in the Book of Mormon accounts involved a volcanic eruption.[823]

The main reason for this is the three-day period of darkness.[824] Geologists who have studied the 3 Nephi 8 account generally agree that nothing except volcanic ash and dust clouds could account for the three days of darkness, as it is described.[825] Not only the darkness, but the excessive lightning, thundering, tempest, and many other features can all be explained by volcanic activity.[826]

In the most recent and thorough analysis by a professional geologist, Jerry Grover Jr. concluded, "In order to account for the destruction described in 3rd Nephi, it is clear that a volcano and a regional earthquake are indicated."[827] Earthquakes are known to trigger volcanic eruptions, especially when a volcano is located on or near a fault line.[828]

After analyzing all the destructive elements mentioned in the Book of Mormon accounts, Grover determined that the best-fit scenario is a strike-slip fault zone, near a coast, with an active volcano nearby.[829] There is at least one fault system in the Americas that meets these criteria: the Veracruz fault system in Mexico.[830] Grover noted, "The Veracruz fault segment . . . is a strike-slip fault, . . . located on and adjacent to the coastal plains . . . [and] has a major volcano sitting directly on the fault system, the volcano San Martín."[831]

In some Book of Mormon geography models, Veracruz, Mexico, is part of the land northward, which experienced greater damage during the cataclysmic events (see 3 Nephi 8:12).[832] Interestingly, while it is impossible to prove the exact timing of a volcanic eruption, current evidence indicates that the San Martín volcano likely experienced an eruption event in the first century AD.[833] Further evidence suggests that during or around the first century AD, Mesoamerica experienced widespread volcanic activity.[834]

Additional evidence comes from ice core samples (see image below) from Greenland and Antarctica. While the estimated dates are still not exact, using ice cores "tends to be fairly good" with margins of error of only a few years.[835] After examining documented dates for volcanic events in four different ice core samples, geologist Benjamin R. Jordan concluded, "There is evidence for large eruptions [somewhere in the world], within the margin of error, for the period of AD 30 to 40."[836]

Ice cores, therefore, offer evidence that there was a major volcanic event close to the timing of Christ's death.[837] Yet ice cores have the drawback of not being able to pinpoint the location of the volcanic events they document from all around the world.[838] A correlation to Mesoamerica, however, is possible, given the evidence already mentioned for extensive volcanic activity around this time. [839]

THE WHY

In graphic detail, the Book of Mormon documents a divinely caused natural disaster occurring at the time of Christ's death that many geologists agree appears to have involved a volcanic eruption, most likely occurring simultaneously with an earthquake along a strike-slip fault line. Thus far, current geologic evidence supports the following conclusions:

1. At least one region in the Americas (Veracruz, Mexico) possessed the necessary geologic characteristics.
2. At least one volcano in that region (San Martín) appears to have erupted in the first century AD.
3. There was further volcanic activity in Mesoamerica in and around the first century AD.
4. Ice core samples indicate that a major volcanic event took place somewhere in the world around AD 30 to 40—around or close to the time of Christ's death.

While none of this can be linked directly to the events described in 3 Nephi, it goes to show that, as with the sign at Christ's birth,[840] nothing in the account given in 3 Nephi 8–10 is scientifically implausible. In fact, the fulfillment of this prophesied volcanic disaster is strikingly realistic, especially its three days of smoky vapor and thick darkness.

Also, like the sign of great light at the time of Christ's birth, the profound darkness at His death and time in the tomb is strongly symbolic. Just as the "excessive light surrounding Christ's birth acts as a kind of morning," the "darkness surrounding Christ's death acts as a kind of evening."[841] Alvin Benson aptly stated, "It appears that the earth was symbolically manifesting its gloom over the death of its creator."[842]

But even the darkest of nights come to an end. The darkness dissipated as the Savior conquered death, and within the year righteous Nephites and Lamanites witnessed the risen, glorified Lord in all His majesty (see 3 Nephi 11).

President Ezra Taft Benson taught, "The record of the Nephite history just prior to the Savior's visit reveals many parallels to our own day as we anticipate the Savior's second coming."[843] This statement warns readers of further societal decay and impending darkness and destruction. But it also enables them to glimpse the grandeur and glory that is to follow for the humble and penitent who come unto Christ.

FURTHER READING

Neal Rappleye, "'The Great and Terrible Judgments of the Lord': Destruction and Disaster in 3 Nephi and the Geology of Mesoamerica," *Interpreter: A Journal of Mormon Scripture 15* (2015): 143–157.

Jerry D. Grover Jr., *Geology of the Book of Mormon* (Vineyard, UT: Grover Publications, 2014).

Benjamin R. Jordan, "Volcanic Destruction in the Book of Mormon: Possible Evidence from Ice Cores," *Journal of Book of Mormon Studies 12,* no. 1 (2003): 78–87.

Bart J. Kowallis, "In the Thirty and Fourth Year: A Geologist's View of the Great Destruction in 3 Nephi," *BYU Studies 37,* no. 3 (1997–1998): 136–190.

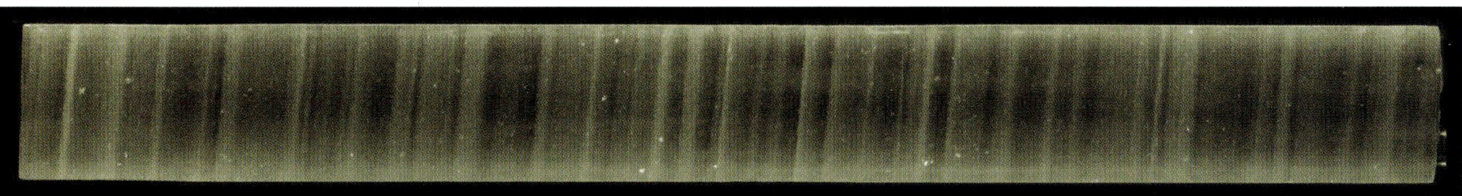

A section of an ice core in which the vertical layers represent individual years and seasons. Ash layers can also determine the presence of volcanic activity.

69

Is There Evidence of Sunken Cities in Ancient America?

"Yea, and the city of Onihah and the inhabitants thereof, and the city of Mocum and the inhabitants thereof, and the city of Jerusalem and the inhabitants thereof; and waters have I caused to come up in the stead thereof." (3 Nephi 9:7)

THE KNOW

After the great destruction recorded in 3 Nephi, the Lord's voice was heard among the people, declaring that the "great city Moroni have I caused to be sunk in the depths of the sea, and the inhabitants thereof to be drowned" (3 Nephi 9:4). The cities of Onihah, Mocum, and Jerusalem suffered similar fates. Concerning them, the Lord declared that "waters have I caused to come up in the stead thereof" (3 Nephi 9:7).

Based on these passages, some may wonder if there is any evidence that cities were flooded in this manner in the ancient Americas. In the 1990s, Roberto Samayoa noticed ruins on an underwater plateau while he was scuba diving in Lake Atitlan, located in the highlands of Guatemala. The site was named Samabaj, which is partly derived from Roberto's own last name, and eventually trained archaeologists began to seriously study the area.[844] A geophysical survey using side sonar scanning revealed even more man-made structures at other underwater locations along Lake Atitlan's southern shore.[845]

Concerning Samabaj, anthropologist John Sorenson noted that the "buildings appear to have been undamaged before their submersion, implying a sudden rise of the water."[846] Journalist Roger Atwood called it an "underwater time capsule unmolested by looters and untouched by urbanization."[847]

Researchers have found "about 30 ancient homes, a plaza, staircases, and even saunas, among the submerged ruins of Samabaj."[848] It also features "no fewer than 16 religious structures," including "at least seven stelas, standing stone markers that often signified power and authority in antiquity."[849] Sonya Medrano, an archaeologist involved with the site's recent underwater excavation and mapping, has described it as "a place of public rituals and pilgrimage."[850]

The sudden rise in water, which left the thirty-acre island submerged under twelve to thirty meters of water, was likely due to local volcanic activity.[851] Based on ceramic remains, Sorenson felt that the ruins were from the "Late Pre-Classic period, probably around the time of Christ,"[852] and Medrano dated "the island's moment of destruction to no later than A.D. 300."[853]

THE WHY

Samabaj offers a perfect example of the type of destruction experienced by the cities of Onihah, Mocum, and Jerusalem, as explained by the voice of the Lord. Rather than sinking into the sea or having a flash flood come crashing down on them from above, the

Lord declared that "waters have I caused to *come up* in the stead thereof" (3 Nephi 9:7; emphasis added). This is exactly what happened at Samabaj—the water level of its surrounding lake quickly arose and submerged it. This underwater settlement, which until recent times lay undetected at the bottom of a popular resort lake, demonstrates that the type of flooding mentioned in 3 Nephi is anything but farfetched.

Interestingly, long before the discovery of Samabaj, several Latter-day Saint scholars identified the region of Lake Atitlan with the waters of Mormon and placed Jerusalem, one of the sunken cities, near its shores.[854] It remains uncertain, however, if Samabaj and its sudden flooding had anything to do with Book of Mormon peoples or the destruction reported in 3 Nephi.

After discussing the symbolic and religious significance that Samabaj's destruction may have held for its inhabitants, Atwood asked, "Did the ancient Maya know why the island was disappearing?"[855] It may be similarly relevant to ask if Book of Mormon peoples knew why their cities were being covered with water. From heaven, the Lord's voice was heard among the people, explaining that this was done "to hide their wickedness and abominations from before my face, that the blood of the prophets and the saints shall not come up any more unto me against them" (3 Nephi 9:7).

This reasoning is actually quite similar to the Lord's justification for sending the flood in Noah's time. The Lord explained to Enoch that He would send the flood because "in [the people's] own abominations have they devised murder, and have not kept the commandments" (Moses 6:28). These "abominations" were first introduced by Cain, who slew his brother Abel (see Moses 5:32). In response to Cain's murder, the Lord declared, "The voice of thy brother's blood cries unto me from the ground" (Moses 5:35).

Thus, in both accounts, the floods were sent because of "abominations" that are scripturally linked with the shedding of innocent blood—blood that symbolically calls out from the ground for divine justice.[856] The Lord wanted the people to understand that He was bound by His own law to exact justice for the spilling of innocent blood. The rising waters symbolically hid the people's wickedness and abominations from before the face of the Lord,[857] while at the same time symbolically cleansing the earth from sin.[858]

FURTHER READING

John L. Sorenson, *Mormon's Codex: An Ancient American Book* (Salt Lake City and Provo, UT: Deseret Book and FARMS, 2013), 133–135, 647–648, 664.

John L. Sorenson, "The Submergence of the City of Jerusalem in the Land of Nephi," *Insights 22*, no. 155 (2002): 2–3.

Why Did Jesus Christ Compare Himself to a Hen?

"How oft have I gathered you as a hen gathereth her chickens under her wings. . . ." (3 Nephi 10:4)

THE KNOW

After the great calamities and destruction among the Nephites, they experienced "thick darkness upon all the face of the land" (3 Nephi 8:10),[859] and in response to these afflictions, "there was great mourning and howling and weeping among all the people" (3 Nephi 8:23). It is in this setting of anguish and suffering that the voice of Jesus Christ was "heard . . . upon all the face of this land" (3 Nephi 9:1).

As part of His message of redemption, Jesus declared, "how oft have I gathered you as a hen gathereth her chickens under her wings" (3 Nephi 10:4). This metaphor was repeated four times in three successive verses, and was even used in three different tenses: "how oft *have* I gathered you and nourished you" (3 Nephi 10:4, speaking to those of the fallen cities), followed by "how oft *would* I have gathered you" (3 Nephi 10:5, speaking of those in Jerusalem), and concluding with "how oft *will* I gather you" (3 Nephi 10:6, speaking to the spared members of the House of Israel; emphasis added for all verses). Clearly, this repeated metaphor was of transcendent—even eternal—significance.[860]

Jane Allis-Pike explained, "For a metaphor to be meaningful, the reader must have a familiarity with the objects used for comparison."[861] For people living in ancient America, *chicken* might have referred to an actual chicken,[862] or it could have been a loan-shift term for a fowl with similar features in the New World.[863] Turkeys, for example, were prevalent in ancient America,[864] took special care to protect their young,[865] and played a significant role in religious thought.[866]

Whatever species of fowl was represented here by the words *hen* and *chickens*,[867] Allis-Pike explained that Jesus Christ can be represented by a mother bird in His role as "creator of this earth," His "desire to protect his young" (those who become His children through covenant), His willingness to "[use] his body to shield his beloved 'children' from endless death and hell," and His "proactive care in the nurture of his 'children.'"[868]

She concluded:

> Like the hen that hurries her chicks together, Christ focuses on "gather[ing]" his "children." This gathering comes in the form of teaching them to follow him, to accept the gospel, to learn the plan of salvation, and receive the saving priesthood ordinances.[869]

The chicks that need to be gathered, on the other hand, meaningfully represent the house of Israel. "The Book of Mormon peoples are one branch of the house of Israel. They have a long-standing history and covenant relationship with the Savior and his gospel. They know the Savior as the chicks know their mother."[870]

THE WHY

The underlying purpose of this metaphor was "to remind and teach the people of the true nature and conditions of their covenant relationship with [Jesus Christ]."[871] Not only does it convey the historical assurance of "Christ's desire to protect his people," but it also "underscores the fact that they must want his protection."[872] This can be seen in Christ's twice-repeated statement, "how oft would I have gathered you," followed by the emphatic declaration: "yet ye would not" (3 Nephi 10:5).

Christ's hen metaphor is explained further in Alma's open invitation that "whosoever will come may come and partake of the waters of life freely; and whosoever will not come the same is not compelled to come" (Alma 42:27).[873] Like a mother hen, Jesus Christ is ever concerned for the physical and spiritual needs of His children. And because His infinite Atonement stretches wide as eternity, He will always remain capable of providing shelter and protection to all who willingly come unto Him. He promises and affirms, "how oft will I gather you" (3 Nephi 10:6).

It should also be recognized that even though this metaphor pertains to God's dealings with the house of Israel, His efforts here and now at gathering and including His children within His covenant are boundless. All who are willing to be "baptized in the name of the Lord, as a witness before him that ye have entered into a covenant with him" will be immediately enfolded and included in His loving arms (Mosiah 18:10). Brent L. Top invited:

> May we exercise greater faith in the arms of the Lord—His arms of power, His arms of love, and His arms of mercy. May we allow Him to cradle and carry and comfort us in those arms. In turn, our arms—our determination and our devotion—will be strengthened. . . . May we all be "clasped in the arms of Jesus."[874]

FURTHER READING

Henry B. Eyring, "'Come Unto Me,'" *Ensign*, May 2013, 22–25.

Jane Allis-Pike, "'How Oft Would I Have Gathered You as a Hen Gathereth Her Chickens': The Power of the Hen Metaphor in 3 Nephi 10: 4–7," in *Third Nephi: An Incomparable Scripture*, ed. Andrew C. Skinner and Gaye Strathearn (Salt Lake City and Provo, UT: Deseret Book and Neal A. Maxwell Institute for Religious Scholarship, 2012), 57–74.

Clifford P. Jones, "The Great and Marvelous Change: An Alternate Interpretation," *Journal of the Book of Mormon and Other Restoration Scripture 19*, no. 2 (2010): 50–63.

Why Has 3 Nephi Been Called "the Focal Point, the Supreme Moment" in the Book of Mormon?

"Behold, I am Jesus Christ, whom the prophets testified shall come into the world." (3 Nephi 11:10)

THE KNOW

When Christ appeared to the Nephites, His first words were, "I am Jesus Christ, whom the prophets testified shall come into the world" (3 Nephi 11:10). In his book *Christ and the New Covenant*, Elder Jeffrey R. Holland said of this moment, "That appearance and that declaration constituted the focal point, the supreme moment, in the entire history of the Book of Mormon."[875] This statement is profoundly true at many levels.

In one important sense, the prophetic anticipation of the Book of Mormon culminates in the appearances of the resurrected Jesus marvelously reported in 3 Nephi 11–27. As Elder Holland further explained, "It was the manifestation and the decree that had informed and inspired every Nephite prophet for the previous six hundred years, to say nothing of their Israelite and Jaredite forefathers for thousands of years before that."[876]

A look at the early chapters of the Book of Mormon demonstrates how important this moment was. Nephi had recorded, quoting Isaiah, that the Lord wanted Isaiah to "make the heart of this people fat, and make their *ears* heavy, and shut their *eyes*—lest they see with their *eyes*, and hear with their *ears*, and *understand* with their heart, and be converted and be healed" (2 Nephi 16:10 and Isaiah 6:10; emphasis added). Isaiah asked, "Lord, how long?" and God told him, "Until the cities be wasted without inhabitant, and the houses without man, and the land be utterly desolate" (2 Nephi 16:11 and Isaiah 6:11).

After the great destruction at the time of the Crucifixion, Christ spoke to the people. He told them about all the cities that had been completely leveled by the series of natural disasters that befell several unrighteous Nephite cities (see 3 Nephi 9:2–12). He then asked the survivors, "will ye not now return unto me, and repent of your sins, and be *converted*, that I may *heal* you?" (3 Nephi 9:13; emphasis added). Thus, after the cities of the Nephites had become "wasted without inhabitant," as Isaiah had said, Christ pled with the people to "be converted" and allow Him to "heal" them.[877]

A voice from God came to the people, and they "did hear the voice, and did *open* their *ears* to hear it; and their *eyes* were towards the sound thereof. . . . And behold, the third time they did *understand* the voice which they heard" (3 Nephi 11:5–6). Mormon seems to have implied that the people finally accepted this healing. After years of closing their eyes, ears, and hearts to God, as Isaiah said, the ears and eyes of the Nephites were opened.[878] They finally understood the gospel in their hearts, allowing themselves to be converted so Christ could heal them.

THE WHY

Mormon masterfully crafted the Book of Mormon to point readers to this "supreme moment" when Christ came to heal His people. Throughout the narrative, Mormon frequently told of how the children of Lehi had, at times, closed themselves off from God.[879] Yet he also interwove through the whole text the idea that Christ would someday come to heal humanity.

As everything in the Book of Mormon had led to this point,[880] Mormon then carefully and deliberately alluded to the words of Isaiah to forcefully illustrate that the pinnacle of the book, that majestic moment, had arrived. With the words, "I am Jesus Christ, whom the prophets testified shall come into the world" (3 Nephi 11:10), Christ had finally come to heal His people, just as the prophets throughout the Book of Mormon had said He would.

It is hard to say enough in praise of 3 Nephi. It has been called a "fifth gospel,"[881] "a resplendent portrait,"[882] "a crowning jewel,"[883] "the pinnacle,"[884] "the climax, the apex,"[885] and even the "first gospel,"[886] as well as "the focal point, the supreme moment, in the entire history of the Book of Mormon."[887] To that, one may also add that it is the inner sanctum of the Book of Mormon, a sacred and infinite template uniting time and all eternity.[888]

As President Ezra Taft Benson said, "It is clear that 3 Nephi contains some of the most moving and powerful passages in all scripture. It testifies of Christ, his prophets, and the doctrines of salvation." President Benson went on to encourage people, especially families, to read 3 Nephi and to "discuss its sacred contents."[889]

This book of scripture is a book of literary and theological contrasts between brilliant light and horrible darkness, death and life, the old and the new, and prideful ambition and humble submission. Above all, this book, named after Christ's chief disciple in the Nephite world, is a treasure trove of testimonies and teachings of the reality of the physical resurrection of Jesus Christ and of His victory over death and hell. His glorious triumph, which is the epitome of the plan of mercy and redemption in the Book of Mormon, is at the same time the supreme gift of joy and salvation to people everywhere.

While it may be easy at times to get bogged down in the details of scripture and to forget what these sacred texts are really about, 3 Nephi reminds readers that Christ and His coming are the "focal point" and the "supreme moment" of the entire Book of Mormon, and indeed of all human existence. Christ is humanity's only hope of ever truly seeing, hearing, and understanding correctly. He is mankind's only hope for healing. In the midst of the mayhem and destruction at the time of the Crucifixion, Christ invited His beloved people to be converted and to allow Him to eternally heal them. 3 Nephi is a potent reminder of the power of Christ to bring sight, understanding, and healing to all the world.

FURTHER READING

Charles Swift, "'So Great and Marvelous Things': The Literary Portrait of Jesus as Divine Lord in 3 Nephi," in *Third Nephi: An Incomparable Scripture*, ed. Andrew C. Skinner and Gaye Strathearn (Salt Lake City and Provo, UT: Deseret Book and Neal A. Maxwell Institute for Religious Scholarship, 2012), 235–260.

Jeffrey R. Holland, *Christ and the New Covenant* (Salt Lake City, UT: Deseret Book, 1997), 249–275.

Robert J. Matthews, "Jesus the Savior in 3 Nephi," in *The Book of Mormon: 3 Nephi 8 Through 30, This Is My Gospel*, ed. Monte S. Nyman and Charles D. Tate Jr. (Provo, UT: BYU Religious Studies Center, 1993), 25–39.

72

Why Did the People Fall Down at the Feet of Jesus?

"And they did fall down at the feet of Jesus, and did worship him." (3 Nephi 11:17)

THE KNOW

When Jesus Christ declared His true identity to the people of Nephi who were gathered around the temple in the land of Bountiful, "the whole multitude *fell to the earth*; for they remembered that it had been prophesied among them that Christ should show himself unto them" (3 Nephi 11:12; emphasis added). Similarly, after they had all gone forth and touched the wounds in His hands, feet, and side, they "did *fall down at the feet of Jesus*, and did worship him" (3 Nephi 11:17; emphasis added). And when Jesus commanded Nephi to come forth, He "bowed himself before the Lord and did *kiss his feet*" (3 Nephi 11:19; emphasis added).

The act of falling at the feet of a ruler and even kissing the ground or his feet was a well-known form of worship in the ancient world called *proskynesis*.[890] In an ancient Near Eastern letter, for example, a vassal showed respect to a Lord through phrases such as "[I am] your slave" and "the dust at your feet" and "I prostrate; at the feet of my king, my lord I fall."[891] An ancient Egyptian liturgical text similarly declared, "As I kiss the ground, even so do I embrace Geb."[892] According to Matthew L. Bowen, this text "prescribes proskynesis, including a ritual embrace of a god (Geb, the earth), as part of a ritualized theophany in a temple setting."[893]

Proskynesis was also known to the ancient Israelites.[894] For instance, in Joseph's dreams, his brothers' sheaves as well as the sun, moon, and stars paid homage to him. This prompted his father to ask, "Shall I and thy mother and thy brethren indeed come to bow down ourselves to thee to the earth?" (Genesis 37:10).[895] Psalms 95:6 reads "O come, let us worship and bow down: let us kneel before the Lord our maker."

New Testament texts—such as Matthew, Mark, Luke, and Revelation—abundantly demonstrate that the early Apostles and followers of Jesus viewed proskynesis as an appropriate mode of worshipping Jesus Christ both before and after His Resurrection.[896]

Furthermore, demonstrations of falling to the earth in ritual prostration are evident in several Book of Mormon settings (in addition to 3 Nephi 11).[897] In Lehi's dream of the tree of life, those who pressed forward and held to the rod of iron eventually "came forth and *fell down* and partook of the fruit of the tree" (1 Nephi 8:30; emphasis added). Bowen remarked, "The people of this third group are the true worshipers, and the tree of which they partake is functionally the true God, Jesus Christ."[898]

When King Benjamin reported the words "delivered unto him by the angel," he looked upon the multitude and saw that the people "had fallen to the earth. . . . And they had viewed themselves in their own carnal state, even less than the dust of the earth" (Mosiah 4:1–2). On this, Hugh Nibley commented:

> This was the kind of proskynesis at which Benjamin aimed! The proskynesis was the falling to the earth (literally, "kissing the ground") in the presence of the king by which all the human race on the day of the coronation demonstrated its submission to divine authority; it was an unfailing part of the Old World New Year's rites as of any royal audience.[899]

THE WHY

Exploring the meaning of proskynesis in both its Old World and Book of Mormon contexts can help readers better understand what this ritual demonstration meant to those who worshiped Jesus Christ at the temple in the land of Bountiful.

For example, the phrase "[I am] . . . the dust at your feet" from the ancient Egyptian letter parallels the response of the people who, after hearing King Benjamin's speech, fell to the earth and considered themselves as "even less than the dust of the earth" (Mosiah 4:2).[900] Bowen rhetorically asked:

> What is the lesson here? Since, as King Benjamin says, we "cannot say that [we] are even as much as the dust of the earth" (Mosiah 2:25), we are to "get down there and realize what [we] are," as Nibley puts it. King Benjamin revives the lessons from the biblical account of the fall and its nameplay on Adam: the man (ha-*ʾadām*, "humanity") was taken from ha-*ʾadāmāh* ("earth," "ground," "soil," Genesis 2:7; 3:19).[901]

Thus by falling to the ground, those who worshiped Christ at Bountiful ritually signified that their bodies were created from the dust of the earth, that they were mortal and fallen, and that they were willingly humbling themselves in the presence of their Creator.[902]

From a story in the New Testament, readers learn of a woman who washed the feet of Jesus with her tears, and "kissed his feet, and anointed them with the ointment" (Luke 7:38). Bowen explained, "Her physical proskynesis in kissing the feet of Jesus was a profound demonstration of the love of God and literally fulfilled the injunction of Psalm 2 to 'kiss the Son' or even (in an emended reading) to 'kiss his [Yahweh's] feet.'"[903]

Likewise, when Nephi (who may well have been familiar with such language found in many of the Psalms) "bowed himself before the Lord and did kiss his feet" at the temple in Bountiful (3 Nephi 11:19), it can be seen as a prescribed act of devotion for Him whose feet had "trodden the winepress alone,"[904] and whose feet bore the "prints of nails" of crucifixion,[905] and whose beautiful feet "bringeth good tidings of good."[906]

In what can be seen as an act of proskynesis to His Father, Jesus Christ Himself submissively "fell on his face, and prayed" while suffering the agonies of the Atonement in Gethsemane (Matthew 26:39). He also washed the feet of His Apostles in an act of humility and service (see John 13:4–16). Those who fall at the feet of Him who "descended below all things"[907] and "kiss his feet . . . [and] bathe his feet with their tears"[908] show their willingness to follow His example of service, humility, and obedience.

Worshipful prostration is an enduring symbol of love and devotion for deity. Nephi taught that the "right way is to believe in Christ . . . wherefore ye must bow down before him, and worship him with all your might" (2 Nephi 25:29). In 3 Nephi 19, Jesus again went a little distance away from the large assembly that had gathered on His second day at the temple of Bountiful, "and bowed himself to the earth," expressing profound gratitude to the Father (3 Nephi 19:19). Joseph Smith and Sidney Rigdon learned that before the throne of God "all things bow in humble reverence, and give him glory forever and ever" (D&C 76:93).

From the examples of those who worshipped Jesus Christ at the temple in Bountiful, readers can learn how to appropriately show reverence for the Lord when they eventually meet Him in person and behold His resurrected body. Of the eternal importance of bowing before our Lord and Master, Elder Neil L. Andersen has unambiguously testified, "I witness that Jesus Christ is the Savior of the world. He suffered and died for our sins and rose the third day. He is resurrected. In a future day, every knee will bow and every tongue confess that He is the Christ."[909]

Elder Neal A. Maxwell has beautifully taught that while Christ rejoices in our genuine goodness and achievements, "any assessment of where we stand in relation to Him tells us that we do not stand at all! We kneel!" and soon "all flesh shall see Him together. All knees shall bow in His presence, and all tongues confess His name. Knees which never before have assumed that posture for that purpose will do so then—and promptly."[910]

FURTHER READING

Dean M. Davies, "The Blessings of Worship," *Ensign*, November 2016.

Matthew L. Bowen, "'They Came and Held Him by the Feet and Worshipped Him': Proskynesis before Jesus in Its Biblical and Ancient Near Eastern Context," *Studies in the Bible and Antiquity* 5 (2013): 63–68.

Matthew L. Bowen, "'They Came Forth and Fell Down and Partook of the Fruit of the Tree': Proskynesis in 3 Nephi 11:12–19 and 17:9–10 and Its Significance," in *Third Nephi: An Incomparable Scripture* (Salt Lake City and Provo, UT: Deseret Book and Neal A. Maxwell Institute for Religious Scholarship, 2012), 107–130.

Matthew L. Bowen, "'And Behold, They Had Fallen to the Earth': An Examination of Proskynesis in the Book of Mormon," *Studia Antiqua* 4, no. 1 (2005): 91–110.

Hugh Nibley, *An Approach to the Book of Mormon, The Collected Works of Hugh Nibley, Volume 6* (Salt Lake City and Provo, UT: Deseret Book and FARMS, 1988), 259–310.

Why Did Jesus Deliver a Version of the Sermon on the Mount at the Temple in Bountiful?

"And blessed are all they who do hunger and thirst after righteousness, for they shall be filled with the Holy Ghost." (3 Nephi 12:6)

THE KNOW

During Christ's visit to the peoples of the Book of Mormon, he presented teachings to them that closely resemble what He taught in the Sermon on the Mount as recorded in the Gospel of Matthew (see 3 Nephi 12–14; Matthew 5–7). Some have argued that the similarities between the Sermon on the Mount in the New Testament and the "Sermon at the Temple" in Bountiful in the Book of Mormon are evidence that Joseph Smith simply plagiarized from the Bible.[911]

Yet there are several elements present in the 3 Nephi text that distinguish it from the version in Matthew. These differences are significant and set it apart as a distinct and powerful testament of its own. For instance, in this setting Jesus declared that the law had been fulfilled, instead of pointing toward a future fulfillment (see 3 Nephi 12:18; cf. Matthew 5:18). He also taught that as a glorified being, He was perfect like the Father (see 3 Nephi 12:48; cf. Matthew 5:48), and thus omitted "thy kingdom come" in the Lord's Prayer (see 3 Nephi 13:10; cf. Matthew 6:10).[912] He also specifically spoke of the Nephite "senine" instead of the Jewish "farthing."[913]

The teachings of the Sermon on the Mount were an important set of teachings that are likely older than the Gospel of Matthew itself.[914] It is therefore not surprising that they are presented in various writings and settings. A similar, but selectively shorter, body of teachings is found in Luke 6:17–49, which is often referred to as "the Sermon on the Plain." The exact relationship between these two texts is debated,[915] but they arguably represent two occasions in which Jesus propounded similar teachings, a smaller set to the crowd out on a field.

The two versions in the New Testament have notable differences,[916] including the omission of all the material in Matthew 6 in the Luke version. John W. Welch noted, "Missing from this speech in Luke are all of the elements that one would expect to be reserved for the closer circle of disciples."[917] The different settings may very well be what lies behind the difference here. One was given on a "plain"—an open space where anyone might pass by. The other was given on a "mountain"—perhaps symbolic of the "mountain of the Lord" (Isaiah 2:2) and synonymous with the temple.[918]

Some scholars have noted the parallels between the Sermon on the Mount and the ancient temple. Georg

Strecker, for example, refers to the Beatitudes as "the conditions that must be fulfilled in order to gain entrance to the holy of holies."[919] Hans Dieter Betz compared the Beatitudes of the Sermon with the initiation rituals of ancient "mystery" religions.[920]

Betz also argued that the Sermon's literary function was as a philosophical *epitome*, a distillation or summary of Jesus's teachings prepared for a specific purpose. He explained that it was "not intended for outsiders or beginners, but for the advanced students [to help] 'those who have made some advance in the survey of the entire system . . . to fix in their minds under the principal headings an elementary outline of the whole treatment of the subject.'"[921] This is not unlike temple teachings, which are usually reserved for those who are more advanced in their learning.

Welch has proposed that the Sermon on the Mount contains twenty-five stages, each related to the temple.[922] The temple connections are further enhanced in the Book of Mormon, where not only the setting at the temple is explicit, but the sequence of events both before and after the material parallel to Matthew evokes temple imagery, doubling the amount of temple themes identified in the Nephite version of the sermon.[923]

THE WHY

The preceding information can help readers understand why a version of the Sermon on the Mount would appear in the Book of Mormon. These reasons may include:

- The likelihood that the teachings upon which the Sermon on the Mount is based, and which are older than the Matthew text, were taught in diverse places to different audiences.
- The giving of the Sermon was modified to be appropriate for the particular audience. The textual differences between the examples available are appropriate for each audience. Specifically, the Sermon at the Temple in 3 Nephi has such modifications as would be expected for a post-Resurrection version of the Sermon.
- The Sermon may have served as a set of temple teachings, information that Jesus would have wanted all worthy and prepared disciples to learn.

The version of the Sermon that we find in 3 Nephi is not simply copied verbatim out of the New Testament, nor is it haphazardly pieced together in the Book of Mormon text. There are some key differences that, if analyzed carefully, can be seen to have real theological significance. Welch noted:

> These differences convey significant theological information. First, the Sermon at the Temple clarified that all things under the law of Moses had been entirely fulfilled in Jesus' mortal life, death, atonement, and resurrection. . . . Second, the Sermon at the Temple speaks from a frame of reference in which Jesus had become glorified with God. Jesus had already ascended to the Father, and thus he could well command his listeners in Bountiful to be perfect as he or as God is perfect (see 3 Nephi 12:48).[924]

In the 3 Nephi version, there is an emphasis on obeying these teachings because they were given explicitly as commandments in a covenant-making setting. There is also a strong emphasis in the Book of Mormon version on coming unto Christ through the ordinances that He had taught and given them.

The Sermon at the Temple in 3 Nephi renders this vital body of teachings from the Savior in the right place with the right words, presenting a version of the Lord's teachings that should not be skimmed over as familiar or redundant. It should be studied and pondered as the treasure that it truly is.

FURTHER READING

Valérie Triplet-Hitoto, "Audience Astonishment at the Sermon on the Mount and the Sermon at the Temple," in *The Sermon on the Mount in Latter-day Scripture,* ed. Gaye Strathearn, Thomas A. Wayment, and Daniel L. Belnap (Salt Lake City and Provo, UT: Deseret Book and BYU Religious Studies Center, 2010), 42–58.

A. Don Sorenson, "The Problem of the Sermon on the Mount and 3 Nephi," *FARMS Review 16*, no. 2 (2004): 117–148.

John W. Welch, *Illuminating the Sermon at the Temple and Sermon on the Mount* (Provo, UT: FARMS, 1999).

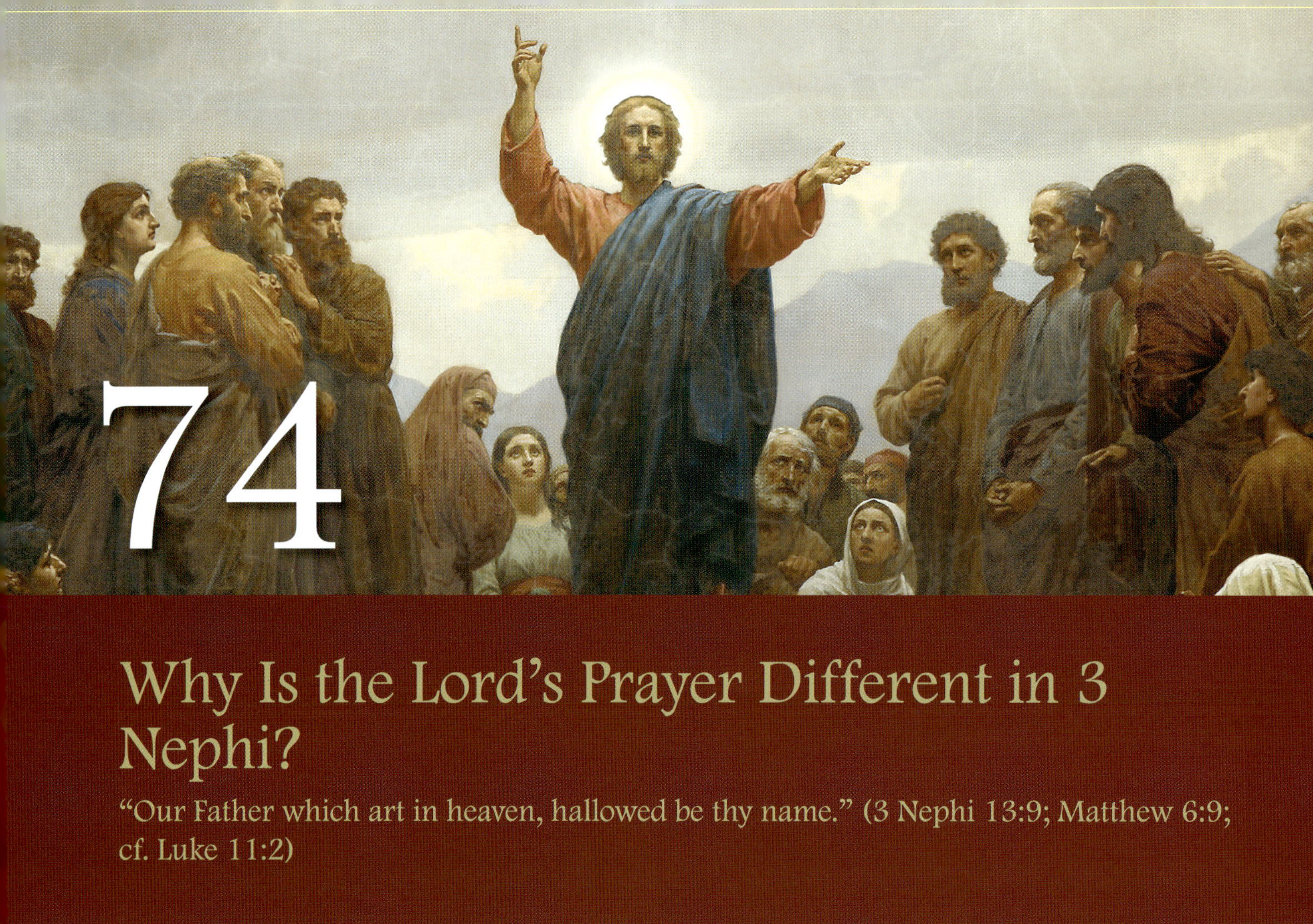

74

Why Is the Lord's Prayer Different in 3 Nephi?

"Our Father which art in heaven, hallowed be thy name." (3 Nephi 13:9; Matthew 6:9; cf. Luke 11:2)

THE KNOW

According to Donald W. Parry, "Nowhere in all of the Book of Mormon is the subject of prayer taught and emphasized in such a concentrated fashion as it is in 3 Nephi 11–20." Here, among the resurrected Lord's teachings at this time, "approximately sixty verses are dedicated to the subject of prayer and . . . eleven prayers are offered."[925] This includes the teaching on prayer in Sermon at the Temple (in 3 Nephi 13:5–13), where Christ gave the Nephites a version of what is called the "Lord's Prayer."

The New Testament Gospels include two slightly different versions of the Lord's Prayer, one in the Sermon on the Mount (see Matthew 6:9–13) and another in Luke 11:2–4. The Didache, an early Christian text generally dated to the first century AD,[926] also has a version of the prayer (see Didache 8). When compared with the versions found among the early Christians, the Lord's Prayer at Bountiful is unique (see table on page 185).[927] The Book of Mormon version is missing two key phrases, and it includes an extended ending of praise not included in the version in Luke.

Thy Kingdom Come: Every version of the Lord's Prayer in the Old World includes the petition, "thy kingdom come." New Testament scholar Hans Betz explained, "God's kingdom . . . is established in heaven, but not yet, at least not fully, on earth." Of course, only "God himself can make his kingdom come."[928] This petition, however, is omitted from the prayer the risen Lord gave to the Nephites.

"Daily" Bread: Each Old World version of the prayer likewise includes a plea for "our daily bread." While the request seems straightforward enough, the exact meaning of this phrase is actually uncertain, because the Greek term translated as "daily" (*epiousion*) "is notoriously difficult" to translate.[929] John W. Welch has argued that in context with "thy kingdom come," it "is unlikely to be a request 'for ordinary food.'"[930] Several possibilities exist, but one interpretation is that it is "a reference to the expected messianic banquet."[931]

The Hymn of Praise: The Lord's Prayer at Bountiful includes the ending, "For thine is the kingdom, and the power, and the glory, forever. Amen." This ending, called by scholars a *doxology* or "hymn of praise," is missing from the version in Luke and from the earliest Greek manuscripts of Matthew. Thus, many scholars conclude that it was not part of the original version in Matthew either.[932] If this is true, then among canonical versions of the Lord's prayer, the version in 3 Nephi may be unique

Luke 11:2–4	Matthew 6:9–13	3 Nephi 13:9–13	Didache 8
Our Father which art in heaven, Hallowed be thy name.	Our Father which art in heaven, Hallowed be thy name.	Our Father which art in heaven, hallowed be thy name.	Our Father who art in heaven, hallowed be Thy name.
Thy kingdom come. Thy will be done, as in heaven, so in earth.	Thy kingdom come. Thy will be done in earth, as it is in heaven.	Thy will be done in earth as it is in heaven.	Thy kingdom come. Thy will be done on earth, as it is in heaven.
Give us day by day our daily bread.	Give us this day our daily bread.		Give us today our daily (needful) bread,
And forgive us our sins; for we also forgive every one that is indebted to us.	And forgive us our debts, as we forgive our debtors.	And forgive us our debts, as we forgive our debtors.	and forgive us our debt as we also forgive our debtors.
And lead us not into temptation; but deliver us from evil.	And lead us not into temptation, but deliver us from evil:	And lead us not into temptation, but deliver us from evil.	And bring us not into temptation, but deliver us from the evil one (or, evil).
	For thine is the kingdom, and the power, and the glory, for ever. Amen.	For thine is the kingdom, and the power, and the glory, forever. Amen.	For Thine is the power and the glory for ever.

for including this detail, though it is also in the non-canonical Didache.

THE WHY

The uniqueness of the Nephite version of the Lord's Prayer can be easy to miss or underappreciate. Too often, readers assume that the two prayers are identical or that the differences are minimal, insignificant, or inconsequential. Careful analysis of the differences suggests it was likely adapted by the Lord to fit the specific circumstances of His visit to the people in Bountiful.

God's Kingdom Had, in One Important Sense, Just Come: As Heather Hardy has carefully shown, "with the arrival of the resurrected Jesus at the temple in Bountiful, God's kingdom is inaugurated upon the earth."[933] John W. Welch explained, "there was no need in Bountiful for Jesus to instruct the people to pray, 'Thy kingdom come' . . . for God's kingdom had already come both in heaven through Christ's victory over death and on earth that day in their midst."[934]

The Bread of Life Is Given: If this original plea was in reference to the bread of the messianic banquet, as some scholars have proposed, then this omission could also be due to the fact that for the Nephites, Jesus Christ, the Bread of Life, had specifically come. The exclusion of this clause would "reflect the postresurrectional setting of the Sermon at the Temple."[935] Indeed, the risen Lord Himself miraculously supplied bread for the partaking of the sacrament (see 3 Nephi 20:3–7), perhaps typologically imitating the feast of heavenly bread that will be had in the end times.

A Praiseworthy Setting: There is some early evidence hinting that, whether originally included in the Matthew prayer or not, Jesus likely included a hymn of praise when He prayed at least on some occasions in Judea.[936] Regardless of its inclusion or exclusion in Matthew, however, Welch has proposed that the sacred setting in Bountiful—at the temple—may explain its inclusion when the Lord gave the prayer there.[937] According to Welch, "the longer doxology would be appropriate in a sacred setting with an inner circle of followers."[938]

Specifically, evidence from rabbinical sources indicate that a "doxological acknowledgment of the kingdom and glory of God was in regular usage in the temple at the time of Jesus."[939] When the high priest spoke the name of the Lord, "the people answered . . . not with a simple 'amen,' but also with praises of God—mentioning such divine attributes as his glory, power, kingdom, and everlasting dominion—before the concluding amen."[940]

Similarly, one scholar suggested, "Perhaps the original function of the 'doxology' in the Lord's Prayer was that of a response by the worshiping congregation."[941] Such would have certainly been appropriate for the resurrected Lord's Prayer given at the temple.

By studying the differences in the Nephite edition of the Lord's Prayer—and, in fact, the whole Sermon at the Temple—readers can come to appreciate the Lord's sensitivity to the particular circumstances in which His teachings on prayer and other topics were given.[942] Rather than a simple cut-and-paste job from the Gospel of Matthew, the Lord carefully and subtly adapted His teachings in ways that are meaningfully sophisticated, situationally appropriate, and spiritually inspiring.[943]

Individuals and communities who follow the Lord can be confident that He is likewise aware of their specific needs and unique circumstances when they come unto Him and cry out, "Our father which art in heaven, hallowed be thy name."

FURTHER READING

Robert L. Millet, "The Praying Savior: Insights from the Gospel of 3 Nephi," in *Third Nephi: An Incomparable Scripture,* ed. Andrew C. Skinner and Gaye Strathearn (Salt Lake City and Provo, UT: Deseret Book and Neal A. Maxwell Institute for Religious Scholarship, 2012), 131–146.

John W. Welch, *Illuminating the Sermon at the Temple and the Sermon on the Mount* (Provo, UT: FARMS, 1999), 79–82, 206–208.

Donald W. Parry, "'Pray Always': Learning to Pray as Jesus Prayed," in *The Book of Mormon: 3 Nephi 9–30, This Is My Gospel* (Provo, UT: BYU Religious Studies Center, 1993), 137–148.

John W. Welch, "The Lord's Prayer," *Ensign*, January 1976.

75

Why Did Jesus Say that Some Well-Intended People Will Be Told to Depart?

"Not every one that saith unto me, Lord, Lord, shall enter into the kingdom of heaven; but he that doeth the will of my Father who is in heaven." (3 Nephi 14:21; Matthew 7:21)

THE KNOW

As Jesus Christ continued to present His "Sermon at the Temple," a version of the Sermon on the Mount (see Matthew 5–7) that He gave to the Book of Mormon peoples,[944] He declared that some people attempting to enter the kingdom of heaven would be told to "depart" (3 Nephi 14:23; Matthew 7:23). They would not be allowed to enter, despite having come to the Lord after proclaiming to have done many things in His name. Although this approach may seem harsh to some, it makes more sense if one understands how Jesus was using covenant and temple language that His audience would have recognized and understood.

The Lord declared:

> Not every one that saith unto me, Lord, Lord, shall enter into the kingdom of heaven; but he that doeth the will of my Father who is in heaven.
>
> Many will say to me in that day: Lord, Lord, have we not prophesied in thy name, and in thy name have cast out devils, and in thy name done many wonderful works?
>
> And then will I profess unto them: I never knew you; depart from me, ye that work iniquity. (3 Nephi 14:21–23; cf. Matthew 7:21–23)

For many readers, this passage is difficult to comprehend, as the people who will be told to depart had apparently been doing good works in the name of the Lord—something that tends to be characteristic of faithful believers. However, Jesus acted as if their use of His name had been tantamount to taking it in vain and suggested that they will not be able to enter because they "work iniquity" instead of doing His Father's will. It helps to recognize that other passages in the scriptures likewise command the wicked to depart. Not coincidentally, these scriptures are laced with covenantal and temple imagery.

For example, the last part of 3 Nephi 14:23/ Matthew 7:23 echoes the words of Psalms 6:8: "Depart from me, all ye workers of iniquity." Hosea 8:1–2 uses similar language and prophesies against those who "shall cry unto me, 'My God, we know thee,'" referring to those who take part in "the house of the Lord," but who have "transgressed my covenant, and trespassed against my law."

Jesus stated that He is the "way" and that "no man cometh unto the Father, but by me" (John 14:6). This was spoken in the context of "my Father's house" (John 14:2)—or, in other words, the house of the Lord.

There are several scriptural passages that declare the importance of knowing or being known by the Lord. While the word *know* may not seem particularly significant, it may often be related to covenantal language. Jesus said that He is "the good shepherd" and that "[I] know my sheep, and am known of mine" (John 10:14).[945] John W. Welch argued that the verb *know* may have a covenantal meaning here, as it does elsewhere in the scriptures.

For example, when God spoke of Abraham's faithfulness in keeping the way of the Lord, He described His covenant relationship with Abraham by declaring "I know him" (Genesis 18:19). Welch explained that "the Sermon on the Mount, therefore, seeks to restore the old covenant between God and Israel, by which God knew (or recognized) Israel and the Israelites knew God (see Hosea 13:4; Jeremiah 24:7)."[946]

Some interesting parallel ideas that involve using the name of the Lord and entering the temple (and by association, the "kingdom of heaven") can be found in Psalms 24. Psalms 24 is a "temple entry" psalm that presents a group of people who are seeking the face of the Lord (see Psalms 24:6)[947] by passing through the gates of the temple (see Psalms 24:7) to ascend "the hill of the Lord" (Psalms 24:3). When attempting to pass through the temple gates, they essentially used the name of "the Lord" as a password (Psalms 24:8), as David J. Larsen has very ably propounded.[948]

Psalms 24:3–4 records the question of the temple-goers: "Who shall ascend into the hill of the Lord?" The requirements are given: "He that hath clean hands and a pure heart [cf. 3 Nephi 12:8; Matthew 5:8], who hath not lifted up his soul unto vanity, nor sworn deceitfully."

Some scholars have suggested that the last clauses make reference to taking the Lord's name in vain, meaning performing actions in the Lord's name illegitimately.[949] Also, the reference to swearing likely signifies taking an oath in the Lord's name. The verse indicates that doing so "deceitfully" will bar the petitioner from ascending to the temple and seeing the face of God.

THE WHY

Comparing Psalm 24 with 3 Nephi 14:21–23 (cf. Matthew 7:21–23) helps clarify that Jesus was using the language of the temple in these verses, as He did throughout the Sermon on the Mount (and, more particularly, the Sermon at the Temple).[950] When Jesus pronounced these sayings regarding those who would say "Lord, Lord" in the hope of entering through the gates of the kingdom of God, He knew that His audience, being familiar with temple language and practices, would understand what He meant.

It appears that Jesus was, as was Hosea (Hosea 8:1–2), directing His comments toward those who officiated in the temple but who had fallen away from correct practice because they were acting in God's name illegitimately, perhaps because they had broken their covenants. This is likely the context in which Jesus saw the Jewish leadership, and perhaps some among the Book of Mormon peoples as well. They claimed to act with the authority of God, but in actuality were using His name in vain. In order to enter His kingdom, the use of His name alone, without the required righteousness and faithful covenant relationship, will not gain them access.

These verses testify that the Lord knows those who follow Him in righteousness. They are recognized by Him. They follow His way and do His Father's will and not their own. Those who use His name must depart from wickedness or, unfortunately, depart from Him. By choosing their own path, the wicked unavoidably depart from the Lord's path.

When followers of Christ follow His covenantal path faithfully, as taught in the Sermon on the Mount and at the Temple, then they will come to know Jesus Christ (see John 17:3) and will do the will of the Father; Christ will then covenantally know them and claim them as His own in His kingdom. Those who choose another path will have to depart, as they have already chosen a way that is not the one that leads to eternal life.

When Jesus says that He does not "know" these people, the problem is not that He doesn't know who they are or what they have done. Obviously, He knows them all too well. What is lacking is their being known to Him as sacred covenant makers, observers, and keepers.

FURTHER READING

David J. Larsen, "Ascending into the Hill of the Lord: What the Psalms Can Tell Us about the Rituals of the First Temple," in *Ancient Temple Worship: Proceedings of the Expound Symposium*, 14 May 2011, ed. Matthew B. Brown, et al. (Salt Lake City and Orem, UT: Eborn Books and The Interpreter Foundation, 2014), 171–188.

John W. Welch, *Illuminating the Sermon at the Temple and the Sermon on the Mount* (Provo, UT: FARMS, 1999).

What Makes 3 Nephi the Holy of Holies of the Book of Mormon?

"Enter ye in at the strait gate; for wide is the gate, and broad is the way, which leadeth to destruction, and many there be who go in thereat; Because strait is the gate, and narrow is the way, which leadeth unto life, and few there be that find it." (3 Nephi 14:13–14; Matthew 7:13–14)

THE KNOW

At the pinnacle of the history recorded in the Book of Mormon, readers find in 3 Nephi the story of the resurrected Jesus Christ, who descended from heaven to teach the people at the temple in Bountiful. The magnitude and sacred content of 3 Nephi 11–26 has brought John W. Welch to call it the "holy of holies" of the Book of Mormon.[951]

A careful analysis of the text reveals that it can be seen as a literary counterpart to the physical holy of holies of the ancient temple. The book depicts a temple setting where Jesus Christ descended from heaven to the temple in the Nephite city of Bountiful (see 3 Nephi 11). With the people gathered around, Christ taught them from that sacred edifice. His words were replete with temple-related terms and imagery, although these are not often noticed. Jesus both opened and closed His initial sermon speaking about building upon the rock, "evoking images of the temple and its eternal stability."[952]

At the temple, Jesus taught a version of the Sermon on the Mount, a set of teachings that contains many subtle references to the temple. Welch explained how the Sermon on the Mount (and 3 Nephi's "Sermon at the Temple") presents principles in a way that can be seen as an escalating path of ascent, leading adherents toward heaven.[953] Welch noted how the sermon begins on a mountain (compare the "mountain of the Lord's house," Isaiah 2:2) and ends by talking metaphorically "about the wise man who builds upon that mountain, by not only hearing but actually patterning his house of righteousness after God's holy house."

The culmination of the sermon is marked by the pronouncement of the words *enter*, an invitation to enter the kingdom of God, or, otherwise, *depart* (see 3 Nephi 14:21–23; Matthew 7:21–23).[954] The ultimate entrance requirement is found in the instruction, "Not everyone that saith unto me, Lord, Lord, shall enter into the kingdom of heaven; but he that doeth the will of my Father who is in heaven" (3 Nephi 14:21; Matthew 7:21). Regarding the significance of this final principle, Welch commented:

> If entrance into the presence of God is the end to which the Sermon on the Mount and the Sermon at the Temple both lead, readers should

> consider the profound connections between the heart of 3 Nephi and the inner sanctum of the temple.[955]

With this perspective in mind, one can make a comparison between the holy of holies of the ancient temple and the events recounted in the book of 3 Nephi (see table on page 191).[956]

THE WHY

Although the scriptural passages regarding the temple and the work of the high priest in the Old Testament can be somewhat obscure and are symbolic of future realities, the account of Christ's appearance at the temple in 3 Nephi is a living manifestation of those ancient symbols. Studying the Sermon at the Temple (or the Sermon on the Mount) from this perspective can give one a greater appreciation for the Sermon and also for the temple, both ancient and modern.

Many readers may not notice how much the Book of Mormon teaches about the temple and how central the temple, its precepts, and its ordinances are to the book's message. In the words of Welch:

> One of [the Book of Mormon's] precepts is clearly the centrality of the temple. The book of 3 Nephi lays forth a holy template for how one may dwell forever in the house of the Lord Jesus Christ, the Son of God and the great and eternal High Priest of all mankind.[957]

Reflecting his own attitude toward 3 Nephi, Welch explained, "When I go to the temple, I think of that as being my trip this month or week to Bountiful; what I experience at the temple is my opportunity to come as close as I can to what happened in 3 Nephi."[958]

For Latter-day Saints, going to the temple is a sacred experience; it offers an opportunity to step out of the world and into the presence of divinity. In ancient Israel, the Holy of Holies was a sacred space where the Lord dwelt; it was so sacred that only the high priest was permitted to enter. The sacred record in 3 Nephi invites all people to come unto Christ and be perfected in Him: "Therefore I would that ye should be perfect even as I, or your Father who is in heaven is perfect" (3 Nephi 12:48). Seeing 3 Nephi this way can help all people to envision coming into the holy presence of God.

When 3 Nephi is seen as the holy of holies, reading it becomes an opportunity for readers to disengage the world and to consecrate their lives to loving and serving the true and living God. We learn from its pages: "For where your treasure is, there will your heart be also. . . . No man can serve two masters; . . . Ye cannot serve God and Mammon. . . . Seek ye first the kingdom of God and his righteousness, and all these things shall be added unto you" (3 Nephi 13:21, 24, 33; Matthew 6:21, 24, 33).

FURTHER READING

John W. Welch, "Seeing Third Nephi as the Holy of Holies of the Book of Mormon," *Journal of the Book of Mormon and Other Restoration Scripture 19*, no. 1 (2010): 36–55; also published in *Third Nephi: An Incomparable Scripture*, ed. Andrew C. Skinner and Gaye Strathearn (Salt Lake City and Provo, UT: Deseret Book and Neal A. Maxwell Institute for Religious Scholarship, 2012), 1–33.

John W. Welch, *Illuminating the Sermon at the Temple and the Sermon on the Mount* (Provo, UT: FARMS, 1999).

Element	Holy of Holies	3 Nephi
Presence of God	The Lord would appear there (Leviticus 16:2)	Jesus appeared to the people at the temple (11:8–12)
Word of the Lord	God's word comes forth from his presence in the first person (Leviticus 26; Psalm 17:2; Isaiah 6:1)	Jesus spoke face-to-face in the first person to the people gathered at the temple (11:9–10)
High Priesthood	Only anointed high priests had access to Holy of Holies	Jesus ordained his disciples to higher priesthood (18:37; Moroni 2:1–3)
Covenant	Resting place of the ark of the covenant containing Ten Commandments	Jesus taught about the Ten Commandments and caused people to participate in covenants (18:10)
Shewbread	Priests ate the showbread, which represented manna, the bread from heaven	Christ gave disciples the sacrament, representing his body "shown" unto them (18:7)
The Divine Name	High Priest wore the name of the Lord on his forehead when he went in to the Holy of Holies (Exodus 28:36; cf. Numbers 6:27)	People took upon themselves the name of Christ when they partook of the sacrament (18:11; Moroni 4:3)
Purity	Participants needed to have "clean hands and a pure heart" (Psalm 24:3–4)	Jesus emphasized the need for purity/worthiness when participating in sacred ordinances (18:28–29)
Blessing	High Priest offered the priestly blessing (Numbers 6:24–26)	Jesus blessed the multitude and fulfilled the words of the priestly blessing (19:25)
White Garments	The High Priest wore white linen garments on the Day of Atonement (Leviticus 16:4)	Jesus wore exceedingly white garments (19:25)
Angels	Cherubim represented angels of the Lord's presence; Isaiah saw fiery seraphim (Isaiah 6:2, 6; cf. Psalm 104:4)	Angels appeared multiple times, "encircled about as if it were by fire" (19:14; 17:24; 27:30)

77

Why Is the Sermon at the Temple Echoed throughout the Rest of 3 Nephi?

"Blessed are the Gentiles, because of their belief." (3 Nephi 16:6)

THE KNOW

In 3 Nephi 12–14, Jesus gave the discourse known as the Sermon at the Temple.[959] However, as 3 Nephi continues forward, it becomes apparent that words and phrases from the sermon are scattered throughout the rest of the text.[960] One might initially wonder why these teachings and concepts are repeated throughout 3 Nephi. John W. Welch argued that the sermon is not quoted at random, but that the subsequent chapters in 3 Nephi were carefully crafted as a way to shed light on the sermon itself.[961]

For example, in 3 Nephi 16, Christ taught, "Blessed are the Gentiles, because of their belief" but warned, "wo, saith the Father, unto the unbelieving of the Gentiles" (3 Nephi 16:6, 8). He then stated that "if the Gentiles will repent and return [unto the Father], they shall be numbered among [the people of the house of Israel]" who shall not be allowed to "tread" the Gentiles down (3 Nephi 16:13–14). However, if the Gentiles reject the covenant, the house of Israel "shall tread them down, and they shall be as salt that hath lost its savor, which is thenceforth good for nothing but to be cast out, and to be trodden under foot of my people, O house of Israel" (3 Nephi 16:15).[962]

This assumes an awareness that Jesus's teaching that if His decisples did not live up to their role as the salt of the earth, they would be "trodden under foot by men" (3 Nephi 12:13) also applies to the Gentiles.[963] In this way, Jesus explained what is involved in and what it means for the "salt to lose its savor." He stated that when the Gentiles "reject the fulness of my gospel, and shall be lifted up in the pride of their hearts above all nations . . . and shall be filled with all manner of lyings, and of deceits, and of mischiefs, and all manner of hypocrisy, and murders, and priestcrafts, and whoredoms, and of secret abominations," that is when they would be "trodden under foot" (3 Nephi 16:10, 15).

It is clear that the repetition here of words from 3 Nephi 12–14 is not haphazard or coincidental. Indeed, 3 Nephi systematically repeats material from the Sermon at the Temple, but in reverse order:

1. If the salt shall lose its savor (12:13)
   2. Be the light unto men (12:14–16)
      3. Think not that I am come to destroy the law or the prophets (12:17)
         4. In me it hath all been fulfilled (12:18)
         4. The law is fulfilled (15:4–6, 8)

3. I do not destroy the prophets (15:6–7); keep the law and the prophets (15:9–10)
2. Ye are a light unto this remnant (15:12), as I fufill my covenant (15:13–16:14)
1. Those who will not turn to Christ will be as salt that has lost its savor (16:15)[964]

The same is true two chapters later, at the end of 3 Nephi 18:

1. No disputations (11:28), blessed are ye (12:1)
2. Let your light so shine (12:16)
3. Ask, and it shall be given (14:7)
4. Built upon a rock (14:24), not upon the sand (14:26)
4. Built upon my rock (18:12), not upon a sandy foundation (18:13)
3. Ask . . . it shall be given (18:20)
2. Hold up your light that it may shine (18:24)
1. Blessed are ye, no disputations (18:34).[965]

According to an ancient literary practice called Seidel's Law, elements in ancient texts were often repeated in reverse order as a way of demonstrating that the author was quoting from something else.[966] This is a textbook example of that style, showing that 3 Nephi consciously uses and explains the Sermon at the Temple.

THE WHY

The careful integration of the Sermon at the Temple throughout 3 Nephi provides a means of understanding seemingly obscure parts of the text, as noted above, but it does something else as well. Welch noted, "It may strike readers as . . . redundant for Jesus to have quoted himself so often, but in doing so he taught his people the central importance of this primary sermon, which was to be remembered and used with precision, in some cases 'nothing varying' from the words that Jesus himself had used (3 Nephi 19:8)."[967]

Through His quotations of these established doctrines, Jesus was "referring back to the fuller teachings that he had already given, precisely because those words had been accepted by these people by way of covenant (3 Nephi 18:10)."[968]

Christ's decision to deliver the sermon in a temple setting likely gave the sermon even more weight. "Thus, the reuse of these holy words by Jesus would have deeply impressed the Nephite audience, indelibly recommitting them to follow these teachings."[969] Ultimately, "the use of these materials throughout 3 Nephi supports the idea that the sermon was immediately accepted as scripture, no doubt the most sacred scripture these people had ever known."[970]

The appearance of the Sermon at the Temple so often in 3 Nephi is a witness of its importance. It was not just an interesting sermon Jesus gave before moving on to more important things; it was the core of His message. Far from being a sign of clumsy redundancy, these repetitions invite readers to connect and apply the Sermon more carefully and deliberately. But it is also an invitation to read all of 3 Nephi more carefully, allowing the words of Jesus in that book to explain the Sermon, in greater fullness, so that all readers may come to understand Jesus's "sermon of sermons" in all its purpose and power.

FURTHER READING

John W. Welch, "Echoes from the Sermon on the Mount," in *The Sermon on the Mount in Latter-day Scripture*, ed. Gaye Strathearn, Thomas A. Wayment, and Daniel L. Belnap (Salt Lake City and Provo, UT: Deseret Book and BYU Religious Studies Center, 2010), 312–340; reprinted as "Reusages of the Words of Christ," *Journal of Book of Mormon Studies and Other Restoration Scripture 22*, no. 1 (2013): 63–71.

Jeffrey R. Holland, *Christ and the New Covenant* (Salt Lake City, UT: Deseret Book, 1997), 249–275.

Robert J. Matthews, "Jesus the Savior in 3 Nephi," in *The Book of Mormon: 3 Nephi 8 Through 30, This Is My Gospel*, ed. Monte S. Nyman and Charles D. Tate Jr. (Provo, UT: BYU Religious Studies Center, 1993), 25–39.

Why Did Jesus Minister to the People One by One?

"And he took their little children, one by one, and blessed them, and prayed unto the Father for them." (3 Nephi 17:21)

THE KNOW

When Jesus ministered to individuals among the Jews, His blessings were often accompanied by acts of physical contact. For instance, "when He healed Peter's mother-in-law of a fever, Jesus '*touched* her hand.' . . . Jesus again 'put forth his hand, and *touched*' a man with leprosy to make him whole. . . . He *touched* the eyes of two blind men as He healed them. . . . He healed deafness and a speech impediment when He put His fingers 'into' a man's ears. . . . He 'put his hands upon' a blind man. . . . He healed a demoniac child when He 'took him by the hand and lifted him up' . . . [and He] healed Jarius' daughter when He 'took her by the hand' and raised her from the dead."[971]

Richard Holzapfel has explained:

> Third Nephi, sometimes referred to as the fifth Gospel in Latter-day Saint circles, describes Christ's post-Resurrection ministry to the Nephites in terms similar to those used in the four New Testament Gospels. It emphasizes the individual experiences of the Nephite people with the resurrected Messiah, noting their direct physical contact with as well as His laying on of hands as the symbolic act of transmitting authority and power.[972]

For example, when Christ first appeared to the people at the temple in the land of Bountiful, He invited them to feel His side, as well as His hands and feet, "and this they did do, going forth *one by one* until they had all gone forth" (3 Nephi 11:15; emphasis added). Later Jesus asked the people to bring forth any who were sick or afflicted, "and he did heal them *every one*" (3 Nephi 17:9; emphasis added). After this, Jesus prayed for the people and then "took their little children, *one by one*, and blessed them, and prayed unto the Father for them" (3 Nephi 17:21; emphasis added).

Jesus "touched with his hand the disciples whom he had chosen, *one by one*" and "gave them power to give the Holy Ghost" (3 Nephi 18:36–37; emphasis added). And in His parting blessing, Jesus "spake unto his disciples, *one by one*," asking them what they desired of Him after He went back to the Father (3 Nephi 28:1; emphasis added). The Savior's personal touch was a strong and memorable part of His presence and loving ministry.

Concerning Christ's pattern of intimately ministering to individuals, Holzapfel noted, "According to the Book of Mormon model, ministering often occurs 'one by one' as disciples come in contact with the Savior and with one another. In many cases a personal 'touch' is a symbolic means of transmitting God's love and power to an individual."[973]

The transmission of priesthood authority and the performance of priesthood ordinances are particularly symbolic of Christ's concern for individuals.[974] Paul the Apostle taught that every person must individually "work out your own salvation with fear and trembling" (Philippians 2:12). President Russell M. Nelson similarly affirmed, "Only as an individual can one be baptized and receive the Holy Ghost. Each of us is born individually; likewise, each of us is 'born again' individually."[975] It is thus through the ordinances of the priesthood, administered one by one to every child of God who is willing to accept them, that Jesus Christ is able to "draw all men unto [Him]" (3 Nephi 27:15).

THE WHY

John W. Welch has noted that "under the old law, entrance into the Holy of Holies and into the presence of the Lord was the unique privilege of the High Priest,"[976] which stands in sharp contrast to the individual immediacy of the Savior's contact with people in 3 Nephi. Jesus Christ's resurrected visitation to nearly "two thousand and five hundred souls" at the temple in Bountiful signified a dramatic expansion of the availability of His presence (3 Nephi 17:25).

Welch explained that the high priest's "privilege of entering into the presence of God foreshadowed or typified the same honor that will come to all of God's righteous children" and that Christ's Sermon at the Temple "extended the covenantal promise of this sacred privilege to all worthy men and women, who will stand someday in the literal presence of God."[977] Holzapfel similarly concluded, "As disciples of Jesus Christ, we should recognize that Jesus swept away the legalistic regulations of the Mosaic code and touched those who had been considered 'untouchable' under the law."[978]

Christ's visitation to the people in Bountiful thus sends a very personal message to every reader of the Book of Mormon: Jesus Christ is a living, resurrected, and glorified being, and He has made Himself personally available to all those who are willing to come fully unto Him. This pattern continues into the latter days, as the Lord has invited us to "seek the face of the Lord always" (D&C 101:38) and has promised, "the days will come that you shall see him; for he will unveil his face unto you, and it shall be in his own time, and in his own way, and according to his own will" (D&C 88:68; cf. 93:1). These invitations are evidence that in His own time and way, Christ will personally visit all who come unto Him.

Significantly, it was in the Holy of Holies of the temple or tabernacle that Jehovah had revealed His presence to the high priest in ancient Israel, just as it was at the temple that Jesus revealed Himself to the people at Bountiful. It was at the temple that He taught them and ministered unto them one by one, and it was at the temple that He administered sacred priesthood ordinances.

Temples continue to be sacred spaces where the Lord or His authorized servants personally and individually minister to God's children. President Howard W. Hunter taught, "Temples are sacred for the closest communion between the Lord and those receiving the highest and most sacred ordinances of the holy priesthood."[979] Concerning His temples in modern times, the Lord has declared, "my presence shall be there, for I will come into it, and all the pure in heart that shall come into it shall see God" (D&C 97:16).

Jesus Christ's pattern of ministering one by one to all of God's children—especially in the precincts of holy temples and through the ordinances of the holy priesthood—ultimately shows His boundless love for every individual. Concerning Christ's visitation to the Nephites, Hugh Nibley remarked, "He appears entirely to individuals. He always appears to individuals. That's what atonement is. He greets them one by one, he gives them the signs and tokens one by one, he converses with them one by one, he blesses the children one by one."[980] Elder Ronald A. Rasband concluded, "Certainly, there is a very profound and tender personal message here. Jesus Christ ministers to, and loves us all, one by one."[981]

FURTHER READING

David A. Bednar, "One by One," *New Era*, July 2016, 38–40.

John W. Welch, "Seeing Third Nephi as the Holy of Holies of the Book of Mormon," *Journal of the Book of Mormon and Other Restoration Scripture 19*, no. 1 (2010): 36–55.

Richard Neitzel Holzapfel, "One by One: The Fifth Gospel's Model of Service," in *A Book of Mormon Treasury: Gospel Insights from General Authorities and Religious Educators* (Provo, UT: BYU Religious Studies Center, 2003), 378–388.

Ronald A. Rasband, "One by One," *Ensign*, November 2000.

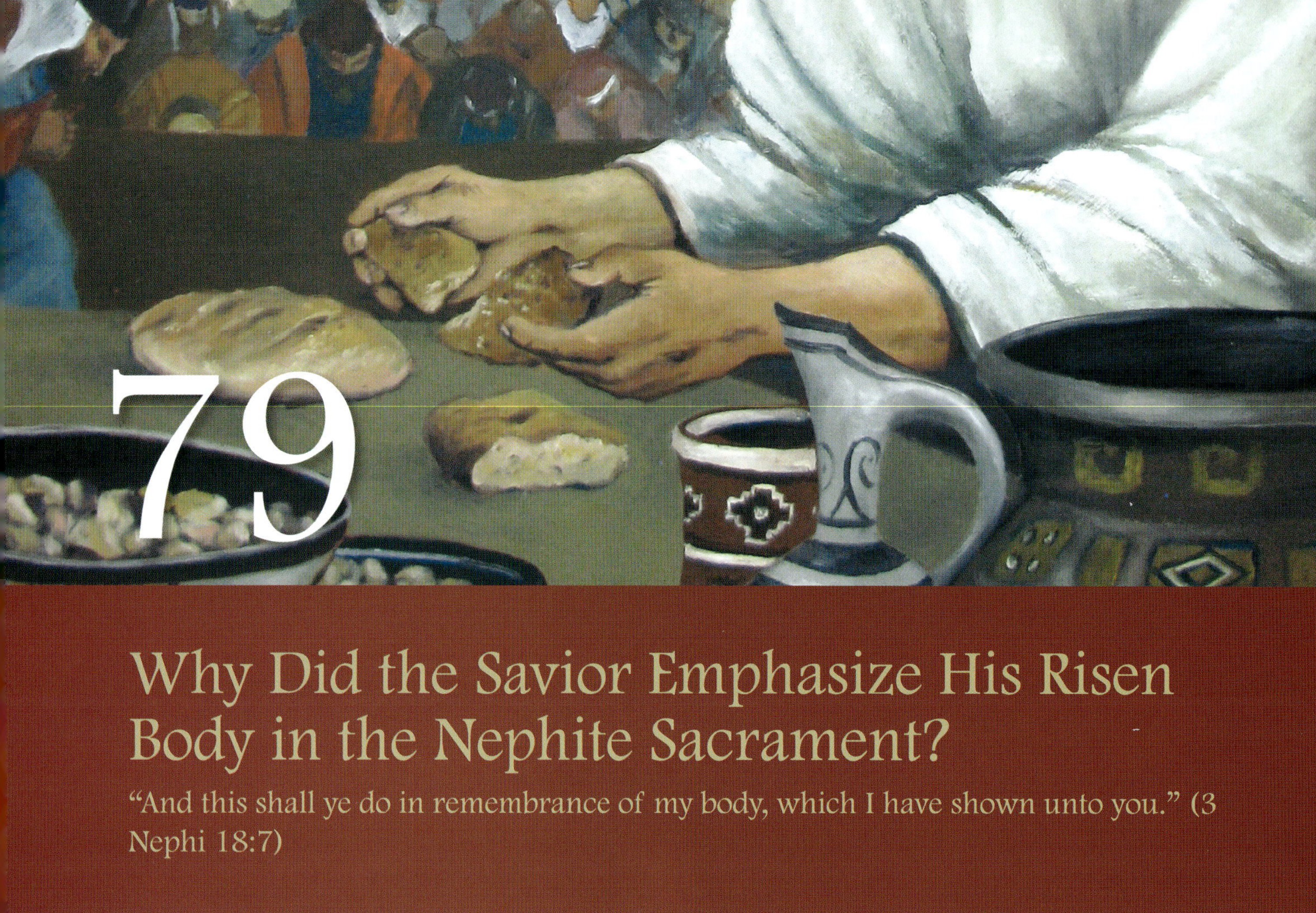

79

Why Did the Savior Emphasize His Risen Body in the Nephite Sacrament?

"And this shall ye do in remembrance of my body, which I have shown unto you." (3 Nephi 18:7)

THE KNOW

According to the Apostle Paul, when the Savior first administered the sacrament to His disciples in Judea, He took the broken bread and said, "Take, eat: this is my body, *which is broken for you*: this do in remembrance of me" (1 Corinthians 11:24; emphasis added). In his Gospel account, Luke used somewhat softer language: "This is my body *which is given for you*: this do in remembrance of me" (Luke 22:19; emphasis added).[982] Both, however, evoke the image of sacrifice. To the Old World disciples, the bread represented the body *given* and *broken* in sacrifice on their behalf.

In contrast, when the Lord first administered the sacrament to the Nephites, He instructed, "this shall ye do in remembrance of my body, *which I have shown unto you*" (3 Nephi 18:7; emphasis added). The body *shown* unto the Nephites was not the broken, sacrificed, mortal body of Jesus, but rather it was the resurrected, glorified body of the risen Lord. As John W. Welch noted, "when we partake of the bread, we should remember that we eat not only in remembrance of the body that has been broken for us—that's the New Testament language" but also "in remembrance of the physical, tangible body" with which the Nephites had direct, physical experience.[983]

Here the Savior was calling the Nephites to remember His physical and painful sacrifice as well as His triumphant resurrection. As S. Kent Brown pointed out, "his body, of course, is the first thing he allows people access to," but this access was "to touch the scars in his hands and his feet and his side,"[984] all of which were physical reminders that His glorious body had been broken and sacrificed.

Furthermore, it seems that the Savior drew on the Nephites' cultural background in order to make the moment as memorable and impactful as possible. As Mark Wright noted, "He bade them first to thrust their hands into his side, and secondarily to feel the prints in his hands and feet (3 Nephi 11:14)." In contrast, when appearing to His Apostles in the Old World after His Resurrection, "he invited them to touch solely his hands and feet (Luke 24:39–40)."[985] While this subtle detail may seem trivial, Wright explained that in Mesoamerican cultures, humans were sacrificed by having their hearts removed while alive, through "a large incision directly below the ribcage."[986]

Thus, Wright explained, "To a people steeped in Mesoamerican culture, the sign that a person had been ritually sacrificed would have been an incision on their side—suggesting they had had their hearts removed."[987] While righteous Nephites themselves would not have participated in human sacrifice, its prevalence within surrounding cultures could well have had some effect on their processing of this amazing experience.[988]

Hence, Wright reasoned that by inviting the Nephites to first "thrust your hands into my side" (3 Nephi 11:14), Christ "may have been communicating with them according to their cultural language."[989] When being asked to remember the body shown to them, surely the Nephites couldn't help but recall this vivid experience as they touched the tangible tokens that Jesus's resurrected body still bore as a result of His infinite atoning sacrifice.

THE WHY

The Savior's invitation to the Nephites to remember the body they were shown is another instance where He subtly yet appropriately adapted His instructions to reflect unique aspects of the Nephite experience. This adaption began at the very moment He showed His body to them—with the invitation to first feel the wound on His side thereby personalizing and maximizing the impact of their experience with His resurrected body.[990]

Perhaps as they thrust their hand into the Savior's side, some Nephites remembered the words of Amulek, who taught the Atonement would "bring about the bowels of mercy, which overpowereth justice, and bringeth about means unto men that they may have faith unto repentance" (Alma 34:15).[991] For followers of Christ today, the wound on Christ's side, emphasized in 3 Nephi 11, can serve as a reminder that, as Elder D. Todd Christofferson taught, "bring[ing] about the bowels of mercy" was "the intent of Christ's suffering—the ultimate manifestation of His love."[992]

For Latter-day Saints today, the Savior's administration of the sacrament to the Nephites is the ultimate source of the sacrament prayers heard each Sunday.[993] Thus, when partaking of the bread and water each week, "we celebrate the sacrament, not only of the Lord's supper, but also of the Lord's appearance in 3 Nephi."[994] Book of Mormon readers, therefore, have the privilege of remembering not only the broken, sacrificed body, but also the victorious, risen body shown to the people at Bountiful.

The call to remember the body shown also evokes the Nephites as witnesses of the Resurrection. It was a physical, tangible body—which they had felt and experienced, one by one.[995] He had not laid the body down after His ascension, as some Christians believe (cf. 3 Nephi 15:1). Thus, 3 Nephi provides a scriptural witness that Jesus retained His physical body. Welch noted, "Now that's incomparable, and there are a lot of things like that in 3 Nephi that we only get from 3 Nephi."[996]

FURTHER READING

Daniel C. Peterson, John W. Welch, Robert L. Millet, Richard Dilworth Rust, Grant Hardy, and S. Kent Brown, "3 Nephi Conference Panel Discussion," in *Third Nephi: An Incomparable Scripture*, ed. Andrew C. Skinner and Gaye Strathearn (Salt Lake City and Provo, UT: Deseret Book and Neal A. Maxwell Institute for Religious Scholarship, 2012), 373–391.

John W. Welch, "Our Nephite Sacrament Prayers," in *Reexploring the Book of Mormon: A New Decade of Research*, ed. John W. Welch (Salt Lake City and Provo, UT: Deseret Book and FARMS, 1992), 286–289.

Why Did Jesus Allude to the Priestly Blessing in Numbers 6?

"And it came to pass that Jesus blessed them as they did pray unto him; and his countenance did smile upon them, and the light of his countenance did shine upon them." (3 Nephi 19:25)

THE KNOW

In 3 Nephi 19, the record recounts a remarkable experience that the people had with Jesus Christ as He prayed with and blessed them. The description of what Jesus did when He blessed those gathered parallels certain words in the "priestly blessing" that God commanded Aaron, the high priest, to pronounce upon the people of Israel in Numbers 6:23–27. In a very literal sense, Jesus fulfilled the petition of the traditional priestly blessing.

The passage in Numbers 6:23–27 features the Lord directing Moses to have his brother Aaron, the high priest, "bless the children of Israel" using the following words:

> The Lord bless thee, and keep thee:
> The Lord make his face shine upon thee, and be gracious unto thee:
> The Lord lift up his countenance upon thee, and give thee peace. (Numbers 6:24–26)

As part of the giving of this blessing, the Lord also declared that "they shall put my name upon the children of Israel" (Numbers 6:27).

This blessing was an important part of the religious practices of ancient Israel and is still a key ritual in modern Judaism. Its significance can be seen through the many biblical passages that borrow from its language, especially in mentions of the Lord lifting up the light of His countenance.[997] Furthermore, archaeological digs in Jerusalem have uncovered the priestly blessing written on small, rolled-up sheets of silver placed in amulets dating from the late seventh century BC (the oldest portion of scripture ever discovered).[998] These finds attest to the antiquity and popularity of the blessing's use.[999]

Anciently, the priestly blessing was performed on the Day of Atonement, following the sacrifices realized on that day. Matthew J. Grey noted that the ritual included "a communal prayer, a priestly prayer of intercession, and the priest raising his hands above his head to bless the congregation."[1000]

There are many similarities between the ancient Israelite practice of the priestly blessing and what Christ did and said among the Book of Mormon people in 3 Nephi 19. There, as Grey noted:

> The resurrected Jesus appears to a Nephite congregation assembled at the temple, has them kneel in communal

> prayer, offers his own intercessory prayer to the Father on their behalf, and returns to "bless them," thus allowing the congregation to experience the full spiritual reality in ritual-communion with God through the intercession of Jesus, the Great High Priest.[1001]

3 Nephi 19:25 recounts that Jesus blessed them and "his countenance did smile upon them, and the light of his countenance did shine upon them." This follows much of Numbers 6:25–26 very closely ("The Lord make his face shine upon thee . . . The Lord lift up his countenance upon thee"). Significantly, some modern translations of Numbers 6 have the pentitioner asking "may the Lord smile on you,"[1002] just as Jesus's "countenance did smile" upon the Nephites.

The expression "let his face shine" is "a Hebrew idiom for 'smile.'"[1003] Additionally, biblical scholar M. I. Gruber has explained that the phrase in verse 26, "lift up his countenance," should be rendered idiomatically as "smile."[1004] With this in mind, we can see Jesus's performance of the priestly blessing in 3 Nephi 19, in which His countenance smiles upon the people, as a very appropriate expression of the Hebrew meaning behind our modern English translations of Numbers 6:25–26.

The transfiguration of the audience's faces and clothing after Jesus's blessing is also worth mentioning. 3 Nephi 19:25 states that "they were as white as the countenance and also the garments of Jesus," whereas, presumably, they were not so previously. Although neither a transfiguration of this sort nor white clothing are mentioned in connection with the blessing in Numbers 6, these things are often part of scriptural accounts of persons who have met the Lord face-to-face.

For example, after Moses spoke with the Lord on Mount Sinai, his face shone so brightly that he had to wear a veil when he returned to speak with the children of Israel (see Exodus 34:32–35). Although Exodus 33:23 inexplicably indicates otherwise, Exodus 33:11 declares that "the Lord spake unto Moses face to face, as a man speaketh unto his friend." Similarly, when Jesus spoke to the Father on the so-called Mount of Transfiguration, He was transfigured so that "his face did shine as the sun, and his raiment was white as the light" (Matthew 17:2). Such a transfiguration seems to be a feature of face-to-face encounters with Deity.

THE WHY

3 Nephi 19 contains the incredible account of Jesus praying with and for the Book of Mormon people and blessing them in a miraculous manner. As He blessed them, Jesus followed what the "priestly blessing" of Numbers 6:23–27 says that the Israelite high priest was supposed to ask for as he blessed the children of Israel.

The high priest was to bless them that the Lord would make His face "shine" upon them, that He would "lift up" His face upon them. Both of these expressions can be understood to mean that God would show His divine approval toward His covenant people, or that He would "smile" upon them, as Jesus did to the people gathered at the temple in Bountiful. Jesus was acting then as the great High Priest (see Hebrews 4:14–16), come to bless this remnant of the house of Israel.

The fact that Jesus would come to these people, bless them, and smile upon them is evidence that the Lord remembers all of His people and that He keeps His covenants to bless them. Jesus truly fulfilled the words of the blessing, as He was "gracious" unto them and gave them "peace" (as promised in Numbers 6:25–26).

The efficaciousness of Jesus's blessing can be seen in the fact that all present were transfigured in His presence to the point that they temporarily became like Him in appearance and were "purified" as He is pure (3 Nephi 19:28). This act was yet another testament to the people that Christ truly loved and cared for them.

This scriptural account is a testimony to modern readers of one of the Book of Mormon's explicitly stated purposes: that it will make known to the house of Israel "the covenants of the Lord, that they are not cast off forever" (Book of Mormon, Title Page).

FURTHER READING

Dana M. Pike, "Israelite Inscriptions from the Time of Lehi," in *Glimpses of Lehi's Jerusalem,* ed. John W. Welch, David Rolph Seely, and Jo Ann H. Seely (Provo, UT: FARMS, 2004), 213–215.

William J. Adams Jr., "Lehi's Jerusalem and Writing on Silver Plates," in *Pressing Forward with the Book of Mormon: The FARMS Updates of the 1990s,* ed. John W. Welch and Melvin J. Thorne (Provo, UT: FARMS, 1999), 23–26.

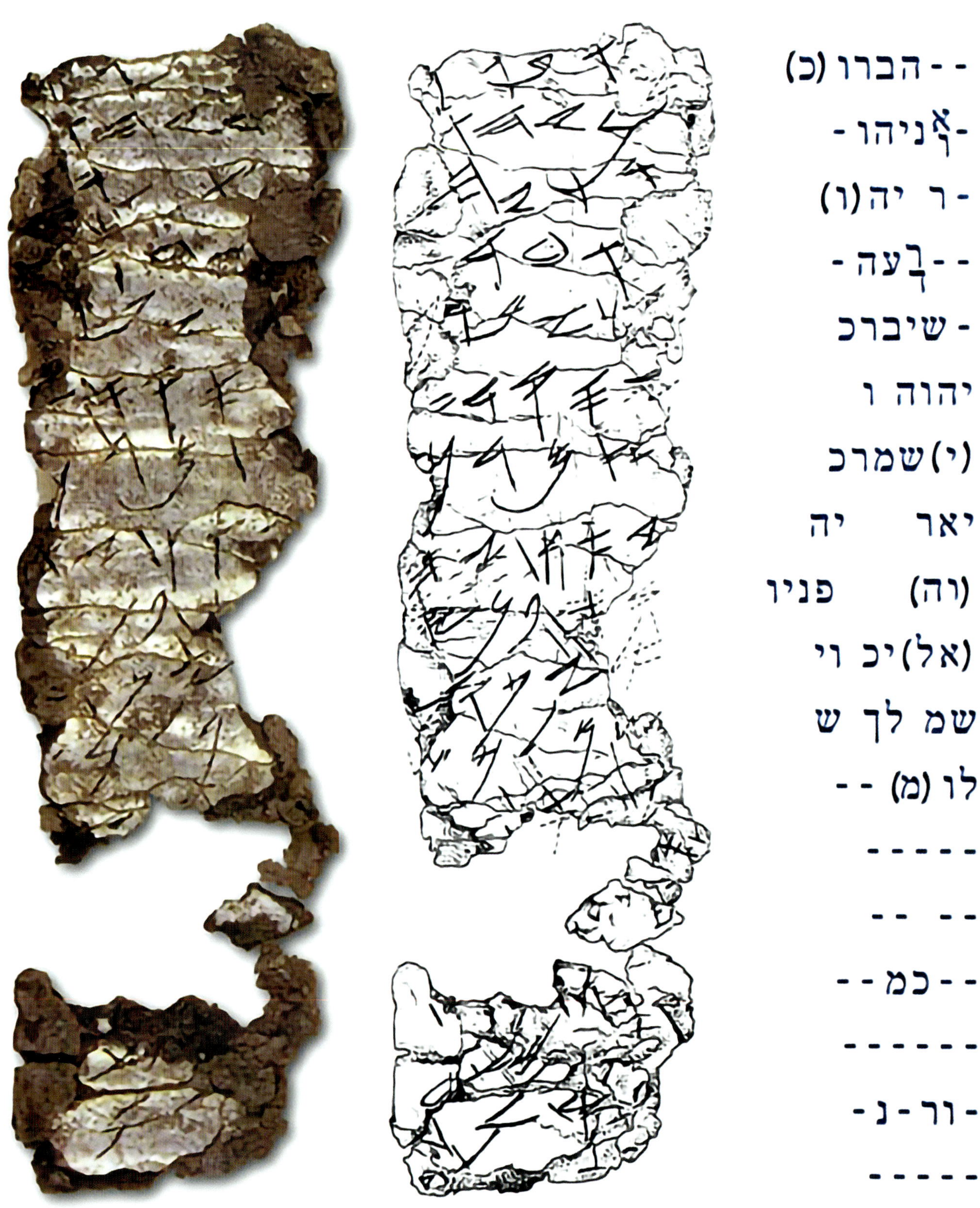
- - הברו(כ)
-אניהו -
-ר יה(ו)
- -בעה -
-שיברכ
יהוה ו
(י)שמרכ
יאר יה
(וה) פניו
(אל)יכ וי
שמ לך ש
לו(מ) - -
- - - - -
- - - -
- -כמ - -
- - - - - -
-ור-נ-
- - - - -

81

Why Is 3 Nephi Important for Understanding the Godhead?

"Father, I pray unto thee for them, and also for all those who shall believe on their words, that they may believe in me, that I may be in them as thou, Father, art in me, that we may be one." (3 Nephi 19:23)

THE KNOW

For nearly two millennia, Christians across the world have wrestled with the exact nature of God the Father and the Lord Jesus Christ—struggling to understand and articulate both Their oneness and Their individuality.[1005] On the other hand, Latter-day Saints—starting with Joseph Smith—have maintained that They are two separate, individual divine Beings who are one in purpose.[1006]

While this doctrine is commonly traced back to the First Vision today, no direct historical documentation has survived of Joseph Smith specifically using that manifestation as he taught about the Godhead,[1007] although he may well have done so. A number of other places in scripture also articulate clearly the separate personages of the Father and the Son.[1008] Latter-day Saint theologian Blake Ostler explained, "the Book of Mormon and Mormon scriptures have always carefully balanced the unity with the distinctness of the divine persons."[1009]

Ostler's statement is especially true of 3 Nephi. During His visit among the Nephite peoples, the Savior frequently made reference to His Father, described His relationship with Him, and is depicted as praying to and otherwise interacting with the Father. As a result, 3 Nephi provides some of the clearest descriptions of the relationship between the Father and the Son.

Theologians David L. Paulsen and Ari D. Bruening have identified five different ways 3 Nephi depicts the Father and the Son as separate, individual beings (see table on p. 202).[1010]

While several passages in 3 Nephi speak of the oneness of the Father and the Son (see 3 Nephi 11:27, 36; 20:35; 28:10), Jesus clarified the nature of this oneness when He prayed with His disciples. He prayed that His disciples may be one with Him just as He and the Father are one (see 3 Nephi 19:23, 29; cf. John 17:11, 21–23).

Paulsen and Bruening thus concluded, "3 Nephi contains extensive and persuasive evidence that Jesus Christ and His Father are distinct persons." They also conclude that 3 Nephi "provides strong evidence that the Father and Son are one" only "in a social . . . sense, involving two persons," and that "the analogy for oneness appears to be . . . that of purification, alignment, and divine in dwelling within a community."[1011]

Paulsen and Bruening feel that these conclusions can be extended to the rest of the Book of Mormon.[1012] Still, they wisely cautioned, "we should not assume that every prophet-writer shares the same idea of

Ways Father and Son Are Differentiated in 3 Nephi	
1. Christ Speaking of God as "My Father"	3 Nephi 14:21; 27:16; 28:10
2. Christ Praying to the Father	3 Nephi 17:14; 19:19–20
3. Christ Obeying the Father	3 Nephi 15:14; 16:16
4. Christ's Ascension to the Father	3 Nephi 15:1; 17:4; 18:27; 26:15
5. Other Ways Father and Son Are Distinguished	3 Nephi 11:35; 15:24; 16:6; 20:26

God's oneness" and may even need to admit that some Book of Mormon "prophets . . . did not have as full an understanding of the Godhead" prior to Christ's coming among them.[1013] This is especially true since Nephite conceptions of Deity—like the Israelites, and later the Jews and Christians—were likely shaped in some ways by broader cultural concepts.[1014]

THE WHY

All of this helps explain why 3 Nephi's witness about the members of the Godhead is so important. Instead of getting potentially limited and culturally influenced understandings of different prophets, "3 Nephi is the most relevant because it recounts the resurrected Christ's interactions with God the Father and includes Christ's own explicit teachings about his relationship to God the Father," and also "contains the personal teachings of the Son regarding himself."[1015]

Understanding the Godhead is no trivial matter. In a discourse given toward the end of his life, the Prophet Joseph Smith taught, "It is necessary for us to have an understanding of God."[1016] The greatest understanding of God comes from Deity Himself. Joseph Smith had personal encounters with both the Father and the Son on multiple occasions throughout his life. For most Latter-day Saints and other readers of the Book of Mormon today, 3 Nephi offers the most direct witness from the Lord Himself regarding His own nature, His Father's nature, and their relationship.

From the Savior Himself in 3 Nephi comes the powerful, unmistakable witness that He and His Father are two separate, individual beings perfectly united with each other and the Holy Ghost in purpose, purity, and love.

FURTHER READING

David L. Paulsen and Ari D. Bruening, "The Social Model of the Trinity in 3 Nephi," in *Third Nephi: An Incomparable Scripture,* ed. Andrew C. Skinner and Gaye Strathearn (Salt Lake City and Provo, UT: Deseret Book and Neal A. Maxwell Institute for Religious Scholarship, 2012), 191–233.

Blake T. Ostler, *Of God and Gods, Exploring Mormon Thought*, vol. 3 (Salt Lake City, UT: Greg Kofford Books, 2008), 257–320.

Ari B. Bruening and David L. Paulsen, "The Development of the Mormon Understanding of God: Early Mormon Modalism and Other Myths," *FARMS Review of Books 13*, no. 2 (2001): 109–169.

82

Why Did Jesus Mix Micah and Isaiah?

"And behold, ye are the children of the prophets; and ye are of the house of Israel; and ye are of the covenant which the Father made with your fathers, saying unto Abraham: And in thy seed shall all the kindreds of the earth be blessed." (3 Nephi 20:25)

THE KNOW

On His second day among the Nephites, reported in 3 Nephi 20:10–23:5, Jesus quoted extensively from Micah and Isaiah, so much so that exactly half of the verses in Jesus's speech come from these prophets.[1017] These quotations often make the sermon difficult to follow.[1018] Yet these quotations stress the importance of covenants, which was exactly the principle Christ was teaching in what Victor Ludlow has called "the Father's Covenant People Sermon."[1019]

This assertion is borne out by the repetition of specific words and phrases.[1020] For example, in these two chapters alone, the word *covenant* appears sixteen times, *the Father* appears thirty-nine times, and *the people* appears thirty-five times, indicating that the discourse revolves emphatically around the Father's covenant with His people, the house of Israel.[1021]

Jesus began the speech by mentioning that part of God fulfilling His covenant with Israel would be that Israel would be gathered and the descendants of Lehi would receive their inheritance in the Americas (see 3 Nephi 20:12–14). Jesus quoted from Micah 5:8–9 and 4:12–13 to explain the destruction that the covenant people will bring upon the Gentiles who reject that covenant (see 3 Nephi 20:15–20).[1022] He emphasizes that establishing His people in the New World was one way in which God would fulfill His covenant with Abraham and Jacob. God would bless the whole world, including the Gentiles, through His covenant people (see 3 Nephi 20:21–29).

Christ used Isaiah 52:1–3, 6–15 in the same way. Christ said that when the people of the Old World accept Him and His new covenant, He will "give unto them Jerusalem for the land of their inheritance" (3 Nephi 20:33). Christ will bless them with the blessings of the covenant by freeing Jerusalem from slavery or "redeeming it."[1023] Christ will do this by "making bare his holy arm," or fighting for Jerusalem, such that the entire earth will know that God has brought salvation to His people, living up to His end of the covenant (3 Nephi 20:34–35).[1024] Those who are not part of the covenant, who are metaphorically referred to as "the uncircumcised," will not be able to enter Jerusalem (3 Nephi 20:36).[1025] Christ will fulfill His covenant to free the people from the symbolic slavery they have labored under, and Jehovah will be their king (see 3 Nephi 20:37–40).[1026]

His people will restore the temple, complete with its "vessels," and the "covenant which the Father hath covenanted with his people [will] be fulfilled" (3 Nephi

20:41–46).[1027] The Gentiles will then become part of the covenant, allowing them to bring the gospel to the descendants of Lehi, thus fulfilling the covenant with them as well (see 3 Nephi 21:1–7). Christ quoted Isaiah 52 to emphasize the work His servant will do to bring the covenant to the Gentiles (see 3 Nephi 21:8, 10). The Savior concluded by commenting on Micah 5:8–15, showing the devastation that would fall on those Gentiles if they reject the covenant (see 3 Nephi 21:12–22).[1028]

Even the structure of the speech connects it to covenants. This speech, like many others in the Book of Mormon, is chiastic,[1029] and in chiasms, the center point is often the most important.[1030] The central point of this sermon is the sign of God's covenant with His people, the coming forth of the Book of Mormon. This signifies that God's covenant with His people is the main point of the speech. This structure and the centrality of covenants begins to make sense of the seemingly choppy use of Micah and Isaiah (see table on p. 205).

THE WHY

As Christ concluded this instructive speech, He spoke about something that applies directly to people living in the world today. He explained that if the Gentiles joined the covenant, they would assist in the gathering of Israel, allowing God's covenant to be fulfilled (see 3 Nephi 21:22–29).[1031]

In 3 Nephi 22:1–23:5, Christ then quoted Isaiah 54 to reassure His people of the everlasting nature of His covenant with them and to speak warmly of the many blessings that will be given to covenant keepers. He reminded them that "the mountains shall depart and the hills be removed, but my kindness shall not depart from thee, neither shall the covenant of my peace be removed" (3 Nephi 22:10).

For some, Christ's covenants with His people in the Old Testament and Book of Mormon may seem buried in the remote past, with little application to people today. However, Christ reminded His people that His covenants are eternal, and that the Gentiles of the latter days would actively participate in those covenants.

3 Nephi 20–22 persuasively illustrates that covenants are central to God's dealings with His people in all periods of time. Even after all that the Nephites had done, Christ reminded His people that He had never forgotten the covenants He made with them, and that He never would. The center point of Jesus's words on this occasion speak of the coming forth of the Book of Mormon in these the latter days as a sign that God has again set His hand to honor and fulfill the covenants He made with His covenant people in past dispensations.

As Jesus introduced Himself to the people gathered at the temple in Bountiful, He said, "Behold, I am Jesus Christ, whom the prophets testified shall come into the world" (3 Nephi 11:10). He drew significantly and purposefully from the prophetic writings of Micah and Isaiah, Israelite prophets who lived about a hundred years before the time of Lehi. Jesus used those prophecies to show the Nephites that some of these prophecies remained yet to be fulfilled. He expounded and contextualized these prophecies clearly and brilliantly, assuring these people that He, His Father, and His covenant people would work together to bring to pass the Father's glorious work.

The Book of Mormon reminds all who read it of the reliability of God. The Nephites certainly knew that mortals fail.[1032] Governments come and go, people are sometimes "quick to do iniquity, and . . . slow to do good" (Helaman 12:4). But the righteous Nephites knew with assurance that they could always rely on Christ to keep His covenants with them, even when all else failed. Modern readers can confidently take the same solace from the Book of Mormon. No matter how long ago Christ made these covenants with His people, they still apply to people today. Christ always kept His covenants with the Nephites, and He will always keep His covenants with those of the new and everlasting covenant today.

FURTHER READING

Victor L. Ludlow, "The Father's Covenant People Sermon: 3 Nephi 20:10–23:5," in *Third Nephi: An Incomparable Scripture*, ed. Andrew C. Skinner and Gaye Strathearn (Salt Lake City and Provo. UT: Deseret Book and Neal A. Maxwell Institute for Religious Scholarship, 2012), 147–174.

Joseph Fielding McConkie, "The Doctrine of a Covenant People," in *The Book of Mormon: 3 Nephi 8 Through 30, This is My Gospel*, ed. Monte S. Nyman and Charles D. Tate Jr. (Provo, UT: BYU Religious Studies Center, 1993), 357–377.

A The Father and Son work together (3 Nephi 20:10)

B Isaiah's words are written, therefore search them (v. 11)

C Isaiah's words and the Father's covenant with Israel will be fulfilled (v. 12)

D Scattered Israel to be gathered (v. 13)

E America an inheritance for the Nephites/Lamanites (v. 14)

F Gentiles to repent & receive blessings (v. 15–20; cf. Micah 5:8–9; 4:12–13)

G A New Jerusalem and the Lord's covenant with Moses, the Gentiles, etc. (v. 21–29)

H Gospel preached and Zion established; the marred servant (v. 30–44; cf. Isaiah 52:1–14)

I Kings shall be speechless (v. 45; cf. Isaiah 52:15)

J Covenant fulfillment and the work of the Father (v. 46)

K A key sign to be given when things are "about to take place" (3 Nephi 21:1)

L Gentiles learn of scattered Israel (v. 2)

M These things in the Book of Mormon to come from Gentiles to you (Lamanites/Nephites) (v. 3)

N Sign of the Father's covenant with the house of Israel (v. 4)

M' These works in the Book of Mormon to come from Gentiles to you (Lamanites/Nephites) (v.5)

L' Some Gentiles to be with Israel (v. 6)

K' Sign as Lamanites begin to know that the work "hath commenced" (v. 7)

J' Work and covenant of the Father (v. 7)

I' Kings shall be speechless (v. 8; cf. Isaiah 52:15)

H' A great and marvelous work; the marred servant (v. 9–10; cf. Isaiah 52:14)

G' Moses, the Gentiles and covenant Israel (v. 11)

F' Unrepentant Gentiles will be cut down (v. 12–21; cf. Micah 5:8–15)

E' America an inheritance for the righteous (v. 22–23)

D' Gentiles to help in the gathering of Israel and a New Jerusalem (v. 24–25)

C' Father's work with his people (v. 26–27)

A' The Father and Son work together (v. 28–29)

B' Isaiah's portrayal of Zion (Isaiah 54); search his words. (3 Nephi 22; 23:1–3)

83

Who Is the Servant Spoken of by Christ?

"But behold, the life of my servant shall be in my hand; therefore they shall not hurt him, although he shall be marred because of them." (3 Nephi 21:10)

THE KNOW

On His second day of visiting the people at Bountiful, Jesus Christ prophesied, "But behold, the life of my servant shall be in my hand; therefore they shall not hurt him, although he shall be marred because of them" (3 Nephi 21:10). The servant spoken of in this passage relates to four poems—known to biblical scholars as the "servant songs"—that are found in the book of Isaiah.[1033] Similar to 3 Nephi 21:10, the introduction to Isaiah's fourth servant song speaks of a servant whose "visage was so marred more than any man" (Isaiah 52:14).

The servant in these poems "has variously been interpreted as referring to corporate Israel, a historical figure such as the prophet Isaiah, a royal servant, a priestly servant, or a second Moses."[1034] Latter-day Saints have typically understood the servant as a reference to Jesus Christ or Joseph Smith.[1035] Some scholars have even proposed that "the servant can refer to both Israel and a number of individuals who have suffered and been persecuted while engaged in God's work."[1036]

In addition to these interpretations, Gaye Strathearn and Jacob Moody have suggested that the servant mentioned in 3 Nephi 21:10 can be meaningfully interpreted as the Book of Mormon itself. They argued that Christ's reference to the servant should be seen as part of a "single thematic unit, structured in a chiastic pattern and centering on the writings of Isaiah."[1037] This literary unit focuses on the gathering of Israel, and at "the very heart of [its] chiastic structure" Jesus Christ described the coming forth of the Book of Mormon as a sign of the gathering.[1038]

Strathearn and Moody proposed that in this context Jesus made "three deliberate statements that show his discussion of the Book of Mormon is in fact linked to the servant prophecy in the previous chapter."[1039]

The Servant Will Cause Astonishment

In the first, Jesus quoted Isaiah 52:15, which depicts rulers being astonished at the servant's message, "for that which had not been told them shall they see; and that which they had not heard shall they consider" (Isaiah 52:15). Christ then immediately added a latter-day prophecy about the Book of Mormon, wherein the Father would provide a "great and a marvelous work" among the people that some would not believe, "although a man shall declare it unto them" (3 Nephi 21:9).[1040]

The Servant Will Be in My Hand

In His second statement, found in 3 Nephi 21:10, Jesus explicitly mentioned that the "life of my servant shall be in my hand." This not only parallels the words *my servant* found in Isaiah 52:13, but it also thematically corresponds to Isaiah 53, which demonstrates that the Lord was aware of and perhaps able to remove the servant's suffering, if He so desired (see Isaiah 53:10–11). Similarly, the Book of Mormon will come forth "out of the earth . . . by the hand of the Lord, and none can stay it" (Mormon 8:26).[1041]

The Servant Will Be Marred

Christ's third statement declared that "they shall not hurt" the servant "although he shall be marred because of them" (3 Nephi 21:10), just as Isaiah prophesied "his visage was so marred more than any man" (Isaiah 52:14). Even though the Book of Mormon has been repeatedly maligned by critics—metaphorically marring its appearance—the text's influence, according to Strathearn and Moody, "continues to increase throughout the world."[1042]

Immediately following this statement, the Lord declared, "I will show unto them that my wisdom is greater than the cunning of the devil" (3 Nephi 21:10). Interestingly, in a context directly dealing with the Book of Mormon, this phrase is quoted verbatim in Doctrine and Covenants 10, thus adding even further evidence for a correlation.[1043]

Strathearn and Moody suggested that in identifying the servant in Isaiah with the Book of Mormon, Jesus was "using a literary device called personification, which applies human attributes to inanimate objects."[1044] This interpretation is not without merit, for in many ways the Book of Mormon can be seen as a type or symbol of Jesus Christ.

Richard Rust, for example, concluded, "As with the fruit of the tree of life, the Book of Mormon itself is considered of great worth. Indeed, as the word of God, it figures Christ the Word. It is also a treasure, typifying Christ 'in whom are hid all the treasures of wisdom and knowledge.'"[1045] Todd Parker similarly described the coming forth of the Book of Mormon as "a typification, or a shadow, or a symbol, of the coming of Christ."[1046]

Following a chart developed by Robert Norman, Parker noted a series of similarities between Christ and the Book of Mormon. For instance, the coming forth of both Jesus Christ and the Book of Mormon was heralded by an angel. Both "came forth in a time of apostasy to restore truth." Both were buried "in a stone receptacle." Both came forth after "a stone was moved away." An angel was sent to both to oversee their "coming forth from the tomb." The first person to see both of them were "forbidden to touch them." And the truthfulness of both were proclaimed by "twelve special witnesses."[1047]

THE WHY

While theirs is not the only valid understanding of this text, Strathearn and Moody's interpretation of 3 Nephi 21:10 certainly provides a rich and meaningful contribution.[1048] Recognizing that the Book of Mormon acts as a servant of the Lord amplifies the truth that it literally embodies the words of Christ (see 2 Nephi 33:10–11). Concerning the coming forth of the Book of Mormon, the Lord declared, "he that believeth not my words believeth not my disciples" (Ether 4:10) and similarly "he that will not believe my words will not believe me—that I am" (Ether 4:12; cf. 3 Nephi 28:34).

Like Jesus Christ and Joseph Smith and so many other servants of the Lord, the Book of Mormon has been largely rejected, persecuted, and, in a sense, marred by the world. And yet, like all servants who are persecuted for His sake, the Lord's hand upholds and supports the Book of Mormon so that it will ultimately withstand its enemies (see 3 Nephi 12:11; cf. Matthew 5:11). Elder Jeffrey R. Holland declared:

> For 179 years this book has been examined and attacked, denied and deconstructed, targeted and torn apart like perhaps no other book in modern religious history—perhaps like no other book in any religious history. And still it stands. . . . I testify that one cannot come to full faith in this latter-day work—and thereby find the fullest measure of peace and comfort in these, our times—until he or she embraces the divinity of the Book of Mormon and the Lord Jesus Christ, of whom it testifies.[1049]

Having been written at the command of Jesus Christ by servants of Jesus Christ, the Book of Mormon aptly functions as composite "servant" to convey the words of Christ. Concerning the authority of His servants to proclaim His words, the Lord has declared "whether by mine own voice or by the voice of my servants, it is the same" (D&C 1:38).

FURTHER READING

Gaye Strathearn and Jacob Moody, "Christ's Interpretation of Isaiah 52's 'My Servant' in 3 Nephi," *Journal of the Book of Mormon and Other Restoration Scripture 18*, no. 1 (2009): 4–15.

Terry B. Ball, "Isaiah's 'Other' Servant Songs," in *The Gospel of Jesus Christ in the Old Testament*, ed. D. Kelly Ogden et al. (Provo, UT: BYU Religious Studies Center, 2009), 207–218.

Richard Dilworth Rust, "'All Things Which Have Been Given of God . . . Are the Typifying of Him': Typology in the Book of Mormon," in *Literature of Belief: Sacred Scripture and Religious Experience*, ed. Neal E. Lambert (Provo, UT: BYU Religious Studies Center, 1981), 233–244.

84

Why Did Jesus Quote All of Isaiah 54?

"For thy maker, thy husband, the Lord of Hosts is his name; and thy Redeemer, the Holy One of Israel—the God of the whole earth shall he be called." (3 Nephi 22:5; Isaiah 54:5)

THE KNOW

At the conclusion to His great covenant speech, Jesus quoted Isaiah 54 in its entirety (see 3 Nephi 22).[1050] It was custom in the ancient Near East to conclude a covenant with promised blessings. As such, Jesus seems to have quoted the chapter as a way of promising blessings at the end of His covenant to the people. In doing so, He readdressed Isaiah 54 to the Nephites, helping them apply it directly to their own circumstances. Careful study illustrates how it may have had a strong impact on Christ's audience, effectively showing them the blessings God was promising them.

Isaiah 54 begins with an analogy about women and barrenness (see 3 Nephi 22:1; Isaiah 54:1). The formerly desolate woman will have to "enlarge the place of [her] tent" in order to fit all the children she will eventually bear (3 Nephi 22:2; Isaiah 54:2).[1051] Isaiah explained that this is symbolic of Israel, who will flourish such that there will not be room for them (see 3 Nephi 22:3; Isaiah 54:3).[1052] Though Isaiah was originally addressing the people of his own time, these verses would likely have brought hope to the Nephites. Just as Israel would flourish after facing disaster and desolation of war, the Nephites would also flourish after the disasters that had befallen them as described in 3 Nephi 8.[1053] They too would spread out again across the land and "inhabit" the cities the destruction left "desolate," as Isaiah had said.

Isaiah then continued with the image of the barren woman, telling Israel that the pain and shame of the past would be erased. Just as a widow could get married again to her husband's brother, called a "redeemer," so Israel would someday be symbolically remarried to the Lord through covenants, despite suffering in the past (see 3 Nephi 22:4–6; Isaiah 54:4–6).[1054] For the Nephites, the shame of the past was fresh, as they had recently rejected the covenant with the Lord. But the Lord assured them that He, "the God of the whole earth," would covenant with them as well, despite their rejection of past covenants (3 Nephi 22:5; Isaiah 54:5).

Isaiah then stated that it might have seemed like the Lord had "forsaken" them "for a moment . . . but with everlasting kindness" He would "have mercy on" them (3 Nephi 22:7–8; Isaiah 54:7–8). Just as Christ promised that the earth would not be destroyed again by a flood, so He promised that He would not punish His people again in such a devastating way.[1055]

The same "mountains" and "hills" that had been covered up in Noah's flood would eventually crumble to dust.[1056] Yet God's covenantal "kindness" would "not depart from" them, "and the covenant" of His "peace" would never "be removed" (3 Nephi 22:7–10; Isaiah 54:7–10). The Nephites may have felt like God had "forsaken" them when they experienced the destruction of so many of their cities. "Mountains" had literally "departed" and "hills" had literally been "removed" when the great destruction fell upon the Nephites (3 Nephi 8:9–12). So these verses would have emphasized the truly permanent nature of God's covenantal peace compared to even the seemingly permanent mountains.

Isaiah then told those who were "tossed with tempest" that their wealth would return to them and be even greater than anyone could imagine (3 Nephi 22:11–12; Isaiah 54:11–12).[1057] For people who had literally experienced a "great and terrible tempest," it would be encouraging to know God would rebuild their lives (3 Nephi 8:6). 3 Nephi 22:13 (cf. Isaiah 54:13) states that "all thy children shall be taught of the Lord; and great shall be the peace of thy children." When Isaiah said the children would be "taught of the Lord,"[1058] he may have meant that they would be "taught about the Lord." However, this phrase could also mean "taught by the Lord," which is exactly what happened when Christ was among the Nephites (3 Nephi 17:11).[1059]

Finally, Isaiah stated that the people would be established in righteousness and peace, and that no foreign or domestic enemies would triumph over them.[1060] The Lord was the one who created the blacksmiths who make weapons and the soldiers who used them, so He would certainly be able to protect His people (see 3 Nephi 22:14–17; Isaiah 54:14–17).[1061] For a society that had been steeped in war and rebellion for so many years and that had just been completely destroyed, this assurance of protection would likely have been an unimaginable relief.

THE WHY

Nephi, the son of Lehi, said that he "did liken all scriptures unto us, that it might be for our profit and learning" (1 Nephi 19:23). Yet for some modern readers of the Book of Mormon, relating the scriptures to themselves may seem difficult to do. Thankfully in 3 Nephi 22, Jesus Himself showed how this could be done.[1062] Christ quoted a chapter of Isaiah that would have related to them on both a literal and figurative level, showing the Nephites how some parts of the scriptures could connect directly to their lives.

Thus, Christ's use of the scriptures provides a pattern for readers of the Book of Mormon today. There are often occasions where events described in the scriptures parallel events in modern life. On those occasions, Christ seems to suggest, one can easily "liken" the scriptures directly to one's own life. If one finds oneself in a difficult corporate environment, for example, the story of Daniel's dealings with his colleagues might be instructive (see Daniel 6). Isaiah's pleas to help the poor seem like they were written yesterday (see Isaiah 3). For anyone who has taken on new responsibilities and feels overwhelmed, Peter's experience taking the lead of the early Christian Church is encouraging (see Acts 1).

Christ showed the Nephites, and all who read the Book of Mormon, that the scriptures can apply directly to them. When Jesus quoted Isaiah 54 to the Nephites, it was at least half a millennium old and had been written in the Old World under totally different circumstances.[1063] Yet it applied precisely to their circumstances. In the same way, the scriptures can still apply directly to the modern reader. Though parts of the scriptures were written in the remote past, they are not remote texts.

Just as Isaiah 54 applied directly to the Nephites, it applies to readers today. The Lord wants modern readers to see that they can claim all of these blessings as their own according to their faithfulness. Christ used this chapter as a covenantal conclusion: a promise of blessings to the Nephites. Modern readers can, and should, claim these blessings as well.

FURTHER READING

Cynthia L. Hallen, "The Lord's Covenant of Kindness: Isaiah 54 and 3 Nephi 22," in *Isaiah in the Book of Mormon,* ed. Donald W. Parry and John W. Welch (Provo, UT: FARMS, 1998), 313–349.

Victor L. Ludlow, "The Father's Covenant People Sermon: 3 Nephi 20:10–23:5," in *Third Nephi: An Incomparable Scripture,* ed. Andrew C. Skinner and Gaye Strathearn (Salt Lake City and Provo, UT: Deseret Book and Neal A. Maxwell Institute for Religious Scholarship, 2012), 147–174.

Joseph Fielding McConkie, "The Doctrine of a Covenant People," in *The Book of Mormon: 3 Nephi 8 Through 30, This Is My Gospel,* eds. Monte S. Nyman and Charles D. Tate Jr. (Provo, UT: BYU Religious Studies Center, 1993), 357–377.

85

Why Would Jesus Call Isaiah's Words Great?

"Yea, a commandment I give unto you that ye search these things diligently; for great are the words of Isaiah." (3 Nephi 23:1)

THE KNOW

Even casual readers of the Book of Mormon are sure to notice: "Book of Mormon prophets . . . quoted extensively from Isaiah."[1064] This tradition begins with the very first prophet-writer, Nephi, who, of all Book of Mormon prophets, used Isaiah most frequently. As Nephi read the words of Isaiah, he may have developed a personal affinity to Isaiah, who Nephi said "saw my Redeemer, even as I have seen him" (2 Nephi 11:2). Nephi saw in Isaiah a congenial prophet who had seen much of what he himself had seen in his own sweeping vision (1 Nephi 11–14).[1065]

Abinadi, too, seems to have personally identified with some of Isaiah's writing, experiencing himself what it is like to be "despised and rejected of men" (Mosiah 14:3; Isaiah 53:3).[1066] In addition to those who quoted Isaiah extensively, many other Book of Mormon prophets seem to have subtly quoted, paraphrased, and alluded to Isaiah's words.[1067]

When the resurrected Savior ministered to the Nephites, He also quoted from Isaiah.[1068] The risen Lord then made an unprecedented endorsement: "great are the words of Isaiah" (3 Nephi 23:1; cf. 20:11).[1069]

Great could mean a variety of things. In Hebrew, *gadol* ("great") "refers to things that are large in size, weight, or number; . . . to things of great significance or influence; to extraordinary events; and to God."[1070] Isaiah's words could thus be called "great" because his is the largest book in the Old Testament, because his prophecies are the most expansive and far-reaching, or because they are the most profound, sublime, and exalted. In line with this possibility, the Savior explained that Isaiah "spake as touching *all things* concerning my people" (3 Nephi 23:2; emphasis added).

Like Nephi and Abinadi, the Savior may also have had more personal reasons for calling Isaiah great. Biblical scholars have found that Isaiah "accounts for most of the [Old Testament] quotations and allusions in the [New Testament]."[1071] Additionally, "More than half the [Old Testament] quotations attributed to Jesus himself are from Isaiah, suggesting that he identified closely with the book and possibly also with the prophet himself."[1072]

Though they look very different in English, the very names *Isaiah* and *Jesus* "are similar in form and meaning."[1073] The Hebrew names are *Yesha'yahu* (Isaiah), meaning "salvation/deliverance of Yahweh [Jehovah]," and *Yeshua* (Jesus), meaning "the Lord is salvation, deliverance, help."[1074] Finally, while the subject continues to be debated in some circles, many scholars would agree that "Isaiah's Servant was central to Jesus' self-understanding."[1075]

This closeness and self-understanding may be evidenced in 3 Nephi, where immediately after commanding the Nephites to "search" the great words of Isaiah, which "have been and shall be" fulfilled, the Savior then commanded: "Therefore give heed to *my* words" (3 Nephi 23:1–4; emphasis added). As one Latter-day Saint scholar noticed, "Jesus positions his teachings to the Nephites as parallel to Isaiah."[1076]

THE WHY

Isaiah's writings continue to have a powerful impact on Jews, Christians, and Latter-day Saints throughout the world. Terry B. Ball noted:

> With his prophecies preserved not only in the Old Testament, but also in the New Testament, the Book of Mormon, and the Doctrine and Covenants, Isaiah's ministry continues to bless and instruct students of the scriptures.[1077]

The pervasive presence of his words in all of the standard works is a testament of their "everlasting worth to all people" in all ages.[1078] Indeed, the words of Isaiah are great in terms of impact and influence.

While those of many faith traditions have recognized the great worth of Isaiah's writings, Book of Mormon readers have not only the Savior's endorsement of Isaiah but additional quotation and commentary on Isaiah from the Lord Himself in 3 Nephi 20–22.

Latter-day Saints also benefit from Nephi's, Jacob's, and Abinadi's quotation, likening, and commentary on Isaiah, along with that of Joseph Smith and other latter-day prophets.[1079] The Book of Mormon also provides an added witness that the Savior felt a strong personal connection to Isaiah and his writings.

It is important to recognize, however, that after endorsing Isaiah specifically, the Lord expanded the command to all prophets: "Search the prophets, for many there be that testify of these things" (3 Nephi 23:5). Thus, the great Isaiah may be a categorical representative of the prophets—all of whom are significant and should be searched.

In this light, it is interesting that in both the New Testament and the Book of Mormon, the next most cited books from the Old Testament after Isaiah are Deuteronomy (from the Law), and the Psalms (from the Writings). Deuteronomy, Isaiah, and the Psalms may thus be thought to represent the Law, the Prophets, and the Writings—the entire corpus of the Old Testament. Thus, while the Lord singled out Isaiah as particularly important, all scripture should be searched, pondered, and applied in the lives of disciples of Christ everywhere (see John 5:39; 2 Timothy 3:16).

FURTHER READING

Garold N. Davis, "Pattern and Purpose of the Isaiah Commentaries in the Book of Mormon," in *Mormons, Scripture, and the Ancient World: Studies in Honor of John L. Sorenson,* ed. Davis Bitton (Provo, UT: FARMS, 1998), 277–303.

Kent P. Jackson, "Teaching from the Words of the Prophets (3 Nephi 23–26)," in *Book of Mormon, Part 2: Alma 30 to Moroni, Studies in the Scriptures,* Volume 8, ed. Kent P. Jackson (Salt Lake City, UT: Deseret Book, 1988), 196–207.

Why Did Jesus Give the Nephites Malachi's Prophecies?

"And it came to pass that he commanded them that they should write the words which the Father had given unto Malachi, which he should tell unto them." (3 Nephi 24:1)

THE KNOW

The words of Malachi, one of the later Old Testament prophets,[1080] were important enough that the Father commanded Jesus to supply the Nephites with Malachi's words (see 3 Nephi 24:1; 26:2). The likely reason for this is because Malachi's words tell "about those who will be destroyed in the Second Coming and those who will survive the Second Coming. So the text fits . . . very profoundly into the overall context and [Jesus's] whole message"[1081] in this section of 3 Nephi.

After miraculously providing bread and wine in administering the sacrament to the multitude, Jesus began in 3 Nephi 20 (and continued in the following chapters) to expound on what would happen to the house of Israel in the latter days, according to the words of the prophets. In 3 Nephi 21, Jesus then gave the sign of the commencement of the final dispensation of the work of the Lord—the coming forth of the Book of Mormon. In 3 Nephi 22, He quoted Isaiah 54 to give the Lord's promises to those in the latter-days—the fulfillment of the covenants He had made with Israel.[1082]

After Jesus had described the last days and the blessings that would be given to the faithful, the question remained, "who may abide the day of his coming, and who shall stand when he appeareth?" (3 Nephi 24:2; Malachi 3:2). Malachi 3–4 (3 Nephi 24–25) provides answers to this question. These chapters indicate that it will not be:

- those who are "sorcerers," "adulterers," "false swearers," "those that oppress the hireling in his wages," those who oppress "the widow" and orphans, those who "turn aside the stranger," or those who fear not the Lord (3 Nephi 24:5; Malachi 3:5)
- those who have "gone away from mine ordinances, and have not kept them" (3 Nephi 24:7; Malachi 3:7)
- those who have robbed God (in "tithes and offerings") (3 Nephi 24:8–9; Malachi 3:8–9)
- those who have "spoken against" God (3 Nephi 24:13; Malachi 3:13)

3 Nephi 24:18 (cf. Malachi 3:18) reveals the positive answer: Those who will abide the day of His coming are those who "discern between the righteous and the wicked, between him that serveth God and him that serveth him not." As Kent P. Jackson observed, "Malachi's revelation drew a stark contrast between

those who are humble and receptive to the Lord's will and those who are not."[1083]

THE WHY

Just as Jesus had commanded the people to "search" diligently the words of Isaiah (3 Nephi 23:1) to learn of things to come, Jesus also desired that the Book of Mormon peoples, as well as the future readers of the book, had Malachi's words.

President Ezra Taft Benson reminded Latter-day Saints that the events leading up to the Savior's visit in 3 Nephi reveal the pattern that will be followed before the Savior's Second Coming.[1084] Kent P. Jackson agreed, "The Savior's visit to the Americas provides a pattern that will be followed on a worldwide scale at his second coming. . . . Just as in ancient America, the period preceding Christ's coming will be characterized by wickedness, wars, and social chaos."[1085]

It has been commonly recognized that this gives 3 Nephi and the sacred events recorded therein greater meaning and relevance to readers today. A parallel, though often unrecognized, implication is that it made prophecies about the Second Coming meaningful to the Nephites. As Aaron P. Schade and David Rolph Seely noted, "Malachi's words given to the Nephites in 3 Nephi were as relevant to them as they are to us today."[1086]

Hence, when the Savior gave the Nephites the words of Malachi, it was not only for future generations (see 3 Nephi 26:2). Jackson explained:

> The relevance of this section of Malachi to Jesus' audience seems clear. Those who did not trust the prophetic announcements of his coming—and thus did not prepare—were cut off. Yet those who were faithful enjoyed the Savior's presence, even then. . . . As Malachi foretold, the day of the Lord's coming is one of destruction for the wicked, while for the righteous it will be a day of unimaginable blessings. . . . What could better describe what the Nephites had gone through and were then experiencing?[1087]

Malachi's words, of course, are important for readers today, but are also already available in the Old Testament. Having them juxtaposed with the experience of the Nephites in 3 Nephi adds support to Malachi's stern warning. The Savior's quotation of Malachi is preceded with an account that leaves little doubt as to just how dreadful the day of the Lord will be for the wicked (see 3 Nephi 25:5; Malachi 4:5). It also accentuates the majesty and splendor enjoyed by the righteous when "the Lord whom ye seek shall suddenly come to his temple" (3 Nephi 24:1; Malachi 3:1).

As a powerfully suitable conclusion to His covenant sermon, Jesus could not have selected a more riveting text than Malachi 3–4 with which to end His second day of instruction among the Nephites. What remained, logically and eschatologically, on that day was for Jesus to "expound all things, even from the beginning until the time that he should come in his glory, . . . even until the elements should melt with fervent heat, and the earth should be wrapt together as a scroll, and the heavens and the earth should pass away," when all people would be judged by God and come forth accordingly in the resurrection (3 Nephi 26:3), thus wrapping up precisely from where Malachi left off.

FURTHER READING

Aaron P. Schade and David Rolph Seely, "The Writings of Malachi in 3 Nephi: A Foundation for Zion in the Past and Present," in *Third Nephi: An Incomparable Scripture*, ed. Gaye Strathearn and Andrew C. Skinner (Salt Lake City and Provo, UT: Deseret Book and Neal A. Maxwell Institute for Religious Scholarship, 2012), 261–278.

Kent P. Jackson, "Teachings from the Words of the Prophets," in *Book of Mormon, Part 2: Alma 30 to Moroni*, *Studies in Scripture: Volume 8*, ed. Kent P. Jackson, (Salt Lake City, UT: Deseret Book, 1988), 196–207.

Why Are Children so Prominent in 3 Nephi?

"And it came to pass that he did teach and minister unto the children of the multitude of whom hath been spoken, and he did loose their tongues, and they did speak unto their fathers great and marvelous things, even greater than he had revealed unto the people; and he loosed their tongues that they could utter." (3 Nephi 26:14)

THE KNOW

In 3 Nephi, Christ often focused on children, just as He did in His mortal ministry.[1088] He blessed them individually (see 3 Nephi 17:21). He talked about the importance of children in the Plan of Salvation (see 3 Nephi 26:2–5).[1089] He quoted passages from Isaiah (see 3 Nephi 22:13; Isaiah 54:13) and Malachi (see 3 Nephi 25:6; Malachi 4:6) referring to children, and He caused angels to encircle and minister unto them (see 3 Nephi 17:22–24).

One reason why children appear so often in 3 Nephi may be that Mormon felt the people had become pure like children. In classic ancient Near East fashion, Mormon makes this point by referring to King Benjamin's speech on becoming as a child.

When Mormon summarized what Jesus did while He was with the Nephites, he recorded that Jesus "*healed* all their *sick*, and their *lame*, and opened the eyes of their *blind* and unstopped the ears of the *deaf*, and even had done *all manner of cures* among them, and *raised a man from the dead*" (3 Nephi 26:15; emphasis added). This comment is remarkably similar to King Benjamin's prophecy that the Messiah would be "*healing* the *sick*, *raising the dead*, causing the *lame* to walk, the *blind* to receive their sight, and the *deaf* to hear, and *curing all manner of diseases*" (Mosiah 3:5; emphasis added). In classic ancient Israelite fashion, Mormon appears to have used this description as a literary "red flag" to signal that the reader should read the passage with King Benjamin's speech in mind.[1090]

Shortly after the passage to which Mormon alluded, King Benjamin stated that the people needed to "humble themselves and become as little children" (Mosiah 3:18).[1091] He also said that people needed to become "as a child, submissive, meek, humble, patient, full of love, willing to submit to all things which the Lord seeth fit to inflict upon him, even as a child doth submit to his father" (Mosiah 3:19).[1092]

To become like little children, the Nephites had to see their children for who they really were. This is exactly what happens in 3 Nephi 26:16, as the children of the multitude said "marvelous things; and the things which they did utter were forbidden that there should not any man write them." Regarding this event, Elder Lynn G. Robbins noted,

> Perhaps more than opening the mouths of babes, the Lord was opening the eyes and ears of their

> astonished parents. Those parents had been granted the extraordinary gift of a glimpse into eternity and of beholding the true identity and premortal stature of their children. Would that not forever change the way the parents saw and treated their children?[1093]

The experience not only transformed how the parents saw the children, but it also changed the way they saw themselves. Shortly after this, the disciples of Jesus began to baptize people, and they also experienced things "which are not lawful to be written" (3 Nephi 26:17–18), just as the children had before. Finally, the people had become like their little children, as King Benjamin had said so many years earlier, and what Christ had reiterated only days earlier: "ye must repent, and become as a little child" (3 Nephi 11:37).

The result of this hallowed moment was that both parents and children had experienced things that were too sacred to record.[1094] Such holy revelations would have been especially suited to the temple. Perhaps these people had glimpsed the eternal nature of the family and had received assurances that their families could be bound together both on earth and in heaven.

THE WHY

As Mormon connected and compared King Benjamin's speech with Christ's visit to the Nephites, he emphasized the significance of children and of becoming childlike. One reason for Christ and Mormon's emphasis on children was likely a very practical one, signaled to the reader by the allusion to King Benjamin's earlier speech. In Mosiah's time, those who began to fight against the Church were those "that could not understand the words of king Benjamin, being little children at the time he spake unto his people" (Mosiah 26:1).

Christ knew if He wanted to perpetuate a Zion-like society for many years to come, He needed to engage personally with the children of this society, one by one.[1095] This way, even if they could not remember His words, as in the case of King Benjamin, they would at least remember how they felt when He was with them.[1096] This would ensure that the children would not fall away from the gospel as they got older.[1097]

However, there is another possible reason for this emphasis on children. In a world that habitually abuses or ignores children, Christ wanted to remind the Nephites, and the modern reader, of the significance of childhood.[1098] As Elder M. Russell Ballard stated:

> He said to behold them [children]. To me that means that we should embrace them with our eyes and with our hearts; we should see and appreciate them for who they really are: spirit children of our Heavenly Father, with divine attributes. When we truly behold our little ones, we behold the glory, wonder, and majesty of God, our Eternal Father. . . . They are receptive to the truth because they have no preconceived notions; everything is real to children. . . . Their souls are endowed naturally with divine potential that is infinite and eternal.[1099]

Children are central to Christ's plan of salvation. It is only through becoming like children and submitting to the Father that God's children can ever hope to have eternal increase. The Book of Mormon reminds its readers of the nobility of children and their importance in the plan of salvation. Christ's interactions with children teach all readers of the Book of Mormon to see children for who they really are, and as each person becomes more like a little child, the Savior helps all who accept Him to see themselves for who they really are and to see the eternal potential of all people.

FURTHER READING

Robert A. Rees, "Children of the Light: How the Nephites Sustained Two Centuries of Peace," in *Third Nephi: An Incomparable Scripture*, ed. Andrew C. Skinner and Gaye Strathearn (Salt Lake City and Provo, UT: Deseret Book and Neal A. Maxwell Institute for Religious Scholarship, 2012), 309–328.

M. Gawain Wells, "The Savior and the Children in 3 Nephi," *Journal of Book of Mormon Studies 14*, no. 1 (2005): 62–73.

Why Is 3 Nephi Sometimes Called the "Fifth Gospel"?

"Verily, verily, I say unto you, this is my gospel." (3 Nephi 27:21)

THE KNOW

While describing the contents of the Book of Mormon in a First Presidency message in 2004, President Gordon B. Hinckley said, "It contains what has been described as the fifth Gospel, a moving testament of the New World concerning the visit of the resurrected Redeemer on the soil of this hemisphere."[1100] In April 1904, B. H. Roberts mentioned that some debated whether "fifth Gospel" was an appropriate designation of 3 Nephi, demonstrating that the idea originated at least a century earlier than President Hinckley's use of the term.[1101]

Gospel literally means "good news," and so in one sense 3 Nephi is a "gospel" because—along with Matthew, Mark, Luke, and John—it declares the good news of Christ's Atonement and Resurrection.[1102] As a literary genre, though, *gospel* is somewhat difficult to define.[1103] Broadly speaking, gospels are texts that focus on the life, teachings, and miracles of Jesus.

Beyond the four canonical Gospels, there are additional early Christian texts dubbed "gospels," such as the Gospel of Mary, the Infancy Gospel of James, the Gospel of Nicodemus (The Acts of Pilate), the Gospel of the Ebionites, the Gospel of the Hebrews, the Gospel of the Nazareans, the Gospel of Thomas, and the Gospel of Philip. Some of these deal mostly with the post-Resurrection acts and teachings of Christ, similar to 3 Nephi.[1104] Hugh Nibley compared the 3 Nephi account with many of these early Christian post-Resurrection traditions and felt that 3 Nephi fit so naturally within that body of literature that "with the title removed, any scholar would be hard put to detect its irregular origin."[1105]

Nibley's work might suggest that 3 Nephi is a "Gospel" within the meaning and tradition given to that genre by early Christians. Yet the designation as a fifth Gospel carries greater weight, suggesting it belongs within the same class as the four canonized Gospels, which, as New Testament scholar Christopher M. Tuckett observed, are quite different from the non-canonized Gospels.[1106]

The four Gospels are, of course, somewhat different within themselves, but a number of points neatly suggest that 3 Nephi has a place alongside them. Some examples include:

- Much like Matthew and Luke, 3 Nephi begins with the fulfillment of prophesied signs of the Savior's birth (see 3 Nephi 1; cf. Matthew 1–2; Luke 1–2).[1107]
- Matthew, Mark, Luke, and John all mention John the Baptist, the forerunner sent to prepare the way

for Christ in the Old World (see Matthew 3; Mark 1; Luke 3; John 1). 3 Nephi likewise records the ministry of a forerunner who baptized among the Nephites—the prophet Nephi, son of Nephi (see 3 Nephi 7:15–26).[1108]

- Just as Jesus did, Nephi cast out devils, healed the sick, and even raised his brother from the dead. As the Savior's New World forerunner, Nephi performed his miracles "in the name of Jesus" (3 Nephi 7:19–22). Thus, as New Testament scholar Krister Stendahl put it, 3 Nephi "transposes the ministry of Jesus into a ministry of Nephi, a man of miracles in the name of Jesus."[1109]
- Matthew, Mark, and Luke all record the Father bearing witness of the Son,[1110] as does 3 Nephi (see 3 Nephi 11:7).
- Just as all four Gospels document the death and crucifixion of Jesus,[1111] 3 Nephi records the fulfillment of prophesied signs confirming the Savior's death and three days in the tomb (see 3 Nephi 8–10).[1112] The 3 Nephi account may even help clarify the timeline of Christ's entombment, since the account of the destruction adds information about the timing and duration of Christ's death.[1113]
- Just as the New Testament Gospels record the teachings of the Savior during His earthly ministry, 3 Nephi records the teachings of the resurrected Lord.[1114] This includes the Sermon at the temple (see 3 Nephi 12–14),[1115] which parallels the Sermon on the Mount (see Matthew 5–7) and Sermon on the Plain (see Luke 6:17–49), the clarification of teachings recorded in John about His "other sheep,"[1116] and the institution of the sacrament.[1117]
- The Nephite record stands as a fifth witness of the bodily resurrection of Christ (see 3 Nephi 11) in a way that exceeds the all other Gospels, canonical[1118] and non-canonical.[1119]

Several more points of comparison could be made.[1120] Yet just as the New Testament Gospels have key differences that ought to be noticed, 3 Nephi is different from the other four Gospels in important respects. As Latter-day Saint gospel scholar Andrew C. Skinner noted, the Savior "said and did things of which the four Gospels have no record, and for which 3 Nephi is our treasured source."[1121] Key among these are the post-Resurrection nature of the Savior's ministry and the emphasis on the temple in Christ's teachings.[1122]

THE WHY

Many have attempted to imitate the Gospels and have failed miserably.[1123] Yet 3 Nephi offers an authentic fifth Gospel that "complements and supplements the four biblical Gospels."[1124] As Skinner pointed out, it is unique among Gospel accounts in possessing material "reviewed and edited by the Savior himself."[1125]

In the October 2016 general conference, Brian K. Ashton similarly taught, "Jesus's visit to the Nephites after His Resurrection was carefully organized to teach us the things of greatest importance."[1126] Thus, disciples of Christ can be confident that "3 Nephi contains those matters that the Savior himself felt were and are most important."[1127]

In July 1838, the Prophet Joseph Smith taught, "The fundamental principles of our religion are the testimony of the apostles and prophets concerning Jesus Christ, that he died, was buried, and rose again the third day, and ascended up into heaven."[1128]

President Ezra Taft Benson taught that the Book of Mormon "is the keystone in our witness of Christ,"[1129] a point Elder Gary E. Stevenson reiterated recently.[1130] While the entire Book of Mormon is saturated with various testimonies of Christ, the gospel of 3 Nephi is the preeminent reason that the Book of Mormon stands as a keystone witness of Christ's divinity.

By detailing the post-Resurrection appearance and ministry of Jesus Christ in the Americas, "3 Nephi stands as an independent witness of the linchpin doctrine of the entire Christian faith—the bodily Resurrection of the Lord Jesus Christ."[1131] It is a Gospel not of the mortal Jesus but of the risen Lord.[1132] In a time of ever-increasing skepticism about who Jesus was and who He claimed to be, the Book of Mormon, as Latter-day Saint author Michael R. Ash observed, "is a unique second witness to the divinity of Christ and the reality of the Resurrection."[1133]

"Truly, 3 Nephi is worthy of the designation Fifth Gospel—the capstone of all Gospel accounts," Skinner concluded.[1134] It is a Gospel the world desperately needs now—a Gospel that has the potential to soften hearts, change minds, and convert people to the Lord. Skinner resolved, "For this Fifth Gospel we should be forever grateful and perhaps much more active in filling the earth with its contents."[1135]

FURTHER READING

Andrew C. Skinner, *Third Nephi: The Fifth Gospel* (Springville, UT: Cedar Fort, 2012).

Monte S. Nyman, *Book of Mormon Commentary,* 6 vols. (Orem, UT: Granite, 2003), vol. 5.

John W. Welch, *Illuminating the Sermon at the Temple and Sermon on the Moun*t (Provo, UT: FARMS, 1999).

Hugh Nibley, *The Prophetic Book of Mormon, The Collected Works of Hugh Nibley, Volume 8* (Salt Lake City and Provo, UT: Deseret Book and FARMS, 1989), 407–434.

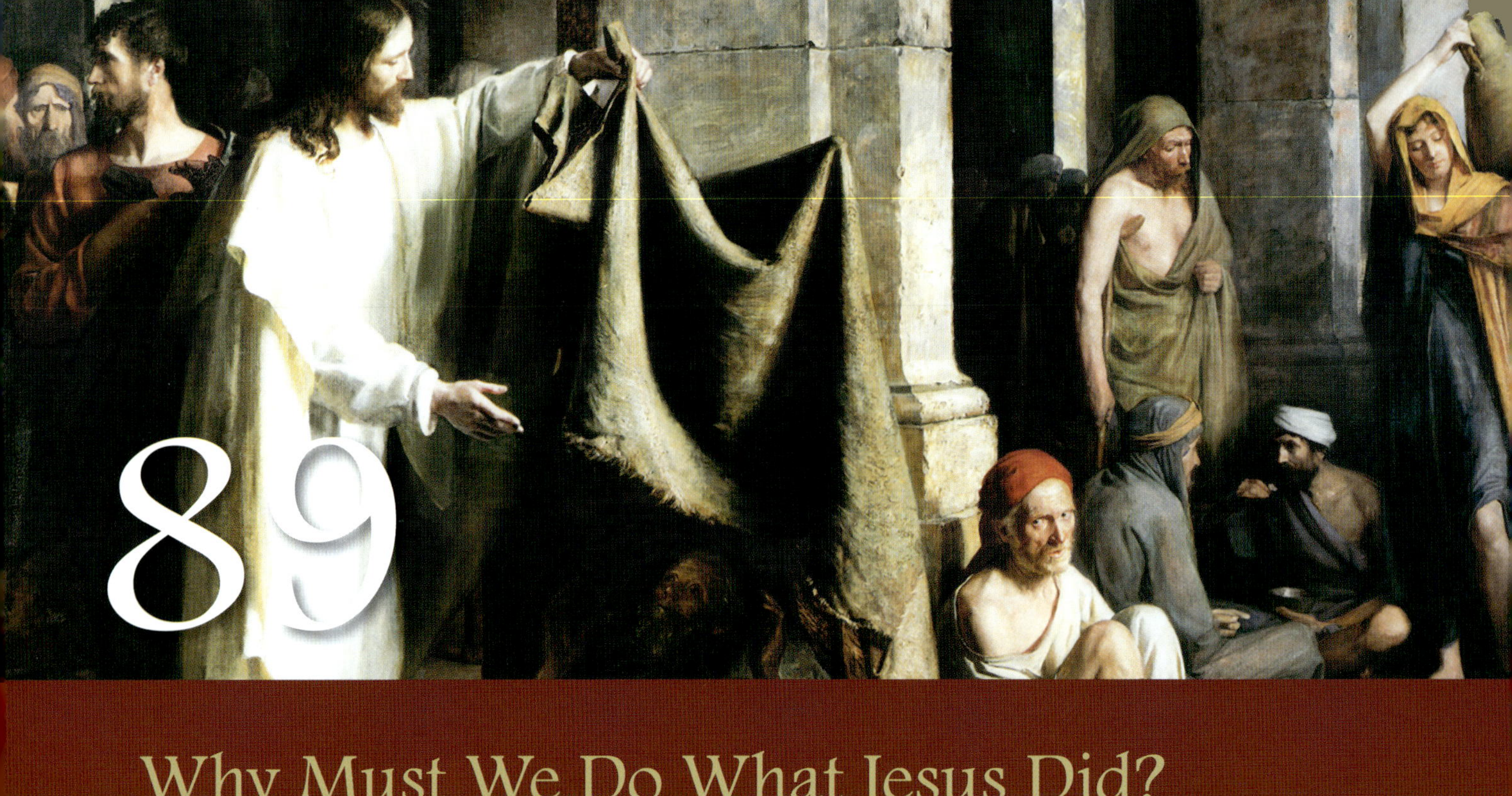

89

Why Must We Do What Jesus Did?

"Therefore, if ye do these things blessed are ye, for ye shall be lifted up at the last day." (3 Nephi 27:22)

THE KNOW

As part of His discourse concerning the name of His Church, Jesus declared, "ye know the things that ye must do in my church; for the works which ye have seen me do that shall ye also do; for that which ye have seen me do even that shall ye do" (3 Nephi 27:21).

Jesus followed this repeated injunction with a promised blessing: "Therefore, if ye do these things blessed are ye, for ye shall be lifted up at the last day" (3 Nephi 27:22). This commandment and its contingent blessing should prompt readers to pause and carefully review what works Jesus did during His ministry among the Nephites.

For instance, Christ's first action was to descend out of the heavens and visit His temple, thus establishing the temple as the sacred symbol of His presence (3 Nephi 11:8). He then "stretched forth His hand" and testified to the people that He was "Jesus Christ, whom the prophets testified shall come into the world" (3 Nephi 11:9–10).[1136] In this way, Jesus affirmed the recorded testimonies of the prophets who came before Him and demonstrated the importance of testifying of sacred truths.

After this, Christ said, "Arise and come forth unto me" (3 Nephi 11:14). This simple statement profoundly captures the essence of the Gospel. Just like the people at Bountiful, all of God's children are invited to come unto Christ by learning of His teachings and then experiencing Him for themselves by the power of the Holy Ghost (see Moroni 10:5; cf. Alma 32:28–35).

Jesus then allowed the people to "thrust their hands into his side, and . . . feel the prints of the nails in his hands and in his feet" (3 Nephi 11:15). Allowing hundreds of individuals to experience physical contact with His divine body provided a powerful testimony of His Resurrection.

Throughout the rest of His three-day ministry among the people, Jesus ordained priesthood holders, instituted the sacrament, healed the sick and the afflicted, blessed the children, prayed for the people, taught important doctrines, defined His gospel, and revealed the name of His Church, among other things (see chart on p. 221 for a comprehensive list).

THE WHY

On September 22 and 23, 1832, Joseph Smith received a revelation from the Lord that declared, "your minds in times past have been darkened because of unbelief, and because you have treated lightly the things you have received" (D&C 84:54).[1137] The Lord further declared that this "vanity and unbelief have brought the whole church under condemnation" and that they would remain under condemnation until they "repent and remember the new covenant, even the Book of Mormon . . . not only to say, but to *do* according to that which I have written" (D&C 84:55, 57; emphasis added).[1138]

This revelation demonstrates how crucial it is for the Church and its members to actually do—and not just say—what the Book of Mormon teaches. Moreover, Jesus's emphatic repetition in 3 Nephi 27:21 makes it abundantly clear just what teachings in the text are most fundamentally important to follow: "for the works which ye have seen me do that shall ye also do; for that which ye have seen me do even that shall ye do."

Paying careful attention to the things Jesus did in 3 Nephi can help explain why Latter-day Saints strive to worship as they do.[1139] For example, why do Church members regularly attend sacrament meetings and bear their testimonies? That is what Jesus did on His first day in Bountiful, proclaiming "this shall ye always do" (3 Nephi 18:11; 3 Nephi 11:10–11).

Why do Church members regularly read their scriptures? That is what Jesus did, reciting the words of Isaiah to the people and commanding them to "search these things diligently" (3 Nephi 23:1). Why do Church members pray often in their families? That is what Jesus did, saying "as I have prayed among you even so shall ye pray in my church" (3 Nephi 18:16). Why do Church members sustain living prophets and Apostles? That is what Jesus did, declaring that the people should "give heed unto the words of these twelve whom I have chosen" (3 Nephi 12:1).

Jesus's visitation among the Nephites gives an extended portrait of His life and teachings.[1140] Those who study His example carefully will discover sacred patterns of ministry as well as profound insights concerning His divine character and personality. They will feel His love for them as individuals, as families, as communities, and as nations. And upon recognizing His eternal love and goodness, they will be "filled with desire" to truly know Him and follow Him in all things (3 Nephi 19:24).

President Howard W. Hunter taught,

> Let us follow the Son of God in all ways and in all walks of life. Let us make him our exemplar and our guide. We should at every opportunity ask ourselves, "What would Jesus do?" and then be more courageous to act upon the answer. . . . To the extent that our

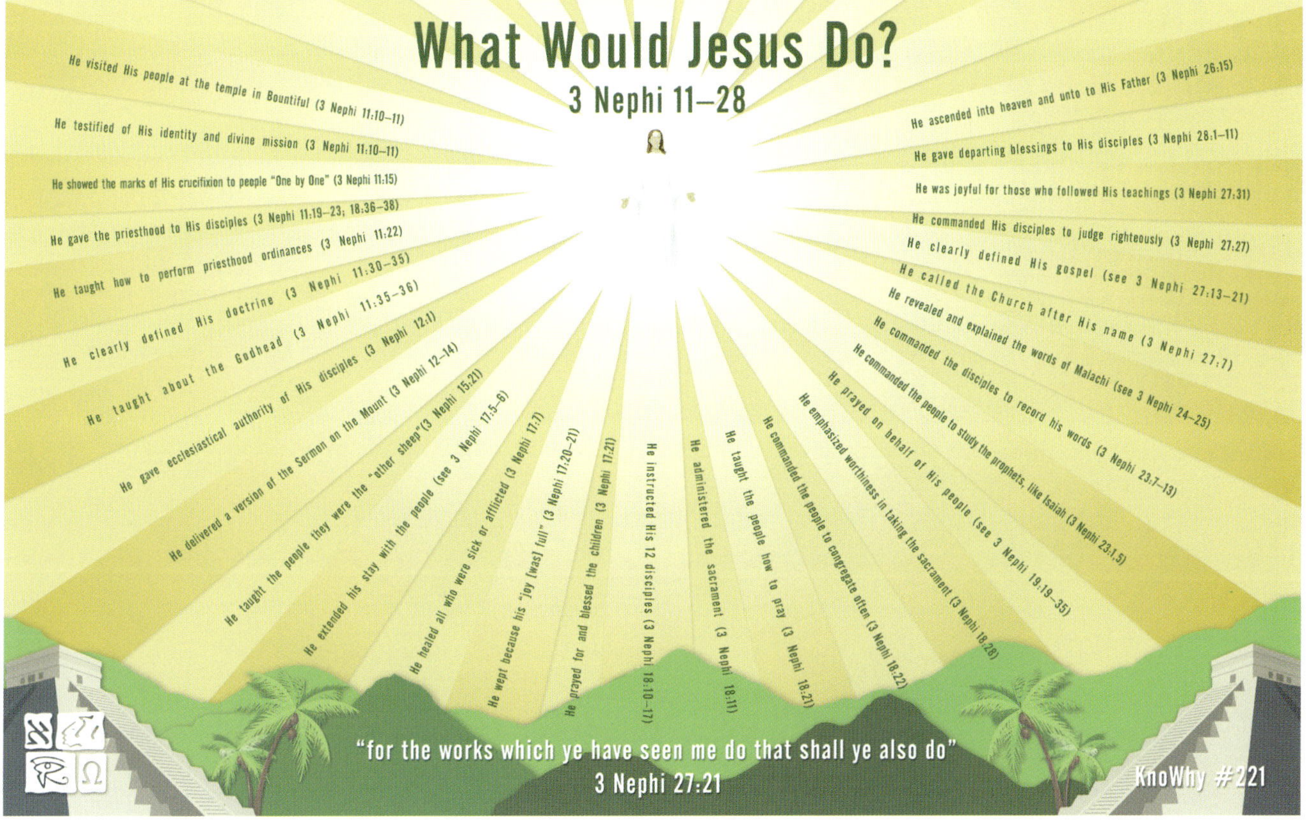

> mortal powers permit, we should make every effort to become like Christ—the one perfect and sinless example this world has ever seen.[1141]

FURTHER READING

Howard W. Hunter, "What Manner of Men Ought Ye to Be?" *Ensign*, May 1994.

Ezra Taft Benson, "Cleansing the Inner Vessel," *Ensign*, May 1986.

90

Why Did Mormon End 3 Nephi with Such Serious Woes?

"Wo unto him that spurneth at the doings of the Lord; yea, wo unto him that shall deny the Christ and his works!" (3 Nephi 29:5)

THE KNOW

At the conclusion of the record of Christ's visit to the Book of Mormon lands, Mormon added a short message directed to future Gentile readers (comprising 3 Nephi 29–30). Mormon pronounced a series of "woes" against those Gentiles who would reject his words and deny the plans and promises of Christ contained therein.

In 3 Nephi 29:5–7, Mormon repeated the phrase "Wo unto him" several times. He exclaimed, "wo unto him that":

- spurneth at the doings of the Lord
- shall deny the Christ and his works
- shall deny the revelations of the Lord
- shall say the Lord no longer worketh by revelation, or by prophecy, or by gifts, or by tongues, or by healings, or by the power of the Holy Ghost
- shall say at that day, to get gain, that there can be no miracle wrought by Jesus Christ

He concluded his list with the warning, "He that doeth this shall become like unto the son of perdition, for whom there was no mercy, according to the word of Christ!" (3 Nephi 29:7). This form of warning is known as a "simile curse," a form of curse using "like" or "as," which is well known from Old Testament and other ancient Near Eastern covenant-treaty texts.[1142]

Donald W. Parry has noted that the "woe unto" statements in the Book of Mormon[1143] are also an example of a recognized genre of prophetic pronouncement known as the "woe oracle," found in many of the prophetic books of the Old Testament[1144] and also in the New Testament.[1145] There are approximately forty examples of this formula in the Book of Mormon.[1146] Parry explained that the "woe oracle" is "often part of a judgment speech . . . used to pronounce anguish and distress upon a person or group of people."[1147]

Woes were pronounced by prophets and by the Lord Jesus Himself when warning those who act out in rebellion against God's plans, especially against His promises to His covenant people. They announce, as it were, an impending doom upon such offenders.

For example, in the first of several "woes" against the Jewish leadership of His day, Jesus exclaimed, "But woe unto you, scribes and Pharisees, hypocrites! For ye shut up the kingdom of heaven against men: for ye neither go in yourselves, neither suffer ye them that are entering to go in" (Matthew 23:13).

THE WHY

3 Nephi 29–30 was written by Mormon as a conclusion to the record of the visit of Christ to the Americas, directed specifically to the Gentiles who would receive these words in the latter days. The record is meant to act as a sign to the Gentiles that the Lord has begun to fulfill His covenant with the children of Israel "concerning their restoration to the lands of their inheritance" (3 Nephi 29:1).

Mormon foresaw that some of the Gentiles who would receive the Book of Mormon would doubt that the Lord would truly fulfill His word. They would believe that His "coming unto the children of Israel" would be delayed and that the words spoken by the prophets and by Christ Himself would be "vain" (3 Nephi 29:2–3).

Mormon's purpose in adding this addendum to the record in 3 Nephi was to declare that "the Lord remembereth his covenant unto them," that He would do for His covenant people "that which he hath sworn" (3 Nephi 29:8), and that the Lord would wield "the sword of his justice" against all those who denied or opposed His plans.

Although Mormon's warnings are bold in decrying those who would work against the Lord and His people, he ultimately offered these offenders the promise of the Lord's forgiveness. He announced that through repentance and baptism, they could receive the "remission of your sins," the companionship of the Holy Ghost, and the opportunity to be "numbered with my people who are of the house of Israel" (3 Nephi 30:2).

Readers may note the sincerity of the Lord's promises to the Gentile readers when Mormon emphasizes that it was Jesus Christ Himself who "commanded" Mormon to add these words to his conclusion. The seriousness of the offenses addressed in the "woes," augmented by the simile curse that "he that doeth this shall become like unto the son of perdition" (3 Nephi 29:7), underscores the idea that anyone can be forgiven of his or her sins. The Lord will extend His mercy to all who hear His word, are willing to change their ways, and are willing to enter into a covenant with Him.

FURTHER READING

John W. Welch, "Counting to Ten," *Journal of Book of Mormon Studies 12*, no. 2 (2003): 42–57, 113–114.

Donald W. Parry, "Hebraisms and Other Ancient Peculiarities in the Book of Mormon," in *Echoes and Evidences of the Book of Mormon,* ed. Donald W. Parry, Daniel C. Peterson, and John W. Welch (Provo, UT: FARMS, 2002), 156–189.

Mark J. Morrise, "Simile Curses in the Ancient Near East, Old Testament, and Book of Mormon," *Journal of Book of Mormon Studies 2,* no. 1 (1993): 124–138.

4 Nephi

91

Why Did the Peace Last so Long in 4 Nephi?

"And surely there could not be a happier people among all the people who had been created by the hand of God." (4 Nephi 1:16)

THE KNOW

The historical era recorded in 4 Nephi has been described as the "most glorious, happy, progressive, and enlightened time in all the combined Jaredite, Nephite, and Lamanite civilizations."[1148] Mormon reported, "And surely there could not be a happier people among all the people who had been created by the hand of God" (4 Nephi 1:16). Andrew C. Skinner explained, "In forty-nine short verses we are shown the practical workings of the law of the celestial kingdom, the true order of heaven on earth, and the ideal pattern of welfare service."[1149]

Mormon's rather sparse summary, however, may cause readers to wonder exactly how the Nephites sustained nearly two centuries of uninterrupted peace.[1150] While Mormon gave a brief description of the societal features that resulted from and sustained such peace,[1151] Robert A. Rees has suggested that this lasting stability was at least partly due to the dramatic poignancy of the events surrounding Christ's visitation. Rees said:

> Had you been a child during this momentous time, imagine what your life would be like for the remainder of your days; imagine the stories you would tell to others about that all-encompassing darkness that enshrouded you in night and how, in your moment of deepest despair, the light came, first as a voice and then as a ray that blossomed into a person as bright as the sun, and how His light flowed into your eyes and into your heart, making your whole body as luminous as sunlight.[1152]

Such experiences would certainly have left lasting impressions and are an indication that "loving, blessing, and teaching the children must have been an integral part of [Christ's] mission."[1153] Those who were children at the time of Christ's visitation would have grown up to be the parents and grandparents of the rising generations. Rees proposed that "these great events, these powerful personal narratives of light overpowering the darkness, would have been told and retold" among the people.[1154]

Moreover, it seems likely that these sacred stories would have been transmitted to rising generations as faithful Saints "[continued] in fasting and prayer, and in meeting together oft both to pray and to hear the word of the Lord" (4 Nephi 1:12).[1155]

As children and grandchildren partook of the sacrament and worshiped with those who had participated in the profound events of Christ's ministry, they too would have felt the power of Christ's love and mercy.[1156] They would have heard the stories of His supernal prayers and miraculous healings.[1157] They would have listened to the testimonies of those who had personally seen and heard and felt the resurrected Savior.[1158] In this spirit of unity, they would have gained their own testimonies of the goodness of Christ.

THE WHY

While societies in every age have sought the key to lasting peace and happiness, few have obtained it.[1159] Some have turned solely to large-scale social reforms or sweeping legislative actions. Yet while such efforts sometimes accomplish much good, they tend to lack the personalized concern and transformative love that emanates from Jesus Christ and His Atonement.

Elder Dale G. Renlund emphasized that "the greater the distance between the giver and the receiver, the more the receiver develops a sense of entitlement."[1160] Notably, as each successive generation in 4 Nephi became further removed from those who had personal contact with the Savior, they also became further removed from His peace, love, and joy.[1161] Mormon eventually reported that the people "did dwindle in unbelief and wickedness, from year to year" (4 Nephi 1:34).[1162]

Yet concerning those who remained righteous, Nephi the son of Lehi prophesied, "the Son of Righteousness shall appear unto them; and he shall heal them, and they shall have peace with him, until three generations shall have passed away" (2 Nephi 26:9). The phrase "have peace *with* him" (emphasis added) suggests that the first three generations were in some way *accompanied by* Jesus. While Nephi's statement certainly relates to spiritual unity, Mormon confirmed its literal fulfillment when reporting that after Christ's three-day visitation, He "did show himself unto them oft, and did break bread oft, and bless it, and give it unto them" (3 Nephi 26:13).

Whereas worldly institutions tend to increasingly distance receivers from their givers, the divine institution of the sacrament is intended to remove the gap between individual receivers and their true Giver, Jesus Christ. It allowed the rising generations in 4 Nephi to feel in their hearts what their ancestors felt and, perhaps on occasion, to experience Christ's personal visitation for themselves.

Indeed, Mormon's only explicit explanation for how the people obtained such peace and happiness was "because of the love of God which did dwell in the hearts of the people" (4 Nephi 1:15).[1163] This love—which Moroni called "the pure love of Christ" (Moroni 7:47)—was surely bestowed on faithful believers in accordance with Christ's sacramental promise: "ye shall have my Spirit to be with you" (3 Nephi 18:11).

Thankfully, the Lord in His abundant mercy has restored the blessings of the sacrament in the latter days (see D&C 20:75–79). President Dallin H. Oaks taught, "The ordinance of the sacrament makes the sacrament meeting the most sacred and important meeting in the Church. It is the only Sabbath meeting the entire family can attend together."[1164] This unifying ordinance allows each worthy individual and each righteous family to draw near to Jesus so they, like the blessed generations in 4 Nephi, can "have peace *with* him" (2 Nephi 26:9; emphasis added) and be "filled with the love of God" (4 Nephi 1:15).

FURTHER READING

Robert A. Rees, "Children of Light: How the Nephites Sustained Two Centuries of Peace," in *Third Nephi: An Incomparable Scripture*, ed. Andrew C. Skinner and Gaye Strathearn (Salt Lake City and Provo, UT: Deseret Book and Neal A. Maxwell Institute for Religious Scholarship, 2012), 309–328.

M. Gawain Wells, "The Savior and the Children in 3 Nephi," *Journal of Book of Mormon Studies 14*, no. 1 (2005): 62–73, 129.

Lindon J. Robinson, "'No Poor Among Them,'" *Journal of Book of Mormon Studies 14*, no. 1 (2005): 86–97, 130.

Byron R. Merrill, "There Was No Contention," in *The Book of Mormon: Fourth Nephi, From Zion to Destruction,* ed. Monte S. Nyman and Charles D. Tate Jr. (Provo, UT: BYU Religious Studies Center, 1995), 167–183.

Mormon

What Do We Know about Mormon's Upbringing?

"I perceive that thou art a sober child, and art quick to observe." (Mormon 1:2)

THE KNOW

Concerning Mormon's record of his own life and ministry, Grant Hardy commented, "Finally, after three hundred pages with Mormon as our guide, we meet the man himself."[1165] While limited in details, Mormon's sketch of his formative years provides important clues concerning his personality and character. This information is particularly valuable because no other writer has influenced the text of the Book of Mormon more than Mormon himself,[1166] the prophet-historian who abridged the record into its current form.[1167]

Mormon declared that he was a "descendant of Nephi" and that his "father's name was Mormon" (Mormon 1:5). John L. Sorenson has proposed that Mormon likely "would have been the ranking member of his generation in a senior lineage or 'house' within the Nephite faction."[1168] Mormon's statement of lineage, therefore, helps establish him as a rightful heir and worthy record keeper.[1169]

Ammaron, the previous record keeper, must have had enough interaction with Mormon to assess that Mormon (at ten years of age) was a "sober child"[1170] who was "quick to observe"[1171] (Mormon 1:2). Because of Mormon's favorable qualities, Ammaron commissioned Mormon to retrieve the Nephite records when he turned "twenty and four years old" (Mormon 1:3) and to "engrave on the plates of Nephi all the things that ye have observed concerning this people" (Mormon 1:4).[1172]

Although Mormon didn't directly express it, readers can appropriately assume that being given such a lofty responsibility at such a tender age would have profoundly influenced him as a youth. Indeed, by the age of fifteen, Mormon was "visited of the Lord, and tasted and knew of the goodness of Jesus" (Mormon 1:15).[1173] At the age of sixteen, Mormon was chosen as the leader of the Nephite armies (see Mormon 2:1–2). Apparently, Ammaron, the Lord, and Mormon's people all saw something extraordinary in his capacity and character as a young man.

As far as secular learning goes, Mormon reported that when he was about ten years old, "I began to be learned somewhat after the manner of the learning of my people" (Mormon 1:2).[1174] The fact that this statement was in the context of Ammaron's commission for him to become the next Nephite record keeper hints that at least some of Mormon's learning was literary in nature. At age eleven, Mormon was "carried by [his] father into the land southward, even to the land of Zarahemla" (Mormon 1:6).[1175] And throughout his military career, Mormon traveled among the lands of his people in order to defend them from the attacks of the Lamanites.[1176]

These types of details suggest that from at an early age, Mormon gained military, geographic, and literary education—all crucial disciplines of knowledge for a prophet-historian in training. As Richard Holzapfel suggested, "Mormon had the best education his culture could furnish."[1177]

Sorenson similarly concluded, "Young Mormon came to maturity in the midst of a society revolutionizing itself. Because of his lofty priestly connections, his noble lineage, and the consequent high degree of literacy he must have commanded, he was thrust into a leadership role with which no average sixteen-year-old would ever have been entrusted."[1178]

A careful analysis of Mormon's childhood thus demonstrates that education, travel, military leadership, emotional maturity, profound spiritual experiences, and unflagging righteousness in the face of adversity helped shape the prophet whose record would eventually "sweep the earth as with a flood" (Moses 7:62).[1179]

THE WHY

Modern readers—especially young people—can learn much from Mormon's stalwart example. Marilyn Arnold has commented, "It was nothing short of miraculous that a child born and reared in a society glutted with iniquity could remain spiritual, loving, and tender-hearted."[1180] Elder Jeffrey R. Holland similarly concluded, "His faith, his hope, and his charity were irrepressible."[1181] Mormon's life thus aptly illustrates President Thomas S. Monson's teaching that the righteous must sometimes dare to stand alone.[1182]

For instance, right after noting that he was "fifteen years of age," Mormon reported that he "did endeavor to preach unto this people" (Mormon 1:15–16). Then, in what must have been sorely disheartening, Mormon was "forbidden . . . [to] preach" because the people "wilfully rebelled against their God" (Mormon 1:16). Like many righteous young people, Mormon desired with his whole heart to serve a mission, but circumstances—specifically others' choices, over which he had no control—denied him the opportunity.

Being one of the few faithful members of his community and also being forbidden to formally share his most deeply held values, he must have been terribly lonely. When he finally was able to preach to the people, Mormon reported that "it was in vain" because the people "did harden their hearts against the Lord their God" (Mormon 3:3). Mormon personally experienced rejection, and he knew what it felt like to stand alone in defense of the truth.

The way Mormon's apparent education and advanced literacy prepared him for his prophetic calling is also instructive. To young people, President Gordon B. Hinckley taught, "Do not short-circuit your education."[1183] Elder Russell M. Nelson similarly declared, "Because of our sacred regard for each human intellect, we consider the obtaining of an education to be a religious responsibility."[1184] Like Mormon, each child of God should educate and prepare themselves to do great, even seemingly impossible things while in mortality.[1185] As Elder Richard G. Scott declared, "Our Heavenly Father did not put us on earth to fail but to succeed gloriously."[1186]

It may have been tempting for those who rejected Mormon's message to see him as a failure. In fact, Mormon himself at times seemed to have been deeply discouraged, even declaring at one point that "my joy was vain" because the people would not repent (Mormon 2:13). Yet readers of the Book of Mormon today recognize that Mormon's mission was one of the greatest and most miraculous accomplishments in the history of the world. Elder Neil L. Andersen taught, "With our mortal eyes, we cannot judge the effect of our efforts, nor can we establish the timetable. When you share the love of the Savior with another, your grade is always an A+."[1187]

While certainly excruciating in the moment, Mormon's life experiences gave him a unique capacity to compile the records of his people and to interpret them in a way that would resonate with modern readers.[1188] As Thomas W. Mackay described it, "Mormon's humanity, his anguish, and his individuality all resound from the pages of the book."[1189] Grant Hardy similarly described Mormon's voice as "sorrowful, humane, moralistic, and precise."[1190] It is this informed and compassionate voice—prepared, refined, and purified by the Lord—that continues to guide readers of the Book of Mormon throughout the world.

FURTHER READING

Matthew L. Bowen, "'O Ye Fair Ones'—Revisited," *Interpreter: A Journal of Mormon Scripture 20* (2016): 315–344.

Thomas S. Monson, "Dare to Stand Alone," *Ensign*, November 2011, 60–67.

Richard Neitzel Holzapfel, "Mormon, the Man and the Message," in *The Book of Mormon: Fourth Nephi, From Zion to Destruction*, ed. Monte S. Nyman and Charles D. Tate Jr. (Provo, UT: BYU Religious Studies Center, 1995), 117–131.

Why Did Mormon Write so Little about His Own Time Period?

"And upon the plates of Nephi I did make a full account of all the wickedness and abominations; but upon these plates I did forbear to make a full account of their wickedness and abominations, for behold, a continual scene of wickedness and abominations has been before mine eyes ever since I have been sufficient to behold the ways of man." (Mormon 2:18)

THE KNOW

By the time Mormon began documenting scenes and events from his own time, his commentary had become terse and despairing. An example of this is Mormon 2, which begins in the 326th year since Christ's birth (see Mormon 2:2) and passes quickly through the intervening years to the 350th (see Mormon 2:28). The whole book of Mormon (see Mormon 1–6) covers a span of sixty-four years, including the entirety of Mormon's adult life, in the space of approximately eleven pages in our modern printed Book of Mormon (averaging fewer than one-fourth page per year).

The brevity of Mormon's writings regarding his own time is surprising when compared to the depth of his coverage of the era of Alma, Helaman, and Captain Moroni in the book of Alma, which covers only thirty-eight years in 161 pages (averaging 4.13 pages per year).[1191] After covering other eras—even times wrought by war and violence, such as the "War Chapters" of the book of Alma—in such exhaustive detail, why did Mormon write so briefly about his own time?

There are a few possible reasons.

Running Out of Time

First, he was probably running out of time. If Mormon began the abridgment of the Nephite records in about the year AD 350, when the period of peace began, then he probably didn't get to his own record until the war with the Lamanites had recommenced in the 360th year (see Mormon 3:4).[1192] The destruction of the Nephite people would not be far away. Mormon was getting older—he was likely around fifty years old at this time—and was weary from war and preaching to his people in vain (see Mormon 3:3). He may have been worried about how much longer he would live to finish his record.

Occupied with War

Furthermore, after the war recommenced in AD 360, Mormon was almost constantly involved in battles with the Lamanites until the end of his life. When he was active in the wars, he was often having to flee to new areas, build up fortifications and make other war preparations, and occupy himself with many other duties. He did have a hiatus of approximately thirteen years when he refused to lead the Nephite armies due to their wickedness (see Mormon 3:11; 5:1). While this no doubt afforded him some time to work on his recordkeeping duties, it is clear in his record that during those years he was weary and worn from all the warfare and wickedness that surrounded him.

Emotional Difficulty

Most of all, though, it appears that Mormon was reluctant to write about the happenings of his own time because of the great pain and anguish he felt for the demise of the Nephite people. Mormon specifically stated that he was sparing readers some details as he abridges his own history on the plates because "a continual scene of wickedness and abominations has been before mine eyes" and "my heart has been filled with sorrow because of their wickedness, all my days" (Mormon 2:18–19).[1193]

Later, Mormon added that he was only writing "a small abridgment," because he dared not "give a full account of the things which I have seen." Such was the case because he was apparently commanded not to by the Lord, and "also that ye [the future Gentile readers] might not have too great sorrow because of the wickedness of this people" (Mormon 5:9). Mormon made it clear that he did "not desire to harrow up the souls of men" by describing in too much detail "the awful scene of blood and carnage" (Mormon 5:8) that played out as his people were swept from off the land. The "blood and carnage" was so rampant that he, perhaps even unconsciously, repeated that phrase multiple times in his record.[1194]

THE WHY

Not long before abridging his own record, Mormon had recently reached what must have been a spiritual pinnacle as he reviewed and abridged the account of the Savior's ministry to the Nephite people (see 3 Nephi 11–26) and the two-century-long era of peace that followed His visit (see 4 Nephi).[1195] To recount the subsequent fall of those happy and righteous people to the depths of depravity that he saw all around him in his day must have been utterly heartbreaking for Mormon.[1196]

When he saw so many of them fail to repent and turn to the Lord and then be killed by the thousands, he could not contain his sorrow. He noted that "my sorrow did return unto me again, and I saw that the day of grace was passed with them, . . . for I saw thousands of them hewn down in open rebellion against their God, and heaped up as dung upon the face of the land" (Mormon 2:15). He lamented that "my heart has been filled with sorrow because of their wickedness, all my days" (Mormon 2:19).

Mormon was a righteous individual in a wicked society, a "sober" man (Mormon 1:2, 15), sensitive to the Spirit and the ways of the Lord. He knew the blessings that could come from keeping the covenants of the Lord and walking in His ways. When he was only fifteen years old he had been "visited of the Lord, and tasted and knew of the goodness of Jesus" (Mormon 1:15).[1197]

He spent most of his life honoring the commandment of the Lord to write the history of his people. Mormon was careful to follow the instructions given to him by God regarding what the message of his record should be. He put enough detail into his book that future generations would be well aware of the lessons to be learned from the destruction of his people, without submerging them in the profound anguish that he experienced at the loss of the "fair ones" whose history he recorded.

FURTHER READING

Richard Neitzel Holzapfel, "Mormon, the Man and the Message," in *The Book of Mormon: Fourth Nephi, From Zion to Destruction,* ed. Monte S. Nyman and Charles D. Tate Jr. (Provo, UT: BYU Religious Studies Center, 1995), 117–131.

E. Dale LeBaron, "Ether and Mormon: Parallel Prophets of Warning and Witness," in *The Book of Mormon: Fourth Nephi, From Zion to Destruction*, ed. Monte S. Nyman and Charles D. Tate Jr. (Provo, UT: BYU Religious Studies Center, 1995), 153–165.

Andrew C. Skinner, "The Course of Peace and Apostasy," in *Book of Mormon, Part 2: Alma 30 to Moroni, Studies in Scripture, Volume 8*, ed. Kent Jackson (Salt Lake City, UT: Deseret Book, 1988), 227–228.

94

Why Is the Ten-Year Peace Treaty Important?

"And it came to pass that the Lamanites did not come to battle again until ten years more had passed away." (Mormon 3:1)

THE KNOW

After briefly reporting on twenty-four continuous years of war and wickedness, Mormon said that the Nephites entered into a treaty with the Lamanites in the 350th year (see Mormon 2:28).[1198] The terms of the treaty required the Nephites to forfeit all their territory in the land southward (see Mormon 2:29), but it brought peace for ten full years in return (see Mormon 3:1). Assuming that the Nephites' festival schedule reset when they started counting their years from Christ's birth, this would have been a jubilee year.[1199] The jubilee year was an additional sabbatical year observed at the end of the seventh seven-year sabbatical period.[1200]

According Robin J. DeWitt Knauth, "The Year of Jubilee . . . is the last layer in the extension of the Sabbath principle."[1201] Being the pinnacle of the sabbatical system, the jubilee year came every fifty years.[1202] It is easy to imagine that a people who saw significance in calendrical cycles of seven would surely have noticed that this jubilee year in the 350th year was not just any jubilee—it was the seventh jubilee since the birth of Christ (350 being 7 x 50).[1203]

Given the decadence and wickedness among both the Nephites and the Lamanites, it is hard to say whether the symbolic importance of that year was widely recognized.[1204] Mormon, no doubt, was aware, and as the chief captain of the Nephite armies, he was probably instrumental in negotiating the terms and timing of the treaty.

Resting the land was central to both the jubilee law in general and to this treaty in particular. The jubilee was intended to be "a year of 'rest' for the land." It was also a time when "land was to be restored to its original inherited line of ownership."[1205] It therefore seems significant that at a time when land was supposed to be restored to its proper owner, large portions of Nephite and Lamanite lands were reallocated under the terms of this ten-year treaty, as they "did get the lands of their inheritance divided" (Mormon 2:28). Any Nephites who still celebrated the jubilee could not have missed the significance: in the Lord's eyes, they were no longer the proper owners of any land south of the narrow neck.

This reality probably wasn't what Mormon would have hoped for in an ideal world, though he still likely welcomed the respite from combat that this extended jubilee season and treaty afforded. Mormon had taken command of the Nephite armies in his mid-teens (see Mormon 2:2). He was now forty years old and was battle-worn after spending the better part of his life at war. Somewhere amid all the warfare and wickedness, Mormon must have found time to marry and father a son, Moroni. As the 350th year approached, he was likely eager to celebrate the jubilee season in peace with his family and other righteous followers.

The extended period of peace also afforded him other opportunities. For one, Mormon took advantage of the time to preach repentance unto the people, although it was to no avail (see Mormon 3:2–3). It was probably during this time that Mormon wrote his epistle on faith, hope, and charity (see Moroni 7) and also did the bulk of his work on the Nephite record, exploring the vast historical archive with which he had been entrusted, formulating the narrative he wanted to tell, and abridging and condensing that material into much of the Book of Mormon.

Moroni was probably a teenager during this time of peace, working under his father as an apprentice, learning the history of his people, and preparing for his role as the final Nephite record keeper and abridger. Given that Mormon was busy commanding the armies before the treaty, and Mormon and Moroni would both become embroiled again in war after the peace treaty expired, these were likely important, formative years for Moroni.

THE WHY

This ten-year treaty is a subtle detail, considering how rapidly Mormon passed over those years. The casual Book of Mormon reader can easily feel overwhelmed by the horrific accounts of war and wonder how Mormon, the leading military commander, would have had time to write such an extensive record of his people's history. The treaty provided an important—perhaps even essential—window of opportunity for Mormon to focus on his record keeping. Given the importance of the Book of Mormon in inspiring millions to come unto Christ, the Lord Himself was no doubt instrumental in bringing about this vital period of peace.

The timing—in the seventh jubilee year—was also significant. The jubilee year was a time of peace, rest, prosperity, forgiveness, and blessings.[1206] For their final jubilee before their complete destruction, the Nephites were granted an extended period of peace. Yet that peace came at the cost of all their territory in the land southward. The loss of land at a time when the land should be redeemed should serve as a powerful warning for modern-day readers: just as the Nephites lost their land, so can mighty nations of today fall if they turn away from God and succumb to evil.

The treaty was also a testament to the good that righteous leaders can do, even in times of wickedness. As commander of the army, Mormon managed to bring peace to his people for ten full years—and at an important juncture in their history, namely the seventh jubilee since the coming of Christ. Though the people ultimately failed to take advantage of the opportunity to repent that this period of peace afforded them, it would be a mistake to dismiss it as a failure.

Although the peace did not last, to obtain a full decade of peace in the face of perpetual war and total annihilation was a major accomplishment. No doubt it served as a blessing that strengthened Mormon's people. The efforts of Mormon and potentially other righteous Nephite leaders involved in the negotiations should not be devalued, as they underscore the unremitting importance of choosing righteous leaders.

Perhaps most impressively, the treaty was also evidence of the Lord's mercy. Despite the Nephites' wickedness and their prophesied fate of destruction drawing nearer, it was not too late for them to change course. In this special jubilee year, the Lord "had spared them, and granted unto them a chance for repentance" (Mormon 3:3) and to thereby obtain forgiveness.

Unfortunately, "the people failed to recognize that the period of peace they had experienced had come to them . . . as a merciful blessing from God to give them an opportunity to repent."[1207] Today, even as the world drifts further away from the Lord's standards, the opportunity for individuals and society as a whole to repent and change course is not lost, but time may be growing short.

FURTHER READING

John W. Welch and J. Gregory Welch, "Benjamin's Themes Related to Sabbatical and Jubilee Years," in *Charting the Book of Mormon: Visual Aids for Personal Study and Teaching* (Provo, UT: FARMS, 1999), chart 91.

Terrence L. Szink and John W. Welch, "King Benjamin's Speech in the Context of Ancient Israelite Festivals," in *King Benjamin's Speech: "That Ye May Learn Wisdom,"* ed. John W. Welch and Stephen D. Ricks (Provo, UT: FARMS, 1998), 193–199.

95

Why Did the Lamanites Sacrifice Women and Children to Idols?

"And they did . . . take many prisoners both women and children, and did offer them up as sacrifices unto their idol gods." (Mormon 4:14)

THE KNOW

While capturing the city Teancum, the Lamanites took many women and children as prisoners and sacrificed them to idols (see Mormon 4:14). Although human sacrifice was likely practiced in earlier times among the Lehites, this is the first time it's specifically recorded in the Book of Mormon.[1208] This shocking event may come as a gut-wrenching surprise to the reader. One wonders why anyone would commit such a senselessly violent act.

Yet human sacrifice happened often in the ancient world.[1209] It appears to have been common during times of apostasy in ancient Israel for people to cause their children to "pass through the fire to Molech" (2 Kings 23:10).[1210] This appears to have been a form of human sacrifice.[1211]

Child sacrifice also has a long tradition in ancient Mesoamerica, where children were sometimes sacrificed to honor a new king.[1212] The earliest evidence stretches back into early Olmec times (1600–1000 BC), where bone fragments from several newborn infants showing clear signs of being sacrificed and dismembered were discovered in a pond at Cerro el Manatí in Veracruz, Mexico.[1213] Similarly, at the Maya site of Colha, Belize, thirty decapitated skulls, including ten from children, were deposited in a pit dating to AD 800 to 850.[1214]

Based on known ancient practices, there are a number of reasons why the Lamanites might have chosen to perform human sacrifice at this time. One possible reason was because a high-status Lamanite (or many high-status Lamanites) may have died in attempts to take the city of Teancum. This might have prompted the companions of these high-status individuals to kill the women and children of the city to serve as wives and servants in the afterlife. This kind of practice was common in the ancient Near East.[1215]

In the ancient Egyptian town of Abydos, for example, the body of a ruler named Djer was discovered, surrounded by the bodies of women who were likely his wives, concubines, or maids.[1216] A similar situation was found at the ancient Mesopotamian city of Ur, where large numbers of attendants, both male and female, had been sacrificed and were buried with the Sumerian queen Puabi to accompany her into the afterlife.[1217]

Similar practices are found in pre-Columbian America.[1218] At a place called Cahokia, near St. Louis, the body of a ruler was found surrounded by fifty-three women who had been sacrificed.[1219] In Mayan, Toltec, and Teotihuacan culture, one also sees women and children offered as sacrifices in a similar way. In some of these cases, it appears that the people being sacrificed had little connection to the dead leader.[1220]

The Lamanites may have also felt that such a sacrifice would help win the war by persuading an idol to fight for them. In the Old Testament, the "the king of Moab . . . took his eldest son that should have reigned in his stead, and offered him for a burnt offering upon the wall." The king offered his child to the Moabite god Chemosh in the middle of battle in order to ensure that he would win the war he was fighting (see 2 Kings 3:26–27).[1221] This implies that he thought the god would fight for him. The Lamanites may also have felt that sacrificing children would help them win. In a related practice, people at Carthage, in North Africa, performed child sacrifice as an assurance that business ventures would succeed.[1222]

Another possibility is that the individuals were sacrificed to obtain war trophies from their body parts, a prevalent practice in pre-columbian North, Central, and South America that often coincided with cannibalism.[1223] Archaeological evidence of cannibalism in Mesoamerica has been suggested for infant sacrifices dating as far back as early Olmec times (1600–1000 BC).[1224]

One final possibility is that the Lamanite warriors thought the sacrifices would help their crops grow. During a time of war, as existed in Mormon 4, crops were often destroyed, causing famine.[1225] This meant that the productivity of the surviving crops became even more important. In Mesoamerica, children were sacrificed during times of famine because people felt that this would increase crop yield.[1226]

THE WHY

One might wonder at first how human sacrifice and idolatry could have been practiced by the children of Lehi after the glorious period of peace described in 4 Nephi. However, it is likely that when Mormon wrote about peace in "all the land" (4 Nephi 1:13), he meant all the land of the Nephites and Lamanites.[1227] If this is the case, then many wicked and idolatrous practices, including human sacrifice, could have been preserved by the Lehites' neighbors and then later reintroduced into Lehite society.[1228]

From the Lamanites, similar practices seem to have spread to the Nephites. It is possible that this chapter of Mormon was written around the same time as Moroni 9, a letter from Mormon to his son. The Nephites would eventually commit heinous crimes, similar to yet even worse than those of the Lamanites (see Moroni 9:10). This suggests that both the Lamanites and Nephites allowed negative influences from neighboring cultures to influence them.

This can serve as a reminder to modern readers of the Book of Mormon that negative influences from surrounding cultures can have a harmful impact on those who believe in Christ. It cautions readers to separate themselves from the negative influences that surround them, something the children of Lehi failed to do.

The Book of Mormon teaches that the shedding of innocent blood is among the most abominable of all sins (see Alma 39:5). A people once so blessed and chosen of God descended to the depths of the worst depravity: killing innocent women and children in the name of false gods. While such acts seem deplorable and unthinkable to many, the descent to such actions begins with a single step. Once one loses the companionship of the Holy Ghost, it is a slippery slope to becoming "past feeling" (Moroni 9:20).

The adversary works hard to push the children of men past feeling so that they willfully break the commandments of God. Not only was the sacrifice of women and children breaking the commandments of God, but it made a mockery of the ultimate sacrifice of the Son of God. Jesus Christ sacrificed Himself so that we would not have to suffer the same fate. The sacrifice of the Son of God was an infinite and eternal sacrifice to break the bands of death and bring salvation to the children of men.[1229]

FURTHER READING

Brant A. Gardner, *Second Witness: Analytical & Contextual Commentary on the Book of Mormon*, 6 vols. (Salt Lake City, UT: Greg Kofford Books, 2007), 6:81–82.

96 What Was Mormon's Purpose in Writing the Book of Mormon?

"And for this intent shall they go—that they may be persuaded that Jesus is the Christ, the Son of the living God." (Mormon 5:14)

THE KNOW

The meaning of any text can be greatly clarified if the fundamental purposes or goals of its primary author are known. The Book of Mormon is no different. Those readers who want to deepen their understanding of its message would do well to pay attention to Mormon's selection of source material, his frequent editorial comments, and his own explicit statements about why he was writing his record.[1230] Mormon sprinkled clues about his purposes and source selection throughout the Book of Mormon that can be easy to miss. A number of things can be learned about Mormon's primary goals and purposes by gathering these clues.

To Fulfill Prophecy

Mormon declared that he was creating his record so "that the prayers of those who have gone hence, who were the holy ones, should be fulfilled according to their faith" (3 Nephi 5:14). Mormon likely had past prophets like Enos in mind here (see Enos 1:13–18). In this sense, Mormon's purpose was to fulfill prophecy "according to the will of God" (3 Nephi 5:14).

To Testify of the Land of Promise

After analyzing Mormon's primary sources, John L. Sorenson asserted that one of Mormon's major editorial aims was to affirm Lehi's blessing upon the land: "Inasmuch as ye will keep my commandments ye shall prosper in the land" (Jarom 1:9).[1231] Sorenson further noted that "overwhelmingly, Mormon's writings depict the Nephites poised on the edge of destruction due to their failure to meet the condition of Lehi's law of survival."[1232] Such narrative episodes aptly serve as a warning to modern audiences who are similarly threatened by impending calamities (see D&C 1:17).

To Provide Spiritual Guidance

Richard Holzapfel has argued that "Mormon's motive for writing and editing the Nephite record seems clear. He regularly sought to draw spiritual lessons from the course of Nephite history."[1233] Also, the Book of Mormon provides spiritual guidance as it works as a companion with the Bible, "unto the confounding of false doctrines and laying down of contentions, and establishing peace" (2 Nephi 3:12; cf. Mormon 7:9).

To Record Whatever the Spirit Impressed Upon Him

In Words of Mormon, readers learn that Mormon was writing for a "wise purpose; for thus it whispereth me, according to the workings of the Spirit of the Lord which is in me" (Words of Mormon 1:7). Interestingly, Mormon then stated, "I do not know all things; but the Lord knoweth all things which are to come; wherefore, he worketh in me to do according to his will" (Words of Mormon 1:7). This suggests that, at least on some levels, even Mormon didn't understand the full purpose of his record. In many cases, he was likely selecting sources and making comments according to the "workings of the Spirit" and not necessarily his own thinking (Words of Mormon 1:7).

To Affirm that Jesus Is the Christ

Mormon said the Book of Mormon would "come forth in [the Lord's] own due time" so that future generations "may be persuaded that Jesus is the Christ, the Son of the living God" (Mormon 5:12, 14). This wording is echoed in Moroni's recapping in the title page of the Book of Mormon, which states that the sacred record would come forth "to the convincing of the Jew and Gentile that Jesus is the Christ" (Book of Mormon Title Page).[1234]

These repeated thesis statements, written after the abridging of the books of 3 and 4 Nephi, suggest that the most fundamental purpose of Mormon's record was to persuade or convince future audiences that Jesus is the Christ. As Brant A. Gardner put it, "Mormon did not write to convince us that the Messiah's doctrine is true, but rather that Jesus is the Messiah."[1235]

THE WHY

These various examples help demonstrate that Mormon's editorial goals were sometimes layered and complex—and likely developed and changed over time as he worked. Grant Hardy recognized that "as a historian, [Mormon] needs to present an overview of Nephite history that is true to his sources; as a writer, he wants to construct a narrative that is aesthetically pleasing and compelling; and as a moralist, he takes responsibility for teaching correct doctrine and providing spiritual guidance."[1236] To this it can be added that, as a prophet, he sought to accurately portray the mind and will of the Lord. Yet whether writing as a prophet, historian, literary artist, or moralist, Mormon's overarching purpose was clearly intent on helping future generations "believe in Christ" (Mormon 7:10).

Mormon seemed to understand that the fulfillment of his various narrative goals and the overall persuasiveness of his record was strongly tied to its status as authentic history.[1237] Hardy explained, "Generally Mormon is a practitioner of narrative theology; that is, he relies on stories to convince readers of the power of God, the consequences of sin, the reality of prophecy, and so forth."[1238] Yet for these stories to have their full persuasive effect, they must necessarily be true. Stephen O. Smoot explained,

> The legitimacy of the most important theological claims of the Book of Mormon hinges on whether the attending story that conveys the doctrine actually happened. . . . The Book of Mormon, accordingly, must be historical and read as history in order for it to really contain the fullness of the theological power it claims to have.[1239]

For example, readers would naturally struggle to accept the Book of Mormon as the fulfillment of prophecy if they doubted that its prophets were real historical individuals. The blessings on the land of promise could hardly be taken seriously if the narratives that demonstrate their historical fulfillment never actually took place. Its doctrinal teachings, such as faith and repentance, would lose their potency if none of its stories of redemption or faith-evoked miracles really happened. And most importantly, the text's status as a second witness of Jesus Christ would be seriously undermined if Christ never actually visited the Americas and ministered at the temple in Bountiful.[1240]

It can thus be seen that Mormon's various purposes could only be accomplished if the Book of Mormon were accepted as the legitimate historical document that it is. Its stories of faith, repentance, sacrifice, service, miracles—and especially its account of Jesus Christ's resurrected ministry—are so powerful because they are historically, and not just metaphorically or symbolically, true.

Mormon's "urge for historical accuracy," however, shouldn't lead readers to conclude that the portrayal of history itself is what will do the convincing.[1241] Rather his recorded stories and inspired commentary serve as vehicles for personal revelation. Moroni's famous promise, for instance, explicitly exhorts and invites readers to ask God the Eternal Father about the truthfulness of the record, and it ensures that if they do so in sincerity and faith in the name of Jesus Christ, "he will manifest the truth of it . . . by the power of the Holy Ghost" (Moroni 10:4).

Because the power of the Holy Ghost will unequivocally testify to the historical reality and spiritual message of the Book of Mormon, it therefore stands as a valid witness of God's influence and interaction with His children.[1242] To believe in the truth of its stories is to believe in the divinity, resurrection, and miraculous power of Jesus Christ. To follow its messages and commandments is to follow the words, inspiration, and "Spirit of Christ" (Moroni 7:16) and to "come unto him, and be perfected in him" (Moroni 10:32).

FURTHER READING

John L. Sorenson, "Mormon's Sources," *Journal of the Book of Mormon and Other Restoration Scripture 20*, no. 2 (2011): 2–15.

Grant Hardy, *Understanding the Book of Mormon: A Reader's Guide* (New York, NY: Oxford University Press, 2010), 89–120.

Brant A. Gardner, "Mormon's Editorial Method and Meta-Message," *FARMS Review 21*, no. 1 (2009): 83–105.

Richard Neitzel Holzapfel, "Mormon, the Man and the Message," in *The Book of Mormon: Fourth Nephi, From Zion to Destruction*, ed. Monte S. Nyman and Charles D. Tate Jr. (Provo, UT: BYU Religious Studies Center, 1995), 117–131.

97

How Could so Many People Have Died at the Battle of Cumorah?

"And Lamah . . . and Gilgal . . . and Limhah . . . and Jeneum . . . and Cumenihah, and Moronihah, and Antionum, and Shiblom, and Shem, and Josh, had fallen with their ten thousand each." (Mormon 6:14)

THE KNOW

In the final battle at the Hill Cumorah, the Lamanites completely decimated the Nephites. Mormon stated that the Lamanites killed roughly 230,000 of his people.[1243] At first, this number may seem impossibly large. One wonders how an army of 230,000 people could exist during a time when the entire population of the world was probably only around 206 million.[1244] It is impossible to know exactly why these numbers are so high, but there are a few possibilities.

1. Mormon May Have Exaggerated

The first thing to consider is that ancient texts often exaggerate population sizes.[1245] In the Old Testament, for example, 600,000 Israelite males are said to have left Egypt (see Exodus 12:37).[1246] When one considers the women and children that left at the same time, this would mean that about 2.5 million Israelites left Egypt at the same time. Since the entire population of Egypt at the time was likely only 2.8 million, these numbers seem to be clearly exaggerated.[1247] It is therefore possible that Mormon, like other ancient historians, simply exaggerated when talking about numbers this large.[1248]

2. A Thousand May Not Actually Mean a Thousand

It is also possible that "ten thousand" represents a military unit and not an exact number of soldiers. In Hebrew, the word *eleph* can mean the literal number 1,000, but it can also mean a military squad.[1249] If this is the case, each military commander could simply have been in charge of ten "squads" of unknown numbers, putting the number of casualties much lower than they might seem at first.[1250]

3. The Army May Actually Have Been Massive

While it is important to be aware of these different possibilities, some evidence suggests that these figures are accurate. The population of pre-Columbian America was much larger than many people assume. In fact, during many periods, the Americas were more populous than Europe.[1251] Thus, 230,000 casualties may have been a reasonable figure in Mormon's day. The Book of Mormon's own population data is consistent with this figure. As one examines the occasions when population size is mentioned throughout the Book of Mormon, and assumes normal population growth, 230,000 deaths in the final battle at Cumorah is not problematic.[1252]

One sees this from the size of actual armies in pre-Columbian America. In Mesoamerica, for example, even after rounding down significantly to account for the above-mentioned tendency of authors to exaggerate, the Aztecs gathered more than 300,000 people for a war against a neighboring kingdom, and this was not noted as a remarkable event. The Quiche, similarly, were able to put an army of 232,000 men into the field, even though many refused to fight.[1253] This demonstrates that the casualty figures cited by Mormon are at least feasible.

4. 230,000 Could Represent the Entire Population

One disturbing possibility presented by Mormon 6 is that most of the Nephite population, including women and children, fought in this battle and were killed.[1254]

Mormon stated:

> [All] my people, with their wives and their children, did now behold the armies of the Lamanites marching towards them; and with that awful fear of death which fills the breasts of *all* the wicked, did they await to receive them. (Mormon 6:7; emphasis added)

Later, Mormon lamented, "O ye fair *sons* and *daughters,* ye *fathers* and *mothers,* ye *husbands* and *wives,* ye fair ones, how is it that ye could have fallen!" (Mormon 6:19; emphasis added). Although it is impossible to say for sure, these verses strongly imply that the entire population fought the Lamanites, and that the 230,000 figure represents that.[1255]

THE WHY

As one examines these possible answers to the question of such high casualty figures, interesting implications arise:

1. If the numbers are exaggerated, this is a reminder to the reader that the Book of Mormon was written like many other ancient texts.
2. If the word *thousand* actually represents military units instead of a number, this gives the reader a fresh insight into the translation of the Book of Mormon.
3. If the numbers are accurate, this shows attention to accuracy of details that is exceptional for an ancient text.
4. If the number actually represents the whole population, this reminds the reader of the tragic nature of this final battle of the Book of Mormon.

There are two overarching approaches one can take when reading the Book of Mormon. One approach is to assume that the book is false, stating that each confusing element in the book proves it to be a fraud. The other is have faith, give the book the benefit of the doubt, look at it through an ancient lens, and realize that ancient texts are rarely as clear-cut as modern readers would prefer. This second approach means that readers of the Book of Mormon need to read it in the same way they might read other ancient sacred texts. They need to be patient with the book, consider it thoughtfully, and not dismiss details that seem strange as a sign that the book is not authentic.

Exploring difficulties and potential solutions available—rather than dismissing them out of hand—creates opportunities to learn, discover, grow, and ultimately increase in faith. If something about the Book of Mormon seems confusing, out of place, or unexpected, this simply means that the Book of Mormon joins the Bible as a book that needs to be pondered and considered carefully if one is to understand seeming oddities in the text.

Whether there were 23,000 killed or 230,000 killed, the destruction was an absolute tragedy and a horror for Mormon and Moroni to witness. This is the appalling climax of action for the whole Book of Mormon narrative. A people who were blessed and righteous for so long ultimately destroyed themselves in senseless acts of violence and carnage.

In a day when senseless acts of violence frequently trouble modern nations, it is easy to imagine the emotional effect on the Nephites. Similarly, wars raging across the earth today kill millions. If the modern reader feels compassion and heartbreak for the victims and families of wars and shootings that people throughout the world experience, then how much more should the reader feel compassion and heartbreak for the destruction of the chosen and blessed Nephites? Yet if the reader feels such poignancy for the Nephites, how much more should they now turn with compassion to those suffering the ravages of war and violence today? And if the reader is filled with compassion for those suffering today, consider how much more God weeps and is heartbroken over the destruction of His children (see Moses 7:29, 32).

FURTHER READING

James E. Smith, "How Many Nephites?: The Book of Mormon at the Bar of Demography," in *Book of Mormon Authorship Revisited*, ed. Noel B. Reynolds (Provo, UT: FARMS, 1997), 255–293.

James E. Smith, "Nephi's Descendants? Historical Demography and the Book of Mormon," *Review of Books on the Book of Mormon* 6, no. 1 (1994): 284–294.

98

How Did Mormon React to Seeing His People Slain?

"O ye fair ones, how could ye have departed from the ways of the Lord!" (Mormon 6:17)

THE KNOW

"O ye fair ones," Mormon lamented, as he reflected upon the destruction of his people. "How could ye have departed from the ways of the Lord! . . . how could ye have rejected that Jesus, who stood with open arms to receive you! Behold," he mourned, "if ye had not done this, ye would not have fallen. But behold, ye are fallen, and I mourn your loss" (Mormon 6:17–18).

Mormon's "soul was rent with anguish" as he witnessed "the slain of [his] people" (Mormon 6:16). That anguish pours out onto the page as one reads his sorrowful lament:

> O ye fair
> sons and daughters,
> ye fathers and mothers,
> ye husbands and wives,
> ye fair ones,
> how is it that ye could have fallen!
> But behold, ye are gone,
> and my sorrows cannot bring your return. (Mormon 6:19–20)

Perhaps because mourning the loss of a loved one is among the most universal aspects of human experience, laments are among the earliest forms of literature in the world, going back to at least the third millennium BC.[1256] "From ancient Sumer," wrote Nancy C. Lee, a religious studies professor, "the laments of poets and singers still resonate with the agony of those who today suffer from war and deprivations."[1257]

The same could be said of Jeremiah's lamentations on the fall of Jerusalem and its people to the Babylonians in 586 BC (see Lamentations). Or consider the example centuries later when the Savior lamented over the city's unwillingness to follow the Lord (see Matthew 23:37; Luke 13:34).[1258]

In the ancient Near East, funeral laments "are typically characterized by short [exclamatory] phrases of the kind 'Oh, my son!',"[1259] not unlike Mormon's sorrowful refrain: *O ye fair ones!* In ancient funeral laments, this exclamation is followed by "narrative passages which contrast the gloriously depicted past of the deceased with the mournful present,"[1260] just as Mormon did:

> how could ye have departed from the ways of the Lord! . . . how could ye have rejected that Jesus, who stood with open arms to receive you! . . . But

behold, ye are fallen, and I mourn your
loss. (Mormon 6:17–18)

As he wrote these words, Mormon was probably envisioning the glorious era of peace and prosperity initiated by the personal visit of the resurrected Lord, which he had read about in the Nephite record. This stark contrast no doubt added to the tragic sting of death that surrounded him.

Ancient poets also applied the forms of funeral laments to whole cities in city laments, "as if the city were a deceased person."[1261] Jeremiah did this as he lamented the destruction of Jerusalem from which Lehi had fled (see Lamentations). Centuries later, the Savior too would lament, "O Jerusalem!" (Matthew 23:37; Luke 13:34).

Mormon similarly applied the form not only to the destruction of an entire city, but the genocide of his people. Like the laments of Jesus, Jeremiah, and other ancient poets and prophets, Mormon's lament powerfully evokes agony and suffering that readers today can readily feel and relate to.

"When relevant," funeral laments would often include curses "directed at those responsible for the death of the deceased."[1262] Mormon, however, knew it was the Nephites who were to blame for their own destruction. And so, he concluded with this ominous warning:

> And the day soon cometh that your mortal must put on immortality,
> and these bodies which are now moldering in corruption must soon become incorruptible bodies;
> and then ye must stand before the judgment-seat of Christ,
> to be judged according to your works;
> and if it so be that ye are righteous,
> then are ye blessed with your fathers who have gone before you.
> O that ye had repented before this great destruction had come upon you.
> But behold, ye are gone,
> and the Father, yea, the Eternal Father of heaven, knoweth your state; and he doeth with you according to his justice and mercy. (Mormon 6:21–22)

Instead of cursing the Lamanites, whom he could have blamed for the death of his people, Mormon invited the Lamanites to repent and receive the gospel (see Mormon 7), to "lay down your weapons of war, and delight no more in the shedding of blood" and "believe in Jesus Christ, that he is the Son of God" (Mormon 7:4–5).[1263]

THE WHY

Mormon's careful variation from traditional lament forms is important.[1264] He did not curse the Lamanites, nor even blame them for his people's destruction, though that would have been easy to do. Instead, he recognized that his people had only themselves and their own wickedness to blame. So he warned that they would soon stand before God in judgment, and he hoped for the best, trusting that God would judge "according to his justice and mercy" (Mormon 6:22). As for the descendants of those who were his enemies (the Lamanites), he invited them to come unto Christ.

Mormon was deeply affected by the tragedy of his people's fall and destruction. The carnage he witnessed is hard to fathom. Mormon's lament was not merely for the loss of a loved one, like that of a funeral lament, but rather for the loss of a people—his people—the Nephites, the "fair ones."[1265]

Despite witnessing what was no doubt emotionally and psychologically traumatizing, Mormon set a worthy example to follow in his final words. His people were wicked, yet he loved them deeply and greatly grieved their loss. He did not seek to blame others, despite his sorrow, and he loved his enemies, inviting them to come unto Christ and put an end to the needless bloodshed.

Readers today can learn to similarly love even those who err, accept personal responsibility for their own choices, and accept the consequences of divine judgments. Instead of blaming others, even those who mourn can find comfort in loving their enemies, praying for those who have despitefully used them, and inviting them to come unto Christ.

FURTHER READING

Matthew L. Bowen, "'O Ye Fair Ones'—Revisited," *Interpreter: A Journal of Mormon Scripture 20* (2016): 315–344.

Matthew L. Bowen, "'O Ye Fair Ones': An Additional Note on the Meaning of the Name Nephi," *Insights: A Window on the Ancient World 23*, no. 6 (2003): 2.

Thomas W. Mackay, "Mormon and the Destruction of Nephite Civilization (Mormon 3–9)," in *Book of Mormon, Part 2: Alma 30 to Moroni, Studies in Scripture, Volume 8*, ed. Kent P. Jackson (Salt Lake City, UT: Deseret Book, 1988), 231–244.

99

Why Did Moroni Write so Many Farewells?

"Behold I, Moroni, do finish the record of my father, Mormon." (Mormon 8:1)

THE KNOW

Turning the page of Mormon's concluding farewell in Mormon 7, readers are introduced to a new author: "Behold I, Moroni, do finish the record of my father, Mormon" (Mormon 8:1). Full of sorrow, Moroni explained that his father was killed by the Lamanites and that he remained "alone to write the sad tale of the destruction of [his] people" (Mormon 8:3). Moroni's remarks in Mormon 8–9 not only finish his father's record,[1266] but they also seem to function as his own farewell.[1267]

Readers may wonder why Moroni would deliver a farewell address and then later go on to include an abridgment of the book of Ether, ten more chapters of a book bearing his own name, and two more farewell endings, one in Ether 12:38–41 and the other in Moroni 10:34. One consideration is that as time progressed, his circumstances and perspectives may have changed and the agony of defeat may have dimmed and healed. In any event, Moroni may have welcomed the opportunity to convey different concluding messages that he felt the Book of Mormon deserved.[1268]

First Farewell

At first, in Mormon 8–9, Moroni explained his uncertainty about the future, declaring "whether they will slay me, I know not" (Mormon 8:3) and "how long the Lord will suffer that I may live I know not" (Mormon 8:5). He reported that he couldn't even write the intent of the record because he didn't have "room upon the plates," and as for "ore I have none, for I am alone" (Mormon 8:5). These verses may indicate that when writing his initial farewell, Moroni was feeling at a loss. He was running out of space and out of time, and he felt duty-bound to conclude his father's record in case he suffered an untimely death.[1269]

Under this sense of urgency, Moroni laid down the law. He issued a series of warnings to protect the record (see Mormon 8:14–22); he prophesied about the conditions when the Lord would bring the record forth (see Mormon 8:26–30); he testified to future peoples (see Mormon 8:35; 9:1, 7, 30); he asked a number of penetrating questions; and he declared four attestations of judgment ("still, still, still, still," Mormon 9:14). He then challenged any who would oppose him ("who can stand?" "who can deny?" "who will despise?" Mormon 9:2–26); he stated almost two dozen commandments (see Mormon 9:27–31); he validated his work with attestations (see Mormon 9:31–35); and he concluded with three pleas that Jesus would nonetheless answer the prayers of the righteous Saints, remember His covenant with the House of Israel, and bless them (see Mormon 9:37).

Second Farewell

In the ensuing years, Moroni must have eventually found enough ore to create additional plates.[1270] At some point, he assumed that he would add only the book of Ether, so he wrote his second farewell, including it in Ether 12. Here he was much less legalistic and much more conciliatory. Perhaps he had been sobered by the fate that befell not only the Jaredites but also his own people. Here he wanted the Gentiles and his brethren, the Lamanites, to know that he loved them (see Ether 12:38), that he had seen Jesus and learned from Him (see Ether 12:39), and that he commended Jesus unto them—that the grace of the Father and the Son may abide with them forever, as the Holy Ghost bears record (see Ether 12:41).

Final Farewell

After finishing his abridgment of the Jaredite history, Moroni returned a third time, reporting: "I had supposed not to have written more, but I have not as yet perished. . . . Wherefore, I write a few more things, contrary to that which I had supposed" (Moroni 1:1–4). He further explained, "I write a few more things, that perhaps they may be of worth unto my brethren, the Lamanites, in some future day, according to the will of the Lord" (Moroni 1:4).[1271] His submission "to the will of the Lord" is telling, suggesting that the Lord was involved—either through inspiration or direct revelation—in his decision to add his final chapters to the record.[1272]

At this point, Moroni included in his record the sacred words to be used in performing priesthood ordinances (see Moroni 2–6), and he copied three items from his father, Mormon, that are of great worth, regarding grace, gifts, faith, hope, love (see Moroni 7); baptism (see Moroni 8); and the atrocities for which the Nephites were obliterated (see Moroni 9).

Finally, he ended with a series of exhortations, begging people to remember, to ask, to deny not, and to come unto Christ, to be perfect in him by the grace of God (see Moroni 10:32) and successful before the judgment bar of the great Jehovah (see Moroni 10:34). Here, Moroni affirmed that God's grace offers the way for all to become sanctified and no more confounded (see Moroni 10:31, 33).[1273]

THE WHY

Moroni wrote his first farewell in the 400th year (see Mormon 8:6), approximately fifteen years after the final battle at Cumorah (see Mormon 6:5), and his final farewell was delivered after the 420th year (see Moroni 10:1), twenty years after his first farewell.[1274] The lengthy gap between these conclusions is significant. For a substantial amount of time, Moroni was likely uncertain what would happen to him, and after his initial farewell, he had twenty years to think about the record and what he might add to its pages.

When readers recognize that Moroni's three farewells were written at different stages of his life and in the context of different record-keeping projects, they can better understand the purpose and meaning of each one. In the first, he spoke with the voice of justice. In the second, he found himself moved by sympathy. As Steve Walker has observed, "Through this [second] closing scenario, stunned at the finality of it, we are staring over the shoulder of Moroni as he stares over the shoulder of the eyewitness, Ether, stupefied by the utter senselessness of this total destruction."[1275]

In the third, Moroni turned the matter over to the will and grace of God. As Elder M. Russell Ballard pointed out, "the Restoration is not an event, but it continues to unfold."[1276] So too, with Moroni: his endings for the Book of Mormon also unfolded as he was able to revisit and add point upon point to his concluding messages.

Moroni's three separate farewells provide readers with three different opportunities to understand the purposes of the Book of Mormon through the eyes of Moroni, its last author and record keeper. As a solemn warning to us today, Mark D. Thomas poetically described Moroni as a "holy wanderer on the border of life and death, on the boundary of meaning and meaninglessness, [who] passes a note to us regarding the collapse of our own house on the top of our own final Cumorah."[1277]

Remarkably, and in spite of the depravity of his own situation, Moroni was ultimately able to deliver a message of redemption, a promise that readers could be forgiven and become "holy, without spot" (Moroni 10:33). As Walker concluded, "That bottom-line hope, stunning amid the otherwise grim finalities, dramatizes the literary reach of the" entire Book of Mormon.[1278]

FURTHER READING

James E. Faulconer, "Sealings and Mercies: Moroni's Final Exhortations in Moroni 10," *Journal of the Book of Mormon and Other Restoration Scripture* 22, no. 1 (2013): 4–19.

Steve Walker, "Last Words: 4 Nephi–Moroni," in *The Reader's Book of Mormon*, ed. Robert A. Rees and Eugene England, 7 vols. (Salt Lake City, UT: Signature Books, 2008), 7: vii–xxii.

Mark D. Thomas, "Moroni: The Final Voice," *Journal of Book of Mormon Studies 12*, no. 1 (2003): 88–99, 119–120.

Sidney B. Sperry, "Moroni the Lonely: The Story of the Writing of the Title Page to the Book of Mormon," *Journal of Book of Mormon Studies 4*, no. 1 (1995): 255–259.

How Can the Book of Mormon Survivors Give Us Hope?

"I even remain alone to write the sad tale of the destruction of my people." (Mormon 8:3)

THE KNOW

Hugh Nibley once described the Book of Mormon as a "tragic book" that begins and ends with destruction and lone survivors.[1279] Its prophetic authors had great cause to mourn, yet the fact that its message of hope in Christ was conveyed by those who had witnessed and survived the worst of human depravity only strengthens its spiritual power. As Steve Walker expressed, "If ever hope were earned, it is this optimism pervading the Book of Mormon narrative, even in the face of the end of all things."[1280]

Lehi, Nephi, and Jacob

When Lehi was called as a prophet, he was shown "great and marvelous things . . . concerning the destruction of Jerusalem" (1 Nephi 1:18). Years later, Nephi not only revealed that this destruction had taken place (see 2 Nephi 25:10), but he saw that in the future his own people would suffer a similar fate: "O the pain, and the anguish of my soul for the loss of the slain of my people! For I, Nephi, have seen it, and it well nigh consumeth me before the presence of the Lord" (2 Nephi 26:7).

Lehi's son Jacob wrote that his people were "wanderers, cast out from Jerusalem, born in tribulation, in a wilderness, and hated of our brethren, which caused wars and contentions; wherefore, we did mourn out our days" (Jacob 7:26). In light of such sobering statements, Lisa Hawkins and Gordon Thomasson noted that "Lehi's entire family can be considered survivor-witnesses of a sort, fleeing from . . . Jerusalem to save Lehi's life."[1281] Yet Lehi, Nephi, and Jacob all rejoiced in Christ and the plan of salvation on numerous occasions, even in the midst of sorrow and suffering.[1282]

Alma the Elder

Alma can be seen as a survivor-witness of Abinadi's prophecies and tragic martyrdom. After risking his own life by pleading on Abinadi's behalf, Alma went into hiding, wrote down Abinadi's words, and used them to gather a following (see Mosiah 17:2–4). Sadly, Alma's followers were forced to flee into the wilderness to escape King Noah's soldiers, only to fall into bondage under Amulon and his Lamanite army a short time later. In the midst of these trying circumstances, the Lord declared to His people that He would ease their burdens so that they could "*stand as witnesses for me hereafter*, and that ye may know of a surety that I, the Lord God, do visit my people in their afflictions" (Mosiah 24:14; emphasis added).[1283]

Alma the Younger and Amulek

While witnessing the terrible martyrdom of women and children by fire, "Amulek said unto Alma: Behold, perhaps they will burn us also. And Alma said: Be it according to the will of the Lord. But, behold, our work is not finished; therefore they burn us not" (Alma 14:12–13).[1284] Alma and Amulek survived this ordeal when others didn't so that they could witness of and testify against the "the chief judge, and the lawyers, and priests, and teachers" who had committed such terrible crimes.[1285] While Alma and Amulek were being persecuted by their captors, an earthquake caused the surrounding prison walls to fall, and "every soul within the walls thereof, save it were Alma and Amulek, was slain" (Alma 14:28).[1286]

Mormon

Mormon's lament for the destruction of his people is filled with terrible anguish: "O ye fair sons and daughters, ye fathers and mothers, ye husbands and wives, ye fair ones, how is it that ye could have fallen! But behold, ye are gone, and my sorrows cannot bring your return" (Mormon 6:19–20).[1287] As a survivor-witness, Mormon declared, "I did stand as an idle witness to manifest unto the world the things which I saw and heard" (Mormon 3:16).[1288] Yet, despite such sorrow, Mormon also stated that he was "filled with charity" (Moroni 8:17) which "rejoiceth in the truth, beareth all things, believeth all things, hopeth all things, endureth all things" (Moroni 7:45).

Ether and Moroni

For years, Ether hid himself in the "cavity of a rock" while he witnessed and recorded the entire destruction of his people (see Ether 13:18–24). Similarly, Moroni explained, "I even remain alone to write the sad tale of the destruction of my people" (Mormon 8:3).[1289] Yet at the very end, these faithful survivor-witnesses saw a bright future beyond death.

Ether could say, "Whether the Lord will that I be translated, or that I suffer the will of the Lord in the flesh, it mattereth not, if it so be that I am saved in the kingdom of God" (Ether 15:34). And in his final words, Moroni remarked, "I soon go to rest in the paradise of God, until my spirit and body shall again reunite, and I am brought forth triumphant through the air" (Moroni 10:34).

THE WHY

In a remarkable study on those who have survived terrible atrocities, Terrence Des Pres explained that having their story told is "enormously important to people facing extinction. In the survivor's own case . . . it becomes a way to transcend the helplessness which withers hope and self-respect."[1290] This certainly seems to be the case with the Book of Mormon prophets who, in the midst of tragic episodes of grief and suffering, diligently recorded their experiences for future generations.[1291]

In our own day, millions suffer from having experienced or witnessed terrible things. Soldiers who experience combat often suffer from post-traumatic stress disorder (PTSD).[1292] Countless individuals struggle with feelings of depression, loneliness, heartache, disappointment, disinterest, and a number of other personal sorrows, mental limitations, and emotional scars. Some of these feelings are due to severe chemical imbalances. Others may be caused by different circumstances out of an individual's control. And sometimes those who suffer simply don't have good answers for why they feel so unhappy.[1293]

The Book of Mormon offers a powerful message of hope to those who for whatever reason have cause to mourn. It shows that while the suffering of its prophetic survivors was real and acute, their overwhelming sorrow was ultimately "swallowed up in the joy of Christ" (Alma 31:38). They mourned for the pain and suffering of their people, but they also looked to the future with hope. They knew that by witnessing and recording these sad experiences, they could help future generations avoid unnecessary sorrows. President Dallin H. Oaks taught that the "Lord will not only consecrate our afflictions for our gain, but He will use them to bless the lives of countless others."[1294]

In each case, the Book of Mormon's sad tales of human atrocities help us refocus our minds and hearts on Jesus Christ—whose infinite sacrifice gives meaning and purpose to our very existence. Not only did Christ experience His own excruciating trials, but through His divine power, He willingly witnessed and participated in our suffering in a way that is personal to each of us.[1295] He is the ultimate survivor-witness. He descended below all things, witnessed the worst of death and hell,[1296] and yet rose again with hope and "healing in His wings."[1297] Elder Jeffrey R. Holland taught, "It is only an appreciation of this divine love that will make our own lesser suffering first bearable, then understandable, and finally redemptive."[1298]

FURTHER READING

Jeffrey R. Holland, "Like a Broken Vessel," *Ensign*, November 2013, 40–42.

Gordon C. Thomasson, "The Survivor and the Will to Bear Witness," in *Reexploring the Book of Mormon: A Decade of New Research,* ed. John W. Welch (Provo, UT: FARMS, 1992), 266–268.

Lisa Bolin Hawkins and Gordon Thomasson, "I Only Am Escaped Alone to Tell Thee: Survivor Witnesses in the Book of Mormon" *FARMS Preliminary Reports* (1984): 1–13.

Are There Other Ancient Records Like the Book of Mormon?

"It shall be brought out of the earth, and it shall shine forth out of darkness, and come unto the knowledge of the people; and it shall be done by the power of God." (Mormon 8:16)

THE KNOW

For some, the story of the coming forth of the Book of Mormon has seemed too bizarre and fanciful to be believable. This was especially true at the time of its publication in 1830. People were suspicious of the claim that an ancient book written on golden plates had been revealed to a young farmer. It has taken nearly two centuries of archaeological discoveries to fully demonstrate that the details of the buried Nephite record fit in exceptionally well with hidden books from all over the ancient world.

Hidden Records

Many passages in the Book of Mormon speak of it and other records being hidden up, often in the earth, in order to come forth to the world at a later time.[1299] According to John A. Tvedtnes, "The concept of hiding books for future generations to discover is [also] evident in a large number of early documents from the ancient Near East, whence came the peoples of the Book of Mormon."[1300] The reports and legends contained in these documents stretch back to Adam himself.

Two rabbis reportedly discovered a record hidden by Adam, and they said that a divine power stopped them from fully reading it.[1301] In response, another rabbi explained that God "does not desire that so much should be revealed to the world, but when the days of the Messiah will be near at hand . . . it will be revealed to all, as it is written."[1302] In "an early Jewish text . . . Moses instructed Joshua on how to preserve the books (parchments) he was leaving in his charge . . . and [to] deposit them in earthen jars until the day of recompense."[1303] The Dead Sea Scrolls (some of which were found in earthen jars), the Nag Hammadi texts, and a host of other documents confirm that many ancient records really were preserved for future generations.[1304]

Metallic Plates, Stone Boxes, and Sealed Documents

The idea that the Book of Mormon was engraved onto golden plates and buried in a stone box, along with other sacred relics, was ridiculed by some people in the nineteenth century.[1305] Yet today, according to H. Curtis Wright, "literally thousands of metal documents" have been discovered from "all over the ancient world."[1306] These include a variety of documents made from gold and gold alloys, some of which are from ancient America.[1307] The discovery of ancient hidden relics, many of them also made from precious materials, is also significant.[1308]

An ancient Egyptian temple text "describes how to inscribe a text on a gold or silver lamella (plate) and place it 'in a clean box.'"[1309] That such boxes were actually used to preserve documents and sacred relics is now widely attested throughout the ancient world.[1310] For instance, in 1854, "six small inscribed plates (gold, silver, bronze, tin, and lead, with one alabaster) were found in a stone box buried beneath [Sargon II's] palace foundation."[1311] In a 1933 excavation at "Persepolis, two pairs of [inscribed] plates (one silver and one gold in each pair) were found in stone boxes placed in the foundation corners of the palace."[1312] And "in 1965 a set of nineteen inscribed gold plates was found in a bronze box."[1313]

Another seeming peculiarity of the Book of Mormon is that a portion of its plates were sealed.[1314] Legal scholar John W. Welch has pointed out that a number of ancient documents were also preserved in two parts—one part sealed and the other open—with both parts bound together in some fashion.[1315] These two-part documents were often legal in nature, validated by witnesses, and intentionally preserved for safe-keeping. These features have remarkable correspondences with the Book of Mormon.[1316]

Mountains, Caves, and Angels

Mountains often symbolize temples or holy sanctuaries.[1317] Likely in relation with this theme, the Book of Mormon reports that several sacred revelations—including the Book of Mormon itself—were received, recorded, or buried in association with mountains or hills.[1318] Historical accounts indicate that many Nephite records were preserved in a hillside cave,[1319] and the Book of Mormon itself emphasizes that it would be "brought out of the *earth*" (Mormon 8:16; emphasis added). Joseph Smith said that an angel named Moroni had responsibility for the plates and that Moroni led him to their buried location on a hill near his family's farm (see Joseph Smith—History 1:21–54).

Many ancient documents were also found or reportedly hidden in mountains or caves. For instance, the Cologne Mani Codex indicates that "an angel brought Enosh to a mountain and instructed him to write on bronze tablets and hide his record." In Russia, "twelve small gold plates" were reportedly found "in a hill."[1320] In the Masonic tradition, the prophet Enoch "inscribed his revelation on a gold plate that he concealed in a temple he constructed inside a mountain."[1321] And in a number of ancient texts, buried or hidden records or relics were guarded by an angel or some sort of divine power.[1322]

The large set of documents collectively referred to as the Dead Sea Scrolls were found in caves surrounding the Dead Sea. In ancient Mesoamerica, caves held deep mythological symbolism and were often considered to be sacred.[1323] In 2005, Holley Moyes and James Brady noted that "only in the last decade have caves been widely recognized as ritual spaces by Mesoamerican archaeologists. Since caves in Mesoamerica were used almost exclusively for ritual, they provide an unrivaled context for studying pre-Columbian religion."[1324] The Book of Mormon's emphasis on caves and sacred records coming forth out of the earth fits right in with these findings.[1325]

THE WHY

In light of post-1830 discoveries from all over the world, and especially from the Middle East, it can be seen that the Book of Mormon is at home in the ancient world. Doubled and witnessed legal documents, engraved golden plates, sealed records, stone boxes, sacred hillside repositories, caches of precious relics—all of these things are abundantly attested to in antiquity, both archaeologically and textually.

Not only can such discoveries strengthen our faith in the Book of Mormon, but they can also help us better understand and appreciate it. For instance, in our day it takes only a few moments to digitally upload or download what would have been a virtual wagonload of documents in the ancient world! Recognizing that Nephite prophets had to find precious ore, forge their own plates, carefully engrave each character, haul the heavy plates to safe locations, and create durable containers to protect them should increase our gratitude for the sacred writings they recorded and preserved.

The Book of Mormon is a testament to the faith and love of the Nephite prophets. The prophet Enos said he prayed that the Lord "would preserve a record of my people, the Nephites . . . that it might be brought forth at some future day" (Enos 1:13). In response, the Lord promised to fulfill this request in His "own due time" (Enos 1:16). He also revealed to Enos that "Thy fathers have also required of me this thing; and it shall be done unto them according to their faith; for their faith was like unto thine" (Enos 1:18).

These verses show that the Book of Mormon exists today because ancient prophets were concerned for future generations whom they would never meet in mortality. They truly cared about us. In turn, we ought to deeply care about them. Only when we recognize and accept the Book of Mormon as an ancient record can we gain the fullest understanding and appreciation for its sacred messages and the prophets who wrote them.

FURTHER READING

John A. Tvedtnes, *The Book of Mormon and Other Hidden Books: Out of Darkness unto Light* (Provo, UT: FARMS, 2000).

John W. Welch, "Doubled, Sealed, Witnessed Documents: From the Ancient World to the Book of Mormon," in *Mormons, Scripture, and the Ancient World: Studies in Honor of John L. Sorenson,* ed. Davis Bitton (Provo, UT: FARMS, 1998), 391–444.

H. Curtis Wright, "Ancient Burials of Metal Documents in Stone Boxes," in *By Study and Also By Faith: Essays in Honor of Hugh W. Nibley*, 2 vols., ed. John M. Lundquist and Stephen D. Ricks (Salt Lake City and Provo, UT: Deseret Book and FARMS, 1990), 2:273–334.

Paul R. Cheesman, *Ancient Writing on Metal Plates: Archaeological Findings Support Mormon Claims* (Bountiful, UT: Horizon, 1985).

102

Why Did Moroni Conclude His Father's Record with Twenty-two Commands?

"O then despise not, and wonder not, but hearken unto the words of the Lord, and ask the Father in the name of Jesus for what things so ever ye shall stand in need. Doubt not, but be believing." (Mormon 9:27)

THE KNOW

Moroni concluded his thoughts at the end of his father's book—Mormon 9—by issuing a long list of admonitions to "those who do not believe in Christ" (Mormon 9:1). In Mormon 9:27–31, depending on how you divide the sentences in this literary unit,[1326] there are twenty-two distinct commandments:

1. despise not
2. wonder not
3. hearken unto the words of the Lord
4. ask the Father in the name of Jesus
5. doubt not
6. be believing
7. begin as in times of old
8. come unto the Lord with all your heart
9. work out your own salvation with fear and trembling before God
10. be wise in the days of your probation
11. strip yourselves of all uncleanness
12. ask not, that ye may consume it on your lusts
13. ask with a firmness unshaken that ye will yield to no temptation
14. serve the true and living God
15. see that ye are not baptized unworthily
16. see that ye partake not of the sacrament of Christ unworthily
17. see that ye do all things in worthiness
18. do it in the name of Jesus Christ
19. condemn me not because of mine imperfection
20. neither [condemn] my father
21. neither [condemn] them who have written before him[1327]
22. give thanks unto God. . . .

Might it be possible that the number of imperatives on this list was not random but served in some purposeful way?

For one thing, compositions that are twenty-two lines or items long appear in Hebrew literature, with that number corresponding to the number of letters in the Hebrew alphabet.[1328] As there is strong evidence for the presence of other Hebrew literary phenomena in the Book of Mormon, Moroni's list of twenty-two commands might be something loosely comparable, at least in length, to an alphabetical acrostic—a composition in which each line or item begins with and features a letter of the alphabet.

In the Bible, several examples can be found in which a Hebrew scribe composed an acrostic consisting, generally, of twenty-two lines, each line beginning with the corresponding letter of the Hebrew alphabet. Alphabetical acrostics appear in Proverbs 31:10–31; Lamentations 1, 2, 3, and 4; and Psalms 25, 34, 37, 111, 112, 119, and 145.

Psalms 119 is perhaps the most famous acrostic, both because of its length and because the letters of the Hebrew alphabet are made explicit in our Bibles as a type of heading to the twenty-two strophes. Within each strophe are eight lines, each of which (in the Hebrew text of the psalm) begins with the corresponding letter of the Hebrew alphabet. So, for example, the eight verses of the first strophe all begin with the first letter of the Hebrew alphabet, א (aleph). The lines of the next strophe all begin with ב (beth), and so on.

Lamentations 2 is a more straightforward example. It has exactly twenty-two verses, and each verse starts with the next letter of the Hebrew alphabet.

Acrostics were likely used in ancient times as a mnemonic device or memorization tool to help individuals more easily memorize and recite compositions. A modern example of this is the acrostic often cited by young biology students—"King Philip Came Over from Great Spain"—as a memory tool to recall biology's taxonomic hierarchy: kingdom, phylum, class, order, family, genus, species.[1329]

In addition, this number may have been significant in Moroni's eyes for other reasons. For example, the author of the Book of Jubilees found it significant that there were twenty-two things created by God during the six days of Creation, and there were twenty-two patriarchs between Adam and Jacob. The author thus implied that the number twenty-two was "blessed and holy." Thus, some Jews considered the number twenty-two to be a sacred number, although that belief is not attested to in available sources earlier than the second century BC.

THE WHY

While it is impossible to know if Moroni's list of twenty-two commandments was actually an acrostic or not—as we only have his text in Joseph Smith's English translation—there are reasons to suspect that Moroni might have been evoking here a type of ancient Hebrew literary form. The fact that a number of Hebrew literary practices exist in the Book of Mormon is widely acknowledged.[1330] And in Mormon 9:32–33, directly after the list of twenty-two commands, Moroni described his affinity for using the Hebrew language. There he explained that the Nephite authors in his time wrote in "reformed Egyptian" characters because there was not enough room on the plates to write in Hebrew, but that "if we could have written in Hebrew, behold, ye would have had no imperfection in our record."[1331]

Thus, it is apparent that Nephite scribes such as Mormon and Moroni had a knowledge of the Hebrew language and of Hebrew scribal practices and desired to use them. Because we can assume that Moroni would have known the Hebrew alphabet, it is not hard to imagine that he would also have been able to recognize alphabetic acrostics on the plates of brass and applied or adapted that form in his own writing to give his writing a sense of traditional form and composition.

The presence of famous lists with each item beginning with repeated grammatical elements was well-known to readers of texts such as the Ten Commandments. These repetitions served as scribal devices to help ensure the accuracy and completeness of the text. They helped audiences take notice of these lists and to remember their contents. In drawing on a traditional compositional device such as this, numbered lists also conveyed a sense of authority, veneration, and assurance that the hand of the Lord stood behind such passages and the blessings promised in return to those who would obey their injunctions (see Mormon 9:37).

Thus, there are multiple reasons why Moroni may have given twenty-two commandments at the end of his first farewell text. Whatever the case may be, Moroni wanted his audience to pay special attention to these directions. The twenty-two points he listed were meant to help future readers cease despising the words of Christ and begin to believe in the power of Christ's salvation. Moroni taught them to prepare themselves to come unto Christ, to be worthy for baptism, and to serve God, enduring to the end, so that they could enjoy all the blessings of the Father's ancient covenant with the house of Israel: "May he bless them forever, through faith on the name of Jesus Christ. Amen" (Mormon 9:37).

FURTHER READING

Donald W. Parry, "Hebraisms and Other Ancient Peculiarities in the Book of Mormon," in *Echoes and Evidences of the Book of Mormon,* ed. Donald W. Parry, Daniel C. Peterson, and John W. Welch (Provo, UT: FARMS, 2002), 155–189.

John A. Tvedtnes, "Since the Book of Mormon Is Largely the Record of a Hebrew People, Is the Writing Characteristic of the Hebrew Language?" *Ensign*, October 1986, 65.

Ether

Why Does the Book of Ether Begin with Such a Long Genealogy?

"And Aaron was a descendant of Heth, who was the son of Hearthom." (Ether 1:16)

THE KNOW

At the beginning his record of the Jaredites, Moroni included a genealogy that descends in reverse chronological order from Ether, the last record-keeper, to Jared, one of the founders of Jaredite civilization (see Ether 1:6–32). Such a genealogy seems unusually long for the Book of Mormon, compared to the much shorter genealogies typically found elsewhere in the Nephite text.[1332] The sudden appearance of such a lengthy genealogy, in reverse order, may be important to understanding the book of Ether.

Grant Hardy has proposed that "the genealogical list in the first chapter provides the framework" for the rest of the book of Ether.[1333] From Ether 1:33 to Ether 11:23, each king is discussed in exact reverse order to the way he appears in the list.[1334] For example, Jared is the last person to appear in the list (see Ether 1:32), and he is the first one discussed in the narrative (see Ether 1:33), as one might expect. This pattern continues throughout the entire book of Ether, never missing a name or getting them out of order, despite all the additional names of people and places in between (see chart on p. 262).

The list in Ether 1 is similar to the king lists attested to in the ancient Near East and similar dynastic histories in pre-Columbian Mesoamerica. Comparable to the lengthy list in Ether 1, the Hittite king list is thirty names long.[1335] A Mayan example has thirty-three names.[1336] Genealogies in the Bible usually start at the beginning and document descendants until arriving in the present.[1337] However, king lists in reverse chronological order, called *retrograde king lists*, are often found in the ancient Near East and may have been the style of king list adopted by the Jaredites.[1338] Mesoamerican dynastic histories also usually start with the most recent ruler and then trace the lineage backward through their ancestors.[1339] In both the Old and New Worlds, the purpose of these lineage lists was to establish authority.[1340]

THE WHY

With this background information in mind, modern readers can appreciate why Moroni began the Jaredite record by laying out the royal lineage of the prophet Ether, the original author of the work. This established the authority of Ether and the authoritative nature of his record. By making that king list the organizing principle of the Jaredite story, Moroni authoritatively tied the origins of the Jaredite civilization back to the divine guidance given to the brother of Jared in Ether 1:35 and Ether 3:8–16

Moreover, Moroni skillfully employed the king list as a subtle organizing principle for his book of Ether. The occurrence of the names on this list in Ether 1:6–32 is in perfect reverse order in Ether 6:1–11:23, despite many details and additional names of people and cities that were added. This is impressive evidence that the book of Ether was carefully crafted by Moroni, based on a well-organized underlying Jaredite narrative. The writing of this book was certainly something that required a great deal of time and attention to detail to compose. As Grant Hardy has noted, "If [Joseph Smith] were composing as he went along," repurposing this king list in its opposite order would have been "quite the feat of memory."[1341]

Studying details such as these allows readers to better understand and relate to the ancient authors of the Book of Mormon. It may be easy to think of the authors of the Book of Mormon as distant from readers today. They're people from the remote past, who may seem difficult to relate to in modern times. Yet on occasion, the curtain gets pulled back, and the modern reader can almost sit with the authors and compilers and observe their manners and methods as they work. The book of Ether is one of those occasions. One can almost see Ether referring to the king list as he crafted his twenty-four-gold-plate record of the Jaredites. One can also observe Moroni as he interspersed his own editorial commentaries into the Jaredite story as it unfolded (see Ether 1:1–6; 3:17–20; 4:1–6:1; 8:18–26; 12:6–41).

Experiences like these allow the reader to connect with these ancient authors in new and unique ways. Seeing how they worked under adverse circumstances can be a reminder that they were ordinary people that God strengthened as they made decisions about what to include and how to include it.

One can only imagine how Joseph Smith felt when he read Ether for the first time and saw how intricate the work was. Yet one can read the book with the same wonder today. Elder Craig C. Christensen put it well:

> For many of us, a witness of the Prophet Joseph Smith begins as we read the Book of Mormon. I first read the Book of Mormon from cover to cover as a young early-morning seminary student. With my vivid boyish imagination, I decided to read as if I were Joseph Smith, discovering the truths in the Book of Mormon for the very first time. It had such an impact on my life that I continue to read the Book of Mormon in that way. I often find that doing so deepens my appreciation for the Prophet Joseph and for the truths restored in this precious book.[1342]

FURTHER READING

John L. Sorenson, *Mormon's Codex: An Ancient American Book* (Salt Lake City and Provo, UT: Deseret Book and Neal A. Maxwell Institute for Religious Scholarship, 2013), 198–218.

John L. Sorenson, "The Book of Mormon as a Mesoamerican Record," in *Book of Mormon Authorship Revisited: The Evidence for Ancient Origins,* ed. Noel B. Reynolds (Provo, UT: FARMS, 1997), 418–429.

John L. Sorenson, *An Ancient American Setting for the Book of Mormon* (Salt Lake City and Provo, UT: Deseret Book and FARMS, 1985), 50–56.

The Genealogy from Jared to Ether

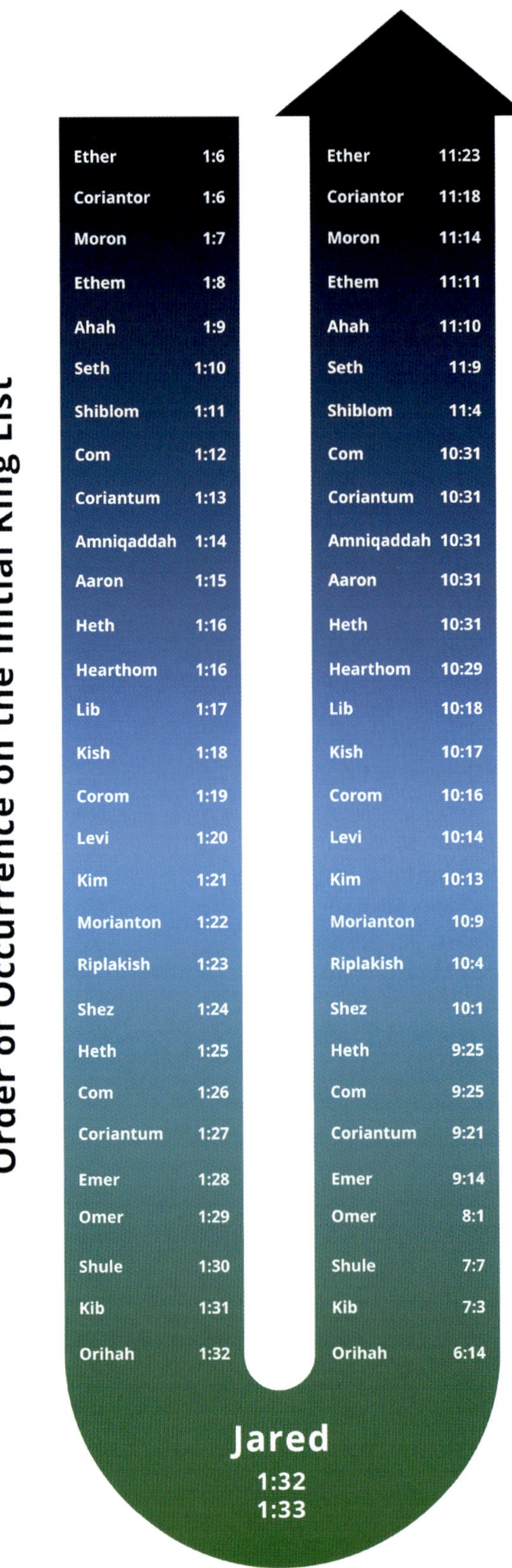

104

Where Does the Word *Deseret* Come From?

"And they did also carry with them deseret, which, by interpretation, is a honey bee." (Ether 2:3)

THE KNOW

When the brother of Jared and his companions traveled, they "did also carry with them deseret, which, by interpretation, is a honey bee" (Ether 2:3). This is the only time in the Book of Mormon where the text gives a definition for a Jaredite word.[1343] But it has proven difficult to know where in the ancient Near East the word came from. "Until possible language affinities for Jaredite names can be determined, all suggestions for etymologies of Jaredite names must remain more speculative than substantive."[1344] The word *deseret* does not translate as "bee" in any known ancient Mesopotamian language.

Hugh Nibley, however, proposed a possible Egyptian explanation for the origins of the word. Nibley's argument was well summarized by Stephen Parker in the *Encyclopedia of Mormonism*:

> In Egyptian, *dšrt* means the red crown (of the king of Lower Egypt). The Egyptian word for bee is *bt*. In the discussion of the sign *dšrt*, Alan Gardiner, in *Egyptian Grammar*, states that [the glyph for the *dšrt* crown] was used to replace [the glyph for bee] in two Egyptian titles where [the bee glyph] was used to mean the . . . King of Lower Egypt. . . . This substitution of [the *dšrt* crown] for [the bee] has led Nibley to associate the Egyptian word *dšrt* and the Book of Mormon word deseret.[1345]

It is generally assumed that the brother of Jared and his companions left from Mesopotamia, so an Egyptian explanation for the word may seem odd at first.[1346] However, evidence for beekeeping in ancient Mesopotamia is basically nonexistent. According to Ronan J. Head, "In a culture that has produced literally hundreds of thousands of extant cuneiform tablets detailing every conceivable aspect of life, including agriculture, the silence on beekeeping is striking."[1347] Thus, if the Jaredites left from Mesopotamia, they must have gotten their bees from an outside culture.

As far back as 3300 BC, there are clear cultural connections between Egypt and Mesopotamia.[1348] If the Jaredites got their bees through some exchange with Egypt, this could explain both why they used an Egyptian term as well as the reason the word is defined in the text. Beekeeping would have been unfamiliar to

Jared and his family as Mesopotamians, thus they would have needed to adopt a foreign word (*deseret*).

While Nibley's proposal is brilliant, it is "almost too brilliant," according to Kevin Barney.[1349] Barney alternatively suggested *deseret* is connected to the Hebrew word for bee, *deborah* (*dbrh*), with the final -*t* being the older form of the word.[1350] Barney admits that he does not "have a similar solution" for the substitution from *b* to *s*, but it is possible that the word could be related to Hebrew because of a small mistake in pronunciation or spelling.[1351]

THE WHY

As he abridged Mosiah's translation of the plates of Ether, Moroni must have been struck by the idea that the Jaredites had carried with them "deseret." Wanting to be clear about this remarkable point, Moroni provided the translation of this word as "a honey bee." He then explained that the Jaredites had carried "swarms of bees" and "seeds of every kind" with them into the valley of Nimrod, perhaps because he knew the importance of honey bees for crop pollination. This would have prepared the group to do what the Lord commanded them to do: move into an unsettled land.

As bees can symbolize hard work, the mention of bees here would be appropriate, considering the amount of work needed to make the Jaredite migration a success. For similar reasons, the word *deseret* became common among Latter-day Saint pioneers in Utah. It was the original name the Saints gave to the Utah territory, and to this day remains the name of a thrift store, newspaper, book publisher, and credit union.[1352]

For Latter-day Saints, a honeybee "is symbolic of work and industry."[1353] It evokes parallels with other cases in the Bible and Book of Mormon where lands of promise have been called lands of milk and *honey* (see Exodus 3:8; 1 Nephi 17:5).

Whatever the ancient origins of *deseret* in the Book of Mormon may be, the modern usage among members of The Church of Jesus Christ of Latter-day Saints poses a striking repetition of ancient history. Nibley noted that the earliest Egyptians came from a more fertile area to a desert region and called it "the land of the bee" and used the *dšrt* crown as a symbol for their new settlement. It is therefore, "a very picturesque coincidence that when the Lord's people migrated to a promised land in these latter days, they called the land Deseret and took for the symbol of their society and their government the honeybee."[1354] Nibley continued:

> The book of Ether is of course directly responsible for this, but it is hard to see how the book can have produced such a striking repetition of history without itself having a real historical basis.

While there is more to explore about the origins of *deseret* and the practices of beekeeping in the ancient world, Nibley soundly concluded:

> When a historical record of any period names persons and institutions that actually existed, it is always assumed that the record insofar as those things are concerned has authentic ties with the past. Both *deseret* and the honeybee seem quite at home in the twilight world of prehistory, alternately concealing and explaining each other, but never very far apart. The numerous ties and parallels that in the end must clear up the matter still await investigation. Suffice it for the present to show that such evidence does exist.[1355]

FURTHER READING

Hugh Nibley, *Lehi in the Desert/The World of the Jaredites/There Were Jaredites, The Collected Works of Hugh Nibley: Volume 5* (Salt Lake City and Provo, UT: Deseret Book and FARMS, 1988), 189–194.

Stephen Parker, "Deseret," in *Encyclopedia of Mormonism*, 4 vols., ed. Daniel H. Ludlow (New York: Macmillan, 1992), 1:370–371.

Kevin L. Barney, "On the Etymology of Deseret," *BCC Papers 1*, no. 2 (November 2006): 1–11.

Why Did Moroni Use Temple Imagery While Telling the Brother of Jared Story?

"Wherefore, having this perfect knowledge of God, he could not be kept from within the veil; therefore he saw Jesus; and he did minister unto him." (Ether 3:20)

THE KNOW

The account of the brother of Jared seeing the finger and then the spirit body of the premortal Jesus Christ is well-known to readers of the Book of Mormon. What may sometimes go unnoticed is the extensive use of temple imagery throughout this visionary account in Ether 3. Moroni described the event in language that recalls the revelatory experiences of other prophets, such as Moses and Isaiah, and also that of the high priests who officiated in the ancient Israelite temple. This language indicates that Moroni likely viewed the brother of Jared's experience as parallel to the temple worship that would be performed among the Israelites and Nephites.

Several elements of the brother of Jared's visionary experience resemble descriptions of the work of ancient prophets and priests, especially in the context of the ancient Israelite temple. The brother of Jared, for example, had sixteen shining stones, comparable to the sixteen precious stones the high priest wore on his priestly vestments. He was able to pass through, or see within, the veil, as did the high priest in the temple rituals. He saw the Lord, as did ancient prophets, priests, and kings (see table starting on p. 266 for further details and examples).

THE WHY

There are many points in common between what ancient Israelite high priests did in temples—and similarly, what prophets did on high mountains—and the account in Ether 3 of what happened to the brother of Jared. Why would Moroni describe this event in words that are so reminiscent of ancient temple ceremonies and rituals?

There are, generally speaking, many parallels between the various temple and visionary accounts of this type throughout the scriptures. Individuals blessed to participate in a temple or mountain visionary experience are often taken through the same processes and shown similar things.

Regarding the relationship between these types of texts and the temple endowment, Elder Neal A. Maxwell stated:

> According to the Prophet Joseph Smith, the crucial holy endowment was administered to Moses "on the mountaintop." President Joseph Fielding Smith expressed the belief that Peter, James, and John also received the holy endowment on a mountain, the Mount of Transfiguration. Nephi, too, was caught up to an exceedingly

high mountain (see 1 Nephi 11:1) and was instructed not to write or speak of some of the things he experienced there (see 1 Nephi 14:25).[1356]

Similarly, M. Catherine Thomas has insightfully suggested that "the brother of Jared received his endowment on the top of mount Shelem."[1357] It is possible that Moroni understood this to be the case, based on his awareness of similar mountain-top or temple experiences of prophets like Nephi (see 1 Nephi 11–14) and of the people at the temple in Bountiful (see 3 Nephi 11), and that he deliberately emphasized the concepts that would lead readers to recognize parallels between the brother of Jared's experience and the rites and ordinances of the temple.

Indeed, the Lord Himself told the brother of Jared that these things would come forth in the Lord's "own due time" (Ether 3:24, 27). This points to a time when a fullness of eternal truths regarding the gospel of Jesus Christ, the house of the Lord, and the ordinances of salvation and exaltation would be restored and revealed again to mankind.

FURTHER READING

M. Catherine Thomas, "The Brother of Jared at the Veil," in *Temples in the Ancient World: Ritual and Symbolism*, ed. Donald W. Parry (Salt Lake City and Provo, UT: Deseret Book and FARMS, 1994), 388–398.

Kent P. Jackson, "'Never Have I Showed Myself unto Man': A Suggestion for Understanding Ether 3:15a," *BYU Studies 30*, no. 3 (1990): 71–76.

Ether 3	Ancient Temple
"exceeding height" of mount Shelem (v. 1)	• Temple was metaphorically "the mountain of the Lord's house" (see Isaiah 2:2; Micah 4:1)[1359] • "Shelem" may have reference to the peace offering and priestly atoning sacrifices[1360]
"sixteen small stones" (v. 1)	• High priest wore sixteen stones on his priestly vestments (see Exodus 28)[1361]
"did carry [the stones] in his hands upon the top of the mount" (v. 1)	• High priest carried incense into the temple in a censer shaped like a hand (see Leviticus 16:12–13; Numbers 16:46)[1362] • "And with these thou shalt clothe Aaron, thy brother, and his sons with him and shalt anoint them and *fill their hands* and sanctify them that they may be my priests" (Exodus 28:41; Jubilee Bible 2000; emphasis added) • "Then flew one of the seraphims unto me, having a live coal in his hand" (Isaiah 6:6)
"encompassed about by the floods" (v. 2)	• "Molten sea" outside the temple represented the primeval waters/floods (Psalms 24:2; 29:3, 10; 93:3)[1363]

Concern over fallen nature (see v. 2)	• Sacrifices, high priest entering temple symbolized redemption from fall[1364] • Interior of temple reflects the Garden of Eden[1365]
Saw the Lord's finger (see v. 6)	• Moses receives stone tablets, "written with the finger of God" (Exodus 31:18; cf. Daniel 5:5) • Moses sees God's "back parts" (Exodus 33:23) • Moses, Aaron, Aaron's sons, and seventy elders saw God's feet (see Exodus 24:9–10)
Fell down before the Lord (see v. 6)	• Moses "fell down before the Lord" (Deuteronomy 9:18, 25) • Moses and Aaron "fell upon their faces" when the Lord spoke with them (Numbers 16:22, 45; 20:6) • Joshua "fell to the earth on his face before the ark of the Lord" (Joshua 7:6) • Ezekiel fell down before the Lord (see Ezekiel 1:28; 3:23; 43:1; 44:4)[1366]
Was struck with fear; feared being smitten (see vv. 6, 8)	• Israel afraid of the Lord at Sinai (see Exodus 20:18–21; cf. Mosiah 4:1–2) • Moses, Aaron, Aaron's sons, and seventy elders saw God, expected that they would be struck down (see Exodus 24:9–11; cf. Genesis 16:13; 32:30; Judges 13:22) • Moses was "afraid of the anger" of the Lord (Deuteronomy 9:19) • Isaiah saw the Lord and said, "Woe is me! for I am undone" (Isaiah 6:5)

Saw the Lord (see v. 13)	• Jacob saw God face to face at Peniel (see Genesis 32:30) • Moses, Aaron, Aaron's sons, and seventy elders saw the Lord (see Exodus 24:9–10) • Moses spoke to Lord face to face in the tent of meeting (see Exodus 33:11; Numbers 12:8; cf. Moses 1) • Lord appeared to Solomon in the tent of meeting (see 2 Chronicles 1:7; 1 Kings 3:5; 9:2; 11:9) • Isaiah saw the Lord in the temple (see Isaiah 6) • People seek the face of the God of Jacob at the temple (see Psalms 24:6) • Joshua, the high priest, stood before the Lord (see Zechariah 3)
"Could not be kept from beholding within the veil" (vv. 19–20)	• Moses saw God's "back parts" on Sinai after God removed His hand (Exodus 33:23) • Aaron to come "within the veil" with his hands full of incense/coal (Leviticus 16:11–12, 15; cf. 16:2) • Priests to do the work "within the veil" (Numbers 18:6) • Ark of the covenant was kept "within curtains" (2 Samuel 7:2) • Jesus passed through the veil of the heavenly temple (see Hebrews 6:19–20; 9:3; 10:20)[1367]
Shown God's work of creation (see vv. 15, 18, 25–26)	• Moses shown the Creation (see Moses 1:27–3:25) • Abraham shown the Creation (see Abraham 3–5) • Depiction of the Creation may have been a part of ancient Israelite temple worship[1368]
Given "two stones" that would "magnify to the eyes of men" his writings (vv. 23–24, 28)	• Priests were to carry the two stones of the Urim and Thummim in their priestly vestments (see Exodus 28:30) • Many priests, also prophets and kings, used the Urim and Thummim[1369]

Why Do so Many of Mormon's Teachings Appear in Ether 4 and 5?

"And blessed is he that is found faithful unto my name at the last day, for he shall be lifted up to dwell in the kingdom prepared for him from the foundation of the world. And behold it is I that hath spoken it. Amen." (Ether 4:19)

THE KNOW

Ether 4 and 5 present Moroni's conclusion to the awe-inspiring account of the brother of Jared's vision of the premortal Christ. Moroni had a number of editorial comments to make to future Gentile readers of this account, including how they could prepare themselves to receive all that the Lord had revealed to the brother of Jared. He wanted them to understand how they could come to believe in his words—and in the words of Christ—as well as what they needed to do in order to receive the blessings that were promised to believers.

As he made these comments in Ether 4–5, Moroni repeated and made use of many of the themes and verbal expressions used by his father, Mormon. For example, Moroni wrote in Ether 4:11 that by the "Spirit he shall know that these things are true; for it persuadeth men to do good."[1369] Mormon similarly stated, "For behold, the Spirit of Christ is given to every man, that he may know good from evil; wherefore, I show unto you the way to judge; for every thing which inviteth to do good, and to persuade to believe in Christ, is sent forth by the power and gift of Christ" (Moroni 7:16).

Furthermore, toward the end of his writings, Moroni again rehearsed these same principles: "And whatsoever thing is good is just and true; wherefore, nothing that is good denieth the Christ, but acknowledgeth that he is" (Moroni 10:6).

The following chart illustrates several of the many intertextual uses in Moroni's writings in Ether 4–5 and Moroni 10 of distinctive words and doctrinal themes previously written by Mormon in Moroni 7.

THE WHY

The material presented here provides an extensive example of intertextuality between two Book of Mormon writers. It is, perhaps, natural to expect that Moroni would know and use the words of his father, the great prophet-redactor-historian, Mormon. BYU professor of law W. Cole Durham Jr. commented on the relationship between the two:

> The scriptures provide only a limited account of Moroni's family relationships and focus solely on father and son, but the glimpses suggest a tie rich with natural affection, strengthened by mutual concern for the ministry.[1370]

Durham noted how these ties affected the content and style of Moroni's writing:

> The very structure of Moroni's writings reflects a profound respect for his father. His initial writings (Morm. 8 and Morm. 9) were intended to do no more than complete his father's record. Later, when Moroni added his own book, approximately two-thirds of its space was devoted to a presentation of his father's teachings and letters.[1371]

Moroni chose to emphasize several of his father's important teachings, including the central themes of faith, hope, and charity, and the need to come unto Christ. As Durham noted, "These themes are prevalent both in the writings of Mormon which Moroni quotes and also throughout Moroni's portion of the Book of Mormon."[1372]

Just as Moroni shared with future readers these teachings of Christ that his father had emphasized, he also passed these principles on in his role as mentor to Joseph Smith. As the Prophet's mother recorded, at the time Joseph beheld the plates, "the angel showed him, by contrast, the difference between good and evil, and likewise the consequences of both obedience and disobedience to the commandments of God, in such a striking manner, that the impression was always vivid in his memory until the very end of his days."[1373]

FURTHER READING

W. Cole Durham Jr., "Moroni," *Ensign*, June 1978.

Parallel Element	Moroni 7 (Mormon)	Ether 4–5 (Moroni)	Moroni 10 (Moroni)
Addressed to specific audience	To the church, the peaceable followers of Christ (7:3)	To the Gentiles (4:6, 13)	To the Lamanites (10:1)
Must have faith, hope, and/or charity to be part of church/kingdom	. . . that have obtained a sufficient *hope* by which ye can enter into the rest of the Lord . . . until ye shall rest with him in *heaven*" (7:3) "for if ye have not *faith* in him then ye are not fit to be numbered among the people of his *church* (7:39)	. . . blessed is he that is found *faithful* unto my name at the last day, for he shall be lifted up to dwell in the *kingdom* . . . (4:19)	And except ye have *charity* ye can in nowise be saved in the *kingdom* of God; neither can ye be saved in the *kingdom* of God if ye have not *faith*; neither can ye if ye have no *hope* (10:21)

Discerning good from evil; all that is good (every good gift) comes from God; anything that is good invites to come to Christ and not deny Him; good people work by the "power and gift(s)" of Christ/God	Wherefore, a man being evil cannot do that which is good; neither will he give a *good gift.* Wherefore, all things which are *good cometh of God*; and that which is evil cometh of the devil; For behold, the Spirit of Christ is given to every man, that he may know good from evil; wherefore, I show unto you the way to judge; for every thing which *inviteth to do good, and to persuade to believe in Christ,* is sent forth by the *power and gift* of Christ; wherefore ye may know with a perfect knowledge it is of God. But whatsoever thing *persuadeth men to do evil, and believe not in Christ, and deny him*, and serve not God, then ye may know with a perfect knowledge it is of the devil. . . . Wherefore, I beseech of you, brethren, that ye should search diligently in the light of Christ that ye may know good from evil; (7:5–19)	For because of my Spirit he shall know that these things are true; for it *persuadeth men to do good.* And whatsoever thing *persuadeth men to do good* is of me; for *good cometh of none save it be of me.* I am the same that *leadeth men to all good* (4:11–12)	And whatsoever thing is good is just and true; wherefore, *nothing that is good denieth the Christ, but acknowledgeth that he is.* And I would exhort you, my beloved brethren, that ye remember that *every good gift cometh of Christ.* And wo be unto the children of men if this be the case; for there shall be none that doeth good among you, no not one. For if there be one among you that doeth good, he shall work by the *power and gifts of God.* (10:6, 18, 25)
Pray unto Father with "heart"	. . . *pray unto the Father* with all the energy of *heart* . . . (7:48)	. . . yea, when ye shall *call upon the Father* in my name, with a broken *heart* and a contrite spirit . . . (4:15)	. . . *ask God, the Eternal Father*, in the name of Christ … ye shall ask with a sincere *heart*, with real intent . . . (10:4)
By the Spirit, one can know the truth	. . . the way to judge is as plain, that ye may *know* with a perfect knowledge . . . For behold, the *Spirit of Christ* is given to every man, that he may *know* good from evil (7:15–16)	For because of my *Spirit* he shall *know* that these things are *true* . . . (4:11)	. . . he will manifest the *truth* of it unto you, by the power of the *Holy Ghost.* And by the power of the Holy Ghost ye may *know* the *truth* of all things (10:4–5)

God will provide witnesses	Wherefore, by the *ministering of angels*, and by *every word which proceeded forth out of the mouth of God*, men began to exercise faith in Christ; For behold, [the angels] are subject unto [Christ], to minister according to the word of his command, *showing themselves* unto them of strong faith and a firm mind in every form of godliness. And the office of their ministry is to call men unto repentance ... to prepare the way among the children of men, by *declaring the word of Christ* unto the chosen vessels of the Lord, that they *may bear testimony of him*. (7:25, 29–31)	And unto three shall [the plates] be shown by the power of God; wherefore they shall know of a surety that these things are true. And in *the mouth of three witnesses* shall these things be established; and the *testimony of three, and this work*, in the which shall be shown forth the power of God and also his word, of which *the Father, and the Son, and the Holy Ghost bear record*—and all this shall stand as a *testimony* against the world at the last day. (5:3–4)	And I exhort you to remember these things; for the time speedily cometh that ye shall know that I lie not, for ye shall see me at the bar of God; and the *Lord God will say unto you*: Did I not declare my words unto you, which were written *by this man*, like as one crying from the dead, yea, even as one speaking out of the dust? And *God shall show unto you*, that that which I have written is true. (10:28–29)
The problem of unbelief	But whatsoever thing persuadeth men to do evil, and *believe not* in Christ, and deny him, and serve not God, then ye may know with a perfect knowledge it is of the devil (7:17)	And now, after that, they have all dwindled in *unbelief* . . . the knowledge which is hid up because of *unbelief*. . . . and it hath not come unto you, because of *unbelief*. Behold, when ye shall rend that veil of *unbelief* which doth cause you to remain in your awful state of wickedness, and hardness of heart, and blindness of mind. . . . (4:3, 13–15)	. . . all these gifts of which I have spoken, which are spiritual, never will be done away, even as long as the world shall stand, only according to the *unbelief* of the children of men. if the day cometh that the power and gifts of God shall be done away among you, it shall be because of *unbelief*. (10:19, 24)

Why Were Three Key Witnesses Chosen to Testify of the Book of Mormon?

"In the mouth of three witnesses shall these things be established." (Ether 5:4)

THE KNOW

The prophet Nephi foresaw that the gold plates of the Book of Mormon would be "hid from the eyes of the world" and that "the eyes of none shall behold it save it be that three witnesses shall behold it, by the power of God" and "none other . . . shall view it, save it be a few according to the will of God" (2 Nephi 27:12–13). Moroni further declared that "in the mouth of three witnesses shall these things be established" (Ether 5:4).

In response to these and other revelations,[1374] Oliver Cowdery, Martin Harris, and David Whitmer, accompanied by Joseph Smith, went into the woods to pray for a special witness of the Book of Mormon.[1375] In the resulting vision,[1376] which occurred near the end of June 1829, these men were visited by the angel Moroni, who presented the gold plates to their view and "turned over the leaves one by one, so that [they] could see them, and discern the engravings thereon distinctly."[1377]

In this remarkable shared experience, they all heard a voice from heaven confirming the truthfulness of the record[1378] and were then shown the sword of Laban, the Liahona, the Urim and Thummim, and the breastplate.[1379]

A careful analysis of this experience and the lives of these Three Witnesses can strengthen faith that Christ's Church has been restored to the earth through the Prophet Joseph Smith.[1380]

The solemn testimony of these three additional witnesses "has appeared in every edition of the Book of Mormon from the beginning."[1381] Each of these specific men sacrificed much to help with the translation and publication of the Book of Mormon, and it's likely this is a significant part of why they were chosen (see Ether 5:2).[1382] Importantly, throughout their lives and even during periods of estrangement from the Church, none of these witnesses ever denied his testimony.[1383]

Oliver Cowdery acted as Joseph's primary scribe,[1384] and throughout his ministry served as a "second witness of many critical events in the restoration of the gospel."[1385] For instance, during the period of translation, he, with Joseph Smith, received the Aaronic and Melchizedek Priesthoods from angelic messengers.[1386]

Shortly after rejoining the Church, and in a public speech recorded by Reuben Miller, Cowdery stated, "I beheld with my eyes. And handled with my hands the gold plates from which [the Book of Mormon] was translated. I also beheld the Interpreters. That book is true."[1387] According to

Richard L. Anderson, throughout Cowdery's life, "He told the same simple story of the vision, whether under privation, persecution, resentment against the translator of the Book of Mormon, ridicule by non-Mormons, or knowledge of imminent death."[1388]

On his deathbed, Oliver Cowdery said to Jacob Gates: "I am a dying man, and what would it profit me to tell you a lie? I know . . . that this Book of Mormon was translated by the gift and power of God. My eyes saw, my ears heard, and my understanding was touched, and I know that whereof I testified is true. It was no dream, no vain imagination of the mind—it was real."[1389]

Whereas Oliver Cowdery sacrificed considerable time and energy to help with the translation process, Martin Harris fronted "the entire cost of the publication of the Book of Mormon" by mortgaging "most of his property."[1390] Harris also spent considerable time and energy seeking to authenticate the characters on the gold plates.[1391]

When asked by the twelve-year-old William Glenn if he had indeed seen the plates and the angel, Harris declared, "Gentlemen, do you see that hand? Are you sure you see it? Are your eyes playing you a trick or something? No. Well, as sure as you see my hand so sure did I see the angel and the plates."[1392] With similar conviction, and often using similar analogies with concrete descriptions, Martin Harris reaffirmed his testimony over and over throughout his long life.[1393]

David Whitmer took the time to escort Joseph Smith and Oliver Cowdery to Fayette, where the Whitmer family graciously hosted Joseph Smith, his wife Emma, and Oliver Cowdery throughout a major portion of the translation process. This willing sacrifice placed considerable strain on the Whitmers.[1394]

David Whitmer, the most interviewed of the witnesses, claimed that throughout his life "thousands came to inquire" and, according to Anderson, "over fifty of these conversations are reported in reasonable detail in contemporary diaries, letters, and newspapers, supplemented by later recollections."[1395] Anderson described Whitmer as "Impeccable in reputation, consistent in scores of recorded interviews, obviously sincere, and personally capable of detecting delusion—no witness is more compelling than David Whitmer."[1396]

Although Whitmer was the only one of the Three Witnesses who never mended his broken ties with the Church, his deathbed testimony stands as a final stamp of certitude of his lifelong conviction: "if God ever uttered a truth, the testimony I now bear is true. I did see the angel of God, and I beheld the glory of the Lord, and he declared the record true."[1397]

THE WHY

The Lord has declared that "in the mouth of two or three witnesses shall every word be established" (D&C 6:28). This principle was the basis of ancient Israelite law (see Deuteronomy 19:15; 2 Corinthians 13:1),[1398] and witnesses still play a crucial role in legal systems throughout the modern world.[1399] In a typical serious legal setting, the testimonies of witnesses help a jury or a judge to establish facts and "reach conclusions about the relative persuasiveness of the evidence."[1400] For these same reasons, God provided three key witnesses to testify of His work through the miracle of the Book of Mormon.[1401]

According to Steven C. Harper, the witnesses to the Book of Mormon provide "some of the most compelling evidence in favor of its miraculous revelation and translation."[1402] In particular, the Three Witnesses support Joseph Smith's original testimony with the following jointly related facts: (1) three other individuals beheld the gold plates for themselves; (2) at the same time, they "were also introduced to the angel who was involved in revealing the plates"; (3) they heard a voice from heaven confirming the record's truthfulness; and (4) they viewed the ancient artifacts that accompanied the plates.[1403]

The joint testimony of these witnesses may be especially important for the modern age, with its increasingly skeptical attitude toward religion and any claims of divine manifestations.[1404] As Anderson explained, "One cannot dismiss the experience easily, for each man so testifying impressed his community with his capacity and unwavering honesty, and all three consistently reaffirmed the experience in hundreds of interviews throughout their lives."[1405]

Furthermore, these men were each stubborn in their own way and demonstrated on multiple occasions that they were willing to follow the path that they individually felt was right, even under heavy adverse pressures.[1406] They were not the type to be easily swayed or duped.[1407]

As described by President Ezra Taft Benson, the testimony of the Three Witnesses was part of the Lord's "built in . . . proof system of the Book of Mormon."[1408] Moroni declared that accompanying these three earthly witnesses would be three heavenly witnesses—"the Father, and the Son, and the Holy Ghost"—and that at the last day these combined witnesses would "stand as a testimony against the world" (Ether 5:4).

FURTHER READING

Neal Rappleye, "'Idle and Slothful Strange Stories': Book of Mormon Origins and the Historical Record,"

Interpreter: A Journal of Mormon Scripture 20 (2016): 21–37.

Alexander L. Baugh, "The Testimony of the Book of Mormon Witnesses," in *A Reason for Faith: Navigating LDS Doctrine & Church History*, ed. Laura Harris Hales (Salt Lake City and Provo, UT: Deseret Book and BYU Religious Studies Center, 2016), 45–58.

Larry E. Morris, "The Experience of the Three Witnesses," in *Revelations in Context: The Stories Behind the Sections of the Doctrine and Covenants*, ed. Matthew McBride and James Goldberg (Salt Lake City, UT: The Church of Jesus Christ of Latter-day Saints, 2016), 25–28.

Richard Lloyd Anderson, "Personal Writings of the Book of Mormon Witnesses," in *Book of Mormon Authorship Revisited: The Evidence for Ancient Origins*, ed. Noel B. Reynolds (Provo, UT: FARMS, 1997), 39–60.

Richard Lloyd Anderson, *Investigating the Book of Mormon Witnesses* (Salt Lake City, UT: Deseret Book, 1981).

108

Where Did the Brother of Jared Get the Idea of Shining Stones?

"And thus the Lord caused stones to shine in darkness, to give light unto men, women, and children, that they might not cross the great waters in darkness." (Ether 6:3)

THE KNOW

When the brother of Jared expressed his concern about the lack of light in the barges the Lord had instructed his people to build, the Lord responded, "What will ye that I should do that ye may have light in your vessels?" (Ether 2:23). In response to this invitation, the brother of Jared "did molten out of a rock sixteen small stones; and they were white and clear, even as transparent glass" (Ether 3:1).[1409] He then asked the Lord to "touch these stones . . . with thy finger, and prepare them that they may shine forth in darkness" (Ether 3:4). As petitioned, the Lord touched them "one by one" (Ether 3:6), which caused them to "shine in darkness, to give light unto men, women, and children, that they might not cross the great waters in darkness" (Ether 6:3).

Hugh Nibley asked, "But who gave the brother of Jared the idea about stones in the first place? It was not the Lord, who left him entirely on his own; and yet the man went right to work as if he knew exactly what he was doing. Who put him on to it?"[1410] While stones that emit light may seem like an absurdity to some modern readers, legends of their existence and importance were widely spread throughout the ancient world.[1411]

Drawing on a substantial body of ancient texts, John A. Tvedtnes has connected the shining stones in Ether to such items as the Urim and Thummim, glowing idols, teraphim, sanctuary stones, and medieval glowing stones.[1412] Tvedtnes concluded, "The account of the stones used to provide light in the Jaredite barges fits rather well into a larger corpus of ancient and medieval literature."[1413]

Of particular relevance is the way that shining stones were directly linked to Noah's ark. In the Bablyonian Talmud, for example, one Jewish commentator reported that the Lord instructed Noah to "Set therein precious stones and jewels, so that they may give thee light, bright as the noon."[1414] Another ancient Jewish rabbi explained, "During the whole twelve months that Noah was in the Ark he did not require the light of the sun by day or the light of the moon by night, but he had a polished gem which he hung up."[1415]

These Jewish explanations are notable when considering that Ether explicitly draws a parallel between the Jaredite vessels and Noah's ark: "there was no water that could hurt them, their vessels being tight like unto a dish, and also they were tight *like unto the ark of Noah*" (Ether 6:7; emphasis added).[1416]

Considering that his people were already constructing barges after the manner of Noah's ark, it is possible that the brother of Jared knew something of the stones that illuminated Noah's vessel when thinking of a potential source of light for the barges of his own people.[1417] Nibley thus argued that the brother of Jared was simply "following the pattern of Noah's ark, for in the oldest records of the human race the ark seems to have been illuminated by just such shining stones."[1418]

THE WHY

An awareness of the ancient sources that discuss the shining stones and Noah's ark may offer additional insights about the story of the brother of Jared. For instance, rather than just drawing on the boundless limits of his own creative imagination, the brother of Jared may have been intentionally demonstrating his faith in the miraculous deliverance of Noah and his family—including the precious stones that, according to a variety of ancient sources, granted them light amidst the deluge. As the brother of Jared likened the sacred story of Noah's salvation to his own people, he thought of a similar solution to his own vexing problem.[1419]

In several ways, this story also helps demonstrate the pattern of the Lord's interaction with His children. In some cases, God will freely grant His children blessings or solutions, simply because they have the faith to ask (see Ether 2:19–21). In other situations, the Lord requires initiative, creativity, and diligent striving on the part of those seeking blessings. Elder Jeffrey R. Holland taught, "Clearly the brother of Jared was being tested. The Lord had done His part—miraculously, profoundly, ingeniously. Unique, resolutely seaworthy ships for crossing the ocean had been provided. . . . Now He wanted to know what the brother of Jared would do about incidentals."[1420]

The story about these stones is also deeply layered with rich symbolism. M. Catherine Thomas, for example, suggested that the stones "evoke the Urim and Thummim" as well as the "white stone mentioned in Revelation 2:17."[1421] Thomas R. Valletta noted that like the Liahona, the stones "typologically led the Jaredites to the promised land by the power of Christ."[1422] Robert E. Clark saw the transparent stones—initially devoid of light—as a reflection of the brother of Jared's "own limitations, his own emptiness" that needed to be "filled with light."[1423] Thomas, likewise, viewed them as supplying "not only practical light, but spiritual light as well."[1424]

With these interpretations in mind, it is noteworthy that the stones only received their light after the Lord touched them "one by one with his finger" (Ether 3:6). In this sense, it can be understood that the light that provides revelation, that reveals one's true identity, that acts as a constant guide through darkness and danger, and that fills the emptiness of the mortal heart with true joy and divine purpose can be activated only through personal contact with Jesus Christ.[1425] Ultimately, the brother of Jared believed that stones could shine with light because he had faith in Jesus Christ—the true "light and life of the world" (3 Nephi 11:11).

FURTHER READING

John A. Tvedtnes, "Glowing Stones in Ancient and Medieval Lore," *Journal of Book of Mormon Studies 6*, no. 2 (1997): 99–123.

Hugh Nibley, *Lehi in the Desert/The World of the Jaredites/There Were Jaredites, The Collected Works of Hugh Nibley, Volume 5* (Salt Lake City and Provo, UT: Deseret Book and FARMS, 1988), 358–379.

Hugh Nibley, *An Approach to the Book of Mormon, The Collected Works of Hugh Nibley, Volume 6* (Salt Lake City and Provo, UT: Deseret Book and FARMS, 1988), 337–358.

Why Is the Book of Ether an Epic?

"Wherefore, he came to the hill Ephraim, and he did molten out of the hill, and made swords out of steel for those whom he had drawn away with him; and after he had armed them with swords he returned to the city Nehor, and gave battle unto his brother Corihor, by which means he obtained the kingdom and restored it unto his father Kib." (Ether 7:9)

THE KNOW

In 1952, Hugh Nibley pointed out that that the book of Ether has many similarities with epic poetry from all over the world.[1426] Epics are long poems that stem from oral tradition that are about heroic figures or the history of a nation, and Nibley argued that the book of Ether was originally an epic.[1427] Since modern archaeological evidence suggests that writing spread across Mesoamerica between 900 and 500 BC, there may not have been a written history of the Jaredite kings until late Jaredite times.[1428] So like the epic poetry to which Nibley has compared the book of Ether, Jaredite history might have largely been based on oral tradition.[1429]

In cultures where writing is not common, oral stories are created in ways that make them easy to remember. This naturally leads to similar methods for creating oral stories across many cultures, leading to many similarities in stories told by various cultures, which Nibley noticed are also present in Ether.[1430]

In the early 1930s, Milman Parry went to southern Europe to observe how people composed long-form oral poetry, similar to the epics Nibley talked about.[1431] Parry observed singers in different regions and asked them to recite oral poems. He found some people who said they could recite something "word for word" every time after only hearing it once. However, when Parry actually recorded them reciting these works, he found that the stories they recited were somewhat different every time.[1432]

This was because these bards, rather than memorizing multiple poems in their entirety, had simply memorized a certain number of phrases and conventions that they could modify and recombine at will, allowing them to tell a practically infinite number of stories about actual historical events by simply changing how they employed the conventions.[1433] This explains how a bard could hear the story once and then be able to repeat it in a way very similar to the way it was given. He did not have to memorize the entire story; he simply had to memorize which conventions had been stitched together and how those conventions had been changed to match each story.[1434]

THE WHY

One might initially assume that epics cannot be historically reliable. However, Nibley pointed out that epics often paint an accurate picture of the world they represent. For example, the book of Ether depicts brothers fighting over a kingdom (see Ether 7:9), as do other epics. This is likely a common occurrence in epics because it was a common occurrence in history.[1435] Nibley also noticed that Ether contains a scene of one king fighting another king to the death. Again, this was probably a common theme in history.[1436] As Nibley observed, "it is [the real world] and not the poet's imagination which furnishes him with his characters and images."[1437]

As with much of the rest of the Book of Mormon, Ether is a carefully crafted work, yet it is also historically reliable.[1438] In the modern era, many people assume that a work must either be one or the other. The Book of Mormon is a reminder that a work can be both a beautifully stirring work of sacred literature and an accurate depiction of events. The Book of Mormon is a beautiful literary creation that can, like the Bible, speak to the reader in profound ways thousands of years after its composition, yet it also accurately depicts the events it describes.

Because epics have this characteristic, the reader can step into the ancient world and get a taste of what life might have been like for the Nephites or the Jaredites. The Book of Mormon, like many ancient texts, is valuable as a window on the past, but as a divinely inspired text, it also teaches the reader timeless lessons specifically tailored to the times in which the modern reader lives.

FURTHER READING

Daniel C. Peterson, "Ether, Book of," in *Book of Mormon Reference Companion*, ed. Dennis L. Largey (Salt Lake City, UT: Deseret Book 2003), 252–254.

David B. Honey, "Ecological Nomadism versus Epic Heroism in Ether: Nibley's Works on the Jaredites," *Review of Books on the Book of Mormon 2*, no. 1 (1990): 143–163.

Hugh Nibley, *Lehi in the Desert/The World of the Jaredites/There Were Jaredites, The Collected Works of Hugh Nibley: Volume 5* (Salt Lake City/Provo, UT: Deseret Book and FARMS, 1988), 285–423.

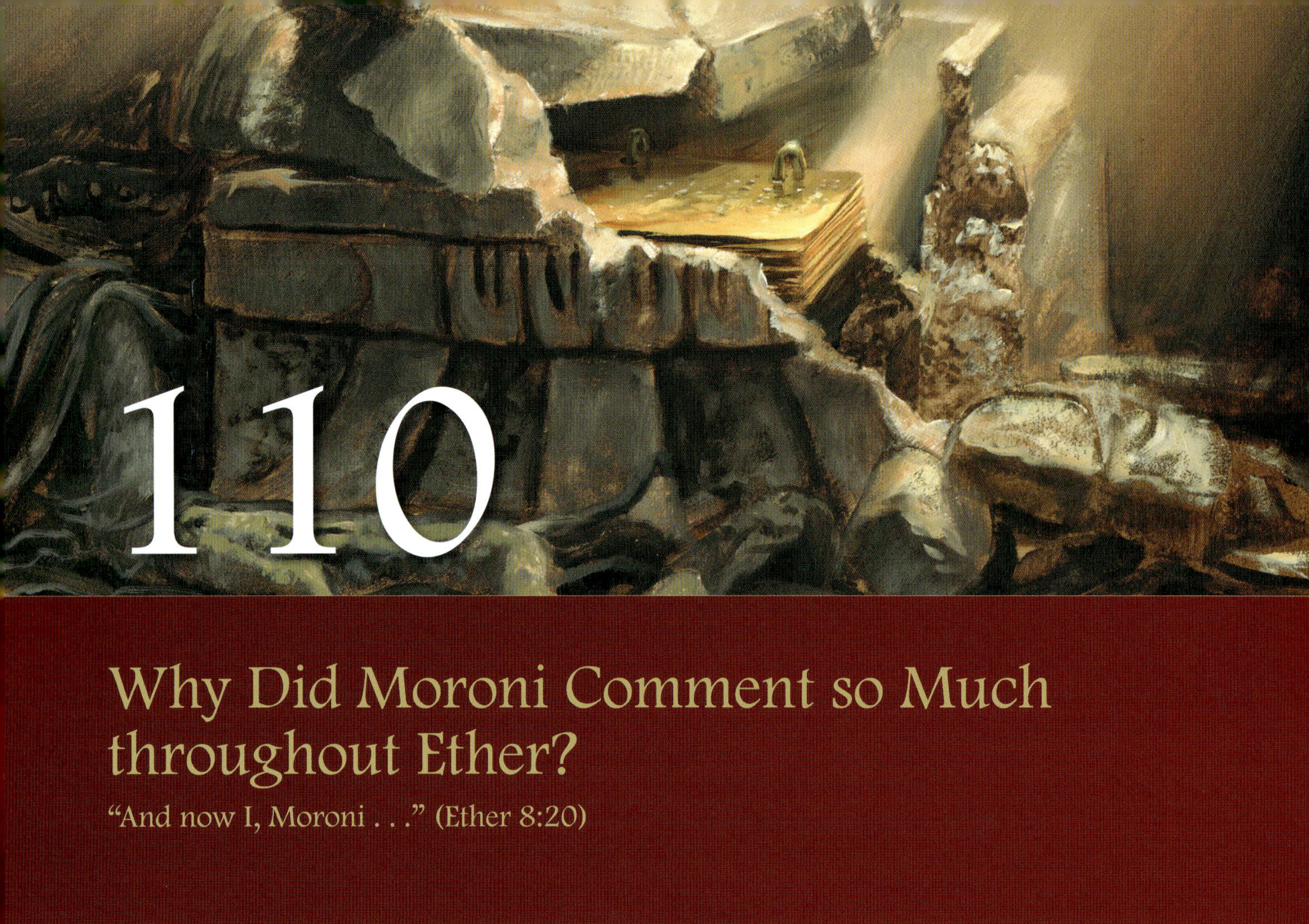

110

Why Did Moroni Comment so Much throughout Ether?

"And now I, Moroni . . ." (Ether 8:20)

THE KNOW

In describing the book of Ether, Book of Mormon scholar Grant Hardy observed, "Moroni maintains a more pervasive narrator presence" than his father, Mormon.[1439] Moroni broke in to comment on the Jaredite narrative at five points: Ether 1:1–6; 3:17–20; 4:1–6:1; 8:18–26; 12:6–41.[1440] In the book of Ether alone, the phrase "I, Moroni" appears eleven times. In contrast, the phrase "I, Mormon" appears only three times outside Mormon's own writing about his own lifetime.[1441] Moroni used Mormon's classic phrase "and thus we see" only once.[1442]

Why were Mormon's and Moroni's approaches so different?

One possible explanation is that Mormon wrote with some sense of security, while Moroni was constantly unsure of his own safety and whether he would have any time to write more. Mormon had an entire decade to compile and abridge the Book of Mormon when the Nephites and Lamanites made a ten-year peace treaty around AD 350.[1443] It would have provided an opportunity to carefully craft his narrative to make the points he wanted to make. His characteristic "and thus we see" served his purposes perfectly without breaking into the text as obviously. In addition, he likely believed he would have enough time to write about his own life, and thus did not feel the need to break into the text with personal comments as often.

Moroni, on the other hand, appears to have been surprised that he survived long enough to write anything after his abridgment of Ether. He states, "Now I, Moroni, after having made an end of abridging the account of the people of Jared, I had supposed not to have written more, but I have not as yet perished" (Moroni 1:1). Moroni's uncertainty about how much time he had left may be reflected in the way he commented on the Jaredite record.[1444]

When one removes Moroni's five comments from Ether, the remaining text flows flawlessly.[1445] Ether 12–13 is a good example of this. When Ether 12:5 and 13:2 are combined, they read like they belong back to back: "Ether did prophesy great and marvelous things unto the people, which they did not believe, because they saw them not. . . . For behold, they rejected all the words of Ether; for he truly told them of all things, from the beginning of man."

This evidence suggests that Moroni did not heavily edit the original Jaredite record while interspersing light commentary like his father did, but rather left the Jaredite record more or less intact. He seems to have only lightly edited it while occasionally inserting large blocks of personal commentary all at once. In Hardy's words,

Moroni's "treatment of the [the Jaredite record] reads like a lightly edited chronicle."[1446] Ultimately, "Moroni does not appear to be reworking his source material to any appreciable extent; in contrast to his father's abridging."[1447]

THE WHY

The seamlessness of the text that one sees when Moroni's asides are removed is a subtle witness to the Book of Mormon's authenticity. Joseph would often dictate long portions of the Book of Mormon, stop translating for a while, and then pick up exactly where he left off without asking anyone where he had stopped the session before.[1448] Dictating an aside as long as Ether 12 from memory and then getting back to the narrative without asking where he had left off would be a remarkable feat of memory if he were not actually translating something.

Even more significant, however, is what this says about Moroni. It is hard to comprehend what it was like to write and abridge so much of the Book of Mormon with death constantly hanging over his head. Moroni seemed uncertain about when his life would end, as he included multiple endings and persistently inserted his own thoughts into Ether.[1449] And yet despite the incredibly difficult circumstance under which he worked, Moroni was still able to produce page after page of beautiful scripture.

Despite the constant probability of death, Moroni, "finished his father's inspired abridgment of the Nephite millennial-long history; . . . he abridged the writings of Ether, . . . he recorded the lengthy writings of the brother of Jared on the gold plates and sealed them up." After that:

> He wandered alone about the land for many years, not only concerned about his personal safety, but also fully aware of his responsibility to preserve the plates until he was commanded to hide them in the earth. Finally, after traveling extensively and fulfilling priesthood responsibilities, he deposited the plates in a hillside in what is now western New York state. What Moroni accomplished has blessed many people and will yet bless many more.[1450]

FURTHER READING

Mark D. Thomas, "Moroni: The Final Voice," *Journal of Book of Mormon Studies 12*, no. 1 (2003): 88–99.

H. Donl Peterson, "Moroni, the Last of the Nephite Prophets," in *The Book of Mormon: Fourth Nephi, From Zion to Destruction*, ed. Monte S. Nyman and Charles D. Tate Jr. (Provo, UT: BYU Religious Studies Center, 1995), 235–249.

John W. Welch, "Preliminary Comments on the Sources Behind the Book of Ether," *FARMS Preliminary Reports* (1986).

Why Did Snakes Infest Jaredite Lands During a Famine?

"And there came forth poisonous serpents also upon the face of the land, and did poison many people." (Ether 9:30)

THE KNOW

During the reign of Heth, prophets warned the people that a "great famine" would come if they did not repent (Ether 9:28). At the behest of Heth himself, the people refused to believe the prophets, instead persecuting them and casting them out (see Ether 9:29). As predicted, "there began to be a great dearth upon the land . . . for there was no rain upon the face of the earth" (Ether 9:30).

In the wake of the great dearth, or famine, a seemingly odd sequence of events followed. First, the land was infested by "poisonous serpents," which "did poison many people." Next, "flocks began to flee" southward, and the serpents followed the flocks. The serpents then stopped and "hedge[d] up the way," preventing people from passing into the land southward (Ether 9:31–33; cf. Ether 10:19).

Strange as it might seem, this series of events may be entirely natural. In times of drought, snakes typically migrate into populated areas in search of water or prey.[1451] If an area has a lot of venomous snakes, incidents of people being bitten and "poisoned" by snakes naturally increases.[1452]

If a drought persists, then snakes, along with other animals, continue to migrate in their search for water, which is likely what Ether interpreted as the flocks "flee[ing] before the poisonous serpents" (Ether 9:31). The flocks were likely migrating both to escape the infestation of snakes and the drought, with some animals perishing as they migrated (see Ether 9:32).[1453]

When Ether indicated that the serpents did "pursue them no more" (Ether 9:33), it was probably because the snake migration ended. The snakes probably stopped when they found a wet habitat with plenty of water available.[1454] If a river or otherwise wet habitat lay between the Jaredites and the land southward, then a large population of snakes would settle there and make it difficult to pass through to the land southward (see map on p. 284 for one possible scenario).[1455]

The whole scenario becomes more extreme if the famine was caused by regional volcanic activity, which "can cause droughts or significant cooling on a regional scale far from the volcanic eruption."[1456] According to geologist Jerry Grover, one of the many effects of volcanic eruptions on the local ecology is to kill or significantly reduce the bird population.[1457]

Several birds of prey not only feed on snakes themselves, but also compete with snakes for the same prey, such as rodents and lizards.[1458] The temporary "decimation of these species would eliminate serious predators on snakes as well as removing competition for snake prey."[1459] As a result, snake populations would skyrocket, further enabling them to prevent passage through regions with a wet habitat.[1460]

THE WHY

In the past, some have considered the story in Ether 9:28–33 about poisonous serpents too incredible to be believable. Yet the details turn out to be ecologically sound. As Brant A. Gardner noted, "what otherwise appears to be a fanciful tale contains surprising touches of authenticity."[1461]

John A. Tvedtnes similarly commented, "the story of the poisonous serpents which plagued the Jaredites has a ring of truth about it."[1462] The event cannot be confidently correlated externally to any particular natural disaster—in part because Jaredite chronology is too imprecise to determine when to look for it.[1463] Nonetheless, the series of events is more true to life than a superficial reading might initially suggest, providing yet another example that illustrates the benefits of patient investigation over shallow reading.

There is also an important spiritual lesson to be learned. Just as the Jaredites faced a famine because of wickedness, so individuals and societies risk spiritual famines when they cut themselves off from the Lord. In so doing, they may naturally find themselves surrounded by spiritual serpents—those who are toxic to healthy and happy spiritual lives. Such noxious influences may create barriers that "hedge up the way" back to the Lord.

Fortunately, no barrier is so great the Atonement cannot "destroy" it, just as the serpents were eventually destroyed (see Ether 10:19).[1464] Just as the famine ended when the Jaredites repented (see Ether 9:35), so too can sincere repentance end the spiritual famines faced by individuals and societies, destroying barriers that keep God's children from returning into His loving arms and letting His light shine through.[1465]

FURTHER READING

Jerry D. Grover Jr., *Geology of the Book of Mormon* (Vineyard, UT: Grover Publications, 2014), 206–210.

Brant A. Gardner, *Second Witness: Analytical and Contextual Commentary on the Book of Mormon*, 6 vols. (Salt Lake City, UT: Greg Kofford Books, 2007), 6:265–267.

John A. Tvedtnes, "Notes and Communications—Drought and Serpents," *Journal of Book of Mormon Studies* 6, no. 1 (1997): 70–72.

N
W
E
S
Land
Northward
Land
Southward

112

Why Did Riplakish Construct a Beautiful Throne?

"And he did erect him an exceedingly beautiful throne." (Ether 10:6)

THE KNOW

Riplakish, the tenth Jaredite king, was a vain and wicked ruler who "did erect him an exceedingly beautiful throne" (Ether 10:6).[1466] While it is difficult to determine the exact timing, it is safe to say that this story about an extravagant throne dates to very early in pre-Columbian America.[1467] Latter-day Saint archaeologist John E. Clark confirms, "The earliest civilization in Mesoamerica is known for its elaborate stone thrones."[1468]

Known to scholars as the Olmec (ca. 1700–400 BC),[1469] the first Mesoamerican civilization began constructing thrones of stone between 1350 and 1000 BC.[1470] Such thrones were usually made of a single, large, altar-like stone, ornamentally carved with three-dimensional depictions of the rulers themselves seated in cave-like openings (see example on p. 286).[1471]

According to art historian Mary Ellen Miller, some thrones may have been painted or otherwise adorned in "brilliant colors."[1472] One such depiction of an elaborate, multi-color throne appears in a wall painting from the late Middle Preclassic period (ca. 800–500 BC) at Oxtotitlan, Mexico, that strongly resembles an Olmec throne from the site of La Venta ("Altar 4").[1473]

The massive stones used to make these thrones, as well as the Olmec's colossal stone heads, could weigh up to forty tons and were transported as far as ninety km (about fifty-six miles).[1474] "The sheer labor requirements involved in these operations," explained Christopher A. Pool, "attest to the exceptional power of the rulers who commissioned them."[1475]

"The altar-throne was an integral part of the apparatus of Olmec rulers," declared Richard Adams.[1476] Mary E. Pye explained that the thrones functioned "as markers in the social and political hierarchy."[1477] According to James Porter, Olmec "thrones played a role in the careers of Olmec leaders commensurate with their impressive appearance as sculptures."[1478]

John E. Clark, writing with Arlene Colman, noted that construction of massive thrones was one of the ways Olmec kings memorialized themselves (along with colossal stone heads and full-figure statues).[1479] Olmec thrones served as "seats of power," symbolically positioning rulers as seated between the human and divine realms,[1480] and legitimizing their high status by establishing continuity back to founding ancestors.[1481] They also positioned "the ruler, both figuratively and contextually, in control of agricultural fertility," where he could control "the arrival of the rains and, by extension, the continued agricultural bounty of the lands."[1482]

THE WHY

To construct an "exceedingly beautiful throne" required that Riplakish have sufficient power to harness a massive labor force. Riplakish is depicted as the second king following a famine that had decimated the Jaredite kingdom (see Ether 9:28–35).[1483] His father had begun to rebuild the kingdom (see Ether 10:1–4), and by the time Riplakish took over the kingdom he wielded considerable power. He burdened the people with burdens "grievous to be borne" and forced them to "labor continually" (Ether 10:5–6).

Kerry Hull proposed that in constructing an elaborate throne, Riplakish likely intended to establish himself as controlling the rains and other elements central to successful agricultural growth, since he was ruling so soon after a famine (see Ether 9:28–35).[1484] It would also have made ties back to important or founding ancestors, memorialized Riplakish in stone, and depicted him as seated between the earth and the supernatural or divine realm. Thus, by erecting a beautiful throne, Riplakish positioned himself as both a political and a religious leader.

Riplakish's effort to portray himself as a great leader and spiritual guide was boldly denounced by the prophet Ether, who said, "Riplakish did not do that which was right in the sight of the Lord" (Ether 10:5). Ultimately, those efforts did not fool Riplakish's people either. After Riplakish reigned for forty-two years, "the people did rise up in rebellion against" him, and he "was killed, and his descendants were driven out of the land" (Ether 10:8). When this happened, Riplakish's throne may have been defaced and mutilated to delegitimize his successors, as was typical when an Olmec ruler was deposed.[1485]

The book of Ether's overall portrayal of the construction of an elegant and elaborate throne very early in ancient American history is entirely correct, even though, as John E. Clark put it, "American prejudices against native tribes in Joseph's day had no room for kings or their tyrannies."[1486] This led Clark to ask, "How did Joseph Smith get this detail right?"[1487] However one wishes to answer that question, the study of early pre-Columbian thrones sheds considerable light on the story of Riplakish.

FURTHER READING

John L. Sorenson, *Mormon's Codex: An Ancient American Book* (Salt Lake City and Provo, UT: Deseret Book and Neal A. Maxwell Institute for Religious Scholarship, 2013), 515– 518.

Brant A. Gardner, *Second Witness: Analytical and Contextual Commentary on the Book of Mormon*, 6 vols. (Salt Lake City, UT: Greg Kofford Books, 2007), 6:269–273.

John E. Clark, "Archaeology, Relics, and Book of Mormon Belief," *Journal of Book of Mormon Studies 14*, no. 2 (2005): 45–46.

Why Does the Book of Mormon Include the Rise and Fall of Two Nations?

"Except they should repent the Lord God would execute judgment against them to their utter destruction; And . . . would send or bring forth another people to possess the land, by his power, after the manner by which he brought their fathers." (Ether 11:20–21)

THE KNOW

Although typically thought of as a Nephite record, the Book of Mormon actually describes the rise and fall of two peoples. It begins with Lehi in Jerusalem, follows his family's journey to the promised land, and chronicles the history of their descendants. A small part of the book describes the rise and fall of an earlier people, the Jaredites, whose prophets had warned them that unless they repented, "the Lord God would execute judgment against them to their utter destruction" and then "bring forth another people to possess the land" (Ether 11:20–21).

The history of Mesoamerica also shows the rise and fall of two major cultures during parallel time periods (see chart on p. 288).[1488] John E. Clark, a Latter-day Saint and prominent Mesoamerican archaeologist, noted, "The two-civilizations requirement used to be a problem for the Book of Mormon, but it no longer is now that modern archaeology is catching up."[1489]

Scholars refer to the first civilization as the Olmec, which arose in the mid-second millennium BC and collapsed around 400 BC.[1490] According to Clark, "the earliest developments of Jaredites and Olmecs are hazy, but from about 1500 BC onward their histories are remarkably parallel." From there, "The alternations between city building and population declines, described for the Jaredites, correspond quite well with lowland Olmec developments."[1491]

Clark has further noted, "In eastern Mesoamerica, Olmec civilization was replaced by the lowland Maya, who began building cities in the jungles of Guatemala about 500 to 400 BC."[1492] The preclassic Maya "experienced peaks and troughs of development, with a mini-collapse about AD 200."[1493] While the final Nephite battles are fought in the fourth century AD, the beginnings of their fall are sown ca. AD 200–210, when after reaching the height of prosperity, religious corruption and social stratification again sets in and proves to be divisive (see 4 Nephi 1:24–29).

John L. Sorenson has pointed out that, corresponding with the annihilation of the Nephites, many Mesoamerican cities were abandoned, destroyed, then rebuilt by invaders in the fourth century AD.[1494] This led Sorenson to conclude, "The picture derived from archaeology thus agrees basically with the Book of Mormon story of the Nephites' retreat."[1495]

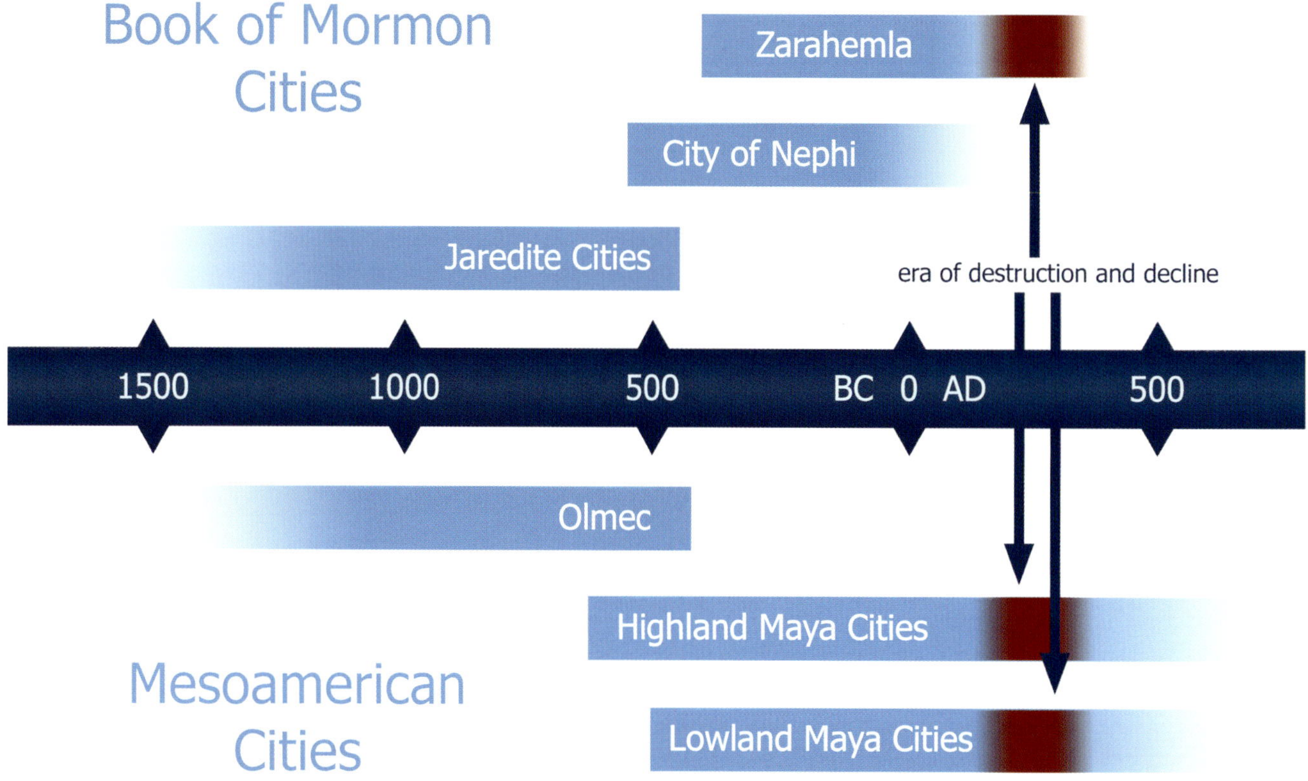

THE WHY

While the geography of the Book of Mormon is not known with certainty, "the correspondences between the Book of Mormon and cycles of Mesoamerican civilization are striking."[1496] It would be a mistake to assume that the Jaredites *are* the Olmec and that the Nephites/Lamanites *are* the Maya. Rather, the consistency in their cycles of civilization suggests that Jaredite and Nephite history could have unfolded within the broader context of Mesoamerican history.[1497]

Significantly, "The Olmecs . . . were not identified as a real culture until 1942, and archaeologists did not know their true age until 1967."[1498] Lacking awareness of early Mesoamerican civilizations and their chronologies, early critics naturally criticized the Book of Mormon's presentation of a twofold civilization.[1499] But as Clark rightly argued, "If early critics cannot be faulted for failing to predict these discoveries, the Book of Mormon should not be denigrated for getting them right."[1500]

By telling the stories of both Nephite and Jaredite societies and their destructions, the Book of Mormon drives home its powerful warning for modern readers. As Steven C. Walker observed, "It is because what happened to the Jaredites happens to the Nephites" that, "more presciently, we sense its potential for ourselves."[1501] The Book of Mormon is a divinely appointed warning for the modern day, *twice* illustrating the downfall that awaits societies that succumb to wickedness and corruption.

Whether Book of Mormon peoples were in Mesoamerica or somewhere else, the archaeology of the Olmec and preclassic Maya confirms that the collapse of civilization is more than just a cautionary tale. This is further affirmed with the rise and fall of post-Book of Mormon Mesoamerican civilizations like Teotihuacan,[1502] the Classic Maya,[1503] the postclassic Maya, and the Aztec.[1504]

The kingdoms of Israel and Judah, and the great empires that once conquered them—Egypt, Assyria, Babylon, Persia, Macedonia, and Rome—all testify of the same fate. Archaeology and history literally the world over attest to the rise and fall of great civilizations, providing a second witness alongside the Book of Mormon, assuring modern readers "that complete deterioration of civilization, and even utter annihilation, are possibilities for even the seemingly invincible United States" and other world powers of the modern age.[1505]

Yet while the history of the world is filled with seemingly invincible civilizations that subsequently became ancient history, only the Book of Mormon diagnoses the root of the problem, and only the Book of Mormon has the antidote. Many factors can contribute to the rise and fall of civilizations, but only adherence to the principles taught by Jesus Christ, as found in 3 Nephi and elsewhere in scripture, can stem the tide of social decay and stave off destruction.

FURTHER READING

John L. Sorenson, *Mormon's Codex: An Ancient American Book* (Salt Lake City and Provo, UT: Deseret Book and Neal A. Maxwell Institute for Religious Scholarship, 2013), 499–595.

John E. Clark, "Archaeological Trends and Book of Mormon Origins," in *The Worlds of Joseph Smith: A Bicentennial Conference at the Library of Congress*, ed. John W. Welch (Provo, UT: BYU Press, 2006), 89–93.

John E. Clark, "Archaeology, Relics, and Book of Mormon Belief," *Journal of Book of Mormon Studies 14*, no. 2 (2005): 48–49.

John L. Sorenson, *Images of Ancient America: Visualizing Book of Mormon Life* (Provo, UT: FARMS, 1999), 192–217.

John L. Sorenson, *An Ancient American Setting for the Book of Mormon* (Salt Lake City and Provo, UT: Deseret Book and FARMS, 1985), 108–137.

Why Must a Trial of Faith Precede a Witness of Truth?

"Wherefore, dispute not because ye see not, for ye receive no witness until after the trial of your faith." (Ether 12:6)

THE KNOW

Although faith plays an important narrative and doctrinal role in many Book of Mormon stories, Ether 12 provides one of its most profound discourses on the topic, rivaled only by Alma 32. After noting Ether's diligent efforts to preach and prophesy "great and marvelous things" to the Jaredites, Moroni reported that "they did not believe, because they saw them not" (Ether 12:5).

Using this narrative detail as a springboard for his famous discourse, Moroni explained, "I would show unto the world that *faith is things which are hoped for and not seen*" (Ether 12:6; emphasis added). This strongly resembles Alma's definition: "if ye have *faith ye hope for things which are not seen*, which are true" (Alma 32:21; emphasis added). Moroni concluded, "wherefore, dispute not because ye see not, for ye receive no witness until after the trial of your faith" (Ether 12:6).[1506]

In order to demonstrate the truth of this principle, Moroni drew on a number of episodes in the Book of Mormon. He wrote, for instance, that it was by faith that "Alma and Amulek . . . caused the prison to tumble to the earth" (Ether 12:13). It was by faith that "Ammon and his brethren . . . wrought so great a miracle among the Lamanites" (Ether 12:15). And it was because of the great faith of the brother of Jared that the Lord "could not withhold anything from his sight" (Ether 12:21).[1507]

However, instead of explicitly making the connection in each case, Moroni expected readers to recall how the characters in each story received a witness of God's power only after their trials. For example, Alma and Amulek were literally on trial (see Alma 14:5, 18–20); were made to witness the suffering of the righteous (see Alma 14:9–14); and were thrown into prison, beaten, and deprived of food, water, and clothing (Alma 14:18–26). Only *after* suffering these depravities did the Lord deliver them by causing the prison walls to fall on their enemies.[1508]

When it was known among the people of Zarahemla that the sons of Mosiah were going to preach to the Lamanites, Ammon said that "they laughed us to scorn" (Alma 26:23). During the fourteen years of their ministry, Ammon recalled that their "hearts were depressed" (Alma 26:27), they "suffered every privation" (Alma 26:28), they were "cast out, and mocked, and spit upon, and smote upon our cheeks . . . stoned, and taken and bound with strong cords, and cast into prison" (Alma 26:29). Only *after* suffering these trials were they able to receive the "fruits of [their missionary] labors" (Alma 26:31).[1509]

When the brother of Jared was concerned about journeying across the ocean in darkness, the Lord asked, "What will ye that I should do that ye may have light in your vessels?" (Ether 2:23). Rather than simply supplying the brother of Jared with a solution to his problem, the Lord required preliminary action, creativity, and then faith in the Lord's power. Only *after* the brother of Jared "did molten out of a rock sixteen small stones" (Ether 3:1) and had faith to ask the Lord to cause them to shine did he see "the finger of the Lord" (Ether 3:6) and then was shown "all things" (Ether 3:26).[1510]

THE WHY

Moroni's discourse on faith demonstrates why the stories in the Book of Mormon are so important. It is a natural impulse to want to see or hear or feel something before accepting that it is true. The Lord reverses this inclination, requiring faith and obedience before giving empirical or miraculous confirmations of the truth. As several Book of Mormon scholars have put it, "Believing without seeing will result in greater seeing."[1511] This kind of "faith—faith that is not dependent upon mortal sight—opens the spiritual eyes to greater views of the things of God."[1512]

D. Kelly Ogden and Andrew C. Skinner explained, "We know our mortal vision is extremely limited; there is a wide spectrum of waves and rays all around us that our eyes, incredible instruments as they are, do not see. In spiritual matters we see not with our eyes but with our spirits. Our spirit, enhanced and quickened or accelerated by the Spirit of God, can see and understand far beyond any mortal capacity."[1513]

It must also be recognized that the goal of faith is not simply to obtain a singular spiritual witness after the completion of a singular trial. Rather it is a process. Alma taught that faith in the word of God begins as a small seed, and that those who plant the seed in their hearts can receive an initial witness of its truth as its goodness begins to grow within them (see Alma 32:30).[1514] If nourished by "faith with great diligence, and with patience" (Alma 32:41), this seed will eventually "take root in you" (Alma 32:42) and become a fully developed "tree springing up unto everlasting life" (Alma 32:41).[1515]

Each step of the faith journey is filled with trials and uncertainty, yet for those who diligently and patiently exercise faith unto obedience, the Lord will provide frequent spiritual witnesses and assurances of the truth. Elder David A. Bednar taught that "the faith that fuels this ongoing process develops, evolves, and changes. As we again turn and face forward toward an uncertain future, assurance leads to action and produces evidence, which further increases assurance." He further explained that this "helix is like a coil, and as it spirals upward it expands and widens."[1516]

Thus the purpose of trials and testing is far more than to provide a prerequisite to receiving answers to questions. It is to develop spiritual character—to "become what our Heavenly Father desires us to become."[1517] Catherine Thomas proposed, "Faith progresses from one's having confidence in God to God's having confidence in that person and permitting him or her to witness and even to administer divine power, as did Moses, Alma, Amulek, Nephi and Lehi, Ammon, the three Nephite disciples, and those . . . like the brother of Jared . . . whose inner spiritual capacity was so well-developed from obedience."[1518]

In a world struggling with doubt and disbelief in spiritual things, the Book of Mormon stands as a shining beacon of hope. Its teachings—delivered by inspired prophets—help readers understand the process of acquiring faith and discern the evidence of its effects in their own lives. Its faith-filled stories help increase confidence that exercising faith during periods of trial and testing will eventually result in profound blessings, spiritual witnesses, and essential personal growth.

FURTHER READING

David A. Bednar, "Seek Learning by Faith," *Ensign*, September 2007, 61–68.

Robert L. Millet, "Faith," in *Book of Mormon Reference Companion*, ed. Dennis L. Largey (Salt Lake City, UT: Deseret Book, 2003), 260–264.

Jeffrey R. Holland, "Rending the Veil of Unbelief," in *A Book of Mormon Treasury: Gospel Insights from General Authorities and Religious Educators* (Provo, UT: BYU Religious Studies Center, 2003), 47–66.

115

How Could Shiz Move and Breathe after Being Beheaded?

"And it came to pass that after he had smitten off the head of Shiz, that Shiz raised up on his hands and fell; and after that he had struggled for breath, he died." (Ether 15:31)

THE KNOW

During the final Jaredite battle, the great king Coriantumr cut off the head of his opponent, Shiz.[1519] But "after he had smitten off the head of Shiz . . . Shiz raised up on his hands and fell; and after that he had struggled for breath, he died" (Ether 15:31). A man struggling for breath without a head is hard to imagine (and most people would not want to). However, this strange event is supported by medical research.

Dr. M. Gary Hadfeld, a professor of neuropathology, discovered a possible medical explanation for Shiz's actions. He stated that "Coriantumr was obviously too exhausted to do a clean job. His stroke evidently strayed a little too high. He must have cut off Shiz's head through the base of the skull, at the level of the midbrain."[1520] If this was the case, then Shiz's strange death scene makes sense.

Hadfield explained, "Shiz's death struggle illustrates the classic reflex . . . when the upper brain stem . . . is disconnected from the brain."[1521] Certain muscles in the arms and legs contract, and this could have caused Shiz to raise up on his hands. This also explains why Shiz would "struggle for breath." Hadfield stated that this botched decapitation "would also cause his rib cage to expand and contract automatically, as it does in all of us when we are sleeping."[1522] This would have made it sound like Shiz was "struggling for breath." This type of neural phenomenon was first reported in 1898, many years after the publication of the Book of Mormon.[1523]

Hadfield noted that "the event obviously astonished both Ether and Moroni, who chronicled it." This is likely why they both would have felt compelled to include it. Even though Moroni would have been familiar with war and the head injuries that go with it, he still "singled out this extraordinary occurrence to include in his abridgment. Perhaps Ether and Moroni had concluded that Shiz's last-minute 'pushup,' . . . was due to an unconquerable spirit, an unwillingness to die."[1524] Even in death, Shiz's bloodlust knew no bounds.

THE WHY

In the past, some have considered this story to be utterly unbelievable. Yet the details turn out to be scientifically sound. This grisly event is uncomfortably true to life, showing yet another example of the benefits of patient investigation over shallow reading.

In addition, this uncomfortably gruesome detail, described as the "most graphic passage in scripture," reminds the reader of the brutality of war.[1525] Moroni chose a brutal decapitation as one of the major events with which to end the book of Ether. He could have left out such an uncomfortable detail, but both Ether and Moroni chose to include it. Moroni may have wanted to emphasize the brutality and hopelessness of this war.

Catherine Thomas put it well:

> In reflection of the utter . . . perishability of their lives and works, [Coriantumr and Shiz] held onto nothing but their swords; no security offered itself. The relentless law of the harvest rolled upon them, and they lived out their remaining days like specters in a terrifying nightmare of anger—sickness, howling, stench, and blood. The lives they had chosen had filled them, not with desire for peace and abundant, thriving life, but with hatred and self-destruction. The ultimate end of evil is death.[1526]

Most readers of the Book of Mormon only like to remember the glorious aspects of war in the Book of Mormon. Moroni does not allow this luxury. Ether 15 portrays an exhausted Coriantumr, covered with blood and mud, so tired that he cannot quite execute a proper decapitation. The brutality of this scene offers a stark reminder that war is always horrific, and that people should not forget the ultimate ending to such senseless conflict. This lesson was not lost on Moroni, who had seen his entire civilization destroyed through war. In the modern world, which is still steeped in warfare, it should also not be lost on readers today.

FURTHER READING

Craig James Ostler, "Shiz," in *Book of Mormon Reference Companion*, ed. Dennis L. Largey (Salt Lake City, UT: Deseret Book, 2003), 722.

M. Gary Hadfield, "The 'Decapitation' of Shiz," in *Pressing Forward with the Book of Mormon: The FARMS Updates of the 1990s*, ed. John W. Welch and Melvin J. Thorne (Provo UT: FARMS, 1999), 266–268.

M. Gary Hadfield, "Neuropathology and the Scriptures," *BYU Studies 33*, no. 2 (1993): 313–328.

Moroni

116

Why Did Moroni Keep Writing?

"Now I, Moroni, after having made an end of abridging the account of the people of Jared, I had supposed not to have written more, but I have not as yet perished." (Moroni 1:1)

THE KNOW

After finishing the book of Ether, Moroni wrote ten more chapters, even though he had not planned on doing so (see Moroni 1:1). One may wonder why Moroni would have done this when his life was so bleak and uncertain. After all, his people had been killed, and he had already completed his father's work of abridging the Nephite and Jaredite records. Among many other reasons, he may have written these chapters to explain more fully something at which his father had only hinted.[1527]

In his account of Christ's visit to the Americas, Mormon mentioned that Jesus laid His hands on His disciples and "gave them power to give the Holy Ghost" (3 Nephi 18:36–37). Mormon promised to later demonstrate how this was fulfilled and how the disciples were able to give the gift of the Holy Ghost (see 3 Nephi 18:37). While Mormon alluded to the giving of the Holy Ghost several times, he did not provide some of the details about this event that the reader might like to have.[1528]

Thankfully for all readers of the Book of Mormon, Moroni seems to have noticed this gap, and he decided to deliver on his father's promise.[1529] To do this, he reported Christ's exact words to His disciples, showing "that the record is true" (3 Nephi 18:37).[1530] This may be the reason for Moroni 2. Moroni finally told his readers about "the words of Christ, which he spake unto his disciples . . . saying: Ye shall call on the Father in my name . . . and after ye have done this ye shall have power that to him upon whom ye shall lay your hands, ye shall give the Holy Ghost" (Moroni 2:1–2).

Although it is impossible to be sure of this, it is likely that Moroni assisted Mormon in his work.[1531] If this is the case, he may have recalled that his father never fulfilled this particular promise to his readers. After living long enough to abridge the book of Ether, another loose end his father had left behind, Moroni may have decided to tie up this loose end as well. This would explain why this note on the gift of the Holy Ghost was one of the first things he wrote. He may have wanted to make sure that, no matter what else happened, his father's promise was fulfilled.

THE WHY

Even though Moroni's life was almost unimaginably difficult, he still continued to write, even after finishing the abridgment of Ether. Knowing that it was only through these plates that the gospel would eventually come to the Lamanites, Moroni may have been driven to personally bear witness and to finish what his father started.[1532]

Moroni's dedication is both inspirational and instructive for the modern reader. It is likely that Moroni was inspired by his father's dedication and that this is part of what drove him to finish what his father had started.[1533] In modern times, parents can also inspire children by their dedication to the cause of Christ, helping them to carry on traditions of discipleship.

As Elder K. Brett Nattress taught:

> I don't know if anything in this world could bring more happiness and joy than to know that our children know the Savior, to know that they know "to what source they may look for a remission of their sins." That is why, as members of the Church, "we preach of Christ" and we testify of Christ (2 Nephi 25:26). That is why we pray with our children every day. That is why we read the scriptures with them every day. That is why we teach them to serve others. . . . As we devote ourselves to these simple patterns of discipleship, we empower our children with the love of the Savior and with divine direction and protection as they face the fierce winds of the adversary. [1534]

FURTHER READING

Hugh Nibley, *Teachings of the Book of Mormon*, 4 vols. (American Fork and Provo, UT: Covenant Communications and FARMS, 2004), 4:220–221.

Byron R. Merrill, "Moroni[2]," in *Book of Mormon Reference Companion*, ed. Dennis L. Largey (Salt Lake City, UT: Deseret Book, 2003), 557.

Gary Layne Hatch, "Mormon and Moroni: Father and Son," in *The Book of Mormon: Fourth Nephi, From Zion to Destruction*, ed. Monte S. Nyman and Charles D. Tate Jr. (Provo, UT: BYU Religious Studies Center, 1995), 105–116.

Where Did Moroni Get the Sacramental Prayers?

"The manner of their elders and priests administering the flesh and blood of Christ unto the church; and they administered it according to the commandments of Christ." (Moroni 4:1)

THE KNOW

Moroni 4–5 present the prayers that the Nephites used in administering the sacrament of the Lord's Supper. Although these prayers, as known to Moroni, were recorded here centuries after the visit of Christ to the Book of Mormon peoples, Moroni indicated that the "elders and priests" of his time "administered it according to the commandments of Christ" in a manner that Moroni claimed was "true" (Moroni 4:1).

Although readers rarely notice the intricate textual interdependency between Moroni 4–5 and 3 Nephi 18, the words of the sacramental prayers in Moroni 4–5 can clearly be traced, for the most part, directly to the very words Jesus Christ used when He administered the sacrament during His post-Resurrection ministry, as recorded in 3 Nephi 18.

There are other records of Nephite covenant-making/renewal ceremonies that appear to have had influence on the sacramental prayers in their final form, especially the grand speech given by King Benjamin in Mosiah 1–5. The chart that follows shows parallels between Mosiah 5, 3 Nephi 18, and Moroni 4–5.

From the chart's comparison, it is clear that the sacrament prayers, as they were known in the time of Moroni, ritually recalled the words that Jesus Christ spoke when He introduced the sacrament to the Book of Mormon people. The language is slightly modified, in that "they" is used instead of "ye," and Jesus's references to Himself (for example, "me," "my body," "I have") are changed to refer to Christ in the third person (for example, "him," "the body of thy Son," "he hath"), as Jesus was no longer present and the prayers are directed to the Father.[1535]

Because the Nephites met often and partook of the sacrament immediately after the visitations of Christ among them, it would seem likely that the ceremonial form of the sacrament prayers crystalized very soon in the ministry of Nephi, the disciple of Jesus. One particularly noteworthy phrase appears in the prayers as found in Moroni 4–5 that was not included in the recorded words of Christ in 3 Nephi 18: "that they are willing to take upon them the name of thy Son" (Moroni 4:3). As shown in the table below, that phrase parallels King Benjamin's words as he put his people under covenant to take upon themselves the name of Christ (see Mosiah 5:8) about 125 years before the appearance of Christ at the temple in Bountiful.

Mosiah 5	3 Nephi 18	Moroni 4–5
	this ye shall do [partake of the bread] in remembrance of my body (18:7)	that they may eat in remembrance of the body of thy Son (4:3)
I would that ye should take upon you the name of Christ (5:8)	and it shall be a testimony unto the Father (18:7)	and witness unto thee, O God, the Eternal Father, that they are willing to take upon them the name of thy Son (4:3)
	that ye do always remember me (18:7)	that they … always remember him (4:3)
	and if ye do always remember me ye shall have my Spirit to be with you (18:7)	that they may always have his Spirit to be with them (4:3)
we are willing . . . to be obedient to [God's] commandments in all things that he shall command us (5:5)	this [partaking of the wine] doth witness unto the Father that ye are willing to do that which I have commanded you (18:10)	and witness unto thee, O God, the Eternal Father, that they are willing to . . . keep his commandments which he hath given them (4:3)
	and ye shall do it in remembrance of my blood, which I have shed for you, that ye may witness unto the Father that ye do always remember me (18:11)	that they may do it in remembrance of the blood of thy Son, which was shed for them; that they may witness unto thee, O God, the Eternal Father, that they do always remember him (5:2)
	and if ye do always remember me ye shall have my Spirit to be with you (18:11)	that they may have his Spirit to be with them (5:2)

THE WHY

The sacrament prayers used in the time of Moroni were closely based on the very words that Christ Himself spoke when He visited the Book of Mormon peoples. The words of Christ were likely used to replace the language of an already rich history of covenant-making rituals among the Nephites, but the replacement still preserved some of the verbiage from their traditional covenant-renewal ceremony. As John W. Welch noted, "It seems that Nephite texts and traditions have combined and coalesced beautifully into the final sacrament prayers in Moroni 4–5."[1536]

Readers may note that the prayers used by the modern Church today, as found in Doctrine and Covenants 20:76–79, are almost exactly the same words recorded in Moroni 4–5. It is significant that these words are essentially the words that Christ spoke when He introduced the ordinance Himself in 3 Nephi 18. The prayers recorded by Moroni demonstrate an effort to keep the prayers as close to Jesus's own words as possible.

Moroni was careful to record these precious sacrament prayers precisely, because they were sacred, were based on the actual words of the resurrected Lord Jesus Christ, and conveyed through the sacramental ordinance the powers of the sacrificed body and atoning blood of Christ. In addition, those words also communicated the power of the Holy Ghost and aligned the will of the Father with ordinary men and women who seek to keep His commandments. To serve these holy purposes, Moroni was careful to convey the words of these prayers with solemn exactness.

FURTHER READING

John W. Welch, "Benjamin's Covenant as a Precursor of the Sacrament Prayers," in *King Benjamin's Speech: "That Ye May Learn Wisdom,"* ed. John W. Welch and Stephen D. Ricks (Provo, UT: FARMS, 1998), 295–314.

John W. Welch, "From Presence to Practice: Jesus, the Sacrament Prayers, the Priesthood, and Church Discipline in 3 Nephi 18 and Moroni 2–6," *Journal of Book of Mormon Studies* 5, no. 1 (1996): 119–139.

Richard Lloyd Anderson, "The Modern-Text Theory," *Review of Books on the Book of Mormon* 6, no. 1 (1994): 379–417.

John W. Welch, "Our Nephite Sacrament Prayers," in *Reexploring the Book of Mormon: A Decade of New Research*, ed. John W. Welch (Salt Lake City and Provo, UT: Deseret Book and FARMS, 1992), 286–289.

Richard Lloyd Anderson, "Religious Validity: The Sacrament Covenant in Third Nephi," in *By Study and Also by Faith: Essays in Honor of Hugh Nibley*, 2 vols., ed. John M. Lundquist and Stephen D. Ricks (Salt Lake City and Provo, UT: Deseret Book and FARMS, 1990), 2:1–51.

What Can an Ancient Christian Text Tell Us about Moroni's Writings?

"And the church did meet together oft, to fast and to pray, and to speak one with another concerning the welfare of their souls." (Moroni 6:5)

THE KNOW

In 1873, a Greek Orthodox bishop named Philotheos Bryennios was studying in a monastery in Constantinople when he came across an unusual ancient manuscript.[1537] It was called *The Teaching of the Twelve Apostles* or the *Didache* (the Greek word for "teaching") and was unlike anything most people had ever seen. It contained instructions on how Christians from as early as the end of the first century were to perform ordinances and how the church was to conduct itself.

In 1830, more than forty years before Bryennios made his groundbreaking discovery, the Book of Mormon was published with a similar collection in Moroni 3–6. Like the *Didache*, these chapters contained notes on ordinances and church conduct.[1538] The similarities between the two texts are striking and shed light on the founding and organization of Christ's Church in both the Old World and the New.

Moroni 3, for example, contains instructions on how appointed leaders (called "elders") were to ordain "priests" and "teachers." One finds the same thing in Didache 15:1, which describes how the community was to appoint worthy and meek men to serve as "bishops" and "deacons" to carry on "the ministry of the prophets and teachers."[1539] Similarly, Moroni 4 and 5 contain two sacrament prayers, one for the bread and one for the wine. Didache 9:1–5 also contains separate prayers, one for the cup of wine and the other for the broken bread.[1540]

Moroni 6 also contains a number of elements that are similar to the Diadache. Moroni 6:1–4 discusses details related to the performance of baptism, as does Didache 7:1–4.[1541] Moroni 6:5–6 then states, "And the church did meet together oft, to fast and to pray, and to . . . partake of bread and wine, in remembrance of the Lord Jesus." Didache 14:1 similarly states, "But on the Lord's day, after you have gathered together, break bread and give thanks."[1542] Didache 8:1 also mentions fasting often, just as Moroni 6:5 mentions frequent fasting.[1543] The Greek words of Didache 16:2 are naturally translated into English with the same expression Moroni used.[1544] Moroni, quoting the words of Christ in 3 Nephi 18:22, states that they should "meet together oft" and the Didache states "gather together often."[1545]

Moroni 6:7–8 states, "and whoso was found to commit iniquity, and . . . repented not, and confessed not, their names were blotted out. But as oft as they repented and sought forgiveness, with real intent, they were forgiven." Didache 15:3 contains a similar commandment: "Rebuke each other, but do not do so wrathfully, but peaceably, as the gospel commands; but let nobody speak to anyone who mistreats his neighbor, and don't let him be heard by you until he repents."[1546]

THE WHY

The Didache was likely written sometime between AD 60 and 117, making it surprisingly early and roughly the same age as much of the New Testament.[1547] However, when looking at it in isolation, one might wonder how much of the material in the Didache goes back to Jesus Himself and how much might have been created by other early Christians.[1548] The similarities between the Didache in the Old World and the words of Moroni in the Book of Mormon suggest that much of these basic instructions for how to organize and manage the Church and perform ordinances go back to the original Apostles, who received their instructions from Christ Himself.

If this is the case, the similarities between the Didache and Moroni show that Christ cares about the details of the Church. Ordinances and Church structure and conduct are not incidental details to Christ, but they are important elements of the Church that He established. This attention to detail proved to be significant in the early days of the Restoration, as the Book of Mormon appears to have been used as something of a handbook for conducting the Church.[1549] John W. Welch has noted that Oliver Cowdery quoted Moroni 3–6 in a three-page document drafted in June 1829, entitled "Articles of the Church of Christ."[1550] That document discusses primarily instructions for the administration of ordinances and other practices of the Church.[1551]

Thus, the same four chapters of Moroni most closely paralleled in the early Christian Didache are the same chapters that were foundational in the organization of the Restored Church in this dispensation as well. This detail is a reminder of the continuity between the Church of Christ established during His ministry and His Church on the earth today. It also allows us to approach the ordinances of the restored gospel more confidently. When we participate in these ordinances, the distance between us and the ancient followers of Christ narrows, and we can, in some small way, participate in these ordinances with them.

FURTHER READING

Hugh Nibley, *Since Cumorah*, *The Collected Works of Hugh Nibley, Volume 7* (Salt Lake City and Provo, UT: Deseret Book and FARMS, 1988), 174–177.

John W. Welch, "The Book of Mormon as the Keystone of Church Administration," *Religious Educator 12*, no. 2 (2011): 88.

John W. Welch, "Approaching New Approaches," *Review of Books on the Book of Mormon 6*, no. 1 (1994): 152–168.

Why Was Singing Hymns a Part of Nephite Worship Services?

"And their meetings were conducted by the church after the manner of the workings of the Spirit . . . for as the power of the Holy Ghost led them whether to preach, or to exhort, or to pray, or to supplicate, or to sing, even so it was done." (Moroni 6:9)

THE KNOW

In Moroni 6, as part of Moroni's instructions regarding how church "meetings were conducted" (Moroni 6:9), Moroni mentioned singing. Evidently, the Nephite Church, as Moroni knew it, made singing a part of their worship services, as guided by the Holy Ghost. Although the text does not indicate when this practice was officially instituted, there is a long history of the use of music and hymns in Judeo-Christian worship. Nephite worship practices fit nicely into this tradition.

The singing of hymns extends back to the sacred ceremonies of the ancient Israelite temple of Jerusalem and beyond.[1552] Margaret Barker has stated, "The Psalms were the hymn book of the temple, and in them we glimpse something of the ancient liturgy."[1553] The Bible indicates that one of the functions of the priestly tribe of Israel, the Levites, was to sing in the tabernacle and, later, the temple in Jerusalem.[1554]

This practice continued through the development of Judaism and was adopted by the earliest Christians as well. The Jewish group(s) who wrote the Dead Sea Scrolls were clearly interested in composing and singing hymns. Among the scrolls, more texts from the book of Psalms were found than from any other biblical book. Furthermore, many other scrolls containing psalms/hymns not known from the Bible have been found.[1555]

The New Testament depicts the Savior and His Apostles singing a hymn at the end of the Passover meal in which Christ instituted the sacrament of the Lord's Supper (see Matthew 26:30). Paul and James recommended the singing of hymns in their letters to Church members (see Ephesians 5:19; James 5:13). The Apostle John witnessed the singing of hymns in heaven before the throne of God (see Revelation 5:8–9; 14:2–3).

Likewise, the Book of Mormon contains many references to the singing of hymns. Lehi and Nephi, the book's first authors, apparently brought the tradition of singing sacred songs with them when they left Jerusalem. Lehi "saw the heavens open," with God on His throne, "surrounded with numberless concourses of angels in the attitude of singing and praising their God" (1 Nephi 1:8). The plates of brass, from which Nephi read, contained references to singing in the context of worshiping God (see 1 Nephi 21:13; 2 Nephi 22:1–6).

King Benjamin spoke of his desire to "join the choirs above in singing the praises of a just God" (Mosiah 2:28). Alma spoke to the members of the Church in Zarahemla about singing "the song of redeeming love" (Alma 5:9,

26; cf. 26:8, 13). In 3 Nephi 4, after their victory over Zemnarihah, the Nephites "did break forth, all as one, in singing" what was evidently a song that they all knew (see 3 Nephi 4:28–33). When Christ visited the Book of Mormon lands, many of the scriptural passages that He shared mentioned singing praises to God.[1556]

THE WHY

The singing of sacred hymns in Moroni's day was clearly part of the religious tradition of ancient Israel that continued not only into Book of Mormon practice, but also into that of later Jewish and Christian groups. Language from the Psalms can be found throughout the Book of Mormon and New Testament, which shows how memorable and important the words of these hymns were in the lives of ancient Israelites and early Christians. What is interesting to ask is why it was an important part of worship services. Beyond the fact that it was tradition and encouraged by the scriptures, there may be three significant reasons:

1. Composing and singing hymns was believed to be inspired by the Spirit and also to bring the Spirit. A Psalms scroll from Qumran declares that David was given the Spirit and that "he uttered all these [hymns] through prophecy which was given him from before the Most High" (11QPsa 27:4–11).
2. This idea that David's psalms were inspired by the Spirit (by prophecy) appears to have continued into Christian belief.[1557] Furthermore, Barker has suggested that the singing of hymns was a way to invoke the Spirit, or presence, of the Lord.[1558] These notions fit well with Moroni's comment that the Church sing hymns "as the power of the Holy Ghost led them" (Moroni 6:9).
3. Singing hymns was apparently done in imitation of the angels in heaven. Latter-day Saint scholar John Tvedtnes argued that when King Benjamin mentioned wanting to "join the choirs above" (Mosiah 2:28), it is likely that he was speaking at the Nephite celebration of the Israelite Feast of Tabernacles, "when a choir of Levites sang in imitation of the choir of angels."[1559]
4. Lehi had seen the heavenly choir of angels (see 1 Nephi 1:8), as had Alma (see Alma 36:22). The Bible also mentions this angelic singing (see Job 38:7; Luke 2:13–14), and some of the Dead Sea Scrolls indicate that human worshippers were to learn the songs of the angels and sing praises along with them.[1560] This notion survived into later Jewish and Christian texts.[1561]
5. Singing hymns was an expression of gratitude to the Lord for His gift of redemption. The Book of Mormon contains several accounts in which the singing of hymns follows an event in which the Lord has saved an individual or group, or after the discussion of a redemptive act. For example, as mentioned above, when Alma rehearsed with the Church members of Zarahemla the redemption of their fathers from physical and spiritual bondage, he emphasized that their fathers "did sing redeeming love" (Alma 5:9). Similarly, when the Nephites were victorious in battle (see 3 Nephi 4), they praised the Lord for having preserved them and "did break forth . . . in singing" (3 Nephi 4:31).

Along with prayer, the singing of hymns has been a legitimate and central part of the worship of our Father in Heaven for millennia. The Lord told Joseph Smith in this dispensation that He is pleased by the singing of "sacred hymns." His "soul delighteth in the song of the heart" and He considers "the song of the righteous [to be] a prayer unto me." The Lord promised that the singing of such hymns by members of the Church "shall be answered with a blessing upon their heads" (D&C 25:11–12).

FURTHER READING

John A. Tvedtnes, *The Most Correct Book: Insights from a Mormon Scholar* (Salt Lake City, UT: Cornerstone Publishing, 1999), 167–169.

LeGrand L. Baker and Stephen D. Ricks, *Who Shall Ascend into the Hill of the Lord?: The Psalms in Israel's Temple Worship in the Old Testament and in the Book of Mormon* (Salt Lake City, UT: Eborn Books, 2011), 520–537.

120

Why Did Mormon Quote from the Sermon at the Temple?

"A man being evil cannot do that which is good." (Moroni 7:6)

THE KNOW

In 3 Nephi 12–14, Jesus delivered the discourse known as the Sermon at the Temple.[1562] Hundreds of years later, as Mormon delivered the discourse recorded in Moroni 7, Mormon appears to have woven words and phrases from Christ's speech into his own address.[1563] Why are these teachings and concepts repeated throughout Moroni 7, just as they had been repeated throughout the rest of 3 Nephi that follows His ascension?[1564] John W. Welch has argued that Mormon does not quote the sermon at random, but that the chapter was written to shed light on the Sermon and on Christ's explanation of it.[1565]

For example, in 3 Nephi 14:20, Christ taught, "By their fruits ye shall know them." Mormon explains these fruits by saying "by their works ye shall know them" (Moroni 7:5).[1566] Mormon then stated that "A man being evil cannot do that which is good" (Moroni 7:6). As Welch noted, this "declaratively and deliberately answers the rhetorical question" in 3 Nephi 14:6, "Do men gather grapes of thorns?"[1567] Mormon's use of Christ's words clarifies that both good and bad people will show their true colors through their actions.

Mormon promised his hearers, "Whatsoever thing ye shall ask the Father in [Christ's] name, which is good, in faith believing that ye shall receive, behold it shall be done unto you" (Moroni 7:26). This explains and clarifies Christ's statement, "Ask, and it shall be given unto you; seek, and ye shall find; knock, and it shall be opened unto you" (3 Nephi 14:7; see also 3 Nephi 27:29).[1568] Mormon clarifies Christ's statement to show that people cannot get whatever they want simply because they ask for it. People must ask for that which is good, and they must also ask with faith that God will give them what they ask for.

Welch noted that "Mormon's emphasis on 'meekness' (Moroni 7:39, 43, 44), a virtue that was sorely lacking among his people" would have been a particularly painful point for his audience.[1569] Christ stated, "Blessed are the meek, for they shall inherit the earth" (3 Nephi 12:5). The Nephites, far from inheriting the earth, were losing their portion of the earth to the Lamanites as their armies continued to take more and more Nephite land.[1570]

THE WHY

The fact that Mormon wove the sermon at the temple so seamlessly into his speech suggests that he knew this speech very well. It's likely he had recently abridged that part of the Nephite record when he gave the discourse recorded in Moroni 7, leaving it fresh on his mind. In the process, he likely had not just read it once or twice, but had read it enough times that it naturally flowed into how he thought and spoke.

It might be easy to read a chapter of scripture a few times and think that there is nothing more to know about it. Mormon does not seem to have fallen into that trap. He didn't simply read Christ's speech and forget about it. He seems to have gone back to it over and over again. He internalized Christ's great speech such that he could effortlessly integrate it into his own address. Welch notes how remarkable this is:

> These texts from Mormon and Moroni, written more than three hundred years after the sermon was given at the temple in Bountiful, show that the words of Jesus were accepted by the disciples of Christ from the very outset as crystallizing the doctrine of Christ, the gospel of Christ, the will of the Lord, the word of the Lord, his plan of happiness, his path of holiness, the foundation of his new covenant written in the heart, and his covenantal pattern for the life of righteousness.[1571]

In the same way that Mormon carefully studied and internalized the scriptures so many years after they were given, modern readers should make the scriptures a part of themselves. Simply reading through the Book of Mormon once or twice will not do. Sometimes readers could carefully study the logic of individual chapters. At other times they could step back to look at the big picture. On yet other occasions they could look at how individual words are used in the text. Regardless of the approach, the scriptures demand careful study that changes the way readers think, speak, and act. Mormon showed his audience what this kind of scripture study looks like, and modern readers can, and should, study the scriptures in the same way today.

FURTHER READING

John W. Welch, "Reusages of the Words of Christ," *Journal of Book of Mormon Studies and Other Restoration Scripture 22*, no. 1 (2013): 63–71.

John W. Welch, "Echoes from the Sermon on the Mount," in *The Sermon on the Mount in Latter-day Scripture*, ed. Gaye Strathearn, Thomas A. Wayment, and Daniel L. Belnap (Provo, UT: BYU Religious Studies Center and Salt Lake City: Deseret Book, 2010), 320–322.

Jeffrey R. Holland, *Christ and the New Covenant* (Salt Lake City, UT: Deseret Book, 1997), 249–275.

What Does Mormon Teach Us about Ministering as Angels?

"And because he hath done this, my beloved brethren, have miracles ceased? Behold I say unto you, Nay; neither have angels ceased to minister unto the children of men." (Moroni 7:29)

THE KNOW

During his masterful discourse in Moroni 7, Mormon made a seeming detour in his discussion of the role of faith, hope, and charity in the lives of his brothers and sisters of the Church. He reminded them of the role that angels play in ministering the gospel.[1572] This aside may seem out of place at first. However, a close reading shows that Mormon was using the ministering of angels as an example to show his own flock how they should minister to those around them.

> For behold, God knowing all things, being from everlasting to everlasting, behold, he sent angels to minister unto the children of men, to make manifest concerning the coming of Christ; and in Christ there should come every good thing. . . .
>
> Wherefore, by the ministering of angels, and by every word which proceeded forth out of the mouth of God, men began to exercise faith in Christ; and thus by faith, they did lay hold upon every good thing; and thus it was until the coming of Christ. (Moroni 7:22, 25)

Mormon's abridgment of his people's records brims with accounts and testimony of angels of the Lord.[1573] Throughout the scriptures, angels have served to bring forth "knowledge, priesthood, comfort, and assurances from God to mortals."[1574] Mormon knew this; not only from his own personal angelic experiences, but also from the accounts of great faith-building miracles in the lives of his forbearers who testified that God works in the same way "from everlasting to everlasting" in testifying of Christ.

With this in mind, however, it is important to note that his ancient audience lived in a time of great wickedness, a time of wars and rumors of wars. Being a Saint in those days was not easy, but true discipleship was never meant to be easy. Taking it upon himself to provide comfort, Mormon had just reassured them that, "Whatsoever thing ye shall ask the Father in my name, which is good, in faith believing that ye shall receive, behold, it shall be done to you" (Moroni 7:26). But could such a promise really be true in such dangerous and unstable times?

Any guessing as to their thoughts is speculation, but it lends us a potential insight into Mormon's mind when he said a few verses later, "my beloved brethren, have miracles ceased? Behold I say unto you, Nay; neither have angels ceased to minister unto the children of men" (Moroni 7:29).

Mormon testified that even in their day, the presence of miracles was no different.

Miracles still occurred, and angels continued to minister.[1575] They showed themselves "unto them of strong faith and a firm mind in every form of godliness" (Moroni 7:30)—not just to the prophets, but to any who possessed strong faith.[1576] And their office, he continued, was "to call men unto repentance" that "the residue of men may have faith in Christ, that the Holy Ghost may have place in their hearts" (Moroni 7:31–32).

THE WHY

While this message certainly had a profound personal impact on Mormon and his struggling Saints, what does it mean for us today? The answer may be more personal than you think.

In the Book of Mormon, the converted Lamanite king Anti-Nephi-Lehi spoke to his people as they faced certain destruction:

> And the great God has had mercy on us, . . . therefore, *in his mercy he doth visit us by his angels*, that the plan of salvation might be made known unto us as well as unto future generations. (Alma 24:14; emphasis added)

Just a few chapters later, Mormon tells us that the Lamanites treated Ammon and the other sons of Mosiah "*as though they were angels* sent from God to save them from everlasting destruction" (Alma 27:4; emphasis added). As these brethren taught repentance, they were looked upon as angels sent from the Lord. It's important to mention here that the Hebrew word *malakh*, often translated as "angel" in the King James Bible, can also be translated as "messenger," which fits Anti-Nephi-Lehi's use of the word.[1577]

Mormon's lesson in these few short verses was not a tangent. More significantly, it was an example of how they could exercise faith, hope, and charity. He held up the angels of the Lord as a model of what they could become and what they could do. Just as the sons of Mosiah were angels to the people of Ammon, the Saints of Mormon's day could be angels to their own people.

In these latter days, Elder Jeffrey R. Holland has profoundly taught us about angels, seen and unseen, that come from both sides of the veil:

> I have spoken here of heavenly help, of angels dispatched to bless us in time of need. But when we speak of those who are instruments in the hand of God, we are reminded that not all angels are from the other side of the veil. Some of them we walk with and talk with—here, now, every day. Some of them reside in our own neighborhoods. Some of them gave birth to us, and in my case, one of them consented to marry me. Indeed heaven never seems closer than when we see the love of God manifested in the kindness and devotion of people so good and so pure that angelic is the only word that comes to mind.[1578]

Today, we live in difficult times, just as Mormon and his people did. Many of us doubt. Many others seek the Lord in prayer, looking for answers, even miracles, to come in some grand and glorious manner. Sometimes we fail to stop and consider the small and simple ways that the Lord puts people in our path. Other times we overlook the moments that we unknowingly serve as His messengers, and His angels, by following a silent prompting. We overlook the ways in which He whispers, "Don't worry. Keep going. I'm still here. Repent."

What do we learn of angels from Mormon? The glorious reality that the day of miracles has not ceased, and angels—mortal and immortal—still minister to the children of men.

FURTHER READING

Jeffrey R. Holland, "The Ministry of Angels," *Ensign*, November 2008, 29–31.

Sydney S. Reynolds, "A God of Miracles," *Ensign*, May 2001.

Oscar W. McConkie, "Angels," in *Encyclopedia of Mormonism*, 4 vols., ed. Daniel H. Ludlow (New York: Macmillan, 1992), 1:40–42.

Larry Evans Dahl, "Angels, Ministry of," in *Book of Mormon Reference Companion,* ed. Dennis L. Largey (Salt Lake City, UT: Deseret Book, 2003), 59–60.

Why Did Moroni Include Mormon's Condemnation of Infant Baptism?

"But little children are alive in Christ, even from the foundation of the world." (Moroni 8:12)

THE KNOW

Soon after Moroni began his ministry, he received a letter from his father that stated, "if I have learned the truth, there have been disputations among you concerning the baptism of your little children" (Moroni 8:5).[1579] Mormon explained that this situation "grieveth me exceedingly; for it grieveth me that there should disputations rise among you" (Moroni 8:4).

The fact that Mormon "immediately . . . inquired of the Lord concerning the matter" suggests that this theological perversion was a relatively recent development among his people (Moroni 8:7). One important consideration is that Nephite children during Mormon's ministry were in danger of being captured by the Lamanites and offered up as "sacrifices unto their idol gods" (Mormon 4:14).[1580] In this context, it is understandable that the parents may have had an increased anxiety for the welfare of their children.

It's also plausible that infant baptism initially stemmed from outside Nephite culture. Matthew Roper explained that in pre-Columbian America, "Aztec midwives ritually bathed newborn children, invoking the cleansing power of the goddess Chalchiuhtlicue. Implicit in the practice was the assumption that infants may inherit evil and impurity at birth."[1581] Roper concluded, "It is not difficult to imagine that Mormon and Moroni were resisting similar cultural traditions which were making dangerous inroads into the Nephite church of Christ."[1582]

Interestingly, the controversy over infant baptism among the Nephites somewhat parallels the situation in Europe and the Near East, where the "practice of baptizing infants emerged among Christians in the third century A.D. and was controversial for some time."[1583] Origen, one of the early church fathers who defended the practice, "argued that baptism takes away the pollution of birth."[1584]

In both situations, the problem wasn't that belief in the power of priesthood ordinances completely ceased; rather, it was because the people, as Isaiah wrote, "have transgressed the laws, changed the ordinance, [and] broken the everlasting covenant" (Isaiah 24:5). This seems to have been the same development in Mormon's time, who was appalled that his people would "pervert the ways of the Lord after this manner" (Moroni 8:16).[1585]

In response to Mormon's inquiry, Jesus Christ revealed that "the whole need no physician, but they that are sick; wherefore, little children are whole, for they are not capable of committing sin" (Moroni 8:8). This revelation led Mormon to sharply declare, "he that saith that little children need baptism denieth the mercies of Christ, and setteth at naught the atonement of him and the power of his redemption" (Moroni 8:20; cf. Mosiah 3:11, 16).

THE WHY

In Mormon 8:35, Moroni addressed future readers directly, declaring, "Jesus Christ hath shown you unto me, and I know your doing."[1586] With this in mind, it seems quite possible that Moroni included Mormon's letter because he understood, either through vision or through some other spiritual manifestation, that infant baptism would be a heated topic of debate among varying Christian denominations in the latter days.[1587]

If so, its inclusion can be seen as fulfilling an important purpose of the Book of Mormon—to merge with the Bible "unto the confounding of false doctrines and laying down of contentions, and establishing peace" (2 Nephi 3:12).[1588] In this sense, Mormon's letter follows the example of Jesus Christ who, upon visiting the temple at Bountiful, promptly taught the correct manner of baptism. "On this wise," He declared, "shall ye baptize; and there shall be no disputations among you" (3 Nephi 11:22).[1589]

This letter also demonstrates how the Lord works through His chosen prophet to settle doctrinal disputations. Apparently Mormon, although away at war, still had ecclesiastical authority to declare the mind and will of the Lord for the Church. He declared, "Behold, I speak with boldness, having authority from God; and I fear not what man can do" (Moroni 8:16).

And yet Mormon also made it clear that his choice to follow Jesus Christ's commandment was made in love. He explained, "I love little children with a perfect love; and they are all alike and partakers of salvation" (Moroni 8:17). Although it's likely there were parents who felt that without baptism their children were in spiritual danger or would be deprived of blessings, Mormon firmly yet lovingly upheld the commandment he had received from Jesus Christ.[1590] In this way, Mormon was an example of "Reproving betimes with sharpness, when moved upon by the Holy Ghost; and then showing forth afterwards an increase of love" (D&C 121:43).

Thus, Mormon's letter provides doctrinal clarification of essential priesthood ordinances, a model of a prophet receiving revelation for the Church, and an example of how to lovingly yet firmly uphold the commandments of the Lord. Not only did this epistle offer an important template for the early Latter-day Saints, but it continues to be relevant to the many moral disputations and doctrinal controversies that arise in churches and societies today. As Hugh Nibley explained, "The Latter-day Saints have always maintained that guidance both in doctrinal and administrational matters can come to the church only by revelation."[1591]

FURTHER READING

Noel B. Reynolds, "Understanding Christian Baptism through the Book of Mormon," *BYU Studies Quarterly 51*, no. 2 (2012): 3–37.

Tad R. Callister, *The Inevitable Apostasy and the Promised Restoration* (Salt Lake City, UT: Deseret Book, 2006), 221–230.

Matthew Roper, "The Baptism of Little Children in Pre-Columbian Mesoamerica," *Insights: A Window on the Ancient World 23* (2003): 2–3.

123

When Did Mormon Write His Letter Recorded in Moroni 9?

"My beloved son, I write unto you again that ye may know that I am yet alive; but I write somewhat of that which is grievous." (Moroni 9:1)

THE KNOW

Moroni 9 contains a letter from Mormon, written to his son Moroni, which describes the spiritual decline of their people.[1592] Although Mormon never said when he wrote this letter, it may be possible to identify its historical context and the approximate date of its composition by comparing its details with Mormon's own record.[1593] In particular, it appears that the contents of Mormon's letter correlate with the historical events and spiritual themes found in Mormon 4, 5, and 6.

Losses in Battle

In his letter, Mormon stated, "I have had a sore battle with the Lamanites, in which we did not conquer" and in which "we have lost a great number of our choice men" (Moroni 9:2). This battle likely took place during a series of Nephite retreats and losses reported in Mormon 5:3–7, which occurred after Mormon resumed his command of the Nephite armies.

Intense Anger and Hardened Hearts

Mormon also mentioned that the Nephites had "harden[ed] their hearts" against the word of God and that "so exceedingly do they anger that it seemeth me that they have no fear of death; and they have lost their love, one towards another" (Moroni 9:4–5). Likewise, in Mormon 4 we learn that "every heart was hardened" (Mormon 4:11) and that the Nephites "did go against the Lamanites with exceedingly great anger" (Mormon 4:15). In each case, a desire for revenge was a strong motivating factor.

Perseverance

In this letter, Mormon declared, "And now, my beloved son, notwithstanding their hardness, let us labor diligently; for if we should cease to labor, we should be brought under condemnation" (Moroni 9:6). This same theme, of continuing to strive for the Nephites' spiritual welfare despite their wickedness, is found in Mormon 5:1: "And it came to pass that I did go forth among the Nephites, and did repent of the oath which I had made that I would no more assist them."

Prisoners and the Suffering of Women and Children

Mormon reported to Moroni that "the Lamanites have many prisoners, which they took from the tower of Sherrizah; and there were men, women, and children" (Moroni 9:7; cf. Moroni 9:16). The taking of Nephite prisoners was also mentioned in Mormon 4:13–14: "And it came to pass that the Lamanites did . . . take many prisoners both women and children, and did offer them up as sacrifices unto their idol gods." It is also implied in Mormon 4:21.[1594]

Destruction and Desertion

Mormon declared that he knew his people "must perish except they repent" (Moroni 9:22). He also mentioned that "many of our brethren have deserted over unto the Lamanites, and many more will also desert over unto them" (Moroni 9:24). This matches the scene of destruction, desertion, and retreat found in Mormon's own record. As his people lost battles and fled northward, Mormon declared that they "began to be swept off . . . even as a dew before the sun" (Mormon 4:18). Mormon's prediction in Moroni 9:24 that even more Nephites would join the Lamanites was fulfilled in Mormon 6:15, which reports that some Nephites survived their last battle because they "deserted over unto the Lamanites."[1595]

Securing the Records

Mormon wrote to Moroni, "I trust that I may see thee soon; for I have sacred records that I would deliver up unto thee" (Moroni 9:24). In Mormon 4:23, we learn that Mormon "did go to the hill Shim, and did take up all the records which Ammaron had hid up unto the Lord." Then, at the Nephites' final battle with the Lamanites, Mormon reported that he hid these records up at Cumorah, all except "these few plates which I gave unto my son Moroni" (Mormon 6:6).[1596]

Dating the Letter

It is uncertain how long Mormon had been separated from Moroni when he composed his letter. Nor can it be determined how much time transpired between the events reported in his letter and the time of its composition. Yet, despite these uncertainties, several details of the letter suggest that it was written sometime between AD 375 and 380:

1. Mormon's language implies that he was personally involved in a "sore battle" that the Nephites lost (Moroni 9:2). From this detail, we can confidently date Mormon's letter to no earlier than the year 375, when Mormon resumed command of the Nephite armies (see Mormon 5:1).[1597]
2. Mormon's report of a "sore battle" also likely dates his letter to no later than the year 380. This is because after 380, no more battles were reported and the Nephites began to gather at Cumorah for their final conflict (see Mormon 5:6–6:5).
3. Mormon expected to see Moroni "soon" so he could deliver "sacred records" to Moroni (Moroni 9:24). This statement was likely made sometime after Mormon retrieved the records from the hill Shim in the year 375 (see Mormon 4:23) but certainly before the final battle in 385, when Mormon and Moroni were reunited.[1598]
4. Mormon counseled Moroni to continue to labor with the people (see Moroni 9:6). This may reflect Mormon's personal decision to repent of his oath and again lead the Nephites in battle in the year 375 (see Mormon 5:1).
5. Mormon's concern about his people's utter destruction, as well as his comments about Nephites deserting to the Lamanite army (see Moroni 9:3, 22–24), suggest that the Nephites were in the final stages of their struggle against the Lamanites. This, again, fits a time frame of 375–380 very well.

THE WHY

The above analysis indicates that Mormon's letter was composed in a real historical setting that can be reliably approximated through a careful reading of the text. This type of internal consistency and realism provides a subtle evidence of the Book of Mormon's historical authenticity. Mormon was a real person engaged in a terrible military conflict, and his personal letter to his son reflects the horrific circumstances of a specific period of his life and of Nephite history.

Understanding the context of this letter's composition can also help us better understand its contents and why Moroni included it in his record in the first place. In one sense, Mormon's personal letter acts as his final warning for latter-day readers. Mormon declared that if his people were destroyed, it would be because they were "like unto the Jaredites . . . seeking for blood and revenge" (Moroni 9:23). Just as Mormon could look back and see a relationship between his people's impending destruction and the destruction of the Jaredites, modern societies can look to Mormon's record and recognize that they face similar calamities if they don't repent.[1599]

Yet, despite his terrible grief, Mormon's hope for a brighter future shines through.

> My son, be faithful in Christ; and may not the things which I have written grieve thee, to weigh thee down unto death; but may Christ lift thee up, and may his sufferings and death, and the showing his body unto

> our fathers, and his mercy and long-suffering, and the hope of his glory and of eternal life, rest in your mind forever. (Moroni 9:25)

Few people have had more cause to be depressed and without hope than Mormon. His letter not only recounts the terrible atrocities of his people, but it also expresses his growing certainty that they would be destroyed. Recognizing the dismal historical context of Mormon's letter only amplifies its profound message of hope and faith in Jesus Christ. Moroni likely saw this personal and intimate message of hope, in the face of such indescribable horrors, as a fitting summary of the Book of Mormon's primary purpose.[1600]

FURTHER READING

Joseph M. Spencer, "On the Dating of Moroni 8–9," *Interpreter: A Journal of Mormon Scripture 22* (2016): 131–148.

Alan C. Miner, "A Chronological Setting for the Epistles of Mormon to Moroni," *Journal of Book of Mormon Studies 3*, no 2. (1994): 94–113.

Mormon's Life and Nephite Military History[1602]			
Chapter	**Historical Period**	**Years**	**Events**
Mormon 1	Mormon's Youth	321	Commission from Ammaron
		322	Mormon moves to Zarahemla; a short-lived conflict breaks out
		322–325	Peace reigns, but alongside Nephite wickedness; miracles cease
		325	Mormon is visited of the Lord but is forbidden to preach
Mormon 2	The Loss of Zerahemlah	326	Serious war breaks out; Mormon becomes leader of the Nephite armies
		327–330	The Nephites are driven from the land of Zarahemla and relocate in Joshua
		330–344	National depression and false repentance occur; Mormon fulfills Ammaron's commission
	The Loss of the South Lands	345	Joshua falls, and the Nephites are driven into the north lands
		346	A reversal of military fortunes occurs at Shem
		346–349	The Nephites slowly recapture their lost lands in the north
		350	A treaty establishes peace, ceding all the south lands to the Lamanites
Mormon 3		350–359	An era of peace, during which Mormon is sent to preach, but unsuccessfully
	War at the North-South Border	360	The Lamanites declare war, and both nations prepare for conflict
		361	The Nephites win the first battle at Desolation
		362	The Nephites again defend Desolation but this time blasphemously swear vengeance; Mormon steps down from leadership of the armies
Mormon 4		363	A series of conflicts at the north-south border. Nephites begin a war of aggression.
		367	The Nephites succeed in driving the Lamanites from their lands
		367–374	The Lamanites cease their aggressions for a period
	The War of Nephite Eradication	375	War begins again
Mormon 5		375–380	The Nephites lose a series of battles; Mormon retrieves the plates of Nephi and resumes leadership of the Nephite armies
		380	Losses force Mormon to seek reprieve so as to gather at Cumorah
Mormon 6		380–385	The Nephites gather at Cumorah for a final battle; Mormon writes his abridgement
		385	The final battle at Cumorah; Mormon's subsequent death

124

How Will God Manifest the Truth of the Book of Mormon?

"If ye shall ask with a sincere heart, with real intent, having faith in Christ, he will manifest the truth of it unto you, by the power of the Holy Ghost." (Moroni 10:4)

THE KNOW

In his final farewell,[1602] Moroni declared, "And I seal up these records, after I have spoken a few words by way of exhortation unto you" (Moroni 10:2).[1603] James E. Faulconer explained, "Moroni is sealing up his book and sealing his testimony." This final farewell places a "seal on the entire content of the Book of Mormon, and it gives us implicit directions for how we should approach the rest of the book."[1604]

Crucial to the organization of this important final sealing are a series of eight exhortations (each beginning with "I would exhort you"),[1605] the most well-known of which is undoubtedly Moroni 10:4: "And when ye shall receive these things, *I would exhort you* that ye would ask God, the Eternal Father, in the name of Christ, if these things are not true; and if ye shall ask with a sincere heart, with real intent, having faith in Christ, he will manifest the truth of it unto you, by the power of the Holy Ghost" (emphasis added).

This passage, often referred to as "Moroni's promise," prescribes a process for receiving revelation, places conditions and parameters on that process, and then assures that a revelation of truth will ultimately come by the power of the Holy Ghost.[1606] Some may wonder, though, exactly what type of spiritual manifestation they should expect after they "read these things" and "remember how merciful the Lord" is (Moroni 10:3), and then "pursue this course and ask in faith" (Book of Mormon Introduction).

Perhaps anticipating this crucial question, Moroni's next two exhortations (see Moroni 10:7–8) discuss the source of spiritual gifts—the Spirit of Christ—as well as their various manifestations.[1607] He explained "there are different ways that these gifts are administered; but it is the same God who worketh all in all, and they are given by the manifestations of the Spirit of God unto men, to profit them" (Moroni 10:8).

If this principle is applied to Moroni's promise, readers can conclude that they should not confine the expected confirmation of truth to a specific type of spiritual manifestation, but rather should be open to the various ways or gifts through which God communicates inspiration and revelation. Elder David A. Bednar has taught, "Revelations are conveyed in a variety of ways, including, for example, dreams, visions, conversations with heavenly messengers, and inspiration. Some revelations are received immediately and intensely; some are recognized gradually and subtly."[1608]

This teaching helps establish that not every person will receive a spiritual confirmation in exactly the same way. Whereas some may experience a powerful burst of spiritual feeling, others might perceive a restrained but consistent stream of subtle impressions. At one time, a person might receive an answer while on bended knees in solitary prayer, and at another time, may obtain a witness while acting on faith to keep the commandments. Whatever the timing or method, Moroni declared that God only "worketh by power, according to the faith of the children of men" (Moroni 10:7). In all cases, it is faith in Jesus Christ that activates the spiritual witness of truth.

THE WHY

Steven Walker remarked, "The [mournful] quality of Moroni's final section speaks directly to us, and I find myself wondering what I would do in Moroni's sandals. What would I say if I had twelve gold pages to say it on? What would I utter as the cumulative wisdom of so many lifetimes?"[1609] With these questions in mind, readers should recognize the weighty importance of Moroni's final exhortations. His last sermon provides a key to unlocking the spiritual truth of the entire record—a truth that might otherwise be withheld or "sealed up" to individuals because of misunderstanding or unbelief (Moroni 10:2).[1610]

Some may have already received a witness of the truthfulness of the Book of Mormon, but perhaps have not recognized it for what it was. Others might be seeking a specific type of spiritual manifestation and yet overlook how the Spirit works through "diversities of operations" (1 Corinthians 12:6; cf. D&C 46:16).[1611] Those who carefully read the context of Moroni's promise will more fully understand the wide variety of true spiritual manifestations that are given for our benefit. The abundance of these gifts helps us to "deny not the power of God" and to "deny not the gifts of God" (Moroni 10:7–8).

Not only did Moroni provide a sampling of such spiritual gifts and divine manifestations, but he also prefaced his special personal promise by exhorting his readers to "remember how merciful the Lord hath been unto the children of men, from the creation of Adam even down until the time that ye shall receive these things, and ponder it in your hearts" (Moroni 10:3).

Why is this a helpful precondition? By realizing that God is merciful, a person who asks with real intent has increased confidence that God will answer generously, as he has acted mercifully before.[1612] Faulconer asked, "As we read scripture, do we see those mercies? As we read of those mercies, do we recognize them as a prototype for what happens in our own lives?"[1613]

Readers who soberly reflect on the stories of divine guidance and profound conversion found in the Book of Mormon will better recognize the many types of tender mercies and the reality of personal revelations that can lead to their own personal testimonies.[1614] As Elder Jeffrey R. Holland taught, "in some ways [the Book of Mormon] is one long revelation about revelation."[1615]

Although initially given to his "brethren, the Lamanites" (Moroni 10:1), Moroni's final revelation about revelation was eventually expanded to address all his readers, extending into "all the ends of the earth" (Moroni 10:24). He exhorted all to "come unto Christ, and lay hold upon every good gift" (Moroni 10:30), and to this universal audience he gave assurance that "God shall show unto you, that that which I have written is true" (Moroni 10:29). Elder Gary E. Stevenson emphatically declared that this truth applies to every individual. "Each of you," he proclaimed, "can . . . receive a personal witness of this book!"[1616]

FURTHER READING

James E. Faulconer, "Sealings and Mercies: Moroni's Final Exhortations in Moroni 10," *Journal of the Book of Mormon and Other Restoration Scripture 22*, no. 1 (2013): 4–19.

Steve Walker, "Last Words: 4 Nephi–Moroni," in *The Reader's Book of Mormon*, 7 vols., ed. Robert A. Rees and Eugene England (Salt Lake City, UT: Signature Books, 2008), 7:vii–xxii.

John W. Welch, "Doubled, Sealed, Witnessed Documents: From the Ancient World to the Book of Mormon," in *Mormons, Scripture, and the Ancient World: Studies in Honor of John L. Sorenson*, ed. Davis Bitton (Provo, UT: FARMS, 1998), 391–444.

The Book of Mormon and the Latter Days

Is There Precedent for General Conference in the Book of Mormon?

"And now it came to pass that there were a great multitude gathered together, of the people of Nephi, round about the temple which was in the land Bountiful." (3 Nephi 11:1)

THE KNOW

Only two months after the Church was restored on April 6, 1830, the first general conference was held on June 9, 1830, at the Peter Whitmer home in Fayette, New York. In the following years, general conferences were held periodically until the Nauvoo era, when they began to be held consistently twice a year, in April and October. Since that time, the semi-annual general conferences of the Church have grown into international events where millions tune in to hear the words of living prophets and Apostles.[1617]

For a number of religious denominations in America, regular conferences played a significant part of nineteenth-century worship and administrative practices. One such conference likely even contributed to the "unusual excitement" that prompted young Joseph to ask God which church was true (Joseph Smith—History 1:5).[1618] While this background surely influenced early Latter-day Saint conferences, Joseph and other early leaders may have been inspired by more ancient precedents as well.

The Book of Mormon records many instances where all the people were gathered together to hear the counsel of prophets and inspired leaders. At Nephi's request, Jacob preached to the people of Nephi, most likely while they were gathered at the newly built temple (see 2 Nephi 6–10), a tradition Jacob continued after Nephi's death (see Jacob 2–3).

King Benjamin had the people "gathered together" at the temple, where he taught them important gospel principles, shared new revelation, and placed them under covenant (see Mosiah 1–5). Later, when the people of Alma and Limhi joined with the Nephites in Zarahemla, Mosiah "caused that all the people should be gathered together," and they read records together, "thought of the immediate goodness of God," and "did raise their voices and give thanks to God" (Mosiah 25:1, 10).

Alma appears to have hosted conference-like gatherings at Zarahemla and Gideon (see Alma 5–7). Shortly before the Lord appeared to the Nephites, "a great multitude gathered together" in what Clifford P. Jones has argued was "a multitude that purposefully gathered to the temple for a spiritual purpose."[1619] Whatever the original purpose was, it quickly became a spiritual gathering as the crowd witnessed the majesty of the risen Lord descending from heaven (see 3 Nephi 11:3–12). From that point, leaders were called and set apart, ordinances were administered, and spiritual instruction was given over the course of several days (see 3 Nephi 11–26).

The Book of Mormon tradition of gathering to perform religious rituals, to receive counsel and instruction, to make covenants, and to learn new revelation appears to be tied to the ancient Israelite festival tradition. Under the laws in Exodus, it was required in Israel that "three times in the year all thy males shall appear before the Lord," connected with the three times in the year that the holy festivals of unleavened bread (Passover), first fruits (Pentecost), and ingathering (around the Feast of Tabernacles) were celebrated (see Exodus 23:14–17).

Especially at the Feast of Tabernacles at the end of every seventh year, all Israelites were to appear before the Lord to hear the law read "in their hearing." Moses instructed:

> Gather the people together, men, and women, and children, and thy stranger that is within thy gates, that they may hear, and that they may learn, and fear the Lord your God, and observe to do all the words of this law (Deuteronomy 31:10–12).

In the Book of Mormon, Jacob and Benjamin appear to have preached at a gathering during the autumn festival season,[1620] Abinadi seems to have prophesied to a crowd in the city of Nephi during Pentecost,[1621] and Alma apparently taught and counseled his sons during Passover.[1622]

THE WHY

As Latter-day Saints gather every spring and fall from around the world to hear the inspired teachings of the prophets, Apostles, and other leaders, they are following sacred scriptural practices clearly found in the Bible, the Book of Mormon, and the Doctrine and Covenants. Elder Robert D. Hales taught, "Conferences have always been part of the true Church of Jesus Christ."[1623]

Following the teachings and leadership of King Benjamin, Latter-day Saints use conference weekend as an opportunity to remember and reflect, recommit to covenants, spend time with family, and serve others. Following Alma's example, it can make available good moments for parents to counsel with their children and for fathers to give priesthood blessings.

Above all, it is a consecrated time to hear the word of the Lord from His chosen servants, to thoughtfully consider how to apply their counsel in one's life, and to move forward with a resolved determination to live the gospel of Jesus Christ more perfectly. Elder Hales taught, "The greatest blessings of general conference come to us after the conference is over," because after "we gather to hear the words of the Lord . . . we return to our homes to live them."[1624]

"Oh, how we need general conference!" exclaimed Elder Hales. "Through conferences our faith is fortified and our testimonies deepened."[1625] Each conference, God's children across the world once again have the long-standing opportunity to hear the voices of prophets, Apostles, and other inspired leaders, thereby having their faith fortified, devotion deepened, and testimonies renewed.

FURTHER READING

Elder Robert D. Hales, "General Conference: Strengthening Faith and Testimony," *Ensign*, November 2013, 6–8.

Why Should We Take the Time to Give Thanks to God?

"And they gave thanks to God, yea, all their men and all their women and all their children that could speak lifted their voices in the praises of their God." (Mosiah 24:22)

THE KNOW

It doesn't take long while reading the Book of Mormon before encountering followers of Christ who gave heartfelt thanks unto God. For example, after escaping Jerusalem and hiking through the desert for a time and finally reaching a valley that contained flowing water,[1626] Lehi's family must have felt immensely grateful. To show their gratitude, they "built an altar of stones, and made an offering unto the Lord, and gave thanks unto the Lord [their] God" (1 Nephi 2:7).[1627] This touching account is just the first of many faithful demonstrations of gratitude to God, which becomes a major theme throughout the Book of Mormon.

Book of Mormon peoples showed gratitude in a variety of contexts, but most frequently after experiencing some sort of divine rescue. Lehi's family showed thanks because they had escaped the dangers of Jerusalem and had been led to a safe and habitable location, one with both food and fresh, running water.[1628]

Similarly, when the people gathered to hear King Benjamin's speech, they offered sacrifice and burnt offerings "that they might give thanks to the Lord their God" (Mosiah 2:4).[1629] Through these offerings they showed gratitude for the Lord who, among other things, had "brought them out of the land of Jerusalem," and "delivered them out of the hands of their enemies," (Mosiah 2:4). King Benjamin then reaffirmed the importance of this doctrine in his famous sermon, explaining that if he, as a mortal king, merited any thanks from his people, then "O how you ought to thank your heavenly King!" (Mosiah 2:19).

At the waters of Mormon, Alma the Elder taught the people that "every day they should give thanks to the Lord their God" (Mosiah 18:23). Some time later, after being freed from the oppressive bondage caused by Amulon and the Lamanites, Alma's people recognized that "none could deliver them except it were the Lord their God" (Mosiah 24:21). And because of this humble recognition, "they gave thanks to God, yea, all their men and all their women and all their children that could speak lifted their voices in the praises of their God" (Mosiah 24:22).

When the great destructions recorded in 3 Nephi eventually ceased, the people's "mourning was turned into joy, and their lamentations into the praise and thanksgiving unto the Lord Jesus Christ" (3 Nephi 10:10).[1630] After Jesus arrived at the temple in Bountiful, He affirmed the importance of giving thanks by showing gratitude to His Father in prayer: "Father, I thank thee that thou hast given the Holy Ghost" (3

Nephi 19:20) and "hast purified those whom I have chosen, because of their faith" (3 Nephi 19:28).[1631]

These various examples help demonstrate the profound importance that the Book of Mormon places on gratitude. Its stories repeatedly emphasize the Lord's power, which blesses the world and His children in many ways—in delivering them from suffering and bondage, in lending them breath from day to day, and in providing them with a Redeemer who will restore them and give them eternal life. Then it depicts their heartfelt praise, worship, and thanksgiving in response to these wondrous blessings.

THE WHY

Mormon's faithful record emphasizes the Lord's hand in the stories of his people as well as their worthy responses of sacrifice, humble worship, and prayers of thanks. Carefully studying these stories can inspire readers to similarly recognize the Lord's influence in their own lives and find cause for their own expressions of heartfelt gratitude. They too will come to recognize the blessings of God's deliverance from trials, trouble, and tribulation.

President Henry B. Eyring, for example, taught, "The times we will pass through will have in them hard trials, as they did for the people of Alma under the cruel Amulon, who put burdens on their backs too heavy for them to bear."[1632] Like the people of Alma, readers in the latter days can have faith that the Lord will similarly deliver them from their own burdens and trials, and even help them to be "cheerful as well as strong" while enduring them.[1633] As similar blessings flow into their own lives, they can follow the example of Alma's people who collectively "lifted their voices in the praises of their God" (Mosiah 24:22).

In the Book of Mormon narratives preceding Christ's visitation, those who escaped from their enemies or experienced miraculous deliverances often offered animal sacrifices as a sign of their gratitude. When Jesus Christ fulfilled the law of Moses, however, such sacrifices were no longer acceptable as an appropriate form of gratitude and worship. Christ taught that now "ye shall offer for a sacrifice unto me a broken heart and a contrite spirit" (3 Nephi 9:20).[1634]

Such a sacrifice is especially meaningful in the context of sabbath day observance (see D&C 59:8–9). President Eyring described the Sabbath as a day of "gratitude and love."[1635] He further explained, "As we partake of the bread and water, we remember that He suffered for us. And when we feel gratitude for what He has done for us, we will feel His love for us and our love for Him."[1636]

Finally, the Book of Mormon itself is a priceless treasure that should evoke a response of sincere gratitude. President Russell M. Nelson taught that "we have had the Book of Mormon for nearly 200 years. . . . Because of these and other precious scriptures, we know that God is our Eternal Father and that His Son, Jesus Christ, is our Savior and Redeemer. For these spiritual gifts, thanks be to God!"[1637]

FURTHER READING

Henry B. Eyring, "Gratitude on the Sabbath Day," *Ensign*, November 2016, 99–101.

Russell M. Nelson, "Thanks Be to God," *Ensign*, May 2012, 77–79.

Dallin H. Oaks, "Give Thanks in All Things," *Ensign*, May 2003.

127

What Have Women Taught about the Book of Mormon in the Latter Days?

"And now, he imparteth his word by angels unto men, yea, not only men but women also." (Alma 32:23)

THE KNOW

Although women do not play a prominent role in most Book of Mormon stories, their importance and influence is apparent.[1638] Nephi, for instance, foresaw the important role of the virgin Mary in God's plan (see 1 Nephi 11:13–20).[1639] Abish was instrumental in bringing her people to the knowledge of Christ (see Alma 19:17).[1640] And the two thousand stripling warriors helped save the Nephite nation because of the faith and influence of their righteous mothers (see Alma 56:47–48).

Women have also played important roles in the The Church of Jesus Christ of Latter-day Saints in our own gospel dispensation. To acknowledge and appreciate this influence, the Church Historian's Press recently selected and published a collection of discourses given by Latter-day Saint women from 1831 to 2016.[1641] Not only do these talks show the vital contribution women have made to the Church and its people, but they also highlight how Latter-day Saint women have promoted, defended, and utilized the Book of Mormon.

Rachel H. Leatham, for example, was "among the first generation of unmarried women to serve proselytizing missions for the church."[1642] When asked to report on her mission at an overflow meeting during the April session of general conference in 1908, she emphasized the importance of the Book of Mormon. She asked the youth,

> Are we familiar with the ancient record of the inhabitants of this continent, the Book of Mormon? And are we familiar with the great truths that are taught therein and with those books that teach us the beauties of the work in which we are engaged today? I am afraid we are not sufficiently conversant with the principles of the gospel and that we are not as diligent as we should be.[1643]

In 1975, Belle S. Spafford was the General Relief Society President. She had also been "affiliated with the [National Council of Women] for fifty-two years" and had even served as its president.[1644] Drawing on these experiences, she used the Book of Mormon to help explain why women should look to God and His prophetic messengers for spiritual guidance about women's divine role and worth:

> Counseling on the desirability of representative government, King Mosiah made this significant statement: "It is common for the lesser part of the people to desire that which is not right" [Mosiah 29:26]. Now, having this warning from a great Book of Mormon prophet, Latter-day Saints would do well to be particularly careful to weigh the voices of the people in the light of the teachings of our modern-day prophets. Even though the voices may be few, they are usually loud and convincing.
>
> Possessing revealed truth and the words of the prophets as they relate to the responsibility of the Latter-day Saint woman and her role in life, we have an unwavering duty to uphold these teachings in our speech and actions, and to direct our lives in harmony with them.[1645]

In 2012, Judy Brummer shared her powerful conversion story at a devotional in Salt Lake City. "Brummer was among the first wave of missionaries to proselytize primarily in the townships and tribal homelands of black South Africans. Her fluency in Xhosa proved crucial to her missionary work. After her mission, she also helped translate large portions of the Book of Mormon into Xhosa."[1646] Sister Brummer explained that while translating,

> It was so clear. It was almost like I was there. I knew exactly what every word meant in English. So it was easy to translate into Xhosa, which does not happen to me now. I understood [the Book of Mormon] with a clarity that I cannot explain, even the portions from Isaiah. I kept saying to myself, "I feel like there is a lightbulb that lit up in my brain. I am not usually this smart," and I know now that it was a gift from God. I did not do it alone; I had help.[1647]

THE WHY

These are only three samples from many selected teachings and testimonies highlighted by the Church Historian's Press. But they beautifully illustrate how the women of the Church have done so much to promote and share the Book of Mormon with the world. They also show how, beginning with Emma Smith, God has called on women in our dispensation "to expound scriptures, and to exhort the church, according as it shall be given thee by my Spirit" (D&C 25:7).

Even though God called male prophets to write the Book of Mormon,[1648] its message is meant for all people. As the prophet Nephi taught, God invites all people "to come unto him and partake of his goodness; and he denieth none that come unto him, black and white, bond and free, male and female; and he remembereth the heathen; and all are alike unto God, both Jew and Gentile" (2 Nephi 26:33).

In our dispensation, God has called on women to help share the message of the Book of Mormon. Whether sharing in public, in a Church setting, or in our own homes, the effect is the same—the Book of Mormon builds faith and hope in Jesus Christ. By sharing its teachings, women participate in the priesthood responsibility to share the gospel with all the world.[1649] Concerning the joy that comes from this service, Sister Carole M. Stephens explained,

> We are covenant daughters in the Lord's kingdom, and we have the opportunity to be instruments in His hands. As we participate in the work of salvation each day in small and simple ways—watching over, strengthening, and teaching one another—we will be able to join with Ammon, who declared:
>
> "Behold, my joy is full, yea, my heart is brim with joy, and I will rejoice in my God" [Alma 26:11].[1650]

FURTHER READING

Maurine Jensen Proctor, "Serious Reflection Precedes Revelation," *BYU Women's Conference*, May 2006, online at churchhistorianspress.org.

Irina Kratzer, "Decisions and Miracles: And Now I See," *Brigham Young University Women's Conference,* April 2000, online at churchhistorianspress.org.

Lucy Mack Smith, "Where Is Your Confidence in God?" Gathering of Emigrating Saints at Lake Erie, Buffalo, New York, May 1831, online at churchhistorianspress.org.

Art Credits

Page xiv, 2: *Moroni Delivers the Plates to Joseph Smith* © Jorge Cocco.
Page 4: *Moroni 6* © Normandy Poulter and the BYU Virtual Scriptures Group.
Page 7: *Replica 1830 edition of the Book of Mormon ©Jasmin Gimenez Rappleye*, courtesy of Book of Mormon Central.
Page 10: *Battle in the Sidon* © James Fullmer.
Page 12: *Man's Mouth* © Jasmin Gimenez Rappleye, courtesy of Book of Mormon Central.
Page 14: *Zoram (Servant of Laban)* © James Fullmer.
Page 16: *Zoram (descendant of Zoram)* © James Fullmer.
Page 18: *Reenactment of Israelite High Priest praying before the altar* © Daniel Smith.
Page 20: *Messier 106*, courtesy of NASA, ESA, the Hubble Heritage Team (STScI/AURA), R. Gendler, and J. GaBany.
Page 22: *Small Sprout* by Mayur_Ankushe, courtesy of Pixabay.com.
Page 23: *Nephite Declaration of Faith Chart* © John W. Welch, Jasmin Gimenez Rappleye, courtesy of Book of Mormon Central.
Page 24: *Agnus Dei* by Francisco de Zubarán, courtesy of Wikimedia Commons.
Page 27, 29: *Lands of the Book of Mormon* © James Fullmer.
Page 30: *Graphic of the chiasmus in Mosiah 5* © Jasmin Gimenez Rappleye, courtesy of Book of Mormon Central.
Page 32: *The Conversion of Saint Paul* © Luca Giordano, courtesy of Wikimedia Commons.
Page 33: *Chart of chiasmus in Alma 36* © Jasmin Gimenez Rappleye, courtesy of Book of Mormon Central.
Page 36: *Brown seer stone* © Anthony Sweat.
Page 38: *The Angel of Death and the First Passover*. Illustration from Bible Pictures and What They Teach Us by Charles Foster, courtesy of Wikimedia Commons.
Page 40: *Statue Rose* by stux, courtesy of Pixabay.com.
Page 42: *Christus Consolator* by Carl Bloch, courtesy of Wikimedia Commons and Brigham Young University Museum of Art.
Page 44: *Ascension* by John Singleton Copley, courtesy of Wikimedia Commons.
Page 47: *The Plan of Salvation* © Clair Hamaker, courtesy of Book of Mormon Central.
Page 49: *Climbing Together* by sasint, courtesy of Pixabay.com.
Page 51: *Zerahemnah* © James Fullmer.
Page 54: *Helaman* © James Fullmer. *Rocky Mountain Landscape* by Albert Bierstadt, courtesy of Wikimedia Commons.
Page 56: *Joseph's Coat Brought to Jacob* © Domenico Fiasella, courtesy of Wikimedia Commons.
Page 58: *Sketch of Captain Moroni* © Jody Livingston, courtesy of Book of Mormon Central.
Page 61: *Declaration of Independence* by John Trumbull, courtesy of Wikimedia Commons.
Page 64: *Battle in the Sidon* © James Fullmer.
Page 66: *Wars in the Book of Mormon Chart* © John W. Welch, Jasmin Gimenez Rappleye, courtesy of Book of Mormon Central.
Page 67: *Wars in the Book of Mormon Timeline* © John W. Welch, Jasmin Gimenez Rappleye, courtesy of Book of Mormon Central.
Page 68: *Sketch of Nephite fortifications* © Jody Livingston, courtesy of Book of Mormon Central.
Page 70: *Moses Destroys the Tables* by Edward Armitage and the Dalziel brothers, courtesy of Wikimedia Commons.
Page 73: *Toppled statue of Ramesses II* © Stephen O. Smoot, courtesy of Book of Mormon Central.
Page 76: *Shule's sons* © James Fullmer.
Page 78: *Brothers on the Eve of Battle* © Daniel Kaonohi, courtesy of Book of Mormon Central.
Page 80: *Jared's Death* © James Fullmer.
Page 83: *Prison Cell* by Ichigo121212, courtesy of Pixabay.com.
Page 85: *The Battle of Stamford Bridge* by Peter Nicolai Arbo, courtesy of Wikimedia Commons.
Page 87: *Siege of the Stripling Sons* © Brian C. Hailes, courtesy of Book of Mormon Central.
Page 89: *Sketch of soldiers carrying provisions* © Jody Livingston, courtesy of Book of Mormon Central.
Page 91: *Simple Map* © James Fullmer.
Page 93: *Vessel* by Angeleses, courtesy of Pixabay.com.
Page 96: *Teancum* © James Fullmer. *Background image* © Book of Mormon Central.
Page 98: *Lion* by minka2507, courtesy of Pixabay.com.
Page 101: *Nephite Pride Cycle* © John W. Welch, Jasmin Gimenez Rappleye, courtesy of Book of Mormon Central.
Page 102: *Priests Traveling across Kealakekua Bay for First Contact Rituals* by John Webber, courtesy of Wikimedia Commons.
Page 104: *Large Rock* by Atlantios, courtesy of Pixabay.com.
Page 106: *Batalla del Rio Sidon* © Jorge Cocco.
Page 109: *Kishkumen* © James Fullmer.
Page 111: *Temple of the Jaguar, Mirador, Guatemala* © Neal Rappleye, courtesy of Book of Mormon Central.
Page 113: *Hill North of Shilom* © James Fullmer.
Page 115: *Large Rock* by Atlantios, courtesy of Pixabay.com.

Page 117: *Naples-Russel Mound 8*, also known as *Zelph's Mound* © HotWhells53, courtesy of Wikiimedia Commons. This image is licensed through CC BY-SA 3.0 and may be found at https://commons.wikimedia.org/wiki/File:Naples-Russel_Mound_8.jpg.

Page 118: Image from Joseph Smith Papers, showing 'and Nephites' crossed out in History, 1838–1856, vol. 1–A, p. 483. Handwriting of Willard Richards. © By Intellectual Reserve, Inc. Used by permission from The Church of Jesus Christ of Latter-day Saints. This document may be found at https://www.josephsmithpapers.org/paper-summary/history-1838-1856-volume-a-1-23-december-1805-30-august-1834/489.

Page 118: Image from Joseph Smith Papers, showing 'last' crossed out in History, 1838–1856, vol. 1–A, p. 483. Handwriting of Willard Richards. © By Intellectual Reserve, Inc. Used by permission from The Church of Jesus Christ of Latter-day Saints. This document may be found at https://www.josephsmithpapers.org/paper-summary/history-1838-1856-volume-a-1-23-december-1805-30-august-1834/489.

Page 118: Image from Joseph Smith Papers, showing 'hill cumorah' crossed out in History, 1838–1856, vol. 1–A, p. 483. Handwriting of Willard Richards. © By Intellectual Reserve, Inc. Used by permission from The Church of Jesus Christ of Latter-day Saints. This document may be found at https://www.josephsmithpapers.org/paper-summary/history-1838-1856-volume-a-1-23-december-1805-30-august-1834/489.

Page 119: Image from Joseph Smith Papers in History, 1838–1856, vol. 1–A, p. 483. Handwriting of Willard Richards. © By Intellectual Reserve, Inc. Used by permission from The Church of Jesus Christ of Latter-day Saints. This document may be found at https://www.josephsmithpapers.org/paper-summary/history-1838-1856-volume-a-1-23-december-1805-30-august-1834/489.

Page 120: *Ancient Records* © James Fullmer.

Page 123: *Lock* by meineresterampe, courtesy of Pixabay.com.

Page 125: *Sketch of Nephi praying on his garden tower* © Jody Livingston.

Page 127: *2 Nephi 31* © Jorge Cocco.

Page 129: *Gavel* by gimono, courtesy of Pixabay.com.

Page 131: Engraving of *Dante Alighieri and Beatrice Portinari Gaze into the Highest Heaven* by Gustave Doré. Courtesy of Wikimedia Commons. Adapted by Jasmin Gimenez Rappleye.

Page 133: *Zeniff Battle* © James Fullmer.

Page 136: *Mayan Calendar* © Jasmin Gimenez Rappleye, courtesy of Book of Mormon Central.

Page 137: Chart depicting Mayan long count © Jasmin Gimenez Rappleye, courtesy of Book of Mormon Central.

Page 138: *Samuel en la muralla 2* © Jorge Cocco.

Page 140: *I am the Light of the World* © James Fullmer.

Page 142: *Adoration of the Shepherds* by Gerard von Honthorst, courtesy of Wikimedia Commons.

Page 144: *Señales del nacimiento de Jesucristo* © Jorge Cocco.

Page 146: *Saint Paul Writing His Epistles* © Valentin de Boulogne, courtesy of Wikimedia Commons.

Page 149: *The Gadianton robbers and their lamb-skin* © Jasmin Gimenez Rappleye. *Sketch of Gadianton Robbers* © Jody Livingston. *Agnus Dei* © Francisco de Zurbarán, courtesy of Wikimedia Commons.

Page 151: *Zemnarihah Hung* © James Fullmer.

Page 153: *Mormón* © Jorge Cocco.

Page 156: *Teotihuacan* © edaintg0, courtesy of Pixabay.com.

Page 159: *Destruction* from *The Course of Empire* by Thomas Cole, courtesy of Wikimedia Commons.

Page 161: *Whisper* by Kristina Flour , courtesy of Unsplash.com.

Page 163: *Jesus Baptized by John* by William Brassey Hole.

Page 165: *The First Nail (Le premier clou)* © James Tissot.

Page 167: *Timeline Chart* © Jasmin Gimenez Rappleye.

Page 168: *Storm* by EliasSch, courtesy of Pixabay.com.

Page 169: *Ice Core* by National Ice Core Laborartory, courtesy of Wikimedia Commons.

Page 171: *Photograph of Lake Atitlan* © Steven Newton, courtesy of Flickr.com. This image is licensed through CC BY 2.0 and may be found at https://www.flickr.com/photos/26298797@N07/4489148579/.

Page 173: *Hen with Chicks* © Michael Anfang, courtesy of Unsplash.com.

Page 175: *I am the Light of the World* © James Fullmer.

Page 177: *Jesús Sanando* © Jorge Cocco.

Page 179: *Jehu Obelisk* © Steven G. Johnson, courtesy of Wikimedia Commons. This image is licensed through CC BY-SA 3.0 and may be found at https://commons.wikimedia.org/wiki/File:Jehu-Obelisk-cropped.jpg.

Page 180: *The Sermon on the Mount* by Carl Bloch, courtesy of Wikimedia Commons.

Page 182: *Sermon on the Mount* by Henrik Olrick, courtesy of Wikimedia Commons.

Page 185: *The Expulsion of Adam and Eve from Paradise* by Benjamin West, courtesy of Wikimedia Commons.

Page 187: *3D Rendering of the Holy Place, Facing the Entrance to the Holy of Holies in Solomon's Temple* © Brian Olsen, courtesy of Photogent.com.

Page 190: Photo of statue by Didgeman, courtesy of Pixabay.com.

Page 192: *Cristo en America* © Jorge Cocco.

Page 194: *Jesus partiendo el pan* © Jorge Cocco.

Page 196: *Other Sheep* © Matt Warren, courtesy of Book of Mormon Central.

Page 198: Two silver scrolls (one pictured here) inscribed with portions of the Priestly Blessing were found at Ketef Hinnom and dated back to the 7th century B.C. *Scrolls* by Tamar Hayardeni, courtesy of Wikimedia Commons.

Page 199: *Jesus* © James Fullmer.

Page 201: *Micah Exhorts the Israelites to Repent* by Gustave Doré, courtesy of Wikimedia Commons.

Page 204: *Copies of the Book of Mormon* © Jasmin Gimenez Rappleye, courtesy of Book of Mormon Central.

Page 207: *Christ the Redeemer Statue* by ckturistando, courtesy of Unsplash.com.

Page 209: *Prophet Isaiah* by Antonio Balestra, courtesy of Wikimedia Commons.

Page 211: *Jesucristo revisa las planchas* © Jorge Cocco.

Page 213: *Mother, Tell Me* © Megan Rieker, courtesy of Book of Mormon Central.

Page 215: *Copies of the Bible* © Jasmin Gimenez Rappleye, courtesy of Book of Mormon Central.

Page 218: *Jesus Healing the Sick at Bethesda* by Carl Bloch, courtesy of Wikimedia Commons.

Page 219: *What Would Jesus Do Infographic* © Jasmin Gimenez Rappleye, courtesy of Book of Mormon Central.

Page 221: *He aquí soy Jesucristo* © Jorge Cocco.

Page 224: *Dawn on the Land of Desolation* © James Fullmer.

Page 226: *4 Nephi* © Normandy Poulter and the BYU Virtual Scriptures Group.

Page 228: *Words of Mormon* © Normandy Poulter and the BYU Virtual Scriptures Group.

Page 230: *Ammarón y Mormon* © Jorge Cocco.

Page 232: *Words of Mormon* © Normandy Poulter and the BYU Virtual Scriptures Group.

Page 234: *Handshake* by SCY, courtesy of Pixabay.com.

Page 236: *Stone Carving at El Tajin Veracruz Mexico, depicting a scene of human heart sacrifice. Photograph* © Thomas Aleto, courtesy of Flickr.com. Retouched by Jasmin Gimenez Rappleye. This image is licensed through CC BY 2.0 and can be found at https://www.flickr.com/photos/ilhuicamina/410025522.

Page 238: *Mormón termina compendio* © Jorge Cocco.
Page 241: *Mormon* © Normandy Poulter and the BYU Virtual Scriptures Group.
Page 244: *Statue of Woman in Grief* © x1klima, courtesy of Flickr.com. This image is licensed through CC BY-ND 2.0 and can be found at https://www.flickr.com/photos/x1klima/39846456793/.
Page 246: *Moroni* © Normandy Poulter and the BYU Virtual Scriptures Group.
Page 249: *Victory Pose* by Catherine McMahon, courtesy of Unsplash.com.
Page 251: *Replica of the Gold Plates* © David A. Baird. Photograph by Daniel Smith.
Page 254: *Alphabet Graphic* © Zander Sturgill.
Page 256: *The Brother of Jared* © Laci Gibbs, courtesy of Book of Mormon Central.
Page 258: *Graphic with Olmec Heads* © Zander Sturgill.
Page 260: *Genealogy from Jared to Ether* © Jasmin Gimenez Rappleye, courtesy of Book of Mormon Central.
Page 261: *Honeybee* by cocoparisienne, courtesy of Pixabay.com.
Page 263: *Gilbert Arizona Temple* © Jerry Ferguson, courtesy of Flickr.com. This image is licensed through CC BY 2.0 and may be found at https://www.flickr.com/photos/fergusonphotography/11439786235.
Page 267: *De generación en generación* © Jorge Cocco.
Page 271: *Portrait of Oliver Cowdery* by Lewis A. Ramsey, P*ortrait of David Whitmer* by Lewis A. Ramsey, *Portrait of Martin Harris* by Lewis A. Ramsey; courtesy of Wikimedia Commons.
Page 274: *The Brother of Jared* © Laci Gibbs, courtesy of Book of Mormon Central.
Page 276: *Battle of Greeks and Amazons* © Colin; courtesy of Wikimedia Commons. This image is licensed through CC BY-SA 3.0 and can be found at https://commons.wikimedia.org/wiki/File:Battle_of_Greeks_and_Amazons.jpg.
Page 278: *Plates of Ether* © James Fullmer.
Page 280: *Snake* by winterseitler, courtesy of Pixabay.com.
Page 282: *Snake Migration Map* © Jasmin Gimenez Rappleye, courtesy of Book of Mormon Central.
Page 283: *Throne of Napoleon I, 1808* © Stuart Mudie, courtesy of Wikimedia Commons. Retouched by Jasmin Gimenez Rappleye. This image is licensed through CC BY-SA 2.0 and can by found at https://commons.wikimedia.org/wiki/File:Throne_of_Napoleon,_in_the_throne_room_of_Fontainebleau_Palace.jpg.
Page 284: *Altar 4 at La Venta* © Ruben Charles, courtesy of Wikimedia Commons. This image is licensed through CC BY 2.0 and can be found at https://commons.wikimedia.org/wiki/File:Altar_4_La_Venta_(Ruben_Charles).jpg.
Page 285: *Dawn on the Land of Desolation* © James Fullmer.
Page 286: Chart adapted from John E. Clark, "Archaeology, Relics, and Book of Mormon Belief," *Journal of Book of Mormon Studies* 14, no. 2 (2005): 48.
Page 288: *Ether 2:14* © Normandy Poulter and the BYU Virtual Scriptures Group.
Page 290: *Consequences of Two Kings* © Brian C. Hailes, courtesy of Book of Mormon Central.
Page 292: *Jesus Washing the Feet of Apostles* © Wolfgang Sauber, courtesy of Wikimedia Commons. Retouched by Jasmin Gimenez Rappleye. This image is licensed through CC BY-SA 2.0 and may be found at https://commons.wikimedia.org/wiki/File:GNM_-_Fu%C3%9Fwaschung.jpg.
Page 294: *Últimas páginas* © Jorge Cocco.
Page 296: *Eucharist* by dh_creative, courtesy of Pixabay.com.
Page 299: *Jesus Washing the Feet of Apostles* © Wolfgang Sauber, courtesy of Wikimedia Commons. Retouched by Jasmin Gimenez Rappleye. This image is licensed through CC BY-SA 2.0 and may be found at https://commons.wikimedia.org/wiki/File:GNM_-_Fu%C3%9Fwaschung.jpg.
Page 301: *75th Anniversary of Music and the Spoken Word* by MoTabChoir01, courtesy of Wikimedia Commons.
Page 303: *Cristo con los 12* © Jorge Cocco.
Page 305: *I Saw Another Angel Fly* © Jorge Cocco.
Page 307: *Baby* by Pexels, courtesy of Pixabay.com.
Page 309: *Mormon* © James Fullmer.
Page 313: *Copies of the Book of Mormon 2* © Jasmin Gimenez Rappleye, courtesy of Book of Mormon Central.
Page 316, 318: *LDS Conference Center Organ* © Paul Smith, courtesy of Flickr.com. This image is licensed through CC BY-SA 2.0 and can be found at https://www.flickr.com/photos/pncsmith/9197593944/.
Page 320: *Harvest* by Sabrina Ripke Fotografie, courtesy of Pixabay.com.
Page 322: *Mary Elizabeth Rollins Reads the Book of Mormon* © Andrew Knaupp, courtesy of Book of Mormon Central.

About Book of Mormon Central

The vision behind Book of Mormon Central is to bring together, to the extent possible, all available informative resources for the study of the Book of Mormon in one place online and on mobile devices. To accomplish this, we have put together a team of enthusiastic students of the Book of Mormon, consisting of archivists, researchers, writers, editors, reviewers, illustrators, narrators, audio engineers, video engineers, web designers, web and mobile developers, graphic artists, and social media publishers in addition to support personnel. Headquartered in Springville, Utah, our mission is to build enduring faith in Jesus Christ by making the Book of Mormon accessible, comprehensible, and defensible to the entire world.

The *KnoWhys* are only one way we seek to accomplish this. Our website also has an archive consisting of both scholarly and devotional resources, from books and articles to audio and visual tools. New items are added to our archive on a daily basis, and the *Journal of Book of Mormon Studies* called it "an important service to students of the Book of Mormon," opening a door for constructive evaluation and organization of vast amounts of material going forward.[a]

Book of Mormon Central also includes some projects still under development. Examples are our questions- and-answers database, which will provide resources on common questions about the Book of Mormon, and what we call the ScripturePlus app. The ScripturePlus app will be a digital version of the scriptures, available online and through a mobile app, which will help give people access to all the rich resources available through Book of Mormon Central through interfacing with an interactive, hyperlinked text of the Book of Mormon. This dynamic resource will draw readers and researchers repeatedly back into the words of the Book of Mormon itself, not away from it on odd detours or dead ends. Our purpose is to enable all students of the Book of Mormon to have a more enriching and enlightening experience studying and pondering and following the teachings and testimonies found in the Book of Mormon.

We also publish in Spanish and will add additional languages as donor support materializes so non-English speaking Latter-day Saints and other interested persons can freely enjoy the riches of the Book of Mormon, Another Testament of Jesus Christ.

MEET THE TEAM

- John W. Welch, Chairman of the Board. Welch is the Robert K. Thomas Professor of Law at the J. Reuben Clark Law School at Brigham Young University, where he has been on the faculty since 1980. From 1991 to 2018 he was editor-in-chief of *BYU Studies*, the premiere Latter-day Saint academic journal. In 1979 he founded the Foundation for Ancient Research and Mormon Studies (FARMS). From 1988 to 1991 he served as one of the editors for Macmillan's *Encyclopedia of Mormonism*. He was general editor of the *Collected Works of Hugh Nibley*. Welch has made several important discoveries that greatly advanced Book of Mormon studies and Latter-day Saint scholarship in general. As working Chairman, Jack oversees all Book of Mormon Central (BMC) projects, contributes to the *KnoWhys*, and provides insightful guidance.

a. Brian M. Hauglid, Mark Alan Wright, Joseph M. Spencer, and Janiece Johnson, "A Book of Mormon Studies Prospectus," *Journal of Book of Mormon Studies* 25 (2016): 16.

- Kirk Magleby, Executive Director. Magleby was an early FARMS officer from 1980 to 1985. He founded the technology company Nuvek, LLC, in 1983 and continues to serve as its General Manager. He has served on the board of Ancient America Foundation (AAF) and Book of Mormon Archaeological Forum, Inc. (BMAF). He blogs at *Book of Mormon Resources*, where his focus is Mesoamerican geography and archaeology. Kirk runs the business side of BMC and manages a number of external relationships.

- Taylor Halverson, Member of the Executive Committee. Halverson has PhDs in both biblical studies and instructional design. He works at BYU's Center for Teaching and Learning, helping professors and students improve the quality of their output. Halverson has published widely on scripture, is a regular contributor to *Deseret News*, and helps lead important projects at BYU and in the private sector (learn more at taylorhalverson.com). Taylor's inspirational leadership guides particularly BMC's *Come Follow Me*, video, and ScripturePlus initiatives.

- Ruth Schmidt, Member of the Executive Committee. Schmidt has a BS in nursing from U of U and a JD from BYU. She was the first nurse-attorney in the state of Utah and practiced law for a number of years. She keeps BMC organized through timely communication, thoughtful writing and editing, and considerate service. She contributes to conferences and events, the annual art contest, various publications including *KnoWhys*, networking, legal affairs, and internal record keeping. Ruth leads many of our special projects.

- Neal Rappleye, Operations Manager. Rappleye studied history and political science at UVU. He is a widely published Book of Mormon researcher. Neal oversees and contributes to BMC's varied research and writing efforts. He blogs at *Studio et Quoque Fide*.

- Jasmin Gimenez Rappleye; Webmaster, Graphic Designer, Production Coordinator. Jasmin holds a degree in Ancient Near Eastern Studies from BYU. She runs BMC's weekly staff meetings. Her editorial, technological, design, and organizational skills are evident in everything we do.

- Stephen O. Smoot, Researcher and Writer. Smoot holds degrees from BYU in Ancient Near Eastern studies and German studies and an MA from University of Toronto in Near and Middle Eastern Civilizations. He is widely published. Stephen blogs on Latter-day Saint topics at *Ploni Almoni*.

- David J. Larsen, Researcher and Writer. Larsen has a PhD in biblical studies from University of St. Andrews in Scotland. He is widely published, with particular emphasis on the Psalms. David helps BMC understand the profound intertextuality between the Book of Mormon and the Bible.

- Ryan Dahle, Researcher and Writer. Dahle graduated from BYU-Idaho and taught in a public school. He is a meticulous researcher and disciplined documentarian. Ryan writes video scripts and leads BMC's joint project with Charis Legacy Foundation to create Evidence Central.

- Jonathon Riley, Researcher and Writer. Riley holds degrees from BYU and Trinity Western and is pursuing a PhD in biblical studies from Catholic University of America. Jonathon has presented at Society of Biblical Literature (SBL) and led our *KnoWhy* production process.

- Matt Roper, Researcher and Writer. Roper holds a BA in history and an MA in sociology from BYU. He was a FARMS, then a Neal A. Maxwell Institute for Religious Scholarship staff member from 1988 to 2017. Widely published, Matt leads BMC's *KnoWhy* production process.

- Nicole Shepard, Editor and Writer. Shepard studied journalism, English, and cinema at UVU and did research in Northern Ireland. She has contributed to BMC videos, *KnoWhys*, *Come Follow Me* materials, firesides, and blog posts. Nicole also coordinates events.

- Zander Sturgill, Digital Publishing Manager. Sturgill graduated from UVU in digital media and information management. He administrates BMC's social media channels, engineers audio for *KnoWhys* and podcasts, and produces videos. Zander helps BMC tell better stories.

- Matt Cutler, Video Producer. Cutler produces videos for popular global YouTube channels with a specialty in parkour. He is a master of creative video editing. Matt has produced many of BMC's top-performing videos.

- Daniel Smith, Video Producer and User Experience Designer. Smith's passion is helping people visualize the scriptures. He is a well-read and widely traveled biblical scholar. He blogs at Redeemer of Israel and produces the popular Messages of Christ YouTube channel.

- Jared Riddick, Archivist. Riddick has a history education degree from BYU-Idaho and is a graduate student at University of North Texas. He curates BMC's online archive, manages our 2,500-volume research library, and cohosts the *Rare Possessions* podcast.

- Israel Gonzalez, Software Developer. Gonzalez managed software development teams in Chile and helped build up a Spanish-language Book of Mormon digital publishing group. He is the lead administrative console and API developer as well as project manager for ScripturePlus.

- Benji Monroy, Spanish Digital Publishing Manager. Monroy was an on-air media personality in Mexico City. He administrates BMC's Spanish social media channels and produces Spanish videos. Under Benji's leadership, BMC's Spanish media often outperform our English originals.

- Nathan Bryant, Development Director. Bryant has held sales positions in a number of media and technology firms. He administrates our Salesforce database, manages donor relations, and coordinates fundraising events.

- Freelancers. BMC depends on vital services from first-rate freelancers, including Scott Christopher, Amanda Cook, and Soraida Tabla, narrators; Angel Sturgill, image editor; Robert Starling, creative consultant; Nick Galieti, audio engineer and podcaster; Noe Correa, translator; Katie Payne, artist; and Brant Gardner, researcher and writer.

- Spanish. BMC's terrific Spanish team; in addition to Benji, Soraida, and Noe (mentioned above); includes Jesus Inda, translator; Alex Martinez, web developer and tech support; Lily Gutierrez, quality control; Javier Tovar, Latin American liaison; Cecilia Gastelum and Benjamin Monroy, social media managers; Fernando Vazquez, graphic designer; and Melody Monroy, influencer.

- Board of Directors. Jack Welch, Taylor Halverson, Ruth Schmidt, Bob Babcock, Scott Petersen, Tyler Perry, and Lynne Wilson.

- Volunteers. All executives and directors are volunteers. In addition, BMC could not function without the services of hundreds of other faithful volunteers. We benefit from peer reviewers, general reviewers, editors, digitizers, social media admins, artists, and others. Profound thanks to our wonderful volunteers.

Endnotes

1 It is also the fall equinox, which some have argued is evidence of "magical" influence on Joseph Smith. See D. Michael Quinn, *Early Mormonism and the Magic World View*, revised and enlarged edition (Salt Lake City, UT: Signature Books, 1998), 141–144; Dan Vogel, *Joseph Smith: The Making of a Prophet* (Salt Lake City, UT: Signature Books, 2004), 43. Joseph Smith was involved in treasure seeking and other "magical" practices, and perhaps saw significance in this timing. Mark Ashurst-McGee, "Moroni as Angel and as Treasure Guardian," *FARMS Review 18*, no. 1 (2006): 34–100, suggests that Joseph Smith's understanding of Moroni and his mission likely included elements of the "treasure guardian lore," while still recognizing that Moroni was a divine messenger from the Lord. Yet Ashurst-McGee felt the connection to treasure seeking and the timing of Moroni's visits has been overstated (see pp. 92–94). On Joseph Smith and treasure digging, or "magic," see Richard Lyman Bushman, "Joseph Smith and Money Digging," in *A Reason for Faith: Navigating LDS Doctrine and Church History*, ed. Laure Harris Hales (Salt Lake City and Provo, UT: Deseret Book and BYU Religious Studies Center, 2016), 1–5; Brant A. Gardner, *The Gift and Power: Translating the Book of Mormon* (Salt Lake City, UT: Greg Kofford Books, 2011), 3–134.

2 In 1826, Rosh Hashanah was October 2, so none of the Jewish holidays landed on September 22. These dates were checked online at http://www.colelchabad.org/Calendar.htm.

3 See John W. Welch, Neal Rappleye, Stephen O. Smoot, David J. Larsen, and Taylor Halverson, eds., *Knowing Why: 137 Evidences that the Book of Mormon Is True* (American Fork, UT: Covenant Communications, 2017), 80–82, 186–187.

4 Lenet Hadley Read, "Joseph Smith's Receipt of the Plates and the Israelite Feast of Trumpets," *Journal of Book of Mormon Studies 2*, no. 2 (1993): 111.

5 For these and many more, see John W. Welch and J. Gregory Welch, *Charting the Book of Mormon: Visual Aids for Personal Study and Teaching* (Provo, UT: FARMS, 1999), chart 88; cf. charts 89–91. See also Terrence L. Szink and John W. Welch, "King Benjamin's Speech in the Context of Ancient Israelite Festivals," in *King Benjamin's Speech: "That Ye May Learn Wisdom,"* ed. John W. Welch and Stephen D. Ricks (Provo, UT: FARMS, 1998), 160–174.

6 In the Book of Mormon, the allegory of the tame and wild olive trees ends with the Lord instructing His servant to call laborers together for the "last time" to prune and nourish the vineyard in preparation for the final harvest (see Jacob 5:61–77). President Ezra Taft Benson taught that the Book of Mormon is "the instrument which God has designed" for gathering this final harvest of souls (Ezra Taft Benson, "A New Witness for Christ," *Ensign*, November 1984, 7). Read concluded, "it is significant that the golden plates were received on 22 September 1827, coinciding with the beginning of Israel's fall garnering and symbolizing the onset of its final harvest of souls" (Lenet Hadley Read, "The Golden Plates and the Feast of Trumpets," *Ensign*, January 2000).

7 The Book of Mormon was brought forth for the express purpose "to show unto the remnant of the house of Israel what great things the Lord hath done for their fathers; and that they may know the covenants of the Lord, that they are not cast off forever" (Title Page). Read aptly summarized, "On 22 September 1827, Israel's trumpets sounded throughout the world; it was the day the Prophet Joseph Smith received the golden plates, which would help fulfill God's promise to remember Israel in the latter days" (Read, "The Golden Plates and the Feast of Trumpets").

8 As Read rightly pointed out, "much of the fullness of the Lord's truth began with the coming forth of the Book of Mormon." Since that time, much new revelation has come forth. Significantly, "one of the most common symbols of the restored gospel is that of the angel Moroni"—the very messenger who delivered the plates—"portrayed in the act of blowing the trumpet." Truth he proclaimed through "the golden plates is still causing a gathering, is still offering its warnings, and is still acting as harbinger of great things to come" (Read, "Joseph Smith's Receipt of the Plates," 117).

9 In his initial visit, Moroni warned that many of the prophecies of judgment in the final days are near at hand (see Joseph Smith—History 1:27–42, 45). The introduction to Latter-day Saint editions of the Book of Mormon hails the Nephite record as a sign "that The Church of Jesus Christ of Latter-day Saints is the Lord's kingdom once again established on the earth, preparatory to the Second Coming of the Messiah" (Introduction).

10 See Roy A. Prete, "God in History? Nephi's Answer," *Journal of Book of Mormon Studies 14*, no. 2 (2005): 26–37, 71.

11 Joseph Smith further clarified that this was "on the fifteenth day of May, 1829" (Joseph Smith—History 1:72). See also *Saints: The Story of the Church of Jesus Christ in the Latter Days, Volume 1: The Standard of Truth, 1815–1846* (Salt Lake City, UT: The Church of Jesus Christ of Latter-day Saints, 2018), 65–68.

12 Although of great importance, Joseph and Oliver initially refrained from openly sharing this miraculous conferral of authority and their mutually administered ordinations and baptisms. Instead, they kept this sacred experience to themselves, due to the "spirit of persecution which had already manifested itself in [their] neighborhood" (Joseph Smith—History 1:74). For further analysis of Joseph's and Oliver's reasons for safeguarding this spiritual experience, see Steven C. Harper, "Trustworthy History?" *FARMS Review 15*, no. 2 (2003): 288–293; Richard Lyman Bushman, *Joseph Smith: Rough Stone Rolling* (New York, NY: Knopf, 2005), 75–76.

13 Oliver Cowdery, "Letter I," *Messenger and Advocate 1*, no. 1 (1834): 15.

14 Oliver Cowdery commented that after writing and reflecting on the account of 3 Nephi, "the question might be asked, have men authority to administer in the name of Christ, who deny revelations?" This rhetorical question further suggests that it was 3 Nephi that most strongly influenced Joseph's and Oliver's quest for baptism and authority. Cowdery, "Letter I," 15.

15 Recognizing that the book of Mosiah was likely the first portion of the Book of Mormon to be translated (aside from the lost 116 pages), Daniel C. Peterson commented that its pages contain an "important piece of evidence for what the very earliest Latter-day Saints might have known or at least encountered about priesthood." Daniel C. Peterson, "Authority in the Book of Mosiah," *FARMS Review 18*, no. 1 (2006): 150.

16 Michael Hubbard MacKay and Gerrit J. Dirkmaat, *From Darkness unto Light: Joseph Smith's Translation and Publication of the Book of Mormon* (Provo and Salt Lake City, UT: Deseret Book and BYU Religious Studies Center, 2015), 131.

17 When President Martin Van Buren asked wherein the Latter-day Saints "differed in [their] religion from the other religions of the day," Joseph Smith said, "we differed in mode of baptism and the gift of the Holy Ghost by the laying on of hands." Letter to Hyrum Smith and High Council, December 5, 1839, p. 88, online at josephsmithpapers.org. For a brief overview of how the ordinance of baptism was corrupted in the early centuries of Christian history, see Tad R. Callister, *The Inevitable Apostasy and the Promised Restoration* (Salt Lake City, UT: Deseret Book, 2006), 233–236. For a treatment of the separate, but related, topic of disputations over infant baptism in the Book of Mormon, see chapter 122.

18 Scott H. Faulring has noted that "the baptismal prayer in the 1829 Articles and in the 1830 Articles and Covenants begins with the phrase *Having authority given me of Jesus Christ* (3 Nephi 11:25) rather than *Having been commissioned of Jesus Christ*, as it reads today in Doctrine and Covenants 20:73. The prophet Joseph Smith revised the earlier wording in that verse when he published the Articles and Covenants in the first edition of the Doctrine and Covenants in 1835." This suggests that baptismal ordinances in the early Church used the phrasing directly from the Book of Mormon instead of the revised wording in Doctrine and Covenants 20. Scott H. Faulring, "The Book of Mormon: A Blueprint for Organizing the Church," *Journal of Book of Mormon Studies 7*, no. 1 (1998): 66.

19 The importance of receiving authority to baptize would also have been confirmed when Jesus stated that He gave "power" to His disciples so they could "baptize [the people] with water" (3 Nephi 12:1).

20 Peterson, "Authority in the Book of Mosiah," 186, n. 49. Peterson here seems to have been talking specifically about 3 Nephi 7:25, which would have been translated only a short amount of time before the Savior's statements in 3 Nephi 11. See also John W. Welch, "The Miraculous Translation of the Book of Mormon," in *Opening the Heavens: Accounts of Divine Manifestations, 1820–1844*, 2nd ed., ed. John W. Welch (Salt Lake City and Provo, UT: Deseret Book and BYU Press, 2017), 104.

21 For further discussion of baptism and priesthood authority in the Book of Mormon, see Faulring, "A Blueprint for Organizing the Church," 65–66.

22 Bushman, *Rough Stone Rolling*, 74.

23 Joseph B. Wirthlin, "Pondering Strengthens the Spiritual Life," *Ensign*, May 1982.

24 Lucy Mack Smith, *Biographical Sketches of Joseph Smith the Prophet and His Progenitors for Many Generations* (Liverpool, UK: S. W. Richards, 1853), 131.

25 See Faulring, "A Blueprint for Organizing the Church," 65: "They encountered the word baptism in its various forms more than a hundred times in the Nephite record, more often than in the Bible, in fact."

26 Faulring, "A Blueprint for Organizing the Church," 65.

27 Cowdery, "Letter I," 15.

28 Cowdery, "Letter I," 15.

29 See Michael Hubbard MacKay, *Sacred Space: Exploring the Birthplace of Mormonism* (Salt Lake City and Provo, UT: Deseret Book and BYU Religious Studies Center, 2016).

30 Scott H. Faulring, "The Book of Mormon: A Blueprint for Organizing the Church," *Journal of Book of Mormon Studies 7*, no. 1 (1998): 63.

31 John W. Welch, Neal Rappleye, Stephen O. Smoot, David J. Larsen, and Taylor Halverson, eds., *Knowing Why: 137 Evidences that the Book of Mormon Is True* (American Fork, UT: Covenant Communications, 2017), 4–6. See also Scott H. Faulring, "An Examination of the 1829 'Articles of the Church of Christ' in Relation to Section 20 of the Doctrine and Covenants," *BYU Studies 43*, no. 4 (2004): 64.

32 Faulring, "An Examination," 67.

33 Jeffrey G. Cannon, "Build Up My Church," in *Revelations in Context: The Stories Behind the Sections of the Doctrine and Covenants*, ed. Matthew McBride and James Goldberg (Salt Lake City, UT: The Church of Jesus Christ of Latter-day Saints, 2016), 29–32.

34 Doctrine and Covenants 20 is less dependent on the Book of Mormon than the "Articles," but still relies heavily on Book of Mormon language. Faulring, "An Examination," 67, states: "Careful textual comparison of Cowdery's 1829 Articles against this early copy of D&C 20 reveals that Oliver Cowdery's document is far more dependent on the Book of Mormon text than is the latter. Roughly one-fifth of section 20 relies on the Book of Mormon for its text, while more than half of Cowdery's Articles are either direct quotations or paraphrases with slight deviations from the Book of Mormon."

35 See chapter 117. The sacrament prayers were also included in Cowdery's "Articles."

36 John W. Welch, "The Book of Mormon as the Keystone of Church Administration," *Religious Educator 12*, no. 2 (2011): 90. Other early versions of Doctrine and Covenants 20, instead of writing out the exact words of the prayers, simply refer the reader to "Book of Mormon, Page 175" or place the material from Moroni 4–5 and 3 Nephi 11 in quotation marks.

37 For more on this, see John A. Tvedtnes, *The Most Correct Book: Insights from a Book of Mormon Scholar* (Salt Lake City, UT: Cornerstone Publishing, 1999), 304–306.

38 Welch, "Administration," 90.

39 Welch, "Administration," 90.

40 For more on the how the Nephite church operated, showing similarities to the Church today, see Robert E. Parsons, "The Practices of the Church: Moroni 1–6," in *The Book of Mormon, Part 2: Alma 30 to Moroni*, ed. Kent P. Jackson, *Studies in Scripture: Volume 8* (Salt Lake City, UT: Deseret Book, 1988), 282–292.

41 Welch, "Administration," 90. Compare Doctrine and Covenants 20:82 to Mosiah 6:1; 3 Nephi 30:2; Moroni 6:4. Also compare Doctrine and Covenants 20:83 to Mosiah 5:11; 3 Nephi 18:31; Moroni 6:7.

42 For more on some of these topics, see chapters 119, 125. See also Welch, et al., *Knowing Why*, 312–313.

43 This revelation comes from the Book of Commandments 4:5; Robin Scott Jensen, Richard E. Turley Jr., and Riley M. Lorimer, eds., *Revelations and Translations, Volume 2: Published Revelations*, The Joseph Smith Papers (Salt Lake City, UT: Church Historian's Press, 2011). See also Gerald E. Smith, *Schooling the Prophet: How the Book of Mormon Influenced Joseph Smith and the Early Restoration* (Provo, UT: Neal A. Maxwell Institute for Religious Scholarship, 2015), 223 n.5.

44 Welch, "Administration," 112.

45 For more on this, see Tvedtnes, *Most Correct Book*, 299–301.

46 Welch, "Administration," 90.

47 On Nehor's trial and death, see John W. Welch, et al., *Knowing Why*, 248–249.

48 John W. Welch, *The Legal Cases in the Book of Mormon* (Provo, UT: BYU Press and the Neal A. Maxwell Institute for Religious Scholarship, 2008), 274. Welch, *Legal Cases*, 277, has specifically drawn a connection between the cases of Nehor and Korihor: "Indeed, it appears that Korihor's case, like Nehor's case, raised some legal issues that arose for the first time in interpreting the meaning of the law of Mosiah. For example, who was to have jurisdiction over cases of false preaching and blasphemy—the chief judge or the high priest? Was unruly or erroneous speech ever to be punishable under the new law, or could a person only be punished for his overt actions? Without prior experience to direct the judgment of the court, these questions became an issue of first impression for the highest courts in Gideon and Zarahemla."

49 Korihor's denial of God's existence should not be quickly equated with the modern form of atheism that arose largely during the Enlightenment. Whereas atheism today denies the existence of any divine or supernatural being, Korihor affirmed the existence of Satan and angels (see Alma 30:53). Instead, Korihor may be seen as denying the existence of a particular divine being—in this case, the Nephite God. Furthermore, Korihor should be understood as denying the operative power of God in mortal affairs, a denial of God's revelations to prophets, the denial of Christ's coming and Atonement, a purely humanistic ethic, and the reduction of spiritual witnesses to "the effect of a frenzied mind." In short, Korihor's was a functional or behavioral atheism that denied God's involvement in human affairs, not a purely intellectual one that denied His existence altogether.

50 Ze'ev W. Falk, *Hebrew Law in Biblical Times*, 2nd ed. (Provo, UT and Winona Lake, IN: BYU Press and Eisenbrauns, 2001), 55–56.

51 Welch, *Legal Cases*, 292.

52 Welch, *Legal Cases*, 290. Interestingly, an ancient Hittite text spells out curses of blindness and deafness for anyone who speaks evil against the king. "Who takes part in evil against the king and queen, may the oath deities seize him. . . . May they b[li]nd him like the blind man. May they d[eaf]en him like the deaf man. And may they utt[erly] destroy him, a mortal, together with his wives, his sons, and his clan." Billie Jean Collins, trans., "The First Soldiers' Oath," in *The Context of Scripture: Volume I, Canonical Compositions from the Biblical World*, ed. William W. Hallo (Leiden: Brill, 2003), 166. This may parallel Korihor's situation, as Korihor was cursed in a similar manner after speaking against the King of Kings.

53 Welch, *Legal Cases*, 289.

54 This description of Zoram comes from Lehi, who also declared, "Wherefore, because thou hast been faithful thy seed shall be blessed with his seed" (2 Nephi 1:30–31). On one level, it seems that Lehi may have compared Zoram to Jonathan in the Old Testament, who "loved as his own soul" (1 Samuel 18:3) and who said to David, "we have sworn both of us in the name of the Lord, saying, The Lord be between me and thee, and between my seed and thy seed for ever" (1 Samuel 20:42). For an extended comparison between Nephi and David, see Book of Mormon Central, "Why Was the Sword of Laban So Important to Nephite Leaders? (Words of Mormon 1:13)," *KnoWhy 411* (February 27, 2018).

55 See Book of Mormon Central, "Why Did Lehi Divide His People into Seven Tribes? (Jacob 1:13)," *KnoWhy 319* (May 29, 2017). These seven tribes are always listed in the same order, with the Zoramites being placed between the groups affiliated with the Nephites and Lamanites: Nephites, Jacobites, Josephites, Zoramites, Lamanites, Lemuelites, and Ishmaelites" (Jacob 1:13). This middle placement is perhaps symbolic of Zoram's outsider status, as well as the fact that Zoram's descendants weren't fully committed to either the Nephites or the Lamanites throughout the long history of their conflicts.

56 These descendants at least included the dissidents Amalickiah and Ammoron (Alma 54:23), and mostly likely the apostate Zoramites who were named after a man name Zoram (Alma 30:59), who himself was presumably a descendent of the Zoram who accompanied Lehi's journey to the New World. See also Sherrie Mills Johnson, "The Zoramite Separation: A Sociological Perspective," *Journal of Book of Mormon Studies 14*, no. 1 (2005): 76. It should be noted, however, that not all Zoramites throughout the history of the Book of Mormon were wicked (see 4 Nephi 1:36–37).

57 Matthew L. Bowen, "'See That Ye Are Not Lifted Up': The Name Zoram and Its Paronomastic Pejoration," *Interpreter: A Journal of Mormon Scripture 19* (2016): 114.

58 See Bowen, "'See That Ye Are Not Lifted Up'," 125–127.

59 See Bowen, "'See That Ye Are Not Lifted Up'," 128–131.

60 See Bowen, "'See That Ye Are Not Lifted Up'," 132–135.

61 See Bowen, "'See That Ye Are Not Lifted Up'," 135–137.

62 For an example of how the Zoramites' pride led them to be ironically defeated in battle, see Parrish Brady and Shon Hopkin, "The Zoramites and Costly Apparel: Symbolism and Irony," *Journal of the Book of Mormon and Other Restoration Scripture 22*, no. 1 (2013): 40–53. See also chapter 6.

63 Dieter F. Uchtdorf, "Pride and the Priesthood," *Ensign*, November 2010, 56.

64 See Sherrie Mills Johnson, "The Zoramite Separation: A Sociological Perspective," *Journal of Book of Mormon Studies 14*, no. 1 (2005): 77: "The meaning of the name Antionum is not known, but given the focus that the Zoramite culture placed on wealth and materialism, it is interesting to note that when the Nephite system of exchange was standardized at the beginning of the reign of the judges, one of the gold measures was called an antion (equivalent to three shiblons of silver or to one and one-half measures of grain; see Alma 11:15, 19). While we do not know if there is a direct relationship between the words *antion* and *Antionum*, the prospect is intriguing."

65 For a potential wordplay that connects the name of Zoram with the Rameumptom, see Matthew L. Bowen, "'See That Ye Are Not Lifted Up': The Name Zoram and Its Paronomastic Pejoration," *Interpreter: A Journal of Mormon Scripture 19* (2016): 125–127. See also chapter 5.

66 See chapter 7.

67 For a similar condemnation of rich apparel in the Old Testament, see Isaiah 3:18–23; cf. 2 Nephi 13:18–23.

68 Parrish Brady and Shon Hopkin, "The Zoramites and Costly Apparel: Symbolism and Irony," *Journal of the Book of Mormon and Other Restoration* Scripture 22, no. 1 (2013): 43.

69 Brady and Hopkin, "The Zoramites and Costly Apparel," 45. For an analysis of Alma's and Amulek's teachings on this topic, see pp. 45–47.

70 Brady and Hopkin, "The Zoramites and Costly Apparel," 47.

71 For the military implications of this alliance, see chapter 11.

72 The development of these points follows Brady and Hopkin, "The Zoramites and Costly Apparel," 47–50.

73 Brady and Hopkin, "The Zoramites and Costly Apparel," 47. This narrative ends when the Lamanite armies, led by Amalickiah and his brother Ammoron (both of whom were Zoramites; see Alma 54:23), are finally defeated (see Alma 62).

74 See Johnson, "The Zoramite Separation," 74–85, 129–130.

75 For an analysis of how foundational this teaching was in the Book of Mormon, see John L. Sorenson, "Mormon's Sources," *Journal of the Book of Mormon and Other Restoration Scripture 20*, no. 2 (2011): 12. See also Welch, et al., *Knowing Why*, 268–269.

76 In contrast to the Zoramites' emphasis on the outward appearances of wealth and privilege, the righteous among the Nephites "did not wear costly apparel, yet they were neat and comely" (Alma 1:27).

77 Elder Joe J. Christensen, "Greed, Selfishness, and Overindulgence," *Ensign*, May 1999.

78 Brady and Hopkin, "The Zoramites and Costly Apparel," 50.

79 For more information about Korihor, see chapter 4.

80 Hugh Nibley, *Since Cumorah, The Collected Works of Hugh Nibley: Volume 7* (Salt Lake City and Provo, UT: Deseret Book and FARMS, 1988), 293.

81 Alma's belief that the gospel was the best solution to social and political problems was manifest earlier when he resigned from his position as chief judge to preach throughout the land. See Welch, et al., *Knowing Why*, 260–262.

82 Alma brought with him the sons of Mosiah (Ammon, Aaron, Omner, and Himni), Amulek, Zeezrom, and his sons Shiblon and Corianton (Alma 31:6–7).

83 This observation is made and commented on in John W. Welch, "Counting to Ten," *Journal of Book of Mormon Studies 12*, no. 2 (2003): 53–55. *O Lord* occurs in Alma 31:26, 30 (twice), 31 (twice), 32 (twice), 34, and 35 (twice).

84 Rachel Elior, "Early Forms of Jewish Mysticism," in *The Cambridge History of Judaism, Volume Four: The Roman-Rabbinic Period*, ed. Steven T. Katz (New York, NY: Cambridge University Press, 2006), 778; cf. p. 781.

85 Elior, "Early Forms of Jewish Mysticism," 778. Elior quoted the high priest's prayer from Yoma 6.2 more fully on the same page: "An thus he used to say: O the Name . . . , Thy people, the House of Israel, have committed iniquity, transgressed and sinned before Thee. O by the Name, atone, I pray you, for the iniquities and transgressions and sins."

86 Welch, "Counting to Ten," 54: "In addition to his ten supplications to Jehovah with the words O Lord, Alma also speaks the words O God four times in this prayer, but in those four cases he is either speaking about or quoting from the apostate prayers of the Zoramites, and in such a context he would not want to mention the holy name of the true God whom he served and called upon. Hence, Alma shifts his terminology to reflect this shift in meaning."

87 Welch, "Counting to Ten," 54.

88 Alonzo Gaskill, *Miracles of the Book of Mormon: A Guide to the Symbolic Messages* (Springville, UT: Cedar Fort, 2015), 254.

89 Welch, "Counting to Ten," 44–45.

90 For more information on the jubilee year, see Welch, et al., *Knowing Why*, 314–315.

91 See Joseph Thomas Hepworth, "Watermelons, Alma 32, and the Experimental Method," *BYU Studies 23*, no. 4 (Fall 1983): 497–501; Larry E. Dahl, "Faith, Hope, Charity," in *The Book of Mormon: The Keystone Scripture*, ed. Paul R. Cheesman (Provo, UT: BYU Religious Studies Center, 1988), 137–150; Joseph Fielding McConkie and Robert L. Millet, *Doctrinal Commentary on the Book of Mormon*, 4 vols. (Salt Lake City, UT: Bookcraft: 1988–1992), 3:222–239; Elaine Shaw Sorensen, "Seeds of Faith: A Follower's View of Alma 32," in *The Book of Mormon: Alma, the Testimony of the Word*, ed. Monte S. Nyman and Charles D. Tate Jr. (Provo, UT: BYU Religious Studies Center, 1992), 129–139; Virginia H. Pearce, "Trying the Word of God," *Ensign*, May 1995; Janet Thomas, "Good Seed," *New Era*, November 1995.

92 David E. Bokovoy, "The Word and the Seed: The Theological Use of Biblical Creation in Alma 32," *Journal of Book of Mormon Studies 23* (2014): 10.

93 See John W. Welch, Neal Rappleye, Stephen O. Smoot, David J. Larsen, and Taylor Halverson, eds., *Knowing Why: 137 Evidences That the Book of Mormon Is True* (American Fork, UT: Covenant Communications, 2017), 62–63.

94 Bokovoy, "The Word and the Seed," 14.

95 Bokovoy, "The Word and the Seed," 16–17.

96 Bokovoy, "The Word and the Seed," 17.

97 Jenny Webb, "It Is Well that Ye Are Cast Out: Alma 32 and Eden," in *An Experiment on the Word: Reading Alma 32*, ed. Adam S. Miller (Provo, UT: Neal A. Maxwell Institute for Religious Scholarship, 2014), 47.

98 See Welch, et al., *Knowing Why*, 274–276.

99 Many Latter-day Saint and non-Latter-day Saint biblical scholars have come to view the opening chapters of Genesis as a temple text, or a text that attempts to recapture the imagery, order, and symbolism of the temple as a sort of microcosm. For a Latter-day Saint perspective, see Donald W. Parry, "Garden of Eden: Prototype Sanctuary," in *Temples of the Ancient World*, ed. Donald W. Parry (Salt Lake City and Provo, UT: FARMS, 1994), 126–151; Donald W. Parry, "The Cherubim, the Flaming Sword, the Path, and the Tree of Life," in *The Tree of Life: From Eden to Eternity*, ed. John W. Welch and Donald W. Parry (Salt Lake City and Provo, UT: Deseret Book and the Neal A. Maxwell Institute for Religious Scholarship, 2011), 1–24. For a non-Latter-day Saint perspective, see John H. Walton, *The Lost World of Genesis One: Ancient Cosmology and the Origins Debate* (Downers Grove, IL: InterVarsity Press, 2009); John H. Walton, *Genesis 1 as Ancient Cosmology* (Winona Lake, IN: Eisenbrauns, 2011).

100 Bokovoy, "The Word and the Seed," 1.

101 Bokovoy, "The Word and the Seed," 20.

102 This chart was adapted from John W. Welch and J. Gregory Welch, *Charting the Book of Mormon: Visual Aids for Personal Study and Teaching* (Provo, UT: FARMS, 1999), chart 42.

103 See 1 Nephi 11:31–33 (Nephi) and 19:9–10 (Nephi summarizing several prophets); 2 Nephi 9:4–15 (Jacob); 2 Nephi 25:12–13 (Nephi); Mosiah 3:5–10 (Benjamin); Mosiah 15:5–9, 20, and 16:10 (Abinadi); Alma 11:39–41 (Amulek); and Mormon 9:1–14 (Moroni). See also Welch and Welch, *Charting the Book of Mormon*, chart 43.

104 Welch and Welch, *Charting the Book of Mormon*, chart 42.

105 Latter-day Saints typically avoid the language of "creeds" due to an antipathy (beginning with Joseph Smith) toward the classical Christian creeds (see Joseph Smith—History 1:19). However, the word *creed* comes from the Latin *credo*, meaning "I believe." At its very basic definition, a *creed* is a statement of faith or belief not unlike our canonized Articles of Faith. See generally John W. Welch, "'All Their Creeds Were an Abomination': A Brief Look at Creeds as Part of the Apostasy," in *Prelude to the Restoration: From Apostasy to the Restored Church*, ed. Steven C. Harper, et al. (Salt Lake City and Provo, UT: BYU Religious Studies Center and Deseret Book, 2004), 228–249; Lincoln H. Blumell, "Re-reading the Council of Nicaea and Its Creed," in *Standing Apart: Mormon Historical Consciousness and the Concept of Apostasy*, ed. Miranda Wilcox and John D. Young (New York, NY: Oxford University Press, 2014), 196–217.

106 Mark Alan Wright and Brant A. Gardner, "The Cultural Context of Nephite Apostasy," *Interpreter: A Journal of Mormon Scripture 1* (2012): 52: "Perhaps we are seeing clues to the process of apostasy when Amulek is teaching Zoramite outcasts and specifically defines Christ's sacrifice by what it was not."

107 Elaine Adler Goodfriend, "Ethical Theory and Practice in the Hebrew Bible," in *The Oxford Handbook of Jewish Ethics and Morality*, ed. Elliot N. Dorff and Jonathan K. Crane (New York, NY: Oxford University Press, 2013), 48 n.9. Goodfriend specifically cited "the Laws of Hammurabi 230 and 210, and Middle Assyrian Law A55."

108 Ze'ev W. Falk, *Hebrew Law in Biblical Times*, 2nd ed. (Winona Lake, IN and Provo, UT: Eisenbrauns and BYU Press, 2001), 68. Talion is the "eye for an eye" concept, or in the case of murder, a life for a life. For more on talionic justice and the Book of Mormon, see chapter 18.

109 Falk noted, "Hebrew courts did not inflict punishment on ascendants or descendants" (*Hebrew Law*, 68). In relation to vicarious punishment, Goodfriend noted, "Exod 21:31 and Deut 24:16 prohibit this practice" ("Ethical Theory," 48 n. 9).

110 Wright and Gardner, "The Cultural Context of Nephite Apostasy," 51.

111 Wright and Gardner, "The Cultural Context of Nephite Apostasy," 51. See Mary Miller and Karl Taube, *An Illustrated Dictionary of the Gods and Symbols of Ancient Mexico and the Maya* (London, England: Thames and

Hudson, 1993), 42, 46–47; Arthur Demarest, *Ancient Maya: The Rise and Fall of a Rainforest Civilization* (Cambridge, England: Cambridge University Press, 2004), 184–188. Michael D. Coe and Stephen Houston, *The Maya*, 9th ed. (New York, NY: Thames and Hudson, 2009), 89, noted bloodletting is depicted at San Bartolo, dating to ca. first or second century BC. They also mention the attestation of bloodletters from Olmec times. Robert J. Sharer with Loa P. Traxler, *The Ancient Maya*, 6th ed. (Stanford, CA: Standford University Press, 2006), 197 described "a lavish ritual involving feasting, bloodletting, and burning incense" from "the end of the Middle Pre-Classic," ca. 800–500 BC. So bloodletting seems clearly attested in Book of Mormon times. See also Welch, et al., *Knowing Why*, 190–191.

112 Gardner, *Second Witness*, 4:478: "Amulek says 'sacrifice his own blood' because the king's letting of some of his own blood was 'the mortar of ancient Maya ritual life.'"

113 Gardner, *Second Witness*, 4:477, typo silently corrected.

114 Mark Alan Wright, "Axes Mundi: Ritual Complexes in Mesoamerica and the Book of Mormon," *Interpreter: A Journal of Mormon Scripture 12* (2014): 89. See also Miller and Taube, *An Illustrated Dictionary of the Gods and Symbols of Ancient Mexico and the Maya*, 96–97, 144–146.

115 Wright, "Axes Mundi," 89.

116 Micah asks about burnt offerings (often birds), then calves and rams, and then his firstborn, thus providing a sequence of fowl, beast, man. Amulek reverses the order in stressing it will not be man, beast, or fowl. This kind of reversal is what scholars call Seidel's Law. See David Bokovoy, "Inverted Quotations in the Book of Mormon," *Insights: A Window on the Ancient World* 20, no. 10 (October 2000): 2; David E. Bokovoy and John A. Tvedtnes, *Testaments: Links Between the Book of Mormon and the Hebrew Bible* (Tooele, UT: Heritage Press, 2003), 56–60.

117 Robert L. Millet and Joseph Fielding McConkie, *Doctrinal Commentary on the Book of Mormon*, 4 vols. (Salt Lake City, UT: Deseret Book, 1897–1992) 3:250.

118 Tad R. Callister, *The Infinite Atonement* (Salt Lake City, UT: Deseret Book, 2000), 59.

119 D. Kelly Ogden and Andrew C. Skinner, *Verse by Verse: The Book of Mormon*, 2 vols. (Salt Lake City, UT: Deseret Book, 2011), 2:18.

120 Callister, *The Infinite Atonement*, 58. Callister went on to write: "Why was it essential that the Atonement be performed by Jesus, who is "infinite and eternal" (Alma 34:14)? Because the Atonement required power, incredible power, even infinite power. . . . Such power could be exercised only by a being who was infinite, meaning a being who possessed all divine virtues in unlimited measure, and was therefore a God" (p. 67).

121 The Book of Mormon first mentions the Zoramites as a distinct group in Jacob 1:13. In this early instance, the Zoramites seem to be those who are lineally descended from Zoram, who was once a servant to Laban. The next mention of the Zoramites is Alma 30:59, which describes them as a group who had "separated themselves from the Nephites and called themselves Zoramites, being led by a man whose name was Zoram." Ammoron specifically mentioned that he was a "descendent of Zoram" (Alma 54:23), which strongly suggests there was a familial link between the early and later Zoramite groups. For further discussion about Zoramite origins, see John A. Tvedtnes, "Book of Mormon Tribal Affiliation and Military Castes," in *Warfare in the Book of Mormon*, eds. Stephen D. Ricks and William J. Hamblin (Salt Lake City and Provo, UT: Deseret Book and FARMS, 1990), 305–306; Sherrie Mills Johnson, "The Zoramite Separation: A Sociological Perspective," *Journal of Book of Mormon Studies 14*, no. 1 (2005): 76.

122 See chapter 4.

123 See chapter 7.

124 Gardner, *Second Witness*, 4:488–489.

125 The Zoramites played a significant role in three major military conflicts: the battle with Zerahemnah and the two Amalickiahite wars. For details concerning these conflicts, see Welch and Welch, *Charting the Book of Mormon*, chart 137, wars 6–8. For a more complete discussion about the role of apostate groups in the Book of Mormon, see J. Christopher Conkling, "Alma's Enemies: The Case of the Lamanites, Amlicites, and Mysterious Amalekites," *Journal of Book of Mormon Studies 14*, no. 1 (2005): 115–117.

126 For a more detailed commentary on the Lamanites' military offensive in this region, see Gardner, *Second Witness*, 4:566–568. Earlier in the text, Mormon provided geographical information to help readers better understand the logistics of the battles that would be discussed in the following chapters. See Welch et al., *Knowing Why*, 300–302. One statement in particular helps readers recognize a major goal of the Nephites' military strategy: "And it came to pass that the Nephites had inhabited the land Bountiful, even from the east unto the west sea, and thus the Nephites in their wisdom, with their guards and their armies, had hemmed in the Lamanites on the south, that thereby they should have no more possession on the north, that they might not overrun the land northward" (Alma 22:33). The Zoramite defection, therefore, posed a serious threat to the Nephites because the land of Antionum (where the Zoramites resided) bordered the land of Jershon (see Alma 31:3; 43:15; 43:22), and Jershon seemed to be a strategic military route into the northern land of Bountiful (see Alma 27:22). For an example of how the Lamanites intentionally took advantage of multiple military fronts, see Alma 52:10–14.

127 For Jeremiah's prophetic warnings, see Jeremiah 25:28; 27:6–8, 11. For Zedekiah's unsanctioned alliance with the Egyptians, see Ezekiel 17:11–21.

128 The Book of Mormon does report the survival of one son, Mulek. See Welch, et al., *Knowing Why*, 236–237. See also Jeffrey R. Chadwick, "Has the Seal of Mulek Been Found?" *Journal of Book of Mormon Studies 12*, no. 2 (2003): 72–83, 117–118.

129 See Robert F. Smith, "Assessing the Broad Impact of Jack Welch's Discovery of Chiasmus in the Book of Mormon," *Journal of Book of Mormon Studies 16*, no. 2 (2007): 68–73.

130 See John W. Welch, "The Discovery of Chiasmus in the Book of Mormon: Forty Years Later," *Journal of Book of Mormon Studies 16*, no. 2 (2007): 74–87, 99.

131 See, for example, John W. Welch, "Chiasmus in the Book of Mormon," *BYU Studies 10*, no. 3 (1969): 69–83; John W. Welch, "Chiasmus in the Book of Mormon," in *Chiasmus in Antiquity: Structures, Analyses, Exegesis*, ed. John W. Welch (Hildesheim: Gerstenberg Verlag, 1981; reprint Provo, UT: Research Press, 1999), 198–210; John W. Welch, "Parallelism and Chiasmus in Benjamin's Speech," in *King Benjamin's Speech: "That Ye May Learn Wisdom,"* ed. John W. Welch and Stephen D. Ricks (Provo, UT: FARMS, 1998), 315–410.

132 John W. Welch, "Chiasmus in the Book of Mormon," in *Book of Mormon Authorship: New Light on Ancient Origins* (Provo, UT: BYU Religious Studies Center, 1982), 35.

133 Welch, "Chiasmus in the Book of Mormon," 35.

134 Consult Donald W. Parry, ed., *Poetic Parallelisms in the Book of Mormon: The Complete Text Reformatted* (Provo, UT: Neal A. Maxwell Institute for Religious Scholarship, 2007); Carl J. Cranney, "The Deliberate Use of Hebrew Parallelisms in the Book of Mormon," *Journal of Book of Mormon Studies 23* (2014): 140–165.

135 Welch, "The Discovery of Chiasmus in the Book of Mormon," 79–80.

136 John W. Welch, "What Does Chiasmus in the Book of Mormon Prove?" in *Book of Mormon Authorship Revisited: The Evidence for Ancient Origins*, ed. Noel B. Reynolds (Provo, UT: FARMS, 1997), 206.

137 See Welch, "Chiasmus in the Book of Mormon," 49.

138 See chapter 13. See also John W. Welch, "A Masterpiece: Alma 36," in *Rediscovering the Book of Mormon: Insights You May Have Missed Before*, ed. John L. Sorenson and Melvin J. Thorne (Salt Lake City and Provo, UT: Deseret Book and FARMS, 1991), 114–131.

139 Welch, "What Does Chiasmus in the Book of Mormon Prove?" 20.

140 Welch, "What Does Chiasmus in the Book of Mormon Prove?" 210.

141 Allen J. Christenson, "Chiasmus in Mesoamerican Texts," in *Reexploring the Book of Mormon*, 233–235; Allen J. Christenson, ed. and trans., *Popol Vuh: The Mythic Sections—Tales of First Beginnings from the Ancient K'iche'-Maya, Ancient Texts and Mormon Studies 2* (Provo, UT: FARMS, 2000), 12–17; Allen J. Christenson, trans., *Popol Vuh: The Sacred Book of the Maya* (Norman, OK: University of Oklahoma Press, 2003), 46–49. To read the Popul Vuh with chiasmus and other parallelisms incorporated, see Allen J. Christenson, trans., *Popol Vuh: Literal Poetic Version* (Norman, OK: University of Oklahoma Press, 2007). For chiasmus in other ancient Mayan texts, see Kerry Michael Hull, *Verbal Art and Performance in Ch'orti' and Maya Hieroglyphic Writing* (PhD dissertation, University of Texas at Austin, 2003), 175–178, 297–301, 480–481.

142 Welch, "What Does Chiasmus in the Book of Mormon Prove?" 213–214.

143 See Boyd F. Edwards and W. Farrell Edwards, "Does Chiasmus Appear in the Book of Mormon by Chance?" *BYU Studies 43*, no. 2 (2004): 103–130; "When Are Chiasms Admissible as Evidence?" *BYU Studies Quarterly 49*, no. 4 (2010): 131–154.

144 Welch, "What Does Chiasmus in the Book of Mormon Prove?" 221.

145 For what was known of chiasmus at the time, see John W. Welch, "How Much Was Known about Chiasmus in 1829 When the Book of Mormon Was Translated?" *FARMS Review 15*, no. 1 (2003): 47–80.

146 See John W. Welch, "The Miraculous Translation of the Book of Mormon," in *Opening the Heavens: Accounts of Divine Manifestations, 1820–1844*, 2nd ed., ed. John Welch (Salt Lake City and Provo, UT: Deseret Book and BYU Press, 2017), 79–120.

147 Welch, "Chiasmus in the Book of Mormon," 83.

148 Alma's experience is strikingly similar to the ordeals that Mesoamerican ritual specialists undergo in order to become healers and religious leaders. See Mark Alan Wright, "'According to Their Language, unto Their Understanding': The Cultural Context of Hierophanies and Theophanies in Latter-day Saint Canon," *Studies in the Bible and Antiquity 3* (2011): 58–64; Mark Alan Wright, "Nephite Daykeepers: Ritual Specialists in Mesoamerica and the Book of Mormon," in *Ancient Temple Worship: Proceedings of the Expound Symposium*, 14 May 2011, ed. Matthew B. Brown, Jeffrey M. Bradshaw, Stephen D. Ricks, and John S. Thompson (Salt Lake City and Orem, UT: Eborn Books and Interpreter Foundation, 2014), 247–252.

149 S. Kent Brown, "Alma's Conversion: Reminiscences in His Sermons," in *The Book of Mormon: Alma, The Testimony of the Word*, ed. Monte S. Nyman and Charles D. Tate Jr. (Provo, UT: BYU Religious Studies Center, 1992), 141–156; reprinted in S. Kent Brown, *From Jerusalem to Zarahemla: Literary and Historical Studies of the Book of Mormon* (Provo, UT: BYU Religious Studies Center, 1998), 113–127. See also Grant Hardy, *Understanding the Book of Mormon: A Reader's Guide* (New York, NY: Oxford University Press, 2010), 134–137.

150 John W. Welch, "Three Accounts of Alma's Conversion," in *Reexploring the Book of Mormon*, 150–153; Welch and Welch, *Charting the Book of Mormon*, charts 106–107.

151 Welch, "Three Accounts of Alma's Conversion," 152.

152 See John W. Welch, "The Discovery of Chiasmus in the Book of Mormon: Forty Years Later," *Journal of Book of Mormon Studies 16*, no. 2 (2007): 74–87, 99; John W. Welch, "Forty-Five Years of Chiasmus Conversations: Correspondence, Criteria, and Creativity," presentation given at the 2012 FAIR Conference. See chapter 12.

153 John W. Welch, "Chiasmus in the Book of Mormon," *BYU Studies 10*, no. 3 (1969): 69–83. See also John W. Welch, "Chiasmus in the Book of Mormon," in *Book of Mormon Authorship: New Light on Ancient Origins*, ed. Noel B. Reynolds (Provo, UT: BYU Religious Studies Center, 1982; reprint, FARMS, 1996), 33–52; John W. Welch, "Chiasmus in the Book of Mormon," in *Chiasmus in Antiquity: Structures, Analysis, Exegesis*, ed. John W. Welch (Provo, UT: Research Press, 1999), 198–210. Chart adapted from Welch and Welch, *Charting the Book of Mormon*, 132.

154 See John W. Welch, "Chiasmus in Alma 36," *FARMS Preliminary Report* (1989); John W. Welch, "A Masterpiece: Alma 36," in *Rediscovering the Book of Mormon*, 114–131; Hardy, *Understanding the Book of Mormon*, 137–142; Noel B. Reynolds, "Rethinking Alma 36," unpublished paper in authors' possession. The full structure of Alma 36 is also laid out in Donald W. Parry, ed., *Poetic Parallelisms in the Book of Mormon: The Complete Text Reformatted* (Provo, UT: Neal A. Maxwell Institute for Religious Scholarship, 2007), 318–321.

155 Nils Wilhelm Lund, *Chiasmus in the New Testament* (Chapel Hill, NC: University of North Carolina Press, 1942), 40–41, 46.

156 See Earl M. Wunderli, "Criteria of Alma 36 as an Extended Chiasm," *Dialogue: A Journal of Mormon Thought 38*, no. 4 (2005): 97–112; Brant A. Gardner, *Second Witness: Analytical and Contextual Commentary on the Book of Mormon*, 6 vols. (Salt Lake City, UT: Greg Kofford Books, 2007), 4:495–497. Joseph M. Spencer, *An Other Testament: On Typology*, 2nd ed. (Provo, UT: Neal A. Maxwell Institute for Religious Scholarship, 2016), 1–32, argues that while "the text appears to be structured as a chiastically framed narrative" (p. 4), only the beginning and end (vv. 1–5, 26–30) are chiastic, while the core (vv. 13–22) is guided by an entirely different structure.

157 For a criteria evaluation, see Welch, "A Masterpiece," 129–130; Welch, "Chiasmus in Alma 36," 26–35. For an explanation of criteria for judging a chiasm, see John W. Welch, "Criteria for Identifying and Evaluating the Presence of Chiasmus," *Journal of Book of Mormon Studies 4*, no. 2 (1995): 1–14. See also the "Criteria Chart," at chiasmusresources.johnwwelchresources.com. For statistical evaluation, see Boyd F. Edwards and Farrell W. Edwards, "Does Chiasmus Appear in the Book of Mormon by Chance?," *BYU Studies 43*, no. 2 (2004): 103–130; Boyd F. Edwards and Farrell W. Edwards, "Response to Earl Wunderli's 'Critique of Alma 36 as an Extended Chiasm'," *Dialogue: A Journal of Mormon Thought 39*, no. 3 (2006): 164–169.

158 Welch, "A Masterpiece," 116.

159 Welch, "A Masterpiece," 128.

160 Welch, "A Masterpiece," 127–128; Welch, "Chiasmus in Alma 36," 24–25.

161 Welch, "A Masterpiece," 128.

162 Hardy, *Understanding the Book of Mormon*, 140.

163 Hardy, *Understanding the Book of Mormon*, 140– 141,

164 See Welch et al., *Knowing Why*, 240–241.

165 Welch, "A Masterpiece," 118. Welch, "Chiasmus in the Book of Mormon" (1982), 51: "Chiasmus allows Alma to place the very turning point of his entire life exactly at the turning point of this chapter: Christ, because of the effects of the future atonement, belongs at the center of both. Compared with the abrupt antithetic parallelisms found in the recounting of this incident recorded in Mosiah 27, the chiasmus in Alma 36 is monumental and meaningful. The chiastic structure amplifies the significance of Alma's conversion and the centrality of spiritual realities around which it turned." Welch, "Chiasmus in the Book of Mormon" (1999), 207: "it says much for Alma's artistic sensitivities that he succeeds in placing the turning point of his life at the turning point of this chapter. Such effects, it would appear, do not occur without design."

166 Reynolds, "Rethinking Alma 36," 6.

167 Welch, "A Masterpiece," 127.

168 In a similar way, another classic conversion story that has enjoyed very wide appeal is that of Jonah, who resisted the Lord's call for him to serve as

a messenger of the gospel of repentance to the city of Nineveh. As has been recently observed, "the chiastic structure of the book of Jonah suggests that it was intentionally composed to center on Jonah's exclamation of salvation (2:4–6), the physical midpoint as well as spiritual crux of this text." David Randall Scott, "The Book of Jonah: Foreshadowings of Jesus as the Christ," *BYU Studies Quarterly 53*, no. 3 (2014): 173–174.

169 As quoted in John W. Welch, "What Does Chiasmus in the Book of Mormon Prove?" in *Book of Mormon Authorship Revisited*, 206.

170 Welch, "A Masterpiece," 131.

171 For a possible etymology, see "Gazelem," *Book of Mormon Onomasticon*, ed. Paul Y. Hoskisson, online at https://onoma.lib.byu.edu/index.php/GAZELEM.

172 McConkie and Millet, *Doctrinal Commentary on the Book of Mormon*, 3:278; compare Matthew Roper, "Teraphim and the Urim and Thummim," *Insights: A Window on the Ancient World 20*, no. 9 (September 2000): 2; Ray Lynn Huntington, "Gazelem," in *Book of Mormon Reference Companion*, ed. Dennis L. Largey (Salt Lake City, UT: Deseret Book 2003), 284; Gardner, *Second Witness*, 4:512–513.

173 Royal Skousen, *Analysis of Textual Variants of the Book of Mormon*, 6 vols., 2nd ed. (Provo, UT: FARMS and BYU Studies, 2017), 4:2456–2457.

174 Richard Lloyd Anderson, "'By the Gift and Power of God'," *Ensign*, September 1977, 78–85; Richard Van Wagoner and Steve Walker, "Joseph Smith: 'The Gift of Seeing'," *Dialogue: A Journal of Mormon Thought 15*, no. 2 (Summer 1982): 49–68; Stephen D. Ricks, "Notes and Communications—Translation of the Book of Mormon: Interpreting the Evidence," *Journal of Book of Mormon Studies 2*, no. 2 (1993): 201–206; Royal Skousen, "Translating the Book of Mormon: Evidence from the Original Manuscript," in *Book of Mormon Authorship Revisited*, 61–93; Matthew B. Brown, *Plates of Gold: The Book of Mormon Comes Forth* (American Fork, UT: Covenant Communications, 2003); John W. Welch, "The Miraculous Translation of the Book of Mormon," in *Opening the Heavens*, 79–227; Don Bradley, "Written by the Finger of God? Claims and Controversies of Book of Mormon Translation," *Sunstone*, December 2010, 20–29; Brant A. Gardner, *The Gift and Power: Translating the Book of Mormon* (Salt Lake City, UT: Greg Kofford, 2011); Roger Nicholson, "The Spectacles, the Stone, the Hat, and the Book: A Twenty-first Century Believer's View of the Book of Mormon Translation," *Interpreter: A Journal of Mormon Scripture 5* (2013): 121–190; Michael Hubbard MacKay and Gerrit J. Dirkmaat, "Firsthand Witness Accounts of the Translation Process," in *The Coming Forth of the Book of Mormon: A Marvelous Work and a Wonder*, ed. Dennis L. Largey et al. (Salt Lake City and Provo, UT: BYU Religious Studies Center and Deseret Book, 2015), 61–79; Michael Hubbard MacKay and Gerrit J. Dirkmaat, *From Darkness Unto Light: Joseph Smith's Translation and Publication of the Book of Mormon* (Salt Lake City and Provo, UT: BYU Religious Studies Center and Deseret Book, 2015); Stanford Carmack, "Joseph Smith Read the Words," *Interpreter: A Journal of Mormon Scripture 18* (2016): 41–64; Michael Hubbard MacKay and Nicholas J. Frederick, *Joseph Smith's Seer Stones* (Salt Lake City and Provo, UT: BYU Religious Studies Center and Deseret Book, 2016).

175 B. H. Roberts, "Book of Mormon Translation," *Improvement Era*, July 1906, 706–713; Russell M. Nelson, "A Treasured Testament," *Ensign*, July 1993, 61–63; Neal A. Maxwell, "'By the Gift and Power of God'," *Ensign*, January 1997, 36–41; Steven E. Snow, "Joseph Smith in Harmony," *Ensign*, September 2015, 51–57; Quentin L. Cook, "Foundations of Faith," *Ensign*, May 2017, 127–131; *Saints: The Story of the Church of Jesus Christ in the Latter Days*, 31–34, 50, 61–64.

176 "Book of Mormon Translation," online at lds.org.

177 Cornelis Van Dam, *The Urim and Thummim: A Means of Revelation in Ancient Israel* (Winona Lake, IN: Eisenbrauns, 1997); Marc G. Blainey, "Techniques of Luminosity: Iron-Ore Mirrors and Entheogenic Shamanism among the Ancient Maya," in *Manufactured Light: Mirrors in the Mesoamerican Realm*, ed. Emiliano Gallaga M. and Marc G. Blainey (Boulder, CO: University Press of Colorado, 2016), 179–206; John J. McGraw, "Stones of Light: The Use of Crystals in Maya Divination," in *Manufactured Light*, 207–227; Olivia Kindl, "The Ritual Uses of Mirrors by Wixaritari (Huichol Indians)," in *Manufactured Light*, 255–283; Karl Taube, "Through a Glass, Brightly: Recent Investigations Concerning Mirrors and Scrying in Ancient and Contemporary Mesoamerica," in *Manufactured Light*, 285–314; John A. Tvedtnes, "Glowing Stones in Ancient and Medieval Lore," *Journal of Book of Mormon Studies 6*, no. 2 (1997): 99–123; Gardner, *Second Witness*, 4:511; Mark Alan Wright, "Nephite Daykeepers: Ritual Specialists in Mesoamerica and the Book of Mormon," *Ancient Temple Worship: Proceedings of the Expound Symposium*, 14 May 2011 (Orem and Salt Lake City, UT: The Interpreter Foundation and Eborn Books, 2014), 244–246.

178 Dowsing, or using a rod to locate water, oil, graves, ores, or stones, is still practiced in some cultures today.

179 Mark Ashurst–McGee, "A Pathway to Prophethood: Joseph Smith Junior as Rodsman, Village Seer, and Judeo-Christian Prophet" (Master's Thesis, Utah State University, 2000); Gardner, *The Gift and Power*, 3–134.

180 See for instance Exodus 7:9–12; 25:10–22; 29:4–7; Numbers 21:4–9; 2 Kings 5:1–19; 6:1–7; John 9:1–7; Acts 19:11–12. For a discussion, see Helen R. Jacobus et al., ed., *Studies on Magic and Divination in the Biblical World* (Piscataway, NJ: Gorgias, 2013); Richard A. Horsley, *Jesus and Magic: Freeing the Gospel Stories from Modern Misconceptions* (Eugene, OR: Cascade, 2014).

181 See Leviticus 16:8; Numbers 26:55; 33:54; 34:13; Joshua 13:6; 14:1–2; Judges 20:9; 1 Samuel 10:20–21; 14:40–42; 1 Chronicles 24:5, 31; 25:8; 26:13–14; Acts 1:26.

182 The leading historians to advance this thesis are D. Michael Quinn, *Early Mormonism and the Magic World View*, 2nd ed. (Salt Lake City, UT: Signature Books, 1998); John L. Brooke, *The Refiner's Fire: The Making of Mormon Cosmology, 1644–1844* (Cambridge: Cambridge University Press, 1994). For extensive reviews of Quinn and Brooke, see John Gee, "'An Obstacle to Deeper Understanding'," *FARMS Review of Books 12*, no. 2 (2000): 185–224; William J. Hamblin, "That Old Black Magic," *FARMS Review of Books 12*, no. 2 (2000): 225–393; William J. Hamblin, Daniel C. Peterson, and George L. Mitton, "Mormon in the Fiery Furnace: Or, Loftes Tryk Goes to Cambridge," *Review of Books on the Book of Mormon 6*, no. 2 (1994): 3–58.

183 Kerry Muhlestein, "Seeking Divine Interaction: Joseph Smith's Varying Searches for the Supernatural," in *No Weapon Shall Prosper: New Light on Sensitive Issues*, ed. Robert L. Millet (Salt Lake City and Provo, UT: BYU Religious Studies Center and Deseret Book, 2011), 77–91; Samuel M. Brown, "The Reluctant Metaphysicians," *Mormon Studies Review 1* (2014): 115–131; Richard Lyman Bushman, "Joseph Smith and Money Digging," in *A Reason for Faith: Navigating LDS Doctrine and Church History*, ed. Laura Harris Hales (Provo and Salt Lake City, UT: BYU Religious Studies Center and Deseret Book, 2016), 1–6; Eric A. Eliason, "Seer Stones, Salamanders, and Early Mormon 'Folk Magic' in the Light of Folklore Studies and Bible Scholarship," *BYU Studies Quarterly 55*, no. 1 (2016): 73–93.

184 See Welch, et al., *Knowing Why*, 240–241.

185 See Welch, et al., *Knowing Why*, 199–200.

186 For example, multiple eyewitnesses spoke of Joseph translating by placing the seer stone into the bottom of a hat and then burying his face in the hat to block out the light around him. From there he would see words appear in the stone and then dictate those words to his scribe. If this was in fact how Joseph translated a substantial amount of the Book of Mormon, as the historical evidence suggests, then it would have been impossible for him to have cribbed from a nearby Bible or pilfered manuscript as he dictated. For

thoughts along these lines, see Daniel C. Peterson, "Editor's Introduction: Not So Easily Dismissed: Some Facts for Which Counterexplanations of the Book of Mormon Will Need to Account," *FARMS Review 17*, no. 2 (2005): xi–xxiv; Neal Rappleye, "'Idle and Slothful Strange Stories': Book of Mormon Origins and the Historical Record," *Interpreter: A Journal of Mormon Scripture 20* (2016): 21–37.

187 Gordon C. Thomasson and John W. Welch, "The Sons of the Passover," in *Reexploring the Book of Mormon*, 196.

188 Fred O. Francis, "The Baraita of the Four Sons," *Journal of the American Academy of Religion 42*, no. 2 (1974): 290: "We are inclined to believe that the three versions which have come down to us interweave a multitude of allied wisdom traditions into a few strands. . . . Though the possibility of an 'original text' is always intriguing, we take the three versions to be representatives of a broad wisdom tradition—broader than they themselves indicate." Francis, "The Baraita of the Four Sons," 280–297, provides a brief overview and then a side-by-side comparison of the three extant texts that have stemmed from these traditions. Note that while most Passover traditions include four sons, only three of them ask questions. For the rationale of there being four sons (rather than two or three), see Francis, "Baraita of Four Sons," 291–292.

189 See Martin Sicker, *A Passover Seder Companion and Analytic Introduction to the Haggadah* (New York: iUniverse, 2004), 55–64, for an interpretive analysis of this ceremony as found in the Jewish Haggadah.

190 Thomasson and Welch, "Sons of Passover," 197.

191 Thomasson and Welch, "Sons of Passover," 197.

192 Alma's exhortation to Corianton comprises Alma 39–42. Although Alma initially rebuked Corianton (see Alma 39:1–7), Alma's ultimate goal was to help his son repent and "let these things trouble [him] no more" (Alma 42:29). See chapter 16.

193 Thomasson and Welch, "Sons of Passover," 197.

194 See Alma 38:11–14. These warnings to Shiblon can be contrasted with Alma's warnings to Helaman, who despite having been strictly commissioned and commanded to fulfill his charge, was not quite as explicitly or directly warned against sin.

195 See Thomasson and Welch, "Sons of Passover," 197–198: "Many other Passover themes are detectable in Alma 35–42. Alma speaks of 'crying out' (compare Deuteronomy 26:7; Alma 36:18) for deliverance from 'affliction' (compare Deuteronomy 26:6; Alma 36:3, 27; especially the unleavened Passover 'bread of affliction') and from bondage in Egypt (Alma 36:28), from the 'night of darkness' (compare Alma 41:7; Exodus 12:30), and from bitter suffering (Alma 36:18, 21; related to the Passover 'bitter herbs' in Exodus 12:8). The Paschal lamb may parallel some of Alma's references to Christ; and the hardness of Pharaoh's heart (see Exodus 11:10) may parallel Alma's reference to the hardness of his people's hearts (see Alma 35:15). Just as Alma's deliverance was preceded by three days and nights of darkness (see Alma 36:16), so was the first Passover (see Exodus 10:22)."

196 For example, John W. Welch, "A Masterpiece: Alma 36," in *Rediscovering the Book of Mormon*, 114–131; John W. Welch, "Chiasmus in the Book of Mormon," in *Book of Mormon Authorship*, 33–52; John W. Welch, "Criteria for Identifying and Evaluating the Presence of Chiasmus," *Journal of Book of Mormon Studies 4*, no. 2 (1995): 1–14. See also chapter 13. It is noteworthy that Alma spoke to Helaman using a doubled chiastic structure in Alma 36, while he gave to Shiblon only the first half of his conversion account in Alma 38, perhaps because Helaman as the firstborn son was entitled to inherit a double portion of the father's estate. To view Alma's sermons formatted into poetic parallels, see Parry, *Poetic Parallelisms*, 318–336. For a literary evaluation of Alma's rehearsal of his conversion, see Hardy, *Understanding the Book of Mormon*, 137–142.

197 See George S. Tate, "The Typology of the Exodus Pattern in the Book of Mormon," in *Literature of Belief: Sacred Scripture and Religious Experience*, ed. Neal E. Lambert (Provo, UT: BYU Religious Studies Center, 1981), 245–262; S. Kent Brown, "The Exodus Pattern in the Book of Mormon," in *From Jerusalem to Zarahemla: Literary and Historical Studies of the Book of Mormon* (Provo, UT: BYU Religious Studies Center, 1998), 75–98.

198 Russel M. Nelson, "The Exodus Repeated," *Ensign*, July 1999.

199 See McConkie and Millet, *Doctrinal Commentary on the Book of Mormon*, 3:289–291; H. Dean Garrett, "The Three Most Abominable Sins," in *The Book of Mormon: Alma, the Testimony of the Word*, ed. Monte S. Nyman and Charles D. Tate Jr. (Provo, UT: BYU Religious Studies Center, 1992), 157–171.

200 Under biblical law, for example, distinctions were drawn between adultery with a married woman and fornication with an unmarried woman, which was "treated rather leniently." Ze'ev Falk, *Hebrew Law in Biblical Times* (Provo, UT and Winona Lake, IN: Brigham Young University Press and Eisenbrauns, 2001), 71.

201 B. W. Jorgensen, "Scriptural Chastity Lessons: Joseph and Potiphar's Wife; Corianton and the Harlot Isabel," *Dialogue: A Journal of Mormon Thought 32*, no. 1 (1999): 7–34; Michael R. Ash, "The Sin 'Next to Murder': An Alternative Interpretation," *Sunstone*, November 2006, 34–43.

202 Ash, "The Sin 'Next to Murder'," 35.

203 Ash, "The Sin 'Next to Murder'," 35. See also Rodney Turner, "Unpardonable Sin," in *The Encyclopedia of Mormonism*, 4 vols., ed. Daniel H. Ludlow (New York, NY: Macmillan, 1992), 4:1499.

204 For example, Hosea related adultery and apostasy as two manifestations of unfaithfulness—the one toward one's spouse and the other toward one's God. See Hosea 2–3. Ezekiel also used forceful language to describe Israel's apostasy as a form of spiritual adultery (see Ezekiel 16:15–22).

205 Ash, "The Sin 'Next to Murder'," 35.

206 Ash, "The Sin 'Next to Murder'," 36.

207 For a deeper analysis of the early doctrine of resurrection in the Book of Mormon, see A. Keith Thompson, "The Doctrine of Resurrection in the Book of Mormon," *Interpreter: A Journal of Mormon Scripture 12* (2016): 114–115.

208 See Thompson, "Doctrine of the Resurrection," 108–109.

209 See John Hilton III and Jana Johnson, "Who Uses the Word Resurrection in the Book of Mormon and How Is It Used?" *Journal of the Book of Mormon and Other Restoration Scripture 21*, no. 2 (2012): 32–33. It is also notable that after Alma privately taught "concerning the resurrection of the dead, and the redemption of the people," we learn that "many did believe on his words" (Mosiah 18:2–3). This statement makes best sense if the Resurrection was previously unknown or unaccepted among the people in the land of Lehi-Nephi.

210 Abinadi taught among the people of Noah who resided in the land of Lehi-Nephi, whereas Alma continued these teachings in the land of Zarahemla. It is significant that the societies in both locations struggled to accept the doctrine of the Resurrection.

211 See chapter 19.

212 See Welch, et al., *Knowing Why*, 248–249.

213 See Welch, et al., *Knowing Why*, 250–251

214 See Douglas J. Merrell, "The False Priests of the Book of Mormon," in *Selections from the Religious Education Student Symposium 2005* (Provo, UT: BYU Religious Studies Center, 2005): 87–94. See also J. Christopher Conkling, "Alma's Enemies: The Case of the Lamanites, Amlicites, and Mysterious Amalekites," *Journal of Book of Mormon Studies 14*, no. 1 (2005): 113–115.

215 See chapter 16.

216 Thompson, "Doctrine of the Resurrection," 124.

217 Alma specifically points out that eventually all will know that God Himself fully comprehends and controls the timing of the Resurrection: "And when the time cometh when all shall rise, then shall they know that God

knoweth all the times which are appointed unto man" (Alma 40:10). It is also important to consider that Alma 40 is just the beginning of Alma's discourse on the Resurrection. This chapter mainly establishes that, after death, the spirits of the righteous will be "received into a state of happiness," while the spirits of the wicked will be "be cast out into outer darkness" (Alma 40:12–13). Alma 41–42 aims to justify the doctrines of resurrection and judgment that are clearly delineated in Alma 40.

218 For more information concerning the doctrine of resurrection in the Book of Mormon, see chapter 17.

219 At the end of chapter 40, Alma began to describe the Resurrection as the "*restoration* of those things of which has been spoken by the mouths of the prophets" (v. 22; emphasis added). This shift carried over into Alma 41, where Alma mentioned *restoration* or *restored* seventeen times, while only mentioning *resurrection* once. To see how frequently Alma mentioned the Resurrection in relation to other Book of Mormon authors, see John Hilton III and Jana Johnson, "Who Uses the Word Resurrection in the Book of Mormon and How Is It Used?" *Journal of the Book of Mormon and Other Restoration Scripture 21*, no. 2 (2012): 32–33.

220 See Welch, et al., *Knowing Why*, 248–249.

221 Welch, *Legal Cases*, 338–339.

222 Welch, *Legal Cases*, 339.

223 For a general explanation of chiastic parallels, see chapter 12. See also Parry, *Poetic Parallelisms*, xvi–xix; John W. Welch, "Chiasmus in the Book of Mormon," in *Book of Mormon Authorship*, 34–39; John W. Welch, "Criteria for Identifying and Evaluating the Presence of Chiasmus," *Journal of Book of Mormon Studies 4*, no. 2 (1995): 1–14.

224 Formatting follows Welch, *Legal Cases*, 343.

225 Formatting follows Welch, *Legal Cases*, 344. For different formats, see Parry, *Poetic Parallelisms*, 332–333; Welch, "Chiasmus in the Book of Mormon," 48.

226 Welch, "Chiasmus in the Book of Mormon," 49.

227 Welch, *Legal Cases*, 344.

228 Welch, et al., *Knowing Why*, 83–85.

229 John W. Welch, "Counting to Ten," *Journal of Book of Mormon Studies 12,* no. 2 (2003): 57.

230 See 1 Nephi 3:19, Enos 1:1, and Mosiah 1:4.

231 See Royal Skousen, "How Joseph Smith Translated the Book of Mormon: Evidence from the Original Manuscript," *Journal of Book of Mormon Studies 7*, no. 1 (1998): 27–28.

232 See Thomas W. Mackay, "Mormon as Editor: A Study in Colophons, Headers, and Source Indicators," *Journal of Book of Mormon Studies 2*, no. 2 (1993): 107.

233 Alma 39:18; 41:2; 42:5, 8, 11, 13, 15, 16, 31.

234 For general information concerning priesthood responsibilities and temple worship in the Old Testament, see Lawrence H. Schiffman, "Priests," in *Harper's Bible Dictionary*, ed. Paul J. Achtemeier (San Francisco, CA: Harper and Row Publishers, 1985), 821–823.

235 Welch, "Counting to Ten," 57.

236 See Mark Alan Wright, "Axes Mundi: Ritual Complexes in Mesoamerica and the Book of Mormon," *Interpreter: A Journal of Mormon Scripture 12* (2014): 79–96. See also John W. Welch, "The Temple in the Book of Mormon: The Temples at the Cities of Nephi, Zarahemla, and Bountiful," in *Temples of the Ancient World*, ed. Donald W. Parry (Salt Lake and Provo, UT: Deseret Book and FARMS, 1994), 297–387.

237 Welch, "Counting to Ten," 45.

238 Several studies have demonstrated that ten, seven, twenty-four, and fifty are all symbolically significant throughout the text. See Corbin Volluz, "A Study in Seven: Hebrew Numerology in the Book of Mormon," *BYU Studies Quarterly 53*, no. 2 (2014): 57–83; Welch, "Number 24," in *Reexploring the Book of Mormon*, 272–274; Welch, et al., *Knowing Why*, 258–259, 314–315.

239 Volluz, "A Study in Seven," 74: "Perhaps most interestingly, the book of Alma appears to be structured around the number seven and, more specifically, around double the number of seven. This may be particularly appropriate in the book named for Alma, the high priest in the land of Zarahemla, for seven is featured prominently in aspects of the law of Moses with which Alma would have been intimately acquainted (see Alma 30:3). The priestly manual contained in the book of Leviticus is replete with instances of the number seven and its multiples, calling for seven sprinklings or anointings (Lev. 4:6, 17; 8:11; 14:51) and marking off heptadic periods of times of impurity (Lev. 12:2; 13:5, 31), of purification or consecration (Lev. 8:33; 15:19; 16:14, 19), or of sacred time."

240 Welch, "Counting to Ten," 54–55.

241 Because of their different form and negative context, it may seem tempting to rule out the first three instances of plan in Alma 12 as having anything to do with the later seven repetitions of plan of redemption. However, it seems that the ancient literary "rules" concerning repetition were not so rigid or inflexible. Antithetical parallelism, for instance, was common in ancient literature. In this example, all instances have at least one word in common, and in total there are ten instances that conceptually deal with an overarching plan. The fact that early usage of the term plan is directly antithetical to the later usage of plan of redemption suggests that an intentional dichotomy may be at play. Although such an assertion is certainly not provable, the attestation of similar instances and variations within the text supports its viability (see footnote 239).

242 Alma 49:30 implies that Corianton took Alma's teachings to heart, repented of his transgressions, and returned to the ministry: "Yea, and there was continual peace among them, and exceedingly great prosperity in the church because of their heed and diligence which they gave unto the word of God, which was declared unto them by Helaman, and Shiblon, and Corianton, and Ammon and his brethren, yea, and by all those who had been ordained by the holy order of God, being baptized unto repentance, and sent forth to preach among the people."

243 Douglas J. Bell, *Defenders of Faith: The Book of Mormon from a Soldier's Perspective* (Springville, UT: Cedar Fort, 2012), 135.

244 In contrast, the Lamanites were "naked, save it were a skin which was girded about their loins" (Alma 43:20). According to Ross Hassig, *War and Society in Ancient Mesoamerica* (Berkeley and Los Angeles, CA: University of California Press, 1992), 73, Maya of the Classic period (and presumably earlier) generally did not use armor.

245 1 Nephi 4:9 mentions Laban's armor. Mosiah 8:10 mentions the discovery of Jaredite "breastplates" by the Limhite people, and Mosiah 21:7 mentions that the Limhites "put on their armor" as they prepared for battle with the Lamanites. Alma 3:5 notes that the Lamanites were "naked, save it were skin which was girded about their loins, and also their armor, which was girded about them."

246 David E. Spencer, *Captain Moroni's Command: Dynamics of Warfare in the Book of Mormon* (Springville, UT: Cedar Fort, 2015), 14. Alternatively, armor may have been more limited and less protective before Moroni introduced the full ensemble of armor mentioned in Alma 43:19.

247 William J. Hamblin, "Armor in the Book of Mormon," in *Warfare in the Book of Mormon*, eds. Stephen D. Ricks and Williman J. Hamblin (Salt Lake City and Provo, UT: Deseret Book and FARMS, 1990), 404–410, reviews the Nephite system of armor.

248 For a full detailing of passages mentioning and describing fortifications in the Book of Mormon, see John L. Sorenson, "Fortifications in the Book of Mormon Account Compared with Mesoamerican Fortifications," in *Warfare in*

the Book of Mormon, 438–443.

249 See Jacob 7:25; Jarom 1:7. Walls are mentioned in the Land of Nephi (Mosiah 7:10; 9:8; 21:19; 22:6). Based on the "astonished" reaction of the Lamanites (see Alma 49:5; cf. vv. 8–9, 14), it seems none of the cities in the Land of Zarahemla had previously been fortified.

250 Hassig, *War and Society*, 64 and 97, understood a lack of evidence for battle standards as a lack of formal military units and formations.

251 See Hamblin, "Armor in the Book of Mormon," 410–416; John L. Sorenson, *Mormon's Codex: An Ancient American Book* (Salt Lake City and Provo, UT: Deseret Book and Neal A. Maxwell Institute, 2013), 418–419; John L. Sorenson, *Images of Ancient America: Visualizing Book of Mormon Life* (Provo UT: FARMS, 1998), 130–131. Aztec armor is described in Ross Hassig, Aztec *Warfare: Imperial Expansion and Political Control* (Norman, OK: University of Oklahoma Press, 1988), 85–90. According to Dorie Reents-Budet, *Painting the Maya Universe: Royal Ceramics of the Classic Period* (Durham, NC: Duke University Press, 1994), 259, one Mayan vase (K2352) depicts what is likely "a type of body protection stuffed with cotton or reinforced in some other manner, similar to the effective armor worn by the later Aztec." Interestingly, their enemies are depicted wearing nothing but a loin cloth, as pointed out by Gardner, *Second Witness*, 4:575. Hassig, *War and Society in Ancient Mesoamerica*, 82–84, discusses similar armor (specifically the thick, quilted armor) at Teotihuacan as early AD 450. On pp. 197–198 n. 22, Hassig noted that "West Mexican cultures produced realistic ceramic figures, among which well-accoutered warriors are prominent." These warrior figurines "are shown wearing what is described as 'barrel armor' because of its shape, which protects the trunk but not the limbs. Judging by the sewn closures, this armor was constructed of leather or fabric." The dating of these figurines is uncertain, but they are stylistically "attributed to the Late Formative" (Late Preclassic). Hassig pointed out that this artistic style "may well have extended through the Classic," thus urging caution that "the martial traits shown may not be from the Formative era." Although uncertain, the evidence is nonetheless suggestive of fabric, or thick-clothing armor dating to Captain Moroni's time period

252 See chapter 27. Spencer, *Captain Moroni's Command*, 20–32, describes and comments on the fortifications of Captain Moroni, including images of pre-Columbian forts from both North America and Mesoamerica. For a fairly detailed treatment of fortifications in the Heartland region, see David E. Jones, *Native North American Armor, Shields, and Fortifications* (Austin, TX: University of Texas Press, 2004), 50–57, 125–135. He documents Native American forts in the Northeast and Southeast with earthen walls, palisades, and bastion towers, similar to those of Moroni. For examples from Mesoamerica, see James N. Ambrosino, Traci Ardren, and Travis W. Stanton, "The History of Warfare at Yaxuná," in *Ancient Mesoamerican Warfare*, ed. M. Kathryn Brown and Travis W. Stanton (New York, NY: AltaMira Press, 2003), 110–112; Payson D. Sheets, "Warfare in Ancient Mesoamerica: A Summary View," in *Ancient Mesoamerican Warfare*, 291. See also Sorenson, *Mormon's Codex*, 405–410; Sorenson, *Images of Ancient America*, 132–133. For Israelite fortifications compared to Book of Mormon fortifications, see John E. Kammeyer, *The Art of Nephite War* (Far West Publications, 2014), chapter 11.

253 See Sorenson, "Fortifications in the Book of Mormon," 429, table 2. On p. 430, table 3 displays the features of fortifications by period, showing that all the features described in the Book of Mormon are attested to in the Late Preclassic. Sorenson also documents fortifications by region (p. 426–427, table 1). Based on all three lines of data, Sorenson concluded, "Evidently all the features mentioned or inferred above for the Book of Mormon complexes one through five were present already during the Mesoamerican Late Pre-Classic or Proto-Classic periods, the archaeological periods coinciding with the Book of Mormon occurrences. In terms of geography, if we accept for the moment a general spatial correlation between Book of Mormon lands and Mesoamerica, we can see broad agreement. We do not yet have sufficient chronological control to pin down when fortifications appeared in many of the regions of Mesoamerica, but it is generally apparent that known archaeological sites display the right sorts of military technology to agree with the Book of Mormon account" (p. 437). Takeshi Inomata and Daniela Triadan, "Culture and Practice of War in Maya Society," in *Warfare in Cultural Context: Practice, Agency, and the Archaeology of Violence*, ed. Axel E. Nielsen and William H. Walker (Tucson, AZ: University of Arizona Press, 2009), 66–69 also note that fortifications become most common during the Late Preclassic phase; and Hassig, *War and Society in Ancient Mesoamerica*, 32–44 documents fortifications in various regions of Mesoamerica, concluding, "during the Late Formative, the general sophistication of warfare in Mesoamerica increased" (p. 44). For more information, see chapter 27.

254 See Hugh Nibley, *The Prophetic Book of Mormon*, 92–95; William J. Hamblin, "The Importance of Warfare in Book of Mormon Studies," in *Warfare in the Book of Mormon*, 491–492; Sorenson, *Mormon's Codex*, 109–110, 421; Kammeyer, *Art of Nephite War*, chapter 14; Kerry Hull, "War Banners: A Mesoamerican Context for the Title of Liberty," *Journal of Book of Mormon Studies 24* (2015): 84–118. The use of banners in ancient Near Eastern warfare can also be seen in William J. Hamblin, *Warfare in the Ancient Near East to 1600 BC: Holy Warriors at the Dawn of History* (New York, NY: Routledge, 2006), 40, 221, 247, 271, 292, 326, 330. For "standard-bearers" in Egyptian warfare, see Anthony J. Spalinger, *War in Ancient Egypt: The New Kingdom* (Oxford, England: Blackwell Publishing, 2005), 156, 177, 221. For "standards" as a feature of Mesoamerican warfare, see Hassig, *War and Society in Ancient Mesoamerica*, 50–51, 128, 140, 143, 148, 150, 152, 153, 162. For Aztec specifically, see Hassig, *Aztec Warfare*, 5, 42, 57, 58, 96, 97, 283 n. 66, 293 n. 20. For war banners in earlier Mesoamerican warfare, see F. Kent Reilly and James F. Garber, "The Symbolic Representation of Warfare in Formative Period Mesoamerica," in *Ancient Mesoameican Warfare*, 127–128.

255 See Hugh Nibley, *Since Cumorah*, 242; Stephen D. Ricks, "'Holy War': The Sacral Ideology of War in the Book of Mormon and in the Ancient Near East," in *Warfare in the Book of Mormon*, 103–110. See also Sorenson, *Mormon's Codex*, 387–389; Hamblin, *Warfare in the Ancient Near East to 1600 BC*, 107.

256 While it is reported that Moroni's preparations for war "had [never] been known among the children of Lehi" (Alma 49:8) before, that does not mean they were not known within the region among others. For the presence and influence of others in the Book of Mormon, see Welch et al., *Knowing Why*, 119–120; John L. Sorenson, "When Lehi's Party Arrived in the Land, Did They Find Others There?" *Journal of Book of Mormon Studies 1*, no. 1 (1992): 1–34; Matthew Roper, "Nephi's Neighbors: Book of Mormon Peoples and Pre-Columbian Populations," *FARMS Review 15*, no. 2 (2003): 91–128; John Gee and Matthew Roper, "'I Did Liken All Scriptures Unto Us': Early Nephite Understandings of Isaiah and Implications for 'Others' in the Land," in *The Fulness of the Gospel: Foundational Teachings from the Book of Mormon*, ed. Camille Fronk, Brian M. Hauglid, Patty A. Smith, and Thomas A. Wayment (Salt Lake City and Provo, UT: Deseret Book and BYU Religious Studies Center, 2003), 51–65.

257 David A. Bednar, "The Hearts of the Children Shall Turn," *Ensign*, November, 2011, 27.

258 For evidence of the Nephites' righteousness directly leading to success in battle, see Alma 43:45–50.

259 John Bytheway, *Righteous Warriors: Lessons from the War Chapters in the Book of Mormon* (Salt Lake City, UT: Deseret Book, 2004), 13.

260 Russell M. Nelson, "Becoming True Millennials," Worldwide Devotional for Young Adults, January 10, 2016

261 Nelson, "Becoming True Millennials," at lds.org.

262 See generally Delbert R. Hillers, *Treaty–Curses and the Old Testament Prophets* (Rome: Pontifical Biblical Institute, 1964); Noel Weeks, *Admonition and Curse: The Ancient Near Eastern Treaty/Covenant Form as a Problem in Inter-Cultural Relationships* (London: T&T Clark, 2004); Anne Marie Kitz, "An Oath, It's Curse and Anointing Ritual," *Journal of the American Oriental Society 124*, no. 2 (April–June 2004): 315–321; Anne Marie Kitz, "Effective Simile and Effective Act: Psalm 109, Numbers 5, and KUB 26," *The Catholic Biblical Quarterly 69*, no. 3 (July 2007): 440–456; Mary R. Bachvarova, "Oath and Allusion in Alcaeus FR. 129," in *Horkos: The Oath in Greek Society*, ed. Alan H. Sommerstein and Judith Fletcher (Exeter: Bristol Phoenix Press, 2007), 179–188.

263 Joseph A. Fitzmyer, "The Aramaic Inscriptions of Se-fire I and II," *Journal of the American Oriental Society 81*, no. 3 (August–September 1961): 185. Brackets indicate instances where the original text has been broken in the manuscript and the translation restored by the translator. Compare also the treaty between Ashurnirari V and Mati'ilu in James B. Pritchard, ed., *The Ancient Near East: An Anthology of Texts and Pictures*, rev. ed. (Princeton, NJ: Princeton University Press, 2011), 210–212.

264 These texts, which contain multiple explicit simile curses for soldiers who fail their military duties, are very interesting in light of the military context of Alma 44. See Billie Jean Collins, "The First Soldiers' Oath" and "The Second Soldier's Oath," in *The Context of Scripture, Volume I: Canonical Compositions from the Biblical World*, ed. William W. Halo (Leiden: Brill, 2003), 165–168.

265 See Weeks, *Admonition and Curse*, 75–77; Jared L. Miller, trans., *Royal Hittite Inscriptions and Related Administrative Texts*, ed. Mauro Giorgieri (Atlanta, GA: Society of Biblical Literature, 2013), 3.

266 Welch et al., *Knowing Why*, 225–226. See also RoseAnn Benson and Stephen D. Ricks, "Treaties and Covenants: Ancient Near Eastern Legal Terminology in the Book of Mormon," *Journal of Book of Mormon Studies 14*, no. 1 (2005): 48–61, 128–129.

267 See Terrence L. Szink, "Oath of Allegiance in the Book of Mormon," in *Warfare in the Book of Mormon*, ed. Stephen D. Ricks and William J. Hamblin (Salt Lake City and Provo, UT: Deseret Book and FARMS, 1990), 35–45; Mark J. Morrise, "Simile Curses in the Ancient Near East, Old Testament, and Book of Mormon," *Journal of Book of Mormon Studies 2*, no. 1 (1993): 124–138; Donald W. Parry, "Hebraisms and Other Ancient Peculiarities in the Book of Mormon," in *Echoes and Evidences of the Book of Mormon*, ed. Donald W. Parry, Daniel C. Peterson, and John W. Welch (Provo, UT: FARMS, 2002), 156–159.

268 Benson and Ricks, "Treaties and Covenants," 61.

269 Rather than being supplied by modern editors, this editorial comment was actually written by Mormon himself and reveals his understanding about the upcoming section of Nephite history. For information related to the introduction and revision of summary headings, see Bruce R. Satterfield, "Publication History of the Book of Mormon," *Church News*, January 1, 2000.

270 See Thomas W. Mackay, "Mormon as Editor: A Study in Colophons, Headers, and Source Indicators," *Journal of Book of Mormon Studies 2*, no. 2 (1993): 90–109; John A. Tvedtnes, "Colophons in the Book of Mormon," in *Reexploring the Book of Mormon*, 13–17; John A. Tvedtnes, "Colophons in the Book of Mormon," in *Rediscovering the Book of Mormon*, 32–37.

271 Alma 45:19 reports that Alma "was taken up by the Spirit, or buried by the hand of the Lord, even as Moses." This seems to allude to Deuteronomy 34:6, which says that "he [the Lord] buried him in a valley in the land of Moab . . . but no man knoweth of his sepulchre unto this day." These clues suggest the possibility that Alma, like Moses, was translated instead of suffering mortal death. For general information concerning the LDS understanding of translated beings, see Mark L. McConkie, "Translated Beings," in *Encyclopedia of Mormonism*, 4:1485–1486.

272 The events of Alma 45 take place in the nineteenth year of the reign of the judges (Alma 45:2), established by Mosiah in the final year of his reign (see Mosiah 29).

273 See 1 Samuel 8:4–5 for a fuller reasoning of their request: "Then all the elders of Israel gathered themselves together, and came to Samuel unto Ramah, And said unto him, Behold, thou art old, and thy sons walk not in thy ways: now make us a king to judge us like all the nations."

274 For evidence that Samuel's warning likely drew upon a contemporary genre of discourse that decried monarchal abuse, see Jonathan Kaplan, "1 Samuel 8:11–18 as 'A Mirror for Princes,'" *Journal of Biblical Literature 131*, no. 4 (2012): 625–642.

275 Simon Martin and Nikolai Grube, *Chronicle of the Maya Kings and Queens: Deciphering the Dynasties of the Ancient Maya*, 2nd ed. (London, England: Thames and Hudson, 2008), 17.

276 Martin and Grube, *Chronicle of Maya Kings and Queens*, 17.

277 See Mosiah 29:13: "Therefore, if it were possible that you could have just men to be your kings . . . I say unto you, if this could always be the case then it would be expedient that ye should always have kings to rule over you." See also Kaplan, "Samuel 8 as Mirror for Princes," 637.

278 See Welch and Welch, *Charting the Book of Mormon*, chart 137, wars 7–8.

279 Copies of the title of liberty were made and were hoisted on various towers and in cities throughout the land of Zarahemla as symbols of loyalty and solidarity (see Alma 51:20).

280 John A. Tvedtnes has noted a potential Hebraism in Alma 46:19. The earliest rendition of the text reads that Moroni "went forth among the people waving the rent," as in the rent part of the garment. See Royal Skousen, ed., *The Book of Mormon: The Earliest Text* (New Haven, CT: Yale University Press, 2009), 441. This was corrected in later editions to read "the rent part," as in English rent is used to refer to a tear, not a piece of torn fabric. However, biblical Hebrew does have a word that would correspond to rent as a noun for a torn piece of fabric (cf. 1 Kings 11:30). See John A. Tvedtnes, "Hebraisms in the Book of Mormon: A Preliminary Survey," *BYU Studies 11*, no. 1 (1970): 50.

281 For more on the presence of simile curses in the Book of Mormon, see chapter 21.

282 "War Rules," in *The Dead Sea Scrolls Reader: Volume I*, ed. Donald W. Parry and Emanuel Tov (Leiden: Brill, 2013), Col. III, lines 13–14. See also Hugh Nibley, *Since Cumorah*, 242.

283 Kerry Hull, "War Banners: A Mesoamerican Context for the Title of Liberty," *Journal of Book of Mormon Studies 24* (2015): 84–118.

284 Hull, "War Banners," 118.

285 Hull, "War Banners," 117.

286 See chapter 20.

287 The Lord's hand in establishing modern constitutional freedoms is made evident in D&C 101:77–80.

288 Richard L. Bushman, "The Book of Mormon and the American Revolution," in *Book of Mormon Authorship*, 201–202.

289 Ryan W. Davis, "For the Peace of the People: War and Democracy in the Book of Mormon," *Journal of Book of Mormon Studies 16*, no. 1 (2007): 44–45.

290 Davis, "Peace of the People," 44.

291 See John W. Welch, "Democratizing Forces in King Benjamin's Speech," in *Pressing Forward with the Book of Mormon*, ed. John W. Welch and Melvin Thorne (Provo UT: FARMS, 1999), 110–126.

292 See Davis, "Peace of the People," 45. For analysis of Lamanite kingship, see Welch et al., *Knowing Why*, 296–297.

293 Davis, "Peace of the People," 50–51.

294 For an analysis of Mormon's views concerning Moroni's efforts to secure

liberty, see Hardy, *Understanding the Book of Mormon*, 109–110.

295 Davis, "Peace of the People," 54.

296 Nephi was taught this truth early on (see 1 Nephi 4:14), and its consistent repetition throughout the Book of Mormon demonstrates its preeminent status in determining the success or failure of the Nephite civilization.

297 Davis, "Peace of the People," 54–55.

298 See Robert D. Hales, "Preserving Agency, Protecting Religious Freedom," *Ensign*, May 2015, 111–113: "First, we can become informed. Be aware of issues in your community that could have an impact on religious liberty. Second, in your individual capacity, join with others who share our commitment to religious freedom. Work side by side to protect religious freedom. Third, live your life to be a good example of what you believe—in word and deed. How we live our religion is far more important than what we may say about our religion."

299 Robert D. Hales, "Preserving Agency," 113.

300 Adapted from John W. Welch, "Why Study Warfare in the Book of Mormon?" in *Warfare in the Book of Mormon*, 6–15.

301 William J. Hamblin, *Warfare in the Ancient Near East to 1600 BC: Holy Warriors at the Dawn of History* (New York, NY: Routledge, 2006), 11–13,

302 Boyd Seevers, *Warfare in the Old Testament: The Organization, Weapons, and Tactics of Ancient Near Eastern Armies* (Grand Rapids, MI: Kregel Academic, 2013), 20.

303 See generally Ross Hassig, *War and Society in Ancient Mesoamerica*; M. Kathryn Brown and Travis W. Stanton, eds., *Ancient Mesoamerican Warfare* (Walnut Creek, CA: AltaMira Press, 2003). For a broader look at warfare across much of pre-Columbian America, see Axel E. Nielsen and William H. Walker, eds., *Warfare in Cultural Context: Practice, Agency, and the Archaeology of Violence* (Tucson, AZ: University of Arizona Press, 2009).

304 Takeshi Inomata and Daniela Triadan, "Culture and Practice of War in Maya Society," in *Warfare in Cultural Context*, 56.

305 Brant A. Gardner, *Traditions of the Fathers: The Book of Mormon as History* (Salt Lake City, UT: Greg Kofford Books, 2015), 312–313.

306 See chapter 20.

307 Welch, "Why Study Warfare in the Book of Mormon?" 4.

308 See Hugh Nibley, "Warfare and the Book of Mormon," in *Warfare in the Book of Mormon*, 127–145; Bell, *Defenders of Faith*; Kammeyer, *The Nephite Art of War*; Morgan Deane, *Bleached Bones and Wicked Serpents: Ancient Warfare in the Book of Mormon* (self-published, 2014); David E. Spencer, *Captain Moroni's Command* (Springville, UT: Cedar Fort, 2015).

309 Welch, "Why Study Warfare in the Book of Mormon?" 17–18.

310 See chapter 20.

311 See Jacob 7:25; Jarom 1:7; Mosiah 7:10; 9:8; 21:19; 22:6.

312 See John L. Sorenson, "Fortifications in the Book of Mormon Account Compared with Mesoamerican Fortifications," in *Warfare in the Book of Mormon*, 438–443 for all references to fortifications in the Book of Mormon.

313 David E. Spencer, *Captain Moroni's Command: Dynamics of Warfare in the Book of Mormon* (Springville, UT: Cedar Fort, 2015), 25–32, shows images of pre-Columbian forts from both North America and Mesoamerica that are similar to the Book of Mormon descriptions.

314 Ross Hassig, *War and Society*, 44. Interestingly, according to Hassig, the "increasing military professionalism" began ca. 400 BC with the spread of "specialized arms" (p. 30). Besides a few swords made by Nephi early on, it was in Jarom's lifetime (ca. 397–359 BC; see Jarom 1:5, 13) that the Nephites first began to develop "weapons of war" (Jarom 1:8).

315 Hassig, *War and Society*, 32.

316 Takeshi Inomata and Daniela Triadan, "Culture and Practice of War in Maya Society," in *Warfare in Cultural Context*, 66.

317 Sorenson, "Fortifications in the Book of Mormon," 429, table 2. As is sometimes done by Mesoamerican scholars, Sorenson splits the Late Preclassic into two periods: the Late Preclassic (400–50 BC) and the Protoclassic (50 BC–AD 200). He documented thirty fortifications for the Late Preclassic and twenty-six for the Protoclassic. To avoid confusion, since all others we have cited do not follow the Late Preclassic/Protoclassic division, we have combined Sorenson's numbers for the two periods and simply called it Late Preclassic. Since these numbers are from 1990, it is likely that there are now more from all periods of Mesoamerican history.

318 Sorenson, "Fortifications in the Book of Mormon," 430, table 3.

319 See Hassig, *War and Society*, 37; David L. Webster, *Defensive Earthworks at Becan, Camepeche, Mexico* (New Orleans, LA: Middle American Research Institute, Tulane University, 1976), 14–15, 88–91, 94–97. See also John L. Sorenson, "Digging in the Book of Mormon: Our Changing Understanding of Ancient America and Its Scripture," *Ensign*, September 1984; John L. Sorenson, *An Ancient American Setting for the Book of Mormon* (Salt Lake City and Provo, UT: Deseret Book and FARMS, 1985), 261–262; Sorenson, *Images of Ancient America*, 132–133; Daniel Johnson, Jared Cooper, and Derek Gasser, *An LDS Guide to Mesoamerica* (Springville, UT: Cedar Fort, 2008), 101–103 (sidebar); Joseph L. Allen and Blake L. Allen, *Exploring the Lands of the Book of Mormon*, rev. ed. (American Fork, UT: Covenant Communications, 2011), 598–602; Sorenson, *Mormon's Codex*, 405–410.

320 Again, this can be seen in Sorenson, "Fortifications in the Book of Mormon," 430, table 3.

321 For a fairly detailed treatment of fortifications in the Heartland region, see Jones, *Native North American Armor, Shields, and Fortifications*, 50–57, 125–135. Jones documented Native American forts in the Northeast and Southeast with earthen walls, palisades, and bastion towers. Scattered references to Mississippian fortifications can be seen in Charles R. Cobb and Bretton Giles, "War Is Shell: The Ideology Embodiment of Mississippian Conflict," in *Warfare in Cultural Context*, 88–91, mentioning palisades and ditches. Palisades, ditches, and bastions are mentioned in Thomas E. Emerson, "Cahokia Interaction and Ethnogenesis in the Northern Midcontinent," in *The Oxford Handbook of North American Archaeology*, ed. Timothy R. Pauketat (New York, NY: Oxford University Press, 2012), 402; Gregory D. Wilson, "Living with War: The Impact of Chronic Violence in the Mississippian-Period Central Illinois River Valley," in *Oxford Handbook of North American Archaeology*, 527–528; John E. Blitz, "Moundville in the Mississippian World," in *Oxford Handbook of North American Archaeology*, 539. Many earthworks in the region, with ditches and mound-like walls, have been mistaken for fortifications but are in fact not defensive sites. See Meghan C. L. Howey, "Regional Organization in the Northern Great Lakes, AD 1200–1600," in *Oxford Handbook of North American Archaeology*, 292–295; George R. Milner, "Mound-Building Societies of the Southern Midwest and Southeast," in *Oxford Handbook of North American Archaeology*, 438–440. Currently, the earliest evidence for fortifications in this region dates to AD 600–1000 (Jones, *Native North American Armor*, 125), while most evidence postdates AD 1000. According to Milner, "Mound-Building Societies," 445, "The Middle Woodland decline in hostilities is likely real—that is, not a result of poor sampling—because many skeletons have been examined." While the definition of Middle Woodland can vary between scholars, Milner defines it as ca. 200 BC–AD 400 (p. 437).

322 Bytheway, *Righteous Warriors*, 60.

323 M. Russell Ballard, "Be Strong in the Lord, and in the Power of His Might," fireside given at BYU on March 3, 2002.

324 See Ballard, "Be Strong in the Lord"; and Bytheway, *Righteous Warriors*, 59–67.

325 See Welch, *Legal Cases*, 12–13; Noel B. Reynolds, "Nephite Kingship Reconsidered," in *Mormons, Scripture, and the Ancient World: Studies in Honor*

of John L. Sorenson, ed. Davis Bitten (Provo UT: FARMS, 1998), 151–189; Jeffrey M. Bradshaw and Ronan James Head, "The Investiture Panel at Mari and Rituals of Divine Kingship in the Ancient Near East," *Studies in the Bible and Antiquity 4* (2012): 1–2, 25–28; Brant A. Gardner, *Traditions of the Fathers: The Book of Mormon as History* (Salt Lake City, UT: Greg Kofford Books, 2015), 267–268; Stephen Houston and David Stuart, "Of Gods, Glyphs and Kings: Divinity and Rulership among the Classic Maya," *Antiquity 70*, no. 268 (1996): 289–312. See also Welch, et al., *Knowing Why*, 296–297.

326 For other examples of writing delivered by the hand of the Lord, see Alma 10:2 and Daniel 5:5, 24–28.

327 See John A. Tvedtnes, *The Book of Mormon and Other Hidden Books: Out of Darkness Unto Light* (Provo, UT: FARMS, 2000), 33–35; H. Curtis Wright, "Ancient Burials of Metal Documents in Stone Boxes," in *By Study and Also by Faith: Essays in Honor of Hugh W. Nibley*, 2 vols., ed. John M. Lundquist and Stephen D. Ricks (Salt Lake City and Provo, UT: Deseret Book and FARMS, 1990), 2:273–334. For a correlation between the ark of the covenant and the sacred relics among the Nephites, see Don Bradley, "Piercing the Veil: Temple Worship in the Lost 116 Pages," 2012 FairMormon Conference presentation.

328 See William J. Hamblin, "Sacred Writing on Metal Plates in the Ancient Mediterranean," *FARMS Review 19*, no. 1 (2007): 37–54; Tvedtnes, *Book of Mormon and Other Hidden Books*, 145–154.

329 Welch, *Legal Cases*, 13.

330 Welch, *Legal Cases*, 13. For a more nuanced awareness of Nephite legal terminology, see John W. Welch, "Statutes, Judgments, Ordinances, and Commandments," in *Reexploring the Book of Mormon*, 62–65.

331 See RoseAnn Benson and Stephen D. Ricks, "Treaties and Covenants: Ancient Near Eastern Legal Terminology in the Book of Mormon," *Journal of Book of Mormon Studies 14*, no. 1 (2005): 48–61, 128–29; Stephen D. Ricks, "Kingship, Coronation, and Covenant in Mosiah 1–6," in *King Benjamin's Speech*, 233–275.

332 See chapter 23.

333 See Welch et al., *Knowing Why*, 244–245.

334 D. Todd Christofferson, "Religious Freedom—A Cherished Heritage to Defend," Freedom Festival speech, June 26, 2016.

335 Mormon's appraisal of Moroni's actions in this situation is clearly approving (see Alma 51:15–21). See chapter 24. See also Ryan W. Davis, "For the Peace of the People: War and Democracy in the Book of Mormon," *Journal of Book of Mormon Studies 16*, no. 1 (2007): 47: "Leaders like Moroni and Pahoran do not gain power arbitrarily. Rather, they have authority; their ability to use power is invested to them by a larger set of people (see Alma 43:17; 46:34). When kings rule without electoral consent, they may make war for personal reasons or for the benefit of a boisterous or influential minority."

336 Von G. Keetch, "An Example of the Believers," BYU-Idaho Devotional, June 14, 2016. For more information about the dramatized video presentation that Elder Keetch used in his address, see "Video Series Helps Mormons Defend Religious Freedom While Respecting Differences," accessed July 7, 2016 at mormonnewsroom.org.

337 For the Church's declaration of beliefs regarding government and law, see D&C 134. See also Spencer W. McBride, "Of Governments and Laws," in *Revelations in Context: The Stories behind the Sections of the Doctrine and Covenants*, ed. Matthew McBride and James Goldberg (Salt Lake City, UT: The Church of Jesus Christ of Latter-day Saints, 2016), 294–298.

338 For more references to pulling down pride, see Alma 4:19; 51:21; 60:36.

339 See Exodus 34:13; Leviticus 26:30; Judges 6:25, 28, 30; 2 Samuel 22:28; 1 Kings 8:32–33; 2 Kings 10:27; 18:4; 2 Chronicles 14:3; 15:16; 31:1; 34:4; Job 14:2; 40:12; Psalms 18:27; 20:8; 30:3; 37:2; 55:23; 59:11; 107:12; Isaiah 5:15; 14:11–12, 15; 22:19; 25:11–12; 43:14; 63:6; Jeremiah 1:10; 18:7; 24:6; 42:10; 51:40; Lamentations 2:2; Ezekiel 17:24; 26:20; 28:8; 31:18; Obadiah 1:4; Zechariah 10:11.

340 See 1 Nephi 13:9; 14:2, 7; 16:25; 18:17–18; 2 Nephi 1:7, 21; 2:29; 26:15; Jacob 6:7; Enos 1:10; Mosiah 7:28; Alma 4:19; 10:18; 12:6, 37; 13:30; 30:23, 47; 42:29–30; 51:21; Helaman 1:24; 6:5, 25; 14:19; 17:10; 3 Nephi 21:15; Ether 2:11; Moroni 8:14.

341 For similar imagery related to Babylon, see Isaiah 21:9; Revelation 14:8; 18:2; Doctrine and Covenants 1:16.

342 See chapter 112. See also Sorenson, *Mormon's Codex*, 370–371, 577; Robert Sharer, "Time of Kings and Queens," *Expedition 54*, no. 1 (2012): 27–28. For iconography depicting Mesoamerican rulers seated on elevated thrones, see Martin and Grube, *Chronicle of the Maya Kings and Queens*, 15, 60, 62, 77, 135, 143, 147, 149 153, 201.

343 For the comments about the rulers idly sitting on their thrones, see Alma 60:7, 11, 21–22.

344 The concept of dethroning a king is mentioned in Mosiah 29:21.

345 See Welch, et al., *Knowing Why*, 178–179.

346 See Kerry Hull, "War Banners: A Mesoamerican Context for the Title of Liberty," *Journal of Book of Mormon Studies 24* (2015): 84–118.

347 See chapter 23.

348 It is also notable that the phrase lifted up is associated with pride in many Book of Mormon passages. For a few examples, see 2 Nephi 28:12; Jacob 1:16; Mosiah 11:5, 19; Alma 31:25; Helaman 3:34; 3 Nephi 6:10; 4 Nephi 1:24; Mormon 8:28.

349 See Morgan Deane, "Experiencing Battle in the Book of Mormon," *Interpreter: A Journal of Mormon Scripture 23* (2017): 240. For a broader, cross-cultural treatment of this same phenomenon, see Sarah Ralph, ed., *The Archaeology of Violence: Interdisciplinary Approaches* (Albany, NY: State University of New York Press, 2012).

350 Martin and Grube, *Chronicle of the Maya Kings and Queens*, 153.

351 David A. Freidel, Barbara MacLeod, and Charles K. Suhler, "Early Classic Maya Conquest in Words and Deeds," in *Ancient Mesoamerican Warfare*, ed. M. Kathryn Brown and Travis W. Stanton (Oxford, UK: Alta Mira Press, 2003), 196.

352 Geoffrey G. McCafferty, "Ethnic Conflict in Postclassic Cholula, Mexico," in *Ancient Mesoamerican Warfare*, 233. Although this example significantly post-dates Book of Mormon times, it helps demonstrate that ritual desecration was an enduring cultural phenomenon in pre-Columbian Mesoamerica.

353 Martin and Grube, *Chronicle of the Maya Kings and Queens*, 153.

354 Gyles Iannone, "The Rise and Fall of an Ancient Maya Petty Royal Court," *Latin American Antiquity 16*, no. 1 (2005): 39; citing David Stuart, "Historical Inscriptions and the Maya Collapse," in *Lowland Maya Civilization in the Eighth Century A.D.*, ed. Jeremy A. Sabloff and John S. Henderson (Washington, D.C.: Dumbarton Oaks Research Library and Collection, 1991–1992), 346.

355 Ezra Taft Benson, "Beware of Pride," *Ensign*, May 1989.

356 Dieter F. Uchtdorf, "Pride and the Priesthood," *Ensign*, November 2010, 56.

357 See Book of Mormon Central, "Why Did Mormon Say the Children of Men Are Less than the Dust of the Earth? (Helaman 12:7)," *KnoWhy 183* (September 8, 2016).

358 See chapter 72. See also Matthew L. Bowen, "'They Came and Held Him by the Feet and Worshipped Him': Proskynesis before Jesus in Its Biblical and Ancient Near Eastern Context," *Studies in the Bible and Antiquity 5* (2013): 63–68; Matthew L. Bowen, "'They Came Forth and Fell Down and Partook of the Fruit of the Tree': Proskynesis in 3 Nephi 11:12–19 and 17:9–10 and Its Significance," in *Third Nephi: An Incomparable Scripture* (Salt Lake City and Provo, UT: Deseret Book and Neal A. Maxwell Institute for Religious Scholarship, 2012), 107–130; Matthew L. Bowen, "'And Behold, They Had

Fallen to the Earth': An Examination of Proskynesis in the Book of Mormon," *Studia Antiqua 4*, no. 1 (2005): 91–110.

359 For a similar concept, see Matthew 11:11; Luke 7:28; Doctrine and Covenants 50:26.

360 The wording and punctuation here slightly varies from current editions of the Book of Mormon but follows Royal Skousen, ed., *The Book of Mormon: The Earliest Text* (New Haven, CT: Yale University Press, 2009), 464.

361 Robert F. Smith and Stephen D. Ricks, "New Year's Celebrations," in *Reexploring the Book of Mormon*, 209.

362 Taylor Halverson, "In Cover of Darkness and the Turning of the New Year," *Deseret News*, January 1, 2015.

363 Sorenson, *An Ancient American Setting for the Book of Mormon*, 275. See also A. Brent Merrill, "Nephite Captains and Armies," in *Warfare in the Book of Mormon*, 275; John L. Sorenson, "The Book of Mormon as a Mesoamerican Record," in *Book of Mormon Authorship Revisited*, 410; Sorenson, *Images of Ancient America*, 166; Sorenson, *Mormon's Codex*, 194, 441.

364 All quotes from Christenson come from Allen J. Christenson, "Maya Harvest Festivals and the Book of Mormon," *Review of Books on the Book of Mormon 3* (1991): 30. See also Allen J. Christenson, "The Dance of First Beginnings: Contemporary Maya Creation Rituals in a World Context," *BYU Studies 39, no. 2* (2000): 150–172.

365 Halverson, "In Cover of Darkness."

366 Daniel C. Peterson, "May Your New Year Begin Better than Amalickiah's," *Deseret News*, December 29, 2011.

367 Halverson, "In Cover of Darkness."

368 John W. Welch, "Law and War in the Book of Mormon," in *Warfare in the Book of Mormon*, 65.

369 Welch, "Law and War," 66; Stephen D. Ricks, "'Holy War': The Sacral Ideology of War in the Book of Mormon and in the Ancient Near East," in *Warfare in the Book of Mormon*, 108–109; John A. Tvedtnes, "What Were the Ages of Helaman's Stripling Warriors?," *Ensign*, September 1992, 28.

370 As the leader of the Church in Zarahemla, Helaman was the one who could assure the Ammonites that their sons were not bound by their father's covenant. This may be why they chose him as their leader.

371 Welch, "Law and War in the Book of Mormon," 66.

372 Noah Webster, *An American Dictionary of the English Language* (New York: S. Converse, 1828), s.v., "stripling." See also Bytheway, *Righteous Warriors*, 106.

373 See Gardner, *Second Witness*, 4:686.

374 One interesting modern-day application can be seen in Kammayer, *The Art of Nephite War*, chapter 19, which focuses on the application to Latter-day Saint soldiers.

375 Clyde James Williams, "Amalickiah," in *Book of Mormon Reference Companion*, 45.

376 See chapter 30.

377 See Brant A. Gardner, *Traditions of the Fathers: The Book of Mormon as History* (Salt Lake City, UT: Greg Kofford Books, 2015), 188–189.

378 Morris Jastrow Jr., "Avenger of Blood," in *Jewish Encyclopedia*. A *sept* is an archaic term synonymous with clan or family. Compare "Blood-Avenger," in *Encyclopedia Judaica*, jewishvirtuallibrary.org.

379 Ze'ev W. Falk, *Hebrew Law in Biblical Times* (Provo, UT and Winona Lake, IN: BYU Press and Eisenbrauns, 2001), 72.

380 Ludwig Koehler and Walter Baumgartner, *The Hebrew and Aramaic Lexicon of the Old Testament*, 2 vols. (Leiden: Brill, 2001), 1:169.

381 David Ewert, "Avenger of Blood," in *The Oxford Companion to the Bible*, ed. Bruce M. Metzger and Michael D. Coogan (New York, NY: Oxford University Press, 1993), 68; Bernhard W. Anderson, *Understanding the Old Testament*, abridged 4th ed. (Upper Saddle River, NJ: Prentice–Hall, 1998), 430–431. Other duties of a goel included redeeming property, including family sold into debt slavery (see Leviticus 25:25, 47–55; Jeremiah 32:6–12), and marrying the widow of a close family member (see Deuteronomy 25:5–10; Ruth 3–4).

382 For altars as places of refuge, see Welch, et al., *Knowing Why*, 282–283.

383 See chapter 24.

384 See Richard Dilworth Rust, "Book of Mormon Literature," *Encyclopedia of Mormonism*, 1:181–185. See also Hardy, *Understanding the Book of Mormon*, xv, 6–7.

385 See Hardy, *Understanding the Book of Mormon*, 123, 176. See also Kim Ridealgh, "Polite like an Egyptian? Case Studies of Politeness in the Late Ramesside Letters," *Journal of Politeness Research: Language, Behavior, Culture 12*, no. 2 (2016): 247. It should be noted, though, that Mormon was not completely averse to making editorial alterations to recorded epistles. For example, in Helaman's lengthy letter to Moroni, Mormon inserts at least one verse of commentary, likely for the purpose of summarizing information (Alma 55:52).

386 The exchange between Moroni and Ammoron is clearly a military-related epistle; the Book of Mormon also contains examples of two other epistolary forms: pastoral and prophetic. For an analysis of these forms in the Book of Mormon, see Sidney B. Sperry, "Types of Literature in the Book of Mormon: Epistles, Psalms, Lamentations," *Journal of Book of Mormon Studies 4*, no. 1 (1995): 69–80. See also Robert F. Smith, "Epistolary Form in the Book of Mormon," *FARMS Review 22*, no. 2 (2010): 125–126 for a comprehensive list of all Book of Mormon epistles.

387 See Richard Dilworth Rust, *Feasting on the Word: The Literary Testimony of the Book of Mormon* (Salt Lake City and Provo, UT: Deseret Book and FARMS, 1997), 150.

388 Rust, *Feasting on the Word*, 151. For a more formal analysis of Moroni's rhetorical strategy, see Rust, *Feasting on the Word*, 152–153.

389 See Helaman 3:14; Words of Mormon 1:5.

390 See Hardy, *Understanding the Book of Mormon*, 175–177.

391 See Rust, *Feasting on the Word*, 154, for an analysis of the narrative ironies in the Nephites' success against the armies of Ammoron.

392 President Gordon B. Hinckley taught that anger, when controlled, can sometimes be appropriate. See Gordon B. Hinckley, "Slow to Anger," *Ensign*, November 2007, 62–65: "Anger may be justified in some circumstances. The scriptures tell us that Jesus drove the moneychangers from the temple, saying, 'My house shall be called the house of prayer; but ye have made it a den of thieves' (Matthew 21:13). But even this was spoken more as a rebuke than as an outburst of uncontrolled anger."

393 David A. Bednar, "'Chosen to Bear Testimony of My Name,'" *Ensign*, November 2015, 128–131.

394 See chapter 24.

395 See Hugh Nibley, *Since Cumorah,* 291–333; Hugh Nibley, "Warfare and the Book of Mormon," in *Warfare in the Book of Mormon*, 127–145; William J. Hamblin, "The Importance of Warfare in Book of Mormon Studies," in *Warfare in the Book of Mormon*, 481–499, reprinted in *Book of Mormon Authorship Revisited*, ed. Noel B. Reynolds (Provo, UT: FARMS, 1997), 523–543; Kammeyer, *The Nephite Art of War*; John E. Kammeyer, *Warfare in Mesoamerica: Battles in the Book of Mormon* (Far West Publications, 2012); Bell, *Defenders of the Faith*; Deane, *Bleached Bones and Wicked Serpents*; Spencer, *Captain Moroni's Command.*

396 For Nibley's time in the military, see Boyd Jay Petersen, *Hugh Nibley: A Consecrated Life* (Salt Lake City, UT: Greg Kofford Book, 2002), 167–222.

397 Nibley, *Since Cumorah*, 291.

398 Nibley, *Since Cumorah*, 292. The full quote is: "The author writes as one would write—as only one could write—who had gone through a long war as a

front-line observer with his eyes wide open. Everything is strictly authentic, with the proper emphasis in the proper place. Strategy and tactics are treated with the knowledge of an expert: logistics and supply; armaments and fortifications; recruiting and training; problems of morale and support from the home front; military intelligence from cloak and dagger to scouting and patrolling; interrogation, guarding, feeding, and exchange of war prisoners; propaganda and psychological warfare; rehabilitation and resettlement; feelers for peace and negotiations at various levels; treason; profiteering; and the exploitation of the war economy by individuals and groups—it is all there."

399 Kammeyer, *The Nephite Art of War*, 182.

400 Hamblin, "The Importance of Warfare in Book of Mormon Studies," 496.

401 Morgan Deane, *Decisive Battles in Chinese History* (Yardley, PA: Westholme Publishing, 2018).

402 Deane, *Bleached Bones*, 91.

403 Spencer, *Moroni's Command*, 91.

404 For what Joseph Smith could have known about military theory, see Kammeyer, *The Nephite Art of War*, chapter 1.

405 For his experience creating battle simulations, see Spencer, *Moroni's Command*, 4.

406 Spencer, *Moroni's Command*, 91.

407 See Deane, *Bleached Bones*, for application of Book of Mormon war principles to modern military practice and policy. For Latter-day Saint perspectives on war, see Patrick Q. Mason, J. David Pulsipher, and Richard L. Bushman, eds., *War and Peace in Our Time: Mormon Perspectives* (Salt Lake City, UT: Greg Kofford Books, 2012); Duane Boyce, *Even unto Bloodshed: An LDS Perspective on War* (Salt Lake City, UT: Greg Kofford Books, 2015).

408 Kammeyer, *The Nephite Art of War*, 182.

409 A popular Latter-day Saint hymn for youth includes the lines, "We are as the army of Helaman; We have been taught in our youth." See Janice Kapp Perry, "We'll Bring the World His Truth (Army of Helaman)," in *Children's Songbook* (Salt Lake City, UT: The Church of Jesus Christ of Latter-day Saints, 1989), 172.

410 On the probable age of the stripling warriors, see chapter 31.

411 Welch, et al., *Knowing Why*, 268–269.

412 David F. Evans, "Tenacity and Discipleship," *Ensign*, June 2016, 20.

413 See Welch, et al., *Knowing Why*, 305–306. Under Jewish law, those who were exempted from serving on the front lines of battle were still required to serve "in the rear: 'They must furnish water and food and repair the roads'"; see John W. Welch, "Exemption from Military Duty," in *Reexploring the Book of Mormon*, 191.

414 Sorenson, *Mormon's Codex*, 381–425. For a more thorough treatment of logistics in Nephite warfare, see, Kammeyer, *The Nephite Art of War*, 72–80.

415 Gardner, *Traditions of the Fathers*, 294; see also Welch et al., *Knowing Why*, 291–292. According to Kitty F. Emery, "A Zooarchaeological Test for Dietary Resource Depression at the End of the Classic Period in the Petexbatun, Guatemala," *Human Ecology 36*, no. 5 (2008): 620, "the only domestic Maya animal during the classic period was the dog." John L. Sorensen paints a much more complex and potentially expansive picture of animal domestication in ancient Mesoamerica, but in either case there seems to be no evidence of domesticated animals being used in a military context. See Sorenson, *Mormon's Codex*, 309–321. See also Kammeyer, *Nephite Art of War*, 74–75.

416 See Ashley E. Sharpe and Kitty F. Emery, "Differential Animal Use within Three Late Classic Maya States: Implications for Politics and Trade," *Journal of Anthropological Archaeology 40* (2015): 287; Stanley Serafin, Carlos Peraza Lope, and Eunice Uc González, "Bioarchaeological Investigation of Ancient Maya Violence and Warfare in Inland Northwest Yucatan, Mexico," *American Journal of Physical Anthropology 154*, no. 1 (2014): 143; Gardner, *Traditions of Fathers*, 294; Kammeyer, *Nephite Art of War*, 72–74.

417 See Traci Ardren and Justin Lowry, "The Travels of Maya Merchants in the Ninth and Tenth Centuries AD: Investigations at Xuenkal and the Greater Cupul Province, Yucatan, Mexico," *World Archeology 43*, no. 3 (2016): 429: "Both overland and sea transport relied upon human carriers; there were no domesticated pack animals in Classic times and depictions of ancient traders wearing heavy back racks full of items are known from elite pottery and native books."

418 A biblical example of a family member personally carrying supplies to soldiers in the field can be seen in young David taking provisions to his brothers who were marshaled to war against the Philistines (see 1 Samuel 17:23). For a brief treatment of this narrative in the context of siege warfare, see Paul Bently Kern, *Ancient Siege Warfare* (Bloomington, IN: Indiana University Press, 1999), 36.

419 To consider general possibilities for the supply of Nephite armaments, see Kammeyer, *Nephite Art of War*, 75–80; William J. Hamblin and A. Brent Merrill, "Swords in the Book of Mormon," in *Warfare in the Book of Mormon*, 329–351; Paul Y. Hoskisson, "Scimitars, Cimeters! We Have Scimitars! Do We Need Another Cimeter?," in *Warfare in Book of Mormon*, 352–359; William J. Hamblin and A. Brent Merrill, "Notes on the Cimeter (Scimitar) in the Book of Mormon," in *Warfare in Book of Mormon*, 360–364; William J. Hamblin, "The Bow and Arrow in the Book of Mormon," in *Warfare in Book of Mormon*, 365–399; William J. Hamblin, "Armor in the Book of Mormon," in *Warfare in Book of Mormon*, 400–424. It has been suggested by several scholars that Nephite weapons would likely have utilized obsidian for blades and arrow points. However, it seems that during battle these brittle, though very sharp, blades and points would have been prone to breakages and fractures, thus needing to be replaced. See, for example, Marco Antonio Cervera Obregón, "The Macuahuitl: An Innovative Weapon of the Late Post-Classic in Mesoamerica," *Arms & Armour 3*, no. 2 (2006): 145–146. For an argument that the macuahuitl (an ancient Mesoamerican sword with inserts for obsidian blades) was in use during the Book of Mormon times, see Matthew Roper, "Swords and 'Cimeters' in the Book of Mormon," *Journal of Book of Mormon Studies 8*, no. 1 (1999): 37–38. For general information about obsidian as an item of trade and industry in ancient Mesoamerica, see C. E. Ebert, M. Dennison, K. G. Hierth, S. B. McClure and D. J. Kennett, "Formative Period Obsidian Exchange Along the Pacific Coast of Mesoamerica," *Archaeometry 57*, no. 1 (2015): 54–73; Barbara L. Stark, et al., "Economic growth in Mesoamerica: Obsidian consumption in the coastal lowlands," *Journal of Anthropological Archaeology 41* (2016): 263–282.

420 D. Todd Christofferson, "Give Us This Day Our Daily Bread," CES Fireside for Young Adults, delivered at Brigham Young University, January 9, 2011.

421 See chapter 38.

422 L. Whitney Clayton, "Blessed Are All the Pure in Heart," *Ensign*, November 2007, 52–53.

423 Robert F. Smith, "Epistolary Form in the Book of Mormon," *FARMS Review 22*, no. 2 (2010): 127.

424 Larry W. Tippetts, "Toward Emotional Maturity: Insights from the Book of Mormon," *Religious Educator 11*, no. 2 (2010): 96.

425 See chapter 24.

426 Dieter F. Uchtdorf, "Come, Join with Us," *Ensign*, November 2013, 22–23.

427 For pot impurity amid the Jewish community at Elephantine, four centuries before Christ, see Bezazel Porten and Ada Yardeni, "Ostracon Clermont-Ganneau 125: A Case of Ritual Purity," *Journal of the American Oriental Society 113* (1993): 451–456.

428 See also Matthew 15:1–9; 23:26–27. These verses seem to suggest that

while the Pharisees were strict to follow the traditional statutes concerning vessel impurity, they were not following the more weighty commandments of God.

429 See Jacob Neusner, *A History of the Mishnaic Law of Purities, Part 3: Kelim* (Leiden: Brill, 1974): 374–381; Mishnah Kelim 2:1; TB Hullim 24b; Sipra, Shemini 7:6; Jacob Milgrom, *Leviticus 1–16* (New York, NY: Doubleday, 1991), 675.

430 See *Gospel of Thomas 89*:1–2; Gospel Oxyrhynchus fragment 840 2:8. See also Robert W. Funk, Roy W. Hoover, and the Jesus Seminar, eds., *The Five Gospels: The Search for the Authentic Words of Jesus* (New York, NY: Polebridge and Macmillan, 1993), 243.

431 See Welch, et al., *Knowing Why*, 134–135.

432 See Donald W. Parry, "Service and Temple in King Benjamin's Speech," *Journal of Book of Mormon Studies 16*, no. 2 (2007): 45; Donald W. Parry, "Demarcation Between Sacred Space and Profane Space: the Temple of Herod Model," in *Temples of the Ancient World*, 428; Hugh Nibley, *Mormonism and Early Christianity, The Collected Works of Hugh Nibley: Volume 4* (Salt Lake City and Provo UT: Deseret Book and FARMS, 1987), 394.

433 Interestingly, Alma 5:19 reverses the order of hands before hearts: "I say unto you, can ye look up to God at that day with *a pure heart and clean hands*? I say unto you, can you look up, having the image of God engraven upon your countenances?" (emphasis added).

434 Parry, "Demarcation of Space," 414.

435 See David A. Bednar, "Clean Hands and a Pure Heart," *Ensign*, November 2007, 82.

436 John W. Welch, *The Sermon at the Temple and the Sermon on the Mount: A Latter-day Saint Approach* (Salt Lake City and Provo, UT: Deseret Book and FARMS, 1990), 45.

437 See Psalms 24:4–5; D&C 97:21. See also Ezra Taft Benson, "Cleansing the Inner Vessel," *Ensign*, May 1986.

438 See chapter 30.

439 Ted L. Gibbons, "Teancum," in *Book of Mormon Reference Companion*, 753.

440 George Reynolds and Janne Sjodahl, *Commentary on the Book of Mormon*, 7 vols. (Salt Lake City, UT: Deseret Book, 1955–1976), 5:178.

441 Gardner, *Second Witness*, 4:762.

442 Thomas S. Monson, "School Thy Feelings, O My Brother," *Ensign*, November 2009, 68. See also Gordon B. Hinckley, "Slow to Anger," *Ensign*, November 2007, 62–63, 66.

443 See chapter 64.

444 Although Mormon was certainly responsible for recording this historical summary in the Book of Mormon, it is not clear whether he was its original author.

445 For another example of the Book of Mormon's use of chiasmus in its summaries of historical content, see chapter 48.

446 Throughout the Bible and Book of Mormon, the concept of remembrance is often associated with keeping the commandments. See Book of Mormon Central, "Why Did Helaman Want His Sons to Remember to Build upon the Rock? (Helaman 5:12)," *KnoWhy 332* (June 28, 2017); Louis Midgley, "To Remember and Keep: On the Book of Mormon as an Ancient Book," in *The Disciple as Scholar: Essays on Scripture and the Ancient World in Honor of Richard Lloyd Anderson*, ed. Stephen D. Ricks, Donald W. Parry, and Andrew H. Hedges (Provo, UT: FARMS, 2000), 95–137; Louis Midgley, "The Ways of Remembrance," in *Rediscovering the Book of Mormon,* 168–176; Louis Midgley, "'O Man, Remember, and Perish Not' (Mosiah 4:30)," in *Reexploring the Book of Mormon*, 127–129.

447 See Welch, et al., *Knowing Why*, 268–269.

448 See chapter 13.

449 For further examples of how chiasmus can help us better understand the Book of Mormon, see Book of Mormon Central, "What Can We Learn from 10 of the Best Chiasms in the Book of Mormon? Part 1," *KnoWhy 349* (August 7, 2017); Book of Mormon Central, "What Can We Learn from 10 of the Best Chiasms in the Book of Mormon? Part 2," *KnoWhy 352* (August 14, 2017); Book of Mormon Central, "What Can We Learn from 10 of the Best Chiasms in the Book of Mormon? Part 3 (Alma 36:18)," *KnoWhy 355* (August 20, 2017).

450 Joseph B. Wirthlin, "Journey to Higher Ground," *Ensign*, November 2005.

451 See Welch et al., *Knowing Why*, 223–224. See also, Gerrit W. Gong, "Always Remember Him," *Ensign*, May 2016.

452 See "HAGOTH," in *Book of Mormon Onomasticon*, ed. Paul Y. Hoskisson, online at https://onoma.lib.byu.edu/index.php/Main_Page. See also, John A. Tvedtnes, "Curious Hagoth," *Meridian Magazine: Latter-day Saints Shaping Their World*, September 20, 2010.

453 See Sorenson, *Mormon's Codex*, 136–137, 358–360, 630–631, for a proposal of possible ship constructions as well as Hagoth's departure location.

454 Alma 63:9 could be argued to be somewhat ambiguous as to the mode of travel: "And it came to pass that in this year there were many people who went forth into the land northward." Within the immediate context of sea voyages and the building of more ships, it's possible to assume that the people who "went forth" were actually sailing forth. However, it should be remembered that land migration is also part of this context (see Alma 63:4), and that Mormon had just reported that "one other ship also did sail forth; and whither she did go we know not" (Alma 63:8). After this he introduced the next details about migration with the phrase "And it came to pass" (Alma 63:9), which often acts as a marker between separate ideas. It would seem odd for Mormon to explicitly mention "one other ship" (which has a tone of finality to it) and remark on its uncertain fate, and then report an additional seafaring journey without even mentioning that it was by ship. Because of the difficulty of such a reading, it seems much more likely that this chapter's final—though unspecified—mention of a journey northward was by land rather than by sea. This point is relevant because two northward land migrations within a short period of time holds greater implications for Nephite territorial expansion.

455 For an analysis of the term *northward* as used in the Book of Mormon, see Brant A. Gardner, "From the East to the West: The Problem of Directions in the Book of Mormon," *Interpreter: A Journal of Mormon Scripture 3* (2013): 148–149; John L. Sorenson, *Mormon's Map* (Provo, UT: FARMS, 2000), 78–81. See also Welch, et al., *Knowing Why*, 300–301.

456 For a treatment of oceanic voyages in the Americas, see John L. Sorenson, *Transoceanic Voyaging: How Ancient America Became Civilized* (unpublished manuscript, 2013), 11–14; see also Sorenson, *Mormon's Codex*, 150–172.

457 There is textual ambiguity as to whether Hagoth actually boarded any of his vessels. Alma 63:7 reports, "And in the thirty and eighth year, this man [Hagoth] built other ships. And the first ship did also return, and many more people did enter into it; and they also took much provisions, and set out again to the land northward." From this sparse statement, it simply cannot be determined if Hagoth himself was part of the "many more people" who again sailed northward.

458 Russel T. Clement, "Polynesian Origins: More Word on the Mormon Perspective," *Dialogue: A Journal of Mormon Thought 13* (Winter 1980): 91.

459 See Clement, "Polynesian Origins," 92–97; Robert E. Parsons, "Hagoth and the Polynesians," in *The Book of Mormon: Alma, the Testimony of the Word*, ed. Monte S. Nyman and Charles D. Tate Jr. (Provo, UT: BYU Religious Studies Center, 1992), 250–258.

460 See Eric B. Shumway, "Polynesians," *Encyclopedia of Mormonism*,

1:1110–1112; Jerry K. Loveland, "Hagoth and the Polynesian Tradition," *BYU Studies 17*, no. 1 (Autumn 1976): 59–73; Ian G. Barber, "Matakite, Mormon Conversions, and Māori-Israelite Identity Work in Colonial New Zealand," *Journal of Mormon History 41*, no. 3 (July 2015): 167–220; Grant Underwood, "Mormonism, the Maori and Cultural Authenticity," *Journal of Pacific History 35*, no. 2 (2000): 133–146; Louis Midgley, "A Māori View of the Book of Mormon," *Journal of Book of Mormon Studies 8*, no. 1 (1999): 4–11, 77; Louis Midgley, "Māori Latter-day Saint Faith: Some Preliminary Remarks," *Interpreter: A Journal of Mormon Scripture 8* (2014): 45–65; Louis Midgley, "The Māori Stairway to Heaven," *Interpreter: A Journal of Mormon Scripture 12* (2014): 97–110; Louis Midgley, "A Singular Reading: The Maori and the Book of Mormon," in *Mormons, Scripture, and the Ancient World: Studies in Honor of John L. Sorenson*, ed. Davis Bitton (Provo, UT: FARMS, 1998), 245–276.

461 Parsons, "Hagoth and Polynesians," 250–251: "In a letter to the mission president of the Samoan Mission dated September 6, 1972, and signed by N. Eldon Tanner and Marion G. Romney, under the letterhead of the First Presidency, they wrote: 'In your letter of September 6, 1972, you ask if the Polynesian people are Lamanites or Nephites. There has been much speculation about the origin of these people. We have, however, no scriptural evidence or revelation from the Lord that would tell us exactly where these people came from or their background.'"

462 Hardy, *Understanding the Book of Mormon*, 207.

463 For possible linguistic connections related to Hagoth's voyagers, see Brian D. Stubbs and John L. Sorenson, "Was There Hebrew Language in Ancient America? An Interview with Brian Stubbs," *Journal of Book of Mormon Studies 9*, no. 2 (2000): 62; Brian D. Stubbs, "A Few Hundred Hints of Egyptian and Northwest Semitic in Uto-Aztecan," presentation given at the 2006 FairMormon conference; Brian D. Stubbs, *Exploring the Explanatory Power of Semitic and Egyptian in Uto-Aztecan* (Provo, UT: Grover Publications, 2015), 359–362.

464 For example, Nephi discussed the scattering as something that would happen "sooner or later" and elaborated on "all those who shall hereafter be scattered" (1 Nephi 22:3–5).

465 For indications of increasing prosperity tied to migrations and free commerce, see Helaman 6:6–9.

466 Sorenson, *Mormon's Codex*, 51–53.

467 As is implied in Mormon 1:6.

468 For possible implications of northward expansion, see Mark Alan Wright, "Heartland as Hinterland: The Mesoamerican Core and North American Periphery of Book of Mormon Geography," *Interpreter: A Journal of Mormon Scripture 13* (2015): 111–129; Tyler Livingston, "The Book of Mormon and Mesoamerican Travels 'Northward,'" *Book of Mormon Archeological Forum*, January 2011. See also chapter 47.

469 See Welch, et al., *Knowing Why*, 244–245.

470 As noted by Hugh Nibley, all three of these names have plausible Egyptian etymologies. See Hugh Nibley, *Lehi in the Desert/The World of the Jaredites/There Were Jaredites, The Collected Works of Hugh Nibley: Volume 5* (Salt Lake City and Provo, UT: Deseret Book and FARMS, 1988), 22–23.

471 Richard L. Bushman, "The Book of Mormon and the American Revolution," in *Book of Mormon Authorship: New Light on Ancient Origins*, ed. Noel B. Reynolds (Provo, UT: BYU Religious Studies Center, 1982; reprinted by FARMS, 1996), 201.

472 Gardner, *Second Witness*, 5:41.

473 Gardner, *Second Witness*, 5:41–42

474 For a legal analysis of these events and proceedings, see Welch, *Legal Cases*, 311–322.

475 Gardner, *Second Witness*, 5:45.

476 Grant Hardy has noted that the way Mormon clarified the relationship between the Gadianton robbers and the entire destruction of his people is unusually explicit. See Hardy, *Understanding the Book of Mormon*, 162–163.

477 See also Richard Dilworth Rust, "'I Know Your Doing': The Book of Mormon Speaks to Our Times," *Ensign*, December 1988.

478 Russell M. Nelson, "Sustaining the Prophets," *Ensign*, November 2014, 75.

479 Gary E. Stevenson, "Where Are the Keys and Authority of the Priesthood?" *Ensign*, May 2016, 32.

480 See chapter 42.

481 See Alma 51:9: "And it came to pass that there were four thousand of those dissenters who were hewn down by the sword; and those of their leaders who were not slain in battle were taken and cast into prison, for there was no time for their trials at this period."

482 It does not matter where in the story the phrase appears or to what it refers—the simple presence of the phrase shows that one story should be read in light of the other story. See Peter J. Leithart, *Deep Exegesis: The Mystery of Reading Scripture* (Waco, TX: Baylor University Press, 2009), 109–115; Phyllis A. Bird, *Missing Persons and Mistaken Identities: Women and Gender in Ancient Israel* (Minneapolis, MN: Augsburg Fortress, 1997), 198; H. G. M. Williamson, "Isaiah 62:4 and the Problem of Inner-Biblical Allusions," *Journal of Biblical Literature 119* (2000): 734–739.

483 Yairah Amit, *Hidden Polemics in Biblical Narrative*, trans. Jonathan Chipman, BibInt 25 (Leiden: Brill, 2000), 42.

484 See Alma 51:34.

485 Welch, *Legal Cases*, 319.

486 Frances Reynolds, *The Babylonian Correspondence of Esarhaddon and Letters to Assurbanipal and Sin-s̆arru-is̆kun from Northern and Central Babylonia* (SAA 18; Helsinki: Helsinki University Press, 2003), 82. Available online through SAAO: State Archives of Assyria Online "SAA 18 100: Your Son Will Kill You! (ABL 1091)": "When they heard about the [tre]aty of rebellion which [. . .], one o[f them] ap[pealed] to the king before . . . Nabû-s'uma-is'kun and Ṣi[llaya] came and ques[tioned him]: '[What] is your appeal to the king ab[out]?' He (answered): 'It is about Arda-[Mullissi].' Th[ey covered] his face with his cloak and made him stand before Arda-Mul[lissi himself], saying: 'Look! [Your appeal] is being granted, say it with your own mouth!' He said: 'Your son Arda-[Mullissi] will kill you.' They uncovered [his] face, and after Arda-Mu[llissi] had interrogated him, th[ey]" appear to then kill the servant and his family.

487 It is also possible that Kishkumen may have been a formidable opponent. In any attempt to incapacitate Kishkumen, Helaman's servant might have been injured or killed, and Helaman would have been killed shortly thereafter. Killing Kishkumen quickly may have been the only way to save Helaman. In addition, the servant couldn't have let Kishkumen out of his sight to warn other guards because then he might have lost track of him. Because Kishkumen was on his way to kill Helaman, the servant may have not had enough time to warn someone of the plan. The servant's only option was to kill Kishkumen.

488 1 Samuel 17:46 is also a close verbal parallel to the Laban story. See Ben McGuire, "Nephi and Goliath: A Case Study of Literary Allusion in the Book of Mormon," *Journal of the Book of Mormon and Other Restoration Scripture 18*, no. 1 (2009): 16–31.

489 See John W. Welch, "Legal Perspectives on the Slaying of Laban," *Journal of Book of Mormon Studies 1*, no. 1 (1992): 133.

490 Generally, two witnesses were needed before a conviction could be obtained, but the Rabbis concluded that this law did not apply in the case of confessions outside of court and when evidence is physically present. Thus, if this rabbinical ruling actually goes back to earlier times, it is possible that it is being reflected here, because the potential murder weapon was likely physically

present (in Kishkumen's possession) at this point, and because he confessed outside of court without being pressured. One sees something like this as far back as Joshua 7:20–21 when a man named Achan condemned himself by confessing that he had done something worthy of death and was summarily executed. Kishkumen's case is similar to this in some ways. See Welch, *Legal Cases*, 332–333.

491 See Welch, *Legal Cases*, 319: "Apparently, these oath-swearing conspirators—like robbers or outlaws who had placed themselves outside the law and therefore were not entitled to its protections (compare the summary execution of the robber Zemnarihah in 3 Nephi 4:28)—were held incontestably guilty upon arrest. Once again, the law that required more than mere intent must have been satisfied by the element of the conspirator's oath."

492 Hermann Gunkel, *The Legends of Genesis: The Biblical Saga and History*, trans. W. H. Carruth (New York, NY: Schocken Books, 1975), 60–61.

493 See chapter 42.

494 See Matthew G. Wells and John W. Welch, "Concrete Evidence for the Book of Mormon," in *Reexploring the Book of Mormon*, 212–214; John L. Sorenson, "How Could Joseph Smith Write So Accurately about Ancient American Civilization?," in *Echoes and Evidences*, 287–288; John W. Welch, "A Steady Stream of Significant Recognitions," in *Echoes and Evidences*, 372–374.

495 In a letter written to President Heber J. Grant dated March 1, 1932, B. H. Roberts shared some sources from the late eighteenth and early nineteenth century that mentioned the use of cement in the construction of buildings by pre-Columbian Native Americans. A copy of this letter is in the possession of Book of Mormon Central.

496 David S. Hyman, *Precolumbian Cements: A Study of the Calcareous Cements in Prehispanic Mesoamerican Building Construction* (doctoral dissertation, The John Hopkins University, 1970), ii.

497 Hyman, *Precolumbian Cements*, ii; sec. 6, 15.

498 Matthew G. Wells, "Cement in Ancient Mesoamerica: A Survey," unpublished manuscript, October 1991 (updated February 1998), 2. A copy of this report is in the possession of Book of Mormon Central.

499 Coe and Houston, *The Maya*, 81.

500 Coe and Houston, *The Maya*, 81. The full quote mentions "rubble and marl," which is a "lime-rich mud or mudstone which contains variable amounts of clays and silt." See Wikipedia, s.v., "Marl."

501 Coe and Houston, *The Maya*, 81.

502 Rene Millon and James A. Bennyhoff, "A Long Architectural Sequence at Teotihuacán," *American Antiquity 26*, no. 4 (1961): 516–523; Rebecca Sload, "Radiocarbon Dating of Teotihucán Mapping Project TE28," *FAMSI*, 2007, each mention finding charcoal underneath concrete structures that was radiocarbon dated to ca. 50 BC–AD 110, although both dated the use of concrete at their respective sites to later phases of development. For Latter-day Saint discussion connecting Teotihuacán to the land northward, see John L. Sorenson, *An Ancient American Setting for the Book of Mormon* (Salt Lake City and Provo, UT: Deseret Book and FARMS, 1985), 266–267; Allen and Allen, *Exploring the Lands of the Book of Mormon*, 193–213; Gardner, *Traditions of the Fathers*, 327–337.

503 This story is related in Heber J. Grant, Conference Report, April 1929, 129; cited in Matthew Roper, "Exceedingly Expert in the Working of Cement (Howlers #9)," *Ether's Cave: A Place for Book of Mormon Research*, July 1, 2013, online at etherscave.blogspot.com (accessed August 8, 2016). Roberts to Grant, March 1, 1932, identified the antagonist as a Mr. Morgan, brother of John Morgan.

504 Sorenson, *Mormon's Codex*, 322.

505 Sorenson, "How Could Joseph Smith Write So Accurately," 287. Welch, "A Steady Stream," 372–373, differs only slightly in wording: "No one in the nineteenth century could have known that cement, in fact, was extensively used in Mesoamerica beginning largely at this time, the middle of the first century BC."

506 Welch, "A Steady Stream," 274.

507 See Welch, et al., *Knowing Why*, 18–19, 172–174, 178–179, 201–202, 291–293.

508 H. Curtis Wright, "Introduction," in Tvedtnes, *The Book of Mormon and Other Hidden Books*, ix–xii, similarly tells the story of a family in the Midwest that was bombarded with critical material dismissing the ancient practice of writing on metal plates, a practice that was already well-attested to at the time of the criticism.

509 Mormon may be speaking here both metaphorically and literally. See chapter 38.

510 Daniel C. Peterson, "Their Own Worst Enemies," in *The Book of Mormon, Part 2: Alma 30 to Moroni, Studies in Scripture, Volume 8*, ed. Kent P. Jackson (Salt Lake City, UT: Deseret Book, 1988), 103, emphasis in original.

511 Thomas S. Monson, "Constant Truths for Changing Times," *Ensign*, May 2005.

512 1 Nephi 13:36; 15:15; 17:29; 20:21; 2 Nephi 4:35; 8:1; 9:45; 18:14; 28:28; Jacob 7:25; Psalms 18:2, 31, 46; 27:5; 28:1; 31:2–3; 40:2; 42:9; 61:2; 62:2, 7; 71:3; 89:26; 94:22; 95:1; 105:41; Isaiah 8:14; 32:2; 48:21; Deuteronomy 32:4, 15, 18, 31; Exodus 17:6; 33:21–22.

513 1 Nephi 15:15; 2 Nephi 4:35; 2 Nephi 18:14, quoting Isaiah 8:14. Jacob, Nephi's younger brother, also used this imagery (see 2 Nephi 9:45; Jacob 4:15–17; 7:25). See Welch, et al., *Knowing Why*, 156–157.

514 The verse reads: "And the Lord shall be seen over them, and his arrow shall go forth as the lightning: and the Lord God shall blow the trumpet, and shall go with whirlwinds of the south." Regarding God's "arrows," see also Psalms 7:13 (ESV): "He hath also prepared for him the instruments of death; he maketh his arrows fiery shafts." See also Welch et al., *Knowing Why*, 47–48.

515 There are examples in the Bible where it is not the Lord Himself who comes in this manner. See, for example, Isaiah 28:2 (cf. Psalms 18:14; 144:6; Isaiah 66:15; Habakkuk 3:14). In context, the "mighty and strong one" is most likely a reference to the Assyrian army, or perhaps to a specific Assyrian king whom the Lord allows to punish the rebellious Northern Kingdom of Israel (cf. Isaiah 10:5–6). The interesting thing to note here is that Isaiah 14 creates a parallel between a prideful king of Assyria and Lucifer (Isaiah 14:12: "How art thou fallen from heaven, O Lucifer, son of the morning!"). Although Isaiah 14:4 identifies the monarch in question as "the king of Babylon," scholars argue that the likely dating of this passage would indicate that this is a reference to the Assyrian king Sargon II (ca. 722–705 BC). See J. J. M. Roberts, *First Isaiah: A Commentary, Hermeneia: A Critical and Historical Commentary on the Bible* (Minneapolis, MN: Fortress Press, 2015), 207–209. See also Welch et al., *Knowing Why*, 121–123. These make it clear that the association of similar imagery to a Satan-figure is not unprecedented in scripture.

516 One striking example is in Moses 1:12–22, where Satan "came tempting" Moses, asking Moses to worship him after Moses had just seen God in His great glory. When Moses refused, recognizing the difference in glory between God and Satan, the evil one ranted and cried out: "I am the Only Begotten, worship me" (Moses 1:19). Moses continued resisting and called upon God, and then "Satan began to tremble, and the earth shook" before he "departed hence" (Moses 1:21–22).

517 Neil L. Andersen, "Spiritual Whirlwinds," *Ensign*, May 2014, 21.

518 Wilford Woodruff, *Diary*, LDS archives; reproduced in Kenneth W. Godfrey, "The Zelph Story," *BYU Studies 29*, no. 2 (1989): 35.

519 Letter to Emma Smith, June 4, 1834, 58, available online at josephsmithpapers.org; spelling standardized.

520 See Godfrey, "The Zelph Story," 31–56; Donald Q. Cannon, "Zelph Revisited," in *Regional Studies in Latter-day Saint Church History: Illinois*, ed. H. Dean Garrett (Provo, UT: Department of Church History and Doctrine, Brigham Young University, 1995), 97–111; Kenneth W. Godfrey, "What Is the Significance of Zelph in the Study of Book of Mormon Geography?" *Journal of Book of Mormon Studies 8*, no. 2 (1999): 70–79, 88.

521 See Thomas J. Riley, "Joseph Smith, Zelph's Mound, and the Armies of Zion: The Construction of American Indians from Archaeological Evidence in Illinois in the Nineteenth Century," *Illinois Archaeology 5*, no. 1–2 (1993): 25; Kenneth B. Farnsworth, "Lamanitish Arrows and Eagles with Lead Eyes: Tales of the First Recorded Explorations in an Illinois Valley Hopewell Mound," *Illinois Archaeology 22*, no. 1 (2010): 32–33.

522 "History of Joseph Smith," *Times and Seasons 6*, no. 20 (January 1, 1846): 1076.

523 See, for example, Bruce H. Porter and Rod L. Meldrum, *Prophecies and Promises: The Book of Mormon and the United States of America* (New York, NY: Digital Legend Press, 2009), 105–108. For a review of this argument, mentioning many of the same points raised here, see Matthew Roper, "Joseph Smith, Revelation, and Book of Mormon Geography," *FARMS Review 22*, no. 2 (2010): 62–70.

524 Godfrey, "The Zelph Story," 42: "Interestingly, the earlier accounts do not expressly identify Zelph with the Nephites, as do the later accounts." In a late account, written in the 1850s (about twenty years after the event) by Wilford Woodruff, he said Zelph "Had joined the Nephites & fought for them under the direction of the great Onandagus who held sway & command over the Armies of the Nephites." But nothing about the Nephites is mentioned in Woodruff's earlier account, written in 1834, probably within a few months of the events described, and some details in his later account are contradicted by his and the other earlier accounts. None of the other accounts written before Joseph Smith's death mention the Nephites either. The primary source accounts are reproduced in Godfrey, "The Zelph Story," 34–42; Cannon, "Zelph Revisited," 98–102.

525 See *History, 1838–1856*, vol. 1–A, 483, online at the josephsmithpapers.org. Manuscript is in the handwriting of Willard Richards. Also, at the top of the page, both "Nephites" and "Lamanites" originally appeared as an identification of who built the mounds, but were subsequently crossed out: "During our travels we visited several of the mounds which had been thrown up by the ancient inhabitants of this country, ~~Nephites, Lamanite &c~~" (pp. 482–483).

526 Rueben McBride, whose account is generally regarded as the earliest, possibly written within days of the event, simply said Zelph "was killed in battle," while Wilford Woodruff said "he was killed in battle with an arrow." Godfrey, "The Zelph Story," 34, 36; Cannon, "Zelph Revisited," 98, 101.

527 "Extracts from H. C. Kimball's Journal," *Times and Seasons 6*, no. 2 (February 1, 1845): 788. Godfrey, "The Zelph Story," 39, dates the account to "possibly around 1843," as does Mark Alan Wright, "Joseph Smith and Native American Artifacts," in *Approaching Antiquity: Joseph Smith and the Ancient World*, ed. Lincoln H. Blumell, Matthew J. Grey, and Andrew H. Hedges (Salt Lake City and Provo, UT: Deseret Book and BYU Religious Studies Center, 2015), 123–124.

528 Godfrey, "The Zelph Story," 47: "None of the sources before the Willard Richards composition, however, actually say that Zelph died in battle with the Nephites, only that he died 'in battle' when the otherwise unidentified people of Onandagus were engaged in great wars 'among the Lamanites.'"

529 *History, 1838–1856*, vol. 1–A, 483.

530 *History, 1838–1856*, vol. 1–A, p. 483. Notice also that the prepublication manuscript has "*a* great struggle" rather than "*the* [last] great struggle," as in the published version.

531 See Godfrey, "The Zelph Story," 38, 44, 47; Godfrey, "What Is the Significance of Zelph," 73–74, 75 discusses possible meanings of this phrase.

532 *History, 1838–1856*, vol. 1–A, 483. The manuscript also has Onandagus rather than Omandagus.

533 Godfrey, "The Zelph Story," 36. Later interlinear additions add "or East sea" after "Cumorah." See Cannon, "Zelph Revisited," 98.

534 Godfrey, "The Zelph Story," 34; Cannon, "Zelph Revisited," 102; capitalization standardized.

535 For a more detailed discussion of the "History of the Church" account and its textual history, see Godfrey, "The Zelph Story," 42–46; Godfrey, "What Is the Significance of Zelph," 74–75.

536 Godfrey, "The Zelph Story," 47; Godfrey, "What Is the Significance of Zelph," 75. When commenting on what can be concluded from the Zelph accounts, Donald Q. Cannon similarly concluded that we know "these skeletal remains belonged to Zelph, a white Lamanite, who had been a warrior under a leader named Onandagus," but says nothing about the last battles between Nephites and Lamanites, nor Cumorah. See Cannon, "Zelph Revisited," 108.

537 John A. Widtsoe, "Is Book of Mormon Geography Known?" *Improvement Era*, July 1950, 547.

538 Cannon, "Zelph Revisited," 108; emphasis added. For more on what Joseph Smith and his contemporaries believed about Book of Mormon geography, see Matthew Roper, "Limited Geography and the Book of Mormon: Historical Antecedents and Early Interpretations," *FARMS Review 16*, no. 2 (2004): 225–275; Andrew H. Hedges, "Book of Mormon Geography in the World of Joseph Smith," *Mormon Historical Studies 8*, no. 1–2 (2007): 77–89; Matthew Roper, "John Bernhisel's Gift to a Prophet: Incidents of Travel in Central America and the Book of Mormon," *Interpreter: A Journal of Mormon Scripture 16* (2015): 207–253; Matthew Roper, "Joseph Smith, Central American Ruins, and the Book of Mormon," in *Approaching Antiquity*, 141–162.

539 Godfrey, "What Is the Significance of Zelph," 70–79; Cannon, "Zelph Revisited," 107.

540 Cannon, "Zelph Revisited," 107.

541 Mark Alan Wright, "Heartland as Hinterland: The Mesoamerican Core and North American Periphery of Book of Mormon Geography," *Interpreter: A Journal of Mormon Scripture 13* (2015): 126–128. See also Cannon, "Zelph Revisited," 107–108; John L. Sorenson, "Mesoamericans in Pre-Columbian North America," in *Reexploring the Book of Mormon*, 218–219; Robert L. Hall, "Some Commonalities Linking North America and Mesoamerica," in *The Oxford Handbook of North American Archaeology*, ed. Timothy R. Pauketat (New York, NY: Oxford University Press, 2012), 52–63.

542 Wright, "Heartland as Hinterland," 116–118. Given the timing of these migrations in the Book of Mormon (mid-first century BC), it is interesting to note that archaeological findings and radiocarbon dating suggests that the Zelph mound is "a ceremonial mortuary center for regional Hopewellian populations during early portions of the Middle Woodland period (ca. 50 BC–AD 100, uncalibrated)" (Farnsworth, "Lamanitish Arrows," 34). Kenneth Farnsworth and Karen A. Atwell, "Excavations at the Blue Island and Naples-Russell Mounds and Related Hopwellian Sites in the Lower Illinois Valley," *Illinois State Archaeological Survey Research Report 34* (Urbana-Champaign, IL: Prairie Research Institute, University of Illinois, 2015) provides the most extensive and up-to-date archaeological report of the Zelph mound (known as Naples-Russell 8 or just Naples 8) and the surrounding area. The radiocarbon dating of skeletal remains near the surface of the mound, thus "likely one of the final burials placed in this massive mortuary facility," dated to the first century AD (p. 181, 194). Other radiocarbon dates from the nearby area "cluster in the last century BC and the first century AD" (p. 181, 193–197), leading Farnsworth to conclude, "Perhaps as early as 50–0 BC, construction of the Naples 8 earthwork began" (p. 181). This would place the beginning of the Hopewell community that started the mound at about the same time-period

in which Book of Mormon peoples were migrating northward, some of whom could have hypothetically settled in the Illinois River Valley and joined with these Hopewell groups. It is impossible to be certain exactly when Zelph himself dated to based on these findings, but given that remains close to the surface were dated to the first century AD, it seems most likely that Zelph (who was found at a similar depth) dated to this same time-period. Some radiocarbon data (p. 169, 184) suggested that the mound was used in the Late Woodland period (ca. 12th–14th century AD) for cremation ceremonies, leaving the possibility open that Zelph came later, but the primary use of the mound appears to be between 50 BC–AD 100. No current evidence ties the mound to the fourth century AD.

543 Godfrey, "What Is the Significance of Zelph," 77.

544 See Hardy, *Understanding the Book of Mormon*, 90: "Mormon addresses readers every now and again throughout the rest of his history—adding a comment, an explanation, or an interpretation—so we are regularly reminded that we are getting his particular perspective, a guided tour so to speak, of Nephite civilization."

545 John L. Sorenson, "Mormon's Sources," *Journal of Book of Mormon and Other Restoration Scripture 20*, no. 2 (2011): 4.

546 First detected in 1987. See John W. Welch, "Chiasmus in Helaman 6:7–13," in *Reexploring the Book of Mormon*, 230–232. See also Welch, "Significant Recognitions," 346: "since the chiasm encompasses the entire report for the year, this unifying structure strongly suggests that the account was written as a single literary unit that Mormon found on the large plates of Nephi."

547 Formatting deviates slightly from John W. Welch, "A Steady Stream of Significant Recognitions," in *Echoes and Evidences*, 345–346. For more information concerning chiasmus in the Book of Mormon see chapters 12 and 13.

548 Welch, "Significant Recognitions," 346. See also Welch, "Chiasmus in Helaman 6:7–13," 230–232.

549 Welch, "Significant Recognitions," 347.

550 It should be noted that not only does the center of this chiasm invoke names of God, but at the point where the chiasm reversers its order the Lord is described as bringing "Mulek into the land north, and Lehi into the land south" (Helaman 6:10). In other words, the verse explicitly describes the Lord's influence in leading these groups of people into their respective locations—lands where they were currently experiencing peace and prosperity. The clear inference, then, is that the Lord was leading them to prosperity.

551 Sorenson, "Mormon's Sources," 12. On prospering in the Book of Mormon, see Welch, et al., *Knowing Why*, 268–269.

552 For a further treatment of this topic, see Hugh Nibley, *The Prophetic Book of Mormon*, 504–508.

553 Welch, "Significant Recognitions," 347.

554 Welch, "Significant Recognitions," 347.

555 John W. Welch and Kelly Ward, "Thieves and Robbers," in *Reexploring the Book of Mormon*, 248. Interestingly, the names of two notable leaders of the Gadianton robbers—Gaddianton and Giddianhi (each spelled with a double "d" in the original manuscript of the Book of Mormon)—may actually have symbolic significance related to their occupation as robbers. See Matthew L. Bowen, "'Swearing by Their Everlasting Maker': Some Notes on Paanchi and Giddianhi," *Interpreter: A Journal of Mormon Scripture 28* (2018): 164–168; John W. Welch, "Theft and Robbery in the Book of Mormon and Ancient Near Eastern Law," *FARMS Preliminary Report* (1985), 30–31; Welch and Ward, "Thieves and Robbers," 249.

556 Welch and Ward, "Thieves and Robbers," 248.

557 John W. Welch, "Legal and Social Perspectives on Robbers in First-Century Judea," *BYU Studies 36*, no. 3 (1996–1997): 142; citing Bernard S. Jackson, *Theft in Early Jewish Law* (Oxford: Clarendon, 1972), 1–5. See also Kent P. Jackson, "Revolutionaries in the First Century," *BYU Studies 36*, no. 3 (1997): 129–140.

558 Welch, "Legal and Social Perspectives," 148.

559 Welch and Ward, "Thieves and Robbers," 248.

560 It's true that the legal language of Joseph Smith's day did offer a distinction between theft and robbery, but according to Welch, these distinctions were "inconsistent in many ways with usages found in the Book of Mormon." Welch, "Theft and Robbery," 38.

561 Welch, *Legal Cases*, 354.

562 For more on the secret societies in the Book of Mormon, see chapter 65.

563 For more on the tactics of the Gadianton robbers, see chapter 54.

564 Wallace E. Hunt Jr., "The Marketplace," in *Pressing Forward with the Book of Mormon: The FARMS Updates of the 1990s*, ed. John W. Welch and Melvin J. Thorne (Provo UT: FARMS, 1999), 197.

565 J. Eric S. Thompson, *The Rise and Fall of Maya Civilization*, 2nd ed. (Norman, OK: University of Oklahoma Press, 1966), 222, as cited in Hunt, "The Marketplace," 97. Although Mesoamerican scholars see the emergence of a more organized market system as taking place after the period of the Book of Mormon, the issue remains uncertain. See Eleanor M. King and Leslie C. Shaw, "Introduction: Research on Maya Markets," in *The Ancient Maya Marketplace: The Archaeology of Transient Space*, ed. Eleanor M. King (Tucson, AZ: University of Arizona Press, 2015), 27: "The issue needs further investigation, however. Already, scholars have been surprised by how far back in time Maya sociopolitical structures that we thought dated primarily to the Classic actually appeared. We know, too, that economic organization became complex earlier, in the Middle to Late Preclassic."

566 Sylvanus G. Morley and George W. Brainerd, *The Ancient Maya*, 4th ed. (Stanford, CA: Stanford University Press, 1983), 249, as cited in Hunt, "The Marketplace," 97. For further information concerning ancient American markets, see John L. Sorenson, "Nephi's Garden and Chief Market," in *Reexploring the Book of Mormon*, 236–238.

567 Sorenson, "Nephi's Garden and Chief Market," 237.

568 Mark Alan Wright, a Mesoamerican archaeologist, personally communicated the details of this market system to Book of Mormon Central staff on August 5, 2016. See also Deborah L. Nichols, "The Merchant's World: Commercial Diversity and the Economics of Interregional Exchange in Highland Mesoamerica," in *Merchants, Markets, and Exchange in the Pre-Columbian World*, ed. Kenneth G. Hirth and Joanne Pillsbury (Washington, D.C.: Dumbarton Oaks Research Library and Collections, 2013), 104; Leslie C. Shaw and Eleanor M. King, "The Maya Marketplace at Maax Na, Belize," in *The Ancient Maya Marketplace*, 178.

569 See Sorenson, *Mormon's Codex*, 356–357.

570 Shaw and King, "Market Place at Maax Na," 177–181.

571 Sorenson, "Nephi's Garden and Chief Market," 236–237.

572 For information concerning towers, see Sorenson, *Mormon's Codex*, 323–325; Kerry Hull, "War Banners: A Mesoamerican Context for the Title of Liberty," *Journal of Book of Mormon Studies 24* (2015): 106–108. See also Gardner, *Second Witness*, 5:121: "Nephi's tower was almost certainly one of the many low pyramidal structures that archaeologists have found in the majority of Mesoamerican sites from Book of Mormon times on. Those attached to private compounds were lower than the stepped pyramids in public squares used for public rituals, but they were nevertheless similarly constructed, if not nearly so high. Nephi's tower was low enough to allow easy conversation with the crowd (Helaman 7:12–13). In a family compound, such towers would have been suitable for prayer and communion with God."

573 John W. Welch, "Was Helaman 7–8 an Allegorical Funeral Sermon?" in *Reexploring the Book of Mormon*, 239.

574 Welch, "Allegorical Funeral Sermon," 240–241. See also Donald W. Parry, "Symbolic Action as Prophecy in the Old Testament," in *Sperry Symposium Classics: The Old Testament*, ed. Paul Y. Hoskisson (Salt Lake City and Provo, UT: Deseret Book and BYU Religious Studies Center, 2005), 337–355;

Menahem Haran, "From Early to Classical Prophecy: Continuity and Change," *Vetus Testamentum 27*, no. 4 (1977): 358–397.

575 The judges do not seem to be able to bring people to trial themselves. Because of the obvious conflict of interests involved they likely needed to wait for the people to do this, but they could incite a mob to bring someone to trial, as they seem to be attempting here. Welch, *Legal Cases*, 325.

576 Robert J. Matthews, "The Joseph Smith Translation—Historical Source and Doctrinal Companion to the Doctrine & Covenants," in *Ninth Annual Church Educational System Religious Educators' Symposium* (Salt Lake City, UT: The Church of Jesus Christ of Latter-day Saints, 1985), 22.

577 On the symbolism of the number seven, see Corbin Volluz, "A Study in Seven: Hebrew Numerology in the Book of Mormon," *BYU Studies Quarterly 53*, no. 2 (2014): 57–83.

578 It is important to note that Nephi is in Zarahemla at this point, as noted in Helaman 7:10, and that Zarahemla is the city where the Mulekites originally settled as noted in Omni 1:14. Therefore, it is likely that many of these people would be at least partially related to the Mulekites.

579 See Kirsten Nielsen, *Yahweh as Prosecutor and Judge* (Sheffield, England: JSOT, 1978); John W. Welch, "Benjamin's Speech as a Prophetic Lawsuit," in *King Benjamin's Speech*, 225–232. Biblical passages regularly identified as utilizing the prophetic lawsuit literary form include Isaiah 1:2–3, 18–20; Jeremiah 2:4–13; Micah 6:1–8; Hosea 4:1–3; and Malachi 3:5.

580 Welch, *Legal Cases*, 242.

581 See also 2 Nephi 27:14: "Wherefore, the Lord God will proceed to bring forth the words of the book; and in the mouth of as many witnesses as seemeth him good will he establish his word; and wo be unto him that rejecteth the word of God!" See Welch, et al., *Knowing Why*, 134–135.

582 See Joshua 6:18–19, in which the Lord explained that everything that could burn was to be destroyed, and all the precious metals were to be offered to the Lord for use in the Tabernacle.

583 Casting lots was considered to be a valid way of obtaining revelation from the Lord in ancient Israel, and that is what Joshua did to determine the will of the Lord in this case. See Welch, *Legal Cases*, 331.

584 Welch, *Legal Cases*, 332–333.

585 Welch, *Legal Cases*, 93.

586 Welch, *Legal Cases*, 334.

587 Welch, *Legal Cases*, 334.

588 Thomas S. Monson, "Choices," *Ensign*, May, 2016, 86.

589 See Welch, et al., *Knowing Why*, 45–46.

590 Genesis 14:11; 1 Samuel 7:5–9; Jeremiah 14:11; Isaiah 6:5.

591 Isaiah 6:1. It is possible that the experience of Moses in Exodus 19–20 was similar to this as well. See also Joel S. Baden, *The Composition of the Pentateuch: Renewing the Documentary Hypothesis* (New Haven, CT: Yale University Press, 2012), 118.

592 1 Kings 22:19–23; Jeremiah 23:18.

593 Ezekiel 2:10; Isaiah 6:5.

594 Isaiah 6:1–13; Amos 3:7; Habakkuk 2:2.

595 See John W. Welch, "Lehi's Council Vision and the Mysteries of God," reprinted in *Reexploring the Book of Mormon*, 24–25; Stephen D. Ricks, "Heavenly Visions and Prophetic Calls in Isaiah 6 (2 Nephi 16), the Book of Mormon, and the Revelation of John," in *Isaiah in the Book of Mormon*, ed. Donald W. Parry and John W. Welch (Provo, UT: FARMS, 1998), 175–181; David E. Bokovoy, "On Christ and Covenants: An LDS Reading of Isaiah's Prophetic Call," *Studies in the Bible and Antiquity 3* (2011): 29–49; Stephen O. Smoot, "The Divine Council in the Hebrew Bible and the Book of Mormon," *Interpreter: A Journal of Mormon Scripture 27*, no. 2 (2017): 155–180.

596 David E. Bokovoy, "'Thou Knowest That I Believe': Invoking The Spirit of the Lord as Council Witness in 1 Nephi 11," *Interpreter: A Journal of Mormon Scripture 1* (2012): 17.

597 John W. Welch, "The Calling of Lehi as a Prophet in the World of Jerusalem," in *Glimpses of Lehi's Jerusalem*, ed. John W. Welch, David Rolph Seely, and Jo Ann H. Seely (Provo, UT: FARMS, 2004), 421–448; Kevin L. Tolley, "To 'See and Hear'," *Interpreter: A Journal of Mormon Scripture 18* (2016): 139–147.

598 Bokovoy, "'Thou Knowest That I Believe'," 22.

599 See chapter 43. See also John E. Harvey, *Retelling the Torah: The Deuteronomistic Historian's Use of Tetrateuchal Narratives, JSOTSup 403* (New York, NY: T&T Clark, 2004), 61.

600 Joseph B. Wirthlin, "Sunday Will Come," *Ensign*, November 2006.

601 Compare 1 Nephi, where Nephi swears by God and himself (see 1 Nephi 4:32), but God just swears by Himself, as He sometimes does. See, for example, Genesis 22:13, Isaiah 45:23, Jeremiah 22:5, Amos 8:7. God swears by Himself because there is no other higher authority by which He can make an oath and covenant; see Hebrews 6:13.

602 Ricks and Hamblin, *Warfare in the Book of Mormon*.

603 For a study of similar groups, see Kent P. Jackson, "Revolutionaries in the First Century," in *Masada and the World of the New Testament*, ed. John F. Hall and John W. Welch (Provo, UT: BYU Studies, 1997), 129–140; John W. Welch, "Legal and Social Perspectives on Robbers in First-Century Judea," in *Masada and the World of the New Testament*, 141–153; John W. Welch and John F. Hall, *Charting the New Testament* (Provo, UT: FARMS, 2002), chart 3–12; Daniel C. Peterson, "Exploratory Notes on the Futuwwa and Its Several Incarnations," in *Bountiful Harvest: Essays in Honor of S. Kent Brown*, ed. Andrew C. Skinner, D. Morgan Davis, and Carl W. Griffin (Provo, UT: Neal A. Maxwell Institute for Religious Scholarship, 2011), 287–312.

604 For more information on the Gadianton robbers and their secret combinations, see chapter 65. See also David R. Benard, John W. Welch, and Daniel C. Peterson, "Secret Combinations," in *Reexploring the Book of Mormon*, 227–229; John W. Welch and Kelly Ward, "Thieves and Robbers," in *Reexploring the Book of Mormon*, 248–249.

605 Daniel C. Peterson, "The Gadianton Robbers as Guerrilla Warriors," in *Warfare in the Book of Mormon*, 152.

606 Samuel B. Griffith, trans., *Mao Tse-tung on Guerrilla Warfare* (U.S. Marine Corps, 1989), 8.

607 See chapter 59.

608 See Peterson, "The Gadianton Robbers as Guerrilla Warriors," 158–162.

609 Peterson, "The Gadianton Robbers as Guerrilla Warriors," 163.

610 See chapter 34.

611 Peterson, "The Gadianton Robbers as Guerrilla Warriors," 167.

612 Peterson, "The Gadianton Robbers as Guerrilla Warriors," 147.

613 Peterson, "The Gadianton Robbers as Guerrilla Warriors," 167.

614 Daniel C. Peterson, "Not Joseph's, and Not Modern," in *Echoes and Evidences*, 197.

615 Ray C. Hillam, "The Gadianton Robbers and Protracted War," *BYU Studies 15*, no. 2 (1975): 221.

616 Griffith, trans., *Mao Tse-tung on Guerrilla Warfare*, 8.

617 The only other example in the Book of Mormon, also involving the timing of Christ's birth, is Lehi's and Nephi's six-hundred-year prophecy (see 1 Nephi 10:3; 19:8; 2 Nephi 25:19). Samuel's five-year prophecy was particularly unique. Gardner, *Second Witness*, 5:190: "The specificity of this prophecy is unique in the scriptural canon. Other time-specific prophecies (e.g., that the Messiah would be born six hundred years from Lehi's departure from Jerusalem, and that the Nephites would be destroyed in four hundred years) were uttered about a future so distant that no listener would still be alive. Because six hundred and four hundred are round numbers, they also might be understood by the listeners as generic

rather than specific figures. . . . The five-year prophecy, however, is absolute, finite, and testable within the lifetime of virtually all of Samuel's listeners."

618 While Samuel's prophecy in Helaman 14 never mentions the timing of the sign of Christ's death, it is evident from 3 Nephi 8:1–4 that the timing had been revealed to the Nephites at some point. Whether it was Samuel who revealed the timing or someone else is not clear, as it only says that the people "began to look with great earnestness for the sign which had been given by the prophet Samuel" (3 Nephi 8:3). Only the sign, not the timing, is connected to Samuel. Perhaps the timing was revealed by the "just man" who kept the record and "did many miracles in the name of Jesus" (3 Nephi 8:1). It could also have been revealed in some of the "much preaching and prophesying which was sent among them" in the wake of the first sign (3 Nephi 2:10). If it was Samuel, it would appear that Mormon omitted that detail when he copied over Samuel's prophecies, perhaps for the reasons suggested here: the timing did not coincide with a number full of symbolic significance.

619 For general reference and background on the Mesoamerican calendrical systems, including the long count (tun) system, see Mary Miller and Karl Taube, *An Illustrated Dictionary of the Gods and Symbols of Ancient Mexico and the Maya* (London, UK: Thames and Hudson, 1993), 48–54; Kaylee Spencer-Ahrens and Linnea H. Wren, "Arithmetic, Astronomy, and the Calendar," in Lynn V. Foster, *Handbook to Life in the Ancient Maya World* (New York, NY: Oxford University Press, 2002), 250–260; Joel W. Palka, *The A to Z of Ancient Mesoamerica* (Lanham, MA: Scarecrow Press, 2010), 22–23.

620 John E. Clark, "Archaeological Trends and Book of Mormon Origins," in *The Worlds of Joseph Smith: A Bicentennial Conference at the Library of Congress*, ed. John W. Welch (Provo, UT: BYU Press, 2005), 90.

621 Mark Alan Wright, "Nephite Daykeepers: Ritual Specialists in Mesoamerica and the Book of Mormon," in *Ancient Temple Worship*, 253: "The twenty-year katun was subdivided into five-year periods called hotuns, which were often celebrated by royalty and commemorated in monumental inscriptions." See also Prudence M. Rice, "Time, Memory, and Resilience among the Maya," in *Millenary Maya Societies: Past Crises and Resilience*, ed. M. Charlotte Arnauld and Alain Breton (Mesoweb Press, 2013), 13: "The completion of full twenty-year k'atun or their five-year quarters were regularly celebrated by rulers in what Mayanists call 'Period-Ending' (hereafter PE) ceremonies."

622 Sorenson, *An Ancient American Setting for the Book of Mormon*, 274.

623 It is important to note that the Nephites need not be using the Mayan calendar to nonetheless recognize the sacred importance of these numbers in the calendaring of their neighbors, and to even be influenced in such a way as to also give weight and import to time cycles of five, twenty, and four hundred years themselves. Though commonly referred to as the "Maya" calendar system, it was known throughout Mesoamerica and likely had its origins among the Olmec between 500–400 BC. The earliest long count date attested is 36 BC, on Stela 2 in Chiapa de Corzo, confirming its use in Samuel's time. See Gardner, *Second Witness*, 5:177; Foster, *Handbook to Life*, 36–37. Interestingly, Chiapa de Corzo is in Chiapas, Mexico, in the Grijalva River valley, believed by some scholars to be the land of Zarahemla. Chiapa de Corzo is even identified by some scholars as the Nephite city of Sidom. See Sorenson, *An Ancient American Setting for the Book of Mormon*, 5–38, 148–167, 197, 204–206; Allen and Allen, *Exploring the Lands of the Book of Mormon*, 748–749, 770–772; Sorenson, *Mormon's Codex*, 128, 581–585, 592, 597–598.

624 John E. Clark, "Archaeology, Relics, and Book of Mormon Belief," *Journal of Book of Mormon Studies 14*, no. 2 (2005): 47. See also Clark, "Archaeological Trends," 90: "The Book of Mormon records several references to a significant four-hundred-year prophecy, consistent with this idiosyncratic Mesoamerican calendar practice." In addition to Helaman 13:5, 9, see Alma 45:10; Mormon 8:6; Moroni 10:1.

625 Wright, "Nephite Daykeepers," 253.

626 John L. Sorenson, "The Book of Mormon as a Mesoamerican Record," in *Book of Mormon Authorship Revisited*, 409; Sorenson, *Mormon's Codex*, 193, 440–441.

627 The four-hundred-year prophecy appears to have been understood and interpreted as four hundred years from the birth of Christ (see Mormon 8:6–7). Alma 45:10 says "the Nephites . . . in four hundred years from the time that Jesus Christ shall manifest himself unto them, shall dwindle in unbelief."

628 Rice, "Time, Memory, and Resilience," 16.

629 Sorenson, *Ancient American Setting*, 274.

630 Gardner, *Second Witness*, 5:177.

631 Personal communication to Book of Mormon Central staff.

632 Sorenson, *Mormon's Codex*, 439; Rice, "Time, Memory, and Resilience," 13, 16: "For the Maya, time was simultaneously linear and cyclical, an endless—'timeless'—rotation of k'atun, b'ak'tun, and multiple eras of creation (as in the Popol Vuh)." Spencer-Ahrens and Wren, "Arithmetic, Astronomy, and the Calendar," 247: "The cycles dominated Maya thought and resulted in a deterministic view in which history repeated itself. If a given day or period resulted in dreadful consequences once, it would do so again when the day returned or when the cycle repeated itself." Just as with the important numbers themselves (five-, twenty-, and four-hundred-year cycles), the Nephites need not be using the Maya calendar itself in order to have enculturated views of time as cyclical.

633 Spencer-Ahrens and Wren, "Arithmetic, Astronomy, and the Calendar," 257, noted, "each k'atun expressed a prophecy of the future while at the same time embodying the historical past." Samuel seems to be expressing the same concept, only using a baktun rather than a katun.

634 Evidence for these notions of cyclical time may be evident in the Book of Mormon. For instance, notice that twenty years (one katun) after Samuel said "the sword of justice hangeth over this people" (Helaman 13:5), Mormon reported that "the sword of destruction did hang over" the Nephites once again (3 Nephi 2:19).

635 Wright, "Nephite Daykeepers," 253; Rice, "Time, Memory, and Resilience," 13. Again, for Nephites influenced by the surrounding culture, five-, twenty-, or four-hundred-year periods can be deemed important, celebratory occasions without necessarily adopting the "tun" system.

636 See Mark Alan Wright, "'According to Their Language, unto Their Understanding': The Cultural Context of Hierophanies and Theophanies in Latter-day Saint Canon," *Studies in the Bible and Antiquity 3* (2011): 51–65.

637 Raymond Westbrook, "Patronage in the Ancient Near East," *Journal of the Economic and Social History of the Orient 48*, no. 2 (2005): 213. For more on suzerain/vassal relations in the Book of Mormon, see Welch, et al., *Knowing Why*, 296–297, 303–304; RoseAnn Benson and Stephen D. Ricks, "Treaties and Covenants: Ancient Near Eastern Legal Terminology in the Book of Mormon," *Journal of Book of Mormon Studies 14*, no. 1 (2005): 48–61, 128–129.

638 David E. Bokovoy, "Love vs. Hate: An Analysis of Helaman 15:1–4," *Insights: A Window on the Ancient World 22*, no. 2 (2002): 2. This was clarified in 1963, when an ancient Middle Eastern scholar named William L. Moran was reading a text called the Vassal Treaty of Esarhaddon. The Assyrian king Esarhaddon wanted to make sure that those ruling under him would continue to be loyal to his successor, Assurbanipal, so he said to them, "You shall love Assurbanipal as yourselves." To Moran, this seemed like a strange thing to say. As biblical scholar James Kugel put it, "Love? Surely the vassals were not being told to become enamored of the future king's winning personality! It seemed to Moran as if love here must have less to do with emotion than with loyalty, political loyalty." See James L. Kugel, *How to Read the Bible: A Guide to Scripture, Then and Now* (New York, NY: Free Press, 2007), 353.

639 See, for example, Deuteronomy 10:12; 11:1, 13, 22; 30:19–20, which all

equate love with serving God, just as the vassal serves the suzerain.

640 Kugel, *How to Read the Bible*, 354.

641 See also Malachi 1:2–3, where the Hebrew word for *love* can be understood as referring to political alliance. Compare this to a similar statement in Moses 7:20 that makes the point clearer: "But the Lord said unto Enoch: Zion have I blessed, but the residue of the people have I cursed." Those in the covenant are blessed; those outside the covenant are not.

642 Thus, an ancient ruler who was serving under Pharaoh could write to the Pharaoh and say, "My lord, just as I love the king my lord, so [does] the king of Nuhasse [love him, and] the king of Ni'i . . . —all these kings are servants of my lord." This letter directly associates loving the king with being a servant to the king. Another such letter describes a civil war by saying: "Behold the city! Half of it loves the sons of 'Abd-Asirta, half of it [loves] my lord." These examples demonstrate the close relationship between love and loyalty in antiquity. See Kugel, *How to Read the Bible*, 354.

643 Bokovoy, "Love vs. Hate," 2.

644 Bokovoy, "Love vs. Hate," 2.

645 Bokovoy, "Love vs. Hate," 2.

646 For a small sampling of this theme, see 1 Nephi 17:35; 2 Nephi 26:33; Jacob 3:5–8; Enos 1:13; Mosiah 2:21–22; Alma 26:23–26; Helaman 11:9–17; 3 Nephi 10:5–6; Mormon 6:17; Ether 12:33–34; Moroni 7:45–48.

647 Thomas S. Monson, "Love—the Essence of the Gospel," *Ensign*, May 2014, 91.

648 See Jeffrey R. Chadwick, "Dating the Birth of Jesus Christ," *BYU Studies Quarterly 49*, no. 4 (2010): 6–9. Some Latter-day Saints might be surprised to learn that not everyone, including respected authorities and Apostles like Orson Pratt, Hyrum M. Smith, J. Reuben Clark, and Bruce R. McConkie, agrees with the tradition started one hundred years ago by James E. Talmage that Christ was born on April 6, 1 BC, based on Doctrine and Covenants 20:1. The best evidence indicates that Doctrine and Covenants 20:1 was written by John Whitmer as an introduction to the revelation (four days after the fact), and "*X* years since the coming of our Lord and Savior Jesus Christ in the flesh" appears to be Whitmer's fancy way of expressing the date. It is used in the Church historical record by Whitmer in reference to June 12, 1831, for instance. See Chadwick, "Dating the Birth of Jesus Christ," 6–9, 28–29 n.12; Lincoln H. Blumell and Thomas A. Wayment, "When Was Jesus Born? A Response to a Recent Proposal," *BYU Studies Quarterly 51*, no. 3 (2012): 71–72; Steven C. Harper, "Historical Headnotes and the Index of Contents in the Book of Commandments and Revelations," *BYU Studies Quarterly 48*, no. 3 (2009): 57. See also Randall P. Spackman, "Introduction to Book of Mormon Chronology: The Principal Prophecies, Calendars, and Dates," *FARMS Preliminary Reports*, (1993), 70–74; John A. Tvedtnes, "When Was Christ Born?" *Interpreter: A Journal of Mormon Scripture 10* (2014): 13–14; Thomas A. Wayment, "The Birth and Death Dates of Jesus Christ," in *The Life and Teachings of Jesus Christ*, 3 vols., ed. Richard Neitzel Holzapfel and Thomas A. Wayment (Salt Lake City, UT: Deseret Book, 2005), 1:83–85.

649 See Blumell and Wayment, "When Was Jesus Born?" 54–59.

650 See Tvedtnes, "When Was Christ Born?" 17–24. Some Christians (mainly Eastern Orthodox) celebrate Christmas on January 6. See Taylor Halverson, "The Real 12 Days of Christmas and Why April 6 is a Religiously Significant Date," *Deseret News*, December 13, 2014.

651 See Tvedtnes, "When Was Christ Born?" 1–2.

652 See Chadwick, "Dating the Birth of Jesus Christ," 11–14; Wayment, "The Birth and Death Dates of Jesus Christ," 385–387; Blumell and Wayment, "When Was Jesus Born?" 59–62; Tvedtnes, "When Was Christ Born?" 4; Spackman, "Introduction to Book of Mormon Chronology," 48–51. On the other hand, the account in Luke 2 mentioning Cyrenius (see Luke 2:2) would require the story to take place sometime around AD 6–7. This is clearly at odds with the death of Herod, and as such most scholars regard this detail as erroneous. See Blumell and Wayment, "When Was Jesus Born?" 61.

653 For discussions on the dating of the Savior's death, see Chadwick, "Dating the Birth of Jesus Christ," 15–17; Jeffrey R. Chadwick, "Dating the Death of Jesus Christ," *BYU Studies 54*, no. 4 (2015): 135–191; Blumell and Wayment, "When Was Jesus Born?" 64–70; Wayment, "The Birth and Death Dates of Jesus Christ," 391–394; Spackman, "Introduction to Book of Mormon Chronology," 60–61.

654 Wayment, "The Birth and Death Dates of Jesus Christ," 394. See Chadwick, "Dating the Death of Jesus Christ," 139–142, for a review of scholars who agree with this timing. However, Blumell and Wayment, "When Was Jesus Born?" 64–70, urge caution against being too dogmatic about this date. See also chapter 67.

655 See Chadwick, "Dating the Birth of Jesus Christ," 17–18.

656 See Chadwick, "Dating the Birth of Jesus Christ," 17–18.

657 For discussion of these issues from various perspectives, see Wayment, "The Birth and Death Dates of Jesus Christ," 393; Chadwick, "Dating the Birth of Jesus Christ," 18–21, 34–35 nn. 48–51; Blumell and Wayment, "When Was Jesus Born?" 62–64, 76–77 nn. 39–45; Chadwick, "Dating the Death of Jesus Christ," 142–149; Spackman, "Introduction to Book of Mormon Chronology"; Randall P. Spackman, "The Jewish/Lunar Calendar," *Journal of Book of Mormon Studies 7*, no. 1 (1998): 48–59, 71; Randall P. Spackman, *A Source Book for Book of Mormon Chronology* (2010–215); David Rolph Seely, "Chronology, Book of Mormon," in *Book of Mormon Reference Companion*, 196–204; Robert F. Smith, "Book of Mormon Event Structure: The Ancient Near East," *Journal of Book of Mormon Studies 5*, no. 2 (1996): 98–147; John L. Sorenson, "The Nephite Calendar in Mosiah, Alma, and Helaman," in *Reexploring the Book of Mormon*, 173–175; Neal Rappleye, "'The Time is Past': A Note on Samuel's Five-Year Prophecy," *Interpreter: A Journal of Mormon Scripture 29* (2018): 21–30.

658 Blumell and Wayment, "When Was Jesus Born?" 64.

659 See Orson Pratt, "The Latter-day Kingdom of God—Divine Authenticity of the Book of Mormon—External Testimony," *Journal of Discourses 13*, discourse 16, April 10, 1870. See also Orson Pratt, "True Christmas and New Year," *Journal of Discourses 15*, discourse 33, December 29, 1872; Spackman, "Introduction to Book of Mormon Chronology," 48, 53; Wayment, "The Birth and Death Dates of Jesus Christ," 387–388, 393–394; Chadwick, "Dating the Birth of Jesus Christ," 25. Pratt (April 11, 4 BC), Spackman (March 23, 5 BC), Wayment (spring or winter, 5 BC), and Chadwick (December 5 BC) each make different assumptions about Nephite calendaring and chronology.

660 Chadwick, "Dating the Death of Jesus Christ," 190.

661 See chapter 58.

662 See chapter 55.

663 Even though some believed the earth could move at God's command, "and it appeareth unto man that the sun standeth still" (Helaman 12:15), Samuel was clearly talking about something else entirely, as he said they would be able to clearly discern the setting and rising of the sun, and there would still be no darkness (see Helaman 14:4). So the sun would not appear still in this instance. For discussion of Nephite cosmology, see Book of Mormon Central, "Why Did Mormon Say the Children of Men Are Less than the Dust of the Earth? (Helaman 12:7)," *KnoWhy 183* (September 8, 2016).

664 A similar event is prophesied to take place around the time of the Lord's Second Coming: "And it shall come to pass in that day, that the light shall not be clear, nor dark: But it shall be one day which shall be known to the Lord, not day, nor night: but it shall come to pass, that at evening time it shall be light" (Zachariah 14:6–7).

665 Hugh Nibley, *Teachings of the Book of Mormon*, 4 vols. (American Fork and Provo, UT: Covenant Communications and FARMS, 2004), 3:291.

Gardner, *Second Witness*, 5:191–192, critiqued this suggestion and proposed, instead, that it was a volcanic eruption, which would have provided light more locally.

666 "Astronomers Peg Brightness of History's Brightest Star," *National Optical Astronomy Observatory News*, March 5, 2003. This article reports on a supernova documented in AD 1006, not 1054.

667 Gardner, *Second Witness*, 5:191–192: "If a day, a night, and a day of light had occurred in the Old World, the evangelists who noted other signs and miracles of Christ's birth would surely have made it part of their record. We must therefore assume that the lighted night was a New World phenomenon, not a worldwide one. . . . A bright new star would be a good explanation for the Old World phenomenon, but there is still the issue of the differentially described phenomena for the Old and New Worlds. The descriptions point to different underlying events that are described in a similar context."

668 John A. Tvedtnes, "A Modern Example of Night without Darkness," *Insights: An Ancient Window 18*, no. 5 (October 1998): 4.

669 Nigel Waston, "The Tunguska Event," *History Today 58*, no. 7 (July 2008): 7.

670 Tony Phillips, "The Tunguska Impact—100 Years Later," *NASA Science News*, June 30, 2008.

671 Vladimir Rubtsov, *The Tunguska Mystery* (New York, NY: Springer, 2009), 15.

672 Rubtsov, *The Tunguska Mystery*, 13.

673 Tvedtnes, "A Modern Example," 4.

674 Rubtsov, *The Tunguska Mystery*, 21. A Bishop's ring "is a diffuse brown or bluish halo around the Sun," so-called because of its discovery by the Reverend S. Bishop.

675 Rubtsov, *The Tunguska Mystery*, 14.

676 Rubtsov, *The Tunguska Mystery*, 17.

677 Rubtsov, *The Tunguska Mystery*, 17. On p. 18, it is noted that the nearest report to Tunguska is six hundred km away.

678 Rubtsov, *The Tunguska Mystery*, 18,

679 Paul C. Hedengren, "Miracles," in *Encyclopedia of Mormonism*, 2:908.

680 John A. Widtsoe, *Joseph Smith as Scientist: A Contribution to Mormon Philosophy* (Salt Lake City, UT: YMMIA, 1908), 35; Welch, et al., *Knowing Why*, 280–281.

681 Interestingly, Aztec sources report a similar phenomenon ca. AD 1500. Waston, "The Tunguska Event," 7, quoted one source as describing the falling object that caused the Tunguska explosion as a "forked tongue of flames," which is strikingly similar to the account of "an omen of evil" in the Florentine Codex. "Ten years before the Spaniards arrived here, an omen of evil first appeared in the heavens. It was like a *tongue of fire, like a flame,* like the light of dawn. . . . It was there to the east when it thus came forth at midnight; *it looked as if day had dawned, day had broken.* Later, the sun destroyed it when he rose." Florentine Codex, as cited in Gardner, *Second Witness*, 5:192, 238; emphasis added. Gardner pointed out that this account "is historical evidence that people in [Mesoamerica] saw signs in the heavens which made night as bright as day. This passage is not necessarily evidence of the lights themselves, but it documents that at least some Mesoamericans accepted that such phenomenon was possible and that it had a divine significance . . . it is not hard to understand how the Nephites might have likewise believed in and described a similar culturally significant phenomenon" (p. 238).

682 While obviously no explosion was reported in the Book of Mormon, it should be pointed out that (1) the explosion happened in the morning of June 30, 1908, so would not have been seen immediately before nightfall; and (2) the nightlight effect was stronger at greater distances away from the explosion. If a similar, though perhaps smaller-scale phenomena occurred in a remote area somewhere a few hundred miles from Nephite territory, they likely would not have seen, felt, or heard the explosion. In the Tunguska event, the falling object was seen as "a bright bluish-white light in the sky" from six hundred miles away. See Waston, "The Tunguska Event," 7. Such a sight, if seen by Nephite astronomers, could have been understood as one of the "great lights in heaven" or the "many signs and wonders in heaven" foretold by Samuel. Mormon does assure readers that there were other signs leading up to the night without darkness, which nonetheless failed to persuade detractors (see 3 Nephi 1:4–5).

683 Kimberly M. Berkey, "Temporality and Fulfillment in 3 Nephi 1," *Journal of Book of Mormon Studies 24* (2015): 74.

684 See John 1:4–5; 3:19; 8:12; 9:5; 12:46; Mosiah 16:9; Alma 38:9; 3 Nephi 9:18; 11:11; Ether 4:12; D&C 10:70; 11:28; 12:9; 34:2; 39:2; 45:7; 93:2; 103.

685 Neal A. Maxwell, "In Him All Things Hold Together," *BYU Speeches*, March 31, 1991.

686 Maxwell, "In Him All Things Hold Together."

687 Neal A. Maxwell, "Encircled in the Arms of His Love," *Ensign*, November 2002.

688 Robert F. Smith, "Epistolary Form in the Book of Mormon," *FARMS Review 22*, no. 2 (2010): 127. See also chapter 37.

689 See Smith, "Epistolary Form," 132: "Since both the Book of Mormon and the brass (bronze) plates of Laban were written in Egyptian, it might be worthwhile for future researchers to also compare ancient Egyptian epistolography to Book of Mormon letters."

690 Kim Ridealgh, "Polite Like an Egyptian? Case Studies of Politeness in the Late Ramesside Letters," *Journal of Politeness Research 12*, no. 2 (2016): 248.

691 Ridealgh, "Polite like an Egyptian," 261.

692 Ridealgh, "Polite like an Egyptian," 260. Ridealgh added that this introductory phrase seemed intended to "mitigate any possible [Face Threatening Acts] due to the request act."

693 Several variants of this self-referential form accompanied by an imperative request can be found in the Book of Mormon, including some that mirror the Egyptian model more precisely. To modern readers of the text, Moroni wrote: "Behold, I would exhort you that *when ye shall read these things,* . . . that ye would remember how merciful the Lord hath been unto the children of men" (Moroni 10:3; emphasis added); "And *when ye shall receive these things,* I would exhort you that ye would ask God, the Eternal Father, in the name of Christ, if these things are not true" (Moroni 10:4; emphasis added). To Joseph Smith, Moroni wrote, "And now *I, Moroni, have written the words* which were commanded me . . . therefore touch them not in order that ye may translate" (Ether 5:1; emphasis added). To the Gentiles and the house of Israel in the latter days, the Lord declared, "*Therefore, when ye shall receive this record* . . . repent all ye ends of the earth, and come unto me" (Ether 4:17–18; emphasis added). Mormon wrote to his son, Moroni: "And now, my son, I desire that ye should labor diligently, that this gross error should be removed from among you; for, *for this intent I have written this epistle*" (Moroni 8:6; emphasis added). Captain Moroni's imperative request to Chief Judge Pahoran is interesting because, as one of inferior authority, Moroni appealed to the words of God rather than the words of his own letter: "therefore I would that ye should *adhere to the word of God,* and send speedily unto me of your provisions and of your men, and also to Helaman" (Alma 60:34; emphasis added). To Ammoron, Captain Moroni seemed to open up a request formula by making a self-reference to his own letter, but he delayed the request because he doubted the possibility of Ammoron hearkening unto him: "Behold, Ammoron, *I have written unto you* somewhat concerning this war . . . Behold, I would tell you somewhat concerning the justice of God . . . Yea, I would tell you these things if ye were capable of hearkening unto them . . . But as ye have once rejected these things . . . even so I may expect you will do it again" (Alma 54:5–8; emphasis added). When Captain Moroni finally

did get around to stipulating a request for prisoner exchange, he once again self-referenced his own epistle: "*I will close my epistle* by telling you that I will not exchange prisoners, save it be on conditions that ye will deliver up a man and his wife and his children, for one prisoner; if this be the case that ye will do it, I will exchange" (Alma 54:11; emphasis added). A special case can be found in one of Moroni's letters to Pahoran. Moroni "sent a petition, with the voice of the people, unto the governor of the land, *desiring that he should read it,* and give him [Moroni] power to compel those dissenters to defend their country" (Alma 51:15; cf. Alma 60:34). Royal Skousen has proposed that the word *read* should actually be *heed.* This is due to Oliver Cowdrey's misspelling *heed* as *head*, which led the 1830 typesetter to conjecturally insert *read* instead of *heed.* Skousen's conjectural emendation actually seems to align quite nicely with the Egyptian formality of expecting the recipient to fulfill a request in response to the letter itself. For Skousen's textual analysis, see Royal Skousen, *Analysis of Textual Variants of the Book of Mormon*, 6 vols., 2nd ed. (Provo, UT: FARMS and BYU Studies, 2017), 2745–2746.

694 For example, "most noble and chief governor" (3 Nephi 3:2), "exceedingly great praise" (3 Nephi 3:2), "firmness of your people" (3 Nephi 3:2), "noble Lachoneus" (3 Nephi 3:3), "your firmness in that which ye believe to be right" (3 Nephi 3:5), and "your noble spirit in the field of battle" (3 Nephi 3:5).

695 See 3 Nephi 3:3: "it seemeth a pity unto me."

696 See 3 Nephi 3:5: "feeling for your welfare."

697 For example, Giddianhi used the phrases "that which ye suppose to be your right and liberty," "supported by the hand of a god," and "defence of your liberty, and your property, and your country" (3 Nephi 3:2). These words and phrases would certainly have been familiar and perhaps even peculiar to the Nephites' political and religious language. Cf. Alma 43:9, 26; 56:11.

698 See 3 Nephi 3:7: "Or in other words, yield yourselves up unto us, and unite with us and become acquainted with our secret works, and become our brethren that ye may be like unto us—not our slaves, but our brethren and partners of all our substance."

699 For example, Giddianhi preferred to use the pronoun *they* in reference to his own men, thereby excluding himself from the threatening acts of his robbers: "*they* should come down against you" (3 Nephi 3:4; emphasis added), "*they* should visit you with the sword" (3 Nephi 3:6; emphasis added), and "*they* shall not stay *their* hand" (3 Nephi 3:8; emphasis added). On the other hand, when seeking cooperation with the Nephites, Giddianhi used the pronouns *us* and *our*, which included him back into his own party: "yield yourselves up unto *us*, and unite with *us* and become acquainted with *our* secret works" (3 Nephi 3:7; emphasis added).

700 Penelope Brown and Stephen C. Levinson, *Politeness: Some Universals in Language Usage* (New York, NY: Cambridge University Press, 1987), 13.

701 For positive politeness, see Brown and Levinson, *Politeness*, 101. For praise, see pp. 103–105; sympathy, p. 106; in-group language, pp. 107–111; and cooperation, pp. 125–127.

702 For negative politeness, see Brown and Levinson, *Politeness*, 129; for expression of reluctance, see pp. 187–188. It should be noted that in Brown and Levinson's model, "negative face" is not undesirable or bad. It is simply their term for the desire of both speakers and hearers to be unimpeded in their actions. A speaker can actually show politeness for a hearer by appealing to his or her "negative face." This is called "negative politeness."

703 3 Nephi 3:11–12, for example, suggests that Lachoneus, to some degree or another, informed his people concerning Giddianhi's intentions for war.

704 Brown and Levinson, *Politeness*, 71.

705 See Gardner, *Second Witness*, 5:255: "Giddianhi can confidently assume that Zarahemla still holds many sympathizers and that victory will be assured in an all-out battle."

706 See Gardner, *Second Witness*, 5:254: "From the Nephite perspective . . . it would not only mean political and economic submission, but the probable destruction of their religion—the very reasons they feared the order of the Nehors."

707 See 1 Corinthians 12:10; Alma 18:18; D&C 46:23.

708 David A. Bednar, "Quick to Observe," *Ensign*, December 2006, 35.

709 As cited in David A. Bednar, "Quick to Observe," 35.

710 There is some textual ambiguity as to whether or not the Gadianton robbers themselves or the lambskins were dyed in blood. Because "a lamb-skin" is singular and the subject of "dyed in blood" is plural, it seems likely that the bodies of the Gadianton robbers were dyed in blood.

711 Matthew Brown suggested that the lambskin and the blood is a point of emphasis by proposing that 3 Nephi 4:7 forms a chiasm, where the turning point focuses on the lambskin about their loins and their being dyed in blood. See Matthew Brown, "Girded About with a Lambskin," *Journal of Book of Mormon Studies* 6, no. 2 (1997): 127–128.

712 See Enos 1:20; Mosiah 10:8; Alma 3:5; Alma 43:20. The description of a leather or skin girdle is also found in the Old Testament when describing Elijah (see 2 Kings 1:8) and in the New Testament in describing John the Baptist (see Matthew 3:4; Mark 1:6). David condemns his general Joab for pursuing war and putting "the blood of war upon his girdle that was about his loins" (1 Kings 2:5).

713 There are twenty-six occurrences of the word *sheep* in the Book of Mormon. Of those, only Ether 9:18 refers to an actual animal being physically present in a Book of Mormon scene. The other uses of the word *sheep* are used metaphorically when referring to ministry or to Jesus Christ. See for example 1 Nephi 22:25; Mosiah 14:6–7; Alma 5:37–38; Helaman 15:13; 3 Nephi 15:17. The word *lamb* occurs seventy-six times in the Book of Mormon and is most often used metaphorically as a title for Jesus Christ. See for example Nephi's vision in 1 Nephi 11–14, which uses the titles "the Lamb" and "Lamb of God" thirty-nine times; also 2 Nephi 31:4–6; 2 Nephi 33:14; Alma 7:14; Mormon 9:2–6. The idea of garments being washed white through the "blood of the Lamb" is found in Alma 13:11; Alma 34:36; Ether 13:10–11. Other references to lambs would have appeared on the brass plates, as they are quotations of Old Testament passages (see 2 Nephi 15:17 [cf. Isaiah 5:17]; 2 Nephi 21:6 [cf. Isaiah 11:6]; 2 Nephi 30:12 [cf. Isaiah 11:6]; Mosiah 14:7 [cf. Isaiah 53:7]). 3 Nephi 28:22 and 4 Nephi 1:33 both refer to a "suckling lamb," not as a title for Jesus Christ, but still in a metaphorical sense to describe the experience of the Three Nephites in a den of beasts. The phrase *suckling lamb* may be an allusion to 1 Samuel 7:9, where the phrase also occurs.

714 For evidence of sheep in the New World, see Wade E. Miller, *Science and the Book of Mormon: Cureloms, Cumoms, Horse and More* (Laguna Niguel, CA: KCT & Associates, 2010), 43–48; Wade E. Miller and Matthew Roper, "Animals in the Book of Mormon: Challenges and Perspectives," *BYU Studies Quarterly* 56, no. 4 (2017): 156. For evidence of the remains of a young domestic sheep in western New York, see William A. Ritchie, *The Archeology of New York State* (Garden City, NY: Natural History Press, 1969), 241–243.

715 The presence of the word *lamb* in the Book of Mormon may be an example of loan-shifting. For a further treatment of loan-shifting and possible explanations for the presence of post-Columbian animals in the Book of Mormon, see Neal Rappleye, "'Put Away Childish Things': Learing to Read the Book of Mormon with Mature Historical Understanding," 2017 FairMormon Conference, 22–24; online at https://www.fairmormon.org/wp-content/uploads/2016/11/Rappleye_2017FM_Presentation.pdf. While the Book of Mormon frequently mentions flocks and herds, these flocks are not identified as flocks of sheep. For a discussion on the nature of flocks and herds in the Book of Mormon, see Gardner, *Second Witness*, 2:92–96. An example of the usage of flocks is the story of Ammon at the waters of Sebus, guarding King

Lamoni's flocks. While the text never specifies what kind of animals Ammon was to protect, the flock's susceptibility to scattering may strongly suggest that they were not sheep. See Gardner, *Second Witness*, 4:174–276.

716 See note 713.

717 Lambs were preferred, but not required, for burnt offerings (see Leviticus 1), peace offerings (see Leviticus 3), and sin offerings (see Leviticus 4). However, for a trespass offering (see Leviticus 5:14–19) and for the Passover (see Exodus 12), sheep were indeed required. The Day of Atonement required the sacrifice of both a bullock and a goat to serve as the "scapegoat" (see Leviticus 16).

718 Several scholars have presented evidence to suggest that Nephi and his descendants built a temple after the manner of Solomon, strictly followed the law of Moses, and officiated in the Melchizedek Priesthood. See John W. Welch, "The Temple in the Book of Mormon: The Temples at the Cities of Nephi, Zarahemla, and Bountiful," in *Temples of the Ancient World*, 297–387; John W. Welch, "The Melchizedek Material in Alma 13:13–19," in *By Study and Also by Faith: Essays in Honor of Hugh W. Nibley*, 2:238–272; Daniel C. Peterson, "Priesthood in Mosiah," in *The Book of Mormon: Mosiah, Salvation Only through Christ*, ed. Monte S. Nyman and Charles D. Tate Jr. (Provo, UT: BYU Religious Studies Center, 1991), 187–210.

719 Mosiah 2:3 explicitly states that the Nephites "took of the firstlings of their flocks, that they might offer sacrifice and burnt offerings according to the law of Moses." While the Book of Mormon never indicates which animals they used for which sacrifices, they were clearly using domesticated animals to serve as their sacrificial offering.

720 The Florentine Codex describes the *nonotzaleque* as a group of assassin-like warriors whose distinguishing feature was dressing in jaguar pelts. While this group of Aztec warriors far post-dates Book of Mormon times, Brant Gardner proposes that traces of this Aztec influence can be seen earlier in the chronology. See Gardner, *Second Witness*, 5:11–29.

721 Gardner, *Second Witness*, 5:263.

722 Not only the animal's identity would have been terrifying, but also the blood because of Israelite laws of blood contamination. See Leviticus 6:27; 12:1–5; 17:10–12; 1 Kings 2:5.

723 Ethan Sproat argued that the term *skins* in the Book of Mormon may be a reference to Adam and Eve's "coats of skins," and that the "skins" of the Lamanites is a reference to some item of clothing that asserted their right to authority. Sproat further connects the blood-stained lambskin in 3 Nephi 4 with an actual temple ritual described in 1 Kings 2. See Ethan Sproat, "Skins as Garments in the Book of Mormon: A Textual Exegesis," *Journal of Book of Mormon Studies 24* (2015): 149–158. Matthew Brown suggested that the lambskin they wore may represent a ceremonial apron or ephod, familiar to Israelite temple worship, as well as Mesoamerican royal aprons. See Brown, "Girded About with a Lambskin," 124–151.

724 Brown, "Girded About with a Lambskin," 146–148. Hugh Nibley discusses how in various ancient cultures, the donning of skins or garments transfers to the wearer the powers and virtues of the animal or garment. If the Gadianton robbers subscribed to such belief, they may have been seeking to coopt the power of the Lamb of God. See Hugh Nibley, *Temple and Cosmos, The Collected Works of Hugh Nibley: Volume 12* (Salt Lake City and Provo, UT: Deseret Book and FARMS, 1992), 112–132.

725 Even the fact that he was hanged without a trial makes sense in an ancient context. John W. Welch stated, "Robbers in the ancient world were more than common thieves; they were outsiders and enemies to society itself. As such, the ancients reasoned, they were outlaws, outside the law, and not entitled to legal process. Against bandits and brigands, 'the remedies were military, not legal.'" Thus, Zemnarihah being executed by hanging without a trial would not have been remarkable in the ancient Israelite world. In addition, "In the Temple Scroll from Qumran, the prescribed penalty for one . . . who 'has defected into the midst of nations, and has cursed his people, [and] the children of Israel,' is that he shall be 'hung on a tree.' It should be noted that the Temple Scroll's description of the kinds of cases that deserve hanging fits Zemnarihah's case exactly." Because Zemnarihah had attacked his own people, he was considered to be a traitor, and so was hanged, and not stoned as one might expect. Welch, *Legal Cases*, 352–354. See also John A. Tvedtnes, "More on the Hanging of Zemharihah," in *Pressing Forward with the Book of Mormon*, 208–210.

726 Welch, *Legal Cases*, 354. See also John W. Welch, "The Execution of Zemnarihah," in *Reexploring the Book of Mormon*, 250–251.

727 Welch, *Legal Cases*, 354–355.

728 Numbers 19:11 notes that "He that toucheth the dead body of any man shall be unclean seven days." However, uncleanness of this kind could also have been transferred to the tree that was touching the body of the dead. See Welch, *Legal Cases*, 355–356.

729 See Welch, *Legal Cases*, 355.

730 Such curses recur periodically throughout the Book of Mormon. See, for example, Mosiah 12:13; Alma 44:14. For more information on simile curses, see Delbert R. Hillers, "Treaty-Curses and the Old Testament Prophets," *Biblica et Orientalia 16* (Rome: Pontifical Biblical Institute, 1964); Noel Weeks, *Admonition and Curse: The Ancient Near Eastern Treaty/Covenant Form as a Problem in Inter-Cultural Relationships* (London: T&T Clark, 2004); Anne Marie Kitz, "An Oath, Its Curse and Anointing Ritual," *Journal of the American Oriental Society 124*, no. 2 (April–June 2004): 315–321; Anne Marie Kitz, "Effective Simile and Effective Act: Psalm 109, Numbers 5, and KUB 26," *The Catholic Biblical Quarterly 69*, no. 3 (July 2007): 440–456.

731 See chapters 21, 23.

732 Billie Jean Collins, "The First Soldiers' Oath" in *The Context of Scripture, Volume I: Canonical Compositions from the Biblical World*, ed. William W. Hallo (Leiden: Brill, 2003), 165–166. The brackets in the words in this quotation represent occasions when scholars have to guess what parts of certain words might be. This happens because the clay tablets on which the text is written are sometimes broken in places.

733 Allen J. Christenson, trans., *Popol Vuh: The Sacred Book of the Maya* (Norman, OK: University of Oklahoma Press, 2007), 110.

734 David A. Bednar, "Ask in Faith," *Ensign*, May 2008, 94.

735 Mormon does introduce himself in Words of Mormon 1:1–2, but according to Brant A. Gardner, "Words of Mormon was likely written after [Mormon's introduction] in 3 Nephi." See Gardner, *Second Witness*, 3:72.

736 See 1 Nephi 1:1; Jacob 1:1; Enos 1:1.

737 See William J. Critchlow III, "Manuscript, Lost 116 Pages," *Encyclopedia of Mormonism*, 2:854–855.

738 Gardner, *Second Witness*, 3:71. Gardner further explained: "As the Words of Mormon show, when Mormon needed to make a textual transition, he attempted to smooth it out by providing linking and explanatory material. Mormon probably used a similar technique when he began his record in the initial 116 pages. Mormon could not assume that the reader would understand who he was and how he produced the text (especially when he made editorial comments without further self-identifications) unless he had previously introduced himself, describing his divine call to abridge the records and his purpose in so doing" (p. 72).

739 See the introductory heading for 3 Nephi 1.

740 See Testimony of the Eight Witnesses (found in the introductory pages of the Book of Mormon); Richard Lloyd Anderson, *Investigating the Book of Mormon Witnesses* (Salt Lake City, UT: Deseret Book, 1981). The doctrine of witnesses is a crucial teaching found—both explicitly and thematically—throughout the Book of Mormon. For examples, see 1 Nephi 11:7; 2 Nephi

11:3; 2 Nephi 27:14; 2 Nephi 29:8; Jacob 4:13; Alma 10:12; 3 Nephi 11:16; Ether 5:4. See also Welch, et al., *Knowing Why*, 130–131.

741 Matthew L. Bowen, "'Most Desirable Above All Things': Onomastic Play on Mary and Mormon in the Book of Mormon," *Interpreter: A Journal of Mormon Scripture 13* (2015): 60. See also "Mormon," *Book of Mormon Onomasticon*.

742 Interestingly, Mormon's closing statement actually mirrors the closing formalities of several epistles found in the Book of Mormon. Mormon wrote, "And now I make an end of my saying. . . . I am Mormon, and a pure descendant of Lehi" (3 Nephi 5:19–20). For comparative examples, see Alma 54:14, 24; 58:41; 60:36. See also Robert F. Smith, "Epistolary Form in the Book of Mormon," *FARMS Review 22*, no. 2 (2010): 125–135; Sidney B. Sperry, "Types of Literature in the Book of Mormon: Epistles, Psalms, Lamentations," *Journal of Book of Mormon Studies 4*, no. 1 (1995): 73–74. See also chapter 59. For a treatment of Mormon's digression as a colophon, see John A. Tvedtnes, "Colophons in the Book of Mormon," in *Rediscovering the Book of Mormon* 36.

743 See Welch and Welch, *Charting the Book of Mormon*, chart 144. Moreover, it seems that Mormon intentionally skimmed over several years so that he could insert his message at the conclusion of the twenty-fifth year since the sign of Christ's birth (see 3 Nephi 5:7). It's thus possible that he purposefully aligned the beginning of a new pride cycle with the commencement of a new hotun (five-year) cycle, a prophetic interval of time keeping in the ancient Mesoamerican calendrical system. See chapter 55. Indicating his awareness of short-term cyclical patterns, Mormon soon reported, "thus six years had not passed away since the more part of the people had turned from their righteousness, like the dog to his vomit, or like the sow to her wallowing in the mire" (3 Nephi 7:8). See chapters 45 and 64.

744 M. Russell Ballard, "Beware of False Prophets and False Teachers," *Ensign*, November 1999.

745 See also the Introduction to the Book of Mormon.

746 See Justine M. Shaw, "Maya Sacbeob: Form and Function," in *Ancient Mesoamerica 12* (2001): 268.

747 For instance, see Alfonso Villa Rojas, "The Yaxuna-Cobá Causeway," *Contributions to American Archaeology 2*, no. 9 (1934).

748 Mark Alan Wright, "The Cultural Tapestry of Mesoamerica," *Journal of the Book of Mormon and Other Restoration Scripture 22*, no. 2 (2013): 14.

749 Sorenson, *Mormon's Codex*, 357.

750 Sorenson, *Mormon's Codex*, 357.

751 See Wright, "The Cultural Tapestry of Mesoamerica," 14.

752 See chapter 50. See also Wallace E. Hunt Jr., "The Marketplace," in *Pressing Forward with the Book of Mormon*, 196–200; John L. Sorenson, "Nephi's Garden and Chief Market," in *Reexploring the Book of Mormon*, 236–238.

753 See Francisco Pérez Ruiz, "Recintos amurallados: Una interpretación sobre el sistema defensivo de Chichen Itza, Yucatán," in *XVIII simposio de investigaciones arqueológicas en Guatemala*, 2004, ed. Juan Pedro Laporte, Bárbara Arroyo, and Héctor E. Mejía (Guatemala City: Museo Nacional de Arqueología y Etnología), 882–883. For an English version of this publication, see Francisco Pérez Ruiz, "Walled Compounds: An Interpretation of the Defensive System at Chichen Itza, Yucatan," online at famsi.org.

754 See Shaw, "Maya Sacbeob," 266.

755 Mormon's three-fold description of highways and roads leading from (1) "city to city," (2) "land to land," and (3) "place to place" is interesting because Shaw has argued that the ancient Maya seemed to have grouped their roads into three major categories: (1) local intrasite, (2) core–outlier intrasite, and (3) intersite. See Shaw, "Maya Sacbeob," 262. Although it is uncertain, it's possible that Mormon's description of "place to place" refers to the "local intrasite" roads, that "land to land" refers to "intersite" roads, and that "city to city" is a description of "core–outlier intrasite" roads. Shaw explained that his "proposed groupings appear to have been a reality for the Lowland Maya. Although I do not insist that the Maya themselves would have classified Sacbeob in this manner, and I realize that the measurements and sample are a product of archaeologists' foci, the divisions are apparently related to something in the real world. The groups are possibly related to the distance normally walked by site inhabitants in a day, the length easily traversed by participants in a ritual, or the span over which political control may have been exerted and maintained under certain conditions" (p. 266). Support for the idea that the Nephites at least conceived of one of these categories (a day's journey) comes from Helaman 4:7: "And there they did fortify against the Lamanites, from the west sea, even unto the east; it being a day's journey for a Nephite, on the line which they had fortified and stationed their armies to defend their north country" (emphasis added).

756 Justine M. Shaw, "Roads to Ruins: The Role of Sacbeob in Ancient Maya Society," in *Highways, Byways, and Road Systems in the Pre-Modern World*, ed. Susan E. Alcock, John Bodel, and Richard J. A. Talbert (Chichester, UK: John Wiley & Sons, 2012), 137.

757 This passage is interesting because it is the only symbolic path in the Book of Mormon that is certainly described as being *straight* (meaning not crooked) instead of *strait* (meaning narrow). All other instances of "strai[gh]t" paths are more ambiguous. See Paul Y. Hoskisson, "Straightening Things Out: The Use of Strait and Straight in the Book of Mormon," *Journal of Book of Mormon Studies 12*, no. 2 (2003): 62; Book of Mormon Central, "Is the Path to Eternal Life 'Strait' or 'Straight'? (1 Nephi 8:20)," *KnoWhy 456* (August 7, 2018).

758 See Sorenson, *Mormon's Codex*, 356–357: "Roads were made and used for at least 2,500 years before the Spanish conquest, beginning with the Olmec people at San Lorenzo. Hundreds of miles of them have now been discovered in locations ranging from the state of Zacatecas on the north to Yucatan and Atlantic Guatemala on the south."

759 See "4 Ways the New Maya Discoveries May Relate to the Book of Mormon," Book of Mormon Central Blog, February 5, 2018, online at bookofmormoncentral.org. See also, Brigit Katz, "LiDAR Scans Reveal Maya Civilization's Sophisticated Network of Roads," February 3, 2017, online at smithsonianmag.com; Tom Clynes, "Exclusive: Laser Scans Reveal Maya 'Megalopolis' Below Guatemalan Jungle," February 1, 2018, online at news.nationalgeographic.com.

760 See Wright, "The Cultural Tapestry of Mesoamerica," 14; Michael R. Ash, "Archaeology and the Book of Mormon," online at fairmormon.org; William J. Hamblin, "Basic Methodological Problems with the Anti-Mormon Approach to the Geography and Archaeology of the Book of Mormon," *Journal of Book of Mormon Studies 2*, no. 1 (1993): 193–196.

761 Shaw, "Roads to Ruins," 139.

762 Shaw, "Roads to Ruins," 135.

763 Shaw, "Roads to Ruins," 139.

764 See Welch, et al., *Knowing Why*, 291–293. The Lamanite system of kingship is quite similar to the systems of rulership found among the ancient Maya. And it is likely that, among other things, Lamoni would have traveled to the feast to pay tribute to his father. See Welch et al., *Knowing Why*, 296–297.

765 For evidence that feasts in ancient Mesoamerican societies held both religious and political significance, see Lisa J. LeCount, "Like Water for Chocolate: Feasting and Political Ritual among the Late Classic Maya at Xunantunich, Belize," *American Anthropologist 103*, no. 4 (2001): 935–953; Keith Eppich, "Feast and Sacrifice at El Perú-Waka': The N14-2 Deposit as Dedication," *PARI Journal 10*, no. 2 (Fall 2009):1–19. Although it is impossible to know if the Lamanites held religious feasts, there is good evidence that the Nephites observed the holy days of their Israelite tradition. See Welch, et al.,

Knowing Why, 80–82, 186–187, 207–209, 314–315. See also chapter 15.
766 Shaw, "Roads to Ruins," 134.
767 See chapter 68.
768 See chapter 91.
769 It's likely that ancient American highways were first brought to the attention of the American public by John Lloyd Stephens and Frederick Catherwood more than ten years after the publication of the Book of Mormon. Among the many roads discussed in his travels, Stephens mentioned "a great paved way, made of pure white stone, called in the Maya language Sacbé, leading from Kabah to Uxmal, on which the lords of those places sent messengers to and fro, bearing letters written on the leaves and bark of trees." John L. Stephens, *Incidents of Travel in Yucatan*, 2 vols. (New York, NY: Harper and Brothers, 1843), 1:415. See also John E. Clark, Wade Ardern, and Matthew Roper, "Debating the Foundations of Mormonism: The Book of Mormon and Archaeology," 2005 FairMormon conference presentation, online at fairmormon.org.
770 See, for example, Helaman 3:25–26, 32; 11:20–21; 3 Nephi 6:1–9; Helaman 3:33–34, 36; 4:11–12; 3 Nephi 6:13–18; 2 Nephi 25:9; Helaman 7:13–28; 10:14–17; 3 Nephi 6:20, 23; Helaman 4:1–2, 11, 13; 11:1–6; 3 Nephi 9:1–12; Helaman 4:14–15, 20–26; 11:7–11, 15; 3 Nephi 5:1–6.
771 For another example of a time when the pride cycle manifested itself among the Nephites, see chapter 45.
772 See chapter 50.
773 Joseph A. Callaway and Hershel Shanks, "The Settlement in Canaan: The Period of the Judges" in *Ancient Israel: From Abraham to the Roman Destruction of the Temple*, 3rd ed,, ed. Hershel Shanks (Washington, DC: Biblical Archaeology Society, 2011), 59–83. This point was overstated for many years. Some scholars went so far as to state that there was no conquest from the outside, and that what some considered to be the conquest of Canaan was actually just a massive peasant's revolt. Then the pendulum swung the other direction with people saying there was no civil unrest during the Israelite invasion of Canaan. However, some scholars now argue that an uprising of the poor against the rich was one significant contributing factor, among others, to the conquest of Canaan. For an exploration of these different approaches, see Hershel Shanks, William G. Dever, Baruch Halpern, and P. Kyle McCarter Jr., *The Rise of Ancient Israel* (Washington, DC: Biblical Archaeology Society, 1992).
774 The word used to describe Rahab is almost certainly not the same word used to describe the more affluent or respected prostitutes associated with ancient temples, implying that Rahab was not well off. Lawrence E. Stager, "Forging an Identity: The Emergence of Ancient Israel," in *The Oxford History of the Biblical World*, ed. Michael D. Coogan (New York, NY: Oxford University Press, 1998), 103–104.
775 Patrick Kearon, "Refuge from the Storm," *Ensign*, May 2016, 111–114.
776 Ray C. Hillam, "Secret Combinations," *Encyclopedia of Mormonism*, 3:1290–1291.
777 See Daniel C. Peterson, "Notes on 'Gadianton Masonry'," in *Warfare in the Book of Mormon*, 176–181.
778 Daniel C. Peterson, "Notes and Communications: 'Secret Combinations' Revisited," *Journal of Book of Mormon Studies 1*, no. 1 (1992): 184.
779 For an overview of these claims, see Peterson, "Notes on 'Gadianton Masonry'," 180–181.
780 Gregory L. Smith, "Cracking the Book of Mormon's 'Secret Combinations'?" *Interpreter: A Journal of Mormon Scripture 13* (2014): 93. It should be noted that Smith wasn't the first to identify nineteenth-century documents that used "secret combinations" in a non-Masonic context. For prior successes in this effort, see Peterson, "Notes on 'Gadianton Masonry'," 174–224; Peterson, "'Secret Combinations' Revisited," 184–188; Paul Mouritsen, "Secret Combinations and Flaxen Cords: Anti-Masonic Rhetoric and the Book of Mormon," *Journal of Book of Mormon Studies 12*, no. 1 (2003): 64–77, 116–18; Nathan Oman, "'Secret Combinations': A Legal Analysis," *FARMS Review 16*, no. 1 (2004): 49–73.
781 Noah Webster, *American Dictionary of the English Language* (1828), s.v., "combination."
782 It should be noted, though, that the term *combination* seemed to be predominantly negative in tone, even without secret as a qualifier. See Peterson, "Notes on 'Gadianton Masonry'," 189–190.
783 See John L. Sorenson, *An Ancient American Setting for the Book of Mormon*, 300–301.
784 See Kent P. Jackson, "Revolutionaries in the First Century," in *Masada and the World of the New Testament*, 129–140; John W. Welch, "Legal and Social Perspectives on Robbers in First Century Judea," in *Masada and the World of the New Testament*, 141–153; John W. Welch and John F. Hall, *Charting the New Testament* (Provo, UT: FARMS, 2002), chart 3–12.
785 See Sorenson, *An Ancient American Setting*, 300–310; Bruce W. Warren, "Secret Combinations, Warfare, and Captive Sacrifice in Mesoamerica and the Book of Mormon," in *Warfare in the Book of Mormon*, 225–236.
786 See Sorenson, *An Ancient American Setting*, 304–305. Likewise, Bonnie Erickson found that risk—a key feature of many, though not all, secret societies—is "so important a consideration that it sets similar processes in motion even for societies differing in time, place, goals, and so on." Bonnie H. Erickson, "Secret Societies and Social Structure," *Social Forces 60*, no. 1 (1981): 190. Although the nineteenth-century Freemasons may not have actually been a truly dangerous group, the label of "secret combinations" given to them by their opponents implies they were involved in something illegal or unwholesome. In other words, they were being characterized as a group whose secrecy was made necessary because of risky behavior.
787 Although some similarities do exist, there are also key differences between the Gadianton robbers and nineteenth-century Freemasons. See Peterson, "Notes on 'Gadianton Masonry'," 209–213.
788 Neil L. Andersen, "Faith Is Not by Chance, but by Choice," Ensign, November 2015, 66.
789 Neil L. Andersen, "Never Leave Him," *Ensign*, November 2010, 41.
790 See Peterson, "'Secret Combinations' Revisited," 185–188; David R. Benard, John W. Welch, and Daniel C. Peterson, "'Secret Combinations'," in *Reexploring the Book of Mormon*, 227–229.
791 See Peterson, "'Secret Combinations' Revisited," 184–188; Mouritsen, "Secret Combinations and Flaxen Cords," 64–77, 116–18; Oman, "'Secret Combinations'," 49–73.
792 Smith, "Cracking the Book of Mormon's 'Secret Combinations'?" 93.
793 Although Alexander Campbell was the first to connect the Book of Mormon's Gadianton robbers with the Freemasons, the argument that "secret combinations" was an exclusive term for Freemasons wasn't developed until the twentieth century. See Peterson, "Notes on 'Gadianton Masonry'," 176–181.
794 Elder Jeffrey R. Holland, "The Greatness of the Evidence," *Chiasmus Jubliee*, August 16, 2017, online at bookofmormoncentral.org.
795 See chapter 124.
796 Dieter F. Uchtdorf, "Be Not Afraid, Only Believe," *Ensign*, November 2015, 78.
797 Luke 1:11–20; Matthew 3:13–17; Mark 1:9–11; Luke 3:21–23. Doctrine & Covenants 84:28 presents the idea that John was ordained to the priesthood "by the angel of God at the time he was eight days old."
798 Mark 1:2; cf. Malachi 3:1; 3 Nephi 24:1.
799 Mark 1:3; cf. Isaiah 40:3, cited by Lehi in 1 Nephi 10:8, thus also known to the Nephites.
800 See Matthew 17:12–13; Luke 1:17, 76–77; JST John 1:21–24. Joseph Smith taught that a forerunner who prepares the way for the building up of God's kingdom is called "an Elias." Joseph Fielding Smith, comp. and ed.,

Teachings of the Prophet Joseph Smith (Salt Lake City, UT: Deseret Book, 1977), 335–336.

801 Cf. 1 Nephi 12:1–3, 5; 19:10–11; Helaman 14:20–27. For details on the prophecy and its fulfillment, see chapters 57 and 68.

802 See Matthew 26–27; Mark 14–15; Luke 22–23; John 12–19; Jeffrey R. Chadwick, "Dating the Death of Jesus Christ," *BYU Studies Quaterly 54*, no. 4 (2015): 136–139. According to most scholars, the synoptic Gospels (Matthew, Mark, Luke) differ with John on whether it was the day before Passover (fourteenth of Nisan) or the day of Passover (fifteenth of Nisan). See Lincoln H. Blumell and Thomas A. Wayment, "When was Jesus Born? A Response to a Recent Proposal," *BYU Studies Quaterly 51*, no. 3 (2012): 65; Richard Neitzel Holzapfel, Eric D. Huntsman, and Thomas A. Wayment, *Jesus Christ and the World of the New Testament*, 137–138; Thomas A. Wayment, "The Birth and Death Dates of Jesus Christ," in *The Life and Teachings of Jesus Christ*, 1:391–392; Stanley E. Porter, "Chronology of the New Testament," in *Eerdmans Dictionary of the Bible*, ed. David Noel Freedman (Grand Rapids, MI: Wm. B. Eerdmans, 2000), 249–250. For a reconciliation favoring the fourteenth of Nisan, see Chadwick, "Dating the Death of Jesus Christ," 165–172. For a reconciliation favoring the fifteenth of Nisan, see Craig L. Blomberg, *The Historical Reliability of Gospels*, 2nd ed. (Downers Grove, IL: InterVarsity Press, 2007), 221–225. On the timing of Pilate's governorship, see Emily Cheney, "Pilate, Pontius," in *Eerdmans Dictionary*, 1058.

803 Chadwick, "Dating the Death of Jesus Christ," 156; see also the chart on p. 157. Porter, "Chronology of the New Testament," 250, adds AD 36, but also determines that "27 is too early and 36 too late" to work with other factors. Blumell and Wayment, "When was Jesus Born?" 64–70, expands the range of possible dates based on the possibility of misidentifying the new moon. Chadwick, "Dating the Death of Jesus Christ," 158–165, responds to this argument. Randall P. Spackman, "Introduction to Book of Mormon Chronology: The Principal Prophecies, Calendars, and Dates," *FARMS Preliminary Reports, 1993*, 60–68, plus appendix 2, argued that the Book of Mormon supports a death date in AD 29, but this date has little support from New Testament scholars.

804 Porter, "Chronology of the New Testament," 250. See Chadwick, "Dating the Death of Jesus Christ," 139–142 for documentation that this is the view of most scholars. See also Wayment, "The Birth and Death Dates of Jesus Christ," 393–394; Holzapfel, Huntsman, and Wayment, *Jesus Christ and the World of the New Testament*, 44; John H. Walton and Craig S. Keener, eds., *NIV Cultural Backgrounds Study Bible* (Grand Rapids, MI: Zondervan, 2016), 1593, 1667, 1863–1864; Ben Witherington III, "Images of Crucifixion: Fresh Evidence," *Biblical Archaeological Review 39*, no. 2 (2013): 28; Blomberg, *Historical Reliability of Gospels*, 225: "the only year close to the time of Christ's ministry in which he could have been crucified would have been AD 30. . . . AD 30 turns out to be the very year many scholars have accepted as the year of Christ's death."

805 Porter, "Chronology of the New Testament," 250. See, for example, Paul Barnett, *Jesus and the Rise of Early Christianity: A History of New Testament Times* (Downers Grover, IL: InterVarsity Press, 1999), 155.

806 See chapter 57. See also Jeffrey R. Chadwick, "Dating the Birth of Jesus Christ," *BYU Studies Quaterly 49*, no. 4 (2010): 17–18; Chadwick, "Dating the Death of Jesus Christ," 142–149.

807 Chadwick, "Dating the Death of Jesus Christ," 190.

808 Representing this traditional view and forcefully rejecting the Thursday argument are Blumell and Wayment, "When Was Jesus Born?" 65–66, 78–79 nn. 51–57. For a response, see Chadwick, "Dating the Death of Jesus Christ," 176–177, 179–180 n. 108.

809 See Chadwick, "Dating the Death of Jesus Christ," 172. David B. Cummings, "Three Days and Three Nights: Reassessing Jesus's En-tombment," *Journal of Book of Mormon Studies 16*, no. 1 (2007): 58 also mentions "advocates of Wednesday" as the day of Christ's death.

810 See Chadwick, "Dating the Death of Jesus Christ," 174–177; Cummings, "Three Days and Three Nights," 59.

811 See Chadwick, "Dating the Death of Jesus Christ," 177–182.

812 Chadwick, "Dating the Death of Jesus Christ," 138; Cummings, "Three Days and Three Nights," 60.

813 There is uncertainty on whether the new moon would have been observed on the correct day in AD 30, making it possible that the fourteenth of Nisan (the day before Passover, and most likely day of Crucifixion) was on Thursday (the correct day), or Friday (if the new moon was observed a day late). This would make the fifteenth of Nisan (the first day of Passover) either Friday (the correct day), or Saturday (if the new moon was observed a day late). See Chadwick, "Dating the Death of Jesus Christ," 154–158. Since most scholars favor an AD 30 date and a Friday for the day of Crucifixion, they assume the new moon was not observed on the correct day, and that the fourteenth of Nisan was thus a day late, on Friday. Chadwick's position—that AD 30 is the year, and thus Christ's death happened on a Thursday (the correct day for the fourteenth of Nisan)—seems more consistent. In fact, Blomberg, *Historicity of the Gospels*, 221–225, favors AD 30 precisely because it is the only year the fifteenth of Nisan fell on Friday and, unlike most New Testament scholars, he favors the synoptic Gospels' chronology (Christ dying on the first day of Passover) over that of John's.

814 Cummings, "Three Days and Three Nights," 63; cf. pp. 60–63; Chadwick, "Dating the Death of Jesus Christ," 182–188.

815 Chadwick, "Dating the Death of Jesus Christ," 184; cf. the charts on pp. 186–187. See also figs. 1 and 2 in Cummings, "Three Days and Three Nights," 62–63.

816 Chadwick, "Dating the Death of Jesus Christ," 190; capitalization altered.

817 Chadwick, "Dating the Death of Jesus Christ," 136.

818 Thomas S. Monson, "He Is Risen," *Ensign*, May 2010, 89.

819 Gordon B. Hinckley, "This Glorious Eastern Morn," *Ensign*, May 1996.

820 "The Living Christ: The Testimony of the Apostles," *Ensign*, April 2000; emphasis added.

821 1 Nephi 12:1–3, 5; 19:10–11; Helaman 14:20–27.

822 Hugh Nibley, *Since Cumorah*, 231–238. *Since Cumorah* originally ran as a series in the *Improvement Era* from 1964–1967.

823 Sorenson, *An Ancient American Setting for the Book of Mormon*, 129, 318–323; James L. Baer, "The Third Nephi Disaster: A Geological View," *Dialogue: A Journal of Mormon Thought 19*, no. 1 (Spring 1986): 129–132; Alvin K. Benson, "Geological Upheaval and Darkness in 3 Nephi 8–10," in *The Book of Mormon: Third Nephi 9–30, "This is My Gospel,"* ed. Monte S. Nyman and Charles D. Tate Jr. (Provo, UT: BYU Religious Studies Center, 1993), 59–73; Russell H. Ball, "An Hypothesis concerning the Three Days of Darkness Among the Nephites," *Journal of Book of Mormon Studies 2*, no. 1 (1993): 107–123; John A. Tvedtnes, "Historical Parallels to the Destruction at the Time of the Crucifixion," *Journal of Book of Mormon Studies 3*, no. 1 (1994): 170–186; John Gee, "Notes and Communications—Another Note on the Three Days of Darkness," *Journal of Book of Mormon Studies 6*, no. 2 (1997): 235–244; Bart J. Kowallis, "In the Thirty and Fourth Year: A Geologist's View of the Great Destruction in 3 Nephi," *BYU Studies 37*, no. 3 (1997–1998): 136–190; Benjamin R. Jordan, "'Many Great and Notable Cities Were Sunk': Liquefaction in the Book of Mormon," *BYU Studies 38*, no. 3 (1999): 119–122; Benjamin R. Jordan, "Volcanic and Ice Dating in the New World," *Journal of Book of Mormon Studies 10*, no. 1 (2001): 75; "When Day Turned to Night,"

Journal of Book of Mormon Studies 10, no. 2 (2001): 66–67; "Investigating New World Volcanism at the Time of Christ's Death," *Insights: A Window on the Ancient World 23*, no. 6 (2003): 3–4; Matthew Roper, "A Note on Volcanism and the Book of Mormon," *Insights: The Newsletter of the Neal A. Maxwell Institute for Religious Scholarship 29*, no. 4 (2009): 4; Benjamin R. Jordan, "Volcanic Destruction in the Book of Mormon: Possible Evidence from Ice Cores," *Journal of Book of Mormon Studies 12*, no. 1 (2003): 78–87; Gardner, *Second Witness*, 5:300–312; John L. Lund, *Joseph Smith and the Geography of Book of Mormon* (The Communication Company, 2012), 173–178; Sorenson, *Mormon's Codex*, 641–649; Jerry D. Grover, *Geology of the Book of Mormon* (Vineyard, UT: Grover Publications, 2014); Gardner, *Traditions of the Fathers*, 343–351; Neal Rappleye, "'The Great and Terrible Judgments of the Lord': Destruction and Disaster in 3 Nephi and the Geology of Mesoamerica," *Interpreter: A Journal of Mormon Scripture 15* (2015): 143–157.

824 Kowallis, "In the Thirty and Fourth Year," 173: "One of the common themes that can be found in almost all accounts of explosive volcanic eruptions is the darkness created by the fall of ash. This darkness may last for a few hours or a few days, and the historical descriptions mimic the terminology used in the Book of Mormon." Benson, "Geological Upheaval," 64: "Volcanic ash, smoke, and gases, along with dust and debris rising into the air from a large earthquake, could have produced the 'vapor of darkness' spoken of in 3 Nephi 8:20 and 10:13." Ball, "An Hypothesis concerning the Three Days of Darkness," 113: the "period of darkness was caused by an immense local cloud of volcanic ash."

825 An earthquake in 1811 felt throughout the eastern United States reportedly caused an "awful darkness of the atmosphere"; however, it lasted only briefly. Grover, *Geology of the Book of Mormon*, 156, explained that earthquakes are not known to cause lengthy periods of darkness. "The mists or vapors of darkness are described as being widespread. The only realistic explanation for this phenomenon is a volcanic ash/tephra cloud disseminated as a result of a volcanic eruption. Occasionally during the initial moments of earthquakes, dust can be generated from shaken buildings or by brief release of sometimes pungent soil gases, but these have never been observed in modern earthquakes to last more than a few hours, and the same is indicated for premodern earthquakes by historic anecdote. Earthquake dust has not been observed to inhibit ignition. Volcanic ash distribution has been historically documented to inhibit combustion and last for days at a time." See also Rappleye, "The Great and Terrible Judgments," 153.

826 Kowallis, "In the Thirty and Fourth Year," 136–190; Lund, *Joseph Smith and the Geography of Book of Mormon*, 173–178; Gardner, *Second Witness*, 5:300–312.

827 Grover, *Geology of the Book of Mormon*, 119.

828 Grover, *Geology of the Book of Mormon*, 137.

829 Grover, *Geology of the Book of Mormon*, 139–41.

830 Grover, *Geology of the Book of Mormon*, 139–48.

831 Grover, *Geology of the Book of Mormon*, 148.

832 Sorenson, *Ancient American Setting*, 46; V. Garth Norman, *Book of Mormon–Mesoamerica Geography: History Study Map* (American Fork, UT: ARCON, 2008), 3; Allen and Allen, *Exploring the Lands of the Book of Mormon*, 428–465; Sorenson, *Mormon's Codex*, 508–509; 712–714.

833 Grover, *Geology of the Book of Mormon*, 39; "When Day Turned to Night," 66–67.

834 Sorenson, *Mormon's Codex*, 641–649; Grover, *Geology of the Book of Mormon*, 32–49. Grover's work documents as many as six volcanos active around the first century AD, ranging from central Mexico to southern Guatemala.

835 Jordan, "Volcanic Destruction in the Book of Mormon," 84.

836 Jordan, "Volcanic Destruction in the Book of Mormon," 87.

837 The exact year of Christ's death is also uncertain and highly debated, though most scholars would place it around AD 30. See chapter 67. See also Thomas A. Wayment, "Appendix—The Birth and Death Dates of Jesus Christ," in *The Life and Teachings of Jesus Christ: From Bethlehem through the Sermon on the Mount*, ed. Richard Neitzel Holzapfel and Thomas A. Wayment (Salt Lake City, UT: Deseret Book, 2005), 383–394; Jeffrey R. Chadwick, "Dating the Death of Jesus Christ," *BYU Studies Quarterly 54*, no. 4 (2015): 135–191.

838 Jordan, "Volcanic Destruction in the Book of Mormon," 87: "However, so far it is not possible to determine the exact geographic location of those eruptions."

839 Jordan, "Volcanic Destruction in the Book of Mormon," 87, similarly argued, "the discovery of a volcanic eruption at Tacaná volcano [in Mesoamerica, ca. AD 25–72] during the period in question, combined with the ice-core record, seems to strengthen the argument for an eruption as part of the cause of destruction described in 3 Nephi."

840 See chapter 58.

841 Kimberly M. Berkey, "Temporality and Fulfillment in 3 Nephi 1," *Journal of Book of Mormon Studies 24* (2015): 74.

842 Benson, "Geological Upheaval," 63.

843 Ezra Taft Benson, *A Witness and a Warning: A Modern-day Prophet Testifies of the Book of Mormon* (Salt Lake City, UT: Deseret Book, 1988), 37; cf. p. 20.

844 Roger Atwood, "Lost Island of the Maya," *Archaeology 68*, no. 4 (2015): 42.

845 Based on an unpublished geophysical survey examined by Book of Mormon Central staff.

846 Sorenson, *Mormon's Codex*, 647.

847 Atwood, "Lost Island of the Maya," 42.

848 Atwood, "Lost Island of the Maya," 43.

849 Atwood, "Lost Island of the Maya," 42–43.

850 Atwood, "Lost Island of the Maya," 43.

851 Based on an unpublished geophysical survey. See also Atwood, "Lost Island of the Maya," 42. For information about the natural disasters in 3 Nephi and their likely connection to volcanic and geological activity, see chapter 68.

852 Sorenson, *Mormon's Codex*, 647. According to Sorenson, his proposed Book of Mormon geography "plausibly places the city of Jerusalem on the south shore of the Lake Atitlan. The near agreement in time between the flooding described in the Book of Mormon city and the rise of the lake waters over Samabaj, as well as the seemingly abrupt manner of that rise, is striking." Although the timing of Samabaj's flooding may be too late, Sorenson's geographical correlation is still intriguing and deserves further consideration and exploration.

853 Atwood, "Lost Island of the Maya," 42.

854 Sorenson, *An Ancient American Setting for the Book of Mormon*, 175–176, 223–225; Bruce W. Warren and Thomas Stuart Ferguson, *The Messiah in Ancient America* (Provo, UT: Book of Mormon Research Foundation, 1987), 44; Allen and Allen, *Exploring the Lands of the Book of Mormon*, 637–646, 737–740.

855 Atwood, "Lost Island of the Maya," 45.

856 Notably, it was immediately after the flood in Genesis that the Lord explained the symbolic importance of blood to Noah: "Every moving thing that liveth shall be meat for you. . . . But flesh with the life thereof, which is the blood thereof, shall ye not eat. And surely your blood of your lives will I require; at the hand of every beast will I require it, and at the hand of man; at the hand of every man's brother will I require the life of man" (Genesis 9:4–5).

857 The symbolism of hiding or covering sins from before the Lord's face hearkens back to the story of Adam and Eve, who, after partaking of the fruit of the tree of knowledge, "hid themselves from the presence of the Lord God" (Genesis 3:8). See also 2 Nephi 9:14, Mormon 9:5; Lamentations 1:8; Isaiah

47:3; Revelation 3:18.

858 Some in the Latter-day Saint (and broader Christian) tradition have interpreted the flood as a literal baptism of the earth, but this is not supported doctrinally or historically. See Paul Y. Hoskisson and Stephen O. Smoot, "Was Noah's Flood the Baptism of the Earth?" in *Let Us Reason Together: Essays in Honor of the Life's Work of Robert L. Millet*, ed. Spencer Fluhman and Brent L. Top (Salt Lake City and Provo, UT: Deseret Book, Neal A. Maxwell Institute of Religious Scholarship, and BYU Religious Studies Center, 2016) 163–188.

859 See chapter 68.

860 For other scriptural references to the hen metaphor, see Matthew 23:37–38; Luke 13:34–35; D&C 10:65; 29:2; 43:24.

861 Jane Allis-Pike, "'How Oft Would I Have Gathered You as a Hen Gathereth Her Chickens': The Power of the Hen Metaphor in 3 Nephi 10: 4–7," in *Third Nephi: An Incomparable Scripture*, ed. Andrew C. Skinner and Gaye Strathearn (Salt Lake City and Provo, UT: Deseret Book and Neal A. Maxwell Institute for Religious Scholarship, 2012), 59.

862 Gardner, *Second Witness*, 5:322: the "common assumption is that chickens were a post-conquest introduction into the Americas." However, there is currently not a consensus concerning the timing and details of the chicken's introduction to the Americas. See George F. Carter, "Pre-Columbian Chickens in America," in *Man Across the Sea: Problems of Pre-Columbian Contacts*, ed. Carroll L. Riley, J. Charles Kelley, Campbell W. Pennington, and Robert L. Rands (Austin, TX: University of Texas Press, 1971), 178–218; George F. Carter, "Before Columbus," in *The Book of Mormon: The Keystone Scripture*, ed. Paul R. Cheesman, S. Kent Brown, and Charles D. Tate Jr. (Provo, UT: BYU Religious Studies Center, 1988), 172–176; Alice A. Storey, et al., "Radiocarbon and DNA Evidence for a Pre-Columbian Introduction of Polynesian Chickens to Chile," *PNAS 104*, no. 25 (2007): 10335–10339. For further references, see Allis-Pike, "How Oft Would I Have Gathered You," 60 n. 6.

863 Allis-Pike, "How Oft Would I Have Gathered You," 60: "many ground-feeding birds—quail, chickens, pheasants, turkeys—gather their offspring under their wings, and since the Book of Mormon is a translated work, the words hen and chicken may simply be the English signifiers of a bird that did exist among the Lehites. Regardless of the actual bird the New World survivors knew, we can assume they would have been familiar with a bird that gathered its offspring under its wings." For a more thorough explanation of loan-shifting and translation, see Neal Rappleye, "'Put Away Childish Things': Learning to Read the Book of Mormon with Mature Historical Understanding," 2017 FairMormon Conference, 22–24. For a specific example of turkey as a loan-shifted term for chicken, see Allen J. Christenson, *Popol Vuh: Sacred Book of the Quiché Maya People: Translation and Commentary* (Norman, OK: University of Oklahoma Press, 2007), 87: "In modern Quiché usage, *ak'* refers to chickens, which were introduced by the Spaniards soon after the Conquest. The Precolumbian *ak'* was the domesticated turkey *(Meleagris ocellata)*. Colonial period dictionaries often refer to the turkey as *kitzih ak'* (true *ak*) to distinguish it from the chicken introduced from Europe."

864 See Erin Kennedy Thorton, Kitty F. Emery, David W. Steadman, Camilla Speller, Ray Matheny, and Dongya Yang, "Earliest Mexican Turkeys *(Meleagris gallopavo)* in the Maya Region: Implications for Pre-Hispanic Animal Trade and the Timing of Turkey Domestication," *PLoS ONE 7*, no. 8 (2012): e42630; Benjamin S. Arbuckle and Sue Ann McCarty, "Animals and Inequality in the Ancient World: An Introduction," in *Animals and Inequality in the Ancient World*, ed. Benjamin S. Arbuckle and Sue Ann McCarty (Boulder, CO: University Press of Colorado, 2014), 33; Erin Kennedy Thorton, "Zooarchaeological and Isotopic Perspectives on Ancient Maya Economy and Exchange," *FAMSI*, 2008, 4.

865 See "Wild Turkey Parenting," *eMammal*, September 6, 2013; Karen Davis, "A Mother Turkey and Her Young: 'Their Kind and Careful Parent,'" *Poultry Press 17*, no. 3 (2007): 2: "During the first few weeks of life, young turkeys sleep on the ground under their mother's wings. After a month or so, they leave the ground and fly at night to a large low branch, where they 'place themselves under the deeply curved wings of their kind and careful parent, dividing themselves for that purpose into two nearly equal parties.'"

866 See Ana Luisa Izquierdo y de la Cueva and María Elena Vega Villalobos, "The Ocellated Turkey in Maya Thought," *PARI Journal 16*, no. 4 (2016): 15–23.

867 The English word *hen*, like the Greek word *ornis* in Matthew 23:37, can be used to mean many kinds of female birds, including female turkeys, quail, or pheasants. While the word *chickens* here could well point to the young chicks of regular chickens, the Greek word used in Matthew 23:37 for chickens is *nossia*, which can mean the young offspring of birds generally. In Psalms 83:4 it refers to the chicks of a sparrow, and in Leviticus 12:8, 14:22, and Luke 2:24 it is used in the expression "two young doves."

868 Allis-Pike, "How Oft Would I Have Gathered You," 65.

869 Allis-Pike, "How Oft Would I Have Gathered You," 66.

870 Allis-Pike, "How Oft Would I Have Gathered You," 67.

871 Allis-Pike, "How Oft Would I Have Gathered You," 58.

872 Allis-Pike, "How Oft Would I Have Gathered You," 58.

873 Alma's teaching is directly linked with the hen metaphor in Doctrine and Covenants 10:65–66: "For, behold, I will gather them as a hen gathereth her chickens under her wings, if they will not harden their hearts; Yea, if they will come, they may, and partake of the waters of life freely."

874 Brent L. Top, "The Loving Arms of Christ," *Ensign*, April 2012, 57.

875 Jeffrey R. Holland, *Christ and the New Covenant* (Salt Lake City, UT: Deseret Book, 1997), 250.

876 Holland, *Christ and the New Covenant*, 250.

877 See Gardner, *Second Witness*, 5:316. If this seems like too much weight to put on a few words of the text, remember that intertextual allusion is common in ancient Israelite narrative and requires only a few words. See Peter J. Leithart, *Deep Exegesis: The Mystery of Reading Scripture* (Waco, TX: Baylor University Press, 2009), 109–115; Phyllis A. Bird, *Missing Persons and Mistaken Identities*, 198; H. G. M. Williamson, "Isaiah 62:4 and the Problem of Inner-Biblical Allusions," *Journal of Biblical Literature 119* (2000): 734–739; Yairah Amit, "Hidden Polemics in Biblical Narrative," trans. Jonathan Chipman, *BibInt 25* (Leiden: Brill, 2000), 42.

878 S. Brent Farley, "The Appearance of Christ to the People of Nephi (3 Nephi 11–14)," in *The Book of Mormon, Part 2*, 149.

879 See chapter 45.

880 McConkie, Millet, and Top, *Doctrinal Commentary*, 4:52–53.

881 B. H. Roberts, "The Fifth Gospel," in *Defense of the Faith and the Saints*, 2 vols. (Salt Lake City, UT: Deseret News, 1907–12), cited in Gaye Strathearn, "Nephi, third book of," in *Book of Mormon Reference Companion*, 597–601; N. Eldon Tanner, "Christ in America," *Ensign*, May 1975, 34; Richard Neitzel Holzapfel, "One by One: The Fifth Gospel's Model of Service," in *A Book of Mormon Treasury: Gospel Insights from General Authorities and Religious Educators* (Salt Lake City, UT: Deseret Book, 2003), 379. See chapter 88.

882 Ed J. Pinegar and Richard J. Allen, *Commentaries and Insights on the Book of Mormon*, 2 vols. (American Fork, UT: Covenant Communications, 2003), 2:433.

883 See Strathearn, "Nephi, third book of," 597.

884 See Strathearn, "Nephi, third book of," 597.

885 McConkie, Millet, and Top, *Doctrinal Commentary*, 4:1.

886 Monte Nyman, *Book of Mormon Commentary*, 6 vols. (Orem, UT: Granite, 2003), 5:2–3.

887 Holland, *Christ and the New Covenant*, 250. For an exquisite media

portrayal of the transcendent words and experiences embodied in 3 Nephi, see Mark Mabry, *Another Testament of Christ: Reflections of Christ* (Salt Lake City, UT: Deseret Book, 2009), and its companion DVD with the same title, which was filmed in Honduras and produced by Cameron Trejo.

888 John W. Welch, "3 Nephi as the Holy of Holies of the Book of Mormon," in *Incomparable Scripture*, 31–32. See chapter 76.

889 Ezra Taft Benson, "The Savior's Visit to America," *Ensign*, May 1987, 6.

890 See Hugh Nibley, *An Approach to the Book of Mormon, The Collected Works of Hugh Nibley, Volume 6* (Salt Lake City and Provo, UT: Deseret Book and FARMS, 1988), 304 n. 22; Matthew L. Bowen, "'They Came and Held Him by the Feet and Worshipped Him': Proskynesis before Jesus in Its Biblical and Ancient Near Eastern Context," *Studies in the Bible and Antiquity 5* (2013): 63–68; Matthew L. Bowen, "'They Came Forth and Fell Down and Partook of the Fruit of the Tree': Proskynesis in 3 Nephi 11:12–19 and 17:9–10 and Its Significance," in *Third Nephi: An Incomparable Scripture* (Salt Lake City and Provo, UT: Deseret Book and Neal A. Maxwell Institute for Religious Scholarship, 2012), 107–108: "Proskynesis, very literally 'a kissing in the presence of,' is a term the Greek historian Herodotus (Histories 1.134) originally applied to the ancient Persian custom of 'prostrating oneself before persons and kissing their feet or the hem of their garment [or] the ground.' The word in its broadest sense denotes the 'hierarchical prostration of inferior to superior,' but in a narrower, cultic sense it signifies 'formal submission in the presence of a being from the divine realm.' Hence, proskynesis is widely used by scholars as an umbrella term for similar rites known from Egypt to the Far East, whereby deities, kings, and other persons deified or thought to belong to the divine realm were so acknowledged and reverenced."

891 Bowen, "They Came and Held Him," 68.

892 Bowen, "They Came and Held Him," 68.

893 Bowen, "They Came and Held Him," 66. For a treatment of throne-theophanies, see Blake T. Ostler, "The Throne-Theophany and Prophetic Commission in 1 Nephi: A Form-Critical Analysis," *BYU Studies 26*, no. 4 (1986): 67–95.

894 See Bowen, "They Came and Held Him," 69–73. For an analysis of ritual prayer (including prostration) in Islam and its relationship with Judaic prayer, see Khaleel Mohammed, "The Foundation of Muslim Prayer," *Medieval Encounters 5*, no. 1 (1999): 17–28.

895 See Brent D. Shaw, *Bringing in the Sheaves: Economy and Metaphor in the Roman World* (Toronto, ON: University of Toronto Press, 2013), 398 n. 44. For a treatment of Joseph, the son of Jacob, as a type of Christ, see Andrew C. Skinner, "Finding Jesus Christ in the Old Testament," *Ensign*, June 2002.

896 Bowen, "They Came and Held Him," 73–88; Stuart Bevan, "Proskynesis in the Synoptics: A Textual Analysis of προσκυνέω and Jesus," *Studia Antiqua 14*, no. 1 (2015): 30–43.

897 In addition to the examples of the tree of life and King Benjamin's speech, numerous instances of proskynesis can be found in the Book of Mormon. See Matthew L. Bowen, "'And Behold, They Had Fallen to the Earth': An Examination of Proskynesis in the Book of Mormon," *Studia Antiqua 4*, no. 1 (2005): 91–110.

898 Bowen, "And Behold, They Had Fallen," 96.

899 Nibley, *An Approach to the Book of Mormon*, 304.

900 Bowen, "They Came and Held Him," 68.

901 Bowen, "They Came Forth and Fell Down," 118.

902 See Book of Mormon Central, "Why Did Mormon Say the Children of Men Are Less than the Dust of the Earth? (Helaman 12:7)," *KnoWhy 183* (September 8, 2016).

903 Bowen, "They Came and Held Him," 82.

904 Isaiah 63:3; cf. D&C 76:107; 88:106; 133:50.

905 3 Nephi 11:14; cf. D&C 6:37.

906 Isaiah 52:7; cf. Mosiah 15:15–18; Romans 10:15; 3 Nephi 20:40.

907 D&C 88:6.

908 3 Nephi 17:10.

909 Neil L. Andersen, "What Thinks Christ of Me?" *Ensign*, May 2012, 114.

910 Neal A. Maxwell, "'O, Divine Redeemer,'" *Ensign*, November 1981.

911 For responses to such an argument, see John W. Welch, "Approaching New Approaches," *Review of Books on the Book of Mormon 6*, no. 1 (1994): 152–168; A. Don Sorenson, "The Problem of the Sermon on the Mount and 3 Nephi," *FARMS Review 16*, no. 2 (2004): 117–148.

912 See chapter 74.

913 In Alma 11:7, the senine appears as the smallest gold measure in Alma 11:5–13. For a more extensive elaboration and additional examples, see John W. Welch, *Illuminating the Sermon*, 125–150. To compare differences, see 3 Nephi 12:26; cf. *kodrantes* ("farthing"), Matthew 5:26; *lepton* ("mite"), Luke 12:59.

914 See, for example, Hans Dieter Betz, *Essays on the Sermon on the Mount*, trans. L. L. Welborn (Philadelphia, PA: Fortress Press, 1985), 55–70; Hans Dieter Betz, *The Sermon on the Mount, Hermeneia—A Critical and Historical Commentary on the Bible* (Minneapolis, MN: Fortress Press, 1995), 70–80; Alfred M. Perry, "The Framework of the Sermon on the Mount," *Journal of Biblical Literature 54* (1935): 103–115; Georg Strecker, *The Sermon on the Mount: An Exegetical Commentary*, trans. O. C. Dean Jr. (Nashville, TN: Abingdon, 1988), 55–56, 63, 67–68, 72.

915 See discussion in Neil J. McEleney, "The Beatitudes of the Sermon on the Mount/Plain," *Catholic Biblical Quarterly 43*, no. 1 (1981): 7–8; Robert A. Guelich, "The Antitheses of Matthew V. 21–48: Traditional and/or Redactional?" *New Testament Studies 22* (1976): 446–449.

916 For example, in the Luke account, Jesus states the Beatitudes differently, pronouncing His words directly to the poor, the hungry, and so forth ("Blessed be ye poor . . . Blessed are ye that hunger now," Luke 6:20–21) instead of indirectly as in the version in Matthew ("Blessed are the poor in spirit . . . Blessed are they which do hunger," Matthew 5:3, 6).

917 Welch, *Illuminating the Sermon*, 222.

918 John W. Welch, *The Sermon on the Mount in Light of the Temple* (Burlington, VT: Ashgate, 2009), 15–39. Biblical scholar W. D. Davies suggested that when Matthew indicates that Jesus taught from a mount, "probably no simple geographic mountain is intended. The mountain is the mountain of the New Moses, the New Sinai." W. D. Davies, *The Sermon on the Mount* (New York, NY: Cambridge University Press, 1966), 17.

919 Strecker, *The Sermon on the Mount*, 33.

920 Betz, *Essays on the Sermon on the Mount*, 30.

921 Betz, *Essays on the Sermon on the Mount*, 79. Elsewhere, Betz has proposed that it was an early Christian didache, or set of instructions for new converts, as did Joachim Jeremias. See Betz, *Essays on the Sermon on the Mount*, 55–69; Joachim Jeremias, *The Sermon on the Mount*, trans. Norman Perrin (Philadelphia, PA: Fortress Press, 1963), 22–23. Krister Stendahl, *The School of Matthew and Its Use in the Old Testament* (Ramsey, NJ: Sigler, 1990), 35, similarly proposed the Sermon was "a manual for teaching and administration within the church."

922 See Welch, *The Sermon on the Mount in Light of the Temple.*

923 See Welch, *Illuminating the Sermon*, 47–114. Welch stated, "I shall explore some fifty elements of the Sermon that I have identified—examining in particular their possible roles in establishing or preparing to establish covenant relationships between God and his people—and consider the capacity of those elements to be ritualized" (p. 48).

924 Welch, *Illuminating the Sermon*, 128–129.

925 Donald W. Parry, "'Pray Always': Learning to Pray as Jesus Prayed," in *The Book of Mormon: 3 Nephi 9–30, This Is My Gospel* (Provo, UT: BYU Religious Studies Center, 1993), 137. See also Robert L. Millet, "The Praying Savior: Insights from the Gospel of 3 Nephi," in *Third Nephi: An Incomparable Scripture*, 134: "The Lord offers much precious counsel on prayer in the Book of Mormon."

926 "Didache," in *The Oxford Dictionary of the Christian Church*, 3rd ed. rev., ed. F. L. Cross and E. A. Livingstone (New York, NY: Oxford University Press, 2005), 482: "Although in the past many English and American scholars tended to assign it to the late 2nd cent., most scholars now date it in the 1st cent."

927 The wording of 3 Nephi 13:9–13 in the table varies slightly from the 2013 edition, following instead Royal Skousen, ed., *The Book of Mormon: The Earliest Text* (New Haven, CT: Yale University Press, 2009), 601. The Didache is the Roberts-Donaldson translation, online at earlychristianwritings.com.

928 Hans Dieter Betz, *The Sermon on the Mount, Hermeneia—A Critical and Historical Commentary on the Bible* (Minneapolis, MN: Fortress Press, 1995), 390–391.

929 Welch, *The Sermon on the Mount in the Light of the Temple*, 129. See also Welch, *Illuminating the Sermon at the Temple and the Sermon on the Mount*, 145–146; Betz, *The Sermon on the Mount*, 397–399.

930 Welch, *The Sermon on the Mount in the Light of the Temple*, 129, citing Margaret Barker, *Temple Themes in Christian Worship* (London, UK: T&T Clark, 2007), 208.

931 Betz, *The Sermon on the Mount*, 398.

932 See Thomas A. Wayment, "How New Testament Variants Contribute to the Meaning of the Sermon on the Mount," in *The Sermon on the Mount in Latter-day Scripture*, ed. Gaye Strathearn, Thomas A. Wayment, and Daniel L. Belnap (Salt Lake City and Provo, UT: Deseret Book and BYU Religious Studies Center, 2010), 306–307.

933 Heather Hardy, "'Saving Christianity': The Nephite Fulfillment of Jesus's Eschatological Prophecies," *Journal of Book of Mormon Studies 23* (2014): 22–55, quote on p. 46.

934 Welch, *Illuminating the Sermon*, 128–129.

935 Welch, *Illuminating the Sermon*, 146. Welch discusses other possible reasons for the omission on pp. 145–146.

936 The Didache (ca. first century) does include the doxology, as do early Latin (fourth or fifth century) and Syriac (fifth century) translations of Matthew. For Latin, see Wayment, "How New Testament Variants Contribute," 306, citing manuscript K (p. 311 n. 17). *K* is the designation for *Codex Bobiensis*, which dates to ca. AD 400. See Wikipedia, s.v., "Codex Bobiensis," online at Wikipedia.org. For Syriac, see Bruce M. Metzger, *The Early Versions of the New Testament: Their Origin, Transmission, and Limitations* (New York, NY: Oxford University Press, 1977), 42. Welch, *Illuminating the Sermon*, 206, noted, "it would have been highly irregular at the time of Jesus to end a Jewish prayer without some words in praise of God." Betz, *The Sermon on the Mount*, 414, noted one scholar who thought it downright "unthinkable that a performance of the Lord's Prayer should end abruptly on the word 'temptation.' Rather, the liturgical order was to end a prayer with a spontaneous praise that was cited from memory." Betz also noticed that the doxology "does not show traces of Christian theology," but rather is "Jewish in formulation and theology" (p. 414). Hence, whether it was in the earliest written versions of the Sermon on the Mount or not, the doxology does not appear to be a later Christian development, but rather goes back to the very earliest roots of the Christian tradition. For these and other reasons, according to Welch, *Illuminating the Sermon*, 206, "no one seems to doubt that Jesus probably pronounced a doxology of some kind at the end of his prayers."

937 See chapter 73. The possibility that the Sermon is intended as a temple text has been extended to the Sermon on the Mount for an academic non-Latter-day Saint audience. See Welch, *The Sermon on the Mount in the Light of the Temple*.

938 John W. Welch, "Approaching New Approaches," *Review of Books on the Book of Mormon 6*, no. 1 (1994): 163.

939 Welch, *Illuminating the Sermon*, 81.

940 Welch, *Illuminating the Sermon*, 81.

941 Betz, *The Sermon on the Mount*, 414.

942 Millet, "The Praying Savior," 134, explained that Jesus instructed the Nephites "to pattern their prayers on the Lord's prayer, with those alterations that would reflect the fact that he is now a resurrected, glorified being, the kingdom of God was now in their midst, and they would soon be initiated into the heavenly order of consecration and stewardship."

943 Welch, *Illuminating the Sermon*, 127–150.

944 See chapter 73.

945 Similarly, Psalms 1:6 informs that "the Lord knoweth the way of the righteous: but the way of the ungodly shall perish." Paul, speaking of those Church members who were trying to stay faithful in the face of apostate teachings, told Timothy: "The Lord knoweth them that are his. And, let every one that nameth the name of Christ depart from iniquity" (2 Timothy 2:19).

946 Welch, *The Sermon on the Mount in the Light of the Temple*, 178–179.

947 Although the King James Version reads "that seek thy face, O Jacob," based on the Hebrew of the Masoretic Text, many modern translations render it "who seek the face of the God of Jacob," based on the evidence of alternate Hebrew manuscripts. See, for examples, the NIV, ESV, RSV, NRSV, and others.

948 In Psalms 24:8, they apparently use the name "the Lord" twice when asked the question "Who is the King of glory?" This is similar to Jesus's usage in Matthew 7/3 Nephi 14:21. See also the one who passes through the temple gates coming "in the name of the Lord" in Psalms 118:19–20, 26. For more on the "temple entry" sequence of Psalms 24, see David J. Larsen, "Ascending into the Hill of the Lord: What the Psalms Can Tell Us about the Rituals of the First Temple," in *Ancient Temple Worship: Proceedings of the Expound Symposium*, 14 May 2011, ed. Matthew B. Brown, et al. (Salt Lake City and Orem, UT: Eborn Books and The Interpreter Foundation, 2014), 171–188.

949 See, for example, Gary Holloway, *James and Jude: The College Press NIV Commentary* (Joplin, MO: College Press, 1996), 123. Also, the Jewish Publication Society's translation of the Tanakh (Hebrew Bible) renders the last half of Psalms 24:4 as "Who hath not taken My name in vain, And hath not sworn deceitfully." Taking the Lord's name in vain should probably be understood as performing actions or making covenants "in his name," and doing so unworthily or illegitimately. See Taylor Halverson, "How else might the Lord's name be taken in vain?" *Deseret News*, June 20, 2016.

950 See, generally, Welch, *The Sermon on the Mount in the Light of the Temple*; Welch, *Illuminating the Sermon at the Temple and the Sermon on the Mount*. See also chapter 73.

951 John W. Welch, "Seeing Third Nephi as the Holy of Holies of the Book of Mormon," *Journal of the Book of Mormon and Other Restoration Scripture 19*, no. 1 (2010): 36–55; also published in *Third Nephi: An Incomparable Scripture*, 1–33.

952 Welch, "Seeing Third Nephi," 40–41. The passages mentioned are 3 Nephi 11:38–39 ("this is my doctrine, and whoso buildeth upon this buildeth upon my rock") and 3 Nephi 14:24–27 ("I will liken him unto a wise man, who built his house upon a rock"). The image of "the rock" is an ancient symbol associated with both the Lord and the temple (see, for example, Psalms 94:22; 71:3; Isaiah 25:4; 28:16; 2 Chronicles 3:1).

953 Welch, *The Sermon on the Mount in Light of the Temple*.

954 See Welch, "Seeing Third Nephi," 45. See also chapter 75.

955 Welch, "Seeing Third Nephi," 45.

956 See Welch, "Seeing Third Nephi," 45–52, for a more complete list.

957 Welch, "Seeing Third Nephi," 53.
958 John W. Welch, "3 Nephi Conference Panel Discussion," in *Third Nephi*, 381.
959 See chapter 73.
960 See John W. Welch, "Echoes from the Sermon on the Mount," in *The Sermon on the Mount in Latter-day Scripture*, ed. Gaye Strathearn, Thomas A. Wayment, and Daniel L. Belnap (Salt Lake City and Provo, UT: Deseret Book and BYU Religious Studies Center, 2010), 314–315.
961 Welch, "Echoes," 313–314.
962 Welch, "Echoes," 315.
963 Welch, "Echoes," 315.
964 Welch, "Echoes," 316.
965 Welch, "Echoes," 317.
966 See M. Seidel, *Studies in Scripture* (Jerusalem: Mosad Harav Kook, 1978). See also Dave Bokovoy, "Inverted Quotations in the Book of Mormon," *Insights: A Window on the Ancient World 20*, no. 10 (October 2000): 2; David E. Bokovoy and John A. Tvedtnes, *Testaments: Links Between the Book of Mormon and the Hebrew Bible* (Tooele, UT: Heritage Press, 2003), 56–60.
967 Welch, "Echoes," 319.
968 Welch, "Echoes," 319.
969 Welch, "Echoes," 319.
970 Welch, "Echoes," 319.
971 Richard Neitzel Holzapfel, "One by One: The Fifth Gospel's Model of Service," in *A Book of Mormon Treasury: Gospel Insights from General Authorities and Religious Educators*, 378.
972 Holzapfel, "One by One," 379–380.
973 Holzapfel, "One by One," 387.
974 See Holzapfel, "One by One," 381–384.
975 Russell M. Nelson, "Salvation and Exaltation," *Ensign*, May 2008, 8.
976 John W. Welch, "Seeing Third Nephi as the Holy of Holies of the Book of Mormon," *Journal of the Book of Mormon and Other Restoration Scripture 19*, no. 1 (2010): 45.
977 Welch, "Seeing Third Nephi," 45. For a presentation on the importance of temples after periods of sorrow and destruction, see Jasmin Gimenez, "Temples Rising from Destruction," Book of Mormon Temples Fireside, March 2016, online at bookofmormoncentral.org.
978 Holzapfel, "One by One," 387.
979 Howard W. Hunter, "The Great Symbol of Our Membership," *Ensign*, October 1994.
980 Hugh Nibley, *Teachings of the Book of Mormon*, 4:88.
981 Ronald A. Rasband, "One by One," *Ensign*, November 2000.
982 Both Matthew and Mark merely said, "Take, eat; this is my body" (Matthew 26:26; Mark 14:22).
983 John W. Welch, "3 Nephi Conference Panel Discussion," in *Third Nephi: An Incomparable Scripture*, 381–382.
984 S. Kent Brown, in "3 Nephi Conference Panel Discussion," 381.
985 Mark Alan Wright, "Axes Mundi: Ritual Complexes in Mesoamerica and the Book of Mormon," *Interpreter: A Journal of Mormon Scripture 12* (2014): 91. In the Gospel of John, Thomas demanded that he would not believe unless he could feel the prints from the nails and thrust his hand into Jesus's side, which he was allowed to do (see John 20:25–28). Notice that thrusting his hand into Jesus's side, however, comes after first feeling the nail marks in His hands and feet. In 3 Nephi, Jesus takes the initiative and invites all first to thrust their hands into his side, then to feel the prints of the nails in his hands and feet.
986 Wright, "Axes Mundi," 89.
987 Wright, "Axes Mundi," 91.
988 See chapter 10.
989 Wright, "Axes Mundi," 90–91.
990 Feeling the imprints of the nails in His hands and feet might have attested to the fulfillment of prophecies, long known to the Nephites, that the Lord Jesus Christ would suffer death by crucifixion. See 1 Nephi 11:33; 19:10, 13.
991 For the ancients, emotion was not felt in the heart, but rather in the gut or bowels (*splanchnizomai* means to feel compassion or pity, and it comes from *splanchna,* or the inwards parts and entrails). So Christ showing the incision in His side not only declares His ritual sacrifice, but it demonstrates His emotional and loving sacrifice.
992 D. Todd Christofferson, "Abide in My Love," *Ensign*, November 2016.
993 John W. Welch, "Our Nephite Sacrament Prayers," in *Reexploring the Book of Mormon*, 286–289.
994 Welch, "3 Nephi Conference Panel Discussion," 381.
995 See chapter 78.
996 Welch, "3 Nephi Conference Panel Discussion," 378.
997 See, for example, Psalms 4:6; 31:16; 44:3; 67:1; 80:1, 3, 7, 19; 89:15; Daniel 9:17.
998 See Gabriel Barkay, "The Priestly Benediction on the Silver Plaques," in *Ketef Hinnom: A Treasure Facing Jerusalem's Walls* (Jerusalem: The Israel Museum, 1986); Gabriel Barkay, Andrew G. Vaughn, Marilyn J. Lundberg, and Bruce Zuckerman, "The Amulets from Ketef Hinnom: A New Edition and Evaluation," *Bulletin of the American Schools of Oriental Research 334* (2000): 41–70; Kenton L. Sparks, *Ancient Texts for the Study of the Hebrew Bible: A Guide to the Background Literature* (Peabody, MA: Hendrickson Publishers, 2005), 460. See also William J. Adams Jr., "Lehi's Jerusalem and Writing on Silver Plates," in *Pressing Forward*, 23–26; William J. Adams Jr., "More on the Silver Scrolls from Lehi's Jerusalem," in *Pressing Forward*, 27–28; Dana M. Pike, "Israelite Inscriptions from the Time of Lehi," in *Glimpses of Lehi's Jerusalem*, 213–215. The amulets were found in a burial site, which may suggest that the message on the silver scrolls inside them was meant to help prepare the deceased individuals for the afterlife.
999 John H. Walton and Craig S. Keener, eds., *Cultural Backgrounds Study Bible: Bringing to Life the Ancient World of Scripture* (Grand Rapids, MI: Zondervan, 2016), 242, noted that these scrolls "indicate the authenticity and antiquity of this 'priestly benediction.'"
1000 From a summary of Matthew Grey's presentation, "'Jesus Blessed Them . . . and His Countenance Did Shine Upon Them': Understanding Third Nephi 19 in Light of the Priestly Blessing," given at the September 2008 conference, "Third Nephi: New Perspectives on an Incomparable Scripture," held at Brigham Young University. The brief summary of the presentation can be found in "Scholars Focus Conference on Third Nephi," *Insights: The Newsletter of the Neal A. Maxwell Institute for Religious Scholarship 28*, no. 6 (2008): 3–4, quote on p. 3.
1001 "Scholars Focus Conference on Third Nephi," 3–4. The connection between 3 Nephi 19:25 and Numbers 6:25 is noted in footnote 25a to 3 Nephi 19:25 in the 2013 LDS edition of the Book of Mormon.
1002 See, for example, Numbers 6:25–26 of the New Living Translation, God's Word Translation, and others.
1003 *The New American Bible* (World Bible Publishers, 1976), 143.
1004 M. I. Gruber, "The Many Faces of Hebrew נשא פנים 'lift up the face,'" *Zeitschrift für die alttestamentliche Wissenschaft 95* (1983): 253.
1005 For a discussion of the different approaches to the Trinity within Christianity from a Mormon perspective, see Blake T. Ostler, *Of God and Gods, Exploring Mormon Thought*, vol. 3 (Salt Lake City, UT: Greg Kofford Books, 2008), 195–255. For an attempt to situate Joseph Smith's teachings on the Godhead within this broader conversation on the Trinity, see David L. Paulsen and Brett McDonald, "Joseph Smith and the Trinity: An Analysis and Defense of the Social Model of the Godhead," *Faith and Philosophy 25*, no. 1 (2008): 47–74. For a

conversation on the issue from a Latter-day Saint and an Evangelical perspective, see Craig L. Blomberg and Stephen E. Robinson, *How Wide the Divide? A Mormon and Evangelical in Conversation* (Downers Grover, IL: InterVarsity Press, 1997), 111–142. For defenses of the Latter-day Saint position, see Ostler, *Of God and Gods*, 257–320; Stephen E. Robinson, *Are Mormons Christians?* (Salt Lake City, UT: Bookcraft, 1991), 71–89; Daniel C. Peterson and Stephen D. Ricks, *Offenders for a Word: How Anti-Mormons Play Word Games to Attack the Latter-day Saints* (Salt Lake City, UT: Aspen Books, 1992), 62–69.

1006 Terryl L. Givens, *Wrestling the Angel, Foundations of Mormon Thought: Cosmos, God, Humanity* (New York, NY: Oxford University Press, 2015), 69–74.

1007 James B. Allen, "Emergence of a Fundamental: The Expanding Role of Joseph Smith's First Vision in Mormon Religious Thought," in *Exploring the First Vision*, ed. Samuel Alonzo Dodge and Steven C. Harper (Provo, UT: BYU Religious Studies Center, 2012), 227–260; James B. Allen, "The Significance of Joseph Smith's First Vision in Mormon Thought," in *Exploring the First Vision*, 283–306.

1008 See, for example, Matthew 20:20–23; Mark 13:32; John 14:28; 20:17; Acts 2:33; 7:55–56; 1 Timothy 2:5.

1009 Ostler, *Of God and Gods*, 259.

1010 For analysis of these and other examples, see David L. Paulsen and Ari D. Bruening, "The Social Model of the Trinity in 3 Nephi," in *Third Nephi: An Incomparable Scripture*, 207–212. All examples in the table are taken from this portion of their paper.

1011 Paulsen and Bruening, "The Social Model of the Trinity," 193, 204, 214. Notions of a social, purified, divine community within the members of the Godhead is consistent with Joseph Smith's own teachings on the oneness of the Godhead, which Terryl Givens described as "a covenantal relationship of unity, in which each has separate functions but each can—and does—represent the whole." Givens, *Wrestling the Angel*, 74. See also, Rodney Turner, "One God," in *Book of Mormon Reference Companion*, 622–623.

1012 See Ari B. Bruening and David L. Paulsen, "The Development of the Mormon Understanding of God: Early Mormon Modalism and Other Myths," *FARMS Review of Books 13*, no. 2 (2001): 123–132.

1013 Paulsen and Bruening, "The Social Model of the Trinity," 206, 228.

1014 See Mark Alan Wright and Brant A. Gardner, "The Cultural Context of Nephite Apostasy," *Interpreter: A Journal of Mormon Scripture 1* (2012): 34–38. See also Welch, et al., *Knowing Why*, 212–213. Since Paulsen and Bruening, "The Social Model of the Trinity," 227–228, feel that "Abinadi is a candidate" for a Book of Mormon prophet with "modalist leanings"—modalism being the view that the Father and Son are merely different modes or offices shared by the same divine being—it seems significant that Wright and Gardner, "The Cultural Context," 37, feel that "Abinadi's explanation in Mosiah 15 of how Christ is both the Father and the Son could also be read as an example" of the Maya deity complex, where a single god was "composed of distinctive manifestations in different circumstances." Maya deity complexes and modalism are conceptually very similar.

1015 Paulsen and Bruening, "The Social Model of the Trinity," 193, 212.

1016 "Discourse, 7 April 1844, as Reported by Wilford Woodruff," 133, The Joseph Smith Papers. This is famously known as the King Follett Discourse.

1017 Victor L. Ludlow, "The Father's Covenant People Sermon: 3 Nephi 20:10–23:5," in *Third Nephi: An Incomparable Scripture*, 148.

1018 Part of the difficulty in understanding simply comes from being part of a modern, rather than an ancient, audience. Most members of an ancient audience listening to this speech would likely have understood blessings and curses associated with covenants. See, for example, Leviticus 26 and Deuteronomy 28.

1019 Ludlow, "The Father's Covenant People Sermon," 147.

1020 Specific words matter in Israelite literature, and the Book of Mormon is no exception. See Yairah Amit, *Hidden Polemics in Biblical Narrative*, trans. Jonathan Chipman (Leiden: Brill, 2000), 42.

1021 Ludlow, "The Father's Covenant People Sermon," 149.

1022 Francis I. Andersen and David Noel Freedman, *Micah: A New Translation with Introduction and Commentary, Anchor Bible Commentary 24E* (New York, NY: Doubleday, 2000), 487.

1023 Klaus Baltzer, *Deutero-Isaiah: A Commentary on Isaiah 40–55, Hermeneia—A Critical and Historical Commentary on the Bible*, trans. M Kohl (Minneapolis, MN: Fortress Press, 2001), 384.

1024 Baltzer, *Deutero-Isaiah*, 384.

1025 Baltzer, *Deutero-Isaiah*, 371.

1026 Joseph Blenkinsopp, *Isaiah 40–55: A New Translation with Introduction and Commentary, Anchor Bible Commentary 40* (New York, NY: Doubleday, 2002), 343.

1027 Baltzer, *Deutero-Isaiah*, 370.

1028 Note that He includes some insertions here in 3 Nephi 21:14, 19–20, 22. For more on the themes in Micah, see Delbert R. Hillers, *Micah, Hermeneia—A Critical and Historical Commentary on the Bible* (Minneapolis, MN: Fortress Press, 1984), 70–74.

1029 Ludlow, "The Father's Covenant People Sermon," 166.

1030 Although common in biblical and ancient Near Eastern sources, chiasmus is also common in pre-Columbian America, so it would have been well understood by Christ's audience. In both cases, the central point is the most important. See Allen J. Christenson, "Chiasmus in Mesoamerican Texts," in *Reexploring the Book of Mormon*, 233–235; Allen J. Christenson, ed. and trans., *Popol Vuh: The Mythic Sections— Tales of First Beginnings From the Ancient K'iche'-Maya, Ancient Texts and Mormon Studies 2* (Provo, UT: FARMS, 2000), 12–17; Allen J. Christenson, trans., *Popol Vuh: The Sacred Book of the Maya*, 46–47; Kerry Michael Hull, *Verbal Art and Performance in Ch'orti' and Maya Hieroglyphic Writing* (PhD dissertation, University of Texas at Austin, 2003), 175–178, 297–301, 480–481. For general information about chiasmus in the Book of Mormon, see chapter 12.

1031 Not surprisingly, 3 Nephi 20:29 is very similar to Isaiah 52:12.

1032 See chapter 45.

1033 See Gaye Strathearn and Jacob Moody, "Christ's Interpretation of Isaiah 52's 'My Servant' in 3 Nephi," *Journal of the Book of Mormon and Other Restoration Scripture 18*, no. 1 (2009): 5: "It has long been noted that Isaiah, starting in chapter 41, includes a series of four Servant Songs or poems (42:1–7; 49:1–6; 50:4–9; 52:13–53:12), three of which are also included in the Book of Mormon (see 1 Nephi 21:1–8; 2 Nephi 7:4–9; Mosiah 14–15; 3 Nephi 20:43–45; 21:8–10)." See also Terry B. Ball, "Isaiah's 'Other' Servant Songs," in *The Gospel of Jesus Christ in the Old Testament*, ed. D Kelly Ogden, et al. (Provo, UT: BYU Religious Studies Center, 2009), 207–218.

1034 Strathearn and Moody, "Christ's Interpretation of Isaiah," 7.

1035 See Welch, et al., *Knowing Why*, 59–61, 210–211; Strathearn and Moody, "Christ's Interpretation of Isaiah," 8.

1036 Strathearn and Moody, "Christ's Interpretation of Isaiah," 8.

1037 This unit spans 3 Nephi 20:10–23:5. See Strathearn and Moody, "Christ's Interpretation of Isaiah," 9. For the chiastic structure, see chapter 82.

1038 Strathearn and Moody, "Christ's Interpretation of Isaiah," 11.

1039 See Strathearn and Moody, "Christ's Interpretation of Isaiah," 11.

1040 See Strathearn and Moody, "Christ's Interpretation of Isaiah," 11.

1041 See Strathearn and Moody, "Christ's Interpretation of Isaiah," 12.

1042 See Strathearn and Moody, "Christ's Interpretation of Isaiah," 12.

1043 Doctrine and Covenants 10:42–43: "And behold, you shall publish it as the record of Nephi; and thus I will confound those who have altered my words. I will not suffer that they shall destroy my work; yea, I will show unto them that my wisdom is greater than the cunning of the devil." See Strathearn and Moody,

"Christ's Interpretation of Isaiah," 12.

1044 See Strathearn and Moody, "Christ's Interpretation of Isaiah," 11.

1045 See Richard Dilworth Rust, "'All Things Which Have Been Given of God . . . Are the Typifying of Him': Typology in the Book of Mormon," in *Literature of Belief: Sacred Scripture and Religious Experience*, ed. Neal E. Lambert (Provo, UT: BYU Religious Studies Center, 1981), 233–244.

1046 Todd Parker, "Abinadi: The Message and the Martyr (Part 2)," *FARMS Transcripts* (1996), 2.

1047 Parker, "Abinadi: The Message and the Martyr," 2.

1048 As satisfying as Strathearn and Moody's interpretation of 3 Nephi 21:10 may be, they acknowledged that previous "interpretations have merit" and that Christ's association of these Isaiah passages with the Book of Mormon simply "add[s] another interpretive layer to the servant." See Strathearn and Moody, "Christ's Interpretation of Isaiah," 13.

1049 Jeffrey R. Holland, "Safety for the Soul," *Ensign*, November 2009, 89–90.

1050 See chapter 82.

1051 Klaus Baltzer, *Deutero-Isaiah: A Commentary on Isaiah 40–55, Hermeneia—A Critical and Historical Commentary on the Bible*, trans. M Kohl (Minneapolis, MN: Fortress Press, 2001), 435–436.

1052 Baltzer, *Deutero-Isaiah*, 437.

1053 See chapter 68.

1054 Baltzer, *Deutero-Isaiah*, 443–444.

1055 Joseph Blenkinsopp, *Isaiah 40–55: A New Translation with Introduction and Commentary, Anchor Bible Commentary 40* (New York, NY: Doubleday, 2002), 364.

1056 Cynthia L. Hallen, "The Lord's Covenant of Kindness: Isaiah 54 and 3 Nephi 22," in *Isaiah in the Book of Mormon*, 335.

1057 Blenkinsopp, *Isaiah 40–55*, 365.

1058 Baltzer, *Deutero-Isaiah*, 453.

1059 For more information on this, see chapter 87.

1060 Baltzer, *Deutero-Isaiah*, 456–457.

1061 Baltzer, *Deutero-Isaiah*, 459.

1062 See Welch, et al., *Knowing Why*, 57–58.

1063 It's possible this chapter of Isaiah was not on the plates of brass and was written after Lehi left Jerusalem. If this is the case, Christ would have been giving this chapter to the Nephites for the first time, like He did with the chapters in Malachi. For further discussion on this issue in connection with the Book of Mormon, see John W. Welch, "Authorship of the Book of Isaiah in Light of the Book of Mormon," in *Isaiah in the Book of Mormon*, 423–437; Kent P. Jackson, "Isaiah in the Book of Mormon," in *A Reason for Faith: Navigating LDS Doctrine and Church History*, ed. Laura Harris Hales (Salt Lake City and Provo, UT: Deseret Book and BYU Religious Studies Center, 2016), 69–78. For an Evangelical approach to the issue of Isaiah unity and authorship, see Richard L. Schultz, "Isaiah, Isaiahs, and Current Scholarship," in *Do Historical Matters Matter to Faith? A Critical Appraisal of Modern and Postmodern Approaches to Scripture*, ed. James K. Hoffmeier and Dennis R. Magary (Wheaton, IL: Crossway, 2012), 243–261.

1064 Victor L. Ludlow, "Isaiah, purposes for quoting," in *Book of Mormon Reference Companion*, 341. For the most comprehensive compilation of studies on Isaiah in the Book of Mormon to date, see Parry and Welch, *Isaiah in the Book of Mormon* (Provo, UT: FARMS, 1998). See also Garold N. Davis, "Pattern and Purpose of the Isaiah Commentaries in the Book of Mormon," in *Mormons, Scripture, and the Ancient World: Studies in Honor of John L. Sorenson*, ed. Davis Bitton (Provo, UT: FARMS, 1998), 277–303. For Nephi's treatment of Isaiah specifically, see Joseph M. Spencer, *The Vision of All: Twenty-Five Lectures on Isaiah in Nephi's Record* (Salt Lake City, UT: Greg Kofford Books, 2016). For previous *KnoWhys* discussing Isaiah in the Book of Mormon, see https://knowhy.bookofmormoncentral.org/tags/isaiah.

1065 See John W. Welch, "Getting Through Isaiah with the Help of the Nephite Prophetic View," in *Isaiah in the Book of Mormon*, 19–45; Welch, et al., *Knowing Why*, 99–108. Nephi also claimed a personal ability to understand the words of Isaiah, in part because he lived in the great city of Jerusalem (see 2 Nephi 25:5), where Isaiah had worked and died the previous century.

1066 See Welch et al., Knowing Why, 210–211.

1067 For a listing of all the quotations and paraphrases of Isaiah in the Book of Mormon, see Victor L. Ludlow, "Isaiah in the Book of Mormon," in *Book of Mormon Reference Companion*, 344.

1068 See chapters 82–84.

1069 Kent P. Jackson, "Teaching from the Words of the Prophets (3 Nephi 23–26)," in *Book of Mormon, Part 2*, 196, also describes this statement as an "unprecedented endorsement." McConkie, Millet, and Top, *Doctrinal Commentary*, 4:157, shared a similar sentiment: "It is one thing for the prophets or the Saints to quote the Lord—such is appropriate and necessary. It is quite another for the Lord to quote someone and then command the Saints to search that prophet's writings! What greater recommendation could there be for us to begin a life-long search and study of Isaiah?" See also Nyman, *Book of Mormon Commentary*, 5:349: "Isaiah is the only book of the sixty-six books in the Bible that has been singled out with a commandment to search it."

1070 Dana M. Pike, "'The Great and Dreadful Day of the Lord': The Anatomy of an Expression," *BYU Studies 41*, no. 2 (2002): 150.

1071 Margaret Barker, "Isaiah," in *Eerdmans Commentary on the Bible*, 490. A single chapter from Isaiah (53) is referenced thirty-six different times in eleven different books in the New Testament. See the chart in John H. Walton and Craig S. Keener, eds., *Cultural Backgrounds Study Bible: Bringing to Life the Ancient World of Scripture* (Grand Rapids, MI: Zondervan, 2016), 1203. For discussion of Isaiah 53 in the New Testament and early Christianity, see Peter Stuhlmacher, "Isaiah 53 in the Gospels and Acts," in *The Suffering Servant: Isaiah 53 in Jewish and Christian Sources*, ed. Bernd Janowski, and Peter Stuhlmacher, trans. Daniel P. Bailey (Grand Rapids, MI: Wm. Eerdmans, 2004), 147–162; Otfried Hofius, "The Fourth Servant Song in the New Testament Letters," in *Suffering Servant*, 163–188; Christopher Markschies, "Jesus Christ as a Man before God: Two Interpretive Models for Isaiah 53 in the Patristic Literature and Their Development," in *Suffering Servant*, 225–320; Daniel P. Bailey, "Isaiah 53 in the Codex A Text and 1 Clement 16:3–14," in *Suffering Servant*, 321–323; Daniel P. Bailey, "'Our Suffering and Crucified Messiah' (Dial. 111.2): Justin Martyr's Allusions to Isaiah 53 in his Dialogue with Trypho with Special Reference to the New Edition of M. Marcovich," in *Suffering Servant*, 324–417; Roy F. Melugin, "On Reading Isaiah 53 as Christian Scripture," in *Suffering Servant*, 55–69; Mikeal C. Parsons, "Isaiah 53 in Acts 8: A Reply to Professor Morna Hooker," in *Suffering Servant*, 104–119; Rikki E. Watts, "Jesus' Death, Isaiah 53, and Mark 10:45: A Crux Revisited," in *Suffering Servant*, 125–151; Adrian M. Leske, "Isaiah and Matthew: The Prophetic Influence in the First Gospel," in *Suffering Servant*, 152–169; David A. Sapp, "The LXX, 1QIsa, and MT Versions of Isaiah 53 and the Christian Doctrine of the Atonement," in *Suffering Servant*, 170–192; J. Ross Wagner, "The Heralds of Isaiah and the Mission of Paul: An Investigation of Paul's Use of Isaiah 51–55," in *Suffering Servant*, 193–222; William R. Farmer, "Reflections on Isaiah 53 and Christian Origins," in *Suffering Servant*, 260–280; Richard E. Averbeck, "Christian Interpretations of Isaiah 53," in *The Gospel According to Isaiah 53: Encountering the Suffering Servant in Jewish and Christian Theology*, ed. Darrell L. Bock and Mitch Glaser (Grand Rapids, MI: Kregel Academic, 2012), 33–60; Michael J. Wilkins, "Isaiah 53 and the Message of Salvation in the Gospels," in *Gospel According to Isaiah 53*, 109–132; Darrell Bock, "Isaiah 53 in Acts 8," in *Gospel According to Isaiah 53*, 133–144; Craig A. Evans, "Isaiah 53 in the Letters of Peter, Paul, Hebrews, and John," in *Gospel According to Isaiah 53*,

145–170.
1072 Barker, "Isaiah," 490.
1073 Barker, "Isaiah," 490.
1074 *Yesha'yahu* is composed of *yesha*, which means "help, deliverance, salvation," and then the theophoric *yahu*, meaning Yahweh. *Yeshua* is another form of the name *Yehoshua* (Joshua) and likewise derives from *yasha*. See Ludwig Koehler and Walter Baumgartner, *The Hebrew and Aramaic Lexicon of the Old Testament*, 1:446, 449. See also "Isaiah," "Jesus," and "Joshua," in *Book of Mormon Onomasticon*; definitions cited in the text come from this source.
1075 Barker, "Isaiah," 490. For discussion about *Jesus and Isaiah's Servant*, see Stuhlmacher, "Isaiah 53 in the Gospels and Acts," 147–162; Watts, "Jesus' Death, Isaiah 53, and Mark 10:45," 125–151; Leske, "Isaiah and Matthew," 152–169; Wilkins, "Isaiah 53 and the Message of Salvation," 109–132; Otto Betz, "Jesus and Isaiah 53," in *Suffering Servant*, 70–87; N. T. Wright, "The Servant and Jesus," in *Suffering Servant*, 281–297. As mentioned, this subject remains debated by some scholars. For an example of the alternative—that Jesus did not personally identify with the servant, see Morna D. Hooker, "Did the Use of Isaiah 53 to Interpret His Mission Begin with Jesus?" in *Suffering Servant*, 88–103.
1076 Gardner, *Second Witness*, 5:552.
1077 Terry B. Ball, "Isaiah, life and ministry," in *Book of Mormon Reference Companion*, 341.
1078 McConkie, Millet, and Top, *Doctrinal Commentary*, 4:158.
1079 See Ann Madsen, "Joseph Smith and the Words of Isaiah," in *Isaiah in the Book of Mormon*, 353–367; John S. Thompson and Eric Smith, "Isaiah and the Latter-day Saints: A Bibliographic Survey," in *Isaiah in the Book of Mormon*, 445–509.
1080 The identity of Malachi and the composition of his book as it is in the Bible has long been debated by biblical scholars. It is interesting to note that Jesus quoted only from Malachi 3–4. There are some indications that the book of Malachi as we now have it may be a composite work or may have been redacted by a later editor who modified the books of Haggai and Zechariah to conform to a specific message and to be a con-clusion to the books of the twelve "minor" prophets. Some have called Malachi a literary product, a written interpretation of previous traditions. A number of ancient sources (such as Targum Jonathan, Megillah 15a of the Talmud, and Jerome) suggest that parts or all of Malachi were written by Ezra the scribe, Mordecai, or others. Thus, we may speculate on the possibility that some of the information in the initial chapters of Malachi was already known to the Nephite scribes (perhaps even included on the plates of brass) or that Jesus considered only the last two chapters to be authentic and/or relevant. See J. D. Nogalski, *Literary Precursors to the Book of the Twelve* (Berlin: de Gruyter, 1993), 53; J. D. Nogalski , *Redactional Processes in the Book of the Twelve* (Berlin: de Gruyter, 1993), 191; J. D. Nogalski, "Intertextuality in the Twelve," in *Forming Prophetic Literature: Essays on Isaiah and the Twelve in Honor of John D. W. Watts*, ed. J. W. Watts (Sheffield: Sheffield Academic Press, 1996), 102–124; P. L. Redditt, "The Book of Malachi in Its Social Setting," *Catholic Biblical Quarterly 56* (1994): 241; Karl W. Weyde, *Prophecy and Teaching: Prophetic Authority, Form Problems, and the Use of Traditions in the Book of Malachi* (Berlin: de Gruyter, 2000), 43–45; David L. Petersen, *Zechariah 9–14 and Malachi* (Louisville, KY: Westminster/John Knox, 1995), 2–3.
1081 John W. Welch, "Understanding the Sermon at the Temple: Zion Society (3 Nephi 19–4 Nephi 1)," in Hugh Nibley, *Teachings of the Book of Mormon*, 168.
1082 See chapters 82–85.
1083 Kent P. Jackson, "Teachings from the Words of the Prophets," in *Book of Mormon, Part 2*, 200.
1084 Ezra Taft Benson, *A Witness and a Warning: A Modern-day Prophet Testifies of the Book of Mormon* (Salt Lake City, UT: Deseret Book, 1988), 37; cf. 20.
1085 Jackson, "Teachings from the Words of the Prophets," 201, 206.
1086 Aaron P. Schade and David Rolph Seely, "The Writings of Malachi in 3 Nephi: A Foundation for Zion in the Past and Present," in *Third Nephi: An Incomparable Scripture*, 278. They also make the traditional point: "The visit of Christ to the New World was a type of the second coming. We can learn much from a study of his visit" (p. 261).
1087 Jackson, "Teachings from the Words of the Prophets," 200–201.
1088 See, for example, Matthew 19:14; Mark 10:14; Luke 18:16.
1089 For more on the connection between Christ's statement and the children, see Kent P. Jackson, "Teaching from the Words of the Prophets (3 Nephi 23–26)," in *Book of Mormon, Part 2*, 204–205.
1090 See H. G. M. Williamson, "Isaiah 62:4 and the Problem of Inner-Biblical Allusions," *Journal of Biblical Literature 119* (2000): 734–739; Yairah Amit, *Hidden Polemics in Biblical Narrative*, trans. Jonathan Chipman (Leiden: Brill, 2000), 42.
1091 For more on repeated themes and images as they run through the Book of Mormon, see Ronald D. Anderson, "Leitworter in Helaman and 3 Nephi," in *Helaman through 3 Nephi 8, According to Thy Word*, 241–249.
1092 The parallels with King Benjamin's speech continue throughout the chapter, as those who were baptized in the name of Christ were called after His name (see 3 Nephi 26:21), just as King Benjamin's subjects took the name of Christ upon themselves (see Mosiah 5:10). See Gardner, *Second Witness*, 5:573.
1093 Lynn G. Robbins, "The Righteous Judge," *Ensign*, November 2016.
1094 It is reasonable that these things could not be written not because they were too hard to explain but because they were sacred. When one compares these sections to 3 Nephi 26:11 and 14:6, it seems that Christ is following His own counsel not to parade the sacred before those who are not prepared. This idea is strengthened when one considers the temple themes that run through this portion of the text, from washing through consecration. See John W. Welch, *Illuminating the Sermon at the Temple and Sermon on the Mount*.
1095 M. Gawain Wells, "The Savior and the Children in 3 Nephi," *Journal of Book of Mormon Studies 14*, no. 1 (2005): 70.
1096 Robert A. Rees, "Children of the Light: How the Nephites Sustained Two Centuries of Peace," in *Third Nephi: An Incomparable Scripture*, 320–321.
1097 See chapter 91.
1098 McConkie, Millet, and Top, *Doctrinal Commentary*, 4:171–172.
1099 M. Russell Ballard, "Great Shall Be the Peace of Thy Children," *Ensign*, April 1994, 59.
1100 Gordon B. Hinckley, "Four Cornerstones of Faith," *Ensign*, February 2004. See also Gordon B. Hinckley, "The Cornerstones of Our Faith," *Ensign*, November 1984.
1101 See B. H. Roberts, Conference Report, April 1904, 16.
1102 Gaye Strathern and Andrew C. Skinner, "Introduction," in *Third Nephi: An Incomparable Scripture*, viii: "All five Gospels testify that Jesus is the Christ, the Son of the living God. They are Gospels because they all declare the 'good news' that the atonement of Jesus Christ makes salvation available to all who come unto him with faith, repentance, baptism, the sanctifying power of the Holy Ghost, and by enduring to the end (3 Nephi 27:13–21)." Interestingly, according to Christopher M. Tuckett, "Within first-century Christianity, the term 'gospel' was used to refer to the Christian kerygma centering on in the death and resurrection of Jesus." See Christorpher M. Tuckett, "Introduction to the Gospels," in *Eerdmans Commentary on the Bible*, 989. In 3 Nephi 27:13–15, Jesus likewise defined gospel as centering on His death and resurrection, thus making the Book of Mormon usage authentic to the first-century AD. See also Andrew C. Skinner, "Jesus's Gospel-Defining Discourse in 3 Nephi 27:13–21: Doctrinal Apex of His New World Visit," in *Third Nephi: An Incomparable*

Scripture, 281–307.

1103 See Tuckett, "Introduction to the Gospels," 990–993. See also Christopher Tuckett, "Gospel, Gospels," in *Eerdmans Dictionary of the Bible*, 522–524; Mark Allan Powell, "The Gospels," in *Harper-Collins Bible Dictionary*, revised and updated, ed. Mark Allan Powell (San Francisco, CA: HarperOne, 2011), 338–340.

1104 Tuckett, "Introduction to the Gospels," 989–990, mentions some of these. Literature on the post-Resurrection ministry of Christ in the Old World is frequently considered to be a genre unto itself, called the forty-day literature, since Christ's post-Resurrection ministry was forty days. See Hugh Nibley, *Mormonism and Early Christianity*, 10–44. A listing with information about each of these documents is available at fortydayministry.com.

1105 Hugh W. Nibley, "Two Shots in the Dark," in *Book of Mormon Authorship*, 123; reprinted in Hugh Nibley, *The Prophetic Book of Mormon*, 409.

1106 Tuckett, "Introduction to the Gospels," 990: "Thus the Gospels which were finally placed in the [New Testament] canon are rather different in kind from the ones that were not."

1107 Andrew C. Skinner, *Third Nephi: The Fifth Gospel* (Springville, UT: Cedar Fort, 2012), 5–9. See chapter 58.

1108 See chapter 66.

1109 Krister Stendahl, "The Sermon on the Mount and Third Nephi," in *Reflections on Mormonism: Judaeo-Christian Parallels*, ed. Truman G. Madsen (Provo, UT: BYU Religious Studies Center, 1978), 141.

1110 See Matthew 3:17; 17:5; Mark 1:11; 9:7; Luke 3:22; 9:35.

1111 Matthew 27; Mark 15; Luke 23; John 19.

1112 See Skinner, *Fifth Gospel*, 9–19. See also chapter 68.

1113 David B. Cummings, "Three Days and Three Nights: Reassessing Jesus's Entombment," *Journal of Book of Mormon Studies 16*, no. 1 (2007): 56–63, 86; Jeffrey R. Chadwick, "Dating the Death of Jesus," *BYU Studies Quarterly 54*, no. 4 (2015): 135–191, esp. 183–188. See also chapter 67.

1114 Stendahl, "The Sermon on the Mount and Third Nephi," 141.

1115 See chapter 73.

1116 See John 10:16; cf. 3 Nephi 15:17–24. See also Skinner, *Fifth Gospel*, 74–77; Book of Mormon Central, "Why Did Jesus Say That There Were 'Other Sheep' Who Would Hear His Voice? (3 Nephi 15:21; cf. John 10:16)," *KnoWhy 207* (October 11, 2016).

1117 See 3 Nephi 18:1–10; 20:3–8; cf. Matthew 26:26–28; Mark 14:22–24; Luke 22:19–20. See Skinner, *Fifth Gospel*, 108–110. See also chapter 79.

1118 See Matthew 28; Mark 16; Luke 24; John 20–21.

1119 See Skinner, *Fifth Gospel*, 21–27. See also chapter 79.

1120 For the most detailed treatment of 3 Nephi as a Gospel, see Skinner, *Fifth Gospel*. See also Monte S. Nyman, *Book of Mormon Commentary*, volume 5.

1121 Skinner, *Fifth Gospel*, 20.

1122 See Skinner, *Fifth Gospel*, 37–47; Welch, *Illuminating the Sermon at the Temple and Sermon on the Mount.*

1123 For a discussion of modern imitation gospels in comparison with 3 Nephi, see Richard Lloyd Anderson, "Imitation Gospels and Christ's Book of Mormon Ministry," in *Apocryphal Writings and the Latter-day Saints*, ed. C. Wilfred Griggs (Provo, UT: BYU Religious Studies Center, 1986), 53–107.

1124 Skinner, *Fifth Gospel*, 2.

1125 Skinner, *Fifth Gospel*, 3. In support of this, Skinner cited 3 Nephi 23:7–8.

1126 Brian K. Ashton, "The Doctrine of Christ," *Ensign*, November 2016.

1127 Skinner, *Fifth Gospel*, 3.

1128 Elder's Journal, July 1838, 44, online at josephsmithpapers.org, grammar standardized.

1129 Ezra Taft Benson, "The Book of Mormon: The Keystone of Our Religion," *Ensign*, November 1986, 5.

1130 Gary E. Stevenson, "Look to the Book, Look to the Lord," *Ensign*, November 2016.

1131 Skinner, *Fifth Gospel*, 3.

1132 Strathern and Skinner, "Introduction," viii: "It is not the account of the mortal Christ but the account of the resurrected, glorified Christ."

1133 Michael R. Ash, *Shaken Faith Syndrome: Strengthening One's Testimony in the Face of Criticism and Doubt*, 2nd ed. (Redding, CA: FairMormon, 2013), 125.

1134 Skinner, *Fifth Gospel*, 3.

1135 Skinner, *Fifth Gospel*, 20.

1136 For a treatment of hand gestures in the Book of Mormon, see Welch, et al., *Knowing Why*, 217–218.

1137 Notably, the timing of this revelation happened to fall on the fifth anniversary of Joseph Smith's retrieval of the plates he would translate into the Book of Mormon. For the importance of this date, see chapter 1.

1138 For further discussion of this topic, see Ezra Taft Benson, "Cleansing the Inner Vessel," *Ensign*, May 1986.

1139 See Welch et al., *Knowing Why*, 4–6.

1140 See Charles Swift, "'So Great and Marvelous Things': The Literary Portrait of Jesus as Divine Lord in 3 Nephi," in *Third Nephi: An Incomparable Scripture*, 235–260.

1141 Howard W. Hunter, "What Manner of Men Ought Ye to Be?" *Ensign*, May 1994.

1142 See Donald W. Parry, "Hebraisms and Other Ancient Peculiarities in the Book of Mormon," in *Echoes and Evidences*, 156–159. See also chapters 4, 23, 61.

1143 Note that Jacob pronounces a series of ten woes in 2 Nephi 9:27–38, and Mormon similarly warns against ten grievous sins in 3 Nephi 30. For more on "woe" statements in the Book of Mormon, see Welch, et al., *Knowing Why*, 89–90; John W. Welch, "Counting to Ten," *Journal of Book of Mormon Studies 12*, no. 2 (2003): 42–57, 113–114.

1144 For example, see Isaiah 5:8, 11, 18, 20–22; Amos 5:18; Ezekiel 13:1–9; 34:1–10; 16:23–27; Habakkuk 2:6, 9, 12, 15, 19; Hosea 7:13; Zephaniah 2:5; Zechariah 11:15–17.

1145 For example, see Matthew 11:21; 18:17; 23:23–33; Luke 6:24–26; 42–51; Revelation 8:13; 12:12; 18:10.

1146 For example, see 1 Nephi 1:13; 2 Nephi 9:27; 15:21; 28:15; Jacob 3:3; Mosiah 3:12; Helaman 7:16–27; 13:11–16; 3 Nephi 9:2; 28:4; Moroni 8:16, 21; 10:25, 26.

1147 Parry, "Hebraisms and Other Ancient Peculiarities," 170.

1148 D. Kelly Ogden and Andrew C. Skinner, *Verse by Verse: The Book of Mormon*, 2 vols. (Salt Lake City, UT: Deseret Book, 2011), 2:228.

1149 Andrew C. Skinner, "The Course of Peace and Apostasy: 4 Nephi–Mormon 2," in *Book of Mormon, Part 2*, 218.

1150 For one possible explanation of Mormon's lack of information in 4 Nephi, see Brant A. Gardner, "Mormon's Editorial Method and Meta-Message," *FARMS Review* 21, no. 1 (2009): 99–105.

1151 Mormon reported that the people "had all things common among them" (4 Nephi 1:3). The disciples performed many miracles "in the name of Jesus" (4 Nephi 1:5). The people "did multiply exceedingly fast" and "were married, and given in marriage" (4 Nephi 1:10–11). There were no "envyings, nor strifes, nor tumults, nor whoredoms, nor lyings, nor murders, nor any manner of lasciviousness . . . [nor] robbers, nor murderers, neither were there Lamanites, nor any manner of -ites" (4 Nephi 1:17–18). The picture evoked from this description is one of economic equality, fully active spiritual gifts, loving marriages and families, and the elimination of crime, sin, and unhealthy social distinctions. For further analysis and application of these blessed conditions, see Marlin K. Jensen, "Living after the Manner of Happiness," *Ensign*, December

2002; Lindon J. Robinson, "'No Poor Among Them,'" *Journal of Book of Mormon Studies 14,* no. 1 (2005): 86–97, 130.

1152 Robert A. Rees, "Children of Light: How the Nephites Sustained Two Centuries of Peace," in *Third Nephi: An Incomparable Scripture*, 320–321.

1153 M. Gawain Wells, "The Savior and the Children in 3 Nephi," *Journal of Book of Mormon Studies 14*, no. 1 (2005): 66.

1154 Rees, "Children of Light," 321.

1155 That these meetings were sacramental in nature is partially evidenced by Mormon's introductory statement that "they did not walk any more after the performances and ordinances of the law of Moses" (4 Nephi 1:12). Christ's atoning sacrifice signaled a fulfillment of these Mosaic ordinances and ushered in a higher law accompanied by the ordinance of the sacrament. Moreover, Mormon's use of the phrase "meeting together oft" in 4 Nephi 1:12 mirror's Christ's commandment to "meet together oft" which is found in the sacramental context of 3 Nephi 18:22. Clearly these meetings fulfilled Christ's injunction to "always do these things," which referred to the sacramental meetings and ordinances (3 Nephi 18:12).

1156 See Richard Lloyd Anderson, "Religious Validity: The Sacrament Covenant in Third Nephi," in *By Study and Also By Faith: Studies in Honor of Hugh Nibley*, 2:1–51. See also chapter 79.

1157 For example, those who witnessed Jesus praying for them reported that "no tongue can speak, neither can there be written by any man, neither can the hearts of men conceive so great and marvelous things as we both saw and heard Jesus speak; and no one can conceive of the joy which filled our souls at the time we heard him pray for us unto the Father" (3 Nephi 17:17).

1158 See chapter 78.

1159 See Byron R. Merrill, "There Was No Contention," in *The Book of Mormon: Fourth Nephi, From Zion to Destruction*, ed. Monte S. Nyman and Charles D. Tate Jr. (Provo, UT: BYU Religious Studies Center, 1995), 169: "With periods of peace being so scarce in the narrative, having a time with no contention must have seemed to Mormon a virtually unattainable condition. Considering the circumstances of his day in combination with all the history he had reviewed, Mormon mentions the absence of contention four times in 17 verses as if to convince himself of such a wonderment, to dispel the belief that this is only a heavenly goal, and to reinforce the possibility of a contentionless people."

1160 Dale G. Renlund, "That I Might Draw All Men Unto Me," *Ensign*, May 2016, 39.

1161 Mormon's first indication of social decline was that a "small part of the people . . . had revolted from the church" (4 Nephi 1:20). Upon removing themselves from Christ's covenants and ordinances, they began to be "lifted up in pride," filled with greed, and "divided into classes" (4 Nephi 1:24–26). After "two hundred and ten years had passed away there were many churches . . . which professed to know the Christ, and yet they did deny the more parts of his gospel" (4 Nephi 1:27).

1162 Summarizing Hugh Nibley's assessment of the Nephite downfall, John W. Welch explained that "first they became privatized. Then they became ethnicized—they taught their children to hate the Nephites or the Lamanites. Then they became nationalized, militarized, terrorized, regionalized, tribalized, fragmentized, polarized, pulverized—and eventually vaporized." See John W. Welch, "Understanding the Sermon at the Temple: Zion Society," in Hugh Nibley, *Teachings of the Book of Mormon*, 4:172. For Hugh Nibley's original and more expansive treatment of this topic, see Hugh Nibley, *The Prophetic Book of Mormon*, 530–531.

1163 See John H. Groberg, "The Power of God's Love," *Ensign*, November 2004: "When filled with God's love, we can do and see and understand things that we could not otherwise do or see or understand. Filled with His love, we can . . . avoid contention, renew strength, and bless and help others in ways surprising even to us."

1164 Dallin H. Oaks, "Sacrament Meeting and the Sacrament," *Ensign*, November 2008, 17.

1165 Hardy, *Understanding the Book of Mormon*, 93. Mormon's personal record is technically not the first time he introduced himself in the text, but it is the first time that he discussed his personality, upbringing, and life experiences with any degree of depth. For an analysis of his previous introduction, see chapter 62.

1166 See Hardy, *Understanding the Book of Mormon*, 90: "The somewhat late introduction of a new major voice—an editor working at the end of Nephite civilization—means that everything that follows has to be interpreted from the perspective of Mormon. Careful readers must constantly ask, 'Why would Mormon choose to include this? What might he have omitted? Is there any significance in the way he arranges events or tells particular stories? And who is Mormon anyway?'"

1167 For commentary that clarifies Mormon's role as an abridger, see Brant A. Gardner, "Mormon's Editorial Meta-Message," FairMormon video presentation (time: 3:55–5:24), online at youtube.com.

1168 Sorenson, *Mormon's Codex*, 684. As an alternative to Sorenson's view, Brant A. Gardner has noted, "Maya practice suggests that the literate were most likely nobles outside direct inheritance lines. This is, of course, exactly where my speculation would place Mormon." See Gardner, *Second Witness*, 6:49.

1169 For additional analysis of Mormon's name, heritage, and qualifications as a record keeper, see chapter 62. See also, Gardner, *Second Witness*, 5:272–275.

1170 Mormon's self-assessment agreed with Ammaron's praise: "I, being fifteen years of age and being somewhat of a sober mind" (Mormon 1:15). See also Ogden and Skinner, *Verse by Verse: The Book of Mormon*, 2:234: "Sober usually means possessing an earnestly thoughtful character, temperance, moderation, and showing no extreme qualities of fancy, emotion or prejudice."

1171 See Gardner, *Second Witness*, 6:49: "Ammaron's description of Mormon as 'quick to observe' may mean that he learned quickly or was a bright student. In this case, Ammaron would have meant Mormon's ability to read and write, required traits for a recordkeeper." For a doctrinal application of "quick to observe," see David A. Bednar, "Quick to Observe," *Ensign*, December 2006.

1172 For a plausible relationship between Ammaron and Mormon, see Gardner, *Second Witness*, 6:48.

1173 Mormon's usage of the terms *visited*, *tasted*, and *knew* suggest that his experience with Jesus Christ was likely very personal and revelatory. See M. Catherine Thomas, "The Brother of Jared at the Veil," in *Temples of the Ancient World: Ritual and Symbolism*, 394–397; David A. Bednar, "'If Ye Had Known Me,'" *Ensign*, November 2016, 102–105.

1174 Interestingly, Mormon's introduction mirrors Nephi's self-introduction: "I, Nephi, having been born of goodly parents, therefore I was taught somewhat in all the learning of my father" (1 Nephi 1:1). For a discussion of how Nephi's writings may have influenced Mormon's autobiography, see Matthew L. Bowen, "'O Ye Fair Ones'—Revisited," *Interpreter: A Journal of Mormon Scripture 20* (2016): 333–334. For a broader comparison of Nephi's and Mormon's editorial styles, see Hardy, *Understanding the Book of Mormon*, 91–92; Richard Neitzel Holzapfel, "Mormon, the Man and the Message," in *The Book of Mormon: Fourth Nephi, From Zion to Destruction*, 128–129.

1175 Considering that most eleven-year-olds are capable of walking long distances, the description of Mormon being "carried" by his father may seem rather odd. One possible explanation for this statement is that in ancient Mesoamerica, the social elite were often carried on litters or sedan chairs when traveling on special journeys. Mormon's childhood education, scribal literacy, and precocious military attainments suggest that his father may have been a prominent social figure. See Welch, et al., *Knowing Why*, 291–293.

1176 For examples of Mormon's military travels, see Mormon 2:3–6, 16–17, 20–21; 4:2–3, 19–20; 5:3–7; 6:4.

1177 Holzapfel, "Mormon, the Man and the Message," 129.
1178 Sorensen, *An Ancient American Setting for the Book of Mormon*, 336.
1179 See Ezra Taft Benson, "Flooding the Earth with the Book of Mormon," *Ensign*, October 1988.
1180 Marilyn Arnold, "Mormon," in *Book of Mormon Reference Companion*, 547.
1181 Jeffrey R. Holland, "Mormon: The Man and the Book, Part 1," *Ensign*, March 1978. See also Jeffrey R. Holland, "Mormon: The Man and the Book, Part 2," *Ensign*, April 1978.
1182 Thomas S. Monson, "Dare to Stand Alone," *Ensign*, November 2011, 60–67.
1183 Gordon B. Hinckley, "Four Bs for Boys," *Ensign*, November 1981.
1184 Russell M. Nelson, "Where Is Wisdom?" *Ensign*, November 1992.
1185 See Russell M. Nelson, "Becoming True Millennials."
1186 Richard G. Scott, "How to Obtain Revelation and Inspiration for Your Personal Life," *Ensign*, May 2012, 47. Also quoted in Richard G. Scott, "Learning to Recognize Answers to Prayer," *Ensign*, November 1989.
1187 Neil L. Andersen, "A Witness of God," *Ensign*, November 2016.
1188 For example, Mormon seemed to select texts from what Phyllis Roundy called a "veritable library of engraved documents" in order to provide a supporting witness to the Bible—a book with which he knew modern readers would be familiar (see Mormon 7:9). See Phyllis Ann Roundy, "Mormon," *Encyclopedia of Mormonism*, 2:933.
1189 Thomas W. Mackay, "Mormon and the Destruction of Nephite Civilization," in *The Book of Mormon, Part 2: Alma 30 to Moroni*, 321.
1190 Hardy, *Understanding the Book of Mormon*, 97.
1191 For details regarding the number of years covered per page of the Book of Mormon, see Welch and Welch, *Charting the Book of Mormon*, charts 22–24.
1192 See chapter 94.
1193 Despite this, Mormon had kept a more detailed record of all that happened to his people on the large plates of Nephi, as the prophet Ammaron had instructed (see Mormon 1:4; 2:17; cf. 3 Nephi 5:8–20). The record of Mormon that has come down to us as part of the larger Book of Mormon was a later abridgment of the more detailed record he wrote on the plates of Nephi.
1194 Mormon 2:8; 4:11; 5:8; cf. 3 Nephi 2:11.
1195 See chapter 91.
1196 Mormon describes their abominations in greatest detail in his letter to his son, Moroni, recorded in Moroni 9. He recounts how the Nephites' actions were worse than those of the Lamanites, including rape, murder, torture, and even the eating of human flesh. See Moroni 9:7–13.
1197 See chapter 92.
1198 See chapter 93.
1199 For discussion of the Jubilee in the Book of Mormon, see Welch, et al., *Knowing Why*, 314–318.
1200 See Robin J. DeWitt Knauth, "Sabbatical Year," in *Eerdmans Dictionary of the Bible*, 1147.
1201 Robin J. DeWitt Knauth, "Jubilee, Year of," in *Eerdmans Dictionary*, 743.
1202 Knauth, "Jubilee, Year of," 743, defined the Jubilee as the "50th year in a series of seven Sabbatical Years." However, there is some ambiguity as to whether the jubilee was the forty-ninth year (the seventh sabbatical year) or the fiftieth. Christopher J. H. Wright, "Jubilee, Year of," in *Anchor Bible Dictionary*, ed. David Noel Freedman, 6 vols. (New Haven, CT: Yale University Press, 1992), 3:1025, explained: "Lev 25:8–10 specifies it as the 50th year, though some scholars believe it may have been actually the 49th—i.e., the 7th Sabbatical Year." Terrence L. Szink and John W. Welch, "King Benjamin's Speech in the Context of Ancient Israelite Festivals," in *King Benjamin's Speech: "That Ye May Learn Wisdom,"* 222 n. 162, reasoned: "The inclusive mode of sometimes counting the last year as the first of the next jubilee cycle accounts for the frequent confusion between 49- and 50-year jubilee counts." See also Jack Finegan, *Handbook of Biblical Chronology*, rev. ed. (Peabody, MA: Hendrickson, 1997), 126–130.
1203 There may be evidence in the Dead Sea Scrolls for something similar happening at Qumran. The Calendric Signs scrolls (4Q319) documents a 294-year cycle of six jubilees (of forty-nine years each), correlated to a separate, priestly cycle of six years. See Geza Vermes, trans., *The Complete Dead Sea Scrolls in English*, rev. ed. (New York, NY: Penguin Books, 2004), 365. According to Roger T. Beckwith, *Calendar and Chronology, Jewish and Christian* (Boston, MA: Brill, 2001), 92, "in some manuscripts it was extended to seven jubilees." 4Q319 does mention "[The signs of the] seventh [Jubilee]." (Vermes, *Complete Dead Sea Scrolls*, 369.)
1204 Though few may have known of the significance, the jubilee may have still been widely celebrated as a cultural tradition, much like Christmas today is often celebrated not only by Christians commemorating the birth of Christ, but also others who typically see it as a time of for family and gift giving.
1205 Knauth, "Jubilee, Year of," 743.
1206 For themes of the jubilee year, see Welch and Welch, "Benjamin's Themes Related to Sabbatical and Jubilee Years," in *Charting the Book of Mormon*, chart 91.
1207 McConkie, Millet, and Top, *Doctrinal Commentary*, 4:222.
1208 Gardner, *Second Witness*, 6:81–82.
1209 For more information on human sacrifice in the Book of Mormon, see chapter 10.
1210 See, for example, Leviticus 18:21; Deuteronomy 18:10; 2 Kings 16:3, among others.
1211 Mark S. Smith, *The Early History of God: Yahweh and Other Deities in Ancient Israel*, 2nd ed. (Grand Rapids, MI: William B. Eerdmans, 2002), 171.
1212 Gardner, *Second Witness*, 6:81; 4:249–250. Child sacrifice in ancient Mesoamerica was seen as a means of increasing the status of the surviving ruler. Traci Ardren, "Empowered Children in Classic Maya Sacrificial Rites," *Childhood in the Past: An International Journal 4*, no. 1 (2011): 133–145.
1213 Ortiz C. Ponciano and María del Carmen Rodríguez, "Olmec Ritual Behavior at El Manatí: A Sacred Space," in *Social Patterns in Pre-Classic Mesoamerica*, ed. David C. Grove and Rosemary A. Joyce (Washington, D.C.: Dumbarton Oaks Research Library and Collection, 1999), 248–249.
1214 Virginia Massey, *The Human Skeletal Remains from a Terminal Classic Skull Pit at Colha, Belize*. Papers of the Colha Project, Vol. 3, Texas Archeological Research Laboratory (Austin, TX: University of Texas Press, 1989).
1215 Ellen F. Morris, "Sacrifice for the State: First Dynasty Royal Funerals and the Rites at Macramallah's Rectangle," in *Performing Death: Social Analyses of Funerary Traditions in the Ancient Near East and Mediterranean*, ed. Nicola Laneri (Chicago, IL: The University of Chicago, 2007), 17.
1216 A. Jeffrey Spencer, *Death in Ancient Egypt*, 1st ed. (Westminster, UK: Penguin Books, 1982), 68, 139.
1217 Harriet Crawford, *Sumer and the Sumerians*, 2nd ed. (New York, NY: Cambridge University Press, 2004), 154.
1218 Lawrence Conrad, "The Middle Mississippian Cultures of the Central Illinois Valley," in *Cahokia and the Hinterlands: Middle Mississippian Cultures of the Midwest*, ed. Thomas E. Emerson and R. Barry Lewis (Urbana, IL: University of Illinois, 2000), 130. See also Sorenson, *Mormon's Codex*, 487.
1219 The most notable example of this dates to around AD 1000, but may have been practiced well before this period in this area. See Timothy R. Pauketat, *Ancient Cahokia and the Mississippians* (New York, NY: Cambridge University Press, 2004), 88–93.
1220 Carlos Serrano Sanchez, "Funerary Practices and Human Sacrifice in Teotihuacan Burials," in *Teotihuacan: Art from the City of the Gods*, ed. Kathleen Berrin (San Fransisco, CA: Thames and Hudson, 1993), 113–114. See also

Vera Tiesler, *New Perspectives on Human Sacrifice and Ritual Body Treatments in Ancient Maya Society* (New York, NY: Springer, 2007), 506.

1221 Judges 11:24 notes that this god was named Chemosh.

1222 This seems to have been done during the time period of the Book of Mormon. See Lawrence Stager and Samuel R. Wolff, "Child sacrifice in Carthage—Religious Rite or Population Control?" *Biblical Archaeological Review 10*, no. 1 (January/February 1984): 31–51. See also Joseph A. Green and Lawrence Stager, "Were Living Children Sacrificed to the Gods? Yes," *Archaeology Odyssey 3*, no. 6 (November/December 2000): 29, 31.

1223 Richard J. Chacon and David H. Dye, eds., *The Taking and Displaying of Human Body Parts as Trophies by Amerindians* (New York, NY: Springer, 2007). For the taking of human body parts as trophies in the Book of Mormon, see Welch, et al., *Knowing Why*, 289–290.

1224 Ortiz C. Ponciano and María del Carmen Rodríguez, "Olmec Ritual Behavior at El Manatí: A Sacred Space," in *Social Patterns in Pre-Classic Mesoamerica*, ed. David C. Grove and Rosemary A. Joyce (Washington, D.C.: Dumbarton Oaks Research Library and Collection, 1999), 248–249. Mormon states cannibalism took place after human sacrifice by the Lamanites, specifically, "they feed the women upon the flesh of their husbands, and the children upon the flesh of their fathers" (Moroni 9:8). In 1609, explorer Samuel de Champlain witnessed the taking of war trophies by the Huron, who, after torturing the war captives, cut their body parts up but kept the scalp as a trophy. Similar to what Mormon describes, the Huroans then gave pieces of the deceased's heart to his brother and the other prisoners. See H. P. Biggar, ed., *The Works of Samuel de Champlain*, 6 vols. (Torono: The Camplain Society, 1922–1936), 2:102–103.

1225 Alma 62:35 notes that war and famine were connected in the Book of Mormon.

1226 In ancient Mesoamerica, children were seen to be "magically effective in drawing rain." See Ardren, "Empowered Children," 133–145. See also A. G. Anda, V. Tielser, V. Zabala, and P. Zabala, "Cenotes, espacios sagrados y la practica del sacrificio humano en Yucatan," *Los Investigadores de la Cultura Maya 12*, no. 2 (Campeche: Universidad Autónoma de Campeche, 2004), 228. In the Maya area, excavations show large numbers of children being sacrificed to the Maya rain god, presumably to increase crop yield by petitioning the god for rain. See Bruce Bower, "Belize Cave Was Maya Child Sacrifice Site," *ScienceNews*, April 19, 2016. For similar traditions among the Aztecs, see Philip. P. Arnold, "Eating Landscape: Human Sacrifice and Sustenance in Aztec Mexico," in *Aztec Ceremonial Landscapes*, ed. David Carrasco (Boulder, CO: University of Colorado Press, 1991), 228. This seems to have been done during the time of the Book of Mormon. See Thomas Benjamin, *The Atlantic World: Europeans, Africans, Indians and Their Shared History* (New York, NY: Cambridge University Press, 2009), 13.

1227 Gardner, *Second Witness*, 6:17.

1228 For a thorough review of the topic, see the article by Matthew Roper, "Nephi's Neighbors: Book of Mormon Peoples and Pre-Columbian Populations," *FARMS Review 15*, no. 2 (2003): 91–128.

1229 See chapter 10.

1230 Concerning Mormon's interjected commentaries, Grant Hardy found that there "are more than a hundred such interruptions, distributed evenly throughout Mormon's history." Hardy, *Understanding the Book of Mormon*, 97. He categorized them as follows: (1) comments dealing with the editorial process, (2) summaries, (3) explanatory details, (4) notices of fulfilled prophecies, (5) narrative foreshadowing, (6) intensifying exclamations, and (7) moral generalizations (see pp. 97–98).

1231 John L. Sorenson, "Mormon's Sources," *Journal of the Book of Mormon and Other Restoration Scripture 20*, no. 2 (2011): 12.

1232 Sorenson, "Mormon's Sources," 12.

1233 Richard Neitzel Holzapfel, "Mormon, the Man and the Message," in *The Book of Mormon: Fourth Nephi, From Zion to Destruction*, 119. Importantly, Nephi—whose writings make up a large portion of the Book of Mormon—seemed to share Mormon's approach of drawing out spiritual lessons and insights from real narratives. Roy A. Prete explained, "As might be expected, Nephi does not follow the practice of modern scholars of differentiating between the historical, doctrinal, and philosophical components of his interpretation, but presents an approach that integrates past events and his own experience with prophetic insight and understanding." See Roy A. Prete, "God in History? Nephi's Answer," *Journal of Book of Mormon Studies 14*, no. 2 (2005): 29.

1234 For information about the authorship and composition of the title page, see Clyde J. Williams, "More Light on Who Wrote the Title Page," *Journal of Book of Mormon Studies* 10, no. 2 (2001): 28–29, 70; Sidney B. Sperry, "Moroni the Lonely: The Story of the Writing of the Title Page to the Book of Mormon," *Journal of Book of Mormon Studies 4*, no. 1 (1995): 255–259; David B. Honey, "The Secular as Sacred: The Historiography of the Title Page," *Journal of Book of Mormon Studies 3*, no. 1 (1994): 94–103; Daniel H. Ludlow, "The Title Page," in *The Book of Mormon: First Nephi, The Doctrinal Foundation*, ed. Monte S. Nyman and Charles D. Tate Jr. (Provo, UT: BYU Religious Studies Center, 1988), 19–34.

1235 Brant A. Gardner, "Mormon's Editorial Method and Meta-Message," *FARMS Review 21*, no. 1 (2009): 98–99.

1236 Hardy, *Understanding the Book of Mormon*, 102.

1237 See chapter 62.

1238 Hardy, *Understanding the Book of Mormon*, 119.

1239 Stephen O. Smoot, "*Et Incarnatus Est*: The Imperative for Book of Mormon Historicity," *Interpreter: A Journal of Mormon Scripture 30* (2018): 153.

1240 Eugene England has argued that although "the religious and moral content of the Book of Mormon is indeed what matters most—is the only part that is 'life-changing'—still, I am convinced, through my own professional expertise as a teacher of both fiction and 'true' personal essays, that it matters very much to readers whether they believe that what they are reading is conveying moral and spiritual truth through made-up stories about things that could happen or on the other hand bearing witness fairly accurately of what actually happened to people like themselves." See Eugene England, "Orson Scott Card: The Book of Mormon as History and Science Fiction," *Review of Books on the Book of Mormon 6*, no. 2 (1994): 62–63.

1241 Hardy, *Understanding the Book of Mormon*, 116. Critics of the text may question its plausibility or historicity on intellectual grounds, but the Book of Mormon was never meant to be proven through scientific or historical analysis. President Dallin H. Oaks taught, "In fact, it is our position that secular evidence can neither prove nor disprove the authenticity of the Book of Mormon. Its authenticity depends, as it says, on a witness of the Holy Spirit." See Dallin H. Oaks, "Worthy of Another Look: The Historicity of the Book of Mormon," *Journal of the Book of Mormon and Other Restoration Scripture 21*, no. 1 (2012): 68; originally published in *Historicity and the Latter-day Saint Scriptures*, ed. Paul Y. Hoskisson (Provo, UT: BYU Religious Studies Center, 2001), 237–248.

1242 Concerning its status as a second witness, President Ezra Taft Benson taught, "The Book of Mormon is not on trial—the people of the world, including the members of the Church, are on trial as to what they will do with this second witness for Christ." See Ezra Taft Benson, "A New Witness for Christ," *Ensign*, November 1984.

1243 James E. Smith, "How Many Nephites? The Book of Mormon at the Bar of Demography," in *Book of Mormon Authorship Revisited*, 255–293.

1244 K. Klein Goldewijk and G. van Drecht, "HYDE 3.1: Current and historical population and land cover," in A. F. Bouwman, T. Kram, and K. Klein Goldewijk, "Integrated modelling of global environmental change. An

overview of IMAGE 2.4," *Netherlands Environmental Assessment Agency (MNP)*, Bilthoven, Netherlands.
1245 "In contrast to the texts of other ancient Near Eastern cultures which typically provide relatively little information about the size of their armies, the Bible includes a great deal of information about the number of Israelite troops. Unfortunately, much of this information is problematic. . . . The numbers appear quite high, especially considering the apparent size of the armies of other, better established contemporary nations. . . . This difficulty has led many to discount the biblical numbers altogether, or consider them to be intentional exaggerations. Clearly, the Bible does include exaggerations. . . . Thus, some argue that the biblical numbers often also exaggerate to make certain points, such as glorifying the God of Israel." Boyd Seevers, *Warfare in the Old Testament: The Organization, Weapons, and Tactics of Ancient Near Eastern Armies* (Grand Rapids, MI: Kregel Academic, 2013), 53. Herodotus, the ancient Greek author, is similarly known for his tendency to never let historical accuracy get in the way of a good story. See Lee L. Brice, *Greek Warfare: From the Battle of Marathon to the Conquests of Alexander the Great* (Santa Barbara, CA: ABC-CLIO, 2012), 74.
1246 The Exodus account gives a number that could be read differently (see the next paragraph of this chapter) but the figures in Numbers are much less ambiguous and show clear exaggeration. See Kenneth A. Kitchen, *On the Reliability of the Old Testament* (Grand Rapids, MI: Wm. B. Eerdmans, 2003), 264; James K. Hoffmeier, *Ancient Israel in Sinai: The Evidence for the Authenticity of the Wilderness Tradition* (New York, NY: Oxford University Press, 2005), 153–159.
1247 Carol A. Redmount, "Bitter Lives: Israel in and Out of Egypt," in *The Oxford History of the Biblical World*, 70.
1248 William J. Hamblin, "The Importance of Warfare in Book of Mormon Studies," in *Warfare in the Book of Mormon*, 495–496.
1249 Kitchen, *On the Reliability of the Old Testament*, 264; Hoffmeier, *Ancient Israel in Sinai*, 153–159.
1250 Other ancient cultures used terms like this as well. The Roman military unit *century* was also the word for one hundred, but these units often did not have one hundred people in them. See Smith, "How Many Nephites?" 286.
1251 Charles C. Mann, *1491: New Revelations of the Americas Before Columbus* (New York, NY: Alfred A. Knopf, 2005), 94.
1252 James E. Smith, "Nephi's Descendants? Historical Demography and the Book of Mormon," *Review of Books on the Book of Mormon 6*, no. 1 (1994): 284–294.
1253 Sorenson, *Mormon's Codex*, 397–398.
1254 Smith, "How Many Nephites?" 286.
1255 Sorenson, *Mormon's Codex*, 286.
1256 See F. W. Dobbs-Allsopp, "Lament," in *Eerdmans Dictionary of the Bible*, 784–785.
1257 Nancy C. Lee, *Lyrics of Lament: From Tragedy to Transformation* (Minneapolis, MN: Fortress Press, 2010), 24.
1258 For more on biblical laments, see Lee, *Lyrics of Lament*, 73–179.
1259 Dobbs-Allsopp, "Lament," 784.
1260 Dobbs-Allsopp, "Lament," 785.
1261 Dobbs-Allsopp, "Lament," 785.
1262 Dobbs-Allsopp, "Lament," 785.
1263 For a more thorough review of the traditional literary form that laments take, see Lee, *Lyrics of Lament*, 49–70.
1264 According to Dobbs-Allsopp, "Lament," 785, "there are several literary transformations" of the standard funeral lament in the Old Testament. So it is not surprising or problematic that Mormon breaks form.
1265 The name *Nephite* may literally mean "fair ones." See Matthew L. Bowen, "'O Ye Fair Ones': An Additional Note on the Meaning of the Name Nephi," *Insights: A Window on the Ancient World 23*, no. 6 (2003): 2; Matthew L. Bowen, "'O Ye Fair Ones'—Revisited," *Interpreter: A Journal of Mormon Scripture 20* (2016): 315–344.
1266 In the 1830 edition of the Book of Mormon, Mormon 8–9 comprised a single chapter. See Welch and Welch, *Charting the Book of Mormon*, chart 170.
1267 Moroni explained that at this point he had "but few things to write" (Mormon 8:1) and that he would "write and hide up the records in the earth; and whither I go it mattereth not" (Mormon 8:4). Not only do these statements have a sense of finality to them, but according to Mark D. Thomas, Moroni's farewell followed the "typical Nephite ending formula." See Mark D. Thomas, "Moroni: The Final Voice," *Journal of Book of Mormon Studies 12*, no. 1 (2003): 92.
1268 See Thomas, "Moroni: The Final Voice," 96.
1269 For Mormon's expectation that Moroni would finish the record, see Words of Mormon 1:2.
1270 It seems that during the period of peace between the Nephites and the Lamanites, Moroni may have been an apprentice to his father, helping him with the research and record-keeping responsibilities of composing the Book of Mormon. In this process, Moroni likely would have learned the metallurgical skills necessary to create his own plates. Moreover, the fact that he mentioned a lack of ore in the first place implies that if he had ore, he could make use of it. For a discussion of what may have transpired during the ten years of peace, see chapter 94.
1271 Steve Walker has described this additional material as "some twenty pages of the most densely packed philosophy in all scripture." See Steve Walker, "Last Words: 4 Nephi–Moroni," in *The Reader's Book of Mormon*, ed. Robert A. Rees and Eugene England, 7 vols. (Salt Lake City, UT: Signature Books, 2008), 7: xviii.
1272 There are at least three plausible explanations for why Moroni felt that Ether would be his final writing project. One possibility is that Moroni wasn't sure how much space it would take to finish his abridgment of Ether. In this scenario, he may have written his farewell remarks in Ether 12 to make sure that he gave proper closure to the text. Then when he finished and found he had more room, he included Moroni 1–10. Another possibility is that Moroni had enough room on the plates to add only the book of Ether. Then at some later time he was able to get access to enough ore to make some additional plates and add them to his record. A third possibility is that Moroni had enough room on the plates to begin with, but he believed that the book of Ether was the last thing the Lord wanted him to write. Then after his abridgment, the Lord inspired or explicitly commanded him to write more.
1273 It's possible that it was in direct response to Moroni's insecurities or dissatisfaction with his first ending that the Lord gave him further opportunities to complete the record.
1274 Moroni's choice to conclude his father's record in the 400th year and then conclude his own after the 420th year may correlate to time-keeping practices in ancient America. Mark Wright explained, "The majority of Classic period monuments begin with a 'Long Count,' which begins with a count of baktuns (400 years) and katuns (20 years). Notably, the concluding chapter of the Book of Mormon likewise begins with a count of 'four hundred and twenty years' (Moroni 10:1), perhaps an intentional allusion to the Maya Long Count." See Mark Alan Wright, "Nephite Daykeepers: Ritual Specialists in Mesoamerica and the Book of Mormon," in *Ancient Temple Worship: Proceedings of the Expound Symposium*, 253. See also John E. Clark, "Archaeology, Relics, and Book of Mormon Belief," *Journal of Book of Mormon Studies 14*, no. 2 (2005): 46–47. See also chapter 55.
1275 Walker, "Last Words," xiii. See also Thomas, "Moroni: The Final Voice," 98: "After ending the Nephite record twice with tales of distressing annihilation,

Moroni ends a final time with a message of hope. . . . The three endings can be summarized, in order of appearance in the record, as past destruction 1 (the Nephites), past destruction 2 (the Jaredites), and future restoration."

1276 M. Russell Ballard, "To Whom Shall We Go?" *Ensign* (November 2016): 91.

1277 Thomas, "Moroni: The Final Voice," 99.

1278 Walker, "Last Words," xviii.

1279 Hugh Nibley, *Teachings of the Book of Mormon*, 1:62. From a literary perspective, a comedy is a story where everything starts out well, descends into chaos, but then eventually ends well. Tragedy, on the other hand, is where everything goes from bad, to worse, to unimaginably terrible, and the story does not end well.

1280 Steve Walker, "Last Words: 4 Nephi–Moroni," in *The Reader's Book of Mormon*, 7: xvii.

1281 Lisa Bolin Hawkins and Gordon Thomasson, "I Only Am Escaped Alone to Tell Thee: Survivor Witnesses in the Book of Mormon," *FARMS Preliminary Reports* (1984): 8.

1282 For examples, see 2 Nephi 2:25; 2 Nephi 4:30; 2 Nephi 9:18. See also, Allan D. Rau, "Cheer Up Your Hearts: Jacob's Message of Hope in Christ," *Religious Educator 14*, no. 3 (2013): 49–63.

1283 See Welch, et al., *Knowing Why*, 234–235.

1284 See Book of Mormon Central, "Why Does God Sometimes Allow His Saints to Be Martyred? (Alma 14:11)," *KnoWhy 351* (August 11, 2017).

1285 Welch, *Legal Cases*, 262–263.

1286 See Welch, et al., *Knowing Why*, 280–281.

1287 See chapter 98.

1288 See chapter 96.

1289 See chapter 99. See also Mark D. Thomas, "Moroni: The Final Voice," *Journal of Book of Mormon Studies 12*, no. 1 (2003): 88–99, 119–120.

1290 Terrence Des Pres, "Survivors and the Will to Bear Witness," *Social Research 40*, no. 4 (1973): 678.

1291 See Hawkins and Thomasson, "I Only Am Escaped Alone to Tell Thee," 1–13; Gordon C. Thomasson, "The Survivor and the Will to Bear Witness," in *Reexploring the Book of Mormon*, 266–268.

1292 For the likelihood that several Book of Mormon prophets experienced the emotional and physical scars of war, see Morgan Deane, "Experiencing Battle in the Book of Mormon," *Interpreter: A Journal of Mormon Scripture 23* (2017): 250–252.

1293 For a discussion of mental illness, depression, and hope in Christ, see Jeffrey R. Holland, "Like a Broken Vessel," *Ensign*, November 2013, 40–42.

1294 Dallin H. Oaks, "Give Thanks in All Things," *Ensign*, 2003.

1295 See Dallin H. Oaks, "Strengthened by the Atonement of Jesus Christ," *Ensign*, November 2015, 61–64.

1296 See Psalms 116:3; 2 Nephi 9:10–26; Revelation 1:18.

1297 See 2 Nephi 25:13; 3 Nephi 25:2; Malachi 4:2.

1298 Holland, "Like a Broken Vessel," 40.

1299 See 1 Nephi 20:6; 2 Nephi 27:12, 22, 26–27; 4 Nephi 1:48–49; Mormon 1:2; 4:23; 5:8, 12; 6:6; 8:4; Ether 4:3, 13, 15; 15:11, 33. See also, Book of Mormon Central, "What Were the 'Other Records' Nephi Saw in Vision? (1 Nephi 13:39)," *KnoWhy 376* (October 26, 2017).

1300 John A. Tvedtnes, *The Book of Mormon and Other Hidden Books*, 11.

1301 Joseph Smith had a similar experience. Joseph initially wasn't able to obtain the gold plates because his heart was not right before the Lord. After locating the record, he "tried three times to take them out of the box, but suffered progressively stronger shocks that deprived him of much of his natural strength, until he exclaimed in frustration, 'Why can I not obtain this book?'" H. Donl Peterson, "Moroni—Joseph Smith's Tutor," *Ensign*, January 1992. It took four years of preparation before he was able to receive the plates. See Joseph Smith—History 1:53.

1302 Tvedtnes, *Book of Mormon and Other Hidden Books*, 137.

1303 Tvedtnes, *Book of Mormon and Other Hidden Books*, 20.

1304 Tvedtnes, *Book of Mormon and Other Hidden Books*, 21, 167–174.

1305 See William J. Hamblin, "Metal Plates and the Book of Mormon," in *Pressing Forward with the Book of Mormon*, 20. Although some examples of metal plates had been discovered by Joseph Smith's day, it's likely that knowledge of these discoveries was mainly held by educated scholars and not the general public. See William J. Hamblin, "An Apologist for the Critics: Brent Lee Metcalfe's Assumptions and Methodologies," *Review of Books on the Book of Mormon 6*, no. 1 (1994): 462–470.

1306 H. Curtis Wright, "Introduction," in Tvedtnes, *Book of Mormon and Other Hidden Books*, 20.

1307 See William J. Hamblin, "Sacred Writing on Metal Plates in the Ancient Mediterranean," *FARMS Review 19*, no. 1 (2007): 37–54; H. Curtis Wright, "Ancient Burials of Metal Documents in Stone Boxes," in *By Study and Also By Faith: Essays in Honor of Hugh W. Nibley*, 2:273–334; Paul R. Cheesman, *Ancient Writing on Metal Plates: Archaeological Findings Support Mormon Claims* (Bountiful, UT: Horizon, 1985); Paul R. Cheesman, "Ancient Writing on Metal Plates," *Ensign*, October 1979; H. Curtis Wright, "Metallic Documents of Antiquity," *BYU Studies 10*, no. 4 (1970): 457–477; Daniel Johnson, "Metals and Gold Plates in Mesoamerica," 2010 BMAF presentation, online at bmaf.org; John A. Tvedtnes and Matthew Roper, "One Small Step," *FARMS Review 15*, no. 1 (2003): 160–169; H. Curtis Wright, *Modern Presentism and Ancient Metallic Epigraphy* (Salt Lake City, UT: Wings of Fire Press, 2006).

1308 See Tvedtnes, *Book of Mormon and Other Hidden Books*, 109–126. The reason additional relics are relevant is because the plates were preserved along with the Nephite interpreters and breastplate. And when the Three Witnesses were granted a view of the plates, they also beheld other Nephite relics, including the breastplate, interpreters, Liahona, and sword of Laban (see D&C 17:1).

1309 Tvedtnes, *Book of Mormon and Other Hidden Books*, 36.

1310 See Tvedtnes, *Book of Mormon and Other Hidden Books*, 31–58.

1311 Tvedtnes, *Book of Mormon and Other Hidden Books*, 43.

1312 Tvedtnes, *Book of Mormon and Other Hidden Books*, 44.

1313 Tvedtnes, *Book of Mormon and Other Hidden Books*, 36.

1314 See Title Page; 2 Nephi 26:17; 27:7–21; 30:3; Ether 3:27; 4:5; 5:1; Moroni 10:2.

1315 See John W. Welch, "Doubled, Sealed, Witnessed Documents: From the Ancient World to the Book of Mormon," in *Mormons, Scripture, and the Ancient World: Studies in Honor of John L. Sorenson*, 391–444; John W. Welch and Kelsey D. Lambert, "Two Ancient Roman Plates," *BYU Studies 45*, no. 2 (2006): 55–76

1316 See Welch, et al., *Knowing Why*, 128–129.

1317 See 2 Nephi 12:2–3; cf. Isaiah 2:2–3.

1318 See 1 Nephi 11:1; 1 Nephi 18:3; 2 Nephi 4:25; Mormon 1:3; Mormon 4:23; Mormon 6:6; Ether 4:1; Ether 15:11.

1319 A number of individuals claimed that Joseph Smith and Oliver Cowdery visited a cave that was filled with Nephite records and artifacts. However, it is difficult to tell, from these reports, whether the experience was in vision or whether they visited the cave in person. See Cameron J. Packer, "Cumorah's Cave," *Journal of Book of Mormon Studies 13*, no. 1–2 (2004): 50–57, 170–71.

1320 Tvedtnes, *Book of Mormon and Other Hidden Books*, 129.

1321 Tvedtnes, *Book of Mormon and Other Hidden Books*, 129.

1322 Tvedtnes, *Book of Mormon and Other Hidden Books*, 75–108.

1323 See Diane E. Wirth, "Revisiting the Seven Lineages of the Book of Mormon and the Seven Tribes of Mesoamerica," *BYU Studies Quarterly 52*, no.

4 (2013): 77–88.

1324 Holley Moyes and James E. Brady, "The Heart of Creation, the Heart of Darkness: Sacred Caves in Mesoamerica," *Expedition 47*, no. 3 (2005): 31. See also Holley Moyes, ed., *Sacred Darkness: A Global Perspective on the Ritual Use of Caves* (Boulder, CO: University Press of Colorado, 2012).

1325 Most notably, the Book of Mormon emphasizes that "great and marvelous were the prophecies of Ether" who "dwelt in the cavity of a rock [as] he made the remainder of this record" (Ether 13:13–14).

1326 This block of text begins with a clear forward marker, "O then . . . ," and ends with a plea "that ye may learn to be more wise than we have been," followed by "And now. . . ."

1327 Note that if numbers twenty and twenty-one are separate points in the acrostic, they do not have their own verb but are governed by the verb "condemn" from number nineteen. This, therefore, would appear to be an example of the ellipsis of the verb, also known as "gapping," that is a recurring feature of Hebrew poetry. This phenomenon can be seen in the acrostic Psalms 33, where the verb made in verse 6 is gapped in the second half of the verse. Likewise, in verse 11, the verb stands is gapped in the second half of the verse. Then verse 12 begins with a gapped verbless statement, "Blessed [is] the nation . . ." (see John A. Cook, "Verbal Patterns in the Psalms," 2006 SBL Presentation).

1328 The Hebrew alphabet that would have been known to the Lehites would likely have been what is now known as the "Paleo-Hebrew" alphabet, a variant of the Phoenician alphabet. Regardless, both of these, as well as the later "square-script" Hebrew alphabet, contained twenty-two letters.

1329 Beginning in 1990, scientists added another level of classification above that of kingdom: the domain. Scientists describe three domains of life, currently including Archaea, Bacteria, and Eukarya (with potentially two other domains being Prionobiota and Virusobiota). Biology students will need to update their acrostic mnemonic to "Determined King Philip Came Over from Great Spain."

1330 See, for example, John A. Tvedtnes, "Since the Book of Mormon Is Largely the Record of a Hebrew People, Is the Writing Characteristic of the Hebrew Language?" *Ensign*, October 1986, 65; Donald W. Parry, "Hebraisms and Other Ancient Peculiarities in the Book of Mormon," in *Echoes and Evidences*, 155–189; Andrew C. Smith, "Deflected Agreement in the Book of Mormon," *Journal of the Book of Mormon and Other Restoration Scripture 21*, no. 2 (2012): 40–57; John W. Welch, "Chiasmus in the Book of Mormon," in *Chiasmus in Antiquity: Structure, Analysis, Exegesis*, 198–210; Kerry Muhlestein, "Insights Available as We Approach the Original Text," *Journal of Book of Mormon Studies 15*, no. 1 (2006): 60–65, 63–64; Matthew Bowen, "Onomastic Wordplay on Joseph and Benjamin and Gezera Shawa in the Book of Mormon," *Interpreter: A Journal of Mormon Scripture 18* (2016): 255–273; Matthew L. Bowen, "'They Were Moved With Compassion' (Alma 27:4; 53:13): Toponymic Wordplay on Zarahemla and Jershon," *Interpreter: A Journal of Mormon Scripture 18* (2016): 233–253; Matthew L. Bowen, "Nephi's Good Inclusio," *Interpreter: A Journal of Mormon Scripture 17* (2016): 181–195.

1331 See Welch, et al., *Knowing Why*, 18–19; Neal Rappleye, "Learning Lehi's Language: Creating a Context for 1 Nephi 1:2," *Interpreter: A Journal of Mormon Scripture 16* (2015): 151–159; Stephen D. Ricks and John A. Tvedtnes, "Notes and Communications—Jewish and Other Semitic Texts Written in Egyptian Characters," *Journal of Book of Mormon Studies 5*, no. 2 (1996): 156–163.

1332 See, for example, Mosiah 7:9; Alma 10:2–3, and the heading of 3 Nephi. Omni 1 can be seen as a genealogy as well, but it is not in the same style.

1333 Hardy, *Understanding the Book of Mormon*, 223.

1334 This was first published in Hardy, *The Book of Mormon: A Reader's Edition*, xiii, though he only mentioned twenty-seven, whereas there are actually thirty. See Welch and Welch, *Charting the Book of Mormon*, chart 31.

1335 Bernard Goldman, *The Ancient Arts of Western and Central Asia: A Guide to the Literature* (Ames, IA: Iowa State University Press, 1991), 249.

1336 Ruth J. Krochock, "Written Evidence," in Lynn V. Foster, *Handbook to Life in the Ancient Maya World* (New York, NY: Oxford University Press, 2002), 286. Evidence for such histories does not yet date back to Jaredite times, but this may be due to the limited amount of writing recovered from Jaredite times. There is evidence for writing spreading across Mesoamerica between 900 and 500 BC, so there is no reason such a list couldn't have been written in (late) Jaredite times. See Stephen D. Houston, "Writing in Early Mesoamerica," in *The First Writing: Script Invention as History and Process*, ed. Stephen D. Houston (New York, NY: Cambridge University Press, 2004), 284. See also John Justeson, "Early Mesoamerican Writing Systems," in *The Oxford Handbook of Mesoamerican Archaeology*, 830–831; Javier Urcid, "Scribal Traditions from Highland Mesoamerica (300–1000 AD)," in *The Oxford Handbook of Mesoamerican Archaeology*, 855. It is also important to note that Moroni lived in the late fourth century (early Classic period) and he may have been the one to impose this structure on the record.

1337 See Genesis 5:3–32 or 1 Chronicles 1–9 for classic examples of this style. Matthew 1:1–16 shows a similar style.

1338 K. Lawson Younger Jr., "Ugaritic King List (1.104)," in *The Context of Scripture*, 3 vols., ed. William W. Hallo (Leiden: Brill, 2003), 1:356 n.1.

1339 Gardner, *Second Witness*, 6:164. For numerous examples, see Simon Martin and Nikolai Grube, *Chronicle of the Maya Kings and Queens*, 26–27, 32–4, 37–40, 48, 52, 70–72, 162, 172–173, and several others.

1340 For more information on dynastic histories, see Urcid, "Scribal Traditions from Highland Mesoamerica (300–1000 AD)," 863–865; Krochock, "Written Evidence," 286–291. For a thorough discussion of dynastic or lineage histories and the Book of Mormon, see Sorenson, *Mormon Codex*, 198–218; John L. Sorenson, "The Book of Mormon as a Mesoamerican Record," in *Book of Mormon Authorship Revisited*, 418–429. See also Nehemiah 7:64.

1341 Hardy, *Reader's Edition*, xiii.

1342 Craig C. Christensen, "A Choice Seer Will I Raise Up," *Ensign*, November 2016.

1343 Paul Y. Hoskisson, "Deseret," in *Book of Mormon Reference Companion*, 230.

1344 "Deseret," *Book of Mormon Onomasticon*.

1345 Stephen Parker, "Deseret," in *Encyclopedia of Mormonism*, 1:371. See also Hugh Nibley, *Lehi in the Desert/The World of the Jaredites/There Were Jaredites*, 189–194, for his full discussion of *deseret*.

1346 Sorenson, *An Ancient American Setting for the Book of Mormon*, 119. However, there is some disagreement on when this happened. See Gardner, *Second Witness*, 6:146–149.

1347 Ronan J. Head, "A Brief Survey of Ancient Near Eastern Beekeeping," *FARMS Review 20*, no. 1 (2008): 62.

1348 John N. Postgate, *Early Mesopotamia: Society and Economy at the Dawn of History* (New York, NY: Routledge, 1992), 56.

1349 Kevin L. Barney, "On the Etymology of Deseret," *BCC Papers 1*, no. 2 (November 2006): 3.

1350 Barney, "On the Etymology of Deseret," 5–6.

1351 In proto-Semitic, the parent language of Hebrew and other ancient Near Eastern languages, the word for bee would have been *dvrt*, which could easily be confused for *deseret* (*dšrt*) if one were to read it aloud. In addition, the *b*, *v*, *s*, and *z* letters in two early alphabets could also have been easily confused, causing someone (Moroni?) to write the word as *dšrt* instead of *dbrt*. For a discussion of proto-Semitic, see James L. Kugel, *How to Read the Bible: A Guide to Scripture, Then and Now* (New York, NY: Free Press, 2007), 87–88.

1352 See Val Brinkerhoff, "The Symbolism of the Beehive in Latter-day Saint Tradition," *BYU Studies Quarterly 52*, no. 2 (2013): 140–150.

1353 Jeffrey Ogden Johnson, "Deseret, State of," in *Encyclopedia of Mormonism*,

1:371.

1354 Hugh Nibley, *The World of the Jaredites*, 193.

1355 Hugh Nibley, *The World of the Jaredites*, 193–194.

1356 Neal A. Maxwell, *Lord Increase Our Faith* (Salt Lake City, UT: Bookcraft, 1994), 78.

1357 M. Catherine Thomas, "The Brother of Jared at the Veil," in *Temples in the Ancient World: Ritual and Symbolism*, ed. Donald W. Parry (Salt Lake City and Provo, UT: Deseret Book and FARMS, 1994), 397.

1358 Cf. Isaiah 27:13; 56:7; 65:11; Psalms 24:3; 68:15–16; Zechariah 8:3; Revelation 21:10; 1 Nephi 11:1; Moses 1:1.

1359 See Thomas, "Brother of Jared at the Veil," 388–398.

1360 The high priest had two stones on his shoulders, twelve on his breastplate, and two in the "pouch" of the ephod (the Urim and Thummim) for a total of sixteen stones. It is also interesting to note that ancient traditions regarding the Urim and Thummim describe them as "shining" or emitting light. Josephus indicated that the stones on the priestly vestments functioned by "bright rays" shining out from them (Ant. 3:8 § 9). See also chapter 108.

1361 Lynn and Hope Hilton, *Discovering Lehi: New Evidence of Lehi and Nephi in Arabia* (Springville, UT: Cedar Fort, 1996), 171–177.

1362 See, for example, Edward Curtis and Albert Madsen, *A Critical and Exegetical Commentary on the Books of Chronicles* (Edinburgh: T&T Clark, 2001), 331–332.

1363 John W. Welch, "The Temple in the Book of Mormon: The Temples at the Cities of Nephi, Zarahemla, and Bountiful," in *Temples of the Ancient World*, 366; Donald W. Parry, "Garden of Eden: Prototype Sanctuary," in *Temples of the Ancient World*, 126–151.

1364 See Alex Douglas, "The Garden of Eden, the Ancient Temple, and Receiving a New Name," in *Ascending the Mountain of the Lord: Temple, Praise, and Worship in the Old Testament*, ed. Jeffrey R. Chadwick, Matthew J. Grey, and David Rolph Seely (Salt Lake City and Provo, UT: BYU Religious Studies Center and Deseret Book, 2013), 39–41.

1365 Cf. Judges 13:20; 1 Samuel 5:3–4; Matthew 2:11; Mark 5:22; Luke 5:12; 8:41; 17:16; Revelation 5:8, 13–14; 7:11; 11:15–17; 19:2, 4. For further reading, see Matthew L. Bowen, "'They Came Forth and Fell Down and Partook of the Fruit of the Tree': Proskynesis in 3 Nephi 11:12–19 and 17:9–10 and Its Significance," in *Third Nephi: An Incomparable Scripture*, ed. Andrew C. Skinner and Gaye Strathearn (Provo, UT: Neal A. Maxwell Institute and Deseret Book, 2012), 107–29; Matthew L. Bowen, "They Came and Held Him by the Feet and Worshipped Him": Proskynesis before Jesus in Its Biblical and Ancient Near Eastern Context," *Studies in the Bible and Antiquity* 5 (2013): 63–89. See also chapter 72.

1366 See also Matthew 27:51; Mark 15:38; Luke 23:45; 1 Corinthians 13:12; Alma 19:6; Ether 12:19; D&C 38:8; 67:10; 101:23; 110:1; Moses 7:61.

1367 See Matthew B. Brown, *The Gate of Heaven* (American Fork, UT: Covenant Communications, 1999), 138–139; John Eaton, *Festal Drama in Deutero-Isaiah* (London: SPCK, 1979), 17–18, 42–43; Stephen D. Ricks, "Liturgy and Cosmogony: The Ritual Use of Creation Accounts in the Ancient Near East," in *Temples of the Ancient World*, 118–125.

1368 Leviticus 8:8; Numbers 27:21; Deuteronomy 33:8; 1 Samuel 2:18; 14:41; 23:6, 9–13; 28:6; 30:7–8; Ezra 2:63; Nehemiah 7:65; Hosea 3:4; Mosiah 8:13–18; Alma 37:1–3; Abraham 3:1, 4.

1369 Moroni presents these words as a quotation from memory of the things Jesus Christ commanded him to write (see Ether 5:1). Because the section quoted here is very similar to what Mormon wrote in his letter transcribed in Moroni 7, readers may speculate that either Moroni received a revelation from Christ that had previously been given (at least partially) to his father, that the revelation had originally been given to Mormon and Moroni simply took upon himself the instructions that Christ had given to his father, or that both Mormon and Moroni had been given similar teachings in the revelations that each had received. See also John Gee, "Quotations of the Sealed Portions of the Book of Mormon," *Insights 24*, no. 6 (2004): 2–3.

1370 W. Cole Durham Jr., "Moroni," *Ensign*, June 1978.

1371 Durham, "Moroni."

1372 Durham, "Moroni." See also Mormon 9:27–29; Ether 4:7, 11–19; Ether 12:23–41; Moroni 7; 10:4–23.

1373 Lucy Mack Smith, *History of Joseph Smith* (Salt Lake City, UT: Bookcraft, 1958), 81.

1374 For the role that 2 Nephi 27:12 and Ether 5:2–4 played in generating interest for the Three Witnesses to seek a divine manifestation, see John W. Welch, "The Miraculous Translation of the Book of Mormon," in *Opening the Heavens: Accounts of Divine Manifestations*, 1820–1844, 2nd ed., ed. John W. Welch (Salt Lake City and Provo, UT: Deseret Book and BYU Press, 2017), 101, 113, n. 98. Accompanying the prophetic promises about the Three Witnesses found in the Book of Mormon is also a revelation recorded in Doctrine and Covenants 5:11–15. Moreover, Joseph apparently obtained the Lord's approval before venturing into the woods with the prospective witnesses. See Steven C. Harper, "The Eleven Witnesses," in *The Coming Forth of the Book of Mormon: A Marvelous Work and a Wonder*, 118; Lucy Mack Smith, *History, 1844–1845*, 11, online at josephsmithpapers.org.

1375 For further information regarding the interest and preparations of the witnesses, see Richard Lloyd Anderson, *Investigating the Book of Mormon Witnesses* (Salt Lake City, UT: Deseret Book, 1981), 7–9.

1376 This vision actually took place in two stages. Initially, these companions all joined together in prayer, but after their second failed attempt Martin Harris withdrew himself, "believing . . . that his presence was the cause of [their] not obtaining" the witness they desired. With Martin Harris departed, Joseph Smith, Oliver Cowdery, and David Whitmer jointly experienced the reported vision. Soon after this, Joseph Smith found Martin and joined him in prayer. It wasn't long before Joseph Smith and Martin Harris experienced the same vision the other companions had witnessed. Joseph Smith, *History, 1838–1856*, volume A-1, 24–25, online at josephsmithpapers.org.

1377 *History, 1838–1856*, volume A-1, 25, online at josephsmithpapers.org.

1378 See *History, 1838–1856*, volume A-1, 25, online at josephsmithpapers.org.

1379 For the prophetic promise that they would behold these items, see Doctrine and Covenant 17:1. For a discussion of these items' evidentiary value, see Daniel C. Peterson, "Tangible Restoration: The Witnesses and What They Experienced," 2006 FairMormon Conference presentation, 31–33, online at fairmormon.org.

1380 A few days afterward, the Eight Witnesses handled the plates that were shown to them by Joseph Smith in Manchester, New York.

1381 Peterson, "Tangible Restoration," 2. See also Michael Hubbard MacKay and Gerrit J. Dirkmaat, *From Darkness unto Light: Joseph Smith's Translation and Publication of the Book of Mormon* (Salt Lake City and Provo, UT: Deseret Book and BYU Religious Studies Center, 2015), 151: "Their written statement was included with the manuscript pages of the Book of Mormon and was eventually printed in the back of the published book in 1830."

1382 See Anderson, *Investigating the Book of Mormon Witnesses*, 9.

1383 See Richard Lloyd Anderson, "Book of Mormon Witnesses," *FARMS Transcripts* (1994), 9.

1384 See Welch, "The Miraculous Translation of the Book of Mormon," 99–101.

1385 Richard Lloyd Anderson, "A Brief Biography of Oliver Cowdery," in *Oliver Cowdery: Scribe, Elder, Witness*, ed. John W. Welch and Larry E. Morris

(Provo, UT: Neal A. Maxwell Institute for Religious Scholarship, 2006), 1.
1386 See Steven C. Harper, "Oliver Cowdery as Second Witness of Priesthood Restoration," in *Days Never to Be Forgotten: Oliver Cowdery*, ed. Alexander L. Baugh (Provo, UT: BYU Religious Studies Center, 2009), 73–89.
1387 Welch, "The Miraculous Translation of the Book of Mormon," 159 (document 72). For further information regarding Miller's account of Oliver Cowdery's testimony, see Richard Lloyd Anderson, "Reuben Miller, Recorder of Oliver Cowdery's Reaffirmations," in *Oliver Cowdery*, 401–417.
1388 Anderson, *Investigating the Book of Mormon Witnesses*, 53–54.
1389 Jacob Forsberry Gates (son of Jacob Gates), signed and notarized affidavit, 30 January 1912, LDS Church Archives; published in *Improvement Era* 15, no. 5 (1912): 418–419; as cited in Scott H. Faulring, "The Return of Oliver Cowdery," in *Oliver Cowdery: Scribe, Elder, Witness*, 362.
1390 Gerrit J. Dirkmaat and Michael Hubbard MacKay, "Joseph Smith's Negotiations to Publish the Book of Mormon," in *The Coming Forth of the Book of Mormon*, 168. For more on Martin's role in publishing the Book of Mormon, see Susan Easton Black and Larry C. Porter, *Martin Harris: Uncompromising Witness of the Book of Mormon* (Provo, UT: BYU Studies, 2018), 151–188.
1391 See Richard E. Bennett, "Martin Harris's 1828 Visit to Luther Brandish, Charles Anthon, and Samuel Mitchell," in *The Coming Forth of the Book of Mormon*, 103–115. See also Black and Porter, *Martin Harris*, 90–101.
1392 Statement of William M. Glenn to O. E. Fischbacher, May 30, 1943, Cardston, Alberta, Canada, cit. *Deseret News*, October 2, 1943, as cited in Anderson, *Investigating the Book of Mormon Witnesses*, 116.
1393 See Anderson, *Investigating the Book of Mormon Witnesses*, 118. For a treatment of Martin Harris's final years, see Susan Easton Black and Larry C. Porter, "'Rest Assured, Martin Harris Will Be Here in Time,'" *Journal of the Book of Mormon and Other Restoration Scripture 20*, no. 1 (2011): 5–27; Black and Porter, *Martin Harris*, 415–444.
1394 See Richard Lloyd Anderson, "The Whitmers: A Family That Nourished the Church," *Ensign*, August 1979.
1395 Anderson, *Investigating the Book of Mormon Witnesses*, 79.
1396 Anderson, *Investigating the Book of Mormon Witnesses*, 90.
1397 Journal of Angus Cannon, January 7, 1888. Cf. Cannon's Tabernacle speech, *Deseret Evening News*, February 12, 1888, as cited in Anderson, *Investigating the Book of Mormon Witnesses*, 92.
1398 For treatments of Nephi's use of this ancient legal standard, see Bruce A. Van Orden, "The Law of Witnesses in 2 Nephi," in *The Book of Mormon: Second Nephi, The Doctrinal Structure*, ed. Monte S. Nyman and Charles D. Tate Jr. (Provo, UT: BYU Religious Studies Center, 1989), 307–321; Bruce A. Van Orden, "'We Prophesy of Christ': The Law of Witnesses in 2 Nephi," *Ensign*, February 1990.
1399 See Welch, *Legal Cases*, 89–99 for a discussion of the role of witnesses in ancient Israelite judicial procedures.
1400 John W. Welch, "The Power of Evidence in the Nurturing of Faith," in *Echoes and Evidences*, 31.
1401 Joseph Smith taught that the Three Witnesses were essential elements in building the kingdom of heaven on the earth: "The kingdom of heaven is like unto leaven which a woman took and hid in three measures of meal, until the whole was leavened. It may be understood that the church of the Latter Day Saints, has taken its rise from a little leaven that was put into three witnesses. Behold, how much this is like the parable: it is fast leavening the lump, and will soon leaven the whole." "Letter to the Elders of the Church, 30 November–1 December 1835," 228, online at josephsmithpapers.org.
1402 Harper, "The Eleven Witnesses," 119; also published as "Evaluating the Book of Mormon Witnesses" *Religious Educator 11*, no. 2 (2010): 37.
1403 Neal Rappleye, "'Idle and Slothful Strange Stories': Book of Mormon Origins and the Historical Record," *Interpreter: A Journal of Mormon Scripture 20* (2016): 29.
1404 For a discussion of these increasing trends, see Dallin H. Oaks, "Stand as Witnesses of God," *Ensign*, March 2015, 31–33.
1405 Anderson, *Investigating the Book of Mormon Witnesses*, 53. See also Richard Lloyd Anderson, "The Credibility of the Book of Mormon Translators," in *Book of Mormon Authorship*, 213–237.
1406 With their lives at stake, David Whitmer, Oliver Cowdery, and Hiram Page stood firmly by their testimonies. See Mitchell K. Schaefer, "'The Testimony of Men': William E. McLellin and the Book of Mormon Witnesses," *BYU Studies 50*, no. 1 (2011): 109.
1407 See Anderson, *Investigating the Book of Mormon Witnesses*, 184–190.
1408 Ezra Taft Benson, "The Book of Mormon and the Doctrine and Covenants," *Ensign*, May 1987.
1409 For a discussion of the ancient transparent stones formed through intensive heat, see Hugh Nibley, *Lehi in the Desert/The World of the Jaredites/There Were Jaredites*, 370–371. For a discussion of glass in the ancient world, see Nibley, *The World of the Jaredites*, 216–218.
1410 Hugh Nibley, *An Approach to the Book of Mormon*, 2nd ed. (Salt Lake City, UT: Deseret Book, 1976), 285.
1411 For a treatment of criticisms regarding the shining stones in the Jaredite barges, see Nibley, *An Approach to the Book of Mormon*, 273–274. For the scientific plausibility of shining stones, see Nicholas Read, Jae R. Ballif, John W. Welch, Bill Evenson, Kathleen Reynolds Gee, and Matthew Roper, "New Light on the Shining Stones of the Jaredites," in *Pressing Forward with the Book of Mormon*, 253–255.
1412 John A. Tvedtnes, "Glowing Stones in Ancient and Medieval Lore," *Journal of Book of Mormon Studies 6*, no. 2 (1997): 99–123.
1413 Tvedtnes, "Glowing Stones," 122–123. See also, Nibley, *An Approach to the Book of Mormon*, 290–291: "The few sources that might have been available to the prophet were obscure and garbled accounts in texts that not half a dozen men in the world could read, eked out by classical sources that were entirely meaningless until the discovery of the key—the great Gilgamesh Epic—long after the appearance of the Book of Mormon. That key ties the pyrophilus stone, the Alexander Cycle, the Syrian rites, the Babylonian Flood stories and the Urim and Thummim together in a common tradition of immense antiquity and makes the story of the Jaredite stones not only plausible but actually typical."
1414 *Babylonian Talmud: Tractate Sanhedrin 108b*, trans. H. Freedman, ed. Isidore Epstein (London, UK: Soncino Press, 1935, reprinted 1952, 1956, and 1961), online at come-and-hear.com.
1415 *Midrash Rabbah*, trans. H. Freedman, ed. H. Freedman and Maurice Simon (London, UK: Soncino Press, 1939, reprinted 1951 and 1961), 244, online at archive.org. This glowing stone is referred to as the *tzohar* in Jewish mysticism and is present in the stories of Noah and Abraham. See Rashi on Genesis 6:16, B. Sanhedrin 108b, B. Bava Batra 16b, Zohar 1:11a–11b. See also Howard Schwartz, *Tree of Souls: The Mythology of Judaism* (New York, NY: Oxford University Press, 2004), 85–88, 332, for traditions on this glowing stone.
1416 Hugh Nibley explained, "The description of the ships suggests nothing in the Bible, where aside from its general dimensions (which are symbolic) nothing is said as to how the ark actually looked; but it exactly matches the description of those sacred magur boats in which, according to the oldest Babylonian stories, the hero of the Flood was saved from destruction." See Hugh Nibley, *Since Cumorah*, 209–210. For parallels between the Jaredite barges and the ship in the Babylonian flood story, see Nibley, *An Approach to the Book of Mormon*, 276–281.
1417 Based on the traditional chronology of the Jaredites, the story of Noah and the flood would have been relatively recent history for the Jaredites, who had

departed from the "great tower, at the time the Lord confounded the language of the people" (Ether 1:33). For information concerning the historicity of the tower of Babel, see Michael R. Ash, "Challenging Issues, Keeping the Faith: Is the Tower of Babel Historical or Mythological?" *Deseret News*, September 27, 2010. Ash notes, "When we shine the light of science and scholarship on the Tower of Babel, we find some interesting things. First, the word 'Babel' comes from an Assyro-Babylonian word that means 'Gate of God' and is related to a Hebrew word that means 'confusion.' It appears that the author(s) of the Babel account are engaging in some wordplay to make a particular point about the story. It's also interesting to note that the book of Ether never mentions 'Babel' but simply the 'great tower.'" For an extensive treatment of the Tower of Babel, see Jeffrey M. Bradshaw and David J. Larsen, *In God's Image and Likeness 2: Enoch, Noah, and the Tower of Babel* (Salt Lake City, UT: Eborn Books and The Interpreter Foundation, 2014), 379–434.
1418 Nibley, *An Approach to the Book of Mormon*, 285.
1419 When Moroni gave his lengthy interjection in Ether 12, he provided numerous examples of faithful prophets and then placed the brother of Jared as the capstone example of faith (see Ether 12:20–21). In the same way that the brother of Jared obtained faith by following the example of Noah, readers can obtain faith by following the example of the brother of Jared, whose faith was so strong that "the Lord could not withhold anything from his sight; wherefore he showed him all things, for he could no longer be kept without the veil" (Ether 12:21).
1420 Jeffrey R. Holland, "Rending the Veil of Unbelief," in *A Book of Mormon Treasury: Gospel Insights from General Authorities and Religious Educators*, 55.
1421 M. Catherine Thomas, "The Brother of Jared at the Veil," in *Temples of the Ancient World: Ritual and Symbolism*, 391. For more information about the Urim and Thummim, see Paul Y. Hoskisson, "Urim and Thummim," *Encyclopedia of Mormonism*, 4:1499–1500; Cornelis Van Dam, *The Urim and Thummim: A Means of Revelation in Ancient Israel* (Winona Lake, IN: Eisenbrauns, 1997); Matthew Roper, "Teraphim and the Urim and Thummim," *Insights: A Window on the Ancient World 20*, no. 9 (2000): 2; Stan Spencer, "Reflections of Urim: Hebrew Poetry Sheds Light on the Directors-Interpreters Mystery," *Interpreter: A Journal of Mormon Scripture 14* (2015): 187–207.
1422 Thomas R. Valletta, "Jared and His Brother," in *The Book of Mormon: Fourth Nephi Through Moroni*, 315.
1423 Robert E. Clark, "The Type at the Border: An Inquiry into Book of Mormon Typology," *Journal of Book of Mormon Studies 2*, no. 2 (1993): 75.
1424 Thomas, "The Brother of Jared at the Veil," 391.
1425 The description of Christ touching the stones "one by one" and filling them with light is symbolic of His pattern of personal ministry. See chapter 78.
1426 Nibley, *Lehi in the Desert/The World of the Jaredites/There Were Jaredites*, 285–423.
1427 Nibley, *There Were Jaredites*, 405–408.
1428 See Stephen D. Houston, "Writing in Early Mesoamerica," in *The First Writing: Script Invention as History and Process*, ed. Stephen D. Houston (New York, NY: Cambridge University Press, 2004), 284. See also John Justeson, "Early Mesoamerican Writing Systems," in *The Oxford Handbook of Mesoamerican Archaeology*, 830–831; Javier Urcid, "Scribal Traditions from Highland Mesoamerica (300–1000 AD)," in *The Oxford Handbook of Mesoamerican Archaeology*, 855.
1429 The word *epic* is used loosely here, because many kinds of orally composed works have elements similar to epics, even if they are not epics. See David B. Honey, "Ecological Nomadism versus Epic Heroism in Ether: Nibley's Works on the Jaredites," *Review of Books on the Book of Mormon 2*, no. 1 (1990): 157.
1430 Walter J. Ong, *Orality and Literacy: The Technologizing of the Word* (New York, NY: Routledge, 1982), 137.
1431 Because this work was done in the 1930s, some assume it is outdated today. But the work of Parry, as well as that of Albert Lord in the 1960s, has proven to be definitive in the field, with scholars still referring to it today. Lord and Parry sometimes failed to appreciate the use of old oral patterns in cultures where written texts had become the norm, but besides this criticism, their work is still considered to be definitive today. See Patrick D. Miller, "The Performance of Oral Tradition in Ancient Israel," in *Contextualizing Israel's Sacred Writings: Ancient Literacy, Orality, and Literary Production*, ed. Brian Schmidt (Atlanta: Society of Biblical Literature, 2015), 175–177. One sees examples of oral traditions from all over the world. See Michael Wood, *In Search of the Trojan War* (New York, NY: Facts on File Publications, 1985), 123.
1432 Albert B. Lord, *The Singer of Tales* (Cambridge, MA: Harvard University Press, 1960), 28.
1433 To some extent, this may have been done in the Old Testament. See David M. Gunn, *The Story of King David: Genre and Interpretation* (Sheffield, UK: Sheffield Academic, 1982), 49, 60.
1434 Lord, *Singer of Tales*, 68, 71, 78–81.
1435 Nibley, *There Were Jaredites*, 396.
1436 Nibley, *There Were Jaredites*, 413.
1437 Nibley, *There Were Jaredites*, 286–287
1438 Epic poems such as *Beowulf* and *The Iliad* were thought to have no basis in reality. However, in many cases, archaeological evidence has shown that epics like these are heavily stylized retellings of actual events. See Wood, *In Search of the Trojan War*.
1439 Hardy, *Understanding the Book of Mormon*, 223.
1440 Welch and Welch, *Charting the Book of Mormon*, chart 15.
1441 Hardy, *Understanding the Book of Mormon*, 223.
1442 George A. Horton Jr., "And Thus We See," in *Book of Mormon Reference Companion*, 57–59.
1443 See chapter 94.
1444 Gardner, *Second Witness*, 6:330.
1445 John W. Welch, "Preliminary Comments on the Sources Behind the Book of Ether," *FARMS Preliminary Reports* (1986), 7.
1446 Hardy, *Understanding the Book of Mormon*, 222.
1447 Hardy, *Understanding the Book of Mormon*, 223.
1448 John W. Welch, "The Miraculous Translation of the Book of Mormon," in *Opening the Heaven*, 91.
1449 See chapter 99.
1450 H. Donl Peterson, "Moroni, the Last of the Nephite Prophets," in *The Book of Mormon: Fourth Nephi*, 235.
1451 Jerry D. Grover Jr., *Geology of the Book of Mormon*, 208, mentions a 2007 drought in Sydney, Australia, that caused an infestation of brown snakes in the city and suburban area. Similar occurrences happened the year before (2006) in Lake Havasu, Arizona (with rattlesnakes and sidewinders), and the year before (2005) in Pennsylvania (with rattlesnakes). See Don Ayotte, "More Snakes Slithering into Lake Havasu City Area," *Havasu News*, September 1, 2006; Eric Mayes, "Heat and Drought Bringing Snakes Out of their Dens," *The Daily Item*, August 18, 2005. See also John A. Tvedtnes, "Notes and Communications—Drought and Serpents," *Journal of Book of Mormon Studies 6*, no. 1 (1997): 70–72; Hugh Nibley, *Lehi in the Desert/The World of the Jaredites/There Were Jaredites*, 221.
1452 For lists of the many venomous snakes in the Olmec region (Veracruz and Oaxaca), which many scholars believe to be where the Jaredites were, see Grover, *Geology of the Book of Mormon*, 206–207; Gardner, *Second Witness*, 6:265.
1453 It is important to note that the there is no indication that the animals perished by snakebite. They more likely perished from the drought.
1454 Grover, *Geology of the Book of Mormon*, 208.
1455 If placed in a Mesoamerican setting, rivers stretch across the northern

part of the Isthmus of Tehuantepec, creating an ideal place for the snakes to settle and thus "hedge up the way" blocking off passage to regions southward of the isthmus. See Sorenson, *Mormon's Codex*, map 11; reprinted in Grover, *Geology of the Book of Mormon*, 204. See also the accounts of armies being stopped by snake infestations in Nibley, *The World of the Jaredites*, 221.

1456 Grover, *Geology of the Book of Mormon*, 205. See also Sorenson, *Mormon's Codex*, 645–646. It was the eruption of Indonesia's Mount Tambora in 1815 that caused the Joseph Smith family's crop failure in 1816, forcing them to move from Vermont to New York. See Brandon S. Plewe, ed., *Mapping Mormonism: An Atlas of Latter-day Saint History* (Provo, UT: BYU Press, 2012), 15; *Saints: The Story of the Church of Jesus Christ in the Latter Days, volume 1*, 3–13.

1457 See Grover, *Geology of the Book of Mormon*, 205–206. See also Sorenson, *Mormon's Codex*, 645.

1458 See Grover, *Geology of the Book of Mormon*, 208–210, which lists specific species in the Olmec area that prey on snakes, rodents, and lizards.

1459 Grover, *Geology of the Book of Mormon*, 210.

1460 See Grover, *Geology of the Book of Mormon*, 208.

1461 Gardner, *Second Witness*, 6:267.

1462 Tvedtnes, "Drought and Serpents," 72. See also Neal Rappleye, "'The Great and Terrible Judgments of the Lord': Destruction and Disaster in 3 Nephi and the Geology of Mesoamerica," *Interpreter: A Journal of Mormon Scripture 15* (2015): 152: "The effects of a volcanic eruption on an environment, therefore, carries rather potent explanatory power for an event often mocked as ridiculous or fanciful by modern critics of the text. It is hard to imagine a more perfect geologic, geographic, and ecologic setup for the events described in Ether 9."

1463 There is wide disagreement on Jaredite chronology, which is primarily due to a lack of any confirmable external events to anchor it. John L. Sorenson and David A. Palmer both date the drought event to ca. 2100–2200 BC. See Sorenson, *An Ancient American Setting for the Book of Mormon*, 118; Sorenson, *Mormon's Codex*, 28; David A. Palmer, *In Search of Cumorah: New Evidences for the Book of Mormon from Ancient Mexico*, 2nd ed. (Springville, UT: Cedar Fort, 1999), 128. Yet Brant A. Gardner dates it to more than 1,000 years later, ca. 800–900 BC. See Gardner, *Second Witness*, 6:264; Grover, *Geology in the Book of Mormon*, 202–203 follows Sorenson and Palmer, and thus seeks to link the drought to volcanic events dated to the late third millennium BC.

1464 This is likely the result of two things. First, as the drought ceased (see Ether 9:35), snakes and other animals would return to their natural habitats, and populations would be more evenly distributed. Second, eventually the bird populations would recover and begin to regulate snake populations, reducing them to normal levels. Thus, the serpents would no longer pose a barrier to the land southward (see Ether 10:19).

1465 For a discussion of Christ's outstretched arms always ready to receive those who repent, see chapter 70.

1466 Other Jaredite kings also sat on a "throne," though none others are described as "exceedingly beautiful" or particularly elaborate. See Ether 7:18; 9:5–6; 14:6, 9.

1467 Jaredite chronology lacks any solid external dating, so the dating of events is difficult, and opinions vary widely. David Palmer dates Riplakish's reign to ca. 2020 BC, and John Sorenson dates it to 1900 BC, while John Clark and Joseph Allen both date it to around 1200 BC, and Brant Gardner dates it to sometime close to 800–770 BC. See David A. Palmer, *In Search of Cumorah: New Evidence for the Book of Mormon from Ancient Mexico*, 2nd ed. (Springville, UT: Cedar Fort, 1999), 128; Sorenson, *Mormon's Codex*, 515; John E. Clark, "Archaeology, Relics, and Book of Mormon Belief," *Journal of Book of Mormon Studies 14*, no. 2 (2005): 46; Allen and Allen, *Exploring the Lands of the Book of Mormon*, 120; Gardner, *Second Witness*, 6:273.

1468 Clark, "Archaeology, Relics, and Book of Mormon Belief," 46.

1469 See Clark, "Archaeology, Relics, and Book of Mormon Belief," 48. See also Joel W. Polka, "Olmec," in *The A to Z of Ancient Mesoamerica* (Lenham, MD: Scarecrow Press, 2010), 92–93. For more on connections between the Olmec and the Jaredites, see chapter 113.

1470 John E. Clark and Arlene Colman, "Time Reckoning and Memorials in Mesoamerica," *Cambridge Archaeological Journal 18*, no. 1 (2008): 97. Mary Miller and Karl Taube, *An Illustrated Dictionary of the Gods and Symbols of Ancient Mexico and the Maya* (New York, NY: Thames and Hudson, 1993), 165, dates the earliest thrones to "around 1200 BC."

1471 See examples in Mary Ellen Miller, *The Art of Mesoamerica: From Olmec to Aztec*, 5th edition (New York, NY: Thames and Hudson, 2012), 38–39.

1472 Miller, *The Art of Mesoamerica*, 38.

1473 David C. Grove, "The Middle Preclassic Period Paintings of Oxtotitlan, Guerrero," *FAMSI*, online at http://www.famsi.org/research/grove/index.html. See also David C. Grove, "Olmec Altars and Myths," *Archaeology 26* (1973): 128–135.

1474 Christopher A. Pool, *Olmec Archaeology and Early Mesoamerica* (New York, NY: Cambridge University Press, 2007), 10. Large thrones (previously mislabeled as "altars") were sometimes recarved into the famed Olmec colossal heads. See James B. Porter, "Olmec Colossal Heads as Recarved Thrones: 'Mutilation,' Revolution, and Recarving," *Res: Anthropology and Aesthetics 17–18* (Spring–Autumn 1989): 23–30. For example, Monuments 2 and 53 from San Lorenzo are, according to Ann Cyphers, "clearly recarved from thrones." Ann Cyphers, "From Stone to Symbols: Olmec Art in Social Context at San Lorenzo Tenochtitlán," in *Social Patterns in Pre-Classic Mesoamerica*, ed. David C. Grove and Rosemary A. Joyce (Washington, D.C: Dumbarton Oaks Research Library and Collection, 1999), 163. See also Pool, *Olmec Archaeology*, 121; Richard E. W. Adams, *Prehistoric Mesoamerica*, 3rd ed. (Norman, OK: University of Oklahoma, 2005), 69–70.

1475 Pool, *Olmec Archaeology*, 10.

1476 Adams, *Prehistoric Mesoamerica*, 86.

1477 Mary E. Pye, "Themes in the Art of the Preclassic Period," in *The Oxford Handbook of Mesoamerican Archaeology*, 800.

1478 Porter, "Olmec Colossal Heads as Recarved Thrones," 24.

1479 Clark and Colman, "Time Reckoning," 96; Pool, *Olmec Archaeology*, 10.

1480 Guersney describes the Olmec-style throne at Oxtotitlan, Mexico, as "a celestial throne," depicting a ruler "engaged in supernatural communion through a cosmic portal symbolized by the quatrefoil opening." Julia Guernsey, *Ritual and Power in Stone: The Performance of Rulership in Mesoamerican Izapan–style Art* (Austin, TX: University of Texas Press, 2006), 80.

1481 Susan D. Gillespie, "Olmec Thrones as Ancestral Altars: The Two Sides of Power," in *Material Symbols: Culture and Economy in Prehistory*, ed. John E. Robb (Carbondale, IL: Center for Archaeological Investigations, 1999), 224–253.

1482 Guernsey, *Ritual and Power in Stone*, 80–81. This is because they were thought of as symbolic caves—places from which the Mesoamericans thought rains were to come.

1483 See chapter 111.

1484 Kerry Hull, personal communication to Book of Mormon Central staff.

1485 Grove noted that "some Olmec-style 'monument mutilation' may have taken place at a leader's death." David C. Grove, "Chalcatzingo: A Brief Introduction," *PARI Journal 9*, no.1 (2008): 3. See also David C. Grove, "Olmec Monuments: Mutilation as a Clue to Meaning," in *The Olmec and Their Neighbors: Essays in Honor of Matthew W. Stirling*, ed. Elizabeth P. Benson (Washington, DC: Dumbarton Oaks, 1981), 49–68; Pool, *Olmec Archaeology*, 120–121. There is good evidence of Olmec monument mutilation occurring within some of the proposed time ranges of Riplakish that were done by the ruler's people. Olmec specialist Michael Coe has stated: "Towards the end of the San Lorenzo phase [1150– 900 BC] all of the great basalt monuments of San

Lorenzo had been mutilated. . . . I take this to have been a revolutionary act, for we have no evidence that it was any other than San Lorenzo people themselves who carried out that great act of destruction." Michael D. Coe, "Solving a Monumental Mystery," *Discovery 3*, no. 1 (1967): 25.

1486 Clark, "Archaeology, Relics, and Book of Mormon Belief," 45.

1487 Clark, "Archaeology, Relics, and Book of Mormon Belief," 46.

1488 Chart adapted from John E. Clark, "Archaeology, Relics, and Book of Mormon Belief," *Journal of Book of Mormon Studies 14*, no. 2 (2005): 48; John E. Clark, "Archaeological Trends and Book of Mormon Origins," in *The Worlds of Joseph Smith: A Bicentennial Conference at the Library of Congress*, ed. John W. Welch (Provo, UT: BYU Press, 2006), 91. For the most thorough correlation made to date of the rise and fall of the Olmec and preclassic Maya with Jaredites and Nephites, see Sorenson, *Mormon's Codex*, 499–695. See also Sorenson, *An Ancient American Setting for the Book of Mormon*; Sorenson, *Images of Ancient America*, 192–217. Note that Sorenson's Jaredite chronology differs from Clark's.

1489 Clark, "Archaeology, Relics, and Book of Mormon Belief," 48.

1490 See Clark, "Archaeology, Relics, and Book of Mormon Belief," 48. Joel W. Polka, "Olmec," in *The A to Z of Ancient Mesoamerica*, 92–93, dates the Olmec to 1750–400 BC. Richard E. W. Adams, *Prehistoric Mesoamerica*, 55–56, discusses Olmec chronology and periodization, ca. 1600–300 BC.

1491 Clark, "Archaeology, Relics, and Book of Mormon Belief," 48. Clark, "Archaeological Trends and Book of Mormon Origins," 93: "The Olmec population grows and falls in respectable parallel to that of the Jaredites' reported increase and demise." Gardner, *Traditions of the Fathers*, 406, agreed: "The Olmec and the Jaredites overlap in time depth and geography." However, Gardner used a different chronology for the Jaredites, shifting them a few hundred years forward in time to ca. 1100–200 BC. See Gardner, *Second Witness*, 6:146–149. On his later dating of the collapse of the Jaredites, Gardner pointed out "a [Olmec] related late tradition called the epi-Olmec lasting through 200 BC" (Gardner, *Traditions of the Fathers*, 395). Gardner thus reasoned that "the devastating wars of annihilation in Ether" were part of "the aftermath of the Olmec political collapse" (Gardner, *Second Witness*, 147).

1492 Clark, "Archaeology, Relics, and Book of Mormon Belief," 48. Adams, *Prehistoric Mesoamerica*, 104–109, 132–133, mentions the rise of several regional centers, pyramids, and monumental architecture between 550 and 400 BC.

1493 Clark, "Archaeology, Relics, and Book of Mormon Belief," 48.

1494 Sorenson, *Images of Ancient America*, 210. See also Sorenson, *Ancient American Setting*, 131–137; Sorenson, *Mormon's Codex*, 666–695. Adams, *Prehistoric Mesoamerica*, 210–211, discusses the fall of certain preclassic sites and increased militarization in the late fourth century AD.

1495 Sorenson, *Images of Ancient America*, 210. Converging with the picture painted by Clark and Sorenson, Francisco Estrada-Belli argued, "By 500 BC the Lowland Maya had developed a sophisticated civilization. It reached its peak around AD 100, after which time it underwent a political reorganization, and some centers were abandoned." Francisco Estrada-Belli, *The First Maya Civilization: Ritual and Power Before the Classic Period* (New York, NY: Routledge, 2011), back cover. Estrada-Belli pointed out defensive earthworks that suggest "civil unrest and endemic warfare" plagued declining cities in the centuries after AD 100 (p. 65), culminating in the third and fourth centuries when many preclassic sites were completely abandoned or show evidence of militarized takeover (pp. 127–137). Specifically, Estrada-Belli suggested that El Mirador, after centuries of decline, was fatally attacked sometime around or after AD 300, after which it was rapidly abandoned once and for all (pp. 127–128). He likewise proposed that Cival was under attack around the same time, with its final abandonment occurring around AD 300 (pp. 131–134). Holmul, on the other hand, did not experience total abandonment, but rather underwent a militarized take over from Teotihuacan documented in inscriptions from the late fourth to early fifth centuries AD (pp. 133–137).

1496 Clark, "Archaeology, Relics, and Book of Mormon Belief," 48.

1497 Gardner, *Traditions of the Fathers*, 406–407.

1498 Clark, "Archaeological Trends and Book of Mormon Origins," 91.

1499 Clark, "Archaeological Trends and Book of Mormon Origins," 89–90.

1500 Clark, "Archaeological Trends and Book of Mormon Origins," 91.

1501 Steven C. Walker, "Last Words," in *The Reader's Book of Mormon*, 7:xiii.

1502 On the collapse of Teotihuacan, see Jeffrey R. Parsons and Yoko Sugira Y., "Teotihuacan and the Epiclassic in Central Mexico," in *The Oxford Handbook of Mesoamerican Archaeology*, 309–323.

1503 On the collapse of the Classic Maya, see David Webster, *The Fall of the Ancient Maya: Solving the Mystery of the Maya Collapse* (New York, NY: Thames and Hudson, 2002); David Webster, "The Classic Maya Collapse," in *Oxford Handbook of Mesoamerican Archaeology*, 324–334.

1504 The postclassic Maya and the Aztec empire fell at the hands of the Spanish (and their native allies). See Michel R. Oudijk, "The Conquest of Mexico," *Oxford Handbook of Mesoamerican Archaeology*, 459–467.

1505 Walker, "Last Words," 7:xiii.

1506 M. Catherine Thomas, "Trial of Faith," in *Book of Mormon Reference Companion*, 765, defines a trial of faith as a "period of divine testing of one's confidence in God during which one has the opportunity to demonstrate his faith by obedience and good works, especially when faced with uncertainty, sacrifice, or adversity."

1507 These are only three of the many examples that Moroni provided. For his entire list see, Ether 12:7–31.

1508 See Welch, et al., *Knowing Why*, 280–281.

1509 See Welch et al., *Knowing Why*, 307–309.

1510 For a discussion of the brother of Jared and his great faith, see Jeffrey R. Holland, "Rending the Veil of Unbelief," in *A Book of Mormon Treasury: Gospel Insights from General Authorities and Religious Educators*, 47–66. See also chapters 105 and 108.

1511 McConkie, Millet, and Top, *Doctrinal Commentary*, 4:296. As an example of the superior status of a spiritual witness of truth, Elder Jeffrey R. Holland testified, "I bear witness of . . . restored priesthood keys which unlock the power and efficacy of saving ordinances. I am more certain that those keys have been restored and that those ordinances are once again available through The Church of Jesus Christ of Latter-day Saints than I am certain I stand before you at this pulpit and you sit before me in this conference." See Jeffrey R. Holland, "The Cost—and Blessings—of Discipleship," *Ensign*, May 2014, 8–9.

1512 McConkie, Millet, and Top, *Doctrinal Commentary*, 4:296.

1513 Ogden and Skinner, *Verse by Verse: The Book of Mormon*, 2:277.

1514 For a discussion of how Alma's explanation of developing faith correlates to Creation imagery, see chapter 8.

1515 Robert L. Millet explained that "each time a principle is applied and blessings are realized, turning faith into knowledge, faith in that principle increases. Faith can thus grow from one level to another—'a particle of faith' (Alma 32:27), 'sufficient' faith (3 Nephi 17:8), 'much faith' (Mosiah 27:14), 'strong' faith (Alma 7:17), 'exceeding faith' (Mosiah 4:3), 'exceedingly great faith' (Moroni 10:11)—into 'perfect faith' (2 Nephi 9:23)." See Robert L. Millet, "Faith," in *Book of Mormon Reference Companion*, 262.

1516 David A. Bednar, "Seek Learning by Faith," *Ensign*, September 2007, 63.

1517 Dallin H. Oaks, "The Challenge to Become," *Ensign*, November 2000. In this same address, President Oaks further explained that "the Final Judgment is not just an evaluation of a sum total of good and evil acts—what we have done. It is an acknowledgment of the final effect of our acts and thoughts—what we have become."

1518 M. Catherine Thomas, "A More Excellent Way," in *Book of Mormon, Part 2: Alma 30 to Moroni*, 276.
1519 Decapitating a captive like this would have been common in both the ancient Near East and pre-Columbian America. See Morgan W. Tanner, "Jaredites," *Encyclopedia of Mormonism*, 2:719.
1520 M. Gary Hadfield, "Neuropathology and the Scriptures," *BYU Studies 33*, no. 2 (1993): 325. This understanding assumes that part of the bottom of the head survived, so that Coriantumr did not "smite off" all of the head of Shiz, to which some people have taken objection. However, such a literal reading of the text is unnecessary. See Gardner, *Second Witness*, 6:326, including footnotes.
1521 M. Gary Hadfeld, "The 'Decapitation' of Shiz," in *Pressing Forward with the Book of Mormon*, 266.
1522 M. Gary Hadfield, "My Testimony, as an Academician, of God and of the Church of Jesus Christ of Latter-day Saints," at Mormon Scholars Testify, April, 2010, online at https://www.fairmormon.org/testimonies/scholars/m-gary-hadfield.
1523 See C. S. Sherrington, "Decerebrate Rigidity, and Reflex Coordination of Movements," *Journal of Physiology 22* (1898): 319.
1524 Hadfield, "My Testimony."
1525 Craig James Ostler, "Shiz," in *Book of Mormon Reference Companion*, 722.
1526 Catherine Thomas, "A More Excellent Way (Ether 9–15)," in *The Book of Mormon, Part 2*, 279–280.
1527 Gardner, *Second Witness*, 6:330. See also Gordon C. Thomasson, "The Survivor and the Will to Bear Witness," in *Reexploring the Book of Mormon*, 266–268.
1528 3 Nephi 26:17, 3 Nephi 28:18, and 4 Nephi 1:1 can all be seen as doing this.
1529 Gary Layne Hatch, "Mormon and Moroni: Father and Son," in *The Book of Mormon: Fourth Nephi*, 112.
1530 It is possible that he got these exact words from the three Nephite disciples themselves. See Book of Mormon Central, "Why Was The 3 Nephites' Wish Helpful for Mormon and Moroni? (3 Nephi 28:7)," *KnoWhy 223* (November 6, 2016).
1531 See chapter 94.
1532 McConkie, Millet, and Top, *Doctrinal Commentary*, 4:319.
1533 Byron R. Merrill, "Moroni2," in *Book of Mormon Reference Companion*, 557.
1534 Elder K. Brett Nattress, "No Greater Joy Than to Know That They Know," *Ensign*, November 2016.
1535 For more on this, see John W. Welch, "Our Nephite Sacrament Prayers," in *Reexploring the Book of Mormon*, 287.
1536 Welch, "Our Nephite Sacrament Prayers," 288.
1537 "Didache," in *The Oxford Dictionary of the Christian Church*, 482. The Didache was also one of the books in the highly revered Codex Siniaticus, which was brought from Saint Catherine's monastery by Tischendorff to Germany—but not until the 1860s, a generation after the Book of Mormon was printed in 1830.
1538 For some similarities between the two texts, see Hugh Nibley, *Since Cumorah*, 176.
1539 See M. B. Riddle, "The Teaching of the Twelve Apostles," in *The Ante-Nicene Fathers: Translations of the Writings of the Fathers down to A.D. 325*, ed. Alexander Roberts and James Donaldson, 10 vols. (Grand Rapids, MI: Wm B. Eerdmans Publishing Company, 1951), 7:381.
1540 See Riddle, "The Teaching of the Twelve Apostles," 7:381.
1541 See Riddle, "The Teaching of the Twelve Apostles," 7:379– 380.
1542 For another translation, see Riddle, "The Teaching of the Twelve Apostles," 7:381.
1543 See Riddle, "The Teaching of the Twelve Apostles," 7:379.
1544 See Riddle, "The Teaching of the Twelve Apostles," 7:382.
1545 For another connection between the Didache and the Book of Mormon, see chapter 74.
1546 For another translation, see Riddle, "The Teaching of the Twelve Apostles," 7:381.
1547 See "Didache," 482: "Although in the past many English and American scholars tended to assign it to the late 2nd cent., most scholars now date it in the 1st century."
1548 For the latest volume of studies exploring this important question, see Jonathan A. Draper and Clayton N. Jefford, eds., *The Didache: A Missing Piece of the Puzzle in Early Christianity* (Atlanta: SBL Press, 2015). Chapters in this book discuss approaches to this text as a whole, leadership and liturgy, relations between the Didache and the Gospel of Matthew (including the Sermon on the Mount), early Christian diversity, revelation, and the challenges faced by the dynamics and methodological issues that arise in continuing studies of the Didache.
1549 See Book of Mormon Central, "Was the Book of Mormon Used as the First Church Administrative Handbook? (3 Nephi 27:21–22)," *KnoWhy 72* (April 6, 2016); "Why Did the Lord Quote the Book of Mormon When Reestablishing the Church? (3 Nephi 11:24)," *KnoWhy 282* (March 3, 2017).
1550 See John W. Welch, "The Book of Mormon as the Keystone of Church Administration," *Religious Educator 12*, No. 2 (2011): 88.
1551 See Scott H. Faulring, "An Examination of the 1829 'Articles of the Church of Christ' in Relation to Section 20 of the Doctrine and Covenants," *BYU Studies 43*, no. 4 (2004): 57–91. See also Robin Scott Jensen, Robert J. Woodford, and Steven C. Harper, eds., *The Revelations and Translations*, vol. 1 of the Manuscript Revelation Books series of The Joseph Smith Papers (Salt Lake City, UT: Church Historian's Press, 2009), 23–24.
1552 There are several songs recorded in the Old Testament (and outside of Psalms) that arguably predate Solomon's temple. Examples include Exodus 15:1–18; Numbers 10:35–36; 23–24; Deuteronomy 32–33; Judges 5; 1 Samuel 2:1–10. Gary A. Rendsburg commented further: "From as far back as our sources allow [the third millennium BCE], hymns were part of Near Eastern temple ritual, with their performers an essential component of the temple functionaries." Gary A. Rendsburg, "The Psalms as Hymns in the Temple of Jerusalem," in *Jesus and Temple: Textual and Archaeological Explorations*, ed. James H. Charlesworth (Minneapolis, MN: Fortress Press, 2014), 95. Also, Sigmund Mowinckel, *The Psalms in Israel's Worship*, trans. D. R. Ap-Thomas, 2 vols. (New York, NY: Abingdon, 1962), 2:85–90.
1553 Margaret Barker, *Temple Themes in Christian Worship* (London, UK: T&T Clark, 2007), 137. The word *psalms* in Greek (*psalmoi*) means, simply, "songs." Although many of the Psalms may not have been written or collected until the time of the second temple, most scholars agree that a large number were composed and in use in the first temple period. See, for example, Rendsburg, "The Psalms as Hymns," 100.
1554 See, for example, 1 Chronicles 6:33; 9:33; 15:27; 2 Chronicles 5:12–13; 29:30; 35:15; Ezra 2:40–41; Nehemiah 7:1, 73; 10:28, 39; 11:22. See John A. Tvedtnes, *The Most Correct Book: Insights from a Mormon Scholar* (Salt Lake City, UT: Cornerstone Publishing, 1999), 169. See also the writings of Josephus, such as *Antiquities of the Jews*, 7.12.3; 20.9.6; and the *Mishnah*, Tamid 7:5.
1555 A few examples include the Thanksgiving Hymns (Hodayot), the Songs of the Maskil, the hymns of the War Scroll, and the Songs of the Sabbath Sacrifice. See Bilhah Nitzan, *Qumran Prayer and Religious Poetry* (Leiden: Brill, 1994). Esther Chazon identified more than three hundred psalms, hymns, and prayers among the Dead Sea Scrolls. Chazon, "Hymns and Prayers in the Dead Sea Scrolls," in *The Dead Sea Scrolls after Fifty Years: A Comprehensive Assessment*, ed. James C. VanderKam and Peter W. Flint (Leiden: Brill, 1998), 244–270. See also James H. Charlesworth, *Critical Reflections on the Odes of Solomon*

(Sheffield, UK: Sheffield Academic Press, 1998), 51.
1556 See as examples 3 Nephi 16:18–19; 20:32–34; 22:1.
1557 See Acts 2:29–31.
1558 Barker, *Temple Themes*, 142.
1559 Tvedtnes, *The Most Correct Book*, 169.
1560 See *1QHodayota* 3:22–24; see also *The Songs of the Sabbath Sacrifice*.
1561 For more on this topic, see Tvedtnes, *The Most Correct Book*, 167–169.
1562 See chapter 73.
1563 John W. Welch, "Echoes from the Sermon on the Mount," in *The Sermon on the Mount in Latter-day Scripture*, ed. Gaye Strathearn, Thomas A. Wayment, and Daniel L. Belnap (Salt Lake City and Provo, UT: Deseret Book and BYU Religious Studies Center, 2010), 320–321.
1564 See chapter 77.
1565 Welch, "Echoes," 320.
1566 This is not the only occasion where Mormon uses Christ's sermon. See, for example, Mormon 3:11–15, which clarifies what Christ meant by "swearing." Gary Layne Hatch, "Mormon and Moroni: Father and Son," in *The Book of Mormon: Fourth Nephi*, 108.
1567 John W. Welch, "Reusages of the Words of Christ," *Journal of Book of Mormon Studies and Other Restoration Scripture 22*, no. 1 (2013): 68.
1568 Welch, "Reusages," 68.
1569 Welch, "Reusages," 68.
1570 See chapter 94.
1571 Welch, "Echoes," 321–322.
1572 See also Book of Mormon Central, "Why Does Mormon State that Angels Did Appear unto Wise Men? (Helaman 16:14)," *KnoWhy 187* (September 14th, 2016).
1573 Angelic visitations occurred often in the Book of Mormon, sometimes multiple times. The text tells us of visitations to Nephi (son of Lehi), Sam, Laman and Lemuel, Jacob, King Benjamin, Alma the Younger, the Sons of Mosiah, Amulek, Nephi (son of Helaman), Samuel the Lamanite, the Nephites gathered at the temple at Bountiful, Mormon, and Moroni.
1574 Oscar W. McConkie, "Angels," in *Encyclopedia of Mormonism*, 1:41.
1575 For an in-depth discussion of the role of angels, see Donald W. Parry, *Angels: Agents of Light, Love, and Power* (Salt Lake City, UT: Deseret Book, 2013).
1576 Larry Evans Dahl, "Angels, Ministry of," in *Book of Mormon Reference Companion*, 60.
1577 Francis Brown, S. R. Driver, and Charles Briggs, *A Hebrew and English Lexicon of the Old Testament* (Oxford, UK: Clarendon Press, 1951), 521.
1578 Jeffrey R. Holland, "The Ministry of Angels" *Ensign*, November 2008.
1579 The timing of this letter remains uncertain. After developing thirteen criteria needed to evaluate the date of its composition, Alan C. Miner concluded that both Moroni 8 and 9 were "written sometime within the year between 375 and 376." Alan C. Miner, "A Chronological Setting for the Epistles of Mormon to Moroni," *Journal of Book of Mormon Studies 3*, no. 2 (1994): 111. In a different study, Joseph M. Spencer proposed that "Mormon's first letter was . . . produced in the years 345–50, while his second letter was written in the years 375–80." Joseph M. Spencer, "On the Dating of Moroni 8–9," *Interpreter: A Journal of Mormon Scripture 22* (2016): 144. See chapter 123 for more information.
1580 See chapter 95.
1581 Matthew Roper, "The Baptism of Little Children in Pre-Columbian Mesoamerica," *Insights: A Window on the Ancient World 23* (2003): 2. Upon reviewing several evidences for infant baptism in pre-Columbian America, Roper concluded, "Thus the idea that little children who die unbaptized will suffer torment for their inherited evil or impurity was not peculiar to American discourse in the early 19th century, as some detractors of the Book of Mormon have claimed" (p. 2).
1582 Matthew Roper, "Review of Mormonism: Shadow or Reality?" *Review of Books on the Book of Mormon 4*, no. 1 (1992): 182–183.
1583 Robert E. Parsons, "Infant Baptism, LDS Perspective," in *Encyclopedia of Mormonism*, 2:682.
1584 Keith E. Norman, "Infant Baptism, Early Christian Origins," in *Encyclopedia of Mormonism*, 2:682.
1585 For a discussion of how the Book of Mormon sheds light on the process of apostasy, see John W. Welch, "Modern Revelation: A Guide to Research about the Apostasy," in *Early Christians in Disarray: Contemporary LDS Perspectives on the Christian Apostasy*, ed. Noel B. Reynolds (Provo, UT: BYU Press and FARMS, 2005), 109: "The knowledge and benefit of the covenants of God could become lost simply by neglecting the performance of ordinances, or priesthood functions, or individual covenants as the Lord had taught. Changing and ultimately eliminating the covenant aspect of baptism—for example, by moving to infant baptism in place of the previous outward sign of adult repentance and covenantal admission into the fold of God—would be symptomatic of the loss of one such covenant."
1586 See chapter 99.
1587 For a Latter-day Saint perspective of the various historical views of infant baptism, see Tad R. Callister, *The Inevitable Apostasy and the Promised Restoration* (Salt Lake City, UT: Deseret Book, 2006), 221–230.
1588 See chapter 96.
1589 It should be noted that Christ's clarification about baptism was delivered directly to Nephi and the other disciples whom the Lord chose as leaders of His Church, and not to the congregation as a whole (see 3 Nephi 11:19–22). This precedent helps explain why the Lord worked through Mormon, the presiding Church leader in his time, to settle doctrinal disputations about infant baptism. For a treatment of how the Book of Mormon conveys the mind and will of Jesus Christ, see chapter 83.
1590 On the importance of loving and caring for children, see Neil L. Andersen, "'Whoso Receiveth Them, Receiveth Me,'" *Ensign*, May 2016, 49–52.
1591 Hugh Nibley, *The World and the Prophets, The Collected Works of Hugh Nibley, Volume 3* (Salt Lake City and Provo, UT: Deseret Book and FARMS, 1987), 97.
1592 Moroni also recorded another letter from his father, which is found in Moroni 8. See chapter 121.
1593 For studies on the chronology of this letter, as well as Mormon's letter found in Moroni 8, see Sidney B. Sperry, *Book of Mormon Compendium* (Salt Lake City, UT: Bookcraft, 1975), 491; Alan C. Miner, "A Chronological Setting for the Epistles of Mormon to Moroni," *Journal of Book of Mormon Studies 3*, no 2. (1994): 94–113; Joseph M. Spencer, "On the Dating of Moroni 8–9," *Interpreter: A Journal of Mormon Scripture 22* (2016): 131–148.
1594 Mormon 4:21: "And when they had come the second time, the Nephites were driven and slaughtered with an exceedingly great slaughter; their women and their children were again sacrificed unto idols." See also chapter 95.
1595 After the destruction at Cumorah, Moroni wrote that the Lamanites "put to death every Nephite that will not deny the Christ" (Moroni 1:2). This suggests that denying Christ was necessary for the Nephites to join the Lamanites.
1596 For information about the Hill Cumorah, see chapter 97. See also Book of Mormon Central, "Where Did the Book of Mormon Happen? (2 Nephi 1:8)," *KnoWhy 431* (May 18, 2018); Book of Mormon Central, "How Are Oliver Cowdery's Messenger and Advocate Letters to Be Understood and Used? (Mormon 6:6)," *KnoWhy 453* (July 26, 2018).
1597 Mormon refused to lead the Nephites between the years 362 and 375 (see

Mormon 3:11; 5:1). Only Nephite victories are recorded for the battles that took place between 359 and 362 (see Mormon 3:7–8). Before that, there were ten years of peace between 350 and 359 (see Mormon 3:1). This means that there are no references to lost battles between the years 350 and 375 in which Mormon could have fought. And any losing battle before the year 350 would seem far too removed from the other details of Mormon's letter for it to be plausibly referenced. For the importance of the ten years of peace, see chapter 94.

1598 Although the Book of Mormon was likely part of the "sacred records" to which Mormon was referring, this assumption isn't certain. It's possible, for example, that Mormon may have kept the plates of the Book of Mormon with him (not at Shim) so he could work on finishing it before his people were destroyed.

1599 See "The Family: A Proclamation to the World," *Ensign*, November 1995.

1600 See chapter 100.

1601 This chart is adapted, with a few changes to dates and descriptions, from Spencer, "On the Dating of Moroni 8–9," 136–138.

1602 See chapter 99 for a comparison of Moroni's three separate farewell endings.

1603 For a treatment of sealed documents in the ancient world, see John W. Welch, "Doubled, Sealed, Witnessed Documents: From the Ancient World to the Book of Mormon," in *Mormons, Scripture, and the Ancient World: Studies in Honor of John L. Sorenson*, 391–444.

1604 James E. Faulconer, "Sealings and Mercies: Moroni's Final Exhortations in Moroni 10," *Journal of the Book of Mormon and Other Restoration Scripture 22*, no. 1 (2013): 6. It should also be noted that in the ancient world, introductory material was often located at the end—rather than the beginning—of a document. See, for example, Welch, et al., *Knowing Why*, 180–181.

1605 Concerning the organization of his treatment of Moroni 10, see Faulkner, "Sealings and Mercies," 6: "The first thing I noticed is that the word exhort occurs over and over in this chapter in one form or another. . . . I tried to keep in mind what these exhortations have to do with the fact that Moroni is sealing up his book and sealing his testimony by the things that he teaches here."

1606 As for the viability of this spiritual witness, S. Brent Farley concluded, "The proof, however, is not an empirical test open to the view of all. It is open only to the view of all who perform the test in the specified way; it is a text that affects the soul and the mind. The heart must be 'sincere'; the intent must be 'real.' . . . And it requires faith, a quality difficult to measure for mortals, but which is definitely measurable to God." S. Brent Farley, "Come unto Christ: Moroni 9–10," in *The Book of Mormon, Part 2*, 306.

1607 Moroni exhorted readers to "deny not the power of God" (Moroni 10:7) and then to "deny not the gifts of God" (Moroni 10:8). After this, he provided the following list of spiritual gifts: "teach the word of wisdom" (Moroni 10:9), "teach the word of knowledge" (Moroni 10:10), "exceedingly great faith" (Moroni 10:11), "gifts of healing" (Moroni 10:11), "mighty miracles" (Moroni 10:12), "prophesy concerning all things" (Moroni 10:13), "beholding of angels and ministering spirits" (Moroni 10:14), "all kinds of tongues" (Moroni 10:15), and "the interpretation of languages and divers kinds of tongues" (Moroni 10:16).

1608 David A. Bednar, "The Spirit of Revelation," *Ensign*, May 2011, 88.

1609 Steve Walker, "Last Words: 4 Nephi–Moroni," in *The Reader's Book of Mormon*, 7:xiv.

1610 The concept of being "sealed up" is being used rather loosely here, where it simply means that a spiritual witness of the truthfulness of the Book of Mormon will generally be inaccessible until one asks and seeks in faith. John W. Welch explained, "There seems to be a distinction in Nephi's mind between being 'sealed' and being 'sealed up.' The former, according to the Old World practice, would normally have to do with physically tying the document shut and affixing a wax or clay seal to the closure. The latter has to do with whether or not a portion will be revealed." Welch, "Doubled, Sealed, Witnessed Documents," 423. Just as the sealed portion of the plates is "hid up because of unbelief" (Ether 4:13), so too will a spiritual witness concerning the revealed portion of the text (the Book of Mormon) be hidden or denied until one can "rend that veil of unbelief" that causes "blindness of mind" (Ether 4:15).

1611 For a comparison of Moroni's and Paul's writings on the subject of spiritual gifts, see Falconer, "Sealings and Mercies," 12–15.

1612 See chapter 114.

1613 Faulconer, "Sealings and Mercies," 9.

1614 For the importance of narrative theology in the Book of Mormon, see chapter 96.

1615 Jeffrey R. Holland, "Conclusion and Charge," in *The Book of Mormon: First Nephi*, 320.

1616 Gary E. Stevenson, "Look to the Book, Look to the Lord," *Ensign*, November 2016, 46.

1617 See Kenneth W. Godfrey, "150 Years of General Conference," *Ensign*, February 1981; M. Dallas Burnett, "Conferences, General Conference," in *Encyclopedia of Mormonism*, 1:307–308; Kenneth W. Godfrey, "General Conference," in *Encyclopedia of Latter-day History*, 418–419.

1618 A Methodist regional conference held in 1819 in Phelps, New York, only a few miles down the road from Palmyra, is believed to be a factor in the "unusual excitement" mentioned by Joseph Smith. See Richard Lloyd Anderson, "Joseph Smith's Accuracy in the First Vison Setting: The Pivotal 1818 Palmyra Camp Meeting," in *Exploring the First Vision*, 91–169. For additional discussion of the "unusual excitement" throughout the region leading up to Joseph Smith's First Vision, see Milton V. Backman Jr., "Awakenings in the Burned-Over District: New Light on the Historical Setting of the First Vision," in *Exploring the First Vision*, 171–197; Milton V. Backman Jr., *Joseph Smith's First Vision: Confirming Evidences and Contemporary Accounts*, 2nd ed. (Salt Lake City, UT: Bookcraft, 1980), 53–88; Matthew B. Brown, *A Pillar of Light: The History and Message of the First Vision* (American Fork, UT: Covenant Communications, 2009), 11–23; Steven C. Harper, *Joseph Smith's First Vision: A Guide to the Historical Accounts* (Salt Lake City, UT: Deseret Book 2012), 24–25.

1619 Clifford P. Jones, "The Great and Marvelous Change: An Alternate Interpretation," *Journal of the Book of Mormon and Other Restoration Scripture 19*, no. 2 (2010): 52.

1620 See John S. Thompson, "Isaiah 50–51, the Israelite Autumn Festivals, and the Covenant Speech of Jacob in 2 Nephi 6–10," in *Isaiah in the Book of Mormon*, 123–150; Terrence L. Szink and John W. Welch, "An Ancient Israelite Festival Context," in *King Benjamin's Speech: "That Ye May Learn Wisdom,"* 148–223. See also Welch, et al., *Knowing Why*, 80–82, 186–187.

1621 See John W. Welch, Gordon C. Thomasson, and Robert F. Smith, "Abinadi and Pentecost," in *Reexploring the Book of Mormon*, 135–138. See also Welch, et al., *Knowing Why*, 207–209.

1622 See Gordon C. Thomasson and John W. Welch, "The Sons of the Passover," in *Reexploring the Book of Mormon*, 196–198. See also chapter 15.

1623 Elder Robert D. Hales, "General Conference: Strengthening Faith and Testimony," *Ensign*, November 2013, 6. Elder Hales continued, "Adam gathered his posterity and prophesied of things to come. Moses gathered the children of Israel and taught them the commandments he had received. The Savior taught multitudes gathered both in the Holy Land and on the American continent. Peter gathered believers in Jerusa-lem" (p. 6).

1624 Hales, "General Conference," 7.

1625 Hales, "General Conference," 6.

1626 For a proposal of the physical location of this valley, see George D. Potter, "A New Candidate in Arabia for the 'Valley of Lemuel,'" *Journal of Book of*

Mormon Studies 8, no. 1 (1999): 54–63, 79; S. Kent Brown, "New Light from Arabia on Lehi's Trail," in *Echoes and Evidences*, 60–62; S. Kent Brown, "The Hunt for the Valley of Lemuel," *Journal of Book of Mormon Studies 16*, no. 1 (2007): 64–73, 86–88.
1627 See Welch, et al., *Knowing Why*, 29–30; David Rolph Seely, "Lehi's Altar and Sacrifice in the Wilderness," *Journal of Book of Mormon Studies 10*, no. 1 (2001): 62–69, 80; Brown, "New Light from Arabia on Lehi's Trail," 62–63; S. Kent Brown, "What Were Those Sacrifices Offered by Lehi?" in *From Jerusalem to Zarahemla: Literary and Historical Studies of the Book of Mormon* (Provo, UT: BYU Religious Studies Center, 1998), 2; Hugh Nibley, *An Approach to the Book of Mormon,* 245–246.
1628 See Welch., et al., *Knowing Why*, 20–21; Hugh Nibley, *Lehi in the Desert/The World of the Jaredites/There Were Jaredites*, 84–92.
1629 For information about sacrifices in the Book of Mormon, see Donald W. Parry, "Service and Temple in King Benjamin's Speech," *Journal of Book of Mormon Studies 16*, no. 2 (2007): 45–47; Matthew Roper, "A Black Hole That's Not So Black," *Review of Books on the Book of Mormon 6*, no. 2 (1994): 169–174.
1630 For more information concerning this profound transformation, see Clifford P. Jones, "The Great and Marvelous Change: An Alternate Interpretation," *Journal of the Book of Mormon and Other Restoration Scripture 19*, no. 2 (2010): 50–63. See also, chapter 70.
1631 For a treatment of Christ's prayers among the people at Bountiful, see Robert L. Millet, "The Praying Savior: Insights from the Gospel of 3 Nephi," in *Third Nephi: An Incomparable Scripture*, 131–146; Donald W. Parry, "'Pray Always': Learning to Pray as Jesus Prayed," in *The Book of Mormon: 3 Nephi 9–30, This Is My Gospel*, ed. Monte S. Nyman and Charles D. Tate (Provo, UT: BYU Religious Studies Center, 1993), 137–148.
1632 Henry B. Eyring, "Gratitude on the Sabbath Day," *Ensign*, November 2016, 101.
1633 Eyring, "Gratitude on the Sabbath Day," 101.
1634 See Book of Mormon Central, "Why Did Jesus Tell All People to Sacrifice a Broken Heart and a Contrite Spirit? (3 Nephi 9:19–20)," *KnoWhy 198* (September 29, 2016).
1635 Eyring, "Gratitude on the Sabbath Day," 99.
1636 Eyring, "Gratitude on the Sabbath Day," 100.
1637 Russell M. Nelson, "Thanks Be to God," *Ensign*, May 2012, 79.
1638 See Book of Mormon Central, "Why Are So Few Women Mentioned in the Book of Mormon? (2 Nephi 26:33)," *KnoWhy 391* (December 19, 2017).
1639 See Welch, et al., *Knowing Why*, 37–38.
1640 See Book of Mormon Central, "What Can We Learn from Abish's Member-missionary Work? (Alma 19:17)," *KnoWhy 374* (October 19, 2017).
1641 See Jennifer Reeder and Kate Holbrook, eds., *At the Pulpit: 185 Years of Discourses by Latter-day Saint Women* (Salt Lake City, UT: Church Historians Press, 2017).
1642 Rachel H. Leatham, "God Has Revealed It unto Me," Annual General Conference Outdoor Overflow Meeting, April 1908, online at churchhistorianspress.org.
1643 Leatham, "God Has Revealed It unto Me," online at churchhistorianspress.org.
1644 Belle S. Spafford, "Latter-day Saint Women in Today's Changing World," Brigham Young University Devotional, February 1975, online at churchhistorianspress.org.
1645 Spafford, "Latter-day Saint Women."
1646 Judy Brummer, "Our Father in Heaven Has a Mission for Us," from a devotional given at Salt Lake City, Utah, April 2012, online at churchhistorianspress.org.
1647 Brummer, "Our Father in Heaven."
1648 Book of Mormon Central, "Why Are So Few Women Mentioned in the Book of Mormon? (2 Nephi 26:33)," *KnoWhy 391* (December 19, 2017).
1649 See Thomas S. Monson, "Welcome to Conference," *Ensign*, November 2012: "We affirm that missionary work is a priesthood duty—and we encourage all young men who are worthy and who are physically able and mentally capable to respond to the call to serve. Many young women also serve, but they are not under the same mandate to serve as are the young men. We assure the young sisters of the Church, however, that they make a valuable contribution as missionaries, and we welcome their service.
1650 Carole M. Stephens, "We Have Great Reason to Rejoice," *Ensign*, November 2013.